W9-AEB-126

America's Founding Charters

America's Founding Charters

Primary Documents of Colonial and Revolutionary Era Governance

VOLUME 3

Edited by Jon L. Wakelyn

GREENWOOD PRESS
Westport, Connecticut • London

Library of Congress Cataloging-in-Publication Data

America's founding charters : primary documents of Colonial and Revolutionary era governance /
edited by Jon L. Wakelyn.

    v. cm.

  ISBN 0–313–33155–3 (v. 1 : alk. paper)—ISBN 0–313–33156–1 (v. 2 : alk. paper)—
  ISBN 0–313–33157–X (v. 3 : alk. paper)—ISBN 0–313–33154–5 (set : alk. paper)
1. United States—Politics and government—To 1775—Sources. 2. United States—Politics
and government—1775–1783—Sources. 3. United States—Politics and government—
1783–1809—Sources. I. Wakelyn, Jon L.
  JK54.A64 2006
  342.73009´03—dc22   2006026954

British Library Cataloguing in Publication Data is available.

Library of Congress Catalog Card Number: 2006026954
ISBN: 0–313–33154–5 (set)
     0–313–33155–3 (vol. 1)
     0–313–33156–1 (vol. 2)
     0–313–33157–X (vol. 3)

First published in 2006

Greenwood Press, 88 Post Road West, Westport, CT 06881
An imprint of Greenwood Publishing Group, Inc.
www.greenwood.com

Printed in the United States of America

The paper used in this book complies with the
Permanent Paper Standard issued by the National
Information Standards Organization (Z39.48–1984).

10 9 8 7 6 5 4 3 2 1

Contents

Preface: The Study of Governance   *xv*

VOLUME 1

Introduction: Origins, 1580s–1688   1

PART I: IDEAS ON GOVERNANCE AND FIRST CHARTERS

1. Ideas on Governance   5
   Richard Hakluyt, *A Discourse on Western Planting*, 1584   6
   Sir Walter Raleigh, "Discovery of Guiana," 1596   9
   Sir Walter Raleigh, Preface to *The History of the World*, 1616   11
   Francis Bacon, "Of Plantations," 1625   12
   Francis Bacon, *The New Atlantis*, 1624   14

2. First Charters   18
   Letters Patent to Sir Humphrey Gilbert, June 11, 1578   18
   Charter to Sir Walter Raleigh, March 25, 1584   21

PART II: CHARTERS AND ESSENTIAL GOVERNING DOCUMENTS

3. Virginia, First Settled 1607   27
   First Charter, April 10, 1606   28
   Instructions for the Governing of Virginia, November 20, 1606   33
   Second Charter, May 23, 1609   37
   Third Charter, March 11, 1612   43
   Instructions to Governor George Yeardley, November 18, 1618   49
   Laws Enacted by the First General Assembly, August 2–4, 1619   55
   Constitution for the Council and Assembly of Virginia, July 24, 1621   60
   Proclamation Settling the Affairs of Virginia, May 13, 1625   60

Surrender of Virginia to the Commonwealth of England, March 12, 1651   62

Election of Burgesses, October 1670   64

Appointment of Governor Thomas Culpepper, May 10, 1680   65

4. Massachusetts Bay, 1630 (Including Plymouth, 1620, and Maine, 1622)   67

Charter of New England, November 3, 1620   68

Agreement Between Settlers (Mayflower Compact), November 11, 1620   78

Charter of New Plymouth, 1629   79

Charter of Massachusetts Bay, 1629   82

Organization of the Government of Massachusetts Bay, April 30, 1629   93

Regulation of Laws of Towns, 1636–1649   95

Duties and Privileges of New Plymouth, 1639–1649   95

Book of General Laws and Liberties of Massachusetts, 1647   97

Law Defining a Freeman, May 31, 1660   105

Instructions from King Charles II to Massachusetts, June 28, 1662   106

Law on Admission of Freeman, August 2, 1664   107

Election Law, February 4, 1679   107

5. Maryland, 1634   109

Charter of Maryland, June 20, 1632   109

Act Determining Members of the General Assembly, 1638   116

Petition Against Lord Baltimore, April 4, 1638   117

Acts for Judges and Courts, 1642   118

Council of State Assumes Control of Maryland, March 29, 1652   120

Lord Proprietor Assents to Twelve Laws, July 30, 1659   121

Creation of Somerset County, August 22, 1666   122

Method of Voting for Provincial Officers of Maryland, May 12, 1670   123

6. Connecticut, 1636 (Including New Haven, 1638—Charter, 1662)   125

Fundamental Orders of Connecticut, 1639   125

Structure of Town Government, October 10, 1639   128

Fundamental Agreement of New Haven, June 4, 1639   129

Government of New Haven, October 27, 1643   132

Charter of Connecticut, April 23, 1662   134

Method of Voting for Provincial Officers, 1670   140

General Laws and Liberties of Connecticut, 1672   141

7. Rhode Island, 1637 (Part of Massachusetts Bay; Separate Charter, 1663)   143

Plantation Agreement at Providence, August 27–September 6, 1640   143

Government of Rhode Island, March 16–17, 1641   145

Patent for Providence Plantation, March 14, 1643   146

Acts and Orders Made at the General Court of Election, May 19–21, 1647   148

Charter of Rhode Island and Providence Plantation, July 8, 1663   151

Royal Commission to Rhode Island, April 8, 1665   160

General Assembly Divided into Two Houses, March 27, 1666   161

8. New York, 1663 (Including New Jersey and Delaware)   162

Charter of New York, March 12, 1663/1664   162

Duke of York's Laws, March 1, 1664   165
Duke's Laws Amended, March 1, 1665   169
Duke's Laws: Public Charges, March 1, 1665   171
Duke's Laws: Voters and Townships, March 1, 1665   173
Second Charter of New York, June 29, 1674   174
Charter of Liberties and Privileges, October 30, 1683   177
Division of New York into Shires and Counties, November 1, 1683   180

 9. New Jersey (East Jersey, 1664; West Jersey, 1675; Charter, 1683)   182
Concessions and Agreements, February 10, 1664   182
Order Concerning Voting Privileges in Woodbridge, October 25, 1670   190
Declaration of Meaning of Lords Proprietors, December 6, 1672   190
Charter of Fundamental Laws of West Jersey, March 3, 1676   191
Fundamental Agreement of West Jersey, November 25, 1681   194
Fundamental Constitution of East Jersey, 1683   196

10. Carolinas, 1664 (North Carolina and South Carolina, 1665)   203
Concessions and Agreements, January 11, 1664   203
Charter of the Carolinas, June 30, 1665   214
Fundamental Constitutions of the Carolinas, March 1, 1669   222
Temporary Laws, June 21, 1671   233
Agrarian Laws: Instructions to Governor and Council of Carolina, June 10, 1672   235
Additions and Alterations to the Fundamental Constitutions of 1669,
March 10, 1682   238

11. New Hampshire, 1679 (Settled as Early as 1623)   240
Exeter Combination, 1639; Revoked, 1640   240
General Laws and Liberties, March 16, 1679   241
Commission to Set Up President and Council, September 18, 1679   243

12. Pennsylvania, 1680/1681 (Delaware Mentioned)   249
Charter of Pennsylvania, February 28, 1680/1681   249
Frame of Government with Laws Agreed Upon in England, May 5, 1682   256
Frame of Government of Pennsylvania, April 2, 1683   265

PART III: CONSOLIDATION OF COLONIES AND RESISTANCE: DOMINION STATUS, 1685–1689

13. Dominion of New England   273
Articles of Confederation of the United Colonies of New England, August 29, 1643   273
Massachusetts Bay Argues Against Losing Charter, November 1683   277
Petition of Connecticut to James II, August 24, 1686   280
Instructions to Governor Edmund Andros Concerning Surrender of Rhode Island
and Connecticut Charters, September 13, 1686   282
Recommendation that Connecticut Be Annexed to Dominion of New England,
June 18, 1687   282
Quo Warranto Proceedings Against the Charters of East and West Jersey,
July 7, 1685   283

New Jersey Proprietor Representations and Proposals, June 1687   284
Commission of Governor Andros as Governor of Dominion of New England
(Including New York and New Jersey), April 7, 1688   286

14. Parliament of England's Response to the Glorious Revolution of 1688/89   292
    English Bill of Rights, February 13, 1689   292

VOLUME 2

Introduction: The Colonial and Provincial Growth of American Governance:
Developments and Defense, 1689–1776   297

PART IV: GOVERNMENTAL DEVELOPMENTS DURING THE EIGHTEENTH CENTURY

15. Virginia   301
    Act to Regulate Elections of Burgesses, October 1705   301
    Act Declaring Who Shall Not Hold Office, October 1705   305
    Act Establishing the General Court, October 1705   306
    Act of Naturalization, October 1705   307
    Acts Establishing Ports and Towns, October 1705   308
    Proclamation for Royal Disallowance of Assembly Acts, October 8, 1752   315
    Act for Directing and Regulating the Elections of Burgesses   315

16. Massachusetts Bay   323
    New Charter of Massachusetts Bay, 1691   323
    Queen's Instructions to Governor Dudley, April 6, 1702   331
    Explanatory Charter for Massachusetts Bay, August 26, 1725   339
    Act for Regulating Townships and Choice of Town Officers, January 15, 1742   341
    Act Empowering Selectmen of Lexington to Call Town Meetings, April 27, 1757   342

17. Maryland   343
    Royal Seizure of Maryland Government, July 25, 1689   343
    Instructions to Governor of Maryland, August 26, 1691   347
    Manner of Summoning and Electing Delegates to the Assemblies, 1715   353
    Act to Raise Funds to Pay Colonial Agent, Together with Letter to
    the Governor, May 1, 1739   355
    Act for Advancement of Justice, November 9, 1753   359
    Act for Speedy Publication of the Laws of this Province, November 17, 1753   361

18. Connecticut   363
    Method of Electing Assistants, October 10, 1689   363
    Powers of Governor and Council, May 12, 1698   364
    Division of Assembly into Two Houses, October 13, 1698   364
    Connecticut Freemen Elect Governor, December 1707   365
    Assembly Report on the Plan of Union, October 1754   365

Act to Prevent Bribery and Corruption in Election of Members of
General Assembly, May 1756 369
Assembly Asks Governor to Write to King on Stamp Act Repeal, May 1766 369

19. Rhode Island 371
Petition to the King, January 30, 1689 371
Call to the People of Rhode Island to Assume Their Former Government,
April 23, 1689 372
Voting for Town Officers, June 19, 1715 373
Act to Regulate General Elections, February 1760 374

20. New York 375
Rights and Privileges of Subjects, May 13, 1691 375
Commission of Governor Benjamin Fletcher, March 18, 1692 378
Regulating Elections of Representatives to the General Assembly, May 16, 1699 ... 383
Charter of the City of New York, January 5, 1730 385
Choice of Representation in Westchester County, June 22, 1734 394
Frequent Elections of Representatives to the General Assembly, December 16, 1737 ... 395

21. New Jersey 397
Remonstrance of East Jersey, 1700 397
Instructions to Governor Lord Cornbury, November 16, 1702 399
Petition to Request a Separate Governor, March 18, 1735 412
Commission to Governor Francis Bernard, 1758 413

22. South Carolina 418
Act for Determination of the General Assembly, June 20, 1694 418
Narrative Proceedings of the People of South Carolina, May 1719 419
Instructions for Governor Francis Nicholson, August 30, 1720 423
Acts to Ascertain Manner of Electing Members of the General Assembly,
September 1721 435
Act to Establish County Courts, September 20, 1721 440
Act on Electing Members to the Commons House of Assembly, April 7, 1759 ... 448

23. North Carolina 451
Act for Establishing a Lasting Foundation of Government, July 1711 451
Act Regulating Elections to the Assembly, 1715 453
Address of the Assembly Concerning Repealed Laws, May 7, 1755 455

24. New Hampshire 458
Unsettled State of the Province, March 15, 1689 458
Commission of the Earl of Bellomont, June 18, 1689 460
Right to Choose a Speaker, April 11, 1728 466

25. Pennsylvania 467
Charter for Inhabitants of Germantown, March 30, 1691 467
Commission of Governor Benjamin Fletcher, October 21, 1692 470
Frame of Government, November 7, 1696 474

Charter of Privileges, October 28, 1701 — 479
Act to Regulate the Number of Members of the Assembly, 1705 — 483
Ordinance for Establishing Courts, February 22, 1706 — 487
Act to Amend the Election of Members to the Assembly, March 4, 1745 — 490

26. Delaware — 494
Charter of Delaware, 1701 — 494
Charter of New Castle, May 28, 1724 — 498
Constitution of Delaware, 1776 — 502

27. Georgia — 511
Charter of the Colony, June 9, 1733 — 511
Establishment of Courts, December 12, 1754 — 521
Act Establishing Method of Appointing Constables, March 27, 1759 — 524
Act to Ascertain Manner of Electing Assembly Members, June 9, 1761 — 524

PART V: ESSAYS ON GOVERNANCE AND DEFENSE OF COLONIAL GOVERNMENT

28. Overviews of Colonial Governance — 531
Anonymous, *An Essay upon the Government of the English Plantations*, 1701 — 532
Archibald Kennedy, *An Essay on the Government of the Colonies*, 1752 — 545

29. Defenses of Colonial Governance — 554
James Otis, *A Vindication of the British Colonies*, 1765 — 556
Richard Bland, *An Inquiry into the Rights of the British Colonies*, 1766 — 569
Thomas Jefferson, *A Summary View of the Rights of British America*, 1774 — 580
John Dickinson, *Essay on the Constitutional Power of Great Britain*, 1774 — 589
Henry Laurens, *To South Carolina Committee*, 1775 — 596
James Wilson, *Speech Delivered in the Convention of Pennsylvania*, 1775 — 600
John Adams, *Thoughts on Government*, 1776 — 607

PART VI: PLANS FOR UNITY, DIVIDED COLONIES, AND UNITED INDEPENDENCE

30. Unity Proposed and Deferred — 615
Albany Plan of Union, 1754 — 615
Stephen Hopkins of Rhode Island Defends the Plan, 1754 — 618
Reasons Considered by the Assembly of Connecticut, October 2, 1754 — 621
Massachusetts Opposes the Albany Plan, December 14, 1754 — 623
A Short Reply to Stephen Hopkins by Philolethes, April 10, 1755 — 624

31. Internal Division — 629
Address to People of Granville County, North Carolina, June 6, 1765 — 629
North Carolina Regulators' Advertisement, August 6, 1766 — 630
Petition of Citizens of Rowan and Orange Counties, October 4, 1768 — 630
Impartial Relation of the First Rise and Cause, 1770 — 631
Address of the Mechanics of New York, June 14, 1776 — 636

32. Toward Independence and Unity   637
    Colonies Send Delegates to the Continental Congress, June–September 1774   638
    Suffolk Resolves, Massachusetts, September 9, 1774   643
    Resolution and Declaration of Rights in Continental Congress, October 1774   646
    Mecklenburg Resolves, North Carolina, May 31, 1775   649
    Address of North Carolina Delegates to Continental Congress, June 19, 1775   651
    Congress Advises New Hampshire to Call Provincial Convention to Establish
    a Government, November 3, 1775   654
    Congress Advises South Carolina, November 4, 1775   654
    Instructions to Representatives of Portsmouth, New Hampshire,
    December 25, 1775   654
    Congress Offers Plan to Adopt National Government, May 10, 1776   656
    Congress Approves Preamble by John Adams, May 15, 1776   656
    Declaration of Independence, July 4, 1776   657

VOLUME 3

Introduction: Governance in the Confederation Period, 1776–1787   661

PART VII: THE FIRST STATE CONSTITUTIONS: DEBATES, ADOPTIONS, AND AMENDMENTS

33. New Hampshire, January 5, 1776   665
    General John Sullivan's Plan of Government, December 11, 1775   665
    Constitution, January 5, 1776   668
    To the Freeholders and Inhabitants of New Hampshire, January 30, 1777   669
    Second Constitution, Containing a Bill of Rights and Form of Government,
    October 31, 1783   670

34. South Carolina, March 26, 1776   684
    Constitution, March 26, 1776   684
    Revised Constitution, March 19, 1778   689

35. Virginia, June 29, 1776   698
    George Mason's Plan for the State Constitution, June 10, 1776   698
    Virginia Bill of Rights, June 12, 1776   700
    Constitution, June 29, 1776   701
    Bill to Remove State Government to Richmond, November 11, 1776   704
    Bills Establishing Court of Appeals and High Court of Chancery,
    November 25, 1776   706
    Revised State Laws, June 18, 1779   713

36. New Jersey, July 2, 1776   715
    Constitution, July 2, 1776   715

37. Delaware, September 11, 1776   719
    Constitution, September 11, 1776   719

38. Pennsylvania, September 28, 1776   724
    Proceedings of Convention, September 17–24, 1776   724
    Constitution, September 28, 1776   726
    Minutes of Supreme Executive Council, June 11, 1777   734
    Attempts to Amend Constitution, December 17, 1783–August 1784   735

39. Connecticut and Rhode Island   754
    Act to Set Up Government of Connecticut, 1776   754
    Connecticut Delegates to Congress Must Be Elected by All Freeholders,
    September 1776   755
    Connecticut Legislature Debates Western Lands, October 1783   756
    Connecticut Act to Regulate Appointments to the Superior Court, May 1784   756

40. Maryland, November 11, 1776   758
    Constitution, November 11, 1776   758

41. North Carolina, December 18, 1776   771
    Letter from Samuel Johnson, April 20, 1776   771
    Instructions to Delegates from Mecklenburg to the Provincial Congress,
    November 1776   771
    Constitution, December 18, 1776   774

42. Georgia, February 5, 1777   781
    Constitution, February 5, 1777   781

43. New York, April 20, 1777   788
    Some Proceedings of the Convention, April 1777   788
    Constitution, April 20, 1777   789
    Letter from John Jay to Robert Livingston, April 29, 1777   799

44. Vermont, July 8, 1777   803
    Constitution, July 8, 1777   803
    Constitution Debated, 1786; Revised, March 1787   812

45. Massachusetts, June 16, 1780   822
    Who May Enact a Constitution, September 17, 1776   822
    Vote on Forming Constitution, September 27, 1776   822
    New Salem Rejects Constitution, May 19, 1778   823
    Essex Result, April 29, 1778   824
    Constitution, June 16, 1780   837

PART VIII: THE ARTICLES OF CONFEDERATION: PROPOSED,
DEBATED, AND RATIFIED

46. Drafts of the Articles of Confederation and Discussion
    in the Continental Congress   865
    John Dickinson Draft of the Articles, June 17–July 11, 1776   866
    Thomas Burke of North Carolina Offers Amendments, April 27, 1777   868
    Thomas Burke, Notes on the Proposed Articles, November 1777   869
    Thomas Burke, Remarks Concerning the Proposed Articles, November 15, 1777   871

47. The States and Ratification of the Articles of Confederation   873
    Articles Proposed to the States, November 15, 1777   873
    Congress Urges States to Ratify Articles, November 17, 1777   879
    William H. Drayton of South Carolina, January 20, 1778   880
    Connecticut Urges Revisions and Authorizes Delegates to Ratify Articles, February 1778   888
    Rhode Island Objects to Articles, Yet Authorizes Ratification, February 1778   889
    J. B. Smith to George Bryan, February 3, 1778   891
    Council to Pennsylvania Delegates, April 30, 1778   892
    Nathaniel Scudder to Speaker of New Jersey Assembly, July 13, 1778   892
    General Assembly of Connecticut, May 7, 1779   894
    Instructions of the General Assembly of Maryland, May 21, 1779   894
    Theodorick Bland to Richard Henry Lee, March 5, 1781   896

PART IX: CONTINENTAL CONGRESS AS THE NATIONAL GOVERNMENT

48. Congress at Work and Changes Made in Governance, 1776–1787   899
    Dispute Over New York–New Hampshire Border, August 27, 1779; Congressional Resolution, September 24, 1779   899
    Congress Discusses Executive Committee, February 1781   904
    Plan of Supplemental Acts of Congress, August 1781   905
    New York Delegates to Governor George Clinton, March 29, 1782   906
    David Howell to Governor William Greene, July 30, 1782   908
    Congress Attempts to Discipline David Howell, December 1782   912
    Report by Congress on David Howell, January 14, 1783   913
    Northwest Ordinances of 1784 and 1787   916
    Secretary of Congress to Robert Livingston, March 1, 1786   921

49. Criticism and Defense of Congress Under the Articles   923
    Alexander Hamilton, "The Continentalist," August 1781–July 1782   924
    Unsubmitted Resolutions to Amend Articles, July 1783   931
    Massachusetts Delegates to Governor James Bowdoin, September 3, 1783   935
    Criticism by Richard Price, 1785   938
    Proposed Amendments to the Articles of Confederation, August 7, 1786   941
    Address of the Annapolis Convention, September 4, 1786   943
    James Manning and Nathan Miller to the Governor of Rhode Island, September 28, 1786   945
    James Madison, *The Vices of the Political System of the United States*, April 1787   946
    Benjamin Rush, *On the Defects of the Confederation*, May 1787   951
    Richard Henry Lee to George Mason, May 15, 1787   953

Afterword: The Meaning of Governance in America   957

Essay on Sources Consulted   961

Index   969

Introduction: Governance in the Confederation Period, 1776–1787

Volume III includes the events of Governance from just after the Declaration of Independence in July 1776 to the calling of the Philadelphia Constitutional Convention during the spring of 1787. During these years a new nation was declared; thrust into war; and required to form its own governing systems, state and national. The Continental Congress and the state governments conducted the affairs of the new nation under the first federal constitution, the Articles of Confederation. The years from 1776 to 1787, then, tested the ability of the people and their leaders to create state governments and form national governance in those harrowing and confused times. At the end of the this period, a number of the delegates to the Philadelphia convention planned to write a second national Constitution. It is for the reader to ask whether the documents presented here in Volume III continue the developments of two centuries of governance experience or take the nation into a new realm of governance.

In Volume III Part VII begins with a transition from Volume II just as the Continental Congress called on the colonies to write state constitutions. Those efforts in state making include the calling of conventions, the drafting of the state constitutions, debates about the governance structure in the constitutions, and state ratification of their constitutions. Printed here are all of the first state constitutions, efforts to reform and add to governance in those constitutions, and, for some of the states, second constitutions. The essential years are from 1776 to 1780, when the last of the first state constitutions finally is ratified in the Massachusetts general assembly.

In Volume III Part VIII provides documents that relate to the first federal constitution, the Articles of Confederation. Some of the most cogent debates within the Congress as well as the redrafting of the constitution make up this part. Debates in the states about ratification carry the process down to 1781 when Maryland, at last, gave its consent to the new constitution. Those debates about the ratification of the Articles of Confederation, as seen in the selections chosen from some of the states (there are many, so only the most important are included), pose the questions of whether the government created from this constitution could work in this new, experimental nation and how the states regarded national governance.

In Volume III Part IX provides documents that assess the ability of the federal Congress to govern under the Articles of Confederation. The first section includes documents that show Congress amending its own procedures and creating a new office for governance. One of the most important acts, The Northwest Ordinance, is included because of its central importance to forming governments in the new American territories. The second section includes documents that criticize and defend the actions and, for that matter, inactions of the Confederation Congress under the Articles of Confederation. (Of the many arguments made, only a few key speeches, reports, and pamphlets from each side are included here.) It is for the reader to decide the merits of these arguments, especially whether they built on the precedent of the foundational documents or wanted to create a new governing system. In short, to what extent did these discussions on the success and failure of the Confederation government support the governance traditions that had developed and are shown in the foundational documents that were printed Volumes I and II?

Volume III concludes with a bibliographical essay on the primary sources used in document selection and the secondary sources that cover the background or context of governing events in the period. Also in this volume is an Afterword from the editor that explains the patterns of governance developed in these three volumes. In the Afterword, the editor also takes the opportunity to sum up what the foundation documents have told us about the formation of this country. To what extent, then, do these essential documents on American governance from the years 1578 to 1787 reflect our values and the way we want to be governed now?

Part VII

The First State Constitutions: Debates, Adoptions, and Amendments

Even before the Continental Congress declared independence and acted in behalf of a new nation, that body had called on the colonial governments to meet and adopt state constitutions. Before independence, four state governments (New Hampshire, South Carolina, Virginia, and New Jersey) were formed through written constitutions. Six more states (Delaware, Pennsylvania, Maryland, North Carolina, Georgia, and New York) declared independent governments by writing constitutions during 1776 and 1777. In 1776 both Connecticut and Rhode Island declined to write state constitutions and declared themselves states abiding by their original charters (both state legislatures called their charters constitutions). Not until 1818 did Connecticut and 1842 did Rhode Island conventions adopt their own constitutions. Although not one of the original 13 colonies and not a state until 1791, Vermont wrote a constitution in 1777, which is included in this volume. Massachusetts refused to ratify a state constitution until 1780, but did set up a functioning state government in 1777.

How did these colonies make their state constitutions? It must be remembered that around 1775 many of the colonial governments had begun to fall apart as governors fled and legislatures disbanded. Some colonies filled the vacuum with hastily formed congresses, committees, or new legislatures and it was these governing bodies that called for the drafting of state constitutions. New Hampshire's legislature chose a committee of 12 to draft a constitution, which was debated and then ratified in the legislature. In 1775 South Carolina created a provisional congress, made up of members of the legislature, which debated and passed its constitution. The popularly elected Virginia provisional congress appointed a committee to draft a state constitution, which was debated and then ratified. The New Jersey provisional congress debated a constitution and passed it. The elected Delaware general assembly called a special convention to draft a constitution, which the convention ratified. The colonial legislatures of Rhode Island and Connecticut simply declared themselves state legislatures, which adopted the old charters as constitutions. In Pennsylvania the new provisional legislature called for the election of a constitutional convention and, after vigorous debate, the convention ratified the constitution. Maryland's popularly elected provisional congress called itself a convention, wrote a constitution, and ratified it. A North Carolina provisional congress wrote a draft constitution, the new Council of Safety called for the election of a House of Representatives, and the House debated the draft and ratified it. Georgia's popularly elected provisional congress called for the election of a legislature and the legislature drafted, debated, and ratified a constitution. The New York provisional congress called for an election of another congress whose members were to draft, debate, and eventually ratify the state constitution. Massachusetts citizens elected a popular convention to draft a constitution and submit it to the people for ratification. However, in May 1778 the voters turned down that constitution. It wasn't until 1780 that the state sent a new constitution to the people, which they popularly ratified. Thus, only one state constitution (Massachusetts) received formal popular approval, but in most others popularly elected officials voted for their state constitutions.

What kinds of governance did these new states create? Most of the states had adapted a combination of governance structures from the colonial charters, statute laws made from the colonial experience, and struggles over authority that had marked the colonial and revolutionary periods. A number of the new states wrote bills of rights or charters of liberty as preambles to their constitutions. Aware of the relationships between personal rights and social order, the states wanted to spell out personal freedoms. All of the constitutions placed sovereignty or original power in the hands of the electorate and most expanded the number of those eligible to vote. Though some states temporized over suffrage reform, others such as New Hampshire and Pennsylvania eloquently embraced the people's role in making governance legitimate. All clearly defined the duties of the executive or governor and most narrowly structured the powers of that office. Only New York gave the governor similar authority to that of his colonial predecessor. Budget making and taxing powers went to the popularly elected lower houses of representatives. All of the new constitutions created popularly elected bicameral legislatures save Pennsylvania, which structured a single house. Most of the upper houses, or state senates, also were popularly elected. Few of the states made distinctions over who was eligible to serve in the different branches of government. A thorny issue was how to elect members to the Continental Congress. In most states the legislatures originally selected the national officeholders. The judiciary was in a state of development, with some states emphasizing mainly local justices and others preferring state-wide judicial offices. Some states popularly elected judges and others gave their legislatures appointment authority. Local, county, and town governments retained much of their former power.

Because of the disruptions of war, the new needs brought on by peace, and questions about the boundaries of the Western frontier, the states early on debated changes in their first constitutions. For example, Virginia moved the state capital to Richmond, provided for legislative appointment of local judges, and added a court of appeals. Connecticut and New Hampshire wrote acts to regulate appointments to the superior court. New Hampshire held another convention and added a Bill of Rights to its second constitution. South Carolina revised its constitution in 1778, although its governor attempted to stop the changes out of fear of further loss of executive power. Vermont revised its constitution in 1787. Other states changed their election procedures for members of the Continental Congress. Throughout the period, states such as Connecticut and Maryland debated their constitutional authority over western lands. No state more vigorously discussed changes in its constitution than Pennsylvania, but to little avail. What is clear from this sample of constitution writing and revisions is that the states seriously respected their constitutions as governing documents.

New Hampshire, January 5, 1776

New Hampshire wrote and passed its first state constitution seven months before the United States came into being. General John Sullivan's *Plan of Government* had been the principle document for shaping the constitution. The delegates argued over the right of apportionment, with town members quite worried over their representation in the state legislature. After ratification, new discussions led to a convention in 1783 that wrote and passed a second state constitution, adding a Bill of Rights.

GENERAL JOHN SULLIVAN'S *PLAN OF GOVERNMENT*, DECEMBER 11, 1775

DEAR SIR—Though continually involved in those difficulties which necessarily attend a military life, I can by no means forget the duty I owe to that Province whose generous favour I have so largely shared, and whose generous favours I have so often experienced. Being deeply impressed with gratitude to that truly patriotic Colony and fully sensible that the remaining part of my life ought to be devoted to the interests of my country in general, and that Province in particular, I have stolen a few moments from the busy scenes of war to offer you my thoughts upon a matter which I deem essential to the future welfare of my truly spirited and deserving brethren within that Government. I hear that the Continental Congress has given our Province a power to assume government. But the contents of this letter to the Provincial Congress having never transpired, and my friends at the Continental Congress having never informed me but in general terms that we had liberty to assume government, I must conclude that liberty is given to set up and establish a new form of government, for, as we were properly speaking, a King's Government before, the giving us a power to assume government, would be giving us a license to assume a form of government which we could never obtain. Taking it therefore for granted that the Congress have given us liberty to set up that form of government which will best answer the true end and design thereof, I shall beg leave to offer you my thoughts upon the subject, leaving you to make such use thereof as your wisdom shall direct.

And, as my ideas of government may in some measure differ from many others, I shall beg leave to premise some few things. And in the first place must observe, that all governments are, or ought to be, instituted for the good of the people; and that form of government is most perfect when that design is most nearly and effectually answered.

Secondly, That government which admits of contrary or clashing interests, is imperfect, and must work its own ruin whenever one branch has gained a power sufficient to overrule or destroy the other. And the adding a third, with a separate and distinct interest, in imitation of the *British* Constitution, so much celebrated by those who understand nothing of it, is only like two contending powers calling in a third which is unconnected in interest, to keep the other two in awe, till it can gain in power sufficient to destroy them both. And I may almost venture to prophesy, that the period is now at hand when the *British* nation will too late discover the defects in their much boasted Constitution, and the ruin of that empire evince to the world the folly and danger of establishing a government consisting of different branches, whose interests must ever clash with each other.

Third. That no danger can arise to a State from giving the people a free and full voice in their own government. And that, what is called the prerogative of the Crown, or checks upon the licentiousness of the people, are only the children of designing or ambitious men, no such thing being necessary; for, though many States have been overturned by the rage and violence of the people, yet that spirit of rage and violence has ever been awakened in the first place by the misconduct of their rulers. And, though often carried to the most dangerous heights, so far from being owing to too much power being lodged in the hands of the people, that it is clearly owing to their having too small, and their rulers too extensive a power.

Thus we find Rome enjoyed its liberties until their Dictators and others were clothed with power unknown before, at least in that country, and made in some sort independent of the people; and to this authority, so inconsiderately given, should be charged all the tumults at Rome, and the final ruin of that empire. This uncontrollable power, so much sought after by designing men, is made use of to enslave the people, and either bring about that event, or raises the just indignation of the people to extirpate the tyrant thus seeking their ruin. And it sometimes happens that the resentment is so far carried by the fury of an enraged populace as totally to destroy the remains of government, and leave them in a state of anarchy and confusion, and too often have designing persons taken advantage of this confusion and established tyranny in its place.

I am well convinced that people are too fond of their own ease and quiet to rise up in rebellion against government, unless when the tyranny becomes intolerable. And their fondness for government must clearly appear, from their so often submitting to one tyrant after they had extirpated another, rather than live in a state of anarchy and confusion. I would therefore advise to such a form of government as would admit of but one object to be kept in view, both by the governour and governed, viz, the good of the whole, that one interest should unite the several governing branches, and that the frequent choice of the rulers, by the people, should operate as a check upon their conduct and remind them that a new election would soon honour them for their good conduct, or disgrace them for betraying the trust reposed in them.

I by no means object to a Governor, but would have him freely appointed by the people, and dependent upon them, and his appointment not to continue for a long time unless re-elected—at most not exceeding three years, and this appointment to be made by the freeholders in person, and not by their representatives, as that would be putting too dangerous a power in their hands, and possibly a majority of designing men might elect a person to answer their own particular purpose, to the great emolument of those individuals, and the oppression of their fellow-subjects; whereas, we can never suppose the people to have anything but the true end of government, viz; their own good in view, unless we suppose them idiots or self-murderers. I am likewise much in favour of a Council and House of Representatives, but would have them likewise chosen by the people, and by no means for a longer time than three years; and this mode of choosing would effectually destroy that pernicious power distinguishing Governours, to throw aside those persons who they found would not join them in enslaving the people. The late conduct of Bernard and Hutchinson, and the present unhappy state of the Province I am now in, are striking witnesses of the justice of this observation, nor can I see the least reason for a

Governour having a power to negative a Speaker of the House.

I would have some rule established for making that person incapable of holding either of the above offices, that should, either before or after his election, bribe or treat the voters, with intent either to procure an election or reward the electors for having chosen him. Accusation, if against the Governour, to be tried by the two Houses; and if against either of the other members by the Governour and the other members of both Houses, he having a vote equal to any other member. And in case judgment should pass against the new elected Governour, the old one to remain till a new election be had; and in case he be the same person formerly elected, the President of the Council to supply his place till a new election can be made, which President should be appointed by free vote of the members of the Council, at their first meeting. The infamous practice of bribing people, in Great Britain, to sell their votes and consequently their liberty, must show the danger of permitting so dangerous a practice to be instituted under our Constitution, to prevent which, and to guard against the undue influence of persons in power over votes, I would recommend the Pennsylvania method, viz: that every vote should be rolled up, sealed on the back thereof, be noted that it is a vote for a Governour, which should be deposited in a box prepared for that purpose; and a vote for Counsellors and Representatives, sealed up, noted an the back, brought in as aforesaid, and deposited in separate boxes, provided for the purpose. That all voters having once given in their votes, should pass out, and care be taken that they should not come in again, till the voting was over; or, if it be thought more expedient, to let the clerk of the meeting have a perfect list of all votes, with three columns ruled against there names, one marked for a Governour, one for a Representative, and when a person brings in a vote for one, a mark to be made against his name in that column; and if he brings in for all three at the same time, a mark to be made in each column: which I think will effectually prevent any fraud in voting again. The Representatives' box to be examined in meeting,

and the election declared. The votes given for Counsellors and Governour to be sealed up by the clerk, and forwarded by him to the Capital of the Province, where all the votes being had together, a sworn Committee should examine the whole and declare the elections. This method, though it may appear somewhat troublesome, will not turn out so upon trial; and it is the most effectual method to secure the freedom of voting, and prevent every species of fraud and connivance.

Any persons who offer themselves as candidates for any berth may, agreeably to the method practised in Pennsylvania publish their design in newspapers, or communicate it in any other method they may think proper, or leave the people to find out persons of merit and nominate for themselves. All civil officers should be appointed by the three branches, and all military officers by the Governour and Council, and never superceded in commission but by the same power which created them. All laws negatived by a Governour, if revived afterwards, and passed by a new House and Council, to be assented to by him at all events, as it would be unreasonable to suppose two Houses of Representatives and two sets of Counsellors, possessed of less wisdom, or to have less understanding of the true interests of the people, than a single person has, and that after having a long time to think upon the matter, and to consult their constituents thereon.

And here I must beg leave to observe that however high other people's notions of government may run, and however much they may be disposed to worship a creature of their own creation, I can by no means consent to lodging too much power in the hands of one person, or suffering an interest in government to exist separate from that of the people, or any man to hold an office, for the execution of which he is not in some way or other answerable to that people to whom he owes his political existence.

Time will not permit me to go more largely into the subject, but I must leave you to weigh these hints, and make such improvement thereon as your wisdom shall direct; and though my notions of Government are somewhat singular, yet, I think this plan will be an improvement upon the Constitution, by far the happiest I know of. Where I have supposed a defect in that Constitution, I have taken the freedom to borrow from that of Pennsylvania, and other governments, to supply it; and in some instances have added my own thoughts, which if they have the force of reason in them, will have their weight. If they should not appear to be founded on reason, I must beg you to excuse my giving you trouble, as I sincerely aim to promote the welfare of that Colony, to which I wish the most lasting happiness.

And assure yourself that I am, with much esteem

Your most obedient servant,

JOHN SULLIVAN.

Reference: Nathaniel Bouton (comp. and ed.), *Documents and Records Relating to the Province of New-Hampshire*, Vol. VII (Nashua: Orren C. Moore, 1873).

CONSTITUTION, JANUARY 5, 1776

VOTED, That this Congress take up CIVIL GOVERNMENT for this colony in manner and form following, viz.

WE, the members of the Congress of New Hampshire, chosen and appointed by the free suffrages of the people of said colony, and authorized and empowered by them to meet together, and use such means and pursue such measures as we should judge best for the public good; and in particular to establish some form of government, provided that measure should be recommended by the Continental Congress: And a recommendation to that purpose having been transmitted to us from the said Congress: Have taken into our serious consideration the unhappy circumstances, into which this colony is involved by means of many grievous and oppressive acts of the British Parliament, depriving us of our natural and constitutional rights and privileges; to enforce obedience to which acts a powerful fleet and army have been sent to this country by the ministry of Great Britain, who have exercised a wanton and cruel abuse of their power, in destroying the lives and properties of the colonists in many places with fire and sword, taking the ships and lading from many of the honest and industrious inhabitants of this colony employed in commerce, agreeable to the laws and customs a long time used here.

The sudden and abrupt departure of his Excellency John Wentworth, Esq., our late Governor, and several of the Council, leaving us destitute of legislation, and no executive courts being open to punish criminal offenders; whereby the lives and properties of the honest people of this colony are liable to the machinations and evil designs of wicked men, *Therefore*, for the preservation of peace and good order, and for the security of the lives and properties of the inhabitants of this colony, we conceive ourselves reduced to the necessity of establishing A FORM OF GOVERNMENT to continue during the present unhappy and unnatural contest with Great Britain; PROTESTING and DECLARING that we neaver sought to throw off our dependance upon Great Britain, but felt ourselves happy under her protection, while we could enjoy our constitutional rights and privileges. And that we shall rejoice if such a reconciliation between us and our parent State can be effected as shall be approved by the CONTINENTAL CONGRESS, in whose prudence and wisdom we confide.

Accordingly pursuant to the trust reposed in us, WE DO RESOLVE, that this Congress assume the name, power and authority of a house of Representatives or Assembly for the *Colony of New-Hampshire*. And that said House then proceed to choose twelve persons, being reputable freeholders and inhabitants within this colony, in the following manner, viz. five in the county of Rockingham, two in the county of Strafford, two in the county of Hillsborough, two in the county of Cheshire, and one in the county of Grafton, to be a distinct and separate branch of the Legislature by the name of a COUNCIL for this colony, to continue as such until the third Wednesday in December next; any seven of whom to be a quorum to do business. That such Council appoint their President, and in his absence that the senior counsellor preside; that a Secretary be appointed by both branches, who may be a counssellor, or otherwise, as they shall choose.

That no act or resolve shall be valid and put into execution unless agreed to, and passed by both branches of the legislature.

That all public officers for the said colony, and each county, for the current year, be appointed by the Council and Assembly, except the several clerks of the Executive Courts, who shall be appointed by the Justices of the respective Courts.

That all bills, resolves, or votes for raising, levying and collecting money originate in the house of Representatives.

That at any session of the Council and Assembly neither branch shall adjourn from any longer time than from Saturday till the next Monday without consent of the other.

And it is further resolved, That if the present unhappy dispute with Great Britain should continue longer than this present year, and the Continental Congress give no instruction or direction to the contrary, the Council be chosen by the people of each respective county in such manner as the Council and house of Representatives shall order.

That general and field officers of the militia, on any vacancy, be appointed by the two houses, and all inferior officers be chosen by the respective companies.

That all officers of the Army be appointed by the two houses, except they should direct otherwise in case of any emergency.

That all civil officers for the colony and for each county be appointed, and the time of their continuance in office be determined by the two houses, except clerks of Courts, and county treasurers, and recorders of deeds.

That a treasurer, and a recorder of deeds for each county be annually chosen by the people of each county respectively; the votes for such officers to be returned to the respective courts of General Sessions of the Peace in the county, there to be ascertained as the Council and Assembly shall hereafter direct.

That precepts in the name of the Council and Assembly, signed by the President of the Council, and Speaker of the house of Representatives, shall issue annually at or before the first day of November, for the choice of a Council and house of Representatives to be returned by the third Wednesday in December then next ensuing, in such manner as the Council and Assembly shall hereafter prescribe.

Reference: Francis Newton Thorpe (ed.), *The Federal and State Constitutions, Colonial Charters, and Other Organic Laws of the States*, Vol. IV (Washington: GPO, 1909).

TO THE FREEHOLDERS AND INHABITANTS OF NEW HAMPSHIRE, JANUARY 30, 1777

. . . We proceed to observe that the declaration of independency made the antecedent form of government to be of necessity null and void; and by that act the people of the different colonies slid back into a state of nature, and in that condition they were to begin anew. But has it been so in the government of New Hampshire? I ask how shall we know that independency has been proclaimed, if we only consult the civil economy of this state? In fact, we have no other sign of it but the bare declaration of the Congress. I ask again, what advantage independency has been of to this government, since it had the same legislature before as after the declaration? Think on these matters; and though it is now late, yet that very consideration proves the necessity of dissolving soon the present unconstitutional legislature, and planting the seed anew.

But if it be still asserted that the legislative constitution is founded on independency, it will prove, if anything, that this very constitution established independency itself, before it was proclaimed by the congress. All power originates from the people. A state of independency before a plan of government is formed, supposes the whole right to be vested in them who by a full representation are to rear a new fabric. But it has not been so in the present case, for this very assembly, which was in being before the declaration of independency, has dictated the regulations that took place afterwards. The grossest absurdity, which will appear in one word, [is], viz., the legislature over the people before independency was unconstitutional and deprived them of their rights, yet this very unconstitutional legislature has marked out their liberties for them in the state of independency. As much as to say, an unconstitutional body have made a constitutional one. Would to God that you might carefully weigh these matters, and that every one would measure them by the feelings in his own mind!

There has been for some time a dispute among you as to the right of each incorporated town to a distinct representation. But that it is just seems so plain from the nature of the thing and what has been wrote upon the subject, that there remains but little room for objection. The chief argument now made use of is that if every small incorporated town is represented distinctly, it will be a great expense to the people. The absurdity of this will appear in a few words. . . .

Should any, in the character of a Committee or otherwise, endeavor to compound matters with the people in the aggrieved towns, as an impartial writer I conjure you strenuously to adhere to these two important articles:

1. That you give not up an ace of the rights that the *smallest* town has to a distinct representation, if incorporated—the bare number of individuals being, in this case, out of the question.

2ndly. That as the present assembly is unconstitutional, being the same, virtually, as before the declaration of independency, they do dissolve themselves, after having notified each corporate town to form a new body that may fix on a plan of government, which can be the only proper seal of your concurrence in independency. Thus you will act a consistent part, and secure your palace from being pilfered within while you are filling up the breaches that are made without.

Reference: Frederick Chase, *History of Dartmouth College*, Vol. I (Cambridge, MA: J. Wilson, 1891–1913), 431–433.

SECOND CONSTITUTION, CONTAINING A BILL OF RIGHTS AND FORM OF GOVERNMENT, OCTOBER 31, 1783

Agreed upon by the Delegates of the people of the State of New Hampshire, in Convention, held at Concord, on the first Tuesday of June, 1783; submitted to, and approved of, by the people of said State; and established by their Delegates in Convention, October 31, 1783.

PART I

THE BILL OF RIGHTS

ARTICLE I

All men are born equally free and independent; therefore, all government of right originates from the people, is founded in consent, and instituted for the general good.

II. All men have certain natural, essential, and inherent rights; among which are the enjoying and defending life and liberty—acquiring, possessing and protecting property—and in a word, of seeking and obtaining happiness.

III. When men enter into a state of society, they surrender up some of their natural rights to that society, in order to insure the protection of others; and, without such an equivelant, the surrender is void.

IV. Among the natural rights, some are in their very nature unalienable, because no equivelant can be given or received for them. Of this kind are the Rights of Conscience.

V. Every individual has a natural and unalienable right to worship God according to the dictates of his own conscience, and reason; and no subject shall be hurt, molested, or restrained in his person, liberty or estate for worshipping God in the manner and season most agreeable to the dictates of his own conscience, or for his religious profession, sentiments or persuasion; provided he doth not disturb the public peace, or disturb others in their religious worship.

VI. As morality and piety, rightly grounded on evangelical principles, will give the best and greatest security to government, and will lay in the hearts of men the strongest obligations to due subjection; and as the knowledge of these, is most likely to be propagated through a society by the institution of the public worship of the Deity, and of public instruction in morality and religion; therefore, to promote those important purposes, the people of this state have a right to empower, and do hereby fully empower the legislature to authorize from time to time, the several towns, parishes bodies-corporate, or religious societies within this state, to make adequate provision at their own expense, for the support and maintenance of public protestant teachers of piety, religion and morality:

Provided notwithstanding, That the several towns, parishes, bodies corporate, or religious societies, shall at all times have the exclusive right of electing their own public teachers, and of contracting with them for their support and maintenance. And no portion of any one particular religious sect or denomination, shall ever be compelled to pay towards the support of the teacher or teachers of another persuasion, sect or denomination.

And every denomination of christians demeaning themselves quietly, and as good subjects of the State, shall be equally under the protection of the law: and no subordination of any one sect or denomination to another, shall ever be established by law.

And nothing herein shall be understood to affect any former contracts made for the support of the ministry; but all such contracts shall remain, and be in the same state as if this constitution had not been made.

VII. The people of this State, have the sole and exclusive right of governing themselves as a free, sovereign and independent State, and do, and forever hereafter shall exercise, and enjoy every power, jurisdiction and right pertaining thereto, which is not, or may not hereafter be by them expressly delegated to the United States of America in Congress assembled.

VIII. All power residing originally in, and being derived from the people, all the magistrates and officers of government, are their substitutes and agents, and at all times accountable to them.

IX. No office or place whatsoever in government, shall be hereditary—the abilities and integrity requisite in all, not being transmissible to posterity or relations.

X. Government being instituted for the common benefit, protection, and security of the whole community, and not for the private interest or emolument of any one man, family or class of men; therefore, whenever the ends of government are perverted, and public liberty manifestly endangered, and all other means of redress are ineffectual, the people may, and of right ought, to reform the old, or establish a new government. The doctrine of non-resistance against arbitrary power, and oppression, is absurd; slavish, and destructive of the good and happiness of mankind.

XI. All elections ought to be free, and every inhabitant of the State having the proper qualifications, has equal right to elect, and be elected into office.

XII. Every member of the community has a right to be protected by it in the enjoyment of his life, liberty and property; he is therefore bound to contribute his share in the expense of such protection, and to yield his personal service when necessary, or an equivelent. But no part of a man's property shall be taken from him, or applied to public uses, without his own consent, or that of the representative body of the people. Nor are the inhabitants of this State controllable by any other laws than those to which they, or their representative body have given their consent.

XIII. No person who is conscientiously scrupulous about the lawfulness of bearing arms, shall be compelled thereto, provided he will pay an equivelent.

XIV. Every subject of this State is entitled to a certain remedy, by having recourse to the laws, for all injuries he may receive in his person, property or character, to obtain right and justice freely, without being obliged to purchase it; completely, and without any denial; promptly, and without delay, conformably to the laws.

XV. No subject shall be held to answer for any crime, or offence, until the same is fully and plainly, substantially and formally described to him; or be compelled to accuse or furnish evidence against himself. And every subject shall have a right to produce all proofs that may be favorable to himself: To meet the witnesses against him face to face, and to be fully heard in his defence by himself and counsel. And no subject shall be arrested, imprisoned, despoiled, or deprived of his property, immunities, or privileges, put out of the protection of the law, exiled or deprived of his life, liberty, or estate, but by the judgment of his peers or the law of the land.

XVI. No subject shall be liable to be tried, after an acquittal, for the same crime or offence.—Nor shall the legislature make any law that shall subject any person to a capital punishment, excepting for the government of the army and navy, and the militia in actual service, without trial by jury.

XVII. In criminal prosecutions, the trial of facts in the vicinity where they happen, is so essential to the security of the life, liberty, and estate of the citizen, that no crime or offence ought to be tried in any other county than that in which it is committed; except in cases of general insurrection in any particular county, when it shall appear to the judges of the superior-court, that an impartial trial cannot be had in the county where the offence may be committed, and upon their report, the assembly shall think proper to direct the trial in the nearest county in which an impartial trial can be obtained.

XVIII. All penalties ought to be proportioned to the nature of the offence. No wise legislature will affix the same punishment to the crimes of theft, forgery, and the like, which they do to those of murder and treason; where the same undistinguishing severity is exerted against all offences, the people are led to forget the real distinction in the crimes themselves, and to commit the most flagrant with as little compunction as they do those of the lightest dye. For the same reason a multitude of sanguinary laws is both impolitic and unjust. The true design of all punishments being to reform, not to exterminate mankind.

XIX. Every subject hath a right to be secure from all unreasonable searches and seizures of his person, his houses, his papers, and all his possessions. All warrants, therefore, are contrary to this right, if the cause or foundation of them be not previously supported by oath, or affirmation; and if the order in the warrant to a civil officer, to make search in suspected places, or to arrest one or more suspected persons, or to seize their property, be not accompanied with a special designation of the persons or objects of search, arrest or seizure; and no warrant ought to be issued but in cases, and with the formalities prescribed by the laws.

XX. In all controversies concerning property, and in all suits between two or more persons, except in cases in which it has been heretofore otherwise used and practised, the parties have a right to a trial by jury; and this method of procedure shall be held sacred, unless in causes arising on the high seas, and such as relate to mariners wages, the legislature shall think it necessary hereafter to alter it.

XXI. In order to reap the fullest advantage of the inestimable privilege of the trial by jury, great care ought to be taken that none but qualified persons should be appointed to serve; and such ought to be fully compensated for their travel, time and attendance.

XXII. The Liberty of the press is essential to the security of freedom in a State; it ought, therefore, to be inviolably preserved.

XXIII. Retrospective laws are highly injurious, oppressive and unjust. No such laws, therefore, should be made, either for the decision of civil causes, or the punishment of offences.

XXIV. A well regulated militia is the proper, natural, and sure defence of a State.

XXV. Standing armies are dangerous to liberty, and ought not to be raised or kept up without the consent of the legislature.

XXVI. In all cases, and at all times, the military ought to be under strict subordination to, and governed by the civil power.

XXVII. No soldier in time of peace, shall be quartered in any house without the consent of the owner; and in time of war, such quarters ought not to be made but by the civil magistrate, in a manner ordained by the legislature.

XXVIII. No subsidy, charge, tax, impost or duty shall be established, fixed, laid or levied, under any pretext whatsoever, without the consent of the people, or their representatives in the legislature, or authority derived from that body.

XXIX. The power of suspending the laws, or the execution of them, ought never to be exercised but by the legislature, or by authority derived therefrom, to be exercised in such particular cases only as the legislature shall expressly provide for.

XXX. The freedom of deliberation, speech, and debate, in either house of the legislature, is so essential to the rights of the people, that it cannot be the foundation of any action, complaint, or prosecution, in any other court or place whatsoever.

XXXI. The legislature ought frequently to assemble for the redress of grievances, for correcting, strengthening and confirming the laws, and for making new ones, as the common good may require.

XXXII. The people have a right in an orderly and peaceable manner, to assemble and consult upon the common good, give instructions to their representatives; and to request of the legislative body, by way of petition or remonstrance, redress of the wrongs done them, and of the grievances they suffer.

XXXIII. No magistrate or court of law shall demand excessive bail or sureties, impose excessive fines, or inflict cruel or unusual punishments.

XXXIV. No person can in any case be subjected to law martial, or to any pains, or penalties, by virtue of that law, except those employed in the army or navy, and except the militia in actual service, but by authority of the legislature.

XXXV. It is essential to the preservation of the rights of every individual, his life, liberty, property and character, that there be an impartial interpretation of the laws, and administration of justice. It is the right of every citizen to be tried by judges as impartial as the lot of humanity will admit. It is therefore not only the best policy, but for the security of the rights of the people, that the judges of the supreme (or superior) judicial court should hold their offices so long as they behave well; and that they should have honorable salaries, ascertained and established by standing laws.

XXXVI. Economy being a most essential virtue in all States, especially in a young one; no pension shall be granted, but in consideration of actual services, and such pensions ought to be granted with great caution by the legislature, and never for more than one year at a time.

XXXVII. In the government of this State, the three essential powers thereof, to wit, the legislative, executive and judicial, ought to be kept as separate from, and independent of each other, as the nature of a free government will admit, or as is consistent with that chain of connexion that binds the whole fabric of the constitution in one indissoluble bond of union and amity.

XXXVIII. A frequent recurrence to the fundamental principles of the constitution, and a constant adherence to justice, moderation, temperance, industry, frugality, and all the social virtues, are indispensably necessary to preserve the blessings of liberty and good government; the people ought, therefore, to have a particular regard to all those principles in the choice of their officers and representatives: And they have a right to require of their law-givers and magistrates, an exact and constant observance of them in the formation and execution of the laws necessary for the good administration of government.

Part II

The Form of Government

The people inhabiting the territory formerly called the Province of New Hampshire, do hereby solemnly and mutually agree with each other, to form themselves into a free, sovereign, and independent Body-politic, or State, by the name of the State of New Hampshire.

The General Court

The supreme legislative power within this State shall be vested in the senate and house of representatives, each of which shall have a negative on the other.

The senate and house shall assemble every year on the first Wednesday of June, and at such other times as they may judge necessary; and shall dissolve, and be dissolved, seven days next preceding the said first Wednesday of June; and shall be stiled The General Court of New Hampshire.

The general court shall forever have full power and authority to erect and constitute judicatories and courts of record, or other courts, to be holden in the name of the State, for the hearing, trying and determining all manner of crimes, offences, pleas, processes, plaints, actions, causes, matters and things whatsoever, arising, or happening within this State, or between or concerning persons inhabiting or residing, or brought within the same, whether the same be criminal or civil, or whether the crimes be capital, or not capital, and whether the said pleas be real, personal, or mixed; and for the awarding and issuing execution thereon. To which courts and judicatories are hereby given and granted full power and authority, from time to time to administer oaths or affirmations, for the better discovery of truth in any matter in controversy, or depending before them.

And farther, full power and authority are hereby given and granted to the said general-court, from time to time, to make, ordain and establish all manner of wholesome and reasonable orders, laws, statutes, ordinances, directions and instructions, either with penalties or without; so as the same be not repugnant, or contrary to this constitution, as they may judge for the benefit and welfare of this State, and for the governing and ordering thereof, and of the subjects of the same, for the necessary support and defence of the government thereof; and to name and settle annually, or provide by fixed laws, for the naming and settling all civil officers within this State; such officers excepted, the election and appointment of whom, are hereafter in this form of government otherwise provided for; and to set forth the several duties, powers and limits of the several civil and military officers of this State, and the forms of such oaths or affirmations, as shall be respectively administered unto them for the execution of their several offices and places, so as the same be not repugnant or contrary to this constitution; and also to impose fines, mulcts, imprisonments and other punishments; and to impose and levy proportional and reasonable assessments, rates and taxes, upon all the inhabitants of, and residents within the said State, and upon all estates within the same; to be issued and disposed of by warrant under the hand of the president of this State for the time being, with the advice and consent of the council, for the public service, in the necessary defence and support of the government of this State, and the protection and preservation of the subjects thereof, according to such acts as are, or shall be in force within the same.

And while the public charges of government, or any part thereof, shall be assessed on polls and estates in the manner that has heretofore been practiced; in order that such assessments may be made with equality, there shall be a valuation of the estates within the State taken anew once in every five years at least, and as much oftener as the general-court shall order.

Senate

THERE shall be annually elected by the freeholders and other inhabitants of this State, qualified as in this constitution is provided, twelve persons to be senators for the year ensuing their election; to be chosen in and by the inhabitants of the districts, into which this State may from time to time be divided by the general-court, for that purpose; And the general-court in assigning the number to be elected by the respective districts, shall govern themselves by the proportion of public taxes paid by the said districts; and timely make known to the inhabitants of the State, the limits of each district, and the number of senators to be elected therein; provided the number of such districts shall never be more than ten, nor less than five.

And the several counties in this State, shall, until the general-court shall order otherwise, be districts for the election of senators, and shall elect the following number, viz; Rockingham, five.—Strafford, two.—Hillsborough, two.—Cheshire, two.—Grafton, one.

The senate shall be the first branch of the legislature: And the senators shall be chosen in the following manner, viz.—Every male inhabitant of each town and parish with town privileges in the several counties in this State, of twenty-one years of age and upwards, paying for himself a poll tax, shall have a right at the annual or other meetings of the inhabitants of said towns and parishes, to be duly warned and holden annually forever in the month of March, to vote in the town or parish wherein he dwells, for the senators in the county or district whereof he is a member.

And every person qualified as the constitution provides, shall be considered an inhabitant for the purpose of electing and being elected into any office or place within this State, in that town, parish and plantation where he dwelleth and hath his home.

The selectmen of the several towns and parishes aforesaid, shall, during the choice of senators, preside at such meetings impartially, and shall receive the votes of all the inhabitants of such towns and parishes present and qualified to vote for senators, and shall sort and count the same in the meeting, and in presence of the town-clerk, who shall make a fair record in presence of the selectmen, and in open meeting, of the name of every person voted for, and the number of votes against his name; and a fair copy of this record shall be attested by the selectmen and town-clerk, and shall be sealed up and directed to the secretary of the State, with a superscription expressing the purport thereof, and delivered by said clerk to the sheriff of the county in which such town or parish lies, thirty days at least, before the first Wednesday of June; and the sheriff of each county, or his deputy, shall deliver all such certificates by him received, into the secretary's office, seventeen days at least, before the first Wednesday of June.

And the inhabitants of plantations and places unincorporated, qualified as this constitution provides, who are or shall be required to assess taxes upon themselves towards the support of government, or shall be taxed therefor, shall have the same privilege of voting for senators in the plantations and places wherein they reside, as the inhabitants of the respective towns and parishes aforesaid have. And the meetings of such plantations and places for that purpose, shall be holden annually in the month of March, at such places respectively therein, as the assessors thereof shall direct: Which assessors shall have like authority for notifying the electors, collecting and returning the votes, as the selectmen and town-clerks have in their several towns by this constitution.

And that there may be a due meeting of senators on the first Wednesday of June, annually, the president and three of the council for the time being, shall as soon as may, examine the returned copies of such records; and fourteen days before the said first Wednesday of June, he shall issue his summons to such persons as appear to be chosen senators by a majority of votes, to attend and take their seats on that day: *Provided nevertheless,* That for the first year the said returned copies shall be examined by the president and five of the council of the former constitution of government; and the said president shall in like manner notify the persons elected, to attend and take their seats accordingly.

The senate shall be final judges of the elections, returns, and qualifications of their own members, as pointed out in this constitution, and shall on the said first Wednesday of June annually, determine and declare, who are elected by each district to be senators by a majority of votes: and in case there shall not appear to be the full number returned elected by a majority of votes for any district, the deficiency shall be supplied in the following manner, viz. The members of the house of representatives and such senators as shall be declared elected, shall take the names of such persons as shall be found to have the highest number of votes in each district, and not elected, amounting to twice the number of senators wanting, if there be so many voted for; and out of these shall elect by joint ballot the number of senators wanted for such district: and in this manner all such vacancies shall be filled up in every district of the State, and in like manner all vacancies in the senate, arising by death, removal out of the State, or otherwise, shall be supplied as soon as may be after such vacancies happen.

Provided nevertheless, That no person shall be capable of being elected a senator, who is not of the protestant religion, and seized of a freehold estate in his own right, of the value of *two hundred pounds,* lying within this State, who is not of the age of thirty years, and who shall not have been an inhabitant of this State for seven years immediately preceding his election; and at the time thereof he shall be an inhabitant of the district for which he shall be chosen.

The senate shall have power to adjourn themselves, provided such adjournment do not exceed two days at a time.

The senate shall appoint their own officers, and determine their own rules of proceedings. And not less than seven members of the senate shall make a quorum for doing business; and when less than eight senators shall be present, the assent of five, at least, shall be necessary to render their acts and proceedings valid.

The senate shall be a court with full power and authority to hear and determine all impeachments made by the house of representatives, against any officer or officers of the State, for misconduct or mal-administration in their offices. But previous to the trial of any such impeachment, the members of the senate shall respectively be sworn, truly and impartially to try and determine the charge in question according to evidence. Their judgment, however shall not extend farther than removal from office, disqualification to hold or enjoy any place of honor, trust or profit under this State; but the party so convicted, shall nevertheless be liable to indictment, trial, judgment, and punishment, according to the laws of the land.

House Of Representatives

There shall be in the legislature of this State, a representation of the people annually elected and founded upon principles of equality:—and in order that such representation may be as equal as circumstances will admit, every town, parish, or place, entitled to town privileges, having one hundred and fifty rateable male polls, of twenty-one years of age, and upwards, may elect one representative; if four hundred and fifty rateable polls, may elect two representatives; and so proceeding in that proportion, making three hundred such rateable polls the mean increasing number for every additional representative.

Such towns, parishes or places as have less than one hundred and fifty rateable polls, shall be classed by the general-assembly, for the purpose of chusing a representative, and seasonably notified thereof. And in every class formed for the above-mentioned purpose, the first annual meeting shall be held in the town, parish, or place wherein most of the rateable polls reside; and afterwards in that which has the next highest number, and so on annually by rotation, through the several towns, parishes, or places, forming the district.

Whenever any town, parish, or place entitled to town privileges as aforesaid, shall not have one hundred and fifty rateable polls, and be so situated as to render the classing thereof with any other town, parish or place very inconvenient, the general-assembly may upon application of a majority of the voters in such town, parish, or place, issue a writ for their electing and sending a representative to the general-court.

The members of the house of representatives shall be chosen annually in the month of March, and shall be the second branch of the legislature.

All persons qualified to vote in the election of senators, shall be entitled to vote within the town, district, parish or place where they dwell, in the choice of representatives. Every member of the house of representatives shall be chosen by ballot; and for two years at least next preceding his election, shall have been an inhabitant of this State, shall have an estate within the town, parish or place which he may be chosen to represent, of the value of *one hundred pounds,* one half of which to be a free-hold, whereof he is seized in his own right; shall be at the time of his election, an inhabitant of the town, parish, or place he may be chosen to represent; shall be of the protestant religion, and shall cease to represent such town, parish, or place immediately on his ceasing to be qualified as aforesaid.

The travel of each representative to the general-assembly, and returning home, once in every session, and no more, shall be at the expense of the State, and the wages for his attendance, at the expense of the town, parish, or places he represents; such members attending seasonably and not departing without licence. All intermediate vacancies in the house of representatives, may be filled up from time to time, in the same manner as annual elections are made.

The house of representatives shall be the grand inquest of the State, and all impeachments made by them, shall be heard and tried by the Senate.

All money bills shall originate in the house of representatives, but the senate may propose or concur with amendments as on other bills.

The house of representatives shall have power to adjourn themselves, but no longer than two days at a time.

A majority of the members of the house of representatives shall be a quorum for doing business: But when less than two thirds of the representatives elected shall be present, the assent of two thirds of those members shall be necessary to render their acts and proceedings valid.

No member of the house of representatives or senate, shall be arrested or held to bail on mean process, during his going to, returning from or attendance upon the court.

The house of representatives shall choose their own speaker, appoint their own officers, and settle the rules of proceedings in their own house. They shall have authority to punish by imprisonment, every person who shall be guilty of disrespect to the house in its presence, by any disorderly and contemptuous behavior, or by threatening, or ill treating any of its members; or by obstructing its deliberations; every person guilty of a breach of its privileges in making arrests for debt, or by assaulting any member during his attendance at any session; in assaulting or disturbing any one of its officers in the execution of any order or procedure of the house, in assaulting any witness, or other person, ordered to attend by and during his attendance of the house, or in rescuing any person arrested by order of the house, knowing them to be such. The senate, president and council, shall have the same powers in like cases; provided that no imprisonment by either, for any offence, exceed ten days.

The journals of the proceedings of both houses of the general-court shall be printed and published, immediately after every adjournment, or prorogation; and upon motion made by any one member, the yeas and nays upon any question, shall be taken and entered in the journals.

Executive Power

President

THERE shall be a supreme executive magistrate, who shall be stiled, THE PRESIDENT OF THE STATE OF NEW HAMPSHIRE; and whose title shall be HIS EXCELLENCY.

The PRESIDENT shall be chosen annually; and no person shall be eligible to this office, unless at the time of his election, he shall have been an inhabitant of this State for seven years next preceding, and unless he shall be of the age of thirty years; and unless he shall at the same time, have an estate of the value of *five hundred pounds,* one half of which shall consist of a freehold in his own right within the State; and unless he shall be of the protestant religion.

Those persons qualified to vote for senators and representatives shall within the several towns, parishes or places, where they dwell, at a meeting to be called for that purpose, some day in the month of March, annually, give in their votes for a president to the selectmen, who shall preside at such meeting, and the clerk in the presence and with the assistance of the selectmen, shall in open meeting sort and count the votes, and form a list of the persons voted for, with the number of votes for each person against his name, and shall make a fair record of the same in the town books, and a public declaration thereof in the said meeting; and shall in the presence of said inhabitants, seal up a copy of said list attested by him and the selectmen, and transmit the same to the sheriff of the county, thirty days at least before the first Wednesday of June, or shall cause returns of the same to be made to the office of the secretary of the State seventeen days at least, before said day, who shall lay the same before the senate and house of representatives on the first Wednesday of June, to be by them examined; and in case of an election by a majority of votes through the State, the choice shall be by them declared, and published: But if no person shall have a majority of votes, the house of representatives shall by ballot elect two out of four persons who had the highest number of votes, if so many shall have been voted for; but if otherwise, out of the number voted for; and make return to the senate of the two persons so elected, on which the senate shall proceed by ballot to elect one of them, who shall be declared president.

The president of the State shall preside in the senate, shall have a vote equal with any other member; and shall also have a casting vote in case of a tie.

The president with advice of council, shall have full power and authority in the recess of the general-court, to prorogue the same from time to time, not exceeding ninety days in any one recess of said court; and during the session of said court, to adjourn or prorogue it to any time the two houses may desire, and to call it together sooner than the time to which it may be adjourned, or prorogued, if the welfare of the State should require the same.

In cases of disagreement between the two houses, with regard to the time of adjournment, or prorogation, the president with advice of council, shall have a right to adjourn or prorogue the general-court, not exceeding ninety days, at any one time, as he may determine the public good may require. And he shall dissolve the same seven days before the said first Wednesday of June. And in case of any infectious distemper prevailing in the place where the said court at any time is to convene, or any other cause whereby dangers may arise to the healths or lives of the members, from their attendance, the president may direct the session to be holden at some other the most convenient place within the State.

The president of this State for the time being, shall be commander in chief of the army and navy, and all the military forces of the State by sea and land; and shall have full power by himself, or by any chief commander, or other officer or officers, from time to time, to train, instruct, exercise and govern the militia and navy; and for the special defence and safety of this State, to assemble in martial array, and put in warlike posture, the inhabitants thereof, and to lead and conduct them, and with them to encounter, expulse, repel, resist and pursue by force of arms, as well by sea as by land, within and without the limits of this State, and also to kill, slay, destroy, if necessary, and conquer by all fitting ways, enterprize and means, all and every such person and persons as shall, at any time hereafter, in a hostile manner attempt or enterprize the destruction, invasion, detriment, or annoyance of this State; and to use and exercise over the army and navy, and over the militia in actual service, the law-martial in time of war, invasion, and also in rebellion, declared by the legislature to exist, as occasion shall necessarily require: And surprize by all ways and means whatsoever, all and every such person or persons, with their ships, arms, ammunition, and other goods, as shall in a hostile manner invade, or attempt the invading, conquering, or annoying this State: And in fine, the president hereby is intrusted with all other powers incident to the office of captain-general and commander in chief, and admiral, to be exercised agreeably to the rules and regulations of the constitution, and the laws of the land: Provided that the president shall not at any time hereafter, by virtue of any power by this constitution granted, or hereafter to be granted to him by the legislature, transport any of the inhabitants of this State, or oblige them to march out of the limits of the same, without their free and voluntary consent, or the consent of the general-court, nor grant commissions for exercising the law-martial in any case, without the advice and consent of the council.

The power of pardoning offences, except such as persons may be convicted of before the senate by impeachment of the house, shall be in the president, by and with the advice of the council: but no charter of pardon granted by the president with advice of council, before conviction, shall avail the party pleading the same, notwith-standing any general or particular expressions contained therein, descriptive of the offence or offences intended to be pardoned.

All judicial officers, the attorney-general, solicitor-general, all sheriffs, coroners, registers of probate, and all officers of the navy and general and field-officers of the militia, shall be nominated and appointed by the president and council; and every such nomination shall be made at least seven days prior to such appointment, and no appointment shall take place, unless three of the council agree thereto. The captains and subalterns in the respective regiments shall be nominated and recommended by the field-officers to the president, who is to issue their commissions immediately on receipt of such recommendation.

No officer duly commissioned to command in the militia, shall be removed from his office, but by the address of both houses to the president, or by fair trial in court-martial, pursuant to the laws of the State for the time being.

The commanding officers of the regiments shall appoint their adjutants and quarter-masters; the brigadiers their brigade majors, the major-generals their aids; the captains and subalterns their non-commissioned officers.

The president and council shall appoint all officers of the continental army, whom by the confederation of the United States it is provided that this State shall appoint, as also all officers of forts and garrisons.

The division of the militia into brigades, regiments and companies, made in pursuance of the militia laws now in force, shall be considered as the proper division of the militia of this State, until the same shall be altered by some future law.

No monies shall be issued out of the treasury of this State, and disposed of (except such sums as may be appropriated for the redemption of bills of credit or treasurers' notes, or for the payment of interest arising thereon) but by warrant under the hand of the president for the time being, by and with the advice and consent of the council, for the necessary support and defence of this State, and for the necessary protection and preservation of the inhabitants thereof, agreeably to the acts and resolves of the general-court.

All public boards, the commissary-general, all superintending officers of public magazines and stores, belonging to this State, and all commanding officers of forts and garrisons within the same, shall once in every three months, officially, and without requisition, and at other times, when required by the president. deliver to him an account of all goods, stores, provisions, ammunition, cannon with their appendages, and small arms with their accoutrements, and of all other public property under their care respectively; distinguishing the quantity, and kind of each as particularly as may be; together with the condition of such forts and garrisons; and the commanding officer shall exhibit to the president, when required by him, true and exact plans of such forts, and of the land and sea, or harbour or harbours adjacent.

The president and council shall be compensated for their services from time to time by such grants as the general-court shall think reasonable.

Permanent and honorable salaries shall be established by law for the justices of the superior-court.

Whenever the chair of the president shall be vacant, by reason of his death, absence from the State, or otherwise, the senior senator for the time being, shall, during such vacancy, have and exercise all the powers and authorities which by this constitution the president is vested with when personally present.

Council

Annually on the first meeting of the general-court, two members of the senate and three from the house of representatives, shall be chosen by joint ballot of both houses as a council, for advising the president in the executive part of government, whom the president for the time being, shall have full power and authority to convene from time to time, at his discretion, and the president with the counsellors, or three of them at least, shall and may from time to time hold and keep a council, for ordering and directing the affairs of the State according to the laws of the land.

The qualifications for counsellors, shall be the same as those required for senators. The members of the council shall not intermeddle with the making or trying impeachments, but shall themselves be impeachable by the house, and triable by the senate for mal-conduct.

The resolutions and advice of the council shall be recorded in a register, and signed by the members present, and this record may be called for at any time, by either house of the legislature, and any member of the council may enter his opinion contrary to the resolution of the majority.

And whereas the elections appointed to be made by this constitution on the first Wednesday of June annually, by the two houses of the legislature, may not be completed on that day, the said elections may be adjourned from day to day until the same shall be completed. And the order of the elections shall be as follows: The vacancies in the senate, if any, shall be first filled up; the president shall then be elected, provided there should be no choice of him by the people, and afterwards the two houses shall proceed to the election of the council.

Secretary, Treasurer, Commissary-General, &c

The secretary, treasurer, and commissary-general, shall be chosen by joint ballot of the senators and representatives assembled in one room.

The records of the State shall be kept in the office of the secretary, who may appoint his deputies, for whose conduct he shall be answerable, and he shall attend the president and council, the senate and representatives, in person or by deputy, as they may require.

County-Treasurer, &c

THE county-treasurers, and registers of deeds shall be elected by the inhabitants of the several towns, in the several counties in the State according to the method now practised, and the present laws of the State; and before they enter upon the business of their offices, shall be respectively sworn faithfully to discharge the duties thereof, and shall severally give bond with sufficient sureties, in a reasonable sum for the use of the county,

for the punctual performance of their respective trusts.

Judiciary Power

THE tenure that all commission officers shall have by law in their offices, shall be expressed in their respective commissions. All judicial officers, duly appointed, commissioned and sworn, shall hold their offices during good behavior, excepting those concerning whom there is a different provision made in this constitution: *Provided nevertheless*, The president, with consent of council, may remove them upon the address of both houses of the legislature.

Each branch of the legislature, as well as the president and council, shall have authority to require the opinions of the justices of the superior court upon important questions of law, and upon solemn occasions.

In order that the people may not suffer from the long continuance in place of any justice of the peace, who shall fail in discharging the important duties of his office with ability and fidelity, all commissions of justices of the peace shall become void, at the expiration of five years from their respective dates; and upon the expiration of any commission, the same may, if necessary be renewed, or another person appointed, as shall most conduce to the well-being of the State. The judges of probate of wills, and for granting letters of administration, shall hold their courts at such place or places, on such fixed days, as the convenience of the people may require. And the legislature shall, from time to time, hereafter appoint such times and places, until which appointments, the said courts shall be holden at the times and places which the respective judges shall direct.

All causes of marriage, divorce and alimony, and all appeals from the respective judges of probate, shall be heard and tried by the superior-court, until the legislature shall by law make other provision.

Clerks of Courts

THE clerks of the superior-court of judicature, inferior courts of common pleas, and general sessions of the peace, shall be appointed by the respective courts during pleasure. And to prevent any fraud or unfairness in the entries and records of said courts, no such clerk shall be of counsel in any cause in the court of which he is clerk, nor shall he fill any writ in any civil action whatsoever.

Delegates to Congress

THE delegates of this State to the congress of the United States, shall some time between the first Wednesday of June, and the first Wednesday of September annually, be elected by the senate and house of representatives in their separate branches, to serve in congress for one year, to commence on the first Monday in November then next ensuing. They shall have commissions under the hand of the president, and the great seal of the state; but may be recalled at any time within the year, and others chosen and commissioned, in the same manner, in their stead; and they shall have the same qualifications, in all respects, as by this constitution are required for the president.

No person shall be capable of being a delegate to congress for more than three years in any term of six years; nor shall any person being a delegate, be capable of holding any office under the United States, for which he, or any other for his benefit, receives any salary, or emolument of any kind.

Encouragement of Literature, &c

KNOWLEDGE and learning, generally diffused through a community, being essential to the preservation of a free government; and spreading the opportunities and advantages of education through the various parts of the country, being highly conducive to promote this end; it shall be the duty of the legislators and magistrates, in all future periods of this government to cherish the interest of literature and the sciences, and all seminaries and public schools, to encourage private and public institutions, rewards and immunities for the promotion of agriculture, arts, sciences, commerce, trades, manufactures and natural history of the country; to countenance and inculcate the principles of humanity and general benevolence, public and private charity, industry and economy, honesty and punctuality, sincerity, sobriety, and all social affections, and generous sentiments among the people.

OATH and subscriptions; exclusion from offices; commissions; writs; confirmation of laws; habeas corpus; the enacting stile; continuance of officers; provision for a future revision of the constitution, &c.

Any person chosen president, counsellor, senator, or representative, military or civil officer (town officers excepted) accepting the trust, shall, before he proceeds to execute the duties of his office, make and subscribe the following declaration, viz.

I, A.B., do truly and sincerely acknowledge, profess, testify and declare, that the State of New-Hampshire is, and of right ought to be, a free, sovereign and independent State; and do swear that I will bear faith, and true allegiance to the same, and that I will endeavor to defend it against all treacherous conspiracies and hostile attempts whatever: And I do further testify and declare, that no man or body of men, hath or can have, a right to absolve me from the obligation of this oath, declaration or affirmation; and that I do make this acknowledgment, profession, testimony and declaration, honestly and truly, according to the common acceptation of the foregoing words, without any equivocation, mental evasion, or secret reservation whatever.

So help me GOD.

I, A.B., do solemnly and sincerely swear and affirm, that I will faithfully and impartially discharge and perform all the duties incumbent on me as according to the best of my abilities, agreeably to the rules and regulations of this constitution, and the laws of the State of New-Hampshire.

So help me GOD.

Provided always, When any person chosen or appointed as aforesaid, shall be of the denomination called quakers, or shall be scrupulous of swearing, and shall decline taking the said oaths, such shall take and subscribe them omitting, the word "*swear,*" and likewise the words "*So help me God*" subjoining instead thereof, "*This I do under the pains and penalties of perjury.*"

And the oaths or affirmations shall be taken and subscribed by the president before the senior senator present, in the presence of the two houses of assembly; and by the senate and representatives first elected under this constitution, before the president and three of the council of the former constitution, and forever afterwards before the president and council for the time being and by the residue of the officers aforesaid, before such persons, and in such manner as from time to time shall be prescribed by the legislature.

All commissions shall be in the name of the State of New-Hampshire, signed by the president, and attested by the secretary, or his deputy, and shall have the great seal of the State affixed thereto.

All writs issuing out of the clerk's office in any of the courts of law, shall be in the name of the State of New-Hampshire; shall be under the seal of the court whence they issue, and bear test of the chief, first, or senior justice of the court; but when such justice shall be interested, then the writ shall bear test of some other justice of the court, to which the same shall be returnable; and be signed by the clerk of such court.

All indictments, presentments and informations shall conclude against the peace and dignity of the State.

The estates of such persons as may destroy their own lives, shall not for that offence be forfeited, but descend or ascend in the same manner, as if such persons had died in a natural way. Nor shall any article which shall accidentally occasion the death of any person be henceforth deemed a deodand, or in any wise forfeited on account of such misfortune.

All the laws which have heretofore been adopted, used and approved, in the province, colony, or State of New-Hampshire, and usually practised on in the courts of law, shall remain and be in full force until altered and repealed by the legislature; such parts thereof only excepted, as are repugnant to the rights and liberties contained in this constitution: *Provided* that nothing herein contained, when compared with the twenty-third article in the bill of rights, shall be construed to affect the laws already made respecting the persons or estates of absentees.

The privilege and benefit of the habeas corpus, shall be enjoyed in this State, in the most free, easy, cheap, expeditious and ample manner, and shall not be suspended by the legislature, except upon the most urgent and pressing occasions, and for a time not exceeding three months.

The enacting stile in making and passing acts, statutes and laws, shall be—*Be it enacted by the Senate and House of Representatives in General-Court convened.*

No president, or judge of the superior court, shall hold any office or place under the authority of this State, except such as by this constitution they are admitted to hold, saving that the judges of the said court may hold the offices of justice of the peace throughout the State; nor shall they hold any place or office, or receive any pension or salary, from any other State, government, or power whatever.

No person shall be capable of exercising at the same time, more than one of the following offices within this state, viz. Judge of probate, sheriff, register of deeds; and never more than two offices of profit, which may be held by appointment of the president, or president and council, or senate and house of representatives, or superior or inferior courts; military offices, and offices of justice of the peace excepted.

No person holding the office of judge of the superior court, secretary, treasurer of the State, judge of probate, attorney-general, commissary-general, judge of the maritime court, or judge of the court of admiralty, military officers receiving pay from the continent or this State, excepting officers of the militia occasionally called forth on an emergency; judge of the inferior court of common-pleas, register of deeds, president, professor or instructor of any college, sheriff, or officer of the customs, including naval-officers, shall at the same time have a seat in the senate or house of representatives, or council; but their being chosen or appointed to, and accepting the same, shall operate as a resignation of their seat in the senate, or house of representatives, or council; and the place so vacated shall be filled up.

No person shall ever be admitted to hold a seat in the legislature, or any office of trust or importance under this government, who, in the due course of law, has been convicted of bribery or corruption, in obtaining an election or appointment.

In all cases where sums of money are mentioned in this constitution, the value thereof shall be computed in silver, at *six shillings and eight pence* per ounce.

To the end that there may be no failure of justice, or danger arise to this State from a change of the form of government, all civil and military officers, holding commissions under the government and people of New-Hampshire, and other officers of the said government and people, at the time this constitution shall take effect, shall hold, exercise and enjoy all the powers and authorities to them granted and committed, until other persons shall be appointed in their stead. All courts of law in the business of their respective departments, and the executive, and legislative bodies and persons, shall continue in full force, enjoyment and exercise of all their trusts and employments, until the general-court, and the supreme and other executive officers under this constitution, are designated and invested with their respective trusts, powers and authority.

This form of government shall be enrolled on parchment, and deposited in the secretary's office, and be a part of the laws of the land, and printed copies thereof shall be prefixed to the books containing the laws of this State, in all future editions thereof.

To preserve an effectual adherence to the principles of the constitution, and to correct any violations thereof, as well as to make such alterations therein, as from experience may be found necessary, the general-court shall at the expiration of seven years from the time this constitution shall take effect, issue precepts, or direct them to be issued from the secretary's office, to the several towns and incorporated places, to elect delegates to meet in convention for the purposes aforesaid: The said delegates to be chosen in the same manner, and proportioned as the representatives to the general-assembly; provided that no alteration shall be made in this constitution before the same shall be laid before the towns and unincorporated places, and approved by two thirds of the qualified voters present, and voting upon the question.

Reference: Albert Stillman Batchellor (comp. and ed.), *Early State Papers of New Hampshire*, Vol. XX (Manchester: John B. Clarke, 1891).

34

South Carolina, March 26, 1776

South Carolina also wrote its constitution before independence. Henry Laurens, representing the Charleston faction that wanted to control the legislature, was the constitution's principle author. Internal debates over executive powers led in 1778 to a revised, second state constitution.

CONSTITUTION, MARCH 26, 1776

Whereas the British Parliament, claiming of late years a right to bind the North American colonies by law in all cases whatsoever, have enacted statutes for raising a revenue in those colonies and disposing of such revenue as they thought proper, without the consent and against the will of the colonists. And whereas it appearing to them that (they not being represented in Parliament) such claim was altogether unconstitutional, and, if admitted, would at once reduce them from the rank of freemen to a state of the most abject slavery; the said colonies, therefore, severally remonstrated against the passing, and petitioned for the repeal, of those acts, but in vain; and whereas the said claim being persisted in, other unconstitutional and oppressive statutes have been since enacted by which the powers of admiralty courts in the colonies are extended beyond their ancient limits, and jurisdiction is given to such courts in cases similar to those which in Great Britain are triable by jury; persons are liable to be sent to and tried in Great Britain for an offence created and made capital by one of those statutes, though committed in the colonies; the harbor of Boston was blocked up; people

indicted for murder in the Massachusetts Bay may, at the will of a governor, be sent for trial to any other colony, or even to Great Britain; the chartered constitution of government in that colony is materially altered; the English laws and a free government, to which the inhabitants of Quebec were entitled by the King's royal proclamation, are abolished and French laws are restored; the Roman Catholic religion (although before tolerated and freely exercised there) and an absolute government are established in that province, and its limits extended through a vast tract of country so as to border on the free Protestant English settlements, with design of using a whole people differing in religious principles from the neighboring colonies, and subject to arbitrary power, as fit instruments to overawe and subdue the colonies. And whereas the delegates of all the colonies on this continent, from Nova Scotia to Georgia, assembled in a general Congress at Philadelphia, in the most dutiful manner laid their complaints at the foot of the throne, and humbly implored their sovereign that his royal authority and interposition might be used for their relief from the grievances occasioned by those statutes, and assured His Majesty that harmony between Great Britain and America, ardently desired by the latter, would be thereby immediately restored, and that the colonists confided in the magnanimity and justice of the King and Parliament for redress of the many other grievances under which they labored. And whereas these complaints being wholly disregarded, statutes still more cruel than those above mentioned have been enacted, prohibiting the intercourse of the colonies with each other, restricting their trade, and depriving many thousands of people of the means of subsistence, by restraining them from fishing on the American coast. And whereas large fleets and armies having been sent to America in order to enforce the execution of those laws, and to compel an absolute and implicit submission to the will of a corrupt and despotic administration, and in consequence thereof, hostilities having been commenced in the Massachusetts Bay, by the troops under command of General Gage, whereby a number of peaceable, helpless, and unarmed people were wantonly robbed and murdered, and there being just reason to apprehend that like hostilities would be committed in all the other colonies. The colonists were therefore driven to the necessity of taking up arms, to repel force by force, and to defend themselves and their properties against lawless invasions and depredations. Nevertheless, the delegates of the said colonies assembled in another Congress at Philadelphia, anxious to procure a reconciliation with Great Britain upon just and constitutional principles, supplicated His Majesty to direct some mode by which the united applications of his faithful colonists might be improved into a happy and permanent reconciliation, that in the mean time measures might be taken for preventing the further destruction of their lives, and that such statutes as immediately distressed any of the colonists might be repealed. And whereas, instead of obtaining that justice, to which the colonists were and are of right entitled, the unnatural civil war into which they were thus precipitated and are involved, hath been prosecuted with unremitted violence, and the governors and others bearing the royal commission in the colonies

having broken the most solemn promises and engagements, and violated every obligation of honor, justice, and humanity, have caused the persons of divers good people to be seized and imprisoned, and their properties to be forcibly taken and detained, or destroyed, without any crime or forfeiture; excited domestic insurrections; proclaimed freedom to servants and slaves, enticed or stolen them from, and armed them against their masters; instigated and encouraged the Indian nations to war against the colonies; dispensed with the law of the land, and substituted the law martial in its stead; killed many of the colonists; burned several towns, and threatened to burn the rest, and daily endeavor by a conduct which has sullied the British arms, and would disgrace even savage nations, of the colonies; and whereas a statute hath been lately passed, whereby, under pretence that the said colonies are in open rebellion, all trade and commerce whatsoever with them is prohibited; vessels belonging to their inhabitants trading in, to, or from the said colonies, with the cargoes and effects on board such vessels, are made lawful prize, and the masters and crews of such vessels are subjected by force to act on board the King's ships against their country and dearest friends; and all seizures and detention or destruction of the persons and properties of the colonists which have at any time been made or committed for withstanding or suppressing the said pretended rebellion, and which shall be made in pursuance of the said act, or for the service of the public, are justified, and persons suing for damages in such cases are, on failing in their suits, subjected to payment of very heavy expenses. And whereas large reënforcements of troops and ships have been ordered and are daily expected in America for carrying on war against each of the united colonies by the most vigorous exertions. And whereas in consequence of a plan recommended by the governors, and which seems to have been concerted between them and their ministerial masters to withdraw the usual officers and thereby loosen the bands of government and create anarchy and confusion in the colonies. Lord William Campbell, late governor, on the fifteenth day of September last, dissolved the general assembly of this colony, and no other hath been since called, although by law the sitting and holding of general assemblies cannot be intermitted above six months, and having used his utmost efforts to destroy the lives, liberties, and properties of the good people here, whom by the duty of his station he was bound to protect, withdrew himself from the colony and carried off the great seal and the royal instructions to governors. And whereas the judges of courts of law here have refused to exercise their respective functions, so that it is become indispensably necessary that during the present situation of American affairs, and until an accommodation of the unhappy differences between Great Britain and America can be obtained, (an event which, though traduced and treated as rebels, we still earnestly desire,) some mode should be established by common consent, and for the good of the people, the origin and end of all governments, for regulating the internal polity of this colony. The congress being vested with powers competent for the purpose, and having fully deliberated touching the premises, do therefore resolve:

I. That this congress being a full and free representation of the people of this colony, shall henceforth be deemed and called the general assembly of South Carolina, and as such shall continue until the twenty-first day of October next, and no longer.

II. That the general assembly shall, out of their own body, elect by ballot a legislative council, to consist of thirteen members, (seven of whom shall be a quorum,) and to continue for the same time as the general assembly.

III. That the general assembly and the said legislative council shall jointly choose by ballot from among themselves, or from the people at large, a president and commander-in-chief and a vice-president of the colony.

IV. That a member of the general assembly being chosen and acting as president and commander-in-chief, or vice-president, or one of the legislative council shall vacate his seat in the general assembly and another person shall be elected in his room; and if one of the legislative council is chosen president and commander-in-chief or vice-president, he shall lose his seat and another person shall be elected in his stead.

V. That there be a privy council, whereof the vice-president of the colony shall of course be a member and president of the privy council, and that six other members be chosen by ballot, three by the general assembly, and three by the legislative council: *Provided always,* That no officer in the army or navy in the service of the continent, or of this colony, shall be eligible. And a member of the general assembly, or of the legislative council, being chosen of the privy council, shall not thereby lose his seat in the general assembly, or in the legislative council, unless he be elected vice-president of the colony, in which case he shall, and another person shall be chosen in his stead. The privy council (of which four to be a quorum) to advise the president and commander-in-chief when required, but he shall not be bound to consult them, unless in cases after mentioned.

VI. That the qualifications of president and commander-in-chief, and vice-president of the colony, and members of the legislative and privy council, shall be the same as of members of the general assembly, and on being elected they shall take an oath of qualification in the general assembly.

VII. That the legislative authority be vested in the president and commander-in-chief, the general assembly and legislative council. All money-bills for the support of government shall originate in the general assembly, and shall not be altered or amended by the legislative council, but may be rejected by them. All other bills and ordinances may take rise in the general assembly or legislative council, and may be altered, amended, or rejected by either. Bills having passed the general assembly and legislative council may be assented to or rejected by the president and commander-in-chief. Having received his assent, they shall have all the force and validity of an act of general assembly of this colony. And the general assembly and legislative council, respectively, shall enjoy all other privileges which have at any time been claimed or exercised by the commons house of assembly, but the legislative council shall have no power of expelling their own members.

VIII. That the general assembly and legislative council may adjourn themselves respectively, and the president and commander-in-chief shall have no power to adjourn, prorogue, or dissolve them, but may, if necessary, call them before the time to which they shall stand adjourned. And where a bill has been rejected, it may, on a meeting after adjournment of not less than three days of the general assembly and legislative council, be brought in again.

IX. That the general assembly and legislative council shall each choose their respective speakers and their own officers without control.

X. That if a member of the general assembly or of the legislative council shall accept any place of emolument or any commission except in the militia, he shall vacate his seat, and there shall thereupon be a new election, but he shall not be disqualified from serving upon being reëlected.

XI. That on the last Monday in October next, and the day following, and on the same days of every second year thereafter, members of the general assembly shall be chosen, to meet on the first Monday in December then next, and continue for two years from the said last Monday in October. The general assembly to consist of the same number of members as this congress does, each parish and district having the same representation as at present, viz: the parish of Saint Philip and Saint Michael, Charlestown, thirty members; the parish of Christ Church, six members; the parish of Saint John, in Berkely County, six members; the parish of Saint Andrew, six members; the parish of Saint George Dorchester, six members; the parish of Saint James Goose Creek, six members; the parish of Saint Thomas and Saint Dennis, six members; the parish of Saint Paul, six members; the parish of Saint Bartholemew, six members; the parish of Saint Helena, six members; the parish of Saint James Santee, six members; the parish of Prince George, Winyaw, six members; the parish of Prince Frederick, six members; the parish of Saint John, in Colleton County, six members; the parish of Saint Peter, six members; the parish of Prince William, six members; the parish of Saint Stephen, six members; the district to the eastward of Wateree River, ten members; the district of Ninety-six, ten members; the district of Saxe Gotha, six members; the district between Broad and Saluda Rivers, in three divisions, viz: the Lower district, four members; the Little River district, four members; the Upper or Spartan district, four members; the district between Broad and Catawba Rivers, ten members; the district called the New Acquisition, ten members; the parish of Saint Mathew, six members; the parish of Saint David, six members; the district between Savannah River and the North Fork of Edisto, six members. And the election of the said members shall be conducted as near as may be agreeable to the directions of the election act, and where there are no churches or church wardens in a district or parish, the general assembly, at some convenient time before their expiration, shall appoint places of election and persons to receive votes and make returns. The qualifications of electors shall be the same as required by law, but persons having property, which, according to the rate of the last preceding tax, is taxable at the sums mentioned in the election act, shall be entitled to vote, though it was no actually taxed, having the other qualifications mentioned in that act; electors shall take an oath of qualification, if required by the returning-officer. The qualification of the elected to be the same as mentioned in the election act, and construed to mean clear of debt.

XII. That if any parish or district neglects or refuses to elect members, or if the members chosen do not meet in general assembly, those who do meet shall have the powers of a general assembly; not less than forty-nine members shall make a house to do business, but the speaker or any seven members may adjourn from day to day.

XIII. That as soon as may be, after the first meeting of the general assembly, a president and commander-in-chief, a vice-president of the colony and privy council, shall be chosen in manner and for the time above mentioned, and till such choice be made the former president and commander-in-chief and vice-president of the colony and privy council shall continue to act as such.

XIV. That in case of the death of the president and commander-in-chief, or his absence from the colony, the vice-president of the colony shall succeed to his office, and the privy council shall choose out of their own body a vice-president of the colony, and in case of the death of the vice-president of the colony, or his absence from the colony, one of the privy council (to be chosen by themselves) shall succeed to his office, until a nomination to those offices, respectively, by the general assembly and legislative council for the remainder of the time for which the officer so dying or being absent was appointed.

XV. That the delegates of this colony in the Continental Congress be chosen by the general assembly and legislative council jointly by ballot in the general assembly.

XVI. That the vice-president of the colony and the privy council, or the vice-president and a majority of the privy council for the time being, shall exercise the powers of a court of chancery, and there shall be an ordinary who shall exercise the powers heretofore exercised by that officer in this colony.

XVII. That the jurisdiction of the court of admiralty be confined to maritime causes.

XVIII. That all suits and process depending in any court of law or equity may, if either party shall be so inclined, be proceeded in and continued to a final ending, without being obliged to commence *de noro*. And the judges of the courts of law shall cause jury-lists to be made, and juries to be summoned, as near as may be, according to the directions of the acts of the general assembly in such cases provided.

XIX. That justices of the peace shall be nominated by the general assembly and commissioned by the president and commander-in-chief, during pleasure. They shall not be entitled to fees except on prosecutions for felony, and not acting in the magistracy, they shall not be entitled to the privileges allowed to them by law.

XX. That all other judicial officers shall be chosen by ballot, jointly by the general assembly and legislative council, and except the judges of the court of chancery, commissioned by the president and commander-in-chief, during good behavior, but shall be removed on address of the general assembly and legislative council.

XXI. That sheriffs, qualified as by law directed, shall be chosen in like manner by the general assembly and legislative council, and commissioned by the president and commander-in-chief, for two years only.

XXII. That the commissioners of the treasury, the secretary of the colony, register of mesne conveyances, attorney-general, and powder-receiver, be chosen by the general assembly and legislative council, jointly by ballot, and commissioned by the president and commander-in-chief during good behavior, but shall be removed on address of the general assembly and legislative council.

XXIII. That all field-officers in the army, and all captains in the navy, shall be, by the general assembly and legislative council, chosen jointly by ballot, and commissioned by the president and commander-in-chief, and that all other officers in the army or navy shall be commissioned by the president and commander-in-chief.

XXIV. That in case of vacancy in any of the offices above directed to be filled by the general assembly and legislative council, the president and commander-in-chief, with the advice and consent of the privy council, may appoint others in their stead, until there shall be an election by the general assembly and legislative council to fill their vacancies respectively.

XXV. That the president and commander-in-chief, with the advice and consent of the privy council, may appoint during pleasure, until otherwise directed by resolution of the general assembly and legislative council, all other necessary officers, except such as are by law directed to be otherwise chosen.

XXVI. That the president and commander-in-chief shall have no power to make war or peace, or enter into any final treaty, without the consent of the general assembly and legislative council.

XXVII. That if any parish or district shall neglect to elect a member or members on the day of election, or in case any person chosen a member of the general assembly shall refuse to qualify and take his seat as such, or die or depart the colony, the said general assembly shall appoint proper days for electing a member or members of the said general assembly in such cases respectively;

and on the death of a member of the legislative or privy council, another member shall be chosen in his room, in manner above mentioned, for the election of members of the legislative and privy council respectively.

XXVIII. That the resolutions of the Continental Congress, now of force in this colony, shall so continue until altered or revoked by them.

XXIX. That the resolutions of this or any former congress of this colony, and all laws now of force here, (and not hereby altered,) shall so continue until altered or repealed by the legislature of this colony, unless where they are temporary, in which case they shall expire at the times respectively limited for their duration.

XXX. That the executive authority be vested in the president and commander-in-chief, limited and restrained as aforesaid.

XXXI. That the president and commander-in-chief, the vice-president of the colony, and privy council, respectively, shall have the same personal privileges as are allowed by act of assembly to the governor, lieutenant-governor, and privy council.

XXXII. That all persons now in office shall hold their commissions until there shall be a new appointment in manner above directed, at which time all commissions not derived from authority of the congress of this colony shall cease and be void

XXXIII. That all persons who shall be chosen and appointed to any office or to any place of trust, before entering upon the execution of office, shall take the following oath: "I, A. B., do swear that I will, to the utmost of my power, support, maintain, and defend the constitution of South Carolina, as established by Congress on the twenty-sixth day of March, one thousand seven hundred and seventy-six, until an accommodation of the differences between Great Britain and America shall take place, or I shall be released from this oath by the legislative authority of the said colony: So help me God." And all such persons shall also take an oath of office.

XXXIV. That the following yearly salaries be allowed to the public officers undermentioned: The president and commander-in-chief, nine thousand pounds; the chief justice and the assistant judges, the salaries, respectively, as by act of assembly established; the attorney-general, two thousand one hundred pounds, in lieu of all charges against the public for fees upon criminal prosecutions; the ordinary, one thousand pounds; the three commissioners of the treasury, two thousand pounds each; and all other public officers shall have the same salaries as are allowed such officers, respectively, by act of assembly.

By order of the congress, March 26, 1776.
WILLIAM HENRY DRAYTON, *President.*
Attested:
PETER TIMOTHY, *Secretary.*

Reference: Francis Newton Thorpe (ed.), *The Federal and State Constitutions, Colonial Charters, and Other Organic Laws of the States*, Vol. VI (Washington: GPO, 1909).

REVISED CONSTITUTION, MARCH 19, 1778

Whereas the constitution or form of government agreed to and resolved upon by the freemen of this country, met in congress, the twenty-sixth day of March, one thousand seven hundred and seventy-six, was temporary only, and suited to the situation of their public affairs at that period, looking forward to an accommodation with Great Britain, an event then desired; and whereas the United Colonies of America have been since constituted independent States, and the political connection heretofore subsisting between them and Great Britain entirely dissolved by the declaration of the honorable the Continental Congress, dated the fourth day of July, one thousand seven hundred and seventy-six, for the many great and weighty reasons therein particularly set forth: It therefore becomes absolutely necessary to frame a constitution suitable to that great event.

Be it therefore constituted and enacted, by his excellency Rawlins Lowndes, esq., president and commander-in-chief in and over the State of South Carolina, by the honorable the legislative council and general assembly, and by the authority of the same:

That the following articles, agreed upon by the freemen of this State, now met in general assembly, be deemed and held the constitution and form of government of the said State, unless altered by the legislative authority thereof, which constitution or form of government shall immediately take place and be in force from the passing of this act, excepting such parts as are hereafter mentioned and specified.

I. That the style of this country be hereafter the State of South Carolina.

II. That the legislative authority be vested in a general assembly, to consist of two distinct bodies, a senate and house of representatives, but that the legislature of this State, as established by the constitution or form of government passed the twenty-sixth of March, one thousand and seven hundred and seventy-six, shall continue and be in full force until the twenty-ninth day of November ensuing.

III. That as soon as may be after the first meeting of the senate and house of representatives, and at every first meeting of the senate and house of representatives thereafter, to be elected by virtue of this constitution, they shall jointly in the house of representatives choose by ballot from among themselves or from the people at large a governor and commander-in-chief, a lieutenant-governor, both to continue for two years, and a privy council, all of the Protestant religion, and till such choice shall be made the former president or governor and commander-in-chief, and vice-president or lieutenant-governor, as the case may be, and privy council, shall continue to act as such.

IV. That a member of the senate or house of representatives, being chosen and acting as governor and commander-in-chief or lieutenant-governor, shall vacate his seat, and another person shall be elected in his room.

V. That every person who shall be elected governor and commander-in-chief of the State, or lieutenant-governor, or a member of the privy council, shall be qualified as forthwith; that is to say, the governor and lieutenant-governor shall have been residents in this State for ten years, and the members of the privy council five years, preceding their said election, and shall have in this State a settled plantation or freehold in their and each of their own right of the value of at least ten thousand pounds currency, clear of debt, and on being elected they shall respectively take an oath of qualification in the house of representatives.

VI. That no future governor and commander-in-chief who shall serve for two years shall be eligible to serve in the said office after the expiration of the said term until the full end and term of four years.

VII. That no person in this State shall hold the office of governor thereof, or lieutenant-governor, and any other office or commission, civil or military, (except in the militia,) either in this or any other State, or under the authority of the Continental Congress, at one and the same time.

VIII. That in case of the impeachment of the governor and commander-in-chief, or his removal from office, death, resignation, or absence from the State, the lieutenant-governor shall succeed to his office, and the privy council shall choose out of their own body a lieutenant-governor of the State. And in case of the impeachment of the lieutenant-governor, or his removal from office, death, resignation, or absence from the State, one of the privy council, to be chosen by themselves, shall succeed to his office until a nomination to those offices respectively, by the senate and house of representatives, for the remainder of the time for which the officer so impeached, removed from office, dying, resigning, or being absent was appointed.

IX. That the privy council shall consist of the lieutenant-governor for the time being, and eight other members, five of whom shall be a quorum, to be chosen as before directed; four to serve for two years, and four for one year, and at the expiration of one year four others shall be chosen in the room of the last four, to serve for two years, and all future members of the privy council shall thenceforward be elected to serve two years, whereby there will be a new election every year for half the privy council, and a constant rotation established; but no member of the privy council who shall serve for two years shall be eligible to serve therein after the expiration of the said term until the full end and term of four years: *Provided always,* That no officer of the army or navy in the service of the continent or this State, nor judge of any of the courts of law, shall be eligible, nor shall the father, son, or brother to the governor for the time being be elected in the privy council during his administration. A member of the senate and house of representatives being chosen of the privy council, shall not thereby lose his seat in the senate or house of representatives, unless he be elected lieutenant-governor, in which case he shall, and another person shall be chosen in his stead. The privy council is to advise the governor and commander-in-chief when required, but he shall not be bound to consult them unless directed by law. If a member of the privy council shall die or depart this State during the recess of the general assembly, the privy council shall choose another to act in his room, until a nomination by the senate and house of representatives shall take place. The clerk of the privy council shall keep a regular journal of all their proceedings, in which shall be entered the yeas and nays on every question, and the opinion, with the reasons at large, of any member who desires it; which journal shall be laid before the legislature when required by either house.

X. That in case of the absence from the seat of government or sickness of the governor and lieutenant-governor, any one of the privy council may be empowered by the governor, under his hand and seal, to act in his room, but such appointment shall not vacate his seat in the senate, house of representatives, or privy council.

XI. That the executive authority be vested in the governor and commander-in-chief, in manner herein mentioned.

XII. That each parish and district throughout this State shall on the last Monday in November next and the day following, and on the same days of every succeeding year thereafter, elect by ballot one member of the senate, except the district of Saint Philip and Saint Michael's parishes, Charleston, which shall elect two members; and except also the district between Broad and Saluda Rivers, in three divisions, viz: the Lower district, the Little River district, and the Upper or Spartan district, each of which said divisions shall elect one member; and except the parishes of Saint Matthew and Orange, which shall elect one member; and also except the parishes of Prince George and All Saints, which shall elect one member; and the election of senators for such parishes, respectively, shall, until otherwise altered by the legislature, be at the parish of Prince George for the said parish and the parish of All Saints, and at the parish of Saint Matthew for that parish and the parish of Orange; to meet on the first Monday in January then next, at the seat of government, unless the casualties of war or contagious disorders should render it unsafe to meet there, in which case the governor and commander-in-chief for the time being may, by proclamation, with the advice and consent of the privy council, appoint a more secure and convenient place of meeting; and to continue for two years from the said last Monday in November; and that no person shall be eligible to a seat in the said senate unless he be of the Protestant religion, and hath attained the age of thirty years, and hath been a resident in this State at least five years. Not less than thirteen members shall be a quorum to do business, but the president or any three members may adjourn from day to day. No person who resides in the parish or district for which he is elected shall take his seat in the senate, unless he possess a settled estate and freehold in his own right in the said parish or district of the value of two thousand pounds currency at least, clear of debt; and no non-resident shall be eligible to a seat in the said senate unless he is owner of a settled estate and freehold in his own right, in the parish or district where he is elected, of the value of seven thousand pounds currency at least, also clear of debt.

XIII. That on the last Monday in November next and the day following, and on the same days of every second year thereafter, members of the house of representatives shall be chosen, to meet on the first Monday in January then next, at the seat of government, unless the casualties of war or contagious disorders should render it unsafe to meet there, in which case the governor and commander-in-chief for the time being may, by proclamation, with the advice and consent of the privy council, appoint a more secure and convenient place of meeting, and to continue for two years from the said last Monday in November. Each parish and district within this State shall send members to the general assembly in the following proportions; that is to say, the parish of Saint Philip and Saint Michael's, Charleston, thirty members; the parish of Christ Church, six members; the parish of Saint John's, in Berkely County, six members; the parish of Saint Andrew, six members; the parish of Saint George, Dorchester, six members; the parish of Saint James, Goose Creek, six members; the parish of Saint Thomas and Saint Dennis, six members; the parish of Saint Paul, six members; the parish of Saint Bartholomew, six members; the parish of Saint Helena, six members; the parish of Saint James, Santee, six members; the parish of Prince George, Winyaw, four members; the parish of All Saints, two members; the parish of Prince Frederick, six members; the parish of Saint John, in Colleton County, six members; the parish of Saint Peter, six members; the parish of Prince William, six members; the parish of Saint Stephen, six members; the district to the eastward of Wateree River, ten members; the district of Ninety-six, ten members; the district of Saxe Gotha, six members; the district between Broad and Saluda Rivers, in three divisions, viz: the lower district, four members; the Little River district, four members; the Upper or Spartan district, four members; the district between Broad and Catawba Rivers, ten members; the district called the New Acquisition, ten members; the parish of Saint Matthew, three members; the parish of Orange, three members; the parish of Saint David, six members; the district between the Savannah River and the North Fork of Edisto, six members. And the election of the said members shall be conducted as near as

may be agreeable to the directions of the present or any future election act or acts, and where there are no churches or church-wardens in a district or parish, the house of representatives, at some convenient time before their expiration, shall appoint places of election and persons to receive votes and make returns. The qualification of electors shall be that every free white man, and no other person, who acknowledges the being of a God, and believes in a future state of rewards and punishments, and who has attained to the age of one and twenty years, and hath been a resident and an inhabitant in this State for the space of one whole year before the day appointed for the election he offers to give his vote at, and hath a freehold at least of fifty acres of land, or a town lot, and hath been legally seized and possessed of the same at least six months previous to such election, or hath paid a tax the preceding year, or was taxable the present year, at least six months previous to the said election, in a sum equal to the tax on fifty acres of land, to the support of this government, shall be deemed a person qualified to vote for, and shall be capable of electing, a representative or representatives to serve as a member or members in the senate and house of representatives, for the parish or district where he actually is a resident, or in any other parish or district in this State where he hath the like freehold. Electors shall take an oath or affirmation of qualification, if required by the returning officer. No person shall be eligible to sit in the house of representatives unless he be of the Protestant religion, and hath been a resident in this State for three years previous to his election. The qualification of the elected, if residents in the parish or district for which they shall be returned, shall be the same as mentioned in the election act, and construed to mean clear of debt. But no nonresident shall be eligible to a seat in the house of representatives unless he is owner of a settled estate and freehold in his own right of the value of three thousand and five hundred pounds currency at least, clear of debt, in the parish or district for which he is elected.

XIV. That if any parish or district neglects or refuses to elect members, or if the members chosen do not meet in general assembly, those who do meet shall have the powers of the general assembly. Not less than sixty-nine members shall make a house of representatives to do business, but the speaker or any seven members may adjourn from day to day.

XV. That at the expiration of seven years after the passing of this constitution, and at the end of every fourteen years thereafter, the representation of the whole State shall be proportioned in the most equal and just manner according to the particular and comparative strength and taxable property of the different parts of the same, regard being always had to the number of white inhabitants and such taxable property.

XVI. That all money bills for the support of government shall originate in the house of representatives, and shall not be altered or amended by the senate, but may be rejected by them, and that no money be drawn out of the public treasury but by the legislative authority of the State. All other bills and ordinances may take rise in the senate or house of representatives, and be altered, amended, or rejected by either. Acts and ordinances having passed the general assembly shall have the great seal affixed to them by a joint committee of both houses, who shall wait upon the governor to receive and return the seal, and shall then be signed by the president of the senate and speaker of the house of representatives, in the senate-house, and shall thenceforth have all the force and validity of a law, and be lodged in the secretary's office. And the senate and house of representatives, respectively, shall enjoy all other privileges which have at any time been claimed or exercised by the commons house of assembly.

XVII. That neither the senate nor house of representatives shall have power to adjourn themselves for any longer time than three days, without the mutual consent of both. The governor and commander-in-chief shall have no power to adjourn, prorogue, or dissolve them, but may, if necessary, by and with the advice and consent of the privy council, convene them before the time to which they shall stand adjourned. And where a bill hath been rejected by either house, it shall not be brought in again that session, without

leave of the house, and a notice of six days being previously given.

XVIII. That the senate and house of representatives shall each choose their respective officers by ballot, without control, and that during a recess the president of the senate and speaker of the house of representatives shall issue writs for filling up vacancies occasioned by death in their respective houses, giving at least three weeks and not more than thirty-five days' previous notice of the time appointed for the election.

XIX. That if any parish or district shall neglect to elect a member or members on the day of election, or in case any person chosen a member of either house shall refuse to qualify and take his seat as such, or die, or depart the State, the senate or house of representatives, as the case may be, shall appoint proper days for electing a member or members in such cases respectively.

XX. That if any member of the senate or house of representatives shall accept any place of emolument, or any commission, (except in the militia or commission of the peace, and except as is excepted in the tenth article,) he shall vacate his seat, and there shall thereupon be a new election; but he shall not be disqualified from serving upon being reëlected, unless he is appointed secretary of the State, a commissioner of the treasury, an officer of the customs, register of mesne conveyances, a clerk of either of the courts of justice, sheriff, powder-reviewer, clerk of the senate, house of representatives, or privy council, surveyor-general, or commissary of military stores, which officers are hereby declared disqualified from being members either of the senate or house of representatives.

XXI. And whereas the ministers of the gospel are by their profession dedicated to the service of God and the cure of souls, and ought not to be diverted from the great duties of their function, therefore no minister of the gospel or public preacher of any religious persuasion, while he continues in the exercise of his pastoral function, and for two years after, shall be eligible either as governor, lieutenant-governor, a member of the senate, house of representatives, or privy council in this State.

XXII. That the delegates to represent this State in the Congress of the United States be chosen annually by the senate and house of representatives jointly, by ballot, in the house of representatives, and nothing contained in this constitution shall be construed to extend to vacate the seat of any member who is or may be a delegate from this State to Congress as such.

XXIII. That the form of impeaching all officers of the State for mal and corrupt conduct in their respective offices, not amenable to any other jurisdiction, be vested in the house of representatives. But that it shall always be necessary that two-third parts of the members present do consent to and agree in such impeachment. That the senators and such of the judges of this State as are not members of the house of representatives, be a court for the trial of impeachments, under such regulations as the legislature shall establish, and that previous to the trial of every impeachment, the members of the said court shall respectively be sworn truly and impartially to try and determine the charge in question according to evidence, and no judgment of the said court, except judgment of acquittal, shall be valid, unless it shall be assented to by two-third parts of the members then present, and on every trial, as well on impeachments as others, the party accused shall be allowed counsel.

XXIV. That the lieutenant-governor of the State and a majority of the privy council for the time being shall, until otherwise altered by the legislature, exercise the powers of a court of chancery, and there shall be ordinaries appointed in the several districts of this State, to be chosen by the senate and house of representatives jointly by ballot, in the house of representatives, who shall, within their respective districts, exercise the powers heretofore exercised by the ordinary, and until such appointment is made the present ordinary in Charleston shall continue to exercise that office as heretofore.

XXV. That the jurisdiction of the court of admiralty be confined to maritime causes.

XXVI. That justices of the peace shall be nominated by the senate and house of representatives jointly, and commissioned by the governor and commander-in-chief during pleasure. They shall be entitled to receive the fees heretofore established by law; and not acting in the magistracy, they shall not be entitled to the privileges allowed them by law.

XXVII. That all other judicial officers shall be chosen by ballot, jointly by the senate and house of representatives, and, except the judges of the court of chancery, commissioned by the governor and commander-in-chief during good behavior, but shall be removed on address of the senate and house of representatives.

XXVIII. That the sheriffs, qualified as by law directed, shall be chosen in like manner by the senate and house of representatives, when the governor, lieutenant-governor, and privy council are chosen, and commissioned by the governor and commander-in-chief, for two years, and shall give security as required by law, before they enter on the execution of their office. No sheriff who shall have served for two years shall be eligible to serve in the said office after the expiration of the said term, until the full end and term of four years, but shall continue in office until such choice be made; nor shall any person be eligible as sheriff in any district unless he shall have resided therein for two years previous to the election.

XXIX. That two commissioners of the treasury, the secretary of the State, the register of mesne conveyances in each district, attorney-general, surveyor-general, powder-receiver, collectors and comptrollers of the customs and waiters, be chosen in like manner by the senate and house of representatives jointly, by ballot, in the house of representatives, and commissioned by the governor and commander-in-chief, for two years; that none of the said officers, respectively, who shall have served for four years, shall be eligible to serve in the said offices after the expiration of the said term, until the full end and term of four years, but shall continue in office until a new choice be made: *Provided,* That nothing herein contained shall extend to the several persons appointed to the above offices respectively, under the late constitution; and that the present and all future commissioners of the treasury, and powder-receivers, shall each give bond with approved security agreeable to law.

XXX. That all the officers in the army and navy of this State, of and above the rank of captain, shall be chosen by the senate and house of representatives jointly, by ballot in the house of representatives, and commissioned by the governor and commander-in-chief, and that all other officers in the army and navy of this State shall be commissioned by the governor and commander-in-chief.

XXXI. That in case of vacancy in any of the offices above directed to be filled by the senate and house of representatives, the governor and commander-in-chief, with the advice and consent of the privy council, may appoint others in their stead, until there shall be an election by the senate and house of representatives to fill those vacancies respectively.

XXXII. That the governor and commander-in-chief, with the advice and consent of the privy council, may appoint during pleasure, until otherwise directed by law, all other necessary officers, except such as are now by law directed to be otherwise chosen.

XXXIII. That the governor and commander-in-chief shall have no power to commence war, or conclude peace, or enter into any final treaty without the consent of the senate and house of representatives.

XXXIV. That the resolutions of the late congress of this State, and all laws now of force here, (and not hereby altered,) shall so continue until altered or repealed by the legislature of this State, unless where they are temporary, in which case they shall expire at the times respectively limited for their duration.

XXXV. That the governor and commander-in-chief for the time being, by and with the advice and consent of the privy council, may lay embargoes or prohibit the exportation of any commodity, for any time not exceeding thirty days, in the recess of the general assembly.

XXXVI. That all persons who shall be chosen and appointed to any office or to any place of trust, civil or military, before entering upon the execution of office, shall take the following oath: "I, A. B., do acknowledge the State of South Carolina to be a free, sovereign, and independent State, and that the people thereof owe no allegiance or obedience to George the Third, King of Great Britain, and I do renounce, refuse, and abjure any allegiance or obedience to him. And I do swear [or affirm, as the case may be] that I will, to the utmost of my power, support, maintain, and defend the said State against the said King George the Third, and his heirs and successors, and his or their abettors, assistants, and adherents, and will serve the said State, in the office of—, with fidelity and honor, and according to the best of my skill and understanding: So help me God."

XXXVII. That adequate yearly salaries be allowed to the public officers of this State, and be fixed by law.

XXXVIII. That all persons and religious societies who acknowledge that there is one God, and a future state of rewards and punishments, and that God is publicly to be worshipped, shall be freely tolerated. The Christian Protestant religion shall be deemed, and is hereby constituted and declared to be, the established religion of this State. That all denominations of Christian Protestants in this State, demeaning themselves peaceably and faithfully, shall enjoy equal religious and civil privileges. To accomplish this desirable purpose without injury to the religious property of those societies of Christians which are by law already incorporated for the purpose of religious worship, and to put it fully into the power of every other society of Christian Protestants, either already formed or hereafter to be formed, to obtain the like incorporation, it is hereby constituted, appointed, and declared that the respective societies of the Church of England that are already formed in this State for the purpose of religious worship shall still continue incorporate and hold the religious property now in their possession. And that whenever fifteen or more male persons, not under twenty-one years of age, professing the Christian Protestant religion, and agreeing to unite themselves in a society for the purposes of religious worship, they shall, (on complying with the terms hereinafter mentioned,) be, and be constituted a church, and be esteemed and regarded in law as of the established religion of the State, and on a petition to the legislature shall be entitled to be incorporated and to enjoy equal privileges. That every society of Christians so formed shall give themselves a name or denomination by which they shall be called and known in law, and all that associate with them for the purposes of worship shall be esteemed as belonging to the society so called. But that previous to the establishment and incorporation of the respective societies of every denomination as aforesaid, and in order to entitle them thereto, each society so petitioning shall have agreed to and subscribed in a book the following five articles, without which no agreement or union of men upon pretence of religion shall entitle them to be incorporated and esteemed as a church of the established religion of this State:

1st. That there is one eternal God, and a future state of rewards and punishments.
2nd. That God is publicly to be worshipped.
3nd. That the Christian religion is the true religion.
4th. That the holy scriptures of the Old and New Testament are of divine inspiration, and are the rule of faith and practice.
5th. That it is lawful and the duty of every man being thereunto called by those that govern, to bear witness to the truth.

And that every inhabitant of this State, when called to make an appeal to God as a witness to truth, shall be permitted to do it in that way which is most agreeable to the dictates of his own conscience. And that the people of this State may forever enjoy the right of electing their own pastors or clergy, and at the same time that the State may have sufficient security for the due discharge of the pastoral office, by those who shall be admitted to be clergymen, no person shall officiate as minister of any established church who shall not have been chosen by a majority of the society to which he shall minister, or by persons appointed by the said majority, to choose and

procure a minister for them; nor until the minister so chosen and appointed shall have made and subscribed to the following declaration, over and above the aforesaid five articles, viz: "That he is determined by God's grace out of the holy scriptures, to instruct the people committed to his charge, and to teach nothing as required of necessity to eternal salvation but that which he shall be persuaded may be concluded and proved from the scripture; that he will use both public and private admonitions; as well to the sick as to the whole within his cure, as need shall require and occasion shall be given, and that he will be diligent in prayers, and in reading of the same; that he will be diligent to frame and fashion his own self and his family according to the doctrine of Christ, and to make both himself and them, as much as in him lieth, wholesome examples and patterns to the flock of Christ; that he will maintain and set forwards, as much as he can, quietness, peace, and love among all people, and especially among those that are or shall be committed to his charge. No person shall disturb or molest any religious assembly; nor shall use any reproachful, reviling, or abusive language against any church, that being the certain way of disturbing the peace, and of hindering the conversion of any to the truth, by engaging them in quarrels and animosities, to the hatred of the professors, and that profession which otherwise they might be brought to assent to. No person whatsoever shall speak anything in their religious assembly irreverently or seditiously of the government of this State. No person shall, by law, be obliged to pay towards the maintenance and support of a religious worship that he does not freely join in, or has not voluntarily engaged to support. But the churches, chapels, parsonages, glebes, and all other property now belonging to any societies of the Church of England, or any other religious societies, shall remain and be secured to them forever. The poor shall be supported, and elections managed in the accustomed manner, until laws shall be provided to adjust those matters in the most equitable way.

XXXIX. That the whole State shall, as soon as proper laws can be passed for these purposes, be divided into districts and counties, and county courts established.

XL. That the penal laws, as heretofore used, shall be reformed, and punishments made in some cases less sanguinary, and in general more proportionate to the crime.

XLI. That no freeman of this State be taken or imprisoned, or disseized of his freehold, liberties, or privileges, or outlawed, exiled or in any manner destroyed or deprived of his life, liberty, or property, but by the judgment of his peers or by the law of the land.

XLII. That the military be subordinate to the civil power of the State.

XLIII. That the liberty of the press be inviolably preserved.

XLIV. That no part of this constitution shall be altered without notice being previously given of ninety days, nor shall any part of the same be changed without the consent of a majority of the members of the senate and house of representatives.

XLV. That the senate and house of representatives shall not proceed to the election of a governor or lieutenant-governor, until there be a majority of both houses present.

In the council-chamber, the 19th day of March, 1778.

Assented to.
RAWLINS LOWNDES.
HUGH RUTLEGE.
Speaker of the Legislative Council.
THOMAS BEE,
Speaker of the General Assembly.

Reference: Francis Newton Thorpe (ed.), *The Federal and State Constitutions, Colonial Charters, and Other Organic Laws of the States,* Vol. VI (Washington: GPO, 1909).

35

Virginia, June 29, 1776

In Virginia, George Mason led a disciplined convention to write a Bill of Rights as a preamble to its constitution. It is said that John Adams influenced the authors of the Virginia constitution, especially in the debates about who could hold office in each of the houses of the legislature. A suffrage reform reduced land ownership for voting from 100 to 50 acres. The legislature frequently tinkered with the form of governance in the constitution, perhaps in part because Governor Thomas Jefferson wanted changes that would allow more votes from the West and would make judges popularly elected. In 1776 the Legislature moved the state capital from Williamsburg to the more central location of Richmond, acknowledging the population growth into the backcountry.

GEORGE MASON'S PLAN FOR THE STATE CONSTITUTION, JUNE 10, 1776

A Plan of Government

Laid before the committee of the House, which they have ordered to be printed for the perusal of the members.

1. Let the legislative, executive, and judicative departments, be separate and distinct, so that neither exercise the powers properly belonging to the other.

2. Let the legislative be formed of two distinct branches, who, together, shall be a complete legislature. They shall meet once, or oftener, every year, and shall be called the GENERAL ASSEMBLY OF VIRGINIA.

3. Let one of these be called the Lower House of Assembly, and consist of two delegates, or representatives, chosen for each county, annually; of such men as have resided in the same for one year last past, are freeholders of the county, possess an estate of inheritance of land, in Virginia, of at least one thousand pounds value, and are upwards of twenty four years of age.

4. Let the other be called the Upper House of Assembly, and consist of twenty four members; for whose election, let the different counties be divided into twenty four districts, and each county of the respective district, at the time of the election of its delegates for the Lower House, choose twelve deputies, or sub-electors, being freeholders residing therein, and having an estate of inheritance of lands within the district of at least five hundred pounds value. In case of dispute, the qualifications to be determined by the majority of the said deputies. Let these deputies choose, by ballot, one member for the Upper House of Assembly, who is a freeholder of the district, hath been a resident

therein for one year last past, possesses an estate of inheritance of lands in Virginia of at least two thousand pounds value, and is upwards of twenty eight years of age. To keep up this assembly, by rotation, let the districts be equally divided into four classes, and numbered, at the end of one year after the general election. Let the six members elected by the first division be displaced, rendered ineligible for four years, and the vacancies be supplied in the manner aforesaid. Let this rotation be applied to each division according to its number, and continued in due order annually.

5. Let each House settle its own rules of proceeding direct writs of election for supplying intermediate vacancies; and let the right of suffrage, both in the election of members for the Lower House, and of deputies for the districts, be extended to those having leases for land, in which there is an unexpired term of seven years, and to every housekeeper who hath resided for one year last past in the country, and hath been the father of three children in this country.

6. Let all laws originate in the lower House, to be approved, or rejected, by the Upper House, or to be amended with the consent of the Lower House, except money bills, which in no instance shall be altered by the Upper House, but wholly approved or rejected.

7. Let a Governour, or chief magistrate, be chosen annually, by joint ballot of both Houses; who shall not continue in that office longer than three years successively, and then be ineligible for the next three years. Let an adequate, but moderate salary, be settled on him, during his continuance in office; and let him, with the advice of a Council of State, exercise the executive powers of government, and the power of proroguing or adjourning the General Assembly, or of calling it upon emergencies, and of granting reprieves or pardons, except in cases where the prosecution shall have been carried on by the Lower House of Assembly.

8. Let a Privy Council, or Council of State, consisting of eight members, be chosen by joint ballot of both Houses of Assembly, promiscuously from their members, or the people at large, to assist in the administration of government.

Let the Governour be President of this Council; but let them annually choose one of their own members, as Vice-President, who, in case of the death of absence of the Governour, shall act as Lieutenant-Governour. Let three members be sufficient to act, and their advice be entered of record in their proceedings. Let them appoint their own clerk, who shall have a salary settled by law, and take an oath of secrecy, in such matters as he shall be directed by the Board to conceal, unless called upon by the Lower House of Assembly for information. Let a sum of money, appropriated to that purpose, be divided annually among the members, in proportion to their attendance; and let them be incapable, during their continuance of office, of sitting in either House of Assembly. Let two members be removed, by ballot of their own Board, at the end of every three years, and be ineligible for the three next years. Let this be regularly continued, by rotation, so as that no member be removed before he hath been three years in the Council; and let these vacancies, as well as those occasioned by death or incapacity, be supplied by new elections, in the same manner as the first.

9. Let the Governour, with the advice of the Privy Council, have the appointment of the militia officers, and the government of the militia, under the laws of the country.

10. Let the two Houses of Assembly, by joint ballot, appoint judges of the supreme court, judges in chancery, judges of admirality, and the attorney-general, to be commissioned by the Governour, and continue in office during good behaviour. In case of death or incapacity, let the Governour, with the advice of the Privy Council, appoint persons to succeed in office pro tempore, to be approved or displaced by both Houses. Let these officers have fixed and adequate salaries, and be incapable of having a seat in either House of Assembly, or in the Privy Council, except the attorney-general and the treasurer, who may be permitted to a seat in the Lower House of Assembly.

11. Let the Governour, and Privy Council, appoint justices of the peace for the counties. Let the clerks of all the courts, the sheriffs, and

coroners, be nominated by the respective courts, approved by the Governour and Privy Council, and commissioned by the Governour. Let the clerks be continued during good behaviour, and all fees be regulated by law. Let the justices appoint constables.

12. Let the Governour, any of the Privy Counsellors, judges of the supreme court, and all other officers of government, for mal-administration, or corruption, be prosecuted by the Lower House of Assembly (to be carried on by the attorney-general, or such other person as the House may appoint) in the supreme court of common law. If found guilty, let him, or them, be either removed from office, or for ever disabled to hold any office under the government, or subjected to such pains or penalties as the laws shall direct.

13. Let all commissions run in the name of the Commonwealth of Virginia, and be tested by the Governour, with the seal of the commonwealth annexed. Let writs run in the same manner, and be tested by the clerks of the several courts. Let indictments conclude, Against the peace and dignity of the commonwealth.

14. Let a treasurer be appointed annually, by joint ballot of both houses.

15. In order to introduce this government, let the representatives of the people, now met in Convention, choose twenty four members to be an upper House; and let both Houses, by joint ballot, choose a Governour and Privy Council; the Upper House to continue until the last day of March next, and the other officers until the end of the succeeding session of Assembly. In case of vacancies, the President to issue writs for new elections.

Reference: Robert A. Rutland (ed.), *The Papers of George Mason, 1725–1792,* Vol. I (Chapel Hill: University of North Carolina Press, 1970).

VIRGINIA BILL OF RIGHTS, JUNE 12, 1776

A declaration of rights made by the representatives of the good people of Virginia, assembled in full and free convention; which rights do pertain to them and their posterity, as the basis and foundation of government.

SECTION 1. That all men are by nature equally free and independent, and have certain inherent rights, of which, when they enter into a state of society, they cannot, by any compact, deprive or divest their posterity; namely, the enjoyment of life and liberty, with the means of acquiring and possessing property, and pursuing and obtaining happiness and safety.

SEC. 2. That all power is vested in, and consequently derived from, the people; that magistrates are their trustees and servants, and at all times amenable to them.

SEC. 3. That government is, or ought to be, instituted for the common benefit, protection, and security of the people, nation, or community; of all the various modes and forms of government, that is best which is capable of producing the greatest degree of happiness and safety, and is most effectually secured against the danger of maladministration; and that, when any government shall be found inadequate or contrary to these purposes, a majority of the community hath an indubitable, inalienable, and indefeasible right to reform, alter, or abolish it, in such manner as shall be judged most conducive to the public weal.

SEC. 4. That no man, or set of men, are entitled to exclusive or separate emoluments or privileges from the community, but in consideration of public services; which, not being descendible, neither ought the offices of magistrate, legislator, or judge to be hereditary.

SEC. 5. That the legislative and executive powers of the State should be separate and distinct from the judiciary; and that the members of the two first may be restrained from oppression, by feeling and participating the burdens of the people, they should, at fixed periods, be reduced to a private station, return into that body from which they were originally taken, and the vacancies be supplied by frequent, certain, and regular elections, in which all, or any part of the former members, to be again eligible, or ineligible, as the laws shall direct.

SEC. 6. That elections of members to serve as representatives of the people, in assembly, ought to be free; and that all men, having sufficient evidence of permanent common interest with, and attachment to, the community, have the right of suffrage, and cannot be taxed or deprived of their property for public uses, without their own consent, or that of their representatives so elected, nor bound by any law to which they have not, in like manner, assented, for the public good.

SEC. 7. That all power of suspending laws, or the execution of laws, by any authority, without consent of the representatives of the people, is injurious to their rights, and ought not to be exercised.

SEC. 8. That in all capital or criminal prosecutions a man hath a right to demand the cause and nature of his accusation, to be confronted with the accusers and witnesses, to call for evidence in his favor, and to a speedy trial by an impartial jury of twelve men of his vicinage, without whose unanimous consent he cannot be found guilty; nor can he be compelled to give evidence against himself; that no man be deprived of his liberty, except by the law of the land or the judgment of his peers.

SEC. 9. That excessive bail ought not to be required, nor excessive fines imposed, nor cruel and unusual punishments inflicted.

SEC. 10. That general warrants, whereby an officer or messenger may be commanded to search suspected places without evidence of a fact committed, or to seize any person or persons not named, or whose offence is not particularly described and supported by evidence, are grievous and oppressive, and ought not to be granted.

SEC. 11. That in controversies respecting property, and in suits between man and man, the ancient trial by jury is preferable to any other, and ought to be held sacred.

SEC. 12. That the freedom of the press is one of the great bulwarks of liberty, and can never be restrained but by despotic governments.

SEC. 13. That a well-regulated militia, composed of the body of the people, trained to arms, is the proper, natural, and safe defence of a free State; that standing armies, in time of peace, should be avoided, as dangerous to liberty; and that in all cases the military should be under strict subordination to, and governed by, the civil power.

SEC. 14. That the people have a right to uniform government; and, therefore, that no government separate from, or independent of the government of Virginia, ought to be erected or established within the limits thereof.

SEC. 15. That no free government, or the blessings of liberty, can be preserved to any people, but by a firm allegiance to justice, moderation, temperance, frugality, and virtue, and by frequent adherence to fundamental principles.

SEC. 16. That religion duty which we owe to our Creator, and the manner of discharging it, can be directed only by reason and conviction, not by force or violence; and therefore all men are equally entitled to the free exercise of religion, according to the dictates of conscience; and that it is the mutual duty of all to practise Christian forbearance, love, and charity towards each other.

Reference: Francis Newton Thorpe (ed.), *The Federal and State Constitutions, Colonial Charters, and Other Organic Laws of the States*, Vol. VII (Washington: GPO, 1909).

CONSTITUTION, JUNE 29, 1776

WE, the Delegates and Representatives of the good people of Virginia, do declare the future form of government of Virginia to be as followeth:

The legislative, executive, and judiciary department, shall be separate and distinct, so that neither exercise the powers properly belonging to the other: nor shall any person exercise the powers of more than one of them, at the same time; except that the Justices of the County Courts shall be eligible to either House of Assembly.

The legislative shall be formed of two distinct branches, who, together, shall be a complete Legislature. They shall meet once, or oftener, every year, and shall be called, *The General Assembly of Virginia*. One of these shall be called, *The House of Delegates*, and consist of two Representatives, to be chosen for each county, and for the district of West-Augusta, annually, of such men as actually reside in, and are freeholders of the same, or duly qualified according to law, and also of one Delegate or Representative, to be chosen annually for the city of Williamsburgh, and one for the borough of Norfolk, and a Representative for each of such other cities and boroughs, as may hereafter be allowed particular representation by the legislature; but when any city or borough shall so decrease, as that the number of persons, having right of suffrage therein, shall have been, for the space of seven years successively, less than half the number of voters in some one county in Virginia, such city or borough thenceforward shall cease to send a Delegate or Representative to the Assembly.

The other shall be called *The Senate*, and consist of twenty-four members, of whom thirteen shall constitute a House to proceed on business; for whose election, the different counties shall be divided into twenty-four districts; and each county of the respective district, at the time of the election of its Delegates, shall vote for one Senator, who is actually a resident and freeholder within the district, or duly qualified according to law, and is upwards of twenty-five years of age; and the Sheriffs of each county, within five days at farthest, after the last county election in the district, shall meet at some convenient place, and from the poll, so taken in their respective counties, return, as a Senator, the man who shall have the greatest number of votes in the whole district. To keep up this Assembly by rotation, the districts shall be equally divided into four classes and numbered by lot. At the end of one year after the general election, the six members, elected by the first division, shall be displaced, and the vacancies thereby occasioned supplied from such class or division, by new election, in the manner aforesaid. This rotation shall be applied to each

division, according to its number, and continued in due order annually.

The right of suffrage in the election of members for both Houses shall remain as exercised at present; and each House shall choose its own Speaker, appoint its own officers, settle its own rules of proceeding, and direct writs of election, for the supplying intermediate vacancies.

All laws shall originate in the House of Delegates, to be approved of or rejected by the Senate, or to be amended, with consent of the House of Delegates; except money-bills, which in no instance shall be altered by the Senate, but wholly approved or rejected.

A Governor, or chief magistrate, shall be chosen annually by joint ballot of both Houses (to be taken in each House respectively) deposited in the conference room; the boxes examined jointly by a committee of each House, and the numbers severally reported to them, that the appointments may be entered (which shall be the mode of taking the joint ballot of both Houses, in all cases) who shall not continue in that office longer than three years successively, nor be eligible, until the expiration of four years after he shall have been out of that office. An adequate, but moderate salary shall be settled on him, during his continuance in office; and he shall, with the advice of a Council of State, exercise the executive powers of government, according to the laws of this Commonwealth; and shall not, under any pretence, exercise any power or prerogative, by virtue of any law, statute or custom of England. But he shall, with the advice of the Council of State, have the power of granting reprieves or pardons, except where the prosecution shall have been carried on by the House of Delegates, or the law shall otherwise particularly direct; in which cases, no reprieve or pardon shall be granted, but by resolve of the House of Delegates.

Either House of the General Assembly may adjourn themselves respectively. The Governor shall not prorogue or adjourn the Assembly, during their sitting, nor dissolve them at any time; but he shall, if necessary, either by advice of the Council of State, or on application of a majority of the House of Delegates, call them before the time to which they shall stand prorogued or adjourned.

A Privy Council, or Council of State, consisting of eight members, shall be chosen, by joint ballot of both Houses of Assembly, either from their own members or the people at large, to assist in the administration of government. They shall annually choose, out of their own members, a President, who, in case of death, inability, or absence of the Governor from the government, shall act as Lieutenant-Governor. Four members shall be sufficient to act, and their advice and proceedings shall be entered on record, and signed by the members present, (to any part whereof, any member may enter his dissent) to be laid before the General Assembly, when called for by them. This Council may appoint their own Clerk, who shall have a salary settled by law, and take an oath of secrecy, in such matters as he shall be directed by the board to conceal. A sum of money, appropriated to that purpose, shall be divided annually among the members, in proportion to their attendance; and they shall be incapable, during their continuance in office, of sitting in either House of Assembly. Two members shall be removed, by joint ballot of both Houses of Assembly, at the end of every three years, and be ineligible for the three next years. These vacancies, as well as those occasioned by death or incapacity, shall be supplied by new elections, in the same manner.

The Delegates for Virginia to the Continental Congress shall be chosen annually, or superseded in the mean time, by joint ballot of both Houses of Assembly.

The present militia officers shall be continued, and vacancies supplied by appointment of the Governor, with the advice of the Privy-Council, on recommendations from the respective County Courts; but the Governor and Council shall have a power of suspending any officer, and ordering a Court Martial, on complaint of misbehaviour or inability, or to supply vacancies of officers, happening when in actual service.

The Governor may embody the militia, with the advice of the Privy Council; and when embodied, shall alone have the direction of the militia, under the laws of the country.

The two Houses of Assembly shall, by joint ballot, appoint Judges of the Supreme Court of Appeals, and General Court, Judges in Chancery, Judges of Admarlty, Secretary, and the Attorney-General, to be commissioned by the Governor, and continue in office during good behaviour. In case of death, incapacity, or resignation, the Governor, with the advice of the Privy Council, shall appoint persons to succeed in office, to be approved or displaced by both Houses. These officers shall have fixed and adequate salaries, and, together with all others, holding lucrative offices, and all ministers of the gospel, of every denomination, be incapable of being elected members of either House of Assembly or the Privy Council.

The Governor, with the advice of the Privy Council, shall appoint Justices of the Peace for the counties; and in case of vacancies, or a necessity of increasing the number hereafter, such appointments to be made upon the recommendation of the respective County Courts. The present acting Secretary in Virginia, and Clerks of all the County Courts, shall continue in office. In case of vacancies, either by death, incapacity, or resignation, a Secretary shall be appointed, as before directed; and the Clerks, by the respective Courts. The present and future Clerks shall hold their offices during good behaviour, to be judged of, and determined in the General Court. The Sheriffs and Coroners shall be nominated by the respective Courts, approved by the Governor, with the advice of the Privy Council, and commissioned by the Governor. The Justices shall appoint Constables; and all fees of the aforesaid officers be regulated by law.

The Governor, when he is out of office, and others, offending against the State, either by maladministration, corruption, or other means, by which the safety of the State may be endangered, shall be impeachable by the House of Delegates. Such impeachment to be prosecuted by the Attorney-General, or such other person or persons, as the House may appoint in the General Court, according to the laws of the land. If found guilty, he or they shall be either forever disabled to hold any office under government, or be removed from such office *pro tempore*, or subjected to such pains or penalties as the laws shall direct.

If all or any of the Judges of the General Court should on good grounds (to be judged of by the House of Delegates) be accused of any of the crimes or offences above mentioned, such House of Delegates may, in like manner, impeach the Judge or Judges so accused, to be prosecuted in the Court of Appeals; and he or they, if found guilty, shall be punished in the same manner as is prescribed in the preceding clause.

Commissions and grants shall run, "*In the name of the Commonwealth of Virginia*," and bear test by the Governor, with the seal of the Commonwealth annexed. Writs shall run in the same manner, and bear test by the Clerks of the several Courts. Indictments shall conclude, "*Against the peace and dignity of the Commonwealth.*"

A Treasurer shall be appointed annually, by joint ballot of both Houses.

All escheats, penalties, and forfeitures, heretofore going to the King, shall go to the Commonwealth, save only such as the Legislature may abolish, or otherwise provide for.

The territories, contained within the Charters, erecting the Colonies of Maryland, Pennsylvania, North and South Carolina, are hereby ceded, released, and forever confirmed, to the people of these Colonies respectively, with all the rights of property, jurisdiction and government, and all other rights whatsover, which might, at any time heretofore, have been claimed by Virginia, except the free navigation and use of the rivers Patomaque and Pokomoke, with the property of the Virginia shores and strands, bordering on either of the said rivers, and all improvements, which have been, or shall be made thereon. The western and northern extent of Virginia shall, in all other respects, stand as fixed by the Charter of King James I. in the year one thousand six hundred and nine, and by the public treaty of peace between the Courts of Britain and France, in the year one thousand seven hundred and sixty-three; unless by act of this Legislature, one or more governments be established westward of the Alleghany mountains. And no purchases of lands shall be made of the Indian natives, but on behalf of the public, by authority of the General Assembly.

Reference: Francis Newton Thorpe (ed.), *The Federal and State Constitutions, Colonial Charters, and Other Organic Laws of the States*, Vol. VII (Washington: GPO, 1909).

BILL TO REMOVE STATE GOVERNMENT TO RICHMOND, NOVEMBER 11, 1776

WHEREAS great numbers of the Inhabitants of this Commonwealth must frequently, and of necessity resort to the seat of Government, where General assemblys are convened, Superior Courts are held and the Governor and Council usually transact the executive business of Government, and the equal rights of all the said Inhabitants require that such seat of Government should be as nearly central to all, as may be, having regard only to Navigation the benefits of which are necessary for encouraging the growth of a Town. *And Whereas* it has been found by the experience of some of our Sister States a very distressing circumstance, in times of war, that their seats of Government were so situated as to be exposed to the insults, and injuries of the publick enemy, which *dangers may be avoided* distresses may be prevented in this Commonwealth and equal Justice done to all *the* it's Citizens of this Commonwealth by removing *the* it's seat of Government to the town of in the County of which is more safe and central than any other Town situated on navigable water.

Be it therefore enacted, by the General Assembly of the Commonwealth of Virginia, that six whole squares of ground, surrounded each of them by four streets, and containing all the ground within such streets situate in the said Town of and on an open and airy part thereof shall be appropriated to the use and purpose of public buildings.

And be it further enacted that on one of the said squares shall be erected one house for the use of the General assembly to be called the Capitol which said Capitol shall contain two rooms or apartments for the use of the Senate and their Clerk, and two others for the use of the House of Delegates and their Clerk, and others for the purposes of Conferences, Committees, and a Lobby, of such forms and dimensions as shall be adapted to their respective purposes. *And* on one other of the said squares shall be erected another building to be called the General Courthouse which shall contain two rooms or apartments for the use of the Court of Appeals and its Clerk, two others for the use of the High Court of Chancery and its Clerk, two others for the use of the General Court and its Clerk, two others for the use of the Court of Admiralty and its Clerk, two others for the use of the Privy Council and its Clerk and others for the uses of Grand and petty juries of such forms and dimensions as shall be adapted to their respective purposes, which said houses shall be built in a handsome manner with walls of Brick, and Porticos, where the same may be convenient or Ornamental: on one other of the said Squares, shall be built a house with three apartments for the Ordinary use of the Clerks of the High Court of Chancery, General Court, and Court of Admiralty; each of them to have one of the said apartments: one other house with three apartments, to be used as a land office: and one other for a publick jail with few apartments for the present, but so planned as to admit of addition in future: two other of the said Squares shall be appropriated to the use of the Governor of the Commonwealth for the time being, to be built on hereafter, and one other square shall be appropriated to the use of a publick Market.

And be it further enacted that five persons shall be appointed by joint Ballot of both houses of Assembly to be called the Directors of the publick buildings who, or any three of them, shall be and are hereby empowered to make choice of such squares of ground situate as before directed as shall be most proper and convenient for the said publick purposes; to agree on plans for the said buildings; to employ proper workmen to erect the same; to procure necessary materials for them; and to draw on the Treasurer of this Commonwealth from time to time as the same shall be wanting for any sums of money not exceeding six thousand pounds in the whole; which draughts he is hereby authorized to answer out of any public money which shall be in his hands at the time: and in case of the death of any of the said Directors, or their refusal to act, the Governor is hereby authorized to appoint others in their stead who shall have the same powers as if they had been *chosen* appointed by joint Ballot of both houses as before directed.

And to the end that reasonable satisfaction may be paid and allowed for all such Lotts of ground as by virtue of this Act may be taken and appropriated to the uses aforesaid, *Be it further enacted* that the Clerk of the County of is hereby empowered and required at the desire of the said Directors to issue a writ directed to the Sheriff of the said County, commanding him to summon and impannel twelve able and discreet Freeholders, no ways concerned in interest in the said Lotts of land, nor in any ways related to the Owners or Proprietors thereof to meet at the said Town of on a certain day to be named in the said writ, not under five nor more than ten days from the date thereof who shall be sworne by the said Sheriff, and shall upon their Oaths value and appraise the said Lots of ground in so many several and distinct parcels as shall be owned by several and distinct owners, and according to their respective interests and Estates therein; and if the said valuation can not be completed in one day then the said Sheriff shall adjourn the said Jurors from day to day until the same be completed, and after such valuation and appraisement so made, the said Sheriff shall forthwith return the same under the hands and Seals of the said Jurors to the Clerks office of the said County. And the right and property of the said Owners *of* in the said lots of land shall be immediately divested and be transferred to this Commonwealth in full and absolute dominion, any want of consent or disability to consent in the said owners notwithstanding.

And be it further Enacted, that the Costs and charges of the purchase of the said Lotts of land shall be paid and satisfied by the publick at the next Session of Assembly to the several and respective proprietors or owners thereof according to the valuation made as aforesaid.

And be it further Enacted that it shall and may be lawful for the said Directors and they are hereby required to rent at the publick expence for the use of the Governor such Houses and Lotts of land as may be necessary for his accomodation until buildings for that purpose may with convenience be erected by the Publick.

And Whereas it may be expedient to enlarge the said Town of by laying off an additional number of Lotts to be added thereto and it may also happen that some of the Lands adjacent to the said Town, not yet laid off into Lotts, may be more convenient for the publick uses, Be it therefore enacted that it shall and may be lawful for the of the said town of and they are hereby required to cause two hundred additional lots or half acres of land to be laid off adjacent to such parts of the said Town of as to them shall seem most convenient for the use of those who may chuse to settle in the said Town. And the said Directors shall be at Liberty to appropriate the six squares aforesaid either from among the Lotts now in the said town, or those to be laid off as before directed,

or may have the said Six Squares laid off in any place adjacent to the said Town, and the said Six squares and two hundred Lotts shall thenceforth be added to and be a part of the said town of saving always to the proprietors of the Land so to be laid off into lotts their full right to the said lotts (other than the Six squares aforesaid) when the same shall be laid off.

And Be it further Enacted that from and after the 25th day of December which shall be in the Year of our Lord 1777. the said Court of Appeals, High Court of Chancery, General Court and Court of Admiralty shall thenceforth hold their Sessions in the said General Courthouse: that the first meeting of General Assembly after the same 25th day of December shall in like manner be in the said Capitol, and the Clerks of the two houses of Assembly and of the said several Courts are hereby authorized and required, at some convenient time before hand, to remove, at the publick expence, their several records to the said Offices to be provided and appropriated to them respectively by the said Directors.

Reference: Julian Boyd (ed.), *The Papers of Thomas Jefferson,* Vol. I (Princeton: Princeton University Press, 1930).

BILLS ESTABLISHING COURT OF APPEALS AND HIGH COURT OF CHANCERY, NOVEMBER 25, 1776

For establishing a court of Appeals for finally determining all suits and controversies, be it enacted by the General assembly that at such place as shall be appointed by act of General assembly there shall be holden a court of Appeals, *to consist of the Judges of the High court of Chancery, the Judges of the General court, and the Judges of the court of Admiralty, any nine of them to be a court, to have precedence in the said court according to seniority.*

Every such judge before he enters upon the duties of his office in the said court shall in open court take and subscribe the oath of fidelity to the Commonwealth, and take the following oath of

office, to wit, 'You shall swear that you will well and truly serve this Commonwealth in the office of a judge of the court of Appeals, and that you will do equal right to all manner of people, great and small, high and low, rich and poor, without respect of persons: you shall not take by yourself or by any other any gift, fee, or reward of gold, silver or any other thing directly or indirectly of any person or persons great or small for any matter done or to be done by virtue of your office, except such fees or salary as shall be by law appointed: you shall not maintain by yourself or any other, privily or openly, any plea or quarrel, depending in the courts of this Commonwealth: you shall not delay any person of right for the letters or request of any person, nor for any other cause; and if any letter or request come to you contrary to the law, you shall nothing do for such letter or request, but you shall proceed to do the law, any such letter or request notwithstanding: and finally in all things belonging to your said office, during your continuance therein, you shall faithfully justly and truly, according to the best of your skill and judgment, do equal and impartial justice without fraud, favor, affection or partiality.'

There shall be two sessions of the said court in every year, to wit, one to begin on the 29th. day of March if not Sunday and then on the next day, the other to begin on the 29th. day of August if not Sunday, and then on the next day, to continue each of them six days, Sunday excluded, unless the business depending before them shall be finished in less time; in which case the Judges may adjourn to the next succeeding court.

The said court shall have power to hear and finally determine all suits and controversies whatsoever which shall be brought before them by appeal from the High court of chancery, the General court, or Court of Admiralty, or by writ of error sued out to any decree, judgment, or sentence of either of the said courts: or which shall be adjourned thither from either of the said courts on account of difficulty: but no suit whatsoever shall be originally commenced in the said court of Appeals. If the said court shall at any time be equally divided in opinion on any question coming before them by appeal, the decree, judgment or sentence of the court below on such question shall stand confirmed.

Provided that no appeal shall be allowed to the said court, or writ of error sued thereout, unless the matter in dispute, exclusive of costs, shall be of the value of fifty pounds, or that some Franchise be in question: and that upon all such appeals or writs of error the party prosecuting the same shall give bond and security in the same manner, and shall be liable to the like damages upon the affirmance of the decree, judgment, or sentence, as is provided and directed upon Appeals to, or writs of error sued out of the General court.

The said court of Appeals shall have power to appoint a tip-staff and Cryer, and also a clerk, who shall issue writs of error, upon bond and security given to him, in all cases where the same are hereby allowed to be issued, and shall receive and carefully preserve transcripts of the records upon all such writs, and on Appeals, which shall be transmitted to him by the clerks of the High court of Chancery, the General court and court of Admiralty respectively, entering the names of the parties in a docket in the order he shall receive them, that the suits may be heard in a regular course, without preference to suitors, unless the court for good cause to them shewn, shall order any cause to be heard out of it's turn: the said clerk shall also attend the court during their several sittings, and make due entries of their proceedings; and shall certify their affirmance or reversal of the decree judgment or sentence in each case, with the costs of the party prevailing, to the court where the said decree, judgment or sentence was given; which court shall enter up the same, and execution shall issue thereupon as well for the costs expended in the court of appeals, as the other matters recovered by the decree, judgment or sentence.

No appeal shall be allowed to the said court or writ of error issued until a final judgment be given in the court from whence the appeal is, or to which the writ of error is directed.

Previous to the hearing of each cause in the said court, a clear and concise state of the case of each party, with the points intended to be insisted on, shall be drawn up and signed by the party's counsel and printed copies thereof delivered to each of the Judges for their perusal and consideration, the expence whereof shall be taxed in the bill of costs.

FOR establishing a Court of general Jurisdiction in Chancery, Be it enacted by the General Assembly of the commonwealth of Virginia, That at some certain place to be appointed by Act of General Assembly and at the times hereinafter directed shall be held a principal Court of Judicature for this commonwealth which shall be called the High Court of Chancery and shall consist of three judges to be chosen from time to time, by the joint ballot of both houses of Assembly and commissioned by the Governor, to hold their office so long as they shall respectively demean themselves well therein any two of them to be a court.

Every person so commissioned before he enters upon the duties of his office, shall, in open Court, take and subscribe the oath of fidelity to this commonwealth and take the following oath of office to wit "You shall swear that well and truly you will serve this Commonwealth in the office of Judge of the High Court of Chancery and that you will do equal right to all manner of people great and small, high and low, rich and poor, according to Equity and good conscience and the laws and usages of Virginia without respect of persons, you shall not take by yourself, or by any other, any gift, fee, or reward of gold, silver or any other thing directly or indirectly of any person or persons great or small for any matter done by virtue of your office; except such fees, or salary as shall be by law appointed, you shall not maintain by yourself or any other privily or openly any plea or quarrel depending in the Courts of this Commonwealth, you shall not delay any person of right for the letters or request of any person nor for any other cause, and if any letter or request come to you contrary to law, you shall nothing do for such letter or request but you shall proceed to do the law any such letter or request notwithstanding, and finally in all things belonging to your said office during your continuance therein, you shall faithfully, justly, and truly according to the best of your skill and judgment do equal and impartial justice without fraud, favour, affection or partiality. *So help you God,*" and if any person shall presume to execute the said office without having taken the said oaths he shall forfeit and pay the sum of five hundred pounds for his said offence.

The said Court shall have general jurisdiction over all persons and in all causes in Chancery, whether brought before them by original process, appeal from any inferior Court, Certiorari, or other legal means, but no person shall commence an original suit in the said Court in a matter of less value than ten pounds except it be against the justices of any County, or other inferior Court

or the Vestry of any Parish on pain of having the same dismissed with Costs.

There shall be two Sessions of the said Court in every year, to wit, one to begin on the fifth day of April, if not Sunday, and then on the next day, the other on the fifth day of September if not Sunday, and then on the next day, to continue each of them eighteen days, Sundays excluded, if they shall so long have business to require their attendance, if not they may when the business is dispatched adjourn to the next Court. The said Court shall however be considered as always open so as to grant injunctions, Writs of ne exeat or other process heretofore allowed by the laws to be issued in time of Vacation by the Clerk of the General Court in Chancery.

The said Court shall have power from time to time to appoint a Clerk who shall hold his office during good behaviour and be entitled to such fees or Salary as shall be established by the legislature.

All original process to bring any person to answer any bill, petition, or information in the said Court and all subsequent process thereupon shall be issued and signed by the Clerk in the name of the Commonwealth and bear teste by the first Commissioner of the said Court; shall be returnable to the first or seventeenth day of the Term which shall be next after the suing out such process and may be executed at any time before the return day thereof. And if any process shall be executed so late that the Sheriff hath not reasonable time to return the same before the day of appearance and thereupon any subsequent process shall be awarded the Sheriff shall not execute such subsequent process but shall return the first process by him executed on which there shall be the same proceedings, as if it had been returned in due time, and all Appeals from decrees in Chancery obtained in any inferior Court shall be made to the third day of the next term.

In all Suits in the said Court the following rules and methods shall be observed that is to say—

The Complainant shall file his Bill within one Calendar month after the day of appearance, or may be ruled on the requisition of the defendant to file such Bill and if he fails to do so within one Calendar month after such rule the suit shall be dismissed with costs and upon the Complainants dismissing his Bill, or the defendants dismissing the same for want of prosecution the Complainant shall pay costs to be taxed by the Clerk of the Court: for which costs a subpoena or other process of contempt may issue returnable on any return day.

The Complainant may amend his Bill before the defendant or his Attorney hath taken out a copy thereof, or in a small matter afterwards without paying costs, but if he amend in a material point after such copy obtained, he shall pay the defendant all costs occasioned thereby.

If the defendant shall not appear on the day of appearance (which in all cases shall be the second day after the term to which the subpoena is returnable) an attachment shall be awarded and issued against him returnable to the next term, which being returned executed, if the defendant doth not appear or being brought into Court upon any such process shall obstinately refuse to answer, the Complainants Bill shall be taken pro confesso and the matter thereof decreed accordingly.

The defendant within three calendar months after his appearance and Bill filed shall put in his answer to be filed with the Clerk in the office, at the expiration of which time, if no answer be filed the Clerk upon request shall issue an Attachment returnable to the next court, and if no answer be filed upon the return of such Attachment executed, the Complainants Bill shall be taken as confessed and the matter thereof decreed and if the Attachment be returned not executed, an Attachment with proclamations, and such subsequent process of contempt may issue as was heretofore issued out of the General Court sitting in Chancery in like cases.

No process of contempt shall issue unless the subpena be returned served by a sworn officer or affidavit be made of the service thereof.

Every defendant may swear to his answer before any judges of this or of the General Court or any justice of the peace.

When a cross Bill shall be preferred, the defendant or defendants to the first Bill shall answer thereto, before the defendant or defendants to the cross Bill shall be compellable to answer such cross bill.

The Complainant shall reply or file exceptions within two Calendar months after the answer shall have been put in. If he fails so to do the defendant may give a rule to reply with the Clerk of the Court which being expired, and no replication or exceptions filed the suit shall be dismissed with costs, but the Court may order the same to be retained if they see cause on payment of costs.

If the Complainant's Attorney shall except against any answer as insufficient he may file his exceptions and give rule with the Clerk to make a better answer within two Calendar months, and if within that time the defendant shall put in a sufficient answer the same shall be received without costs, but if any defendant insist on the sufficiency of his answer, or neglect, or refuse to put in a sufficient answer, or shall put in another insufficient answer, the Plaintiff may set down his exceptions to be argued the next term in Court and after the expiration of such rule, or any second insufficient answer put in no further or other answer shall be received, but upon payment of costs.

If upon argument the Complainants exceptions shall be over ruled or the defendants answer adjudged insufficient, the Complainant shall pay to the defendant or the defendant to the Complainant such costs as shall be allowed by the Court.

Upon a second answer adjudged insufficient costs shall be doubled. If a defendant shall put in a third insufficient answer which shall be so adjudged the Complainant may go on with the subsequent process of contempt as if no answer had been put in.

Rules to plead, answer, reply, rejoin or other proceedings not before particularly mentioned, when necessary, shall be given from month to month with the Clerk in his office, and shall be entered in a rule book for the information of all Parties, Attornies or Solicitors concerned therein.

No defendant shall be admitted to put in a rejoinder unless it be filed on or before the expiration of the rule to rejoin, but the Complainant may proceed to the examination of witnesses.

After an Attachment with proclamation returned, no plea or demurrer shall be received, unless by order of Court upon motion.

If the Complainant conceives any plea or demurrer to be naught, either for the matter or manner of it he may set it down with the Clerk to be argued. Or if he thinks the plea good but not true he may take issue upon it and proceed to trial by jury as hath been heretofore used in other causes in Chancery where trial hath been by jury. And if thereupon the plea shall be found false the Complainant shall have the same advantages as if it had been so found by verdict at common Law.

If a plea or demurrer be over ruled, no other plea or demurrer shall be thereafter received but the defendant shall answer the allegations of the Bill.

If the Complainant shall not proceed to reply to, or set for hearing as before mentioned any plea or demurrer before the second Court after filing the same, the Bill may be dismissed of course with costs.

Upon a plea or demurrer, argued, and over ruled, costs shall be paid, as where an answer is judged insufficient, and the defendant shall answer within two Calendar months after, but if adjudged good the defendant shall have his costs.

If any defendant shall obstinately insist on a demurrer after the same hath been over ruled by the Court, and shall refuse to answer, the Bill shall be taken as confessed and the matter thereof decreed.

After any Bill filed and before the defendant hath answered, upon oath made that any of the Complainants witnesses are aged or infirm or going out of the country, the Clerk may issue a commission for taking the examination of such witnesses de bene esse the party praying such commission giving reasonable notice to the adverse party of the time and place of taking the depositions.

All matters of fact material to the determination of the cause which in the course of the proceedings shall be affirmed by the one party and denied by the other, shall be tried by Jury, for which purpose an issue or issues shall be made up by declaration and plea as hath heretofore been used in Chancery when issues have been specially directed to be made up and tried by Jury.

And for rendering the said trials more convenient to parties and witnesses, a venue shall be laid in the Declaration a transcript of the record deliverd to the Clerk of Assise where the said venue is laid and a trial be had before the judge of the same assise in every case in such manner as is directed by law in actions at the common law, saving to the Defendant the same benefit of evidence by his own answer as hath been heretofore allowed in trials before the Court of Chancery. Nevertheless the judges for good cause to them shewn, may direct the venue to be changed in any cause or may order any trial to be had at their bar and not at the Assises.

The judge of Assise shall certifie under his seal upon or with each record transmitted, the verdict which shall be given therein, together with such demurrers, or exceptions to evidence, or to the opinion of the Court as he shall be desired by either party to certifie, which verdict and other certificates the Clerk of Assise shall return in convenient time to the office of the Clerk in Chancery.

When the Postea shall be return'd if the Complainant shall not within one Calendar month thereafter set down the cause for hearing with the Clerk, the Defendant may have the same set down at his request.

The Court in their sittings may regulate all proceedings in the Office and for good cause shewn may set aside any dismissions and reinstate the suits, on such terms as shall appear equitable.

For prevention of errors in entering up the decrees and orders of the court the proceedings of every day shall be drawn up at large by the clerk and read in open court the next day (except those of the last day of each term, which shall be drawn up, read and corrected the same day) and any necessary corrections made therein, when they shall be signed by the presiding judge of the court and preserved among the records.

And for the more entire and better preservation of the records of the court, when any cause shall be finally determined, the clerk shall enter all the pleadings therein and other matters relating thereto, together in a book to be kept for that purpose, so that an entire and perfect record may be made thereof, and those wherein the title to lands is determined shall be entered in separate books to be kept for that purpose only.

The Court in their Sessions or any two of the Judges in vacation may grant writs of Certiorari for removing before them the proceedings on any suit in Chancery depending in any county or other inferior Court, writs of ne exeat to prevent the departure of any defendant out of the Country, until security be given for performing the decree, and writs of Injunction to stay Execution of Judgments obtained in any of the Courts of common Law subject nevertheless to the rules following That is to say

No writ of Certiorari shall be granted to remove any suit unless the matter in dispute be of value sufficient to intitle the High Court of Chancery to original jurisdiction therein: nor unless ten days notice of the motion be given to the adverse party: nor in Vacation but upon such petition and affidavit as are by law directed for writs of Certiorari to be granted by the General Court and in all cases bond and security shall be given for performing the decree of the said High Court of Chancery before the issuing of the Certiorari. Writs of ne exeat shall not be granted but upon a bill filed and affidavits made to the truth of its allegations, which being produced to the Court in term time or to two judges in Vacation they may grant or refuse such writ as to them shall seem just, and if granted, they shall direct to be indorsed thereon in what penalty bond and security shall be required of the defendant.

If the Defendant shall by answer satisfie the Court there is no reason for his restraint; or give sufficient security to perform the Decree the writ may be discharged.

No Injunction shall be granted to stay proceedings in any suit at law, unless the matter in dispute be of value sufficient to admit of original jurisdiction in the said High Court of Chancery,

nor unless the Court in Term time or two judges thereof in Vacation shall be satisfied of the Plaintiffs equity either by affidavit certified at the foot of the Bill that the allegations thereof are true, or by other means, and shall order the same, in which case the Complainant shall enter into bond with sufficient security for paying all money and tobacco and costs due or to become due to the Plaintiff in the action at Law, and also all such costs as shall be awarded against him or her in case the Injunction shall be dissolved.

The said High Court of Chancery shall take cognizance of and hear and determine all suits in Chancery which were depending in the General Court at its last adjournment in the same manner as if the said Suits had been originally commenced in or appeals enterd to the said High Court of Chancery.

If any suit shall be depending or hereafter commenced against any Defendant or Defendants who are out of this country and others within the same having in their hands effects of or otherwise indebted to such absent defendant or defendants and the appearances of such absentees be not entered and security given to the satisfaction of the Court for performing the decrees upon affidavit that such Defendant or defendants are out of the Country, or that upon enquiry at his her or their usual place of abode, he she or they could not be found so as to be served with process, in all such cases the said High Court of Chancery may make any order and require surety if it shall appear necessary to restrain the defendants in this Country from paying, conveying away or secreting the debts by them owing to, or the effects in their hands of such absent defendant or defendants and for that purpose may order such debts to be paid and effects delivered to the said Plaintiff or Plaintiffs upon their giving sufficient security for the return thereof to such persons and in such manner as the Court shall direct. The Court shall also appoint some day in the succeeding term for the absent defendant or defendants to enter his or their appearance to the suit and give security for performing the decree, a copy of which order shall be forthwith published in the Virginia gazette and continued for two months successively and shall also be published on some Sunday immediately after divine service in such Parish Church or Churches as the Complainant shall direct; and another copy shall be Posted at the front doors of the said Court.

If such absent defendant or defendants shall not appear and give such security within the time limited or such further time as the Court may allow them for good cause shewn, the Court may proceed to take such proof as the Complainant shall offer, and if they shall thereupon be satisfied of the Justice of the demand they may order the Bill to be taken as confessed and make such order and decree therein as shall appear just, and may inforce due performance and execution thereof by such ways and means as hath heretofore been used for inforcing other decrees, requiring the Plaintiff or Plaintiffs to give security as the Court shall approve, for abiding such future order as may be made for restoring the estate or effects to the absent defendant or defendants upon his or their appearance and answering the Bill: and if the Plaintiff or Plaintiffs shall refuse to give, or not be able to procure such security the effects shall remain under the direction of the Court in the hands of a receiver or otherwise for so long time, and shall then be finally disposed of in such manner as to the Court shall seem just.

If any defendant or defendants shall be in custody upon any process of contempt, and be brought into Court by virtue of a writ of Habeas corpus or other process, and shall refuse or neglect to enter his or her appearance according to the rules of the Court or appoint an Attorney of the Court to do the same for him, The Court in such case may direct an Attorney to enter an appearance for the Defendant or defendants, and thereupon such proceedings may be had as if he or they had actually entered an appearance; but if such defendant or defendants shall be in custody at the time a decree shall be made, upon Refusal or neglect to enter an appearance or to appoint an Attorney as aforesaid, or shall be forthcoming so as to be served with a copy of the Decree then such defendant or defendants shall be served with such copy before any process shall be taken out to compel the performance thereof.

And if such defendant or defendants shall die in custody before such service, then his Heir, if any real estate be sequestered or affected by such decree, or if only personal estate, his Executor or Administrator shall be served with a copy in a reasonable time after such death shall be known to the Plaintiff and who is such Heir Executor, or Administrator.

If any person or persons who shall be out of the Country at the time any decree is pronounced as aforesaid, shall within seven years from the passing such decree return to this country and appear openly or in case of his or her death if his or her Heir Executor or Administrator shall within the said seven years be and appear openly within this country, the Plaintiff or Plaintiffs their Executors or Administrators shall serve such person or persons so returning or appearing with a copy of the decree within a reasonable time after such return or appearance shall be known to the Plaintiff or Plaintiffs and thereupon such defendants or their representatives may within twelve months after such service, or those defendants not served with a copy, or their representatives, may within seven years after the decree pronounced appear in Court and petition to have the case reheard. And upon their paying down or giving security for payment of such costs, as the Court shall think reasonable, they shall be admitted to answer the Bill, and issue may be joined, and witnesses on both sides examined, and such other proceedings, decree and execution had, as if there had been no former decree in the cause. But if the several defendants or their representatives, upon whom the decree shall be so served shall not within twelve months after such service and the other defendants or their representatives upon whom no such service is made shall not within seven years from the time of the decree pronounced appear and petition to have the cause reheard as aforesaid, and pay or secure to be paid such costs as the Court may think reasonable as aforesaid, All and every decree to be made in pursuance of this Act against any defendant or defendants so failing, shall stand absolutely confirmed against him, her, or them, his, her, or their heirs, Executors and Administrators and all persons claiming under him, her, or them by virtue of any act or conveyance, done or made subsequent to the commencement of the suit. And at the end of such term, the Court may make such further order for quieting the Plaintiff or Plaintiffs in any such suits, in their possession of and title to the Estate and effects so sequestered or made liable, as to them shall seem reasonable.

Reference: Julian Boyd (ed.), *The Papers of Thomas Jefferson,* Vol. I (Princeton: Princeton University Press, 1930).

REVISED STATE LAWS, JUNE 18, 1779

WHEREAS on the late change which hath of necessity been introduced into the form of government in this country it is become also necessary to make corresponding changes in the laws heretofore in force, many of which are inapplicable to the powers of government as now organised, others are founded on principles heterogeneous to the republican spirit, others which, long before such change, had been oppressive to the people, could yet never be repealed while the regal power continued, and others, having taken their origin while our ancestors remained in Britain, are not so well adapted to our present circumstances of time and place, and it is also necessary to introduce certain other laws, which, though proved by the experience of other states to be friendly to liberty and the rights of mankind, we have not heretofore been permitted to adopt; and whereas a work of such magnitude, labour, and difficulty, may not be effected during the short and busy term of a session of assembly:

Be it therefore enacted by the General Assembly of the commonwealth of Virginia, and it is hereby enacted by the authority of the same, That a committee, to consist of five persons, shall be appointed by joint ballot of both houses (three of whom to be a quorum) who shall have full power and authority to revise, alter, amend, repeal, or introduce all or any of the said laws, to form the same into bills, and report them to the next meeting of the general assembly.

And to prevent any delay which may happen in the proceedings of the said committee, by the death or disability of any member thereof, *Be it farther enacted,* That if either of the said members should die, refuse to act, or be disabled by sickness from proceeding in the said work, it shall be lawful for the remaining members to appoint some other person in his stead and place, which person so appointed is hereby declared a member of the said committee, in like manner as if he had originally been appointed by joint ballot of both houses.

And be it farther enacted, That the said committee shall have power to meet at such times and places as they shall think proper for the purpose of proceeding on the said revisal, to appoint a clerk for their ease and assistance in the work, and to send for any copies of records to the clerk in whose custody they are, which such clerk is hereby directed forthwith to transmit to them.

Provided, That such bills so to be prepared and reported by the committee of revisors shall be of no force or authority until they shall have gone through their several readings in both houses of assembly, and been passed by them in such manner and form as if the same had been originally introduced without the direction of this act. they shall have disbursed, before the general assembly of this commonwealth.

And be it farther enacted, That the governour, by and with the advice of the privy council, may, and he is hereby authorised and empowered to form out of the two militia companies in the town of Alexandria, in the county of Fairfax, one artillery company, to consist of fifty matrosses, with proper officers, to be duly exercised at the batteries in the said town twice in every week, and to mount proper guards at the same; and the officers and matrosses of the said company, when on duty, shall receive the same pay and provisions, and be subject to the like rules and regulations, as the other artillery companies in the service of this state receive and are subject to.

And whereas the minute companies formerly raised in this country are already greatly reduced by enlistments into the regular service, and are likely to be more so by future enlistments, so that there remains little prospect of their answering the purposes of their institution, and moreover it will tend to weaken the militia of this commonwealth, and may create discontents, if such broken companies of minute-men continue exempt from militia duty, *Be it therefore enacted, by the authority aforesaid,* That from and after the passing this act all the minute battalions, companies, and parts of companies, throughout this state shall be totally dissolved and discharged, and the said minute-men shall thereafter be considered as militia, and be subject to all such rules and regulations as are or shall be established for the better training and disciplining the militia; and the captains of each minute company shall, and they are hereby required to receive of each man in their respective companies all such arms and other accoutrements as have been provided at the publick expense, and deliver, or cause the same to be delivered, to the county lieutenant of each county, to be disposed of as the governour, with the advice of the council, shall direct.

Reference: William Waller Hening (ed.), *The Statutes at Large, Being a Collection of the Laws of Virginia,* Vol. IX (Richmond: J.&G. Cochran, 1821).

36

New Jersey, July 2, 1776

New Jersey followed the procedure of adoption and form of many other first state constitutions. Unique to New Jersey, however, was that its constitution eliminated all property requirements for voting.

CONSTITUTION, JULY 2, 1776

WHEREAS all the constitutional authority ever possessed by the kings of Great Britain over these colonies, or their other dominions, was, by compact, derived from the people, and held of them, for the common interest of the whole society; allegiance and protection are, in the nature of things, reciprocal ties, each equally depending upon the other, and liable to be dissolved by the others being refused or withdrawn. And whereas George the Third, king of Great Britain, has refused protection to the good people of these colonies; and, by assenting to sundry acts of the British parliament, attempted to subject them to the absolute dominion of that body; and has also made war upon them, in the most cruel and unnatural manner, for no other cause, than asserting their just rights—all civil authority under him is necessarily at an end, and a dissolution of government in each colony has consequently taken place.

And whereas, in the present deplorable situation of these colonies, exposed to the fury of a cruel and relentless enemy, some form of government is absolutely necessary, not only for the preservation of good order, but also the more effectually to unite the people, and enable them to exert their whole force in their own necessary defence: and as the honorable the continental congress, the supreme council of the American colonies, has advised such of the colonies as have not yet gone into measures, to adopt for themselves, respectively, such government as shall best conduce to their own happiness and safety, and the well-being of America in general:— We, the representatives of the colony of New Jersey, having been elected by all the counties, in the freest manner, and in congress assembled, have, after mature deliberations, agreed upon a set of charter rights and the form of a Constitution, in manner following, viz.

I. That the government of this Province shall be vested in a Governor, Legislative Council, and General Assembly.

II. That the Legislative Council, and General Assembly, shall be chosen, for the first time, on the second Tuesday in August next; the members whereof shall be the same in number and qualifications as are herein after mentioned; and shall be and remain vested with all the powers and authority to be held by any future Legislative

Council and Assembly of this Colony, until the second Tuesday in October, which shall be in the year of our Lord one thousand seven hundred and seventy-seven.

III. That on the second Tuesday in October yearly, and every year forever (with the privilege of adjourning from day to day as occasion may require) the counties shall severally choose one person, to be a member of the Legislative Council of this Colony, who shall be, and have been, for one whole year next before the election, an inhabitant and freeholder in the county in which he is chosen, and worth at least one thousand pounds proclamation money, of real and personal estate, within the same county; that, at the same time, each county shall also choose three members of Assembly; provided that no person shall be entitled to a seat in the said Assembly unless he be, and have been, for one whole year next before the election, an inhabitant of the county he is to represent, and worth five hundred pounds proclamation money, in real and personal estate, in the same county: that on the second Tuesday next after the day of election, the Council and Assembly shall separately meet; and that the consent of both Houses shall be necessary to every law; provided, that seven shall be a quorum of the Council, for doing business, and that no law shall pass, unless there be a majority of all the Representatives of each body personally present, and agreeing thereto. Provided always, that if a majority of the representatives of this Province, in Council and General Assembly convened, shall, at any time or times hereafter, judge it equitable and proper, to add to or diminish the number or proportion of the members of Assembly for any county or counties in this Colony, then, and in such case, the same may, on the principles of more equal representation, be lawfully done; anything in this Charter to the contrary notwithstanding; so that the whole number of Representatives in Assembly shall not, at any time, be less than thirty-nine.

IV. That all inhabitants of this Colony, of full age, who are worth fifty pounds proclamation money, clear estate in the same, and have resided within the county in which they claim a vote for twelve months immediately preceding the election, shall be entitled to vote for Representatives in Council and Assembly; and also for all other public officers, that shall be elected by the people of the county at large.

V. That the Assembly, when met, shall have power to choose a Speaker, and other their officers; to be judges of the qualifications and elections of their own members; sit upon their own adjournments; prepare bills, to be passed into laws; and to empower their Speaker to convene them, whenever any extraordinary occurrence shall render it necessary.

VI. That the Council shall also have power to prepare bills to pass into laws, and have other like powers as the Assembly, and in all respects be a free and independent branch of the Legislature of this Colony; save only, that they shall not prepare or alter any money bill—which shall be the privilege of the Assembly; that the Council shall, from time to time, be convened by the Governor or Vice-President, but must be convened, at all times, when the Assembly sits; for which purpose the Speaker of the House of Assembly shall always, immediately after an adjournment, give notice to the Governor, or Vice-President, of the time and place to which the House is adjourned.

VII. That the Council and Assembly jointly, at their first meeting after each annual election, shall, by a majority of votes, elect some fit person within the Colony, to be Governor for one year, who shall be constant President of the Council, and have a casting vote in their proceedings; and that the Council themselves shall choose a Vice-President who shall act as such in the absence of the Governor.

VIII. That the Governor, or, in his absence, the Vice-President of the Council, shall have the supreme executive power, be Chancellor of the Colony, and act as captain-general and commander in chief of all the militia, and other military force in this Colony; and that any three or more of the Council shall, at all times, be a privy-council, to consult them; and that the Governor be ordinary or surrogate-general.

IX. That the Governor and Council, (seven whereof shall be a quorum) be the Court of Appeals, in the last resort, in all clauses of law, as heretofore; and that they possess the power of granting pardons to criminals, after condemnation, in all cases of treason, felony, or other offences.

X. That captains, and all other inferior officers of the militia, shall be chosen by the companies, in the respective counties; but field and general officers, by the Council and Assembly.

XI. That the Council and Assembly shall have power to make the Great Seal of this Colony, which shall be kept by the Governor, or, in his absence, by the Vice-President of the Council, to be used by them as occasion may require: and it shall be called, *The Great Seal of the Colony of New-Jersey.*

XII. That the Judges of the Supreme Court shall continue in office for seven years: the Judges of the Inferior Court of Common Pleas in the several counties, Justices of the Peace, Clerks of the Supreme Court, Clerks of the Inferior Court of Common Pleas and Quarter Sessions, the Attorney-General; and Provincial Secretary, shall continue in office for five years: and the Provincial Treasurer shall continue in office for one year; and that they shall be severally appointed by the Council and Assembly, in manner aforesaid, and commissioned by the Governor, or, in his absence, the Vice-President of the Council. Provided always, that the said officers, severally, shall be capable of being re-appointed, at the end of the terms severally before limited; and that any of the said officers shall be liable to be dismissed, when adjudged guilty of misbehaviour, by the Council, on an impeachment of the Assembly.

XIII. That the inhabitants of each county, qualified to vote as aforesaid, shall at the time and place of electing their Representatives, annually elect one Sheriff, and one or more Coroners; and that they may re-elect the same person to such offices, until he shall have served three years, but no longer; after which, three years must elapse before the same person is capable of being elected again. When the election is certified to the Governor, or Vice-President, under the hands of six freeholders of the county for which they were elected, they shall be immediately commissioned to serve in their respective offices.

XIV. That the townships, at their annual town meetings for electing other officers, shall choose constables for the districts respectively; and also three or more judicious freeholders of good character, to hear and finally determine all appeals, relative to unjust assessments, in cases of public taxation; which commissioners of appeal shall, for that purpose, sit at some suitable time or times, to be by them appointed, and made known to the people by advertisements.

XV. That the laws of the Colony shall begin in the following style, viz. "Be it enacted by the Council and General Assembly of this Colony, and it is hereby enacted by authority of the same:" that all commissions, granted by the Governor or Vice-President, shall run thus—"The Colony of New-Jersey to A. B. &c. greeting:" and that all writs shall likewise run in the name of the Colony: and that all indictments shall conclude in the following manner, viz. "Against the peace of this Colony, the government and dignity of the same."

XVI. That all criminals shall be admitted to the same privileges of witnesses and counsel, as their prosecutors are or shall be entitled to.

XVII. That the estates of such persons as shall destroy their own lives, shall not, for that offence, be forfeited; but shall descend in the same manner, as they would have done, had such persons died in the natural way; nor shall any article, which may occasion accidentally the death of any one, be henceforth deemed a deodand, or in anywise forfeited, on account of such misfortune.

XVIII. That no person shall ever, within this Colony, be deprived of the inestimable privilege of worshipping Almighty God in a manner agreeable to the dictates of his own conscience; nor, under any pretence whatever, be compelled to attend any place of worship, contrary to his own faith and judgment; nor shall any person, within this Colony, ever be obliged to pay tithes, taxes, or any other rates, for the purpose of building or repairing any other church or churches, place or places of worship, or for the maintenance of any minister or ministry, contrary to what he believes to be right, or has deliberately or voluntarily engaged himself to perform.

XIX. That there shall be no establishment of any one religious sect in this Province, in preference to another; and that no Protestant inhabitant of this Colony shall be denied the enjoyment of any civil right, merely on account of his religious principles; but that all persons, professing a belief in the faith of any Protestant sect, who shall demean themselves peaceably under the government, as hereby established, shall be capable of being elected into any office of profit or trust, or being a member of either branch of the Legislature, and shall fully and freely enjoy every privilege and immunity, enjoyed by others their fellow subjects.

XX. That the legislative department of this government may, as much as possible, be preserved from all suspicion of corruption, none of the Judges of the Supreme or other Courts, Sheriffs, or any other person or persons possessed of any post of profit under the government, other than Justices of the Peace, shall be entitled to a seat in the Assembly: but that, on his being elected, and taking his seat, his office or post shall be considered as vacant.

XXI. That all the laws of this Province, contained in the edition lately published by Mr. Allinson, shall be and remain in full force, until altered by the Legislature of this Colony (such only excepted, as are incompatible with this Charter) and shall be, according as heretofore, regarded in all respects, by all civil officers, and others, the good people of this Province.

XXII. That the common law of England, as well as so much of the statute law, as have been heretofore practised in this Colony, shall still remain in force, until they shall be altered by a future law of the Legislature; such parts only excepted, as are repugnant to the rights and privileges contained in this Charter; and that the inestimable right of trial by jury shall remain confirmed as a part of the law of this Colony, without repeal, forever.

XXIII. That every person, who shall be elected as aforesaid to be a member of the Legislative Council, or House of Assembly, shall, previous to his taking his seat in Council or Assembly, take the following oath or affirmation, viz:

"I, A. B., do solemnly declare, that, as a member of the Legislative Council, [or Assembly, as the case may be,] of the Colony of New-Jersey, I will not assent to any law, vote or proceeding, which shall appear to me injurious to the public welfare of said Colony, nor that shall annual or repeal that part of the third section in the Charter of this Colony, which establishes, that the elections of members of the Legislative Council and Assembly shall be annual; nor that part of the twenty-second section in said Charter, respecting the trial by jury, nor that shall annul, repeal, or alter any part or parts of the eighteenth or nineteenth sections of the same."

And any person or persons, who shall be elected as aforesaid, is hereby empowered to administer to the said members the said oath or affirmation.

Provided always, and it is the true intent and meaning of this Congress, that if a reconciliation between Great-Britain and these Colonies should take place, and the latter be taken again under the protection and government of the crown of Britain, this Charter shall be null and void—otherwise to remain firm and inviolable.

In Provincial Congress, New Jersey, Burlington, July 2, 1776. By order of Congress. SAMUEL TUCKER, *Pres.* WILLIAM PATTERSON, *Secretary.*

Reference: Francis Newton Thorpe (ed.), *The Federal and State Constitutions, Colonial Charters, and Other Organic Laws of the States,* Vol. V (Washington: GPO, 1909).

37

Delaware, September 11, 1776

Delaware elected delegates to a constitutional convention, and they wrote a document similar to the other new states, and emphasized the duty of all eligible citizens to vote.

CONSTITUTION, SEPTEMBER 11, 1776

The Constitution, or System of Government, agreed to and resolved upon by the Representatives in full Convention of the Delaware State, formerly styled "The Government of the Counties of New Castle, Kent, and Sussex, upon Delaware," the said Representatives being chosen by the Freemen of the said State for that express Purpose.

ARTICLE 1. The government of the counties of New Castle, Kent and Sussex, upon Delaware, shall hereafter in all public and other writings be called The Delaware State.

ART. 2. The Legislature shall be formed of two distinct branches; they shall meet once or oftener in every year, and shall be called, "The General Assembly of Delaware."

ART. 3. One of the branches of the Legislature shall be called, "The House of Assembly," and shall consist of seven Representatives to be chosen for each county annually of such persons as are freeholders of the same.

ART. 4. The other branch shall be called "The council," and consist of nine members; three to be chosen for each county at the time of the first election of the assembly, who shall be freeholders of the county for which they are chosen, and be upwards of twenty-five years of age. At the end of one year after the general election, the councillor who had the smallest number of votes in each county shall be displaced, and the vacancies thereby occasioned supplied by the freemen of each county choosing the same or another person at a new election in manner aforesaid. At the end of two years after the first general election, the councillor who stood second in number of votes in each county shall be displaced, and the vacancies thereby occasioned supplied by a new election in manner aforesaid. And at the end of three years from the first general election, the councillor who had the greatest number of votes in each county shall be displaced, and the vacancies thereby occasioned supplied by a new election in manner aforesaid. And this rotation of a councillor being displaced at the end of three years in each county, and his office supplied by a new choice, shall be continued afterwards in due order annually forever, whereby, after the first general election, a councillor will remain in trust for three years from the time of his being elected, and a councillor will be displaced, and the same or another chosen in each county at every election.

ART. 5. The right of suffrage in the election of members for both houses shall remain as exercised by law at present; and each house shall choose its own speaker, appoint its own officers, judge of the qualifications and elections of its own members, settle its own rules of proceedings, and direct writs of election for supplying intermediate vacancies. They may also severally expel any of their own members for misbehavior, but not a second time in the same sessions for the same offence, if reelected; and they shall have all other powers necessary for the legislature of a free and independent State.

ART. 6. All money-bills for the support of government shall originate in the house of assembly, and may be altered, amended, or rejected by the legislative council. All other bills and ordinances may take rise in the house of assembly or legislative council, and may be altered, amended, or rejected by either.

ART. 7. A president or chief magistrate shall be chosen by joint ballot of both houses, to be taken in the house of assembly, and the box examined by the speakers of each house in the presence of the other members, and in case the numbers for the two highest in votes should be equal, then the speaker of the council shall have an additional casting voice, and the appointment of the person who has the majority of votes shall be entered at large on the minutes and journals of each house, and a copy thereof on parchment, certified and signed by the speakers respectively, and sealed with the great seal of the State, which they are hereby authorized to affix, shall be delivered to the person so chosen president, who shall continue in that office three years, and until the sitting of the next general assembly and no longer, nor be eligible until the expiration of three years after he shall have been out of that office. An adequate but moderate salary shall be settled on him during his continuance in office. He may draw for such sums of money as shall be appropriated by the general assembly, and be accountable to them for the same; he may, by and with the advice of the privy council, lay embargoes or prohibit the exportation of any commodity for any time not exceeding thirty days in the recess of the general assembly; he shall have the power of granting pardons or reprieves, except where the prosecution shall be carried on by the house of assembly, or the law shall otherwise direct, in which cases no pardon or reprieve shall be granted, but by a resolve of the house of assembly, and may exercise all the other executive powers of government, limited and restrained as by this constitution is mentioned, and according to the laws of the State. And on his death, inability, or absence from the State, the speaker of the legislative council for the time being shall be vice-president, and in case of his death, inability, or absence from the State, the speaker of the house of assembly shall have the powers of a president, until a new nomination is made by the general assembly.

ART. 8. A privy council, consisting of four members, shall be chosen by ballot, two by the legislative council and two by the house of assembly: *Provided,* That no regular officer of the army or navy in the service and pay of the continent, or of this, or of any other State, shall be eligible; and a member of the legislative council or of the house of assembly being chosen of the privy council, and accepting thereof, shall thereby lose his seat. Three members shall be a quorum, and their advice and proceedings shall be entered of record, and signed by the members present, (to any part of which any member may enter his dissent,) to be laid before the general assembly when called for by them. Two members shall be removed by ballot, one by the legislative council and one by the house of assembly, at the end of two years, and those who remain the next year after, who shall severally be ineligible for the three next years. The vacancies, as well as those occasioned by death or incapacity, shall be supplied by new elections in the same manner; and this rotation of a privy councillor shall be continued afterwards in due order annually forever. The president may by summons convene the privy council at any time when the public exigencies may require, and at such place as he shall think most convenient, when and where they are to attend accordingly.

ART. 9. The president, with the advice and consent of the privy council, may embody the militia, and act as captain-general and commander-in-chief of them, and the other military force of this State, under the laws of the same.

ART. 10. Either house of the general assembly may adjourn themselves respectively. The president shall not prorogue, adjourn, or dissolve the general assembly, but he may, with the advice of the privy council, or on the application of a majority of either house, call them before the time they shall stand adjourned; and the two houses shall always sit at the same time and place, for which purpose immediately after every adjournment the speaker of the house of assembly shall give notice to the speaker of the other house of the time to which the house of assembly stands adjourned.

ART. 11. The Delegates for Delaware to the Congress of the United States of America shall be chosen annually, or superseded in the mean time, by joint ballot of both houses in the general assembly.

ART. 12. The president and general assembly shall by joint ballot appoint three justices of the supreme court for the State, one of whom shall be chief justice, and a judge of admiralty, and also four justices of the courts of common pleas and orphans' courts for each county, one of whom in each court shall be styled "*chief justice*," (and in case of division on the ballot the president shall have an additional casting voice,) to be commissioned by the president under the great seal, who shall continue in office during good behavior; and during the time the justices of the said supreme court and courts of common pleas remain in office, they shall hold none other except in the militia. Any one of the justices of either of said courts shall have power, in case of the noncoming of his brethren, to open and adjourn the court. An adequate fixed but moderate salary shall be settled on them during their continuance in office. The president and privy council shall appoint the secretary, the attorney-general, registers for the probate of wills and granting letters of administration, registers in chancery, clerks of the courts of common pleas and orphans' courts, and clerks of the peace, who shall be commissioned as aforesaid, and remain in office during five years, if they behave themselves well; during which time the said registers in chancery and clerks shall not be justices of either of the said courts of which they are officers, but they shall have authority to

sign all writs by them issued, and take recognizances of bail. The justices of the peace shall be nominated by the house of assembly; that is to say, they shall name twenty-four persons for each county, of whom the president, with the approbation of the privy council, shall appoint twelve, who shall be commissioned as aforesaid, and continue in office during seven years, if they behave themselves well; and in case of vacancies, or if the legislature shall think proper to increase the number, they shall be nominated and appointed in like manner. The members of the legislative and privy councils shall be justices of the peace for the whole State, during their continuance in trust; and the justices of the courts of common pleas shall be conservators of the peace in their respective counties.

ART. 13. The justices of the courts of common pleas and orphans' courts shall have the power of holding inferior courts of chancery, as heretofore, unless the legislature shall otherwise direct.

ART. 14. The clerks of the supreme court shall be appointed by the chief justice thereof, and the recorders of deeds, by the justices of the courts of common pleas for each county severally, and commissioned by the president, under the great seal, and continue in office five years, if they behave themselves well.

ART. 15. The sheriffs and coroners of the respective counties shall be chosen annually, as heretofore; and any person, having served three years as sheriff, shall be ineligible for three years after; and the president and privy council shall have the appointment of such of the two candidates, returned for said offices of sheriff and coroner, as they shall think best qualified, in the same manner that the governor heretofore enjoyed this power.

ART. 16. The general assembly, by joint ballot, shall appoint the generals and field-officers, and all other officers in the army or navy of this State; and the president may appoint, during pleasure, until otherwise directed by the legislature, all necessary civil officers not hereinbefore mentioned.

ART. 17. There shall be an appeal from the supreme court of Delaware, in matters of law and equity, to a court of seven persons, to consist of the president for the time being, who shall preside therein, and six others, to be appointed, three by the legislative council, and three by the house of assembly, who shall continue in office during good behavior, and be commissioned by the president, under the great seal; which court shall be styled the *"court of appeals,"* and have all the authority and powers heretofore given by law in the last resort to the King in council, under the old government. The secretary shall be the clerk of this court: and vacancies therein occasioned by death or incapacity, shall be supplied by new elections, in manner aforesaid.

ART. 18. The justices of the supreme court and courts of common pleas, the members of the privy council, the secretary, the trustees of the loan office, and clerks of the court of common pleas, during their continuance in office, and all persons concerned in any army or navy contracts, shall be ineligible to either house of assembly; and any member of either house accepting of any other of the offices hereinbefore mentioned (excepting the office of a justice of the peace) shall have his seat thereby vacated, and a new election shall be ordered.

ART. 19. The legislative council and assembly shall have the power of making the great seal of this State, which shall be kept by the president, or, in his absence, by the vice-president, to be used by them as occasion may require. It shall be called *"The Great Seal of the Delaware State,"* and shall be affixed to all laws and commissions.

ART. 20. Commissions shall run in the name of "The Delaware State," and bear test by the president. Writs shall run in the same manner, and bear test in the name of the chief-justice, or justice first named in the commissions for the several courts, and be sealed with the public seals of such courts. Indictments shall conclude, *"Against the peace and dignity of the State."*

ART. 21. In case of vacancy of the offices above directed to be filled by the president and general assembly, the president and privy council may appoint others in their stead until there shall be a new election.

ART. 22. Every person who shall be chosen a member of either house, or appointed to any office or place of trust, before taking his seat, or entering upon the execution of his office, shall take the following oath, or affirmation, if conscientiously scrupulous of taking an oath, to wit:

"I, A B, will bear true allegiance to the Delaware State, submit to its constitution and laws, and do no act wittingly whereby the freedom thereof may be prejudiced."

And also make and subscribe the following declaration, to wit:

"I, A B, do profess faith in God the Father, and in Jesus Christ His only Son, and in the Holy Ghost, one God, blessed for evermore; and I do acknowledge the holy scriptures of the Old and New Testament to be given by divine inspiration."

And all officers shall also take an oath of office.

ART. 23. The president, when he is out of office, and within eighteen months after, and all others offending against the State, either by maladministration, corruption, or other means, by which the safety of the Commonwealth may be endangered, within eighteen months after the offence committed, shall be impeachable by the house of assembly before the legislative council; such impeachment to be prosecuted by the attorney-general, or such other person or persons as the house of assembly may appoint, according to the laws of the land. If found guilty, he or they shall be either forever disabled to hold any office under government, or removed from office *pro tempore*, or subjected to such pains and penalties as the laws shall direct. And all officers shall be removed on conviction of misbehavior at common law, or on impeachment, or upon the address of the general assembly.

ART. 24. All acts of assembly in force in this State on the 15th day of May last (and not hereby altered, or contrary to the resolutions of Congress or of the late house of assembly of this State) shall so continue, until altered or repealed by the legislature of this State, unless where they are temporary, in which case they shall expire at the times respectively limited for their duration.

ART. 25. The common law of England, as well as so much of the statute law as has been heretofore adopted in practice in this State, shall remain in force, unless they shall be altered by a future law of the legislature; such parts only excepted as are repugnant to the rights and privileges contained in this constitution, and the declaration of rights, &c., agreed to by this convention.

ART. 26. No person hereafter imported into this State from Africa ought to be held in slavery under any pretence whatever; and no negro, Indian, or mulatto slave ought to be brought into this State, for sale, from any part of the world.

ART. 27. The first election for the general assembly of this State shall be held on the 21st day of October next, at the court-houses in the several counties, in the manner heretofore used in the election of the assembly, except as to the choice of inspectors and assessors, where assessors have not been chosen on the 16th day of September, instant, which shall be made on the morning of the day of election, by the electors, inhabitants of the respective hundreds in each county. At which time the sheriffs and coroners, for the said counties respectively, are to be elected; and the present sheriffs of the counties of Newcastle and Kent may be rechosen to that office until the 1st day of October, A.D. 1779; and the present sheriff for the county of Sussex may be rechosen to that office until the 1st day of October, A.D. 1778, provided the freemen think proper to reëlect them at every general election; and the present sheriffs and coroners, respectively, shall continue to exercise their offices as heretofore, until the sheriffs and coroners, to be elected on the said 21st day of October, shall be commissioned and sworn into office. The members of the legislative council and assembly shall meet, for transacting the business of the State, on the 28th day of October next, and continue in office until the 1st day of October, which will be in the year 1777; on which day, and on the 1st day of October in each year forever after, the legislative council, assembly, sheriffs, and coroners shall be chosen by ballot, in manner directed by the several laws of this State, for regulating elections of members of assembly and sheriffs and coroners; and the general assembly shall meet on the 20th day of the same month for the transacting the business of the State; and if any of the said 1st and 20th days of October should be Sunday, then, and in such case, the elections shall be held, and the general assembly meet, the next day following.

ART. 28. To prevent any violence or force being used at the said elections, no person shall come armed to any of them, and no muster of the militia shall be made on that day; nor shall any battalion or company give in their votes immediately succeeding each other, if any other voter, who offers to vote, objects thereto; nor shall any battalion or company, in the pay of the continent, or of this or any other State, be suffered to remain at the time and place of holding the said elections, nor within one mile of the said places respectively, for twenty-four hours before the opening said elections, nor within twenty-four hours after the same are closed, so as in any manner to impede the freely and conveniently carying on the said election: *Provided always,* That every elector may, in a peaceable and orderly manner, give in his vote on the said day of election.

ART. 29. There shall be no establishment of any one religious sect in this State in preference to another; and no clergyman or preacher of the gospel, of any denomination, shall be capable of holding any civil office in this State, or of being a member of either of the branches of the legislature, while they continue in the exercise of the pastorial function.

ART. 30. No article of the declaration of rights and fundamental rules of this State, agreed to by this convention, nor the first, second, fifth, (except that part thereof that relates to the right of suffrage,) twenty-sixth, and twenty-ninth articles of this constitution, ought ever to be violated on any pretence whatever. No other part of this constitution shall be altered, changed, or diminished without the consent of five parts in seven of the assembly, and seven members of the legislative council.

GEORGE READ, *President.*
Attest:
JAMES BOOTH, *Secretary.*
Friday, September 10, 1776.

Reference: Francis Newton Thorpe (ed.), *The Federal and State Constitutions, Colonial Charters, and Other Organic Laws of the States,* Vol. I (Washington: GPO, 1909).

38

Pennsylvania, September 28, 1776

In Pennsylvania radicals seized control of the popularly elected constitutional convention. The delegates added a loyalty oath that required all officeholders to swear allegiance to the constitution. Key parts of the Pennsylvania constitution included a Bill of Rights, a single house legislature, and a commitment to speedy printing and distribution of proceedings of the state legislature. Immediate conflict between the radicals and conservatives led to repeated debate over the state's system of governance.

PROCEEDINGS OF CONVENTION, SEPTEMBER 17–24, 1776

August 24, 26, 27 and 28, 1776

The convention was occupied with the consideration of legislative and executive business.

August 29, 30 and 31, 1776

The committee of the whole reported further progress in the consideration of the frame of government.

September 3d and 4th, 1776

The convention, among other things, made progress in the committee of the whole in the consideration of the frame of government.

Thursday, September 5, 1776

The convention resolved itself into a committee of the whole house, in order to resume the consideration of the frame of government.

Mr, Rittenhouse was called to and assumed the chair; after some time the president resumed the chair, and Mr. Rittenhouse reported from the committee, that they had finished the business referred to them, and were ready to report thereon. Which report was read, and

Ordered, That the president, Mr. Rittenhouse and Mr. Vanhorn, be desired to revise the same, and make such alterations therein in method and stile, without affecting the sense, as they may think proper; and when that is done, to get 400 copies printed for public consideration.

The convention then resumed the consideration of legislative and executive business.

From the 5th to the 16th of September, 1776

The convention was engaged in the consideration of legislative and executive business.

Monday, September 16, 1776

The convention, agreeably to the order of the day, resumed the consideration of the frame of government.

It was moved by Col. Ross and seconded by Mr. Clymer, that the first and second sections of the proposed frame of government be debated upon and amended. Whereupon it was

Resolved, That the further debate on the second section is precluded, because it was fully debated and determined before, as appears by the minutes of the 1st and 2d of August last.

Moved and seconded that the yeas and nays on any question in the frame of government, shall be entered on the minutes, when it shall be required by any four members: But the previous question being put, it was determined that the question be not now put.

September 17, 18, 19, 20, 21, 23 and 24, 1776

The convention was engaged in legislative and executive business, and in considering the frame of government.

Wednesday, September 25, 1776

A letter from the Rev. Messrs. Duffield and Marshall, praying that the clergy of this state may be exempted from the burthen of civil offices, and setting forth their reasons for such exemption, was read, and ordered to lie on the table for consideration.

A letter from the Rev. Messrs. Muhlenberg and Weynberg, praying for an addition to the 47th article of the proposed frame of government, confirming the incorporations for promoting religious and charitable purposes, was read, and ordered to lie on the table.

The House resumed the consideration of the frame of government.

Ordered, That Mr. Cannon, Mr. Jacobs and Mr. Rittenhouse, be appointed to prepare a draft of a preamble to the declaration of rights and frame of government, and of the oaths of allegiance and office to be inserted in the said frame.

In the afternoon the gentlemen appointed to draw up a preamble to the declaration of rights and frame of government, reported an essay for that purpose, which was read and referred for further consideration.

They also reported an essay for the oaths and affirmations of allegiance and of office, which being read and amended, at the table, were approved of, and ordered to be inserted in the frame of government.

Thursday, September 26, 1776

On the 26d September, Col. Matlack, Mr. Jacobs and Col. Thomas Smith, were appointed a committee to bring in a draft of a resolve, for settling and regulating the general election for the present year. On this day the committee reported a draft for that purpose, which was then read and amended: The following is an abstract of this resolution.

Whereas, it is not convenient to hold the next election throughout this state, for choosing the elective officers thereof, on the day on which it will be most convenient to the people to hold their elections for the future; and this convention being desirous that the freemen of this state may, as soon as possible, enjoy the advantages of a free and established government, it is therefore

Resolved, That the next election for representatives, &c. usually chosen on the 1st of October, shall be held for the city and counties respectively, on Tuesday the 5th day of November next.

Provision is made for the election of inspectors, and the appointment of judges and clerks, and making the returns of the election, &c.

Every elector before his vote shall be received, shall take the following oath or affirmation, in stead of that heretofore required, viz.

Reference: The Proceedings Relative to Calling the Convention of 1776 and 1790 (Harrisburg: John S. Wiesting, 1826).

CONSTITUTION, SEPTEMBER 28, 1776

WHEREAS all government ought to be instituted and supported for the security and protection of the community as such, and to enable the individuals who compose it to enjoy their natural rights, and the other blessings which the Author of existence has bestowed upon man; and whenever these great ends of government are not obtained, the people have a right, by common consent to change it, and take such measures as to them may appear necessary to promote their safety and happiness. AND WHEREAS the inhabitants of this commonwealth have in consideration of protection only, heretofore acknowledged allegiance to the king of Great Britain; and the said king has not only withdrawn that protection, but commenced, and still continues to carry on, with unabated vengeance, a most cruel and unjust war against them, employing therein, not only the troops of Great Britain, but foreign mercenaries, savages and slaves, for the avowed purpose of reducing them to a total and abject submission to the despotic domination of the British parliament, with many other acts of tyranny, (more fully set forth in the declaration of Congress) whereby all allegiance and fealty to the said king and his successors, are dissolved and at an end, and all power and authority derived from him ceased in these colonies. AND WHEREAS it is absolutely necessary for the welfare and safety of the inhabitants of said colonies, that they be henceforth free and independent States, and that just, permanent, and proper forms of government exist in every part of them, derived from and founded on the authority of the people only, agreeable to the directions of the honourable American Congress. We, the representatives of the freemen of Pennsylvania, in general convention met, for the express purpose of framing such a government, confessing the goodness of the great Governor of the universe (who alone knows to what degree of earthly happiness mankind may attain, by perfecting the arts of government) in permitting the people of this State, by common

consent, and without violence, deliberately to form for themselves such just rules as they shall think best, for governing their future society; and being fully convinced, that it is our indispensable duty to establish such original principles of government, as will best promote the general happiness of the people of this State, and their posterity, and provide for future improvements, without partiality for, or prejudice against any particular class, sect, or denomination of men whatever, do, by virtue of the authority vested in use by our constituents, ordain, declare, and establish, the following *Declaration of Rights* and *Frame of Government,* to be the CONSTITUTION of this commonwealth, and to remain in force therein for ever, unaltered, except in such articles as shall hereafter on experience be found to require improvement, and which shall by the same authority of the people, fairly delegated as this frame of government directs, be amended or improved for the more effectual obtaining and securing the great end and design of all government, herein before mentioned.

A Declaration of The Rights of the Inhabitants of The Commonwealth, or State of Pennsylvania

I. That all men are born equally free and independent, and have certain natural, inherent and inalienable rights, amongst which are, the enjoying and defending life and liberty, acquiring, possessing and protecting property, and pursuing and obtaining happiness and safety.

II. That all men have a natural and unalienable right to worship Almighty God according to the dictates of their own consciences and understanding: And that no man ought or of right can be compelled to attend any religious worship, or erect or support any place of worship, or maintain any ministry, contrary to, or against, his own free will and consent: Nor can any man, who acknowledges the being of a God, be justly deprived or abridged of any civil right as a citizen, on account of his religious sentiments or peculiar mode of religious worship: And that no authority can or ought to be vested in, or assumed by any power whatever, that shall in any case interfere with, or in any manner controul, the right of conscience in the free exercise of religious worship.

III. That the people of this State have the sole, exclusive and inherent right of governing and regulating the internal police of the same.

IV. That all power being originally inherent in, and consequently derived from, the people; therefore all officers of government, whether legislative or executive, are their trustees and servants, and at all times accountable to them.

V. That government is, or ought to be, instituted for the common benefit, protection and security of the people, nation or community; and not for the particular emolument or advantage of any single man, family, or sett of men, who are a part only of that community; And that the community hath an indubitable, unalienable and indefeasible right to reform, alter, or abolish government in such manner as shall be by that community judged most conducive to the public weal.

VI. That those who are employed in the legislative and executive business of the State, may be restrained from oppression, the people have a right, at such periods as they may think proper, to reduce their public officers to a private station, and supply the vacancies by certain and regular elections.

VII. That all elections ought to be free; and that all free men having a sufficient evident common interest with, and attachment to the community, have a right to elect officers, or to be elected into office.

VIII. That every member of society hath a right to be protected in the enjoyment of life, liberty and property, and therefore is bound to contribute his proportion towards the expence of that protection, and yield his personal service when necessary, or an equivalent thereto: But no part of a man's property can be justly taken from him, or applied to public uses, without his own consent, or that of his legal representatives: Nor can any man who is conscientiously scrupulous of bearing arms, be justly compelled thereto, if he will pay such equivalent, nor are the people bound by any laws, but such as they have in like manner assented to, for their common good.

IX. That in all prosecutions for criminal offences, a man hath a right to be heard by himself and his council, to demand the cause and nature of his accusation, to be confronted with the witnesses, to call for evidence in his favour, and a speedy public trial, by an impartial jury of the country, without the unanimous consent of which jury he cannot be found guilty; nor can he be compelled to give evidence against himself; nor can any man be justly deprived of his liberty except by the laws of the land, or the judgment of his peers.

X. That the people have a right to hold themselves, their houses, papers, and possessions free from search and seizure, and therefore warrants without oaths or affirmations first made, affording a sufficient foundation for them, and whereby any officer or messenger may be commanded or required to search suspected places, or to seize any person or persons, his or their property, not particularly described, are contrary to that right, and ought not to be granted.

XI. That in controversies respecting property, and in suits between man and man, the parties have a right to trial by jury, which ought to be held sacred.

XII. That the people have a right to freedom of speech, and of writing, and publishing their sentiments; therefore the freedom of the press ought not to be restrained.

XIII. That the people have a right to bear arms for the defence of themselves and the state; and as standing armies in the time of peace are dangerous to liberty, they ought not to be kept up; And that the military should be kept under strict subordination to, and governed by, the civil power.

XIV. That a frequent recurrence to fundamental principles, and a firm adherence to justice, moderation, temperance, industry, and frugality are absolutely necessary to preserve the blessings of liberty, and keep a government free: The people ought therefore to pay particular attention to these points in the choice of officers and representatives, and have a right to exact a due and constant regard to them, from their legislatures and magistrates, in the making and executing such laws as are necessary for the good government of the state.

XV. That all men have a natural inherent right to emigrate from one state to another that will receive them, or to form a new state in vacant countries, or in such countries as they can purchase, whenever they think that thereby they may promote their own happiness.

XVI. That the people have a right to assemble together, to consult for their common good, to instruct their representatives, and to apply to the legislature for redress of grievances, by address, petition, or remonstrance.

Plan or Frame of Government
For the Commonwealth or State
of Pennsylvania

SECTION 1. The commonwealth or state of Pennsylvania shall be governed hereafter by an assembly of the representatives of the freemen of the same, and a president and council, in manner and form following—

SECT. 2. The supreme legislative power shall be vested in a house of representatives of the freemen of the commonwealth or state of Pennsylvania.

SECT. 3. The supreme executive power shall be vested in a president and council.

SECT. 4. Courts of justice shall be established in the city of Philadelphia, and in every county of this state.

SECT. 5. The freemen of this commonwealth and their sons shall be trained and armed for its defence under such regulations, restrictions, and exceptions as the general assembly shall by law direct, preserving always to the people the right of choosing their colonels and all commissioned officers under that rank, in such manner and as often as by the said laws shall be directed.

SECT. 6. Every freemen of the full age of twenty-one years, having resided in this state for the space of one whole year next before the day of election for representatives, and paid public taxes during that time, shall enjoy the right of an elector: Provided always, that sons of freeholders of the age of twenty-one years shall be intitled to vote although they have not paid taxes.

SECT. 7. The house of representatives of the freemen of this commonwealth shall consist of persons most noted for wisdom and virtue, to be chosen by the freemen of every city and county of this commonwealth respectively. And no person shall be elected unless he has resided in the city or county for which he shall be chosen two years immediately before the said election; nor shall any member, while he continues such, hold any other office, except in the militia.

SECT. 8. No person shall be capable of being elected a member to serve in the house of representatives of the freemen of this commonwealth more than four years in seven.

SECT. 9. The members of the house of representatives shall be chosen annually by ballot, by the freemen of the commonwealth, on the second Tuesday in October forever, (except this present year,) and shall meet on the fourth Monday of the same month, and shall be stiled, *The general assembly of the representatives of the freemen of Pennsylvania*, and shall have power to choose their speaker, the treasurer of the state, and their other officers; sit on their own adjournments; prepare bills and enact them into laws; judge of the elections and qualifications of their own members; they may expel a member, but not a second time for the same cause; they may administer oaths or affirmations on examination of witnesses; redress grievances; impeach state criminals; grant charters of incorporation; constitute towns, boroughs, cities, and counties; and shall have all other powers necessary for the legislature of a free state or commonwealth: But they shall have no power to add to, alter, abolish, or infringe any part of this constitution.

SECT. 10. A quorum of the house of representatives shall consist of two-thirds of the whole number of members elected; and having met and chosen their speaker, shall each of them before they proceed to business take and subscribe, as well the oath or affirmation of fidelity and allegiance hereinafter directed, as the following oath or affirmation, viz:

I — do swear (or affirm) that as a member of this assembly, I will not propose or assent to any bill, vote, or resolution, which shall appear to me injurious to the people; nor do or consent to any act or thing whatever, that shall have a tendency to lessen or abridge their rights and privileges, as declared in the constitution of this state; but will in all things conduct myself as a faithful honest representative and guardian of the people, according to the best of my judgment and abilities.

And each member, before he takes his seat, shall make and subscribe the following declaration, viz:

I do believe in one God, the creator and governor of the universe, the rewarder of the good and the punisher of the wicked. And I do acknowledge the Scriptures of the Old and New Testament to be given by Divine inspiration.

And no further or other religious test shall ever hereafter be required of any civil officer or magistrate in this State.

SECT. 11. Delegates to represent this state in congress shall be chosen by ballot by the future general assembly at their first meeting, and annually forever afterwards, as long as such representation shall be necessary. Any delegate may be superseded at any time, by the general assembly appointing another in his stead. No man shall sit in congress longer than two years successively, nor be capable of reëlection for three years afterwards: and no person who holds any office in the gift of the congress shall hereafter be elected to represent this commonwealth in congress.

SECT. 12. If any city or cities, county or counties shall neglect or refuse to elect and send representatives to the general assembly, two-thirds of the members from the cities or counties that do elect and send representatives, provided they be a majority of the cities and counties of the whole state, when met, shall have all the powers of the general assembly, as fully and amply as if the whole were present.

SECT. 13. The doors of the house in which the representatives of the freemen of this state shall sit in general assembly, shall be and remain open for the admission of all persons who behave decently, except only when the welfare of this state may require the doors to be shut.

SECT. 14. The votes and proceedings of the general assembly shall be printed weekly during their sitting, with the yeas and nays, on any question, vote or resolution, where any two members require it, except when the vote is taken by ballot; and when the yeas and nays are so taken every member shall have a right to insert the reasons of his vote upon the minutes, if he desires it.

SECT. 15. To the end that laws before they are enacted may be more maturely considered, and the inconvenience of hasty determinations as much as possible prevented, all bills of public nature shall be printed for the consideration of the people, before they are read in general assembly the last time for debate and amendment; and, except on occasions of sudden necessity, shall not be passed into laws until the next session of assembly; and for the more perfect satisfaction of the public, the reasons and motives for making such laws shall be fully and clearly expressed in the preambles.

SECT. 16. The stile of the laws of this commonwealth shall be, "Be it enacted, and it is hereby enacted by the representatives of the freemen of the commonwealth of Pennsylvania in general assembly met, and by the authority of the same." And the general assembly shall affix their seal to every bill, as soon as it is enacted into a law, which seal shall be kept by the assembly, and shall be called, *The seal of the laws of Pennsylvania,* and shall not be used for any other purpose.

SECT. 17. The city of Philadelphia and each county of this commonwealth respectively, shall on the first Tuesday of November in this present year, and on the second Tuesday of October annually for the two next succeeding years, *viz.* the year one thousand seven hundred and seventy-seven, and the year one thousand seven hundred and seventy-eight, choose six persons to represent them in general assembly. But as representation in proportion to the number of taxable inhabitants is the only principle which can at all times secure liberty, and make the voice of a majority of the people the law of the land; therefore the general assembly shall cause complete lists of the taxable inhabitants in the city and each county in the commonwealth respectively, to be taken and returned to them, on or before the last meeting of the assembly elected in the year one thousand seven hundred and seventy-eight, who shall appoint a representation to each, in proportion to the number of taxables in such returns; which representation shall continue for the next seven years afterwards at the end of which, a new return of the taxable inhabitants shall be made, and a representation agreeable thereto appointed by the said assembly, and so on septennially forever. The wages of the representatives in general assembly, and all other state charges shall be paid out of the state treasury.

SECT. 18. In order that the freemen of this commonwealth may enjoy the benefit of election as equally as may be until the representation shall commence, as directed in the foregoing section, each county at its own choice may be divided into districts, hold elections therein, and elect their representatives in the county, and their other elective officers, as shall be hereafter regulated by the general assembly of this state. And no inhabitant of this state shall have more than one annual vote at the general election for representatives in assembly.

SECT. 19. For the present the supreme executive council of this state shall consist of twelve persons chosen in the following manner: The freemen of the city of Philadelphia, and of the counties of Philadelphia, Chester, and Bucks, respectively, shall choose by ballot one person for the city, and one for each county aforesaid, to serve for three years and no longer, at the time and place for electing representatives in general assembly. The freemen of the counties of Lancaster, York, Cumberland, and Berks, shall, in like manner elect one person for each county respectively, to serve as counsellors for two years and no longer. And the counties of Northampton, Bedford, Northumberland and Westmoreland, respectively, shall, in like manner, elect one person for each county, to serve as

counsellors for one year, and no longer. And at the expiration of the time for which each counsellor was chosen to serve, the freemen of the city of Philadelphia, and of the several counties in this state, respectively, shall elect one person to serve as counsellor for three years and no longer; and so on every third year forever. By this mode of election and continual rotation, more men will be trained to public business, there will in every subsequent year be found in the council a number of persons acquainted with the proceedings of the foregoing years, whereby the business will be more consistently conducted, and moreover the danger of establishing an inconvenient aristocracy will be effectually prevented. All vacancies in the council that may happen by death, resignation, or otherwise, shall be filled at the next general election for representatives in general assembly, unless a particular election for that purpose shall be sooner appointed by the president and council. No member of the general assembly or delegate in congress, shall be chosen a member of the council. The president and vice-president shall be chosen annually by the joint ballot of the general assembly and council, of the members of the council. Any person having served as a counsellor for three successive years, shall be incapable of holding that office for four years afterwards. Every member of the council shall be a justice of the peace for the whole commonwealth, by virtue of his office.

In case new additional counties shall hereafter be erected in this state, such county or counties shall elect a counsellor, and such county or counties shall be annexed to the next neighbouring counties, and shall take rotation with such counties.

The council shall meet annually, at the same time and place with the general assembly.

The treasurer of the state, trustees of the loan office, naval officers, collectors of customs or excise, judge of the admirality, attornies general, sheriffs, and prothonotaries, shall not be capable of a seat in the general assembly, executive council, or continental congress.

SECT. 20. The president, and in his absence the vice-president, with the council, five of whom shall be a quorum, shall have power to appoint and commissionate judges, naval officers, judge of the admiralty, attorney general and all other officers, civil and military, except such as are chosen by the general assembly or the people, agreeable to this frame of government, and the laws that may be made hereafter; and shall supply every vacancy in any office, occasioned by death, resignation, removal or disqualification, until the office can be filled in the time and manner directed by law or this constitution. They are to correspond with other states, and transact business with the officers of government, civil and military; and to prepare such business as may appear to them necessary to lay before the general assembly. They shall sit as judges, to hear and determine on impeachments, taking to their assistance for advice only, the justices of the supreme court. And shall have power to grant pardons, and remit fines, in all cases whatsoever, except in cases of impeachment; and in cases of treason and murder, shall have power to grant reprieves, but not to pardon, until the end of the next sessions of assembly; but there shall be no remission or mitigation of punishments on impeachments, except by act of the legislature; they are also to take care that the laws be faithfully executed; they are to expedite the execution of such measures as may be resolved upon by the general assembly; and they may draw upon the treasury for such sums as shall be appropriated by the house: They may also lay embargoes, or prohibit the exportation of any commodity, for any time, not exceeding thirty days, in the recess of the house only: They may grant such licences, as shall be directed by law, and shall have power to call together the general assembly when necessary, before the day to which they shall stand adjourned. The president shall be commander in chief of the forces of the state, but shall not command in person, except advised thereto by the council, and then only so long as they shall approve thereof. The president and council shall have a secretary, and keep fair books of their proceedings, wherein any counsellor may enter his dissent, with his reasons in support of it.

SECT. 21. All commissions shall be in the name, and by the authority of the freemen of the commonwealth of Pennsylvania, sealed with the state seal, signed by the president or vice-president, and attested by the secretary; which seal shall be kept by the council.

SECT. 22. Every officer of state, whether judicial or executive, shall be liable to be impeached by the general assembly, either when in office, or after his resignation or removal for mal-administration: All impeachments shall be before the president or vice-president and council, who shall hear and determine the same.

SECT. 23. The judges of the supreme court of judicature shall have fixed salaries, be commissioned for seven years only, though capable of re-appointment at the end of that term, but removable for misbehaviour at any time by the general assembly; they shall not be allowed to sit as members in the continental congress, executive council, or general assembly, nor to hold any other office civil or military, nor to take or receive fees or perquisites of any kind.

SECT. 24. The supreme court, and the several courts of common pleas of this commonwealth, shall, besides the powers usually exercised by such courts, have the powers of a court of chancery, so far as relates to the perpetuating testimony, obtaining evidence from places not within this state, and the care of the persons and estates of those who are *non compotes mentis*, and such other powers as may be found necessary by future general assemblies, not inconsistent with this constitution.

SECT. 25. Trials shall be by jury as heretofore: And it is recommended to the legislature of this state, to provide by law against every corruption or partiality in the choice, return, or appointment of juries.

SECT. 26. Courts of sessions, common pleas, and orphans courts shall be held quarterly in each city and county; and the legislature shall have power to establish all such other courts as they may judge for the good of the inhabitants of the state. All courts shall be open, and justice shall be impartially administered without corruption or unnecessary delay: All their officers shall be paid an adequate but moderate compensation for their services: And if any officer shall take greater or other fees than the law allows him, either directly or indirectly, it shall ever after disqualify him from holding any office in this state.

SECT. 27. All prosecutions shall commence in the name and by the authority of the freemen of the commonwealth of Pennsylvania; and all indictments shall conclude with these words, *"Against the peace and dignity of the same."* The style of all process hereafter in this state shall be, *The commonwealth of Pennsylvania.*

SECT. 28. The person of a debtor, where there is not a strong presumption of fraud, shall not be continued in prison, after delivering up, *bona fide*, all his estate real and personal, for the use of his creditors, in such manner as shall be hereafter regulated by law. All prisoners shall be bailable by sufficient sureties, unless for capital offences, when the proof is evident, or presumption great.

SECT. 29. Excessive bail shall not be exacted for bailable offences: And all fines shall be moderate.

SECT. 30. Justices of the peace shall be elected by the freeholders of each city and county respectively, that is to say, two or more persons may be chosen for each ward, township, or district, as the law shall hereafter direct: And their names shall be returned to the president in council, who shall commissionate one or more of them for each ward, township, or district so returning, for seven years, removable for misconduct by the general assembly. But if any city or county, ward, township, or district in this commonwealth, shall hereafter incline to change the manner of appointing their justices of the peace as settled in this article, the general assembly may make laws to regulate the same, agreeable to the desire of a majority of the freeholders of the city or county, ward, township, or district so applying. No justice of the peace shall sit in the general assembly unless he first resigns his commission; nor shall he be allowed to take any fees, nor any salary or allowance, except such as the future legislature may grant.

SECT. 31. Sheriffs and coroners shall be elected annually in each city and county, by the freemen; that is to say, two persons for each office, one of whom for each, is to be commissioned by the president in council. No person shall continue in the office of sheriff more than three successive years, or be capable of being again elected during four years afterwards. The election shall be held at the same time and place appointed for the election of representatives: And the commissioners and assessors, and other officers chosen by the people, shall also be then and there elected, as has been usual heretofore, until altered or otherwise regulated by the future legislature of this state.

SECT. 32. All elections, whether by the people or in general assembly, shall be by ballot, free and voluntary: And any elector, who shall receive any gift or reward for his vote, in meat, drink, monies, or otherwise, shall forfeit his right to elect for that time, and suffer such other penalties as future laws shall direct. And any person who shall directly or indirectly give, promise, or bestow any such rewards to be elected, shall be thereby rendered incapable to serve for the ensuing year.

SECT. 33. All fees, licence money, fines and forfeitures heretofore granted, or paid to the governor, or his deputies for the support of government, shall hereafter be paid into the public treasury, unless altered or abolished by the future legislature.

SECT. 34. A register's office for the probate of wills and granting letters of administration, and an office for the recording of deeds, shall be kept in each city and county: The officers to be appointed by the general assembly, removable at their pleasure, and to be commissioned by the president in council.

SECT. 35. The printing presses shall be free to every person who undertakes to examine the proceedings of the legislature, or any part of government.

SECT. 36. As every freeman to preserve his independence, (if without a sufficient estate) ought to have some profession, calling, trade or farm, whereby he may honestly subsist, there can be no necessity for, nor use in establishing offices of profit, the usual effects of which are dependence and servility unbecoming freemen, in the possessors and expectants; faction, contention, corruption, and disorder among the people. But if any man is called into public service, to the prejudice of his private affairs, he has a right to a reasonable compensation: And whenever an office, through increase of fees or otherwise, becomes so profitable as to occasion many to apply for it, the profits ought to be lessened by the legislature.

SECT. 37. The future legislature of this state, shall regulate intails in such a manner as to prevent perpetuities.

SECT. 38. The penal laws as heretofore used shall be reformed by the legislature of this state, as soon as may be, and punishments made in some cases less sanguinary, and in general more proportionate to the crimes.

SECT. 39. To deter more effectually from the commission of crimes, by continued visible punishments of long duration, and to make sanguinary punishments less necessary; houses ought to be provided for punishing by hard labour, those who shall be convicted of crimes not capital; wherein the criminals shall be imployed for the benefit of the public, or for reparation of injuries done to private persons: And all persons at proper times shall be admitted to see the prisoners at their labour.

SECT. 40. Every officer, whether judicial, executive or military, in authority under this commonwealth, shall take the following oath or affirmation of allegiance, and general oath of office before he enters on the execution of his office.

The Oath or Affirmation of Allegiance

I — do swear (or affirm) that I will be true and faithful to the commonwealth of Pennsylvania: And that I will not directly or indirectly do any act or thing prejudicial or injurious to the constitution or government thereof, as established by the convention.

The Oath or Affirmation of Office

I — do swear (or affirm) that I will faithfully execute the office of — for the — of — and will do equal right and justice to all men, to the best of my judgment and abilities, according to law.

SECT. 41. No public tax, custom or contribution shall be imposed upon, or paid by the people of this state, except by a law for that purpose: And before any law be made for raising it, the purpose for which any tax is to be raised ought to appear clearly to the legislature to be of more service to the community than the money would be, if not collected; which being well observed, taxes can never be burthens.

SECT. 42. Every foreigner of good character who comes to settle in this state, having first taken an oath or affirmation of allegiance to the same, may purchase, or by other just means acquire, hold, and transfer land or other real estate; and after one year's residence, shall be deemed a free denizen thereof, and entitled to all the rights of a natural born subject of this state, except that he shall not be capable of being elected a representative until after two years residence.

SECT. 43. The inhabitants of this state shall have liberty to fowl and hunt in seasonable times on the lands they hold, and on all other lands therein not inclosed; and in like manner to fish in all boatable waters, and others not private property.

SECT. 44. A school or schools shall be established in each county by the legislature, for the convenient instruction of youth, with such salaries to the masters paid by the public, as may enable them to instruct youth at low prices: And all useful learning shall be duly encouraged and promoted in one or more universities.

SECT. 45. Laws for the encouragement of virtue, and prevention of vice and immorality, shall be made and constantly kept in force, and provision shall be made for their due execution: And all religious societies or bodies of men heretofore united or incorporated for the advancement of religion or learning, or for other pious and charitable purposes, shall be encouraged and protected in the enjoyment of the privileges, immunities and estates which they were accustomed to enjoy, or could of right have enjoyed, under the laws and former constitution of this state.

SECT. 46. The declaration of rights is hereby declared to be a part of the constitution of this commonwealth, and ought never to be violated on any pretence whatever.

SECT. 47. In order that the freedom of the commonwealth may be preserved inviolate forever, there shall be chosen by ballot by the freemen in each city and county respectively, on the second Tuesday in October, in the year one thousand seven hundred and eighty-three, and on the second Tuesday in October, in every seventh year thereafter, two persons in each city and county of this state, to be called the COUNCIL OF CENSORS; who shall meet together on the second Monday of November next ensuing their election; the majority of whom shall be a quorum in every case, except as to calling a convention, in which two-thirds of the whole number elected shall agree: And whose duty it shall be to enquire whether the constitution has been preserved inviolate in every part; and whether the legislative and executive branches of government have performed their duty as guardians of the people, or assumed to themselves, or exercised other or greater powers than they are intitled to by the constitution: They are also to enquire whether the public taxes have been justly laid and collected in all parts of this commonwealth, in what manner the public monies have been disposed of, and whether the laws have been duly executed. For these purposes they shall have power to send for persons, papers, and records; they shall have authority to pass public censures, to order impeachments, and to recommend to the legislature the repealing such laws as appear to them to have been enacted contrary to the principles of the constitution. These powers they shall continue to have, for and during the space of one year from the day of their election and no longer: The said council of censors shall also have power to call a convention, to meet within two years after their sitting, if there appear to them an absolute necessity of amending any article of the constitution which may be defective, explaining such as may be thought not clearly expressed, and of adding such as are necessary for the preservation of the rights and happiness of the people: But the articles to be amended, and the amendments proposed, and such articles as are proposed to be added or abolished, shall be promulgated at least six months before the day appointed for the election of such convention, for the previous consideration of the people, that they may have an opportunity of instructing their delegates on the subject.

Passed in Convention the 28th day of September, 1776, and signed by their order.

BENJ. FRANKLIN, *Prest.*

Reference: Francis Newton Thorpe (ed.), *The Federal and State Constitutions, Colonial Charters, and Other Organic Laws of the States,* Vol. I (Washington: GPO, 1909).

MINUTES OF SUPREME EXECUTIVE COUNCIL, JUNE 11, 1777

"To the Hon'ble the Representatives of the Freemen of the Commonwealth of Pennsylvania in General Assembly met:

"The Supreme Executive Council of the said Commonwealth beg leave to represent:

"That they are sorry to find the present Constitution of this State so dissatisfactory to any of the well affected Inhabitants thereof, and would gladly concur in any suitable and safe measure for the removal of this uneasiness; That they are of opinion this might be greatly attained by taking the sence of the Majority of the Electors throughout the Counties on the important Question, whether a Convention be holden at some proper time to reconsider the frame of Government formed by the late Convention? That to fix the exact mode of obtaining the mind of the Majority on this subject, most properly belongs to their Representatives; That the Council hope that if some suitable mode of advising & getting the People at large to declare themselves, and if this were advised and published at this time, great ease and relief would be thereby given to some persons who are dissatisfied as aforesaid; and that unanimity in the common cause, so necessary at this time, will be promoted.

"By Order of Council.
"THOMAS WHARTON, jun., President

Reference: Minutes of Supreme Executive Council of Pennsylvania, Vol. XI (Harrisburg: Theodore Fern and Co., 1852).

ATTEMPTS TO AMEND CONSTITUTION, DECEMBER 17, 1783–AUGUST 1784

Wednesday, December 17, 1783

Ordered, That the committee appointed November 19, to enquire whether the constitution has been preserved inviolate, in every part, be instructed to enquire, whether the legislative and executive branches of government have performed their duty, as guardians of the people, or assumed to themselves, or exercised other or greater powers than they are entitled to by the constitution.

Thursday, January 1, 1784

The council resolved itself into a committee of the whole, Mr. M'Allister in the chair, to consider whether the constitution of this state is perfect in all its parts, or whether the same requires any amendment or alteration.

After some time the president resumed the chair, and the chairman delivered in a report, which was read and laid on the table.

Friday, January 2, 1784

The report of the committee of the whole was read, and the following resolution was adopted.

Resolved, That some articles of the constitution of this commonwealth, are materially defective, and absolutely require alteration and amendment.

On motion, Resolved, That a committee be appointed to report those articles of the constitution, which are materially defective and absolutely require alteration and amendment, agreeable to the foregoing resolution. The members chosen, were Mr. Miles, Mr. Fitzsimons, Mr. St. Clair, Mr. Hartley and Mr. Arndt.

Saturday, January 3, 1784

Resolved, That it be an instruction to the committee appointed to report those articles of the constitution, which are materially defective, and absolutely require alteration and amendment, to report the alterations and amendments.

Saturday, January 17, 1784

The committee appointed to enquire, whether the constitution has been preserved inviolate in every part, and whether the legislative and executive branches of government have performed their duty as guardians of the people, or assumed to themselves, or exercised other or greater powers than they are entitled to by the constitution, delivered in a report, in part, which was read and ordered to lie on the table.

The committee appointed the 2d instant, to report those articles of the constitution which are materially defective and absolutely require alteration and amendment, and who were instructed to report the alterations and amendments, delivered in a report, which was read and laid on the table.

Monday, January 19, 1784

The council proceeded to consider the report of the committee on the defects and alterations of the constitution, and the same was read the second time, by paragraphs, considered, amended and adopted, and is in the following words, viz.

Your committee, to whom it was referred to report those articles of the constitution which are defective and the alterations and amendments, beg leave to report,

That by the constitution of the state of Pennsylvania, the supreme legislative power is vested in one house of representatives, chosen by all those who pay public taxes. Your committee humbly conceive, the said constitution to be in this respect materially defective.

1. Because if it should happen that a prevailing faction in that one house was desirous of enacting unjust and tyrannical laws, there is no check upon their proceedings.

2. Because an uncontrolled power of legislation will always enable the body possessing it, to usurp both the judicial and the executive authority, in which case no remedy would remain to the people but by a revolution.

That by the said constitution the supreme executive power is delegated to a council. Your committee conceive the said constitution to be in this respect materially defective.

1. Because the constant sitting of a council is expensive and burthensome.

2. Because a numerous body of men, though possessed of wisdom necessary for deliberation, will never possess the decision necessary for action on sudden emergencies.

3. Because where a council act either weakly or wickedly, there is no individual so accountable to the public, as every man ought to be in such cases.

4. Because a single man would never be able of himself to do such acts as he may persuade a majority of his council to concur in, and support by their numbers.

5. Because the election of the president being by joint ballot of the council and assembly, if a prevailing faction should ever happen in the assembly, so as to lead a considerable majority, the president thus chosen, will have nothing to fear from the legislature, and by influencing the council, would possess exorbitant authority, without being properly accountable for the exercise of it.

That by the said constitution the judges of the supreme court are to be commissioned for seven years only, and are removable (for misbehaviour)

at any time, by the general assembly. Your committee conceive the said constitution to be in this respect materially defective.

1. Not only because the lives and property of the citizens, must in a great degree depend upon the judges, but the liberties of the state are evidently connected with their independence.

2. Because if the assembly should pass an unconstitutional law, and the judges have virtue enough to refuse to obey it, the same assembly could instantly remove them.

3. Because at the close of seven years, the seats of the judges must depend on the will of the council; wherefore the judges will naturally be under an undue bias, in favor of those upon whose will their commissions are to depend.

That great care is taken by the said constitution to establish a rotation in sundry offices, which your committee humbly conceive to be improvident.

1. Because the hope of re-appointment to office, is among the strongest incentives to the due execution of the trust it confers.

2. Because the state is thereby necessarily deprived of the service of useful men for a time, and compelled to make experiment of others, who may not prove equally wise and virtuous.

3. Because the check intended by such principle of rotation, can be of no good effect to repress inordinate ambition, unless it were extended so as to preclude a man from holding any office whatever.

4. Because the privilege of the people in elections, is so far infringed as they are thereby deprived of the right of choosing those persons whom they would prefer.

Your committee having thus briefly stated the leading objection to the constitution, proceed with all possible deference, to point out the articles they recommend to be struck out, and to propose the amendments. And first,

In the bill of rights, section 9; that there be added after the words, "judgment of his peers," *of the vicinage.* Because the verification of the facts in the vicinity where they happen, is one of the greatest securities to life, liberty and happiness.

That as there is no clause in the bill of rights, to prevent retrospective laws being passed, your committee submit the following.

Laws made to punish for actions done before the existence of such laws, are unjust, tyrannical and oppressive, and inconsistent with the fundamental principles of a free government: nor ought any citizen in any case, to be declared guilty of treason or felony by the legislature.

That sections 1 and 2, of the constitution be left out, and the following substituted.

The supreme legislative power within this commonwealth, shall be vested in two separate and distinct bodies of men; the one to be called the legislative council, the other to be called the assembly of the commonwealth of Pennsylvania; who shall meet once, at least, in every year, for the despatch of public business, and shall be stiled the general assembly of Pennsylvania.

In lieu of section 3, we submit the following:

There shall be a principle executive magistrate, who shall be stiled the governor of the commonwealth of Pennsylvania.

That section 5 be altered and stand amended as follows,

The freemen of this commonwealth and their sons shall be trained and armed for its defence, under such regulations, restrictions and exceptions as the general assembly shall by law direct.

Because an uniformity in the constitution and discipline of the militia throughout the United States may be essential to its usefulness, and

Because the general assembly being the representatives of the people, will, in a point so essential to their security and happiness, make the law conformable to the opinion of their constituents, and to the interest of the commonwealth.

That in section 6, two years' residence be inserted instead of one year.

In the room of section 7, the following is submitted:

The general assembly of this commonwealth shall consist of persons most noted for wisdom and virtue, to be chosen by the freemen of every city and county therein respectively, and no person shall be elected unless he shall have resided in the city or county for which he shall be chosen, one year immediately before the said election: Nor shall any member, while he continues such, hold any other office, except in the militia.

Section 8 to be left out, for the reasons given on the principle of rotation.

Sect 9 The members of the general assembly shall be chosen annually, by ballot, by the freemen of this commonwealth, on the second Tuesday in October for ever, and shall meet on the fourth Monday of the same month. They shall be styled the assembly of the commonwealth of Pennsylvania; shall have power to choose their speaker, their other necessary officers, and the treasurer of the state; they shall judge of the elections and qualifications of their own members; may expel a member, but not a second time for the same cause; they may administer oaths or affirmations, on examination of witnesses; impeach state criminals, and may prepare bills to be passed into laws. All money bills shall originate in the assembly only, but they shall not on any occasion annex to or blend with a money bill any matter, clause or thing, not immediately relating thereto, and necessary for imposing, assessing, levying or applying the taxes or supplies to be raised for the support of government, or the current expenses of the state, but shall have all other powers, necessary for one branch of the legislature of a free state or commonwealth.

In section 10, a quorum of the assembly shall consist of two-thirds of the whole number of members elected, but a smaller number shall have power to adjourn from day to day.

And add to the section the following clause,

The members of the legislative council and of the assembly, shall each of them (after they have chosen their president and speaker, and before they proceed to other business) take and subscribe the oath or affirmation of fidelity and allegiance, and the declaration directed to be taken by the members of assembly, in the 10th section of the constitution.

That section 11 stand amended as follows:

Delegates to represent this commonwealth in congress, shall be chosen by the joint ballot of the future general assembly, at their first meeting, annually, for ever. Any delegate may be superseded at any time by the general assembly, appointing another in his stead. No man shall sit in congress more than three years in any term of six years,; and no person, while he holds any office in the gift of congress, shall hereafter be elected to represent this commonwealth in congress.

Section 12, being provided for by section 10, to be left out.

Section 13, instead of "the doors of the house," to insert "the doors of each house."

That section 14 be altered, and stand amended as follows:

The votes and proceedings of the general assembly shall be printed weekly during their sitting, with the yeas and nays on any question, vote or resolution, when any two members require it, except when the vote is taken by ballot. We propose that the remainder of the section be left out.

Because we conceive the entering the dissent on the minutes, with reasons, only tends to foment party disputes, weaken the force of the laws, and impede their execution.

Section 15, we humbly conceive, was always delusory, and if a second branch is agreed to, will be rendered unnecessary.

That section 16 be altered and stand amended as follows:

The stile of the laws of this commonwealth shall be, Be it enacted, and it is hereby enacted by the general assembly of the commonwealth of Pennsylvania, and by the authority of the same.

That section 17 be altered as follows:

Whereas representation in proportion to the number of taxable male inhabitants, is the best principle which can at all times secure liberty, and make the voice of the people the law of the land: Therefore the general assembly shall cause complete lists of the taxable male inhabitants, in the city and each county of the commonwealth respectively, to be taken, and returned to them on or before the last meeting of the general assembly, which shall be elected in the year, who shall in the year appoint a representation in the general assembly, in proportion to the number of taxables in such returns, in the ratio of 1250 taxables for each representative in assembly, and of 2500 taxables for each representative in the legislative council, which representation shall continue for the ensuing seven years, at the end of which term a new return of the taxable male inhabitants shall be made, and a representation agreeably thereto appointed by the said general assembly, and in like manner septennially for ever.

And in order to prevent a too numerous representation, which would be expensive and burthensome, the representatives in assembly shall never exceed 100 in the whole; nor shall the representatives in the legislative council ever exceed 50; to prevent which, the ratio shall be altered from time to time, as the number of taxables increase, so as to preserve an equal representation in proportion to the taxable male inhabitants.

That section 18 be altered as follows:

In order that the freemen of this commonwealth may enjoy the benefit of election as equally as may be, they shall meet annually at such convenient place or places within the city and each county respectively, as the law may hereafter direct, and there choose their representatives and other elective officers; and no inhabitant of this state shall have more than one annual vote for representatives in the assembly and in the legislative council; nor shall any person be admitted to vote except in the city or county in which he shall be an inhabitant.

That section 19 be struck out, and the following substituted:

To the end that the blessings of free and equal government may be extended and secured to the good people of this commonwealth, and that the laws may be more maturely considered, there shall be a legislative council, which for the present and until a return is taken as heretofore directed, shall consist of twenty-nine persons, who shall be chosen by ballot and at the time and at the places appointed for holding the elections for members of assembly, and in the following proportions, that is to say.

The freemen of the city of Philadelphia shall elect	2	persons.
county of Philadelphia,	3	
Chester,	3	
Bucks,	2	
To serve for three years respectively.		

The freemen of the county of Lancaster shall elect	4	persons.
York,	3	
Cumberland,	3	
Berks,	2	
To serve for two years respectively.		
The freemen of the county of Northampton shall elect	2	persons.
Bedford,	1	
Northumberland,	1	
Westmoreland,	1	
Washington,	1	
Fayette,	1	
To serve for one year respectively.		

And at the expiration of the time for which each councillor is chosen to serve, the freemen of the city of Philadelphia and of each county shall respectively elect the same number of councillors for the city and each county respectively, as is herein directed to serve for three years, and so on every third year. Provided, however, that the general assembly shall not be precluded from altering the present number of representatives, agreeably to the principle already laid down in the constitution, with respect to the election of members of assembly, in proportion to the number of male taxables in the city and each county. The legislative council shall be the first branch of the legislature; shall have power to choose a president, and their other necessary officers. The president shall have a casting vote on all questions in that body, but no other vote except when given by ballot. All bills (except money bills) may originate in the legislative council or assembly, and may be altered, amended or rejected by either. They shall sit on their own adjournments, but neither the legislative council or assembly shall have power to adjourn themselves for a longer time than two days, unless by mutual consent. They shall judge of the election and qualifications of their own members; may expel a member, but not a second time for the same cause. They shall be a court with full authority to hear and determine all impeachments against any officer or officers of the government, for misconduct or mal-administration in their offices, either when in office or otherwise, (provided the impeachment shall be prosecuted within one year after their resignation or removal,) and shall take to their assistance (for advice only) the judges of the supreme court; but previous to the trial of every impeachment, the members shall be respectively sworn, truly and impartially to try and determine the cause, according to the evidence; nor shall their judgment extend farther than to removal from office, and disqualification from holding or enjoying any place of honor, trust or profit under the commonwealth; but the party so convicted shall nevertheless be liable to indictment, trial, judgment and punishment, according to the laws of the land.

Not less than two-thirds of the legislative council shall be a quorum to do business, but a smaller number may adjourn from day to day. All vacancies which may happen by death, resignation or otherwise, in the legislative council or assembly, shall be filled up by writ from the president of the one and speaker of the other, directed to the sheriff of the proper county or counties.

The legislative council shall meet at the same time and place with the assembly, and shall have and enjoy all the powers necessary for a distinct branch of a free legislature.

The treasurer of the state, trustees of the loan office, naval officers, collectors of customs or excise, or any part of the public revenue, judge of the admiralty, attorney-general, sheriffs and prothonotaries shall not be capable of a seat in the general assembly or continental congress.

That section 20 be left out, and the following inserted:

The governor shall be chosen annually by the freemen of this commonwealth, qualified as is required to entitle persons to vote for members of assembly, at the same time and place or places, which shall be directed for the choosing of their representatives in the general assembly, where they shall give in their votes by ballot, and elect some fit person, who shall be a freeholder and shall have resided at least seven years in the state next before the time of his election; which votes shall be sorted, cast up and counted, and fair lists, containing the names of the persons voted for, and of the number of votes for each, made by the sheriffs, judges and inspectors, in the same manner as is or may be directed by law for ascertaining the members elected for the general assembly; which lists, signed and sealed by the said sheriffs, judges and inspectors shall be returned by the sheriffs into the office of the secretary of this commonwealth, days at least before the time appointed by the constitution for the meeting of the general assembly, and the said secretary shall, on the first day of the session, lay before the general assembly the said returns, and the two branches together shall forthwith proceed to examine the said returns, and the person having the greatest number of votes shall be by them declared and published to be governor; but if no person shall have a majority of votes, the general assembly shall by joint ballot elect one person out of the two who had the highest number of votes, or if it should so happen that more than two persons had an equal and highest number of votes, then they shall elect one person from the whole of those that have such equal and highest number of votes, and the person so elected shall by them be declared and published to be the governor.

The governor shall be, in virtue of his office, general and commander in chief of the militia and all the forces of the commonwealth, and admiral of the navy of the same: He shall have power to convene the general assembly on extraordinary occasions, and, at his discretion, to grant reprieves and pardons to persons convicted of crimes, other than those that may be convicted on impeachment, or of treason or murder, in which cases he may suspend the execution of the sentence, until it shall be reported to the legislature at their subsequent meeting, and may direct him to pardon, grant further reprieves, or carry the sentence or sentences into execution: He shall have power to appoint and commissionate the judges of the supreme court and the judges of the courts of common pleas, naval officers, judge of the admiralty, the attorney general, and all other officers civil or military, except such as shall be appointed by the general assembly, or chosen by the people,

agreeably to the constitution, whom he shall nevertheless commissionate.

It shall be his duty to inform the general assembly, at every session, of the condition of the commonwealth, as far as respects his department, and to recommend such matters to their consideration as he shall think conducive to its welfare. He shall correspond with the continental congress and with the other states, and transact the business of the state with the officers of government, civil and military. He shall take care that the laws be duly executed, and shall expedite such measures as may be resolved upon by the general assembly.

In case of absence, resignation, removal from office or death of the governor, the president of the legislative council shall execute all the powers vested in the governor, until another governor shall be chosen, or until the governor absent or impeached shall return or be acquitted; and in such case the legislative council shall choose by ballot one of their body to supply the place of the president during the time he shall exercise the authority of the governor.

All bills which have passed the legislative council and assembly shall, before they become laws, be presented to the governor for his revisal, and if, upon revision, he approves thereof, he shall signify his approbation by signing the same; but if he objects to the passing of such bill, he shall return it, together with his objections in writing, to the council or assembly in whichsoever it has originated, who shall enter the said objections at large upon their records, and proceed to reconsider the said bill. But if, after such reconsideration, two-thirds of the legislative council or assembly shall, notwithstanding the said objections, agree to pass the same, it shall, together with the objections, be sent to the other branch of the legislature, where it shall also be reconsidered, and if approved by two-thirds of the members present, it shall have the force of a law, but in all such cases, the votes of both houses shall be determined by yeas and nays, and the names of the persons voting for or against the said bill, shall be entered on their records; and in order to prevent unnecessary delays, if any bill shall not be returned by the governor within days after it shall have been presented, the same shall be a law, unless the general assembly shall by an adjournment render a return within days impracticable, in which case the bill shall be returned on the first day of the meeting of the legislature, after the expiration of the said days.

A secretary shall be elected by the joint ballot of the legislative council and assembly, and shall be commissioned by the governor for the time being. He shall be keeper of the seals of the state, and shall under the direction of a committee of both branches of the legislature, affix the seal to the laws when the same shall be enacted: He shall countersign all commissions signed by the governor, and all orders drawn by him on the treasury of the state, for monies appropriated, as well as all marriage and tavern licenses, and perform the other duties which may be enjoined on him by the constitution or laws of this commonwealth. He shall keep fair records of his proceedings, to be laid before either house of the legislature, when called for, and shall attend the governor or either house when required.

That section 21 be altered, and stand amended as follows:

All commissions shall be in the name of the commonwealth of Pennsylvania, sealed with the state seal, signed by the governor or the person exercising the powers of government for the time, and attested by the secretary.

That section 22 be altered as follows:

Every officer of this commonwealth, whether judicial or executive, shall be liable to impeachment by the assembly, either in office, or at any time within twelve months after removal or resignation, for maladministration; and all impeachments shall be before the legislative council, who shall hear and determine the same.

The judges of the supreme court and of the respective courts of common pleas, shall have fixed salaries; shall be appointed and commissioned by the governor, and shall hold their appointments and salaries during good behaviour; they may be removed by the governor, upon the address of the general assembly, provided that two thirds of each house agree to such address; they shall not be capable of sitting in the continental congress or general assembly, nor to hold any other office, civil or military, nor shall they take or receive any fees or perquisites of any kind.

That section 30 be altered as follows:

Justices of the peace shall be elected by the freeholders of each city and county respectively, that is say, two or more persons may be chosen for each ward, township or district, as the law shall hereafter direct, and their names shall be returned to the governor, who shall commissionate one or more of them for each ward, township or district so returning, for seven years, removable by the governor on the address of the general assembly; but if any city or county, ward, township or district in this commonwealth, shall hereafter incline to change the manner of appointing their justices of the peace, as settled in this article, the general assembly may make laws to regulate the same agreeable to the desire of a majority of the freeholders of the city or county, ward, township or district so applying. No justice of the peace shall sit in the general assembly, unless he first resign his commission, nor shall he be allowed to take any fees nor any allowance or salary, except such as are or may hereafter be granted by law.

That in section 31 "*governor*" be inserted in the room of "*president and council.*"

That in section 33 the following words be struck out, "unless altered or abolished by the future legislature."

Because in our opinion the restriction should be absolute, and not subject to the will of any future general assembly.

That in section 34, instead of "president and council," "*governor*" be inserted.

That in section 40 the words "as established by the convention," be left out.

That section 42 be amended as follows:

Every foreigner of good character, who comes to settle in this state, having first taken an oath or affirmation of allegiance to the same, may purchase or by other just means acquire, hold and transfer land or other real estate; and after two years' residence shall be deemed a free denizen thereof, except that he shall not be capable of being elected a representative in assembly or in the legislative council, or of being elected or appointed to any office of trust until he has resided in the state five years.

That section 47 be left out.

Your committee beg leave to add, that the confused manner in which the constitution is thrown together, is justly exceptionable; at the same time to remark, that their report will be liable to the same objections, because they have thought it their duty to follow the constitution in the order in which it stands, and to propose the alterations and amendments to each in the same order.

Dissentient

1. Because the report is a manifest violation of the 47th section of the constitution under which we are appointed. We think it a duty we owe to ourselves and our constituents, to state fully and circumstantially the proceedings of this council, previously to the decision of the present question, in order that our own characters may stand acquitted and that our constituents, whose happiness, together with our own, is so intimately connected with it, may be enabled to form a proper judgment.

On the 4th December last, the council resolved itself into a committee of the whole, to consider "whether there is a necessity of amending any article of the constitution, which may be defective, explaining such as may be thought not clearly expressed, and of adding such as are necessary for the preservation of the rights and happiness of the people." On the 1st of January, instant, the committee of the whole made report: "That some articles of the constitution of this commonwealth, are materially defective, and absolutely require amendment." Which was read the first time, and ordered to lie on the table. On the 2d of January, the above report was taken up for the second reading, when it was fully debated, and previously to the question being put on it, a member who voted against, and another who voted for the report, expressly and repeatedly declared (which the whole council acquiesced in) "That the decision of this question was to determine absolutely, whether

a convention was to be called or not." Upon the question being put, it appeared that of all the members elected there were but twelve for adopting the report, and ten who were present, against it; and although the minutes of the council say it was carried in the affirmative, yet, as the constitution expressly requires two thirds at least, of all the censors elected, which is eighteen, to concur in proposing changes in the frame of government; we are warranted in saying, *it was determined by more than the number required,* that there does not exist a necessity of making any alterations. Therefore, we consider the appointment of a committee, after this, to bring in propositions for altering the form of government, and all the subsequent proceedings of the council on the subject, as factious, illegal and establishing an alarming precedent. We cannot suppose that an appeal to the people at large, is again intended, for this council is authorised to deliberate and determine upon the propriety of making changes. Besides, that appeal has been repeatedly made, and as often decided with unexampled unanimity in favor of the constitution. It is also inconsistent with the idea of representation, and subversive of all legal and orderly government. If however, this appeal be intended from the council to its constituents, we wish it to be so stated; if to the convention, we have already decided by the constitutional number, that no convention is to be called. Should good order and government be unhinged by this step, we persuade ourselves, that we have as little to fear as those who so violently urge the present measure.

2. Because we consider it as an essential principle in every constitution, that it shall not be lightly changed. Clogs and difficulties have therefore, with great wisdom been thrown in the way of all attempts to change fundamental principles. In ours, the spirit of the constitution requires, that in the course of seven years, faults of so alarming a tendency should be discovered, as to induce two thirds at least, of all the censors elected, to concur in propositions for a change. This we conceive to be a principle essential to the preservation of any constitution whatever, without it, we shall be subject to continual fluctuations, and we fear fall into anarchy or tyranny.

3. Because we are convinced, that the same departure from the rule, which is prescribed by the constitution, for the calling of a convention, will be perverted to authorise that convention, when assembled (by whatever means) to proceed to further and more extravagant innovations (if possible) than any of those which have been hitherto proposed, or at least avowed. If we suffer ourselves to be carried away by the tide of the party prevailing in the place where we happen at present to convene, we fear that the state may be plunged into irretrievable destruction. We may be happy in the preservation of a free constitution; we tremble for the consequences of so wild a departure from the very principles which many of us have sworn to observe, and all of us profess to obey.

4. Because we recollect the present constitution was formed with great harmony, at the most auspicious period of time, when the flame of patriotism shone brightest, when the good people of the state were impressed with no other idea than that of acquiring and maintaining to themselves and their posterity, equal liberty, when no factions were formed with ambitious or mercenary motives. We have seen it support the safety and happiness of the state against a most formidable enemy without, with every embarrassment of a most indefatigable and insidious party within. We hoped, as the constitution had pointed out an orderly mode of reconsidering every part of our proceedings at the end of seven years, that peace and harmony would have prevailed in the review. If we are disappointed, we must ascribe it to those who have undertaken to propose articles for alteration, when no legal body is constituted for making those alterations, and when it has been already decided, upon the principles of the constitution, that a convention shall not be called.

5. Because the present constitution, with all the pretended aults imperfections, which have been so industriously searched out and ascribed to it by men who wanted an excuse for real disaffection or factious views, has stood the test of the most arduous trial, at a time when vigor and energy were indispensably necessary in the execution of measures essential to our safety, among a people of whose purity, in some parts of the state, we cannot boast.

6. Because the alterations proposed will introduce a form of government much more expensive, burthensome and complicated. But what we dread more than expense and delay, they tend to introduce among the citizens new and aristocratic ranks, with a chief magistrate at their head, vested with powers exceeding those which fall to the ordinary lot of kings. We are sufficiently assured, that the good people of Pennsylvania, most ardently love equal liberty, and that they abhor all attempts to lift one class of citizens above the heads of the reast, and much more the elevating any one citizen to the throne of royalty; and herein we are confident we speak not only the language of our constituents, but that we proclaim also the voice of God and nature.

7. Because we have been taught to believe, that many free constitutions have been destroyed for want of the means of reducing them at fixed periods to their first principles. This has been constanty recommended by the greatest and best political writers, is fully established in the 14th section of our bill of rights, and has been wisely provided for by the 47th section of our frame of government. This salutary provision, among others, is now attempted to be destroyed, so that no guard may remain against innovations, no check may be left against the encroachments of power. Hereafter, if the present attempt should succeed, no constitutional mode can be appealed to, upon the most attrocious and alarming abuses of government. Nothing will remain to the people, but the dreadful appeal to arms, to which so many before us have been reduced to the necessity of applying: An appeal frequently unsuccessful, and always dangerous; dangerous even in case of victory, because the conquerors, even under the standard of liberty have so often proved tyrants. A legal mode is infinitely to be preferred, and we think ought always to be preserved.

Joseph Hart, John Smiley,
Samuel Smith, William Finley,
John Whitehill, James Edgar,
Simon Dreisbach, John M'Dowell.
Baltzer Gehr,

Wednesday, January 21, 1784

The following resolution was adopted, yeas 13, nays 9.

Whereas the dissentients to the report of the committee appointed to propose alterations and amendments in the constitution, have among other things, stated that on the 2d of January, when the report of a former committee on the constitution was under consideration, "A member who voted against, and another who voted for the report, expressly and repeatedly declared (which the council acquiesced in) that the descision of this question was to determine absolutely whether a convention was to be called or not." Therefore,

Resolved, That the council did not then, nor at any time since, acquiesce or agree in the opinion, that the vote of the 2d of January, determined the question as to calling a convention.

The following address was then presented to the chair, and on motion, the same was read the second time and adopted, viz.

Friends and fellow citizens,

Agreeably to the trust reposed in us, we have met and seriously deliberated upon those matters submitted to our consideration, by the constitution of this state.

The most weighty subject that has come before us, is the constitution itself. To that therefore, whilst we have not neglected the others, we have principally directed our attention. We have examined it with candor; we have compared it with the constitutions of other states; we have discovered some of its defects; we have suggested the necessity of abolishing such parts of it as are expensive and burthensome, and dangerous to your liberties, and have with great deference thrown out, for your consideration, such alterations as appear to us to be best calculated to secure to you the blessings of free and equal government.

By the report of our committee which accompanies this address, you will perceive that though the majority of this council approve of the alterations, considering them essential to your existence as a free people, it has not yet met with the concurrence of two-thirds of our whole number, which the constitution has made necessary to enable us to call a convention. We are strangers to the motives of the minority, for refusing to give you an opportunity to judge upon a matter, you and we, and all our posterity are so deeply interested in, while by their silence upon the subject of the report, they have confessed that the constitution wants amendment. By refusing to indulge you in a convention for that purpose, they hold up consequences from that meeting that are dishonorable to freemen. They have indeed had the power to prevent it for the present, in the manner pointed out by the constitution:—But their sullen *no* in this council cannot rob you of your birthright.

Is it that they were concerned in the framing of the constitution, and therefore cannot bear that any fault should be found with it? This fondness for the productions of the brain, is a weakness mankind is subject to. But in so momentous a concern, passion and prejudice should, as far as human nature is capable of it, be laid aside, and the arguments offered, weighed with that cool deliberation the subject deserves. Nor can it be in any case, much less in the intricate science of government, upon which so few have had either leisure or opportunity to turn their thoughts, an impeachment of any man's judgment, to say he is mistaken. If errors then have crept in, they ought to be corrected; if there are ambiguities, they should be explained, and if the system itself is wrong it should be altered.

One cannot hesitate a moment in declaring that all these were naturally to be expected from the time and circumstances under which the present constitution was formed. Our political knowledge was in its infancy. The passions of the state were unusually agitated. A large body of militia were busy in preparing to march to another state to oppose the progress of the British army. Another body of citizens to the amount of five thousand were absent, on the same service, in the continental army. Amidst the din of arms and the dread of invasion, and when many wise and able men were necessarily absent, whose advice and assistance would have been of great use, was it reasonable to expect that a constitution could be formed proper for a great and growing state? And if an improper one was formed, which is our decided opinion, shall it not be altered or amended?

Let it not be said, that the constitution has carried us triumphantly through a perilous war; this is far from being the case. We owe all the exertions of Pennsylvania to the virtue of the people. In times of danger, it is well known, the constitution forsook us, and the will of our rulers became the only law. It is well known likewise, that a great part of the citizens of Pennsylvania, from a perfect conviction that political liberty could never long exist under such a frame of government, were opposed to the establishment of it, and that when they did submit to it, a solemn engagement was entered into by its then friends, that after seven years should be expired, and the enemy driven from our coasts, they would concur with them in making the wished for amendments. The seven years have elapsed, and our country now enjoys a favorable to the most temperate deliberations on the subject of government; but a minority in this council, which by the absurdity of its constitution, can in this instance bind the majority, say it is unnecessary. We appeal to your common sense, whether such a conduct is calculated to restore order and mutual confidence. It may be proper here to remark, that this very minority, although near one half of the members present in this council, do not represent one third of you; so that the voice of more than two thirds of the people, if the majority speak your sense, is sunk entirely; and, contrary to all principles, the lesser number binds the greater. What do these men fear from a convention? are they afraid to trust you with the exercise of the inestimable power of choosing a government for yourselves? You cannot, you will not injure yourselves in this business. If the constitution in its present form is most agreeable, you have only to instruct your representa-

tives in the convention to adopt it in all its parts. You are the sovereigns of Pennsylvania. All the power of the state is derived from your votes. Nothing can be obligatory on you which is contrary to your inclinations, or repugnant to your happiness. We do not quote any part of the bill of rights to prove to you that you may call a convention, when and in what manner you please. This privilege is your birth right and no power on earth can deprive you of it. We appeal to you therefore, to decide the great question, whether Pennsylvania shall continue unhappy and distracted under her present constitution, or whether by calling a convention, and amending it, you will restore harmony amongst yourselves and dignity to your government.

We recommend to your serious consideration, the report of our committee, which has been adopted by this council and has become one of its acts. Weigh the reasons upon which it is founded with coolness and deliberation, and suffer not yourselves to be imposed upon, or your passions inflamed by artful men, or by words without meaning. We can have no interest separate from yours; and as to our political principles, when you recollect that all have been the constant opposers of our British foes, and most of us have risked our lives and fortunes, during the whole of the contest, you can entertain no doubt about them. The proposed alterations are not experiments, but are founded on reason and the experience of our sister states. The future welfare of your country is in your hands. If you give her a good government she will be great and free. If you mistake in this point, the die will be cast, and you are sealed up to insignificance or misery.

We have not the most distant prospect, that the gentlemen in the minority will concur in calling a convention to amend the constitution, which we have thought, we hope not improperly, the most important part of our business; and it is that you might have an opportunity to instruct them on that subject, that we have at present suspended our deliberations.

On motion, that the president sign the address, and that it be published with the report, the yeas and nays were as follow:

YEAS

Samuel Miles,	Arthur St. Clair,
Stephen Chambers	William Irvine,
Thomas Fitzsimons,	Anthony Wayne,
Thomas Hartley,	John Arndt,
Fredk. A. Muhlenberg,	James Moore,
Richard M'Allister,	David Espy.

NAYS

Joseph Hart,	Baltzer Gehr,
John Smiley,	James Edgar,
Samuel Smith,	Simon Dreisbach,
William Finley,	John M'Dowell.
John Whitehill,	James Read,

The convention then adjourned until 3 o'clock on Tuesday the 1st of June, next, P.M.

———

A view of the proceedings of the second session of the council of censors, convened at Philadelphia, on the 1st of June, 1784.

Tuesday, June 1, 1784

A number of the members met pursuant to adjournment, but there not being a quorum present, they adjourned from day to day until Friday June 4th, 1784, when a quorum appearing, they proceeded to business, and were engaged until the 5th August following, in the consideration of other subjects than those connected with the constitution.

Tursday, August 5, 1784

Resolved, That the powers of this council do extend to all abuses and deviations from the constitution, which happen as well during the existence of this council, as previous to its being constituted.

The committee appointed to enquire whether the constitution has been preserved inviolate in every part, and whether the legislative and

executive branches of government have performed their duty, as guardians of the people, or assumed to themselves or exercised other or greater powers than they are entitled to by the constitution, delivered in a further report, which was read and ordered to lie on the table.

Wednesday, August 11, 1784

It was resolved, that the council will on Monday the 16th instant, take up for a second reading the said report. Monday the 16th of August, the council proceeded to the consideration of the reports of the said committee, read the 17th of January and the 5th of August, and the same were considered by paragraphs, amended, and on the 3d of August adopted, in the words following, viz.

The committee appointed to enquire "whether the constitution has been preserved inviolate in every part, and whether the legislative or executive branches of government have performed their duty as guardians of the people, or assumed to themselves or exercised other or greater powers than they are entitled to by the constitution," beg leave to report:

That they have examined and investigated the proceedings of the legislative body of this state, and that they find various and multiplied instances of departure from the frame of government. But conceiving it to be the most important and at the same time the least disagreeable part of the duty of the council of censors to bring the administration back to its first principles, they have selected such and so many instances of deviation, as are necessary to illustrate and re-establish the several leading principles of the constitution. These, for perspicuity, they have arranged under the respective section, or clause of the section violated; together with the opinion of the committee thereon, and their reasons for such opinion; and they now submit the whole to the council.

The journals of the general assembly and the laws passed since the revolution, have furnished all the cases referred to; because by the second statute of this commonwealth, in section 3, the acts of assembly of the late province of Pennsylvania, are revived and declared to be law within the state, so far only as they are not repugnant to, or inconsistent with the constitution.

In our enquiries we considered the constitution as a system, which, in establishing the natural rights of individuals, founds all civil power on the authority of the people only, in whom the sovereignty resides, and whose is that sovereignty in its several parts, as the same is delegated to different bodies of the citizens, as their trustees or servants. The exercise of power in the greatest articles of it, those of making laws, and carrying those laws into execution, is, by the three first sections of this grand bulwark of equal liberty, so honorable to the founders of it, and so invaluable to the citizens, by a most marked and decided distribution, assigned to two great branches. The legislative power is vested in the representatives of the people in general assembly, and the executive in a president and council; and from this last, for the greater security of the people, the judicial, of which it is a part, is again severed, and rendered independent of both. Thus wisely precluding an accumulation of power and influence, in the hands of one or of few, which the history of mankind evinces ever to have been subversive of all public justice and private right, and introductive of the capricious, unsteady domination of prejudice, party and self-interest, instead of the government of laws prescribed, promulgated and known.

The legislative, executive and judicial powers of the people being thus severally delegated to different bodies, the convention has carefully guarded against any encroachment of one on the proper authority of either of the other bodies, by making it a principal duty of a council of censors every seventh year to enquire, "Whether the constitution has been preserved inviolate, and whether the legislative and executive branches of government have assumed to themselves, or exercised other or greater powers than they are entitled to by the constitution."

These observations your committee premise to their report, as they are the clew by which they have been able to investigate the fabric.

The supposed doubts and difficulties, the contradictions and absurdities imputed to the constitution, which have been industriously and insidiously suggested to the people, as rendering it an impracticable system of administration, and as justifying acts of government in violation of it, have vanished before us as we proceeded. By thus recurring to the source of all authority, and recognising the distribution of powers, this frame of government, as established by the convention, appears to your committee to be clear in its principles, accurate in its form, consistent in its several parts, and worthy of the veneration of the good people of Pennsylvania, and of all the attachment they have formerly and during this session of the council of censors shewn to it.

Your committee beg leave further to suggest, that the checks and guards provided by the convention upon the proceedings of the legislative body, carry with them a very strong implied censure against the disposing of public money by vote; legislating for individuals, or in any case, by summary resolutions, which should be considered as no more than previous declarations of the sense of the house upon unfinished business; a foundation whereon to raise the superstructure of law, after mature deliberation, and clothed with the solemnities of enacting, which give weight and dignity, as well as public notoriety to the statute. This consideration is the more interesting, as the executive powers, being no longer opposed to the popular interest, and so restricted in this state that they cease to be objects of watchful jealousy.

We believe, with the illustrious Montesquieu, that the representative body is not fit for active resolutions, but for the enacting of laws, and to see whether the laws be duly executed. This latter duty of seeing whether the laws have been duly executed, the convention has assigned to the council of censors: thus wisely providing for a dispassionate review of so important an object, at a distance of time when animosities may have subsided, and calm reason may suffer the law of the land to resume its proper exercise. And we are of opinion with the great Locke, who, speaking of legislative power, lays it down as the fundamental law of all commonwealths, "that the legislative cannot assume to itself a power to rule by extemporary and arbitrary decrees, but is bound to dispense law and justice, and to decide the rights of the subject by promulgated, standing laws, and known authorised judges; and that men give up their natural independence to the society with this trust, that they shall be governed by known laws; otherwise their peace, quiet and property will be in the same uncertainty as in a state of nature."

This practice of entering into personal discussions and hasty votes, too often in contradiction to express laws, solemnly enacted, we fear, has been too much countenanced in some instances *from a determination that the people should experience, practically, what extravagancies a single legislature, unrestrained by the rules of the constitution, may be capable of committing*. And this while people were yet in some degree under the habits of the former vague, undefined and unsystematical proprietary government of the province; when every increase of power, obtained by their representatives from the executive, and every instance in which the force of law could be obtained to a resolve of the house, seemed at least to be favorable to the public interest, have not adverted to the dangerous effects arising to the community from such proceedings, in our present circumstances.

However irregular and inconsistent it may be, in well formed governments, for the representative body to legislate by a hasty vote, and to execute, or to appoint the officers who execute, yet every instance in which the representative body succeeded in such attempts, tended to restrict or counterbalance the enormous influence of a proprietor, having an interest opposed to that of the people; negative on their orderly proceedings in legislation in his own person, and another within his influence; and having almost every officer (from the chief justice of the supreme court downwards) the creature of his power, and the servant of his will; every freeholder for his tenant, a rental from the quit rents, and a fixed revenue for his deputies, which made him and his governors independent of the people and their representatives; and millions of acres to dispose of, as his interest or

ambition might suggest. Thus circumstanced, every opportunity was anxiously embraced of getting the public revenues into the disposition of the assembly or of officers appointed by them; and thus the same body who levied the money from the subject, expended it in some instances by their resolves, without control or accountability. However dangerous the powers of the proprietor may have been, yet your committee believe that these proceedings of the assembly were not the less irregular. They were however practised, and they have unfortunately acquired too great a sanction with the people from custom, and from the popular character of the last assembly before the revolution, and of the committees and council of safety since that period, who, having alone the exercise of every power of government, continued the practice of course.

From similar circumstances, and the continued opposition to the alarming influence of the proprietary power, arose and has been handed down, the usage in general assembly, through a committee of grievances, of extending their deliberations to the cases of individuals, who have been taught to consider an application to the legislature as a shorter and more certain mode of obtaining relief from hardships and losses, than the usual process of law. For as the erecting of a court of chancery would be adding to the weight of the proprietor, by giving him new jurisdiction, as well as the appointment of a new corps of officers, it was deemed expedient to retain the exercise of equitable power in the hands of the assembly; and there is reason to think that favor and partiality have from the nature of public bodies of men, predominated in the distribution of this relief. These dangerous procedures have been too often recurred to since the revolution.

Your committee further observe, that from the peculiar circumstances attending the late struggle with great Britain, examples have been set, which it will be extremely dangerous, and in some cases derogatory to the sovereignty of the state, to suffer to pass into precedents.

We are willing to leave the scale of depreciation and some other acts, *expost-facto*, to be justified by the necessity of the case. But law is well defined to be "a rule prescribed or made before hand." Public monies ought to be appropriated before they are levied. The reward of services should be ascertained when they are prescribed, and neither increased nor diminished afterwards, from favor or prejudice to the party. Innocence and guilt, and all demands by or against the public, ought, in all instances, to be judged by the known and usual course of proceedings; ever preserving, in case of doubts as to fact and law, the sacred right of trial by jury, and the proper tribunals; jury trial being the only instance of judicial power which the people have reserved to themselves.

These considerations your committee offer to the council, to be recommended to the watchful attention of the citizens of the state, as a standing protest of this council of censors against the many violations of the constitution, which are now more generally hinted at, or hereinafter particularly noticed.

We flatter ourselves that by recurring to the line of duty prescribed to the several branches of government by the constitution, the expenses and burthensome length of the sessions of the legislature may be saved to the good people of Pennsylvania.

In some instances it is certainly true that the constitution has been invaded through necessity, in times of extreme danger, when this country was involved in a very unequal struggle for life and liberty, and when good men were induced to hazard all consequences, for the sake of preserving our existence as a people. Yet in a calm review of these proceedings, we think it proper to advert even to such breaches of the constitution, as have been occasioned by the extremest necessity, lest they should be brought into precedent when no such necessity shall exist.

Bill Of Rights

Section 8. "That every member of society hath a right to be protected in the enjoyment of life, liberty and property, and is therefore bound to contribute his proportion towards the expense of that protection, &c.

It is the opinion of this committee, that the acts of assembly, passed within this commonwealth since the revolution, for seizing and taking the goods of the inhabitants of this state, for the use of the army, and for setting prices thereon, are inconsistent with this article, and with the rights of property. See vol. 1, chap. 47, 48, 129, 170 and 178.

Some of the acts of assembly, made to prevent forestalling, were also unconstitutional invasions of the rights of property. See chapters 44, 62, 81, vol. I.

September 28, 1779, The general assembly resolve, "That the salt within the city and liberties, beyond the occasion of a private family, be taken from the proprietors, by the president and council, and that the price thereof be ascertained by council."

It is the opinion of this committee, that the attempts which have been made to regulate the prices of commodities, were absurd and impossible. They tended to produce the very opposite effects to those which they were designed to produce, and were invasions of the right of property. See vol. I, chap. 60.—Journals of assembly, Nov. 22, 1779; Dec. 16, 1777; Jan. 25 and Feb. 14, 1780.

Section 10. "The people have a right to hold themselves, their houses, papers and possessions free from search and seizure, and therefore warrants without oaths or affirmations first made, affording a sufficient foundation for them, and whereby any messenger or officer may be commanded or required to search suspected places, or to seize any person or his property, not particularly described, are contrary to that right, and ought not to be granted."

It is the opinion of this committee that the authority given by the act for county levies and other tax laws, and by the excise laws to the collectors of these taxes, to break open houses in the day time, without oath or affirmation first made, shewing a sufficient foundation for them, is inconsistent with the 10th section of the bill of rights.

Section 11. "That in all controversies respecting property, and in suits between man and man, the parties have a right to trial by jury, which ought to be held sacred."

In the third session of the present assembly, a law has been passed to vest in Isaac Austin a real estate in the city of Philadelphia, claimed and possessed by George Adam Baker, as his freehold. This extraordinary act of assembly moreover commands the sheriff to put Mr. Austin in possession.

It is remarkable that the bill depending on this occasion, was passed after it had been shewn to the house that an action of ejectment, concerning part of the premises, was depending in the court of common pleas of Philadelphia county; an attorney at law having appeared to the action for the defendant, Isaac Austin.

So flagrant an infringement of the sacred rights of a citizen to trial by jury, and so manifest, and withal so wanton a violation of the constitution of this commonwealth, calls for the severest censure of the people and of this council. To their respective constituents it belongs to enquire how their servants in assembly, individually, voted on this occasion. From the journals of the house they will derive full information on the subject.

The Constitution

Section 7, latter clause. "No member of the house of representatives, whilst he continues such, shall hold *any other office*, except in the militia."

It is the opinion of this committee, that members of the general assembly may not hold the office of county treasurer. There have been sundry instances of county treasurers sitting as members of the house of representatives, since the revolution.

Section 9. "The members of the house of representatives shall have power to prepare bills and enact them into laws."

It is the opinion of this committee, that acts of assembly to amend titles to land, which may be defective from the loss of deeds, and from the denial of deeds by the vendors, after the price has been paid, have been too frequently passed, and have too decidedly barred all other persons, who might have pretensions to the same; that the practice is dangerous, that it tempts to fraud, and that in either case they are seldom necessary, as the testimony upon which the house proceeds may now be perpetuated, under a clause of the constitution, as well in the courts of common pleas as in the supreme court, in order to have the effect it ought to have, and no greater. And perhaps it would be better to lodge a chancery power with proper judges, to compel the specific performance of bargains for lands in the latter case. See acts of assembly, vol. I, chap. 122, to confirm lands of T. Beans.—Chap. 123, to confirm lands of T. Summers.—Vol. II, chap. 94, to confirm lands of Percifor Frazer.

By these acts, all claims not made within one year after the passing of them, are for ever barred, saving only *femes covert, infants, &c.* Thus the loss of a deed becomes the advantage of the party, whilst, through mistake, others may be injured by the relief intended by the legislature to the applier, whose neglect in not recording his deeds, has given occasion to the interposition of the house.

It is the opinion of this committee, that the dissolving of the bands of marriage is another very improper exercise of legislative power, and an intrusion upon the judicial branch; and that instead of passing acts occasionally, there should be a power given to proper judges of determining on such applications.

It is the opinion of this committee that acts of assembly for vacating useless highways and roads, are also improper and unconstitutional. There should be an authority lodged with proper courts, to vacate useless roads.

Section 9. "The house of representatives shall have power to judge of the qualifications of their own members."

It is the opinion of this committee, that the general assembly has no right to expel one of its members, charged with crimes not committed as a member, but as a public officer or in his private capacity, until he shall be convicted thereof before his proper judges.

September 9, 1783, Mr.——, a representative in the general assembly for—county, is, first declared guilty of notorious frauds and other enormous crimes; secondly, he is expelled from his seat; thirdly, the attorney general is directed to institute actions against him for fraud and perjury. After such denunciations, would it be possible for the accused to obtain a fair trial? Suppose one of the members of the house were to kill a man, would it be just that the house should anticipate his sentence, and pronounce the homicide to be a malicious murder? Besides, after fixing such an odium on the unhappy manslayer, every member concerned would be interested against a fair hearing. But if, after all, the culprit should be acquitted by his peers, where would be the dignity of the legislature? Examples of this nature from the British house of commons will not serve for precedents in Pennsylvania. The proceedings against Sir Robert Walpole and Sir Richard Steele, in the reign of Queen Ann, and the expulsion of John Wilkes, in the days of George the third, for a libel, reflected dishonor on none but the authors of these violences. Mr.——, whether guilty or not, was a citizen; the example which his case has set is dangerous to all.

Section 9. "The house of representatives may redress grievances."

It is the opinion of this committee that the general assembly, under reports of the committees of grievances, in some instances, has exercised powers inconsistent with the constitution. . . .

Remark

The word grievances seems to have changed its import. Fomerly the excesses and oppressive proceedings of the executive power, and of the courts of justice, were the grievances of England. Such as purveyance, or seizing in an arbitrary manner, provisions and other supplies for the use of the kings household; extorted benevolences to the crown; compositions of knighthood; ship money; levying taxes, after the laws which granted them were expired; monopolies; extra-judicial opinions of judges; denial of bail, where bail was of

right; billeting of soldiers; suspending of law by prerogative; proclamations to alter the law; and such matters as, arising from the undue influence of the crown, could not be remedied without the interposition of parliament—not hardships which will always arise from the operation of general laws, nor even the misdeeds of particular officers, or private men, for which there is an easy and legal remedy; much less inconveniences, to which the negligence of the sufferer himself has subjected him.

Section 9th. "The general assembly may impeach state criminals."

It is the opinion of this committee, that the proceedings and sentence of the general assembly (5th March, 1783,) by which——, late secretary of the supreme executive council, was declared "unworthy of public trust and confidence," were unconstitutional.

——was a public officer, holding at the pleasure of the president and council. He was liable, as other civil officers to an impeachment, and to trial (as an officer) for his misconduct, before the supreme executive council; he was also amenable in the ordinary course of justice. But the constitution of Pennsylvania countenances no undefined and arbitrary powers; such as the house assumed in his case; powers, that may be equally exerted to shelter a set of defaulters and peculators, and to destroy persons obnoxious to the predominant party. In Mr.——'s case there was neither summons, hearing, charge or trial. In short he was condemned unheard.

Section 9. "The house of representatives, shall have all other powers necessary for the legislature of a free commonwealth."

It appears to your committee that the act passed on the 21, January 1777, entitled "An act to enable a smaller number of the members of assembly, than a quorum to collect the absent members, and issue writs for filling vacancies occasiond by neglect or refusal" and the supplement thereto passed the 11 October, 1777, And the act "to amend the several acts of this commonwealth, directing the mode of electing members of the general assembly thereof," passed the 12th September 1782, are deviations from the 9th and

12th sections of the constitution, so far as respects the issuing writs for new elections, and subjecting the members to the payment of charges incurred by sending for absentees.

Section 10. "The members of the house of representatives shall, each of them, before they proceed to business, take and subscribe, as well the oath or affirmation of fidelity and allegiance hereinafter directed, as the following oath or affirmation." Then follows the oath of office.

The oath or affirmation of allegiance is,

"I. A. B. do swear or affirm, that I will be true and faithful to the commonwealth of Pennsylvania; and that I will not directly or indirectly do any act or thing prejudicial or injurious to the commonwealth, or government thereof, as established by the convention." See section 40.

It appears by the journals of the general assembly that on the 5th day of November 1778, and on occasion of the first meeting of a new house, divers members "expressed some scruples with respect to taking the oath or affirmation of allegiance prescribed by the constitution, apprehending they would be thereby precluded from taking measures to obtain the sense of the people with respect to calling a convention &c."

Wherefore the next day, (November 6th,) it was "unanimously agreed that every member might take said oath, with a reservation of full liberty to himself to pursue such measures as he might judge necessary for collecting the sentiments of the people, on the subject of calling a new convention to revise, amend and confirm the constitution; and reserving also full liberty of co-operating, as well with his fellow citizens as with the said convention, if called."

It appears that twenty-five of the representatives in said assembly adopted the reservation above mentioned.

By information which your committee rely on, it appears that some of the members of the first assembly, after the revolution, were admitted to take the oath of allegiance (section 40,) without the words "as established by the constitution."

It is the opinion of this committee, that the admission of members of general assembly in the above instances, upon taking the oaths and affirmations required, with a reservation, were deviations from the constitution of this state.

Section 11. "No person who holds any office in the gift of congress, shall hereafter be elected to represent this commonwealth in congress."

Benjamin Franklin Esq. one of the commissioners of congress, to the court of France, being on the 10th of December 1777, elected to represent Pennsylvania in congress, was a deviation from the above clause.

Section 15th. "To the end that laws, before they are enacted, may be more maturely considered, and the inconvenience of hasty determinations, as much as possible prevented, all bills of a public nature shall be published, and, except on occasions of sudden necessity, shall not be passed into laws until the next session of the general assembly."

Very many bills have been passed hastily, in the same session, in violation of this section.

Thus this important and essential restraint upon the proceedings of the legislature hath been laid aside in many instances, without any apparent necessity.

The postponing of bills to another sitting, is at length so much disregarded that of thirty nine acts of assembly, which were passed during the last session of the present house thirty one of them originated within the same sitting: and with respect to almost all these, so far from any sudden necessity existing for thus hastily passing them, there does not seem to be any considerable motives for thus precipitating more than two or three of them. If the act for regulating the choice of justices of the peace, had become immediately necessary, it was from the neglect of the house, to take up the business earlier.

It is the opinon of this committee, that the 15th section of the constitution, whereby the authority to legislate is laid under peculiar restraints, has been evaded, and in a great measure defeated, by the exercise of a power assumed by the general assembly to make laws, and to alter laws, and to appropriate the lands, goods and money, of the commonwealth, by resolve only; which, so far from being published for consideration, and deferred to the next session, is passed secretly, immediately.

Reference: The Proceedings Relative to Calling the Convention of 1776 and 1790 (Harrisburg: John S. Wiesting, 1826).

39

Connecticut and Rhode Island

Although neither Connecticut nor Rhode Island wrote constitutions until the nineteenth century, both set up a governing system based on their colonial charters. The two states had long elected their governors and were satisfied with governance under the charters. Included here are some of the governance reforms in Connecticut during the 1780s, Including the passage of a law that popularly elected delegates to the Continental Congress. Leaders in the legislature actively debated the state's claim to western lands because members wanted to revise the charter to protect those claims.

ACT TO SET UP GOVERNMENT OF CONNECTICUT, 1776

An Act containing an Abstract and Declaration of the Rights and Privileges of the People of this State, and securing the same.

The People of this State, being by the Providence of God, free and independent, have the sole and exclusive Right of governing themselves as a free, sovereign, and independent State; and having from their Ancestors derived a free and excellent Constitution of Government whereby the Legislature depends on the free and annual Election of the People, they have the best Security for the Preservation of their civil and religious Rights and Liberties. And forasmuch as the free Fruition of such Liberties and Privileges as Humanity, Civility and Christianity call for, as is due to every Man in his Place and Proportion, without Impeachment and Infringement, hath ever been, and will be the Tranquility and Stability of Churches and Commonwealths; and the Denial thereof, the Disturbance, if not the Ruin of both.

PARAGRAPH 1. *Be it enacted and declared by the Governor, and Council, and House of Representatives, in General Court assembled,* That the ancient Form of Civil Government, contained in the Charter from *Charles* the Second, King of *England,* and adopted by the People of this State, shall be and remain the Civil Constitution of this State, under the sole authority of the People thereof, independent of any King or Prince whatever. And that this Republic is, and shall forever be and remain, a free, sovereign and independent State, by the Name of the STATE OF CONNECTICUT.

2. *And be it further enacted and declared,* That no Man's Life shall be taken away: No Man's Honor or good Name shall be stained: No Man's Person shall be arrested, restrained, banished, dismembered, nor any Ways punished: No Man shall be deprived of his Wife or Children: No Man's Goods or Estate shall be taken away from him, nor any Ways indamaged under the Colour of Law, or Countenance of Authority; unless clearly warranted by the Laws of this State.

3. That all the free Inhabitants of this or any other of the United States of *America*, and Foreigners in Amity with this State, shall enjoy the same justice and Law within this State, which is general for the State, in all Cases proper for the Cognizance of the Civil Authority and Court of Judicature within the same, and that without Partiality or Delay.

4. And that no Man's Person shall be restrained, or imprisoned, by any authority whatsoever, before the Law hath sentenced him thereunto, if he can and will give sufficient Security, Bail, or Mainprize for his Appearance and good Behaviour in the mean Time, unless it be for Capital Crimes, Contempt in open Court, or in such Cases wherein some express Law doth allow of, or order the same.

Reference: Francis Newton Thorpe (ed.), *The Federal and State Constitutions, Colonial Charters, and Other Organic Laws of the States,* Vol. I (Washington: GPO, 1909).

CONNECTICUT DELEGATES TO CONGRESS MUST BE ELECTED BY ALL FREEHOLDERS, SEPTEMBER 1776

Instructions to their Representatives, voted by the freemen of a town in Connecticut, at their annual meeting in September 1776.

Gentlemen: Although we repose the highest confidence in your zeal for the publick weal and particular attention to the true interests of your constituents, yet we think it our duty to manifest to you our sentiments respecting a matter which we hope may come under the consideration of the honourable General Assembly of the State of Connecticut the ensuing session, and in our apprehension is of the utmost importance to the people of this State, viz: The mode of electing Delegates to represent this State in the General Congress of America.

The exigency of publick affairs have heretofore seemed to require that they should be nominated and appointed by the General Assembly, which has been done to general satisfaction. America is now declared independent, and is forming into an empire unconnected with any other part of the globe. We think it a duty we owe ourselves and posterity to guard our rights and privileges on every quarter, lest a precedent, founded at first in necessity or accident, should be in time construed to deprive us of one privilege which we deem essential to the preservation of all the rest.

The power of electing Representatives, who, with others, are entrusted with power to declare war and make peace, to form alliances with foreign nations, and to make laws for an extensive empire, (we conceive) can be lodged nowhere in so safe hands as that of the whole body of freeholders in a State. Bribery and corruption, intrigue and undue influence, is much more easily practised upon a few than many; although we have the highest value for our own General Assembly, whose members have heretofore been governed and directed by the most laudable of principles, the love of their country's welfare, yet we are not sure that in all future times the same attention will be paid to the true interest of their constituents, or the same principle be the ruling motive of action; and we must declare to you that we think it a right which unalienably belongs to the freeholders of this State to elect members to represent them in the General Congress of America, and a right and power which posterity cannot be deprived of by any previous or present obligation to others.

We do, therefore, as part of the freeholders of this State, enjoin it upon you as our Representatives in General Assembly, to use your utmost influence that the Assembly do order and direct that such election of Delegates to represent this State in General Congress, be annually made by the freeholders, or freemen at large, and not by their Representatives in General Assembly.

Reference: Peter Force, *American Archives,* 5th Ser., Vol. II (Washington: GPO, 1836), 895.

CONNECTICUT LEGISLATURE DEBATES WESTERN LANDS, OCTOBER 1783

On the Report of a Committee respecting the Inhabitants Settled under the Claim of this State west of Delaware River accepted and approved Whereas a large number of Inhabitants West of Delaware River and within the Charter Limits of this State settled there under the Claim and Jurisdiction of the said State having first with the approbation of the General Assembly thereof purchased the Native Right of Soil and for many Years past have been incorporated and in the exercise of Government under the Laws of the said State, And Whereas by a late Decree of Commissioners appointed for settling a Dispute relative to Jurisdiction between this State and the State of Pensylvania, the Tract of Land possessed by the said Settlers is unexpectedly declared to be within the Jurisdiction of the latter, since which the said Settlers as it is represented notwithstanding their having acquired the Native and Possessory Right as aforesaid and corroborated their Title by vast Labour and expence in reducing the said Lands from a Wilderness State and stood as a Barrier to Pensylvania and other Interior Settlements, through a long distressing War in which most of their Males capable of Labour or Defence have been Slain Circumstances which entituled them to expect as well from the Justice as Clemency of that great and opulent State the fullest Protection for their Persons and to be forever Quieted in their Possessions and for which they lost no Time in applying to its Legislature by Humble Petition, yet notwithstanding to their great astonishment and Distress they find themselves left to the Mercy of Men who Claiming under the Proprietary Title of that State are prosecuting against them Suits of ejectment, and in some Cases entering into their Possessions and Labours by force.

Whereupon Resolved by this Assembly that it will in their Opinion be expedient for the said Settlers as the only Remedy left them to apply to the Honb[le] the Congress of the United States for a Court to be Instituted to try their Right of Soil & Possession, pursuant to the Ninth of the Articles of Confederation, that it will be the Duty of this State to contenance and Patronise them in such Application, and that the Delegates of this State that shall be in Congress be directed to give them all necessary Aid therein, And that his Excellency the Governor be desired to address a full State of their Claims and Sufferings to Congress and sollicit the Protection of that Honorable Body in their behalf until a final adjudication of the Cause shall be had.

Whereas this State has the undoubted and exclusive Right of Jurisdiction and Preemption to all the Lands lying West of the Western Limits of the State of Pensylvania and East of the River Misisipi and extending throughout from the Lattitude 41, to Lattitude 42, & 2 Minits North by Virtue of the Charter Granted by King Charles the second to the late Colony now State of Connecticut bearing Date the 23[d] Day of April A Dom 1662, which Claim and Title to make known for the information of all to the end that they may conform themselves thereto,

Resolved that his Excellency the Governor be desired to Issue his Proclamation declaring and ascerting the Right of this State to all the Lands within the Limits aforesaid and strictly forbiding all Persons to enter or Settle thereon without special Licence and Authority first obtained from the General Assembly of this State.

Reference: Leonard Woods Labaree (comp.), *Public Records of the State of Connecticut* (Hartford: The State, 1943).

CONNECTICUT ACT TO REGULATE APPOINTMENTS TO THE SUPERIOR COURT, MAY 1784

Be it Enacted by the Governor Council and Representatives in General Court Assembled and by the Authority of the same, That no Person shall hereafter be capable of holding the Office of Governor Lieutenant Governor Assistant or Member of the House of Representatives of this State or of Delegate in the Congress of the United States or either of them, and the Office of Judge of the Superior Court at the same Time.

And be it further Enacted by the Authority aforesaid, That the Judges of the Superior Court shall hereafter hold their Offices during the Pleasure of the General Assembly.

Provided nevertheless that nothing in this Act shall be construed to prevent any Judge of the Superior Court appointed at this Assembly from holding for the Term of one Year from the first Day of the Session of the present Assembly, any other Office which he now holds or to which he now stands elected.

Be it further Enacted by the Authority aforesaid that the Lieutenant Governor and Council of this State for the Time being shall be the Supreme Court of Errors in this State, and shall be the Dernier resort of all Matters brought by way of Error or Complaint from the Judgment or Decree of the Superior Court in Matters of Law or Equity, wherein the Rules of Law or the Principles of Equity appear from the files Records and Exhibits of said Court to have been erroneously or mistakenly adjudged and determined; And said Supreme Court are hereby Impowered authorized and enabled to take Cognizance of all such Causes that shall be brought before them as aforesaid and shall be invested with all the Powers Authorities and Jurisdictions necessary and requisite for carrying into complete Execution all their Judgments Decrees and determinations in the Matters aforesaid according to the Laws Customs and Usages of this State; And their Determinations and Decrees shall be final and conclusive to all Concerned.

And be it further Enacted by the Authority aforesaid that the said Supreme Court of Errors shall be held annually at the Place where the General Assembly shall be held to Meet on the Tuesday of the Week next before the stated Sessions of said Assembly. And all Writs returnable to said Court shall be served twelve Days before the Sessions of said Court and returned to the Clerk of said Court before the Day of said Sessions. And the Secretary of this State for the Time being shall (ex Officio) be the Clerk of said Court. And said Court shall have Power to Adjourn from Time to Time and to such Place as they shall think necessary and expedient.

And it is further Provided that the Lieutenant Governor or in his absence the Senior Councillor present shall preside seven of whom shall Constitute a Quorum. . . .

Reference: Leonard Woods Labaree (comp.), *Public Records of the State of Connecticut* (Hartford: The State, 1943).

40

Maryland, November 11, 1776

Debates about Maryland's constitution showed tensions between the interior farmers and the coastal merchants regarding apportioning representation. Maryland included in its constitution a comment on the expectation that quality individuals would lead the state.

CONSTITUTION, NOVEMBER 11, 1776

A Declaration of Rights, and the Constitution and Form of Government agreed to by the Delegates of Maryland, in free and full Convention assembled.

A Declaration of Rights, &C.

THE parliament of Great Britain, by a declaratory act, having assumed a right to make laws to bind the Colonies in all cases whatsoever, and, in pursuance of such claim, endeavoured, by force of arms, to subjugate the United Colonies to an unconditional submission to their will and power, and having at length constrained them to declare themselves independent States, and to assume government under the authority of the people;—Therefore we, the Delegates of Maryland, in free and full Convention assembled, taking into our most serious consideration the best means of establishing a good Constitution in this State, for the sure foundation and more permanent security thereof, declare.

I. That all government of right originates from the people, is founded in compact only, and instituted solely for the good of the whole.

II. That the people of this State ought to have the sole and exclusive right of regulating the internal government and police thereof.

III. That the inhabitants of Maryland are entitled to the common law of England, and the trial by jury, according to the course of that law, and to the benefit of such of the English statutes, as existed at the time of their first emigration, and which, by experience, have been found applicable to their local and other circumstances, and of such others as have been since made in England, or Great Britain, and have been introduced, used and practised by the courts of law or equity; and also to acts of Assembly, in force on the first of June seventeen hundred and seventy-four, except such as may have since expired, or have been or may be altered by acts of Convention, or this Declaration of Rights—subject, nevertheless, to the revision of, and amendment or repeal by, the Legislature of this State: and the inhabitants of Maryland are also entitled to all property, derived to them, from or under the Charter, granted by his Majesty Charles I. to Cæcilius Calvert, Baron of Baltimore.

IV. That all persons invested with the legislative or executive powers of government are the trustees of the public, and, as such, accountable for their conduct; wherefore, whenever the ends of government are perverted, and public liberty manifestly endangered, and all other means of redress are ineffectual, the people may, and of right ought, to reform the old or establish a new government. The doctrine of non-resistance, against arbitrary power and oppression, is absurd, slavish, and destructive of the good and happiness of mankind.

V. That the right in the people to participate in the Legislature is the best security of liberty, and the foundation of all free government; for this purpose, elections ought to be free and frequent, and every man, having property in, a common interest with, and an attachment to the community, ought to have a right of suffrage.

VI. That the legislative, executive and judicial powers of government, ought to be forever separate and distinct from each other.

VII. That no power of suspending laws, or the execution of laws, unless by or derived from the Legislature, ought to be exercised or allowed.

VIII. That freedom of speech and debates, or proceedings in the Legislature, ought not to be impeached in any other court or judicature.

IX. That a place for the meeting of the Legislature ought to be fixed, the most convenient to the members thereof, and to the depository of public records; and the Legislature ought not to be convened or held at any other place, but from evident necessity.

X. That, for redress of grievances, and for amending, strengthening and preserving the laws, the Legislature ought to be frequently convened.

XI. That every man hath a right to petition the Legislature, for the redress of grievances, in a peaceable and orderly manner.

XII. That no aid, charge, tax, fee, or fees, ought to be set, rated, or levied, under any pretence, without consent of the Legislature.

XIII. That the levying taxes by the poll is grievous and oppressive, and ought to be abolished; that paupers ought not to be assessed for the support of government; but every other person in the State ought to contribute his proportion of public taxes, for the support of government, according to his actual worth, in real or personal property, within the State; yet fines, duties, or taxes, may properly and justly be imposed or laid, with a political view, for the good government and benefit of the community.

XIV. That sanguinary laws ought to be avoided, as far as is consistent with the safety of the State: and no law, to inflict cruel and unusual pains and penalties, ought to be made in any case, or at any time hereafter.

XV. That retrospective laws, punishing facts committed before the existence of such laws, and by them only declared criminal, are oppressive, unjust, and incompatible with liberty; wherefore no *ex post facto* law ought to be made.

XVI. That no law, to attaint particular persons of treason or felony, ought to be made in any case, or at any time hereafter.

XVII.nThat every freeman, for any injury done him in his person or property, ought to have remedy, by the course of the law of the land, and ought to have justice and right freely without sale, fully without any denial, and speedily without delay, according to the law of the land.

XVIII. That the trial of facts where they arise, is one of the greasest securities of the lives, liberties and estates of the people.

XIX. That, in all criminal prosecutions, every man hath a right to be informed of the accusation against him; to have a copy of the indictment or charge in due time (if required) to prepare for his defence; to be allowed counsel; to be confronted with the witnesses against him; to have process for his witnesses; to examine the witnesses, for and against him, on oath; and to a speedy trial by an impartial jury, without whose unanimous consent he ought not to be found guilty.

XX. That no man ought to be compelled to give evidence against himself, in a common court of law, or in any other court, but in such cases as have been usually practised in this State, or may hereafter be directed by the Legislature.

XXI. That no freeman ought to be taken, or imprisoned, or disseized of his freehold, liberties, or privileges, or outlawed, or exiled, or in any manner destroyed, or deprived of his life, liberty, or property, but by the judgment of his peers, or by the law of the land.

XXII. That excessive bail ought not to be required, nor excessive fines imposed, nor cruel or unusual punishments inflicted, by the courts of law.

XXIII. That all warrants, without oath or affirmation, to search suspected places, or to seize any person or property, are grievous and oppressive; and all general warrants—to search suspected places, or to apprehend suspected persons, without naming or describing the place, or the person in special—are illegal, and ought not to be granted.

XXIV. That there ought to be no forfeiture of any part of the estate of any person, for any crime except murder, or treason against the State, and then only on conviction and attainder.

XXV. That a well-regulated militia is the proper and natural defence of a free government.

XXVI. That standing armies are dangerous to liberty, and ought not to be raised or kept up, without consent of the Legislature.

XXVII. That in all cases, and at all times, the military ought to be under strict subordination to and control of the civil power.

XXVIII. That no soldier ought to be quartered in any house, in time of peace, without the consent of the owner; and in time of war, in such manner only, as the Legislature shall direct.

XXIX. That no person, except regular soldiers, mariners, and marines in the service of this State, or militia when in actual service, ought in any case to be subject to or punishable by martial law.

XXX. That the independency and uprightness of Judges are essential to the impartial administration of justice, and a great security to the rights and liberties of the people; wherefore the Chancellor and Judges ought to hold commissions during good behaviour; and the said Chancellor and Judges shall be removed for misbehaviour, on conviction in a court of law, and may be removed by the Governor, upon the address of the General Assembly; *Provided,* That two-thirds of all the members of each House concur in such address. That salaries, liberal, but not profuse, ought to be secured to the Chancellor and the Judges, during the continuance of their commissions, in such manner, and at such times, as the Legislature shall hereafter direct, upon consideration of the circumstances of this State. No Chancellor or Judge ought to hold any other office, civil or military, or receive fees or perquisites of any kind.

XXXI. That a long continuance, in the first executive departments of power or trust, is dangerous to liberty; a rotation, therefore, in those departments, is one of the best securities of permanent freedom.

XXXII. That no person ought to hold, at the same time, more than one office of profit, nor ought any person, in public trust, to receive any present from any foreign prince or state, or from the United States, or any of them, without the approbation of this State.

XXXIII. That, as it is the duty of every man to worship God in such manner as he thinks most acceptable to him; all persons, professing the Christian religion, are equally entitled to protection in their religious liberty; wherefore no person ought by any law to be molested in his person or estate on account of his religious persuasion or profession, or for his religious practice; unless, under colour of religion, any man shall disturb the good order, peace or safety of the State, or shall infringe the laws of morality, or injure others, in their natural, civil, or religious rights; nor ought any person to be compelled to frequent or maintain, or contribute, unless on contract, to maintain any particular place of worship, or any particular ministry; yet the Legislature may, in their discretion, lay a general and equal tax, for the support of the Christian religion; leaving to each individual the power of appointing the payment over of the money, collected from him, to the support of any particular place of worship or minister, or for the benefit of the poor of his own denomination, or the poor in general of any particular county: but the churches, chapels, glebes, and all other property now belonging to the church of England, ought to remain to the church of England forever. And all acts of Assembly, lately passed, for collecting monies for building or repairing particular churches or chapels of ease, shall continue in force, and be executed, unless the Legislature shall, by act, supersede or repeal the same: but no county court shall assess any quantity of tobacco, or sum of money, hereafter, on the application of any vestrymen or church-wardens; and every encumbent of the church of England, who hath remained in his parish, and performed his duty, shall be entitled to receive the provision and support established by the act, entitled "An act for the support of the clergy of the church of England, in this Province," till the November court of this present year, to be held for the county in which his parish shall lie, or partly lie, or for such time as he hath remained in his parish, and performed his duty.

XXXIV. That every gift, sale, or devise of lands, to any minister, public teacher, or preacher of the gospel, as such, or to any religious sect, order or denomination, or to or for the support, use or benefit of, or in trust for, any minister, public teacher, or preacher of the gospel, as such, or any religious sect, order or denomination—and every gift or sale of goods, or chattels, to go in succession, or to take place after the death of the seller or donor, or to or for such support, use or benefit—and also every devise of goods or chattels to or for the support, use or benefit of any minister, public teacher, or preacher of the gospel, as such, or any religious sect, order, or denomination, without the leave of the Legislature, shall be void; except always any sale, gift, lease or devise of any quantity of land, not exceeding two acres, for a church, meeting, or other house of worship, and for a burying-ground, which shall be improved, enjoyed or used only for such purpose—or such sale, gift, lease, or devise, shall be void.

XXXV. That no other test or qualification ought to be required, on admission to any office of trust or profit, than such oath of support and fidelity to this State, and such oath of office, as shall be directed by this Convention, or the Legislature of this State, and a declaration of a belief in the Christian religion.

XXXVI. That the manner of administering an oath to any person, ought to be such, as those of the religious persuasion, profession, or denomination, of which such person is one, generally esteem the most effectual confirmation, by the attestation of the Divine Being. And that the people called Quakers, those called Dunkers, and those called Menonists, holding it unlawful to take an oath on any occasion, ought to be allowed to make their solemn affirmation, in the manner that Quakers have been heretofore allowed to affirm; and to be of the same avail as an oath, in all such cases, as the affirmation of Quakers hath been allowed and accepted within this State, instead of an oath. And further, on such affirmation, warrants to search for stolen goods, or for the apprehension or commitment of offenders, ought to be granted, or security for the peace awarded, and Quakers, Dunkers or Menonists ought also, on their solemn affirmation as aforesaid, to be admitted as witnesses, in all criminal cases not capital.

XXXVII. That the city of Annapolis ought to have all its rights, privileges and benefits, agreeable to its Charter, and the acts of Assembly confirming and regulating the same, subject nevertheless to such alteration as may be made by this Convention, or any future Legislature.

XXXVIII. That the liberty of the press ought to be inviolably preserved.

XXXIX. That monopolies are odious, contrary to the spirit of a free government, and the principles of commerce; and ought not to be suffered.

XL. That no title of nobility, or hereditary honours, ought to be granted in this State.

XLI. That the subsisting resolves of this and the several Conventions held for this Colony, ought to be in force as laws, unless altered by this Convention, or the Legislature of this State.

XLII. That this Declaration of Rights, or the Form of Government, to be established by this Convention, or any part or either of them, ought not to be altered, changed or abolished, by the Legislature of this State, but in such manner as this Convention shall prescribe and direct.

This Declaration of Rights was assented to, and passed, in Convention of the Delegates of the freemen of Maryland, begun and held at Annapolis, the 14th day of August, A.D. 1776.

By order of the Convention.

MAT. TILGHMAN, *President.*

The Constitution, or From of Government, &c.

I. THAT the Legislature consist of two distinct branches, a Senate and House of Delegates, which shall be styled, *The General Assembly of Maryland.*

II. That the House of Delegates shall be chosen in the following manner: All freemen, above twenty-one years of age, having a freehold of fifty acres of land, in the county in which they offer to vote, and residing therein—and all freemen, having property in this State above the value of thirty pounds current money, and having resided in the county, in which they offer to vote, one whole year next preceding the election, shall have a right of suffrage, in the election of Delegates for such county: and all freemen, so qualified, shall, on the first Monday of October, seventeen hundred and seventy-seven, and on the same day in every year thereafter, assemble in the counties, in which they are respectively qualified to vote, at the court-house, in the said counties; or at such other place as the Legislature shall direct; and, when assembled, they shall proceed to elect, *viva voce,* four Delegates, for their respective counties, of the most wise, sensible, and discreet of the people, residents in the county where they are to be chosen, one whole year next preceding the election, above twenty-one years of age, and having, in the State, real or personal property above the value of five hundred pounds current money; and upon the final casting of the polls, the four persons who shall appear to have the greatest number of legal votes shall be declared and returned duly elected for their respective counties.

III. That the Sheriff of each county, or, in case of sickness, his Deputy (summoning two Justices of the county, who are required to attend, for the preservation of the peace) shall be the judges of the election, and may adjourn from day to day, if necessary, till the same be finished, so that the whole election shall be concluded in four days; and shall make his return thereof, under his hand, to the Chancellor of this State for the time being.

IV. That all persons qualified, by the charter of the city of Annapolis, to vote for Burgesses, shall, on the same first Monday of October, seventeen hundred and seventy-seven, and on the same day in every year forever thereafter, elect, *viva voce,* by a majority of votes, two Delegates, qualified agreeable to the said charter; that the Mayor, Recorder, and Aldermen of the said city, or any three of them, be judges of the election, appoint the place in the said city for holding the same, and may adjourn from day to day, as aforesaid, and shall make return thereof, as aforesaid: but the inhabitants of the said city shall not be entitled to vote for Delegates for Anne-Arundel county, unless they have a freehold of fifty acres of land in the county distinct from the city.

V. That all persons, inhabitants of Baltimore town, and having the same qualifications as electors in the county, shall, on the same first Monday in October, seventeen hundred and seventy-seven, and on the same day in every year forever thereafter, at such place in the said town as the Judges shall appoint, elect, *viva voce,* by a majority of votes, two Delegates, qualified as aforesaid: but if the said inhabitants of the town shall so decrease, as that a number of persons, having a right of suffrage therein, shall have been, for the space of seven years successively, less than one half the number of voters in some one county in this State, such town shall thenceforward cease to send two Delegates or Representatives to the House of Delegates, until the said town shall have one half of the number of voters in some one county in this State.

VI. That the Commissioners of the said town, or any three or more of them, for the time being, shall be judges of the said election, and may adjourn, as aforesaid, and shall make return thereof, as aforesaid: but the inhabitants of the said town shall not be entitled to vote for, or be elected, Delegates for Baltimore county: neither shall the inhabitants of Baltimore county, out of the limits of Baltimore town, be entitled to vote for, or be elected, Delegates for the said town.

VII. That on refusal, death, disqualification, resignation, or removal out of this State of any Delegate, or on his becoming Governor, or member of the Council, a warrant of election shall issue by the Speaker, for the election of another in his place; of which ten days' notice, at least, (excluding the day of notice, and the day of election) shall be given.

VIII. That not less than a majority of the Delegates, with their Speaker (to be chosen by them, by ballot) constitute a House, for the transaction of any business other than that of adjourning.

IX. That the House of Delegates shall judge of the elections and qualifications of Delegates.

X. That the House of Delegates may originate all money bills, propose bills to the Senate, or receive those offered by that body; and assent, dissent, or propose amendments; that they may inquire on the oath of witnesses, into all complaints, grievances, and offences, as the grand inquest of this State; and may commit any person, for any crime, to the public jail, there to remain till he be discharged by due course of law. They may expel any member, for a great misdemeanor, but not a second time for the same cause. They may examine and pass all accounts of the State, relating either to the collection or expenditure of the revenue, or appoint auditors, to state and adjust the same. They may call for all public or official papers and records, and send for persons, whom they may judge necessary in the course of their inquiries, concerning affairs relating to the public interest; and may direct all office bonds (which shall be made payable to the State) to be sued for any breach of duty.

XI. That the Senate may be at full and perfect liberty to exercise their judgment in passing laws—and that they may not be compelled by the House of Delegates, either to reject a money bill, which the emergency of affairs may require, or to assent to some other act of legislation, in their conscience and judgment injurious to the public welfare—the House of Delegates shall not, on any occasion, or under any pretence, annex to, or blend with a money bill, any matter, clause, or thing, not immediately relating to, and necessary for the imposing, assessing, levying, or applying the taxes or supplies, to be raised for the support of government, or the current expenses of the State: and to prevent altercation about such bills, it is declared, that no bill, imposing duties

or customs for the mere regulation of commerce, or inflicting fines for the reformation of morals, or to enforce the execution of the laws, by which an incidental revenue may arise, shall be accounted a money bill: but every bill, assessing, levying, or applying taxes or supplies, for the support of government, or the current expenses of the State, or appropriating money in the treasury, shall be deemed a money bill.

XII. That the House of Delegates may punish, by imprisonment, any person who shall be guilty of a contempt in their view, by any disorderly or riotous behaviour, or by threats to, or abuse of their members, or by any obstruction to their proceedings. They may also punish, by imprisonment, any person who shall be guilty of a breach of privilege, by arresting on civil process, or by assaulting any of their members, during their sitting, or on their way to, or return from the House of Delegates, or by any assault of, or obstruction to their officers, in the execution of any order or process, or by assaulting or obstructing any witness, or any other person, attending on, or on their way to or from the House, or by rescuing any person committed by the House: and the Senate may exercise the same power, in similar cases.

XIII. That the Treasurers (one for the western, and another for the eastern shore) and the Commissioners of the Loan Office, may be appointed by the House of Delegates, during their pleasure; and in case of refusal, death, resignation, disqualification, or removal out of the State, of any of the said Commissioners or Treasurers, in the recess of the General Assembly, the governor, with the advice of the Council, may appoint and commission a fit and proper person to such vacant office, to hold the same until the meeting of the next General Assembly.

XIV. That the Senate be chosen in the following manner: All persons, qualified as aforesaid to vote for county Delegates, shall, on the first day of September, 1781, and on the same day in every fifth year forever thereafter, elect, *viva voce*, by a majority of votes, two persons for their respective counties (qualified as aforesaid to be elected county Delegates) to be electors of the Senate; and the Sheriff of each county, or, in case of sickness, his Deputy (summoning two Justices of the county, who are required to attend, for the preservation of the peace,) shall hold and be judge of the said election, and make return thereof, as aforesaid. And all persons, qualified as aforesaid, to vote for Delegates for the city of Annapolis and Baltimore town, shall, on the same first Monday of September, 1781, and on the same day in every fifth year forever thereafter, elect, *viva voce*, by a majority of votes, one person for the said city and town respectively, qualified as aforesaid to be elected a Delegate for the said city and town respectively; the said election to be held in the same manner, as the election of Delegates for the said city and town; the right to elect the said elector, with respect to Baltimore town, to continue as long as the right to elect Delegates for the said town.

XV. That the said electors of the Senate meet at the city of Annapolis, or such other place as shall be appointed for convening the Legislature, on the third Monday in September, 1781, and on the same day in every fifth year forever thereafter, and they, or any twenty-four of them so met, shall proceed to elect, by ballot, either out of their own body, or the people at large, fifteen Senators (nine of whom to be residents on the western, and six to be residents on the eastern shore) men of the most wisdom, experience and virtue, above twenty-five years of age, residents of the State above three whole years next preceding the election, and having real and personal property above the value of one thousand pounds current money.

XVI. That the Senators shall be balloted for, at one and the same time, and out of the gentlemen residents of the western shore, who shall be proposed as Senators, the nine who shall, on striking the ballots, appear to have the greatest numbers in their favour, shall be accordingly declared and returned duly elected: and out of the gentlemen residents of the eastern shore, who shall be proposed as Senators, the six who shall, on striking the ballots, appear to have the greatest number in their favour, shall be accordingly declared and returned duly elected: and if two or more on the same shore shall have an equal number of bal-

lots in their favour, by which the choice shall not be determined on the first ballot, then the electors shall again ballot, before they separate; in which they shall be confined to the persons who on the first ballot shall have an equal number: and they who shall have the greatest number in their favour on the second ballot, shall be accordingly declared and returned duly elected: and if the whole number should not thus be made up, because of an equal number, on the second ballot, still being in favour of two or more persons, then the election shall be determined by lot, between those who have equal numbers; which proceedings of the electors shall be certified under their hands, and returned to the Chancellor for the time being.

XVII. That the electors of Senators shall judge of the qualifications and elections of members of their body; and, on a contested election, shall admit to a seat, as an elector, such qualified person as shall appear to them to have the greatest number of legal votes in his favour.

XVIII. That the electors, immediately on their meeting, and before they proceed to the election of Senators, take such oath of support and fidelity to this State, as this Convention, or the Legislature, shall direct; and also an oath "to elect without favour, affection, partiality, or prejudice, such persons for Senators, as they, in their judgment and conscience, believe best qualified for the office."

XIX. That in case of refusal, death, resignation, disqualification, or removal out of this State, of any Senator, or on his becoming Governor, or a member of the Council, the Senate shall, immediately thereupon, or at their next meeting thereafter, elect by ballot (in the same manner as the electors are above directed to choose Senators) another person in his place, for the residue of the said term of five years.

XX. That not less than a majority of the Senate, with their President (to be chosen by them, by ballot) shall constitute a House, for the transacting any business, other than that of adjourning.

XXI. That the Senate shall judge of the elections and qualifications of Senators.

XXII. That the Senate may originate any other, except money bills, to which their assent or dissent only shall be given; and may receive any other bills from the House of Delegates, and assent, dissent, or propose amendments.

XXIII. That the General Assembly meet annually, on the first Monday of November, and if necessary, oftener.

XXIV. That each House shall appoint its own officers, and settle its own rules of proceeding.

XXV. That a person of wisdom, experience, and virtue, shall be chosen Governor, on the second Monday of November, seventeen hundred and seventy-seven, and on the second Monday in every year forever thereafter, by the joint ballot of both Houses (to be taken in each House respectively) deposited in a conference room; the boxes to be examined by a joint committee of both Houses, and the numbers severally reported, that the appointment may be entered; which mode of taking the joint ballot of both Houses shall be adopted in all cases. But if two or more shall have an equal number of ballots in their favour, by which the choice shall not be determined on the first ballot, then a second ballot shall be taken, which shall be confined to the persons who, on the first ballot, shall have had an equal number; and, if the ballots should again be equal between two or more persons, then the election of the Governor shall be determined by lot, between those who have equal numbers: and if the person chosen Governor shall die, resign, move out of the State, or refuse to act, (the General Assembly sitting) the Senate and House of Delegates shall, immediately thereupon, proceed to a new choice, in manner aforesaid.

XXVI. That the Senators and Delegates, on the second Tuesday of November, 1777, and annually on the second Tuesday of November forever thereafter, elect by joint ballot (in the same manner as Senators are directed to be chosen) five of the most sensible, discreet, and experienced men, above twenty-five years of age, residents in the State above three years next preceding the election, and having therein a freehold of lands and tenements, above the value of one thousand pounds current money, to be the Council to the

Governor, whose proceedings shall be always entered on record, to any part whereof any member may enter his dissent; and their advice, if so required by the Governor, or any member of the Council, shall be given in writing, and signed by the members giving the same respectively: which proceedings of the Council shall be laid before the Senate, or House of Delegates, when called for by them or either of them. The Council may appoint their own Clerk, who shall take such oath of suport and fidelity to this State, as this Convention, or the Legislature, shall direct; and of secrecy, in such matters as he shall be directed by the board to keep secret.

XXVII. That the Delegates to Congress, from this State, shall be chosen annually, or superseded in the mean time by the joint ballot of both Houses of Assembly; and that there be a rotation, in such manner, that at least two of the number be annually changed; and no person shall be capable of being a Delegate to Congress for more than three in any term of six years; and no person, who holds any office of profit in the gift of Congress, shall be eligible to sit in Congress; but if appointed to any such office, his seat shall be thereby vacated. That no person, unless above twenty-one years of age, and a resident in the State more than five years next preceding the election, and having real and personal estate in this State above the value of one thousand pounds current money, shall be eligible to sit in Congress.

XXVIII. That the Senators and Delegates, immediately on their annual meeting, and before they proceed to any business, and every person, hereafter elected a Senator or Delegate, before he acts as such, shall take an oath of support and fidelity to this State, as aforesaid; and before the election of a governor, or members of the Council, shall take an oath, "elect without favour, affection, partiality, or prejudice, such person as Governor, or member of the Council, as they, in their judgment and conscience, believe best qualified for the office."

XXIX. That the Senate and Delegates may adjourn themselves respectively: but if the two Houses should not agree on the same time, but adjourn to different days, then shall the Governor appoint and notify one of those days, or some day between, and the Assembly shall then meet and be held accordingly; and he shall, if necessary, by advice of the Council, call them before the time, to which they shall in any manner be adjourned, on giving not less than ten days' notice thereof; but the Governor shall not adjourn the Assembly, otherwise than as aforesaid, nor prorogue or dissolve it, at any time.

XXX. That no person, unless above twenty-five years of age, a resident in this State above five years next preceding the election—and having in the State real and personal property, above the value of five thousand pounds, current money, (one thousand pounds whereof, at least, to be freehold estate) shall be eligible as governor.

XXXI. That the governor shall not continue in that office longer than three years successively, nor be eligible as Governor, until the expiration of four years after he shall have been out of that office.

XXXII. That upon the death, resignation, or removal out of this State, of the Governor, the first named of the Council, for the time being, shall act as Governor, and qualify in the same manner; and shall immediately call a meeting of the General Assembly, giving not less than fourteen days' notice of the meeting, at which meeting, a Governor shall be appointed, in manner aforesaid, for the residue of the year.

XXXIII. That the Governor, by and with the advice and consent of the Council, may embody the militia; and, when embodied, shall alone have the direction thereof; and shall also have the direction of all the regular land and sea forces, under the laws of this State, (but he shall not command in person, unless advised thereto by the Council, and then, only so long as they shall approve thereof); and may alone exercise all other the executive powers of government, where the concurrence of the Council is not required, according to the laws of this State; and grant reprieves or pardons for any crime, except in such cases where the law shall otherwise direct; and may, during the recess of the General Assembly, lay embargoes, to prevent the departure of any shipping, or the exportation of any commodi-

ties, for any time not exceeding thirty days in any one year—summoning the General Assembly to meet within the time of the continuance of such embargo; and may also order and compel any vessel to ride quarantine, if such vessel, or the port from which she may have come, shall, on strong grounds, be suspected to be infected with the plague; but the Governor shall not, under any pretence, exercise any power or prerogative by virtue of any law, statute, or custom of England or Great Britain.

XXXIV. That the members of the Council, or any three or more of them, when convened, shall constitute a board for the transacting of business; that the Governor, for the time being, shall preside in the Council, and be entitled to a vote, on all questions in which the Council shall be divided in opinion; and, in the absence of the Governor, the first named of the Council shall preside; and as such, shall also vote, in all cases, where the other members disagree in their opinion.

XXXV. That, in case of refusal, death, resignation, disqualification, or removal out of the State, of any person chosen a member of the council, the members thereof, immediately thereupon, or at their next meeting thereafter, shall elect by ballot another person (qualified as aforesaid) in his place, for the residue of the year.

XXXVI. That the Council shall have power to make the Great Seal of this State, which shall be kept by the Chancellor for the time being, and affixed to all laws, commissions, grants, and other public testimonials, as has been heretofore practised in this State.

XXXVII. That no Senator, Delegate of Assembly, or member of the Council, if he shall qualify as such, shall hold or execute any office of profit, or receive the profits of any office exercised by any other person, during the time for which he shall be elected; nor shall any Governor be capable of holding any other office of profit in this State, while he acts as such. And no person, holding a place of profit or receiving any part of the profits thereof, or receiving the profits or any part of the profits arising on any agency, for the supply of clothing or provisions for the Army or Navy, or holding any office under the United States, or any of them—or a minister, or preacher of the gospel, of any denomination—or any person, employed in the regular land service, or marine, of this or the United States—shall have a seat in the General Assembly or the Council of this State.

XXXVIII. That every Governor, Senator, Delegate to Congress or Assembly, and member of the Council, before he acts as such, shall take an oath "that he will not receive, directly or indirectly, at any time, any part of the profits of any office, held by any other person during his acting in his office of Governor, Senator, Delegate to Congress or Assembly, or member of the Council, or the profits or any part of the profits arising on any agency for the supply of clothing or provisions for the Army or Navy."

XXXIX. That if any Senator, Delegate to Congress or Assembly, or member of the Council, shall hold or execute any office of profit, or receive, directly or indirectly, at any time, the profits or any part of the profits of any office exercised by any other person, during his acting as Senator, Delegate to Congress or Assembly, or member of the Council—his seat (on conviction, in a Court of law, by the oath of two credible witnesses) shall be void; and he shall suffer the punishment of wilful and corrupt perjury, or be banished this State forever, or disqualified forever from holding any office or place of trust or profit, as the Court may judge.

XL. That the Chancellor, all Judges, the Attorney-General, Clerks of the General Court, the Clerks of the County Courts, the Registers of the Land Office, and the Registers of Wills, shall hold their commissions during good behaviour, removable only for misbehaviour, on conviction in a Court of law.

XLI. That there be a Register of Wills appointed for each county, who shall be commissioned by the Governor, on the joint recommendation of the Senate and House of Delegates; and that, upon the death, resignation, disqualification, or removal out of the county of any Register of Wills, in the recess of the General Assembly, the Governor, with the advice of the Council,

may appoint and commission a fit and proper person to such vacant office, to hold the same until the meeting of the General Assembly.

XLII. That Sheriffs shall be elected in each county, by ballot, every third year; that is to say, two persons for the office of Sheriff for each county, the one of whom having the majority of votes, or if both have an equal number, either of them, at the discretion of the Governor, to be commissioned by the Governor for the said office; and having served for three years, such person shall be ineligible for the four years next succeeding; bond with security to be taken every year, as usual; and no Sheriff shall be qualified to act before the same is given. In case of death, refusal, resignation, disqualification, or removal out of the county before the expiration of the three years, the other person, chosen as aforesaid, shall be commissioned by the Governor to execute the said office, for the residue of the said three years, the said person giving bond and security as aforesaid: and in case of his death, refusal, resignation, disqualification, or removal out of the county, before the expiration of the said three years, the Governor, with the advice of the Council, may nominate and commission a fit and proper person to execute the said office for the residue of the said three years, the said person giving bond and security as aforesaid. The election shall be held at the same time and place appointed for the election of Delegates; and the Justices, there summoned to attend for the preservation of the peace, shall be judges thereof, and of the qualification of candidates, who shall appoint a Clerk, to take the ballots. All freemen above the age of twenty-one years, having a freehold of fifty acres of land in the county in which they offer to ballot, and residing therein—and all freemen above the age of twenty-one years, and having property in the State above the value of thirty pounds current money, and having resided in the county in which they offer to ballot one whole year next preceding the election—shall have a right of suffrage. No person to be eligible to the office of Sheriff for a county, but an inhabitant of the said county above the age of twenty-one years, and having real and personal property in the State above the value of one thousand pounds current money. The Justices aforesaid shall examine the ballots; and the two candidates properly qualified, having in each county the majority of legal ballots, shall be declared duly elected for the office of Sheriff for such county, and returned to the Governor and Council, with a certificate of the number of ballots for each of them.

XLIII. That every person who shall offer to vote for Delegates, or for the election of the Senate, or for the Sheriff, shall (if required by any three persons qualified to vote) before he be permitted to poll, take such oath or affirmation of support and fidelity to this State, as this Convention or the Legislature shall direct.

XLIV. That a Justice of the Peace may be eligible as a Senator, Delegate, or member of the Council, and may continue to act as a Justice of the Peace.

XLV. That no field officer of the militia be eligible as a Senator, Delegate, or member of the Council.

XLVI. That all civil officers, hereafter to be appointed for the several counties of this State, shall have been residents of the county, respectively, for which they shall be appointed, six months next before their appointment; and shall continue residents of their county, respectively, during their continuance in office.

XLVII. That the Judges of the General Court, and Justices of the County Courts, may appoint the Clerks of their respective Courts; and in case of refusal, death, resignation, disqualification, or removal out of the State, or from their respective shores, of the Clerks of the General Court, or either of them, in the vacation of the said Court—and in case of the refusal, death, resignation, disqualification, or removal out of the county, of any of the said County Clerks, in the vacation of the County Court of which he is Clerk—the Governor, with the advice of the Council, may appoint and commission a fit and proper person to such vacant office respectively, to bold the same until the meeting of the next General Court, or County Court, as the case may be.

XLVIII. That the Governor, for the time being, with the advice and consent of the Council, may appoint the Chancellor, and all Judges and Justices, the Attorney-General, Naval Officers, officers in the regular land and sea service, officers of the militia, Registers of the Land Office, Surveyors, and all other civil officers of government (Assessors, Constables, and Overseers of the roads only excepted) and may also suspend or remove any civil officer who has not a commission, during good behaviour; and may suspend any militia officer, for one month: and may also suspend or remove any regular officer in the land or sea service: and the Governor may remove or suspend any militia officer, in pursuance of the judgment of a Court Martial.

XLIX. That all civil officers of the appointment of the Governor and Council, who do not hold commissions during good behaviour, shall be appointed annually in the third week of November. But if any of them shall be reappointed, they may continue to act, without any new commission or qualification; and every officer, though not reappointed, shall continue to act, until the person who shall be appointed and commissioned in his stead shall be qualified.

L. That the Governor, every member of the Council, and every Judge and Justice, before they act as such, shall respectively take an oath, "That he will not, through favour, affection or partiality vote for any person to office; and that he will vote for such person as, in his judgment and conscience, he believes most fit and best qualified for the office; and that he has not made, nor will make, any promise or engagement to give his vote or interest in favor of any person."

LI. That there be two Registers of the Land Office, one upon the western, and one upon the eastern shore: that short extracts of the grants and certificates of the land, on the western and eastern shores respectively, be made in separate books, at the public expense, and deposited in the offices of the said Registers, in such manner as shall hereafter be provided by the General Assembly.

LII. That every Chancellor, Judge, Register of Wills, Commissioner of the Loan Office, Attorney-General, Sheriff, Treasurer, Naval Officer, Register of the Land Office, Register of the Chancery

Court, and every Clerk of the common law courts, Surveyor and Auditor of the public accounts, before he acts as such, shall take an oath "That he will not directly or indirectly receive any fee or reward, for doing his office of, but what is or shall be allowed by law; nor will, directly or indirectly, receive the profits or any part of the profits of any office held by any other person; and that he does not hold the same office in trust, or for the benefit of any other person."

LIII. That if any Governor, Chancellor, Judge, Register of Wills, Attorney-General, Register of the Land Office, Register of the Chancery Court, or any Clerk of the common law courts, Treasurer, Naval Officer, Sheriff, Surveyor or Auditor of public accounts, shall receive, directly or indirectly, at any time, the profits, or any part of the profits of any office, held by any other person, during his acting in the office to which he is appointed; his election, appointment and commission (on conviction in a court of law by oath of two credible witnesses) shall be void; and he shall suffer the punishment for wilful and corrupt perjury, or be banished this State forever, or disqualified forever from holding any office or place of trust or profit, as the court may adjudge.

LIV. That if any person shall give any bribe, present, or reward, or any promise, or any security for the payment or delivery of any money, or any other thing, to obtain or procure a vote to be Governor, Senator, Delegate to Congress or Assembly, member of the Council, or Judge, or to be appointed to any of the said offices, or to any office of profit or trust, now created or hereafter to be created in this State—the person giving, and the person receiving the same (on conviction in a court of law) shall be forever disqualified to hold any office of trust or profit in this State.

LV. That every person, appointed to any office of profit or trust, shall, before he enters on the execution thereof, take the following oath; to wit: "I. A. B., do swear, that I do not hold myself bound in allegiance to the King of Great Britain, and that I will be faithful, and bear true allegiance to the State of Maryland;" and shall also subscribe a declaration of his belief in the Christian religion.

LVI. That there be a Court of Appeals, composed of persons of integrity and sound judgment in the law, whose judgment shall be final and conclusive, in all cases of appeal, from the General Court, Court of Chancery, and Court of Admiralty: that one person of integrity and sound judgment in the law, be appointed Chancellor: that three persons of integrity and sound judgment in the law, be appointed judges of the Court now called the Provincial Court; and that the same Court be hereafter called and known by the name of *The General Court;* which Court shall sit on the western and eastern shores, for transacting and determining the business of the respective shores, at such times and places as the future Legislature of this State shall direct and appoint.

LVII. That the style of all laws run thus; "*Be it enacted by the General Assembly of Maryland:*" that all public commissions and grants run thus: "*The State of Maryland,*" &c. and shall be signed by the Governor, and attested by the Chancellor, with the seal of the State annexed—except military commissions, which shall not be attested by the Chancellor, or have the seal of the State annexed: that all writs shall run in the same style, and be attested, sealed and signed as usual: that all indictments shall conclude, "*Against the peace, government, and dignity of the State.*"

LVIII. That all penalties and forfeitures, heretofore going to the King or proprietary, shall go to the State—save only such, as the General Assembly may abolish or otherwise provide for.

LIX. That this Form of Government, and the Declaration of Rights, and no part thereof, shall be altered, changed, or abolished, unless a bill so to alter, change or abolish the same shall pass the General Assembly, and be published at least three months before a new election, and shall be confirmed by the General Assembly, after a new election of Delegates, in the first session after such new election; provided that nothing in this form of government, which relates to the eastern shore particularly, shall at any time hereafter be altered, unless for the alteration and confirmation thereof at least two-thirds of all the members of each branch of the General Assembly shall concur.

LX. That every bill passed by the General Assembly, when engrossed, shall be presented by the Speaker of the House of Delegates, in the Senate, to the Governor for the time being, who shall sign the same, and thereto affix the Great Seal, in the presence of the members of both Houses: every law shall be recorded in the General Court office of the western shore, and in due time printed, published, and certified under the Great Seal, to the several County Courts, in the same manner as hath been heretofore used in this State.

This Form of Government was assented to, and passed in Convention of the Delegates of the freemen of Maryland, begun and held at the city of Annapolis, the fourteenth of August, A.D. one thousand seven hundred and seventy-six.

By order of the Convention.

M. TILGHMAN, *President*.

Reference: Francis Newton Thorpe (ed.), *The Federal and State Constitutions, Colonial Charters, and Other Organic Laws of the States*, Vol. III (Washington: GPO, 1909).

41

North Carolina, December 18, 1776

North Carolina adopted the Virginia Declaration of Rights in its state constitution. The constitution paid close attention to local rights and the legislature was required to publish a journal of its statutes.

LETTER FROM SAMUEL JOHNSON, APRIL 20, 1776

DEAR SIR:—We have not yet been able to agree on a Constitution. We have a meeting on it every evening, but can conclude on nothing—the great difficulty in our way is how to establish a check on the representatives of the people, to prevent their assuming more power than would be consistent with the liberties of the people—such as increasing the time of their duration, and such like. Many projects have been proposed, too tedious for a letter to communicate. Some have proposed that we should take up the plan of the Connecticut constitution, for a ground-work, but with some amendments—such as that the great officers, instead of being appointed by the people at large, should be appointed by the Assembly—that the judges of our courts should hold their offices during good behavior, &c. After all, it appears to me, that there can be no check on the representatives of the people in a Democracy, but the people themselves; and, in order that the check may be the more efficient, I would have annual elections. . . .

Dear Sir,
Your affectionate brother,

SAM. JOHNSTON.

Reference: Griffith J. McRea, *The Life and Correspondence of James Iredell*, Vol. I (New York: D. Appleton, 1857).

INSTRUCTIONS TO DELEGATES FROM MECKLENBURG TO THE PROVINCIAL CONGRESS, NOVEMBER 1776

At a general Conference of the inhabitants of Mecklenburgassembledat theCourt-houseonthefirst of November, 1776, for the express purpose of drawing up instructions for the present Representatives in Congress the following were agreed to by the assent of the people present and ordered to be signed by John M. Alexander, Chairman chosen to preside for the day in said Conference.

To Waightstill Avery, Hezekiah Alexander, John Phifer, Robert Erwin and Zacheus Wilson, Esquires:

GENTLEMEN: You are chosen by the inhabitants of this county to serve them in Congress or General Assembly for one year and they have agreed to the following Instructions which you are to observe with the strictest regard viz.: You are instructed:

1. That you shall consent to and approve the Declaration of the Continental Congress declaring the thirteen United Colonies free and independent States.

2. That you shall endeavor to establish a free government under the authority of the people of the State of North Carolina and that the Government be a simple Democracy or as near it as possible.

3. That in fixing the fundamental principles of Government you shall oppose everything that leans to aristocracy or power in the hands of the rich and chief men exercised to the oppression of the poor.

4. That you shall endeavor that the form of Government shall set forth a bill of rights containing the rights of the people and of individuals which shall never be infringed in any future time by the law-making power or other derived powers in the State.

5. That you shall endeavour that the following maxims be substantially acknowledged in the Bills of Rights (viz.):

1st. Political power is of two kinds, one principal and superior, the other derived and inferior.

2^d. The principal supreme power is possessed by the people at large, the derived and inferior power by the servants which they employ.

3^d. Whatever persons are delegated, chosen, employed and intrusted by the people are their servants and can possess only derived inferior power.

4th. Whatever is constituted and ordained by the principal supreme power can not be altered, suspended or abrogated by any other power, but the same power that ordained may alter, suspend and abrogate its own ordinances.

5th. The rules whereby the inferior power is to be exercised are to be constituted by the principal supreme power, and can be altered, suspended and abrogated by the same and no other.

6th. No authority can exist or be exercised but what shall appear to be ordained and created by the principal supreme power or by derived inferior power which the principal supreme power hath authorized to create such authority.

7th. That the derived inferior power can by no construction or pretence assume or exercise a power to subvert the principal supreme power.

6. That you shall endeavour that the Government shall be so formed that the derived inferior power shall be divided into three branches distinct from each other, viz.:

The power of making laws
The power of executing laws and
The power of Judging.

7. That the law making power shall have full and ample authority for the good of the people to provide legal remedies for all evils and abuses that may arise in the State, the executive power shall have authority to apply the legal remedies when the judging power shall have ascertained where and upon what individuals the remedies ought to be applied.

8. You shall endeavour that in the original Constitution of the Government now to be formed the authority of officers possessing any branch of derived power shall be restrained; for example,

9. The law making power shall be restrained in all future time from making any alteration in the form of Government.

10. You shall endeavour that the persons in whose hands the law making power shall be lodged, shall be formed into two Houses or Assemblies independent of each other, but both dependent upon the people, viz.:

A Council and General Assembly

11. You shall endeavour that the good people of this State shall be justly and equally represented in the two Houses; that the Council shall consist of

at least thirteen persons, twelve of whom shall be annually chosen by the people in the several districts, and that every person who has a right to vote for members of the General Assembly shall also have a right to vote for member of Council, and that the Council and General Assembly shall every year at their first meeting form one body for the purpose of electing a Governor who shall then be chosen by ballot and that the Governor by virtue of his office shall be a member of Council but shall never vote in Council on the subject of making laws unless when the Council are divided, in which case the Governor shall have the casting vote.

12. That the law making power shall be lodged in the hands of one General Assembly composed of Representatives annually chosen by the people freely and equally in every part of the State according to _____.

13. N.B. Considering the long time that would be taken up and consequent delay of business the choice of a Council by the people would at this time occasion, it is thought best for the dispatch of public business, and this county do assent that after the form of Government shall be agreed to by the people, the present delegates in Congress shall resolve themselves into a General Assembly for one year and that they choose 12 persons, inhabitants residing in the several districts, to form a Council and the persons so chosen shall be possessed of all the powers of a Council for one year as fully as if chosen by the people.

14. You shall endeavour that no officer of the regular troops or collector of public money shall be eligible as a member of General Assembly or if being elected he shall afterwards accept of such office or collectorship he shall thereby vacate his seat. And in general that no persons in arrears for public money shall have a seat in General Assembly.

15. You shall endeavour that the delegates to represent this State in any future Continental Senate shall never be appointed for longer time than one year and shall not be capable to serve more than three years successively and that the Council and General Assembly shall have power to appoint the said delegates for one year and give them instructions and power to bind this State in matters relating to peace and War and mak-

ing treaties for that purpose with Foreign Powers and also for the purposes of General Trade and Commerce of the United States.

16. You shall endeavour that all Treasurers and Secretaries for this State shall be appointed by the General Assembly.

17. You shall endeavour that all Judges of the Court of Equity, Judges of the Court of Appeals and Writs of Error and all Judges of the Superior Courts shall be appointed by the General Assembly and hold their office during one year.

18. You shall endeavour that Trials by Jury shall be forever had and used in their utmost purity.

19. You shall endeavour that any person who shall hereafter profess himself to be an Atheist or deny the Being of God or shall deny or blaspheme any of the persons of the Holy Trinity or shall deny the divine authority of the Old and New Testament or shall be of the Roman Catholic religion shall not sustain hold or enjoy any office of trust or profit in the State of North Carolina.

20. That in all times hereafter no professing christian of any denomination whatever shall be compelled to pay any tax or duty towards the support of the clergy or worship of any other denomination.

21. That all professing christians shall enjoy the free and undisturbed exercise of religion and may worship God according to their consciences without restraint except idolatrous worshipers.

22. You shall endeavour that the form of Government when made out and agreed to by the Congress shall be transmitted to the several counties of this State to be considered by the people at large for their approbation and consent if they should choose to give it to the end that it may derive its force from the principal supreme power.

And after the Constitution and form of Government shall be agreed upon and established [and] the General Assembly formed you shall endeavour that they may exercise the law making power on the following subjects of legislation (viz)

1. You shall endeavour to have all vestry laws and marriage acts heretofore in force totally and forever abolished.

2. You shall endeavour to obtain an attachment law providing for creditors a full and ample

remedy against debtors who run away to avoid payment.

3. You shall endeavour to obtain an appraisement law for the relief of the poor when their goods are sold by execution.

4. You shall endeavour to obtain a law to establish a college in this county and procure a handsome endowment for the same.

5. You shall endeavour to diminish the fees of Clerks in the Superior and Inferior Courts and make the Fee Bill more perspicuous and clear it of all ambiguities.

6. You shall endeavour to obtain a law that Overseers may be elected annually in every county, with power to provide for the poor.

7. You shall endeavour to obtain a law to prevent clandestine marriages, and that Gospel ministers regularly ordained, whether by Bishops, by Presbyteries or by Association of regular ministers, shall have legal authority to marry after due publication of banns where the parties live.

8. You shall endeavour that all Judges and Justices may be impowered and required by law to administer oaths with uplifted hand when the party to be sworn shall desire that the same may be done without the book.

9. You shall endeavour to pass laws for establishing and immediately opening superior and inferior Courts.

10. You shall endeavour to pass a law for establishing a Court of Equity.

11. You shall endeavour to obtain a law for paying the Justices of the County Court.

12. You shall endeavour by law to inforce the attendance of the Judges of the Superior Court, and in case of due attendance to make them _____ allowance.

13. You shall endeavour that so much of the *Habeas Corpus* Act and the Common and Statute law heretofore in force and use and favorable to the liberties of the people shall be continued in force in this State, excluding every idea of the kingly office and power.

14. That persons be chosen annually in every county to collect taxes.

15. That a General and equal land tax be laid throughout the State.

16. That people shall be taxed according to their estates.

17. That sheriff, clerk and register shall be chosen by the freeholders in every county, the register to continue in office during good behaviour, the sheriff to be elected every year. The same person to be capable to be elected every year if all moneys due by virtue of his office shall be faithfully paid up.

18. That men shall be quieted in their titles and possessions and that provision shall be made to secure men from being disturbed by old and foreign claims against their landed possessions.

Test: J. M^cKNIT.

Reference: William L. Saunders (ed.), *The Colonial Records of North Carolina*, Vol. X (10 vols.; Raleigh: State Archives, 1886–1890).

CONSTITUTION, DECEMBER 18, 1776

A Declaration of Rights, &c.

I. That all political power is vested in and derived from the people only.

II. That the people of this State ought to have the sole and exclusive right of regulating the internal government and police thereof.

III. That no man or set of men are entitled to exclusive or separate emoluments or privileges from the community, but in consideration of public services.

IV. That the legislative, executive, and supreme judicial powers of government, ought to be forever separate and distinct from each other.

V. That all powers of suspending laws, or the execution of laws, by any authority, without consent of the Representatives of the people, is injurious to their rights, and ought not to be exercised.

VI. That elections of members, to serve as Representatives in General Assembly, ought to be free.

VII. That, in all criminal prosecutions, every man has a right to be informed of the accusation against him, and to confront the accusers and witnesses with other testimony, and shall not be compelled to give evidence against himself.

VIII. That no freeman shall be put to answer any criminal charge, but by indictment, presentment, or impeachment.

IX. That no freeman shall be convicted of any crime, but by the unanimous verdict of a jury of good and lawful men, in open court, as heretofore used.

X. That excessive bail should not be required, nor excessive fines imposed, nor cruel or unusual punishments inflicted.

XI. That general warrants—whereby an officer or messenger may be commanded to search suspected places, without evidence of the fact committed, or to seize any person or persons, not named, whose offences are not particularly described, and supported by evidence—are dangerous to liberty, and ought not to be granted.

XII. That no freeman ought to be taken, imprisoned, or disseized of his freehold, liberties or privileges, or outlawed, or exiled, or in any manner destroyed, or deprived of his life, liberty, or property, but by the law of the land.

XIII. That every freeman, restrained of his liberty, is entitled to a remedy, to inquire into the lawfulness thereof, and to remove the same, if unlawful; and that such remedy ought not to be denied or delayed.

XIV. That in all controversies at law, respecting property, the ancient mode of trial, by jury, is one of the best securities of the rights of the people, and ought to remain sacred and inviolable.

XV. That the freedom of the press is one of the great bulwarks of liberty, and therefore ought never to be restrained.

XVI. That the people of this State ought not to be taxed, or made subject to the payment of any impost or duty, without the consent of themselves, or their Representatives in General Assembly, freely given.

XVII. That the people have a right to bear arms, for the defence of the State; and, as standing armies, in time of peace, are danger-ous to liberty, they ought not to be kept up; and that the military should be kept under strict subordination to, and governed by, the civil power.

XVIII. That the people have a right to assemble together, to consult for their common good, to instruct their Representatives, and to apply to the Legislature, for redress of grievances.

XIX. That all men have a natural and unalienable right to worship Almighty God according to the dictates of their own consciences.

XX. That, for redress of grievances, and for amending and strengthening the laws, elections ought to be often held.

XXI. That a frequent recurrence to fundamental principles is absolutely necessary, to preserve the blessings of liberty.

XXII. That no hereditary emoluments, privileges or honors ought to be granted or conferred in this State.

XXIII. That perpetuities and monopolies are contrary to the genius of a free State, and ought not to be allowed.

XXIV. That retrospective laws, punishing facts committed before the existence of such laws, and by them only declared criminal, are oppressive, unjust, and incompatible with liberty; wherefore no *ex post facto* law ought to be made.

XXV. The property of the soil, in a free government, being one of the essential rights of the collective body of the people, it is necessary, in order to avoid future disputes, that the limits of the State should be ascertained with precision; and as the former temporary line between North and South Carolina, was confirmed, and extended by Commissioners, appointed by the Legislatures of the two States, agreeable to the order of the late King George the Second, in Council, that line, and that only, should be esteemed the southern boundary of this State as follows: that is to say, beginning on the sea side, at a cedar stake, at or near the mouth of Little River (being the southern extremity of Brunswick county,) and running from thence a northwest course, through the boundary house, which stands in thirty-three degrees fifty-six minutes, to thirty-five degrees north latitude;

and from thence a west course so far as is mentioned in the Charter of King Charles the Second, to the late Proprietors of Carolina. Therefore all the territories, seas, waters, and harbours, with their appurtenances, lying between the line above described, and the southern line of the State of Virginia, which begins on the sea shore, in thirty-six degrees thirty minutes, north latitude, and from thence runs west, agreeable to the said Charter of King Charles, are the right and property of the people of this State, to be held by them in sovereignty; any partial line, without the consent of the Legislature of this State, at any time thereafter directed, or laid out, in anywise notwithstanding:—*Provided always,* That this Declaration of Rights shall not prejudice any nation or nations of Indians, from enjoying such hunting-grounds as may have been, or hereafter shall be, secured to them by any former or future Legislature of this State:—*And provided also,* That it shall not be construed so as to prevent the establishment of one or more governments westward of this State, by consent of the Legislature:—*And provided further,* That nothing herein contained shall affect the titles or possessions of individuals holding or claiming under the laws heretofore in force, or grants heretofore made by the late King George the Second, or his predecessors, or the late lords proprietors, or any of them.

The Constitution, or Form of Government, &C

WHEREAS allegiance and protection are, in their nature, reciprocal, and the one should of right be refused when the other is withdrawn:

And whereas George the Third, King of Great Britain, and late Sovereign of the British American Colonies, hath not only withdrawn from them his protection, but, by an act of the British Legislature, declared the inhabitants of these States out of the protection of the British crown, and all their property, found upon the high seas, liable to be seized and confiscated to the uses mentioned in the said act; and the said George

the Third has also sent fleets and armies to prosecute a cruel war against them, for the purpose of reducing the inhabitants of the said Colonies to a state of abject slavery; in consequence whereof, all government under the said King, within the said Colonies, hath ceased, and a total dissolution of government in many of them hath taken place.

And whereas the Continental Congress, having considered the premises, and other previous violations of the rights of the good people of America, have therefore declared, that the Thirteen United Colonies are, of right, wholly absolved from all allegiance to the British crown, or any other foreign jurisdiction whatsoever: and that the said Colonies now are, and forever shall be, free and independent States.

Wherefore, in our present state, in order to prevent anarchy and confusion, it becomes necessary, that government should be established in this State; therefore we, the Representatives of the freemen of North-Carolina, chosen and assembled in Congress, for the express purpose of framing a Constitution, under the authority of the people, most conducive to their happiness and prosperity, do declare, that a government for this State shall be established, in manner and form following, to wit:

I. That the legislative authority shall be vested in two distinct branches, both dependent on the people, to wit, a *Senate* and *House of Commons.*

II. That the Senate shall be composed of Representatives, annually chosen by ballot, one for each county in the State.

III. That the House of Commons shall be composed of Representatives annually chosen by ballot, two for each county, and one for each of the towns of Edenton, Newbern, Wilmington, Salisbury, Hillsborough and Halifax.

IV. That the Senate and House of Commons, assembled for the purpose of legislation, shall be denominated, *The General Assembly.*

V. That each member of the Senate shall have usually resided in the county in which he is chosen for one year immediately preceding his election, and for the same time shall have possessed, and continue to possess, in the county which he represents, not less than three hundred acres of land in fee.

VI. That each member of the House of Commons shall have usually resided in the county in which he is chosen for one year immediately preceding his election, and for six months shall have possessed, and continue to possess, in the county which he represents, not less than one hundred acres of land in fee, or for the term of his own life.

VII. That all freemen, of the age of twenty-one years, who have been inhabitants of any one county within the State twelve months immediately preceding the day of any election, and possessed of a freehold within the same county of fifty acres of land, for six months next before, and at the day of election, shall be entitled to vote for a member of the Senate.

VIII. That all freemen of the age of twenty-one years, who have been inhabitants of any one county within this State twelve months immediately preceding the day of any election, and shall have paid public taxes, shall be entitled to vote for members of the House of Commons for the county in which he resides.

IX. That all persons possessed of a freehold in any town in this State, having a right of representation, and also all freemen, who have been inhabitants of any such town twelve months next before, and at the day of election, and shall have paid public taxes, shall be entitled to vote for a member to represent such town in the House of Commons:—Provided always, That this section shall not entitle any inhabitant of such town to vote for members of the House of Commons, for the county in which he may reside, nor any freeholder in such county, who resides without or beyond the limits of such town, to vote for a member for said town.

X. That the Senate and House of Commons, when met, shall each have power to choose a speaker, and other their officers; be judges of the qualifications and elections of their members; sit upon their own adjournments from day to day; and prepare bills, to be passed into laws. The two Houses shall direct writs of election for supplying intermediate vacancies; and shall also jointly, by ballot, adjourn themselves to any future day and place.

XI. That all bills shall be read three times in each House, before they pass into laws, and be signed by the Speakers of both Houses.

XII. That every person, who shall be chosen a member of the Senate or House of Commons, or appointed to any office or place of trust, before taking his seat, or entering upon the execution of his office, shall take an oath to the State; and all officers shall also take an oath of office.

XIII. That the General Assembly shall, by joint ballot of both houses, appoint Judges of the Supreme Courts of Law and Equity, Judges of Admiralty, and Attorney-General, who shall be commissioned by the Governor, and hold their offices during good behaviour.

XIV. That the Senate and House of Commons shall have power to appoint the generals and field-officers of the militia, and all officers of the regular army of this State.

XV. That the Senate and House of Commons, jointly at their first meeting after each annual election, shall by ballot elect a Governor for one year, who shall not be eligible to that office longer than three years, in six successive years. That no person, under thirty years of age, and who has not been a resident in this State above five years, and having, in the State, a freehold in lands and tenements above the value of one thousand pounds, shall be eligible as a Governor.

XIV. That the Senate and House of Commons, jointly, at their first meeting after each annual election, shall by ballot elect seven persons to be a Council of State for one year, who shall advise the Governor in the execution of his office; and that four members shall be a quorum; their advice and proceedings shall be entered in a journal, to be kept for that purpose only, and signed by the members present; to any part of which, any member present may enter his dissent. And such journal shall be laid before the General Assembly when called for by them.

XVII. That there shall be a seal of this State, which shall be kept by the Governor, and used by him, as occasion may require; and shall be called,

The Great Seal of the State of North Carolina, and be affixed to all grants and commissions.

XVIII. The Governor, for the time being, shall be captain-general and commander in chief of the militia; and, in the recess of the General Assembly, shall have power, by and with the advice of the Council of State, to embody the militia for the public safety.

XIX. That the Governor, for the time being, shall have power to draw for and apply such sums of money as shall be voted by the general assembly, for the contingencies of government, and be accountable to them for the same. He also may, by and with the advice of the Council of State, lay embargoes, or prohibit the exportation of any commodity, for any term not exceeding thirty days, at any one time in the recess of the General Assembly; and shall have the power of granting pardons and reprieves, except where the prosecution shall be carried on by the General Assembly, or the law shall otherwise direct; in which case he may, in the recess, grant a reprieve until the next sitting of the General Assembly; and may exercise all the other executive powers of government, limited and restrained as by this Constitution is mentioned, and according to the laws of the State. And on his death, inability, or absence from the State, the Speaker of the Senate for the time being— (and in case of his death, inability, or absence from the State, the Speaker of the House of Commons) shall exercise the powers of government after such death, or during such absence or inability of the Governor (or Speaker of the Senate,) or until a new nomination is made by the General Assembly.

XX. That in every case where any officer, the right of whose appointment is by this Constitution vested in the General Assembly, shall, during their recess, die, or his office by other means become vacant, the Governor shall have power, with the advice of the Council of State, to fill up such vacancy, by granting a temporary commission, which shall expire at the end of the next session of the General Assembly.

XXI. That the Governor, Judges of the Supreme Court of Law and Equity, Judges of Admiralty, and Attorney-General, shall have adequate salaries during their continuance in office.

XXII. That the General Assembly shall, by joint ballot of both Houses, annually appoint a Treasurer or Treasurers for this State.

XXIII. That the Governor, and other officers, offending against the State, by violating any part of this Constitution, mal-administration, or corruption, may be prosecuted, on the impeachment of the General Assembly, or presentment of the Grand Jury of any court of supreme jurisdiction in this State.

XXIV. That the General Assembly shall, by joint ballot of both Houses, triennially appoint a Secretary for this State.

XXV. That no persons, who heretofore have been, or hereafter may be, receivers of public the monies, shall have a seat in either House of General Assembly, or be eligible to any office in this State, until such person shall have fully accounted for and paid into the treasury all sums for which they may be accountable and liable.

XXVI. That no Treasurer shall have a seat, either in the Senate, House of Commons, or Council of State, during his continuance in that office, or before he shall have finally settled his accounts with the public, for all the monies which may be in his hands at the expiration of his office belonging to the State, and hath paid the same into the hands of the succeeding Treasurer.

XXVII. That no officer in the regular army or navy, in the service and pay of the United States, of this or any other State, nor any contractor or agent for supplying such army or navy with clothing or provisions, shall have a seat either in the Senate, House of Commons, or Council of State, or be eligible thereto: and any member of the Senate, House of Commons, or Council of State, being appointed to and accepting of such office, shall thereby vacate his seat.

XXVIII. That no member of the Council of State shall have a seat, either in the Senate, or House of Commons.

XXIX. That no Judge of the Supreme Court of Law or Equity, or Judge of Admiralty, shall have a seat in the Senate. House of Commons, or Council of State.

XXX. That no Secretary of this State, Attorney-General, or Clerk of any Court of record, shall have a seat in the Senate, House of Commons, or Council of State.

XXXI. That no clergyman, or preacher of the gospel, of any denomination, shall be capable of being a member of either the Senate, House of Commons, or Council of State, while he continues in the exercise of the pastoral function.

XXXII. That no person, who shall deny the being of God or the truth of the Protestant religion, or the divine authority either of the Old or New Testaments, or who shall hold religious principles incompatible with the freedom and safety of the State, shall be capable of holding any office or place of trust or profit in the civil department within this State.

XXXIII. That the Justices of the Peace, within their respective counties in this State, shall in future be recommended to the Governor for the time being, by the Representatives in General Assembly; and the Governor shall commission them accordingly: and the Justices, when so commissioned, shall hold their offices during good behaviour, and shall not be removed from office by the General Assembly, unless for misbehaviour, absence, or inability.

XXXIV. That there shall be no establishment of any one religious church or denomination in this State, in preference to any other; neither shall any person, on any pretence whatsoever, be compelled to attend any place of worship contrary to his own faith or judgment, nor be obliged to pay, for the purchase of any glebe, or the building of any house of worship, or for the maintenance of any minister or ministry, contrary to what he believes right, or has voluntarily and personally engaged to perform; but all persons shall be at liberty to exercise their own mode of worship:—*Provided,* That nothing herein contained shall be construed to exempt preachers of treasonable or seditious discourses, from legal trial and punishment.

XXXV. That no person in the State shall hold more than one lucrative office, at any one time:—*Provided,* That no appointment in the militia, or the office of a Justice of the Peace, shall be considered as a lucrative office.

XXXVI. That all commissions and grants shall run in the name of the State of North Carolina, and bear test, and be signed by the Governor. All writs shall run in the same manner, and bear test, and be signed by the Clerks of the respective Courts. Indictments shall conclude, *Against the peace and dignity of the State.*

XXXVII. That the Delegates for this State, to the Continental Congress while necessary, shall be chosen annually by the General Assembly, by ballot; but may be superseded, in the mean time, in the same manner; and no person shall be elected, to serve in that capacity, for more than three years successively.

XXXVIII. That there shall be a Sheriff, Coroner or Coroners, and Constables, in each county within this State.

XXXIX. That the person of a debtor, where there is not a strong presumption of fraud, shall not be continued in prison, after delivering up, *bona fide*, all his estate real and personal, for the use of his creditors, in such manner as shall be hereafter regulated by law. All prisoners shall be bailable by sufficient sureties, unless for capital offences, when the proof is evident, or the presumption great.

XL. That every foreigner, who comes to settle in this State, having first taken an oath of allegiance to the same, may purchase, or, by other means, acquire, hold, and transfer land, or other real estate; and after one year's residence, shall be deemed a free citizen.

XLI. That a school or schools shall be established by the Legislature, for the convenient instruction of youth, with such salaries to the masters, paid by the public, as may enable them to instruct at low prices; and all useful learning shall be duly encouraged, and promoted, in one or more universities.

XLII. That no purchase of lands shall be made of the Indian natives, but on behalf of the public, by authority of the General Assembly.

XLIII. That the future Legislature of this State shall regulate entails, in such a manner as to prevent perpetuities.

XLIV. That the Declaration of Rights is hereby declared to be part of the Constitution of this State, and ought never to be violated, on any pretence whatsoever.

XLV. That any member of either House of General Assembly shall have liberty to dissent from, and protest against any act or resolve, which he may think injurious to the public, or any individual, and have the reasons of his dissent entered on the journals.

XLVI. That neither House of the General Assembly shall proceed upon public business, unless a majority of all the members of such House are actually present; and that, upon a motion made and seconded, the yeas and nays, upon any question, shall be taken and entered on the journals; and that the journals of the proceedings of both Houses of the General Assembly shall be printed, and made public, immediately after their adjournment.

This Constitution is not intended to preclude the present Congress from making a temporary provision, for the well ordering of this State, until the General Assembly shall establish government, agreeable to the mode herein before described.

RICHARD CASWELL, *President.*

December the eighteenth, one thousand seven hundred and seventy-six, read the third time, and ratified in open Congress.

By order,

JAMES GREEN, jun. *secretary.*

Reference: Francis Newton Thorpe (ed.), *The Federal and State Constitutions, Colonial Charters, and Other Organic Laws of the States,* Vol. V (Washington: GPO, 1909).

42

Georgia, February 5, 1777

Georgia stressed the importance of suffrage reforms in its first constitution. The Georgia constitution otherwise followed the constitution-making pattern of other Southern states. (There are no known records of its convention's discussions on the proposed state constitution.)

CONSTITUTION, FEBRUARY 5, 1777

Whereas the conduct of the legislature of Great Britain for many years past has been so oppressive on the people of America that of late years they have plainly declared and asserted a right to raise taxes upon the people of America, and to make laws to bind them in all cases whatsoever, without their consent; which conduct, being repugnant to the common rights of mankind, hath obliged the Americans, as freemen, to oppose such oppressive measures, and to assert the rights and privileges they are entitled to by the laws of nature and reason; and accordingly it hath been done by the general consent of all the people of the States of New Hampshire, Massachusetts Bay, Rhode Island, Connecticut, New York, New Jersey, Pennsylvania, the counties of New Castle, Kent, and Sussex on Delaware, Maryland, Virginia, North Carolina, South Carolina, and Georgia, given by their representatives met together in general Congress, in the city of Philadelphia;

And whereas it hath been recommended by the said Congress, on the fifteenth of May last, to the respective assemblies and conventions of the United States, where no government, sufficient to the exigencies of their affairs, hath been hitherto established, to adopt such government as may, in the opinion of the representatives of the people, best conduce to the happiness and safety of their constituents in particular and America in general;

And whereas the independence of the United States of America has been also declared, on the fourth day of July, one thousand seven hundred and seventy-six, by the said honorable Congress, and all political connection between them and the Crown of Great Britain is in consequence thereof dissolved:

We, therefore, the representatives of the people, from whom all power originates, and for whose benefit all government is intended, by virtue of the power delegated to us, do ordain and declare, and it is hereby ordained and declared, that the following rules and regulations be adopted for the future government of this State:

ARTICLE I. The legislative, executive, and judiciary departments shall be separate and distinct, so that neither exercise the powers properly belonging to the other.

ART. II. The legislature of this State shall be composed of the representatives of the people, as is hereinafter pointed out; and the representatives shall be elected yearly, and every year, on the first Tuesday in December; and the representatives so elected shall meet the first Tuesday in January following, at Savannah, or any other place or places where the house of assembly for the time being shall direct.

On the first day of the meeting of the representatives so chosen, they shall proceed to the choice of a governor, who shall be styled "*honorable;*" and of an executive council, by ballot out of their own body, viz: two from each county, except those counties which are not yet entitled to send ten members. One of each county shall always attend, where the governor resides, by monthly rotation, unless the members of each county agree for a longer or shorter period. This is not intended to exclude either member attending. The remaining number of representatives shall be called the house of assembly; and the majority of the members of the said house shall have power to proceed on business.

ART. III. It shall be an unalterable rule that the house of assembly shall expire and be at an end, yearly and every year, on the day preceding the day of election mentioned in the foregoing rule.

ART. IV. The representation shall be divided in the following manner: ten members from each county, as is hereinafter directed, except the county of Liberty, which contains three parishes, and that shall be allowed fourteen.

The ceded lands north of Ogechee shall be one county, and known by the name of Wilkes.

The parish of Saint Paul shall be another county, and known by the name of Richmond.

The parish of Saint George shall be another county, and known by the name of Burke.

The parish of Saint Matthew, and the upper part of Saint Philip, above Canouchee, shall be another county, and known by the name of Effingham.

The parish of Christ Church, and the lower part of Saint Philip, below Canouchee, shall be another county, and known by the name of Chatham.

The parishes of Saint John, Saint Andrew, and Saint James shall be another county, and known by the name of Liberty.

The parishes of Saint David and Saint Patrick shall be another county, and known by the name of Glynn.

The parishes of Saint Thomas and Saint Mary shall be another county, and known by the name of Camden.

The port and town of Savannah shall be allowed four members to represent their trade.

The port and town of Sunbury shall be allowed two members to represent their trade.

ART. V. The two counties of Glynn and Camden shall have one representative each, and also they, and all other counties that may hereafter be laid out by the house of assembly, shall be under the following regulations, viz: at their first institution each county shall have one member, provided the inhabitants of the said county shall have ten electors; and if thirty, they shall have two; if forty, three; if fifty, four; if eighty, six; if a hundred and upward, ten; at which time two executive councillors shall be chosen from them, as is directed for the other counties.

ART. VI. The representatives shall be chosen out of the residents in each county, who shall have resided at least twelve months in this State, and three months in the county where they shall be elected; except the freeholders of the counties of Glynn and Camden, who are in a state of alarm, and who shall have the liberty of choosing one member each, as specified in the articles of this constitution, in any other county, until they have residents sufficient to qualify them for more; and they shall be of the Protestant religion, and of the age of twenty-one years, and shall be possessed in their own right of two hundred and fifty acres of land, or some property to the amount of two hundred and fifty pounds.

ART. VII. The house of assembly shall have power to make such laws and regulations as may be conducive to the good order and well-being of the State; provided such laws and regulations be not repugnant to the true intent and meaning of any rule or regulation contained in this constitution.

The house of assembly shall also have power to repeal all laws and ordinances they find injurious to the people; and the house shall choose its own speaker, appoint its own officers, settle its own rules of proceeding, and direct writs of election for supplying intermediate vacancies, and shall have power of adjournment to any time or times within the year.

ART. VIII. All laws and ordinances shall be three times read, and each reading shall be on different and separate days, except in cases of great necessity and danger; and all laws and ordinances shall be sent to the executive council after the second reading, for their perusal and advice.

ART. IX. All male white inhabitants, of the age of twenty-one years, and possessed in his own right of ten pounds value, and liable to pay tax in this State, or being of any mechanic trade, and shall have been resident six months in this State, shall have a right to vote at all elections for representatives, or any other officers, herein agreed to be chosen by the people at large; and every person having a right to vote at any election shall vote by ballot personally.

ART. X. No officer whatever shall serve any process, or give any other hinderance to any person entitled to vote, either in going to the place of election, or during the time of the said election, or on their returning home from such election; nor shall any military officer, or soldier, appear at any election in a military character, to the intent that all elections may be free and open.

ART. XI. No person shall be entitled to more than one vote, which shall be given in the county where such person resides, except as before excepted; nor shall any person who holds any title of nobility be entitled to a vote, or be capable of serving as a representative, or hold any post of honor, profit, or trust in this State, whilst such person claims his title of nobility; but if the person shall give up such distinction, in the manner as may be directed by any future legislation, then, and in such case, he shall be entitled to a vote, and represent, as before directed, and enjoy all the other benefits of a free citizen.

ART. XII. Every person absenting himself from an election, and shall neglect to give in his or their ballot at such election, shall be subject to a penalty not exceeding five pounds; the mode of recovery, and also the appropriation thereof,

to be pointed out and directed by act of the legislature: *Provided, nevertheless,* That a reasonable excuse shall be admitted.

ART. XIII. The manner of electing representatives shall be by ballot, and shall be taken by two or more justices of the peace in each county, who shall provide a convenient box for receiving the said ballots: and, on closing the poll, the ballots shall be compared in public with the list of votes that have been taken, and the majority immediately declared; a certificate of the same being given to the persons elected, and also a certificate returned to the house of representatives.

ART. XIV. Every person entitled to vote shall take the following oath or affirmation, if required, viz:

"I, A B, do voluntarily and solemnly swear (or affirm, as the case may be) that I do owe true allegiance to this State, and will support the constitution thereof; so help me God."

ART. XV. Any five of the representatives elected, as before directed, being met, shall have power to administer the following oath to each other; and they, or any other member, being so sworn, shall, in the house, administer the oath to all other members that attend, in order to qualify them to take their seats, viz:

"I, A B, do solemnly swear that I will bear true allegiance to the State of Georgia, and will truly perform the trusts reposed in me; and that I will execute the same to the best of my knowledge, for the benefit of this State, and the support of the constitution thereof, and that I have obtained my election without fraud or bribe what ever; so help me God."

ART. XVI. The continental delegates shall be appointed annually by ballot, and shall have a right to sit, debate, and vote in the house of assembly, and be deemed a part thereof, subject, however, to the regulations contained in the twelfth article of the Confederation of the United States.

ART. XVII. No person bearing any post of profit under this State, or any person bearing any military commission under this or any other State or States, except officers of the militia, shall be elected a representative. And if any representative shall be appointed to any place of profit or military commission, which he shall accept, his seat shall immediately become vacant, and he shall be incapable of reëlection whilst holding such office.

By this article it is not to be understood that the office of a justice of the peace is a post of profit.

ART. XVIII. No person shall hold more than one office of profit under this State at one and the same time.

ART. XIX. The governor shall, with the advice of the executive council, exercise the executive powers of government, according to the laws of this State and the constitution thereof, save only in the case of pardons and remission of fines, which he shall in no instance grant; but he may reprieve a criminal, or suspend a fine, until the meeting of the assembly, who may determine therein as they shall judge fit.

ART. XX. The governor, with the advice of the executive council, shall have power to call the house of assembly together, upon any emergency, before the time which they stand adjourned to.

ART. XXI. The governor, with the advice of the executive council, shall fill up all intermediate vacancies that shall happen in offices till the next general election; and all commissions, civil and military, shall be issued by the governor, under his hand and the great seal of the State.

ART. XXII. The governor may preside in the executive council at all times, except when they are taking into consideration and perusing the laws and ordinances offered to them by the house of assembly.

ART. XXIII. The governor shall be chosen annually by ballot, and shall not be eligible to the said office for more than one year out of three, nor shall he hold any military commission under any other State or States.

The governor shall reside at such place as the house of assembly for the time being shall appoint.

ART. XXIV. The governor's oath:

"I, A B, elected governor of the State of Georgia, by the representatives thereof, do solemnly promise and swear that I will, during the term of my appointment, to the best of my skill and judgment, execute the said office faithfully and conscientiously, according to law, without favor, affection, or partiality; that I will, to the utmost of my power, support, maintain, and defend the State of Georgia, and the constitution of the same; and use my utmost endeavors to protect the people thereof in the secure enjoyment of all their rights, franchises, and privileges; and that the laws and ordinances of the State be duly observed, and that law and justice in mercy be executed in all judgments. And I do further solemnly promise and swear that I will peaceably and quietly resign the government to which I have been elected at the period to which my continuance in the said office is limited by the constitution. And, lastly, I do also solemnly swear that I have not accepted of the government whereunto I am elected contrary to the articles of this constitution; so help me God."

This oath to be administered to him by the speaker of the assembly.

The same oath to be administered by the speaker to the president of the council.

No person shall be eligible to the office of governor who has not resided three years in this State.

ART. XXV. The executive council shall meet the day after their election, and proceed to the choice of a president out of their own body; they shall have power to appoint their own officers and settle their own rules of proceedings.

The council shall always vote by counties, and not individually.

ART. XXVI. Every councillor, being present, shall have power of entering his protest against any measures in council he has not consented to, provided he does it in three days.

ART. XXVII. During the sitting of the assembly the whole of the executive council shall attend, unless prevented by sickness, or some other urgent necessity; and, in that case, a majority of the council shall make a board to examine the laws and ordinances sent them by the house of assembly; and all laws and ordinances sent to the council shall be returned in five days after, with their remarks thereon.

ART. XXVIII. A committee from the council, sent with any proposed amendments to any law or ordinance, shall deliver their reasons for such proposed amendments, sitting and covered; the whole house at that time, except the speaker, uncovered.

ART. XXIX. The president of the executive council, in the absence or sickness of the governor, shall exercise all the powers of the governor.

ART. XXX. When any affair that requires secrecy shall be laid before the governor and the executive council, it shall be the duty of the governor, and he is hereby obliged, to administer the following oath, viz:

"I, A B, do solemnly swear that any business that shall be at this time communicated to the council I will not, in any manner whatever, either by speaking, writing, or otherwise, reveal the same to any person whatever, until leave given by the council, or when called upon by the house of assembly; and all this I swear without any reservation whatever; so help me God."

And the same oath shall be administered to the secretary and other officers necessary to carry the business into execution.

ART. XXXI. The executive power shall exist till renewed as pointed out by the rules of this constitution.

ART. XXXII. In all transactions between the legislative and executive bodies the same shall be communicated by message, to be delivered from the legislative body to the governor or executive council by a committee, and from the governor to the house of assembly by the secretary of the council, and from the executive council by a committee of the said council.

ART. XXXIII. The governor for the time being shall be captain-general and commander-in-chief over all the militia, and other military and naval forces belonging to this State.

ART. XXXIV. All militia commissions shall specify that the person commissioned shall continue during good behavior.

ART. XXXV. Every county in this State that has, or hereafter may have, two hundred and fifty men, and upwards, liable to bear arms, shall be formed into a battalion; and when they become too numerous for one battalion, they shall be formed into more, by bill of the legislature; and those counties that have a less number than two hundred and fifty shall be formed into independent companies.

ART. XXXVI. There shall be established in each county a court, to be called a superior court, to be held twice in each year.

On the first Tuesday in March, in the county of Chatham.

The second Tuesday in March, in the county of Effingham.

The third Tuesday in March, in the county of Burke.

The fourth Tuesday in March, in the county of Richmond.

The next Tuesday, in the county of Wilkes.

And Tuesday fortnight, in the county of Liberty.

The next Tuesday, in the county of Glynn.

The next Tuesday, in the county of Camden.

The like courts to commence in October and continue as above.

ART. XXXVII. All causes and matters of dispute, between any parties residing in the same county, to be tried within the county.

ART. XXXVIII. All matters in dispute between contending parties residing in different counties shall be tried in the county where the defendant resides, except in cases of real estate, which shall be tried in the county where such real estate lies.

ART. XXXIX. All matters of breach of the peace, felony, murder, and treason against the State to be tried in the county where the same was committed. All matters of dispute, both civil and criminal, in any county where there is not a sufficient number of inhabitants to form a court, shall be tried in the next adjacent county where a court is held.

ART. XL. All causes, of what nature soever, shall be tried in the supreme court, except as hereafter mentioned; which court shall consist of the chief-justice, and three or more of the justices residing in the county. In case of the absence of the chief-justice, the senior justice on the bench shall act as chief-justice, with the clerk of the county, attorney for the State, sheriff, coroner, constable, and the jurors; and in case of the absence of any of the aforementioned officers, the justices to appoint others in their room *pro tempore*. And if any plaintiff or defendant in civil causes shall be dissatisfied with the determination of the jury, then, and in that case, they shall be at liberty, within three days, to enter an appeal from that verdict, and demand a new trial by a special jury, to be nominated as follows, viz: each party, plaintiff and defendant, shall choose six, six more names shall be taken indifferently out of a box provided for that purpose, the whole eighteen to be summoned, and their names to be put together into the box, and the first twelve that are drawn out, being present, shall be the special jury to try the cause, and from which there shall be no appeal.

ART. XLI. The jury shall be judges of law, as well as of fact, and shall not be allowed to bring in a special verdict; but if all or any of the jury have any doubts concerning points of law, they shall apply to the bench, who shall each of them in rotation give their opinion.

ART. XLII. The jury shall be sworn to bring in a verdict according to law, and the opinion they entertain of the evidence; provided it be not repugnant to the rules and regulations contained in this constitution.

ART. XLIII. The special jury shall be sworn to bring in a verdict according to law, and the opinion they entertain of the evidence; provided it be not repugnant to justice, equity, and conscience, and the rules and regulations contained in this constitution, of which they shall judge.

ART. XLIV. Captures, both by sea and land, to be tried in the county where such shall be carried in; a special court to be called by the chief-justice, or in his absence by the then senior justice in the said county, upon application of the captors or claimants, which cause shall be determined within the space of ten days. The mode of proceeding and appeal shall be the same as in the superior courts, unless, after the second trial, an appeal is made to the Continental Congress; and the distance of time between the first and second trial shall not exceed fourteen days; and all maritime causes to be tried in like manner.

ART. XLV. No grand jury shall consist of less than eighteen, and twelve may find a bill.

ART. XLVI. That the court of conscience be continued as heretofore practiced, and that the jurisdiction thereof be extended to try causes not amounting to more than ten pounds.

ART. XLVII. All executions exceeding five pounds, except in the case of a court-merchant, shall be stayed until the first Monday in March; provided security be given for debt and costs.

ART. XLVIII. All the costs attending any action in the superior court shall not exceed the sum of three pounds, and that no cause be allowed to depend in the superior court longer than two terms.

ART. XLIX. Every officer of the State shall be liable to be called to account by the house of assembly.

ART. L. Every county shall keep the public records belonging to the same, and authenticated copies of the several records now in the possession of this State shall be made out and deposited in that county to which they belong.

ART. LI. Estates shall not be entailed; and when a person dies intestate, his or her estate shall be divided equally among their children; the widow shall have a child's share, or her dower, at her option; all other intestates' estates to be divided according to the act of distribution, made in the reign of Charles the Second, unless otherwise altered by any future act of the legislature.

ART. LII. A register of probates shall be appointed by the legislature in every county, for proving wills and granting letters of administration.

ART. LIII. All civil officers in each county shall be annually elected on the day of the general election, except justices of the peace and registers of probates, who shall be appointed by the house of assembly.

ART. LIV. Schools shall be erected in each county, and supported at the general expense of the State, as the legislature shall hereafter point out.

ART. LV. A court-house and jail shall be erected at the public expense in each county, where the present convention or the future legislature shall point out and direct.

ART. LVI. All persons whatever shall have the free exercise of their religion; provided it be not repugnant to the peace and safety of the State; and shall not, unless by consent, support any teacher or teachers except those of their own profession.

ART. LVII. The great seal of this State shall have the following device: on one side a scroll, whereon shall be engraved, "The Constitution of the State of Georgia;" and the motto, "*Pro bono publico.*" On the other side, an elegant house, and other buildings, fields of corn, and meadows covered with sheep and cattle; a river running through the same, with a ship under full sail, and the motto, "*Deus nobis hæc otia fecit.*"

ART. LVIII. No person shall be allowed to plead in the courts of law in this State, except those who are authorized so to do by the house of assembly; and if any person so authorized shall be found guilty of malpractice before the house of assembly, they shall have power to suspend them. This is not intended to exclude any person from that inherent privilege of every *freeman*, the liberty to plead his own cause.

ART. LIX. Excessive fines shall not be levied, nor excessive bail demanded.

ART. LX. The principles of the *habeas-corpus* act shall be a part of this constitution.

ART. LXI. Freedom of the press and trial by jury to remain inviolate forever.

ART. LXII. No clergyman of any denomination shall be allowed a seat in the legislature.

ART. LXIII. No alteration shall be made in this constitution without petitions from a majority of the counties, and the petitions from each county to be signed by a majority of voters in each county within this State; at which time the assembly shall order a convention to be called for that purpose, specifying the alterations to be made, according to the petitions preferred to the assembly by the majority of the counties as aforesaid.

Done at Savannah, in convention, the fifth day of February, in the year of our Lord one thousand seven hundred and seventy-seven, and in the first year of the Independence of the United States of America.

Reference: Francis Newton Thorpe (ed.), *The Federal and State Constitutions, Colonial Charters, and Other Organic Laws of the States*, Vol. II (Washington: GPO, 1909).

43

New York, April 20, 1777

New York published the proceedings of its constitutional debates, thus providing much information about what the delegates thought important to include in the constitution. The mechanics of New York organized to influence their delegates to the convention and had much to say about proper apportionment of delegates to the state legislature. The New York state constitution gave much power to the governor, unlike most other states, perhaps because John Jay, a supporter of central authority, drafted the document.

SOME PROCEEDINGS OF THE CONVENTION, APRIL 1777

The foregoing appears in the draft as one solid section, but for convenience of reference I have arranged it in paragraphs with appropriate headings. It will be observed that this scheme is quite like the modern election law, but the Convention was not prepared to adopt it, and apparently did not seriously consider it. While it was under consideration the provision for an election by ballot was, on motion of Mr. Morris, stricken out, and elections were required to be held according to the laws of the colony. April 5th, Mr. Jay offered the following substitute for the section:

"And whereas it hath been a prevailing opinion among the good people of this State, that the mode of election by ballot would tend more to preserve the liberty and equal freedom of the people than the manner of voting *viva voce*, and it is expedient that a fair experiment be made as to which of those methods of voting is to be preferred:

"Be it ordained, That as soon as may be after the expiration of the present war between the United States of America and Great Britain, an act or acts be passed by the Legislature of this State for causing all elections hereafter to be held in this State for senators and representatives in assembly to be by ballot and directing the manner in which the same shall be conducted.

"Be it further Ordained, That whenever thereafter the mode of voting by ballot, shall, on experience, appear to be attended with more mischief and less conducive to the safety or interests of this State than the method of voting *viva voce*, it shall be lawful and constitutional for the legislature of this State to abolish the same, providing two thirds of the members present in both houses shall concur therein; and further, that in the meantime all elections for senators and representatives in assembly be made *viva voce*, according to the laws of the colony of New York for regulating elections so far as the same may be consistent with this constitution or according to such laws as by the legislature of this state may for that purpose be enacted."

The Convention unanimously rejected Mr. Morris's motion to strike out the word "senators" whenever it occurred, so that the section would apply only to members of assembly. Gilbert Livingston's motion to strike out the proviso requiring a two-thirds vote of the legislature to restore voting *viva voce* was also rejected.

Reference: Charles Z. Lincoln, *The Constitutional History of New York*, Vol. I (Rochester: The Lawyer Cooperative Publication Co., 1906).

CONSTITUTION, APRIL 20, 1777

Whereas the many tyrannical and oppressive usurpations of the King and Parliament of Great Britain on the rights and liberties of the people of the American colonies had reduced them to the necessity of introducing a government by congresses and committees, as temporary expedients, and to exist no longer than the grievances of the people should remain without redress; And whereas the congress of the colony of New York did, on the thirty-first day of May now last past, resolve as follows, viz:

"Whereas the present government of this colony, by congress and committees, was instituted while the former government, under the Crown of Great Britain, existed in full force, and was established for the sole purpose of opposing the usurpation of the British Parliament, and was intended to expire on a reconciliation with Great Britain, which it was then apprehended would soon take place, but is now considered as remote and uncertain;

"And whereas many and great inconveniences attend the said mode of government by congress and committees, as of necessity, in many instances, legislative, judicial, and executive powers have been vested therein, especially since the dissolution of the former government by the abdication of the late governor and the exclusion of this colony from the protection of the King of Great Britain;

"And whereas the Continental Congress did resolve as followeth, to wit:

"'Whereas His Britannic Majesty, in conjunction with the lords and commons of Great Britain, has, by a late act of Parliament, excluded the inhabitants of these united colonies from the protection of his Crown; and whereas no answers whatever to the humble petition of the colonies for redress of grievances and reconciliation with Great Britain has been, or is likely to be, given, but the whole force of that kingdom, aided by foreign mercenaries, is to be exerted for the destruction of the good people of these colonies; and whereas it appears absolutely irreconcilable to reason and good conscience for the people of these colonies now to take the oaths and affirmations necessary for the support of any government under the Crown of Great Britain, and it is necessary that the exercise of every kind of authority under the said Crown should be totally suppressed, and all the powers of government exerted under the authority of the people of the colonies for the preservation of internal peace, virtue, and good order, as well as for the defense of our lives, liberties, and properties, against the hostile invasions and cruel depredations of our enemies: Therefore,

"'*Resolved*, That it be recommended to the respective assemblies and conventions of the united colonies, where no government sufficient to the exigencies of their affairs has been hitherto established, to adopt such government as shall, in the opinion of the representatives of the people, best conduce to the happiness and safety of their constituents in particular, and America in general.'

"And whereas doubts have arisen whether this congress are invested with sufficient power and authority to deliberate and determine on so important a subject as the necessity of erecting and constituting a new form of government and internal police, to the exclusion of all foreign jurisdiction, dominion, and control whatever; and whereas it appertains of right solely to the people of this colony to determine the said doubts: Therefore,

"*Resolved,* That it be recommended to the electors in the several counties in this colony, by election, in the manner and form prescribed for the election of the present congress, either to authorize (in addition to the powers vested in this congress) their present deputies, or others in the stead of their present deputies, or either of them, to take into consideration the necessity and propriety of instituting such new government as in and by the said resolution of the Continental Congress is described and recommended; and if the majority of the counties, by their deputies in provincial congress, shall be of opinion that such new government ought to be instituted and established, then to institute and establish such a government as they shall deem best calculated to secure the rights, liberties, and happiness of the good people of this colony; and to continue in force until a future peace with Great Britain shall render the same unnecessary; and

"*Resolved,* That the said elections in the several counties ought to be had on such day, and at such place or places, as by the committee of each county respectively shall be determined. And it is recommended to the said committees to fix such early days for the said elections as that all the deputies to be elected have sufficient time to repair to the city of New York by the second Monday in July next; on which day all the said deputies ought punctually to give their attendance.

"And whereas the object of the aforegoing resolutions is of the utmost importance to the good people of this colony:

"*Resolved,* That it be, and it is hereby, earnestly recommended to the committees, freeholders, and other electors in the different counties in this colony diligently to carry the same into execution."

And whereas the good people of the said colony, in pursuance of the said resolution, and reposing special trust and confidence in the members of this convention, have appointed, authorized, and empowered them for the purposes, and in the manner, and with the powers in and by the said resolve specified, declared, and mentioned.

And whereas the Delegates of the United American States, in general Congress convened, did, on the fourth day of July now last past, solemnly publish and declare, in the words following, viz:

"When, in the course of human events, it becomes necessary for one people to dissolve the political bands which have connected them with another, and to assume among the powers of the earth the separate and equal station to which the laws of nature and of nature's God entitle them, a decent respect to the opinions of mankind requires that they should declare the causes which impel them to the separation.

"We hold these truths to be self-evident, that all men are created equal; that they are endowed by their Creator with certain unalienable rights; that among these are, life, liberty, and the pursuit of happiness; that to secure these rights, governments are instituted among men, deriving their just powers from the consent of the governed; that whenever any form of government becomes destructive of these ends, it is the right of the people to alter or to abolish it, and to institute new government, laying its foundation on such principles, and organizing its powers in such form, as to them shall seem most likely to effect their safety and happiness. Prudence, indeed, will dictate that governments long established should not be changed for light and transient causes, and accordingly all experience hath shown that mankind are more disposed to suffer, while evils are sufferable, than to right themselves by abolishing the forms to which they are accustomed. But when a long train of abuses and usurpations, pursuing invariably the same object, evinces a design to reduce them under absolute despotism, it is their right, it is their duty, to throw off such government, and to provide new guards for their future security. Such has been the patient sufferance of these colonies; and such is now the necessity which constrains them to alter their former system of government. The history of the present King of Great Britain is a history of repeated injuries and usurpations, all having in direct object the establishment of an absolute tyranny over these States. To prove this, let facts be submitted to a candid world.

"He has refused his assent to laws, the most wholesome and necessary for the public good.

"He has forbidden his governors to pass laws of immediate and pressing importance, unless suspended in their operation till his assent should be obtained; and when so suspended, he has utterly neglected to attend to them.

"He has refused to pass other laws for the accommodation of large districts of people, unless those people would relinquish the right of representation in the legislature; a right inestimable to them, and formidable to tyrants only.

"He has called together legislative bodies at places unusual, uncomfortable, and distant from the depository of their public records, for the sole purpose of fatiguing them into compliance with his measures.

"He has dissolved representative houses repeatedly, for opposing with manly firmness his invasions on the rights of the people.

"He has refused for a long time, after such dissolutions, to cause others to be elected, whereby the legislative powers, incapable of annihilation, have returned to the people at large, for their exercise; the State remaining in the mean time exposed to all the dangers of invasion from without, and convulsions within.

"He has endeavored to prevent the population of these States; for that purpose obstructing the laws for naturalization of foreigners, refusing to pass others to encourage their migrations hither, and raising the conditions of new appropriations of lands.

"He has obstructed the administration of justice, by refusing his assent to laws for establishing judiciary powers.

"He has made judges dependent on his will alone, for the tenure of their offices, and the amount and payment of their salaries.

"He has erected a multitude of new offices, and sent hither swarms of officers to harass our people and eat out their substance.

"He has kept among us, in times of peace, standing armies, without the consent of our legislatures.

"He has affected to render the military independent of, and superior to, the civil power.

"He has combined with others to subject us to a jurisdiction foreign to our constitution, and unacknowledged by our laws; giving his assent to their acts of pretended legislation:

"For quartering large bodies of troops among us:

"For protecting them, by a mock trial, from punishment for any murders they should commit on the inhabitants of these States:

"For cutting off our trade with all parts of the world:

"For imposing taxes on us without our consent:

"For depriving us, in many cases, of the benefits of trial by jury:

"For transporting us beyond seas, to be tried for pretended offences:

"For abolishing the free system of English laws in a neighboring province, establishing therein an arbitrary government, and enlarging its boundaries, so as to render it at once an example and fit instrument for introducing the same absolute rule into these colonies:

"For taking away our charters, abolishing our most valuable laws, and altering fundamentally the forms of our governments:

"For suspending our own legislatures, and declaring themselves invested with power to legislate for us in all cases whatsoever.

"He has abdicated government here, by declaring us out of his protection, and waging war against us.

"He has plundered our seas, ravaged our coasts, burnt our towns, and destroyed the lives of our people.

"He is at this time transporting large armies of foreign mercenaries to complete the work of death, desolation, and tyranny, already begun with circumstances of cruelty and perfidy scarcely paralleled in the most barbarous ages, and totally unworthy the head of a civilized nation.

"He has constrained our fellow-citizens, taken captive on the high seas, to bear arms against their country, to become the executioners of their friends and brethren, or to fall themselves by their hands.

"He has excited domestic insurrections amongst us, and has endeavored to bring on the inhabitants of our frontiers the merciless Indian savages, whose known rule of warfare is an undistinguished destruction of all ages, sexes and conditions.

"In every stage of these oppressions, we have petitioned for redress in the most humble terms. Our repeated petitions have been answered only by repeated injury. A prince whose character is thus marked by every act which may define a tyrant, is unfit to be the ruler of a free people.

"Nor have we been wanting in attentions to our British brethren. We have warned them from time to time of attempts by their legislature to extend an unwarrantable jurisdiction over us. We have reminded them of the circumstances of our emigration and settlement here. We have appealed to their native justice and magnanimity, and we have conjured them by the ties of our common kindred to disavow these usurpations, which would inevitably interrupt our connection and correspondence. They too have been deaf to the voice of justice and of consanguinity. We must therefore acquiesce in the necessity which denounces our separation, and hold them as we hold the rest of mankind, enemies in war; in peace, friends.

"We, therefore, the Representatives of the United States of America, in general Congress assembled, appealing to the Supreme Judge of the world for the rectitude of our intentions, do, in the name and by the authority of the good people of these colonies, solemnly publish and declare, That these united colonies are, and of right ought to be, free and independent States; that they are absolved from all allegiance to the British Crown, and that all political connection between them and the State of Great Britain is, and ought to be, totally dissolved; and that

as free and independent States they have full power to levy war, conclude peace, contract alliances, establish commerce, and to do all other acts and things which independent States may of right do. And for the support of this declaration, with a firm reliance on the protection of Divine Providence, we mutually pledge to each other our lives, our fortunes, and our sacred honor."

And whereas this convention, having taken this declaration into their most serious consideration, did, on the ninth day of July last past, unanimously resolve that the reasons assigned by the Continental Congress for declaring the united colonies free and independent States are cogent and conclusive; and that while we lament the cruel necessity which has rendered that measure unavoidable, we approve the same, and will, at the risk of our lives and fortunes, join with the other colonies in supporting it.

By virtue of which several acts, declarations, and proceedings mentioned and contained in the afore-cited resolves or resolutions of the general Congress of the United American States, and of the congresses or conventions of this State, all power whatever therein hath reverted to the people thereof, and this convention hath by their suffrages and free choice been appointed, and among other things authorized to institute and establish such a government as they shall deem best calculated to secure the rights and liberties of the good people of this State, most conducive of the happiness and safety of their constituents in particular, and of America in general.

I. This convention, therefore, in the name and by the authority of the good people of this State, doth ordain, determine, and declare that no authority shall, on any pretence whatever, be exercised over the people or members of this State but such as shall be derived from and granted by them.

II. This convention doth further, in the name and by the authority of the good people of this State, ordain, determine, and declare that the supreme legislative power within this State shall be vested in two separate and distinct bodies of men; the one to be called the assembly of the State of New York, the other to be called the senate of the State of New York; who together shall form the legislature, and meet once at least in every year for the despatch of business.

III. And whereas laws inconsistent with the spirit of this constitution, or with the public good, may be hastily and unadvisedly passed: Be it ordained, that the governor for the time being, the chancellor, and the judges of the supreme court, or any two of them, together with the governor, shall be, and hereby are, constituted a council to revise all bills about to be passed into laws by the legislature; and for that purpose shall assemble themselves from time to time, when the legislature shall be convened; for which, nevertheless, they shall not receive any salary or consideration, under any pretence whatever. And that all bills which have passed the senate and assembly shall, before they become laws, be presented to the said council for their revisal and consideration; and if, upon such revision and consideration, it should appear improper to the said council, or a majority of them, that the said bill should become a law of this State, that they return the same, together with their objections thereto in writing, to the senate or house of assembly (in which soever the same shall have originated) who shall enter the objection sent down by the council at large in their minutes, and proceed to reconsider the said bill. But if, after such reconsideration, two-thirds of the said senate or house of assembly shall, notwithstanding the said objections, agree to pass the same, it shall, together with the objections, be sent to the other branch of the legislature, where it shall also be reconsidered, and, if approved by two-thirds of the members present, shall be a law.

And in order to prevent any unnecessary delays, be it further ordained, that if any bill shall not be returned by the council within ten days after it shall have been presented, the same shall be a law, unless the legislature shall, by their adjournment, render a return of the said bill within ten days impracticable; in which case the bill shall be returned on the first day of the meeting of the legislature after the expiration of the said ten days.

IV. That the assembly shall consist of at least seventy members, to be annually chosen in the several counties, in the proportions following, viz:

For the city and county of New York, nine.
The city and county of Albany, ten.
The county of Dutchess, seven.
The county of Westchester, six.
The county of Ulster, six.
The county of Suffolk, five.
The county of Queens, four.
The county of Orange, four.
The county of Kings, two.
The county of Richmond, two.
Tryon County, six.
Charlotte County, four.
Cumberland County, three.
Gloucester County, two.

V. That as soon after the expiration of seven years (subsequent to the termination of the present war) as may be a census of the electors and inhabitants in this State be taken, under the direction of the legislature. And if, on such census, it shall appear that the number of representatives in assembly from the said counties is not justly proportioned to the number of electors in the said counties respectively, that the legislature do adjust and apportion the same by that rule. And further, that once in ever seven years, after the taking of the said first census, a just account of the electors resident in each county shall be taken, and if it shall thereupon appear that the number of electors in any county shall have increased or diminished one or more seventieth parts of the whole number of electors, which, on the said first census, shall be found in this State, the number of representatives for such county shall be increased or diminished accordingly, that is to say, one representative for every seventieth part as aforesaid.

VI. And whereas an opinion hath long prevailed among divers of the good people of this State that voting at elections by ballot would tend more to preserve the liberty and equal freedom of the people than voting *viva voce*: To the end, therefore, that a fair experiment be made, which of those two methods of voting is to be preferred—

Be it ordained, That as soon as may be after the termination of the present war between the United States of America and Great Britain, an act or acts be passed by the legislature of this State for causing all elections thereafter to be held in this State for senators and representatives in assembly to be by ballot, and directing the manner in which the same shall be conducted. And whereas it is possible that, after all the care of the legislature in framing the said act or acts, certain inconveniences and mischiefs, unforseen at this day, may be found to attend the said mode of electing by ballot:

It is further ordained, That if, after a full and fair experiment shall be made of voting by ballot aforesaid, the same shall be found less conducive to the safety or interest of the State than the method of voting *viva voce*, it shall be lawful and constitutional for the legislature to abolish the same, provided two-thirds of the members present in each house, respectively, shall concur therein. And further, that, during the continuance of the present war, and until the legislature of this State shall provide for the election of senators and representatives in assembly by ballot, the said election shall be made *viva voce*.

VII. That every male inhabitant of full age, who shall have personally resided within one of the counties of this State for six months immediately preceding the day of election, shall, at such election, be entitled to vote for representatives of the said county in assembly; if, during the time aforesaid, he shall have been a freeholder, possessing a freehold of the value of twenty pounds, within the said county, or have rented a tenement therein of the yearly value of forty shillings, and been rated and actually paid taxes to this State: *Provided always,* That every person who now is a freeman of the city of Albany, or who was made a freeman of the city of New York on or before the fourteenth day of October, in the year of our Lord one thousand seven hundred and seventy-five, and shall be actually and usually resident in the said cities, respectively, shall be entitled to vote for representatives in assembly within his said place of residence.

VIII. That every elector, before he is admitted to vote, shall, if required by the returning-officer or either of the inspectors, take an oath, or, if of the people called Quakers, an affirmation, of allegiance to the State.

IX. That the assembly, thus constituted, shall choose their own speaker, be judges of their own members, and enjoy the same privileges, and proceed in doing business in like manner as the assemblies of the colony of New York of right formerly did; and that a majority of the said members shall, from time to time, constitute a house, to proceed upon business.

X. And this convention doth further, in the name and by the authority of the good people of this State, ordain, determine, and declare, that the senate of the State of New York shall consist of twenty-four freeholders to be chosen out of the body of the freeholders; and that they be chosen by the freeholders of this State, possessed of freeholds of the value of one hundred pounds, over and above all debts charged thereon.

XI. That the members of the senate be elected for four years; and, immediately after the first election, they be divided by lot into four classes, six in each class, and numbered one, two, three, and four; that the seats of the members of the first class shall be vacated at the expiration of the first year, the second class the second year, and so on continually; to the end that the fourth part of the senate, as nearly as possible, may be annually chosen.

XII. That the election of senators shall be after this manner: That so much of this State as is now parcelled into counties be divided into four great districts; the southern district to comprehend the city and county of New York, Suffolk, Westchester, Kings, Queens, and Richmond Counties; the middle district to comprehend the counties of Dutchess, Ulster, and Orange; the western district, the city and county of Albany, and Tryon County; and the eastern district, the counties of Charlotte, Cumberland, and Gloucester. That the senators shall be elected by the freeholders of the said districts, qualified as aforesaid, in the proportions following, to wit: in the southern district, nine; in the middle district, six; in the western district, six; and in the eastern district, three. And be it ordained, that a census shall be taken, as soon as may be after the expiration of seven years from the termination of the present war, under the direction of the legislature; and if, on such census, it shall appear that the number of senators is not justly proportioned to the several districts, that the legislature adjust the proportion, as near as may be, to the number of freeholders, qualified as aforesaid, in each district. That when the number of electors, within any of the said districts, shall have increased one twenty-fourth part of the whole number of electors, which, by the said census, shall be found to be in this State, an additional senator shall be chosen by the electors of such district. That a majority of the number of senators to be chosen aforesaid shall be necessary to constitute a senate sufficient to proceed upon business; and that the senate shall, in like manner with the assembly, be the judges of its own members. And be it ordained, that it shall be in the power of the future legislatures of this State, for the convenience and advantage of the good people thereof, to divide the same into such further and other counties and districts as shall to them appear necessary.

XIII. And this convention doth further, in the name and by the authority of the good people of this State, ordain, determine, and declare, that no member of this State shall be disfranchised, or deprived of any the rights or privileges secured to the subjects of this State by this constitution, unless by the law of the land, or the judgment of his peers.

XIV. That neither the assembly or the senate shall have the power to adjourn themselves, for any longer time than two days, without the mutual consent of both.

XV. That whenever the assembly and senate disagree, a conference shall be held, in the preference of both, and be managed by committees, to be by them respectively chosen by ballot. That the doors, both of the senate and assembly, shall at all times be kept open to all persons, except when the welfare of the State shall require their debates to be kept secret. And the journals of all their proceedings shall be kept in the manner heretofore accustomed by the general assembly of the colony of New York; and except such parts as they shall, as aforesaid, respectively determine not to make public be from day to day (if the business of the legislature will permit) published.

XVI. It is nevertheless provided, that the number of senators shall never exceed one hundred, nor the number of the assembly three hundred; but that whenever the number of senators shall amount to one hundred, or of the assembly to three hundred, then and in such case the legislature shall, from time to time thereafter, by laws for that purpose, apportion and distribute the said one hundred senators and three hundred representatives among the great districts and counties of this State, in proportion to the number of their respective electors; so that the representation of the good people of this State, both in the senate and assembly, shall forever remain proportionate and adequate.

XVII. And this convention doth further, in the name and by the authority of the good people of this State, ordain, determine, and declare that the supreme executive power and authority of this State shall be vested in a governor; and that statedly, once in every three years, and as often as the seat of government shall become vacant, a wise and descreet freeholder of this State shall be, by ballot, elected governor, by the freeholders of this State, qualified, as before described, to elect senators; which elections shall be always held at the times and places of choosing representatives in assembly for each respective county; and that the person who hath the greatest number of votes within the said State shall be governor thereof.

XVIII. That the governor shall continue in office three years, and shall, by virtue of his office, be general and commander-in-chief of all the militia, and admiral of the navy of this State; that he shall have power to convene the assembly and senate on extraordinary occasions; to prorogue them from time to time, provided such prorogations shall not exceed sixty days in the space of any one year; and, at his discretion, to grant reprieves and pardons to persons convicted of crimes, other than treason or murder, in which he may suspend the execution of the sentence, until it shall be reported to the legislature at their subsequent meeting; and they shall either pardon or direct the execution of the criminal, or grant a further reprieve.

XIX. That it shall be the duty of the governor to inform the legislature, at every session, of the condition of the State, so far as may respect his department; to recommend such matters to their consideration as shall appear to him to concern its good government, welfare, and prosperity; to correspond with the Continental Congress, and other States; to transact all necessary business with the officers of government, civil and military; to take care that the laws are faithfully executed to the best of his ability; and to expedite all such measures as may be resolved upon by the legislature.

XX. That a lieutenant-governor shall, at every election of a governor, and as often as the lieutenant-governor shall die, resign, or be removed from office, be elected in the same manner with the governor, to continue in office until the next election of a governor; and such lieutenant-governor shall, by virtue of his office, be president of the senate, and, upon an equal division, have a casting voice in their decisions, but not vote on any other occasion. And in case of the impeachment of the governor, or his removal from office, death, resignation, or absence from the State, the lieutenant-governor shall exercise all the power and authority appertaining to the office of governor until another be chosen, or the governor absent or impeached shall return or be acquitted: *Provided*, That where the governor shall, with the consent of the legislature, be out of the State, in time of war, at the head of a military force thereof, he shall still continue in his command of all the military force of this State both by sea and land.

XXI. That whenever the government shall be administered by the lieutenant-governor, or he shall be unable to attend as president of the senate, the senators shall have power to elect one of their own members to the office of president of the senate, which he shall exercise *pro hac vice*. And if, during such vacancy of the office of governor, the lieutenant-governor shall be impeached, displaced, resign, die, or be absent from the State, the president of the senate shall, in like manner as the lieutenant-governor, administer the government, until others shall be elected by the suffrage of the people, at the succeeding election.

XXII. And this convention doth further, in the name and by the authority of the good people of this State, ordain, determine, and declare, that the treasurer of this State shall be appointed by act of the legislature, to originate with the assembly; *Provided*, that he shall not be elected out of either branch of the legislature.

XXIII. That all officers, other than those who, by this constitution, are directed to be otherwise appointed, shall be appointed in the manner following, to wit: The assembly shall, once in every year, openly nominate and appoint one of the senators from each great district, which senators shall form a council for the appointment of the said officers, of which the governor for the time being, or the lieutenant-governor, or the president of the senate, when they shall respectively administer the government, shall be president and have a casting voice, but no other vote; and with the advice and consent of the said council, shall appoint all the said officers; and that a majority of the said council be a quorum. And further, the said senators shall not be eligible to the said council for two years successively.

XXIV. That all military officers be appointed during pleasure; that all commissioned officers, civil and military, be commissioned by the governor; and that the chancellor, the judges of the supreme court, and first judge of the county court in every county, hold their offices during good behavior or until they shall have respectively attained the age of sixty years.

XXV. That the chancellor and judges of the supreme court shall not, at the same time, hold any other office, excepting that of Delegate to the general Congress, upon special occasions; and that the first judges of the county courts, in the several counties, shall not, at the same time, hold any other office, excepting that of Senator or Delegate to the general Congress. But if the chancellor, or either of the said judges, be elected or appointed to any other office, excepting as is before excepted, it shall be at his option in which to serve.

XXVI. That sheriffs and coroners be annually appointed; and that no person shall be capable of holding either of the said offices more than four years successively; nor the sheriff of holding any other office at the same time.

XXVII. *And be it further ordained,* That the register and clerks in chancery be appointed by the chancellor; the clerks of the supreme court, by the judges of the said court; the clerk of the court of probate, by the judge of the said court; and the register and marshal of the court of admiralty, by the judge of the admiralty. The said marshal, registers, and clerks to continue in office during the pleasure of those by whom they are appointed as aforesaid.

And that all attorneys, solicitors, and counsellors at law hereafter to be appointed, be appointed by the court, and licensed by the first judge of the court in which they shall respectively plead or practise, and be regulated by the rules and orders of the said courts.

XXVIII. *And be it further ordained,* That where, by this convention, the duration of any office shall not be ascertained, such office shall be construed to be held during the pleasure of the council of appointment: *Provided,* That new commissions shall be issued to judges of the county courts (other than to the first judge) and to justices of the peace, once at the least in every three years.

XXIX. That town clerks, supervisors, assessors, constables, and collectors, and all other officers, heretofore eligible by the people, shall always continue to be so eligible, in the manner directed by the present or future acts of legislature.

That loan officers, county treasurers, and clerks of the supervisors, continue to be appointed in the manner directed by the present or future acts of the legislature.

XXX. That Delegates to represent this State in the general Congress of the United States of America be annually appointed as follows, to wit: The senate and assembly shall each openly nominate as many persons as shall be equal to the whole number of Delegates to be appointed; after which nomination they shall meet together, and those persons named in both lists shall be Delegates; and out of those persons whose names are not on both lists, one-half shall be chosen by the joint ballot of the senators and members of assembly so met together as aforesaid.

XXXI. That the style of all laws shall be as follows, to wit: *"Be it enacted by the people of the State of New York, represented in senate and assembly;"* and that all writs and other proceedings shall run in the name of "The people of the State of New York," and be tested in the name of the chancellor, or chief judge of the court from whence they shall issue.

XXXII. And this convention doth further, in the name and by the authority of the good people of this State, ordain, determine, and declare, that a court shall be instituted for the trial of impeachments, and the correction of errors, under the regulations which shall be established by the legislature; and to consist of the president of the senate, for the time being, and the senators, chancellor, and judges of the supreme court, or the major part of them; except that when an impeachment shall be prosecuted against the chancellor, or either of the judges of the supreme court, the person so impeached shall be suspended from exercising his office until his acquittal; and, in like manner, when an appeal from a decree in equity shall be heard, the chancellor shall inform the court of the reasons of his decree, but shall not have a voice in the final sentence. And if the cause to be determined shall be brought up by writ of error, on a question of law, on a judgment in the supreme court, the judges of that court shall assign the reasons of such their judgment, but shall not have a voice for its affirmance or reversal.

XXXIII. That the power of impeaching all officers of the State, for mal and corrupt conduct in their respective offices, be vested in the representatives of the people in assembly; but that it shall always be necessary that two third parts of the members present shall consent to and agree in such impeachment. That previous to the trial of every impeachment, the members of the said court shall respectively be sworn truly and impartially to try and determine the charge in question, according to evidence; and that no judgment of the said court shall be valid unless it be assented to by two third parts of the members then present; nor shall it extend farther than to removal from office, and disqualification to hold or enjoy any place of honor, trust, or profit under this State. But the party so convicted shall be, nevertheless, liable and subject to indictment, trial, judgment, and punishment, according to the laws of the land.

XXXIV. *And it is further ordained,* That in every trial on impeachment, or indictment for crimes or misdemeanors, the party impeached or indicted shall be allowed counsel, as in civil actions.

XXXV. And this convention doth further, in the name and by the authority of the good people of this State, ordain, determine, and declare that such parts of the common law of England, and of the statute law of England and Great Britain, and of the acts of the legislature of the colony of New York, as together did form the law of the said colony on the 19th day of April, in the year of our Lord one thousand seven hundred and seventy-five, shall be and continue the law of this State, subject to such alterations and provisions as the legislature of this State shall, from time to time, make concerning the same. That such of the said acts, as are temporary, shall expire at the times limited for their duration, respectively. That all such parts of the said common law, and all such of the said statutes and acts aforesaid, or parts thereof, as may be construed to establish or maintain any particular denomination of Christians or their ministers, or concern the allegiance heretofore yielded to, and the supremacy, sovereignty, government, or prerogatives claimed or exercised by, the King of Great Britain and his predecessors, over the colony of New York and its inhabitants, or are repugnant to this constitution, be, and they hereby are, abrogated and rejected. And this convention doth further ordain, that the resolves or resolutions of the congresses of the colony of New York, and of the convention of the State of New York, now in force, and not repugnant to the government established by this constitution, shall be considered as making part of the laws of this State; subject, nevertheless, to such alterations and provisions as the legislature of this State may, from time to time, make concerning the same.

XXXVI. *And be it further ordained,* That all grants of lands within this State, made by the King of Great Britian, or persons acting under his authority, after the fourteenth day of October, one thousand seven hundred and seventy-five, shall be null and void; but that nothing in this constitution contained shall be construed to affect any grants of land within this State, made by the authority of the said King or his predecessors, or to annul any charters to bodies-politic by him or them, or any of them, made prior to that day. And that none of the said charters shall be adjudged to be void by reason of any non-user or misuser of any of their respective rights or privileges between the nineteenth day of April, in the year of our Lord one thousand seven hundred and seventy-five and the publication of this constitution. And further, that all such of the officers described in the said charters respectively as, by the terms of the said charters, were to be appointed by the governor of the colony of New York, with or without the advice and consent of the council of the said King, in the said colony, shall henceforth be appointed by the council established by this constitution for the appointment of officers in this State, until otherwise directed by the legislature.

XXXVII. And whereas it is of great importance to the safety of this State that peace and amity with the Indians within the same be at all times supported and maintained; and whereas the frauds too often practised towards the said Indians, in contracts made for their lands, have, in divers instances, been productive of dangerous discontents and animosities: Be it ordained, that no purchases or contracts for the sale of lands, made since the fourteenth day of October, in the year of our Lord one thousand seven hundred and seventy-five, or which may hereafter be made with or of the said Indians, within the limits of this State, shall be binding on the said Indians, or deemed valid, unless made under the authority and with the consent of the legislature of this State.

XXXVIII. And whereas we are required, by the benevolent principles of rational liberty, not only to expel civil tyranny, but also to guard against that spiritual oppression and intolerance wherewith the bigotry and ambition of weak and wicked priests and princes have scourged mankind, this convention doth further, in the name and by the authority of the good people of this State, ordain, determine, and declare, that the free exercise and enjoyment of religious profession and worship, without discrimination or preference, shall forever hereafter be allowed, within this State, to all mankind: *Provided,* That the liberty of conscience, hereby granted, shall not be so construed as to excuse acts of licentiousness, or justify practices inconsistent with the peace or safety of this State.

XXXIX. And whereas the ministers of the gospel are, by their profession, dedicated to the service of God and the care of souls, and ought not to be diverted from the great duties of their function; therefore, no minister of the gospel, or priest of any denomination whatsoever, shall, at any time hereafter, under any pretence or description whatever, be eligible to, or capable of holding, any civil or military office or place within this State.

XL. And whereas it is of the utmost importance to the safety of every State that it should always be in a condition of defence; and it is the duty of every man who enjoys the protection of society to be prepared and willing to defend it; this convention therefore, in the name and by the authority of the good people of this State, doth ordain, determine, and declare that the militia of this State, at all times hereafter, as well in peace as in war, shall be armed and disciplined, and in readiness for service. That all such of the inhabitants of this State being of the people called Quakers as, from scruples of conscience, may be averse to the bearing of arms, be therefrom excused by the legislature; and do pay to the State such sums of money, in lieu of their personal service, as the same may, in the judgment of the legislature, be worth. And that a proper magazine of warlike stores, proportionate to the number of inhabitants, be, forever hereafter, at the expense of this State, and by acts of the legislature, established, maintained, and continued in every county in this State.

XLI. And this convention doth further ordain, determine, and declare, in the name and by the authority of the good people of this State, that trial by jury, in all cases in which it hath heretofore been used in the colony of New York, shall be established and remain inviolate forever. And that no acts of attainder shall be passed by the legislature of this State for crimes, other than those committed before the termination of the present war; and that such acts shall not work a corruption of blood. And further, that the legislature of this State shall, at no time hereafter, institute any new court or courts, but such as shall proceed according to the course of the common law.

XLII. And this convention doth further, in the name and by the authority of the good people of this State, ordain, determine, and declare that it shall be in the discretion of the legislature to naturalize all such persons, and in such manner, as they shall think proper: *Provided*, All such of the persons so to be by them naturalized, as being born in parts beyond sea, and out of the United States of America, shall come to settle in and become subjects of this State, shall take an oath of allegiance to this State, and abjure and renounce all allegiance and subjection to all and every foreign king, prince, potentate, and State in all matters, ecclesiastical as well as civil.

By order.
LEONARD GANSEVOORT,
President pro tempore.

Reference: Francis Newton Thorpe (ed.), *The Federal and State Constitutions, Colonial Charters, and Other Organic Laws of the States*, Vol. V (Washington: GPO, 1909).

LETTER FROM JOHN JAY TO ROBERT LIVINGSTON, APRIL 29, 1777

TO ROBERT R. LIVINGSTON AND GOUVERNEUR MORRIS
Fish Kill, 29 April 1777
Gentlemen

Your Letter of the 26 Instant was this Evening delivered to me. When I was called last from Convention, a Clause in the Report of the Form of Government had been by a very great Majority agreed to, instituting a Council for the appointment of military and many civil Officers, *including Clerks of Courts*; and though I publicly advocated and voted for that Clause, you express much Surprize at my disapproving a material alteration of it. Had you retained the most distant Idea of the part I took relative to the various modes proposed for the appointment of officers, I am confident you would not have asserted "*that I was fully of opinion to appoint by Judges of the Sup. Court, not only Clerks, but all other civil Officers in the Government.*" Had such a Representation of my opinion relative to the best mode of appointing those officers, fallen from some Persons whom I could name, I should have called it very disengenuous and uncandid.

The Fact was thus. The Clause directing the Governor to *nominate* officers to the Legislature for their approbation being read and debated, was generally disapproved. Many other methods were devised by different Members, and mentioned to the House merely for Consideration. I mentioned several myself, and told the Convention at the Time, that however I might then incline to adopt them, I was not certain but that after considering them, I should vote for their Rejection. While the Minds of the members were thus fluctuating between various opinions, Capt. Platt moved for the only amendment which was proposed to the House for introducing the Judges. I told the House I preferred the amendment to the original Clause in the Report, but that I thought a better mode might be devised. I finally opposed the adoption of Capt. Platts amendment, and well remember that I spent the Evening of that Day with Mr Morris at your Lodgings, in the Course of which I proposed the Plan for the Institution of the Council as it now stands, and after conversing on the Subject, we agreed to bring it into the House the next Day. It was moved and debated and carried with this only amendment, that the Speaker of the General Assembly for the Time being was then (to avoid the Governors having frequent opportunities of a casting Vote) added to the Council.

As to the Alteration in question, vizt. transferring the appointment of Clerks etc of Courts from the Council to the respective Judges, I dislike it for many Reasons which the Limits of a Letter will not admit of being fully enumerated and discussed.

You say that "*great Inconveniencies must arise from suffering Clerks to be independent of such Courts, and of Consequence frequently ignorant, always inattentive.*" If Ignorance and Inattention would by some necessary Consequence unknown to me, characterize all such Clerks as the Council (of which the Governor is President, and consisting of the Speaker of the General assembly and four Senators elected in that House) Should appoint, I grant that the appointment ought to be in other Hands. But I am at a Loss and unable to Conjecture by what subtle Refinement or new Improvement in the Science of Politics it should be discovered, that a Council acknowledged to be competent to the Choice and appointment of the first Judges of the Land, was insufficient to the nomination of clerks of Courts; or from whence it is to be inferred that they, by where will and pleasure the Duration of many other offices is limited by the Constitution, would either appoint or continue in office ignorant or inattentive Clerks more than ignorant or inattentive Judges Sherifs or Justices of the peace. Nor can I percieve why the clerks in chancery appointed by the Council, should be more ignorant and inattentive than the Examiners, who you are content should still be appointed by that Body; unless Ignorance and Inattention be supposed less dangerous and important in the one than the other.

That Clerks should be *dependent* is agreed on all Hands, on whom? is the only question. I think not on the Judges Because

The chancellor, and the Judges of the Sup. Court holding permanent Commissions, will be *tempted* not only to give these appointments to their Children Brothers Relatives and Favorites, but to continue them in Office against the public Good. You I dare say, know Men of too little Probity Abilities and Industry to fill an office well, and yet of sufficient art and attention to avoid such gross Misbehaveour, as might justify loud Clamors against them.

Besides, Men who appoint others to offices, generally have a Partiality for them, and are often disposed, on Principles of Pride as well as Interest, to support them. By the Clerks of Courts being dependent on the Judges Collusion becomes more easy to be practiced, and more difficult to be detected, and instead of publishing and punishing each others Transgressions, will combine in concealing palliating or excusing their mutual Defects or misdemeanours.

From the Clerks, etc. being appointed by the Council, these advantages would result.

The Council might avail themselves of the advice of the Judges without being bound by their Prejudices or interested in their Designs.

Should the Council promote their Favorites at the Expence of the public, that Body, having a new Set of members every Year, a bad officer thus appointed would lose his office on his Patrons being removed from the Council.

It would avoid that odium to which that part of the Constitution will now be exposed vizt. that it was framed by Lawyers, and done with Design to favor the Profession.

The new Clause respecting the licensing of attornies, to speake plain, is in my opinion the most whimsical crude and indigested Thing I have met with.

There will be between thirty and forty Courts in this State, and as that Clause now stands, an Attorney (however well qualified, and licensed by the Sup. Court) must before he can issue a writ in a little Borough or Mayors Court, obtain their Licence also. The Reasons assigned for this, seem to be

That it would be improper for one Court to do this *Drudgery* for the Rest.

That it would be difficult to distinguish which Court it would be most proper to impose it upon.

That the Judges of the inferior Courts might be offended at being relieved from this *Drudgery*, thinking themselves as capable of judging of the Merits of an Attorney as of a Cause; and that they

had equal Right with others to say who shall and who shall not be entitled to Practice.

To say that it would be improper for one to do this *Drudgery* for the Rest, is begging the Question. Other Courts than the Sup. Court *never* had this *Drudgery* to do; and I believe never will have in any part of the World, except in the State and by the Constitution of New York.

Why the Examination and licensing of Attornies should with more Propriety be stiled *a Drudgery*, than striking a Jury, or any other Business incident to the office of Judge, I know not. If it be, I should think it ought not to be multiplied by thirty or forty, and then imposed on all in the State, and compelling an Attorney to sollicit, and pay fees for admission to thirty or forty Courts, when one would have sufficed.

How it should be difficult to distinguish the proper Court for the Purpose, is to me misterious.

The Sup. Court controuls all the Courts in the State which proceed according to the Course of the common Law, and its Jurisdiction is bounded only by the Limits of the State. An Attorney is an officer of a common Law Court. That Court therefore which by the Constitution is made superior to the others, must be supposed most competent not only to the Determination of Causes, but of the Qualification of the attornies who manage them. The lesser Courts cannot be deemed equally qualified for either; and being dependent and inferior in every other Respect, ought not to have *concurrent*, *independent* or *equal* Authority in this. Justice as well as Decency forbids that a Mayor and four Alderman should constitutionally have a Right to refuse Admission to Attornies licensed by the Sup. Court.

Whence is it to be inferred that the Judges of the inferior Courts, unless gratified with this novel unprecedented power, would *complain?* It is not to be found among the Rights enjoyed by them prior to the Revolution; and I much doubt whether, unless within this Fortnight or three Weeks, there was a single man in the State who ever thought of such a Thing.

It would be arrogance in them to expect to be endulged in a Right to examine question and reject the Judgment of the Sup. Court respecting the Qualifications of Attornies, when that very Court is appointed among other Things to correct their Errors in all other Cases, nay in this Case the mere will of these little courts is to be the Law; and an Attorney of Reputation and Eminence in the Sup. Court is without Remedy in Case an inferior Court should unjustly refuse to admit him.

According to the present System an Attorney must, if he chuses to have *general* Licence, obtain admission into the Sup. Court, three Mayors Courts, thirteen inferior Courts of common pleas for Counties, fourteen Courts of Sessions for the peace, and the Lord knows how often, or in how many Courts of oyer and Terminer and Goal Delivery.

Remember that I now predict, that this same Clause which thus gives inferiour Courts uncontrouled and unlimited authority to admit as many Attornies as they please, will fill every County in the State with a Swarm of designing cheating litigious Pettifoggers, who like Leaches and Spiders will fatten on the Spoils of the Poor the Ignorant the Feeble and the unwary.

The Division of the State into Districts for the purpose of facilitating Elections I well remember was agreed to be referred to the Legislature, and I well remember too, several members as well as myself were of Opinion that a short Clause should be inserted in the Constitution, which should give the People a Right Claim on the Legislature for it.

The Connecticut Plan of nominating or holding up Senators, I ever warmly espoused. I thought it bore strong marks of Wisdom and sound Policy. Nor have I forgot that others opposed it; or that I undertook with the Leave of the House, to reduce

it to Writing and offer it to their Consideration. The opinion that the rotatory mode of electing renders it entirely useless, I have neither heard nor can I percieve any Reason for.

The Difficulty of getting any Government at all, you know has long been an apprehension of little Influence on my mind; and always appeared to be founded less in Fact, than in a Design of quickning the Pace of the House.

What the Secretary may have written to Mr. Benson, I know not. I expressed the same Sentiments to him that were inserted in my Letter to Mr Hobart, and no others.

The other parts of the Constitution I approve, and only regret that like a Harvest cut before it was all ripe, some of the Grains have shrunk. Exclusive of the Clauses which I have mentioned, and which I wish had been added; another material one has been omitted, vizt. a Direction that all Persons holding Offices under the Government should swear allegiance to it, and renounce all allegiance and Subjection to foreign Kings Princes and States in all matters ecclesiastical as well as civil. I should also have been for a Clause against the Continuation of domestic Slavery, and the Support and Encouragement of Literature; as well as some other Matters though perhaps of less Consequence.

Though the Birth of the Constitution is in my opinion premature, I shall nevertheless do all in my power to nurse and keep it alive, being far from approving the spartan Law which encouraged Parents to destroy such of their Children as perhaps by some cross accident, might come into the World defective or misshapen.

I am etc.

Reference: Richard B. Morris (ed.), *John Jay: The Making of a Revolutionary*, Vol. I (New York: Harper & Row, 1975).

44

Vermont, July 8, 1777

Although Vermont did not join the Union until 1791 it nevertheless wrote a constitution and thought of itself as part of the New Nation. Its Constitution created a Governing system with near universal manhood suffrage. Vermonters also debated and revised their constitution in 1787. The revised constitution gave greater clarity about the powers of the legislature.

CONSTITUTION, JULY 8, 1777

WHEREAS, all government ought to be instituted and supported, for the security and protection of the community, as such, and to enable the individuals who compose it, to enjoy their natural rights, and the other blessings which the Author of existence has bestowed upon man; and whenever those great ends of government are not obtained, the people have a right, by common consent, to change it, and take such measures as to them may appear necessary to promote their safety and happiness.

And whereas, the inhabitants of this State have (in consideration of protection only) heretofore acknowledged allegiance to the King of Great Britain, and the said King has not only withdrawn that protection, but commenced, and still continues to carry on, with unabated vengeance, a most cruel and unjust war against them; employing therein, not only the troops of Great Britain, but foreign mercenaries, savages and slaves, for the avowed purpose of reducing them to a total and abject submission to the despotic domination of the British parliament, with many other acts of tyranny, (more fully set forth in the declaration of Congress) whereby all allegiance and fealty to the said King and his successors, are dissolved and at an end; and all power and authority derived from him, ceased in the American Colonies.

And whereas, the territory which now comprehends the State of *Vermont*, did antecedently, of right, belong to the government of *New-Hampshire*; and the former Governor thereof, viz. his Excellency *Benning Wentworth*, Esq., granted many charters of lands and corporations, within this State, to the present inhabitants and others. And whereas, the late Lieutenant Governor *Colden*, of *New York*, with others, did, in violation of the tenth command, covet those very lands; and by a false representation made to the court of Great Britain, (in the year 1764, that for the convenience of trade and administration of justice, the inhabitants were desirous of being annexed to that government,) obtained jurisdiction of those very identical lands, *ex-parte*; which ever was, and is, disagreeable to the inhabitants. And whereas, the legislature of *New-York*, ever have, and still continue to disown the good people of this State, in their landed property, which will appear in the complaints hereafter inserted, and in the 36th section of their present constitution, in which is established the grants of land made by that government.

They have refused to make regrants of our lands to the original proprietors and occupants, unless at the exorbitant rate of 2300 dollars fees for each township; and did enhance the quit-rent, three fold, and demanded an immediate delivery of the title derived before, from *New-Hampshire*.

The judges of their supreme court have made a solemn declaration, that the charters, conveyances, &c. of the lands included in the before described premises, were utterly null and void, on which said title was founded: in consequence of which declaration, writs of possession have been by them issued, and the sheriff of the county of Albany sent, at the head of six or seven hundred men, to enforce the execution thereof.

They have passed an act, annexing a penalty thereto, of thirty pounds fine and six months imprisonment, on any person who should refuse assisting the sheriff, after being requested, for the purpose of executing writs of possession.

The Governors, *Dunmore, Tryon* and *Colden,* have made re-grants of several tracts of land, included in the premises, to certain favorite land jobbers in the government of *New-York,* in direct violation of his Britannic majesty's express prohibition, in the year 1767.

They have issued proclamations, wherein they have offered large sums of money, for the purpose of apprehending those very persons who have dared boldly, and publicly, to appear in defence of their just rights.

They did pass twelve acts of outlawry, on the 9th day of March, A.D. 1774, impowering the respective judges of their supreme court, to award execution of death against those inhabitants in said district, that they should judge to be offenders, without trial.

They have, and still continue, an unjust claim to those lands, which greatly retards emigration into, and the settlement of, this State.

They have hired foreign troops, emigrants from *Scotland,* at two different times, and armed them, to drive us out of possession.

They have sent the savages on our frontiers, to distress us.

They have proceeded to erect the counties of Cumberland and Glocester, and establish courts of justice there, after they were discountenanced by the authority of Great Britain.

The free convention of the State of *New-York,* at *Harlem,* in the year 1776, unanimously voted, "That all quit-rents, formerly due to the King of Great Britain, are now due and owing to this Convention, or such future government as shall be hereafter established in this State."

In the several stages of the aforesaid oppressions, we have petitioned his Britannic majesty, in the most humble manner, for redress, and have, at very great expense, received several reports in our favor; and, in other instances, wherein we have petitioned the late legislative authority of *New-York,* those petitions have been treated with neglect.

And whereas, the local situation of this State, from *New-York,* at the extreme part, is upward of four hundred and fifty miles from the seat of that government, which renders it extreme difficult to continue under the jurisdiction of said State.

Therefore, it is absolutely necessary, for the welfare and safety of the inhabitants of this State, that it should be, henceforth, a free and independent State; and that a just, permanent, and proper form of government, should exist in it, derived from, and founded on, the authority of the people only, agreeable to the direction of the honorable American Congress.

We the representatives of the freemen of *Vermont,* in General Convention met, for the express purpose of forming such a government,—confessing the goodness of the Great Governor of the universe, (who alone, knows to what degree of earthly happiness, mankind may attain, by perfecting the arts of government,) in permitting the people of this State, by common consent, and without violence, deliberately to form for themselves, such just rules as they shall think best for governing their future society; and being fully convinced that it is our indispensable duty, to establish such original principles of government, as will best promote the general happiness of the people of this State, and their posterity, and provide for future improvements, without partiality for, or prejudice against, any particular class, sect, or denomination of men whatever,—do, by virtue of authority vested in us, by our constituents, ordain, declare, and establish, the following declaration of rights, and frame of government, to be the CONSTITUTION of this COMMONWEALTH, and to remain in force therein, forever, unaltered, except in such articles, as shall, hereafter, on experience, be found to require improvement, and which shall, by the same authority of the people, fairly delegated, as this frame of government directs, be amended or improved, for the more effectual obtaining and securing the great end and design of all government, herein before mentioned.

Chapter I

A Declaration Of The Rights Of The Inhabitants Of The State Of Vermont

I. THAT all men are born equally free and independent, and have certain natural, inherent and unalienable rights, amongst which are the enjoying and defending life and liberty; acquiring, possessing and protecting property, and pursuing and obtaining happiness and safety. Therefore, no male person, born in this country, or brought from over sea, ought to be holden by law, to serve any person, as a servant, slave or apprentice, after he arrives to the age of twenty-one years, nor female, in like manner, after she arrives to the age of eighteen years, unless they are bound by their own consent, after they arrive to such age, or bound by law, for the payment of debts, damages, fines, costs, or the like.

II. That private property ought to be subservient to public uses, when necessity requires it; nevertheless, whenever any particular man's property is taken for the use of the public, the owner ought to receive an equivalent in money.

III. That all men have a natural and unalienable right to worship ALMIGHTY GOD, according to the dictates of their own consciences and understanding, regulated by the word of GOD; and that no man ought, or of right can be compelled to attend any religious worship, or erect, or support any place of worship, or maintain any minister, contrary to the dictates of his conscience; nor can any man who professes the protestant religion, be justly deprived or abridged of any civil right, as a citizen, on account of his religious sentiment, or peculiar mode of religious worship, and that no authority can, or ought to be vested in, or assumed by, any power whatsoever, that shall, in any case, interfere with, or in any manner controul, the rights of conscience, in the free exercise of religious worship: nevertheless, every sect or denomination of people ought to observe the Sabbath, or the Lord's day, and keep up, and support, some sort of religious worship, which to them shall seem most agreeable to the revealed will of GOD.

IV. That the people of this State have the sole, exclusive and inherent right of governing and regulating the internal police of the same.

V. That all power being originally inherent in, and consequently, derived from, the people; therefore, all officers of government, whether legislative or executive, are their trustees and servants, and at all times accountable to them.

VI. That government is, or ought to be, instituted for the common benefit, protection, and security of the people, nation or community; and not for the particular emolument or advantage of any single man, family or set of men, who are a part only of that community; and that the community hath an indubitable, unalienable and indefeasible right to reform, alter, or abolish, government, in such manner as shall be, by that community, judged most conducive to the public weal.

VII. That those who are employed in the legislative and executive business of the State, may be restrained from oppression, the people have a right, at such periods as they may think proper, to reduce their public officers to a private station, and supply the vacancies by certain and regular elections.

VIII. That all elections ought to be free; and that all freemen, having a sufficient, evident, common interest with, and attachment to, the community, have a right to elect officers, or be elected into office.

IX. That every member of society hath a right to be protected in the enjoyment of life, liberty and property, and therefore, is bound to contribute his proportion towards the expense of that protection, and yield his personal service, when necessary, or an equivalent thereto; but no part of a man's property can be justly taken from him, or applied to public uses, without his own consent, or that of his legal representatives; nor can any man who is conscientiously scrupulous of bearing arms, be justly compelled thereto, if he will pay such equivalent; nor are the people bound by any law, but such as they have, in like manner, assented to, for their common good.

X. That, in all prosecutions for criminal offences, a man hath a right to be heard, by himself and his counsel—to demand the cause and nature of his accusation—to be confronted with the witnesses—to call for evidence in his favor, and a speedy public trial, by an impartial jury of the country; without the unanimous consent of which jury, he cannot be found guilty; nor can he be compelled to give evidence against himself; nor can any man be justly deprived of his liberty, except by the laws of the land or the judgment of his peers.

XI. That the people have a right to hold themselves, their houses, papers and possessions free from search or seizure; and therefore warrants, without oaths or affirmations first made, affording a sufficient foundation for them, and whereby any officer or messenger may be commanded or required to search suspected places, or to seize any person or persons, his, her or their property, not particularly described, are contrary to that right, and ought not to be granted.

XII. That no warrant or writ to attach the person or estate, of any freeholder within this State, shall be issued in civil action, without the person or persons, who may request such warrant or attachment, first make oath, or affirm, before the authority who may be requested to issue the same, that he, or they, are in danger of loosing his, her or their debts.

XIII. That, in controversies respecting property, and in suits between man and man, the parties have a right to a trial by jury; which ought to be held sacred.

XIV. That the people have a right to freedom of speech, and of writing and publishing their sentiments; therefore, the freedom of the press ought not be restrained.

XV. That the people have a right to bear arms for the defence of themselves and the State; and, as standing armies, in the time of peace, are dangerous to liberty, they ought not to be kept up; and that the military should be kept under strict subordination to, and governed by, the civil power.

XVI. That frequent recurrence to fundamental principles, and a firm adherence to justice, moderation, temperance, industry and frugality, are absolutely necessary to preserve the blessings of liberty, and keep government free. The people ought, therefore, to pay particular attention to these points, in the choice of officers and representatives, and have a right to exact a due and constant regard to them, from their legislators and magistrates, in the making and executing such laws as are necessary for the good government of the State.

XVII. That all people have a natural and inherent right to emigrate from one State to another, that will receive them; or to form a new State in vacant countries, or in such countries as they can purchase, whenever they think that thereby they can promote their own happiness.

XVIII. That the people have a right to assemble together, to consult for their common good—to instruct their representatives, and to apply to the legislature for redress of grievances, by address, petition or remonstrance.

XIX. That no person shall be liable to be transported out of this State for trial, for any offence committed within this State.

Chapter II

Plan Or Frame Of Government

SECTION I. THE COMMONWEALTH or STATE of VERMONT, shall be governed, hereafter, by a Governor, Deputy Governor, Council, and an Assembly of the Representatives of the Freemen of the same, in manner and form following.

SECTION II. The supreme legislative power shall be vested in a House of Representatives of the Freemen or Commonwealth or State of *Vermont*.

SECTION III. The supreme executive power shall be vested in a Governor and Council.

SECTION IV. Courts of justice shall be established in every county in this State.

SECTION V. The freemen of this Commonwealth, and their sons, shall be trained and armed for its defence, under such regulations, restrictions and exceptions, as the general assembly shall, by law, direct; preserving always to the people, the right of choosing their colonels of militia, and all commissioned officers under that rank, in such manner, and as often, as by the said laws shall be directed.

SECTION VI. Every man of the full age of twenty-one years, having resided in this State for the space of one whole year, next before the election of representatives, and who is of a quiet and peaccable behaviour, and will take the following oath (or affirmation) shall be entitled to all the privileges of a freeman of this State.

I —— solemnly swear, by the ever living God, (or affirm, in the presence of Almighty God,) that whenever I am called to give my vote or suffrage, touching any matter that concerns the State of Vermont, *I will do it so, as in my conscience, I shall judge will most conduce to the best good of the same, as established by the constitution, without fear or favor of any man.*

SECTION VII. The House of Representatives of the Freemen of this State, shall consist of persons most noted for wisdom and virtue, to be chosen by the freemen of every town in this State, respectively. And no foreigner shall be chosen, unless he has resided in the town for which he shall be elected, one year immediately before said election.

SECTION VIII. The members of the House of Representatives, shall be chosen annually, by ballot, by the freemen of this State, on the first Tuesday of September, forever, (except this present year) and shall meet on the second Thursday of the succeeding October, and shall be stiled the General Assembly of the Representatives of the Freemen of *Vermont*; and shall have power to choose their Speaker, Secretary of the State, their Clerk, and other necessary officers of the house— sit on their own adjournments—prepare bills and enact them into laws—judge of the elections and qualifications of their own members—they may expel a member, but not a second time for the same cause—They may administer oaths (or affirmations) on examination of witnesses—redress grievances—impeach State criminals—grant charters of incorporation—constitute towns, boroughs, cities and counties, and shall have all other powers necessary for the legislature of a free State: but they shall have no power to add to, alter, abolish, or infringe any part of this constitution. And for this present year, the members of the General Assembly shall be chosen on the first Tuesday of March next, and shall meet at the meeting-house, in *Windsor*, on the second Thursday of March next.

SECTION IX. A quorum of the house of representatives shall consist of two-thirds of the whole number of members elected; and having met and chosen their speaker, shall, each of them, before they proceed to business, take and subscribe, as well the oath of fidelity and allegiance herein after directed, as the following oath or affirmation, viz.

I —— do solemnly swear, by the ever living God, (or, I do solemnly affirm in the presence of Almighty God) that as a member of this assembly, I will not propose or assent to any bill, vote, or resolution, which shall appear to me injurious to the people; nor do or consent to any act or thing whatever, that shall have a tendency to lessen or abridge their rights and privileges, as declared in the Constitution of this State; but will, in all things, conduct myself as a faithful, honest representative and guardian of the people, according to the best of my judgment and abilities.

And each member, before he takes his seat, shall make and subscribe the following declaration, viz.

I do believe in one God, the Creator and Governor of the universe, the rewarder of the good and punisher of the wicked. And I do acknowledge the scriptures of the old and new testament to be given by divine inspiration, and own and profess the protestant religion.

And no further or other religious test shall ever, hereafter, be required of any civil officer or magistrate in this State.

SECTION X. Delegates to represent this State in Congress shall be chosen, by ballot, by the future General Assembly, at their first meeting, and annually, forever afterward, as long as such representation shall be necessary. Any Delegate may be superceded, at any time, by the General Assembly appointing another in his stead. No man shall sit in Congress longer than two years successively, nor be capable of re-election for three years afterwards; and no person who holds any office in the gift of the Congress, shall, thereafter, be elected to represent this State in Congress.

SECTION XI. If any town or towns shall neglect or refuse to elect and send representatives to the General Assembly, two thirds of the members of the towns, that do elect and send representatives, (provided they be a majority of the inhabited towns of the whole State) when met, shall have all the powers of the General Assembly, as fully and amply, as if the whole were present.

SECTION XII. The doors of the house in which the representatives of the freemen of this State, shall sit, in General Assembly, shall be and remain open for the admission of all persons, who behave decently, except only, when the welfare of this State may require the doors to be shut.

SECTION XIII. The votes and proceedings of the General Assembly shall be printed, weekly, during their sitting, with the yeas and nays, on any question, vote or resolution, where one-third of the members require it; (except when the votes are taken by ballot) and when the yeas and nays are so taken, every member shall have a right to insert the reasons of his votes upon the minutes, if he desire it.

SECTION XIV. To the end that laws, before they are enacted, may be more maturely considered, and the inconveniency of hasty determination as much as possible prevented, all bills of public nature, shall be first laid before the Governor and Council, for their perusal and proposals of amendment, and shall be printed for the consideration of the people, before they are read in General Assembly, for the last time of debate and amendment; except temporary acts, which, after being laid before the Governor and Council, may (in case of sudden necessity) be passed into laws; and no other shall be passed into laws, until the next session of assembly. And for the more perfect satisfaction of the public, the reasons and motives for making such laws, shall be fully and clearly expressed and set forth in their preambles.

SECTION XV. The style of the laws of this State shall be,—"Be it enacted, and it is hereby enacted, by the Representatives of the Freemen of the State of *Vermont*, in General Assembly met, and by the authority of the same."

SECTION XVI. In order that the Freemen of this State might enjoy the benefit of election, as equally as may be, each town within this State, that consists, or may consist, of eighty taxable inhabitants, within one septenary or seven years, next after the establishing this constitution, may hold elections therein, and choose each, two representatives; and each other inhabited town in this State may, in like manner, choose each, one representative, to represent them in General Assembly, during the said septenary or seven years; and after that, each inhabited town may, in like manner, hold such election, and choose each, one representative, forever thereafter.

SECTION XVII. The Supreme Executive Council of this State, shall consist of a Governor, Lieutenant-Governor, and twelve persons, chosen in the following manner, viz. The Freemen of each town, shall, on the day of election for choosing representatives to attend the General Assembly, bring in their votes for Governor, with his name fairly written, to the constable, who shall seal them up, and write on them, votes for the Governor, and deliver them to the representative chosen to attend the General Assembly; and, at the opening of the General Assembly, there shall be a committee appointed out of the Council and Assembly, who, after being duly sworn to the faithful discharge of their trust, shall proceed to receive, sort, and count, the votes for the Governor, and declare the person who has the major part of the votes, to be Governor, for the year ensuing. And if there be no choice made, then the Council and General Assembly, by their joint ballot, shall make choice of a Governor.

The Lieutenant Governor and Treasurer, shall be chosen in the manner above directed; and each freeman shall give in twelve votes for twelve councillors, in the same manner; and the twelve highest in nomination shall serve for the ensuing year as Councillors.

The Council that shall act in the recess of this Convention, shall supply the place of a Council for the next General Assembly, until the new Council be declared chosen. The Council shall meet annually, at the same time and place with the General Assembly; and every member of the Council shall be a Justice of the Peace for the whole State, by virtue of his office.

SECTION XVIII. The Governor, and in his absence, the Lieutenant or Deputy Governor, with the Council—seven of whom shall be a quorum—shall have power to appoint and commissionate all officers, (except those who are appointed by the General Assembly,) agreeable to this frame of government, and the laws that may be made hereafter; and shall supply every vacancy in any office, occasioned by death, resignation, removal or disqualification, until the office can be filled, in the time and manner directed by law or this constitution. They are to correspond with other States, and transact business with officers of government, civil and military; and to prepare such business as may appear to them necessary to lay before the General Assembly. They shall sit as judges to hear and determine on impeachments, taking to their assistance, for advice only, the justices of the supreme court; and shall have power to grant pardons, and remit fines, in all cases whatsoever, except cases of impeachment, and in cases of treason and murder—shall have power to grant reprieves, but not to pardon, until the end of the next session of the Assembly: but there shall be no remission or mitigation of punishment, on impeachments, except by act of legislation. They are also, to take care that the laws be faithfully executed. They are to expedite the execution of such measures as may be resolved upon by General Assembly; and they may draw upon the Treasurer for such sums as may be appropriated by the House: they may also lay embargoes, or prohibit the exportation of any commodity for any time, not exceeding thirty days, in the recess of the House only: they may grant such licences as shall be directed by law, and shall have power to call together the General Assembly, when necessary, before the day to which they shall stand adjourned. The Governor shall be commander-in-chief of the forces of the State; but shall not command in person, except advised thereto by the Council, and then, only as long as they shall approve thereof. The Governor and Council shall have a Secretary, and keep fair books of their proceedings, wherein any Councillor may enter his dissent, with his reasons to support it.

SECTION XIX. All commissions shall be in the name of the freemen of the State of *Vermont*, sealed with the State seal, signed by the Governor, and in his absence, the Lieutenant Governor, and attested by the Secretary; which seal shall be kept by the Council.

SECTION XX. Every officer of State, whether judicial or executive, shall be liable to be impeached by the General Assembly, either when in office, or after his resignation, or removal for mal-administration. All impeachments shall be before the Governor or Lieutenant Governor and Council, who shall hear and determine the same.

SECTION XXI. The supreme court, and the several courts of common pleas of this State shall, besides the powers usually exercised by such courts, have the powers of a court of chancery, so far as relates to perpetuating testimony, obtaining evidence from places not within this State, and the care of persons and estates of those who are *non compotes mentis,* and such other powers as may be found necessary by future General Assemblies, not inconsistent with this constitution.

SECTION XXII. Trials shall be by jury; and it is recommended to the legislature of this State to provide by law, against every corruption or partiality in the choice, and return, or appointment, of juries.

SECTION XXIII. All courts shall be open, and justice shall be impartially administered, without corruption or unnecessary delay; all their officers shall be paid an adequate, but moderate, compensation for their services; and if any officer shall take greater or other fees than the laws allow him, either directly or indirectly, it shall ever after disqualify him from holding any office in this State.

SECTION XXIV. All prosecutions shall commence in the name and by the authority of the freemen of the State of *Vermont,* and all indictments shall conclude with these words, "against the peace and dignity of the same." The style of all process hereafter, in this State, shall be,—The State of *Vermont.*

SECTION XXV. The person of a debtor, where there is not a strong presumption of fraud, shall not be continued in prison, after delivering up, *bona fide,* all his estate, real and personal, for the use of his creditors, in such manner as shall be hereafter regulated by law. All prisoners shall be bailable by sufficient securities, unless for capital offences, when the proof is evident or presumption great.

SECTION XXVI. Excessive bail shall not be exacted for bailable offences: and all fines shall be moderate.

SECTION XXVII. That the General Assembly, when legally formed, shall appoint times and places for county elections, and at such times and places, the freemen in each county respectively, shall have the liberty of choosing the judges of inferior court of common pleas, sheriff, justices of the peace, and judges of probates, commissioned by the Governor and Council, during good behavior, removable by the General Assembly upon proof of maladministration.

SECTION XXVIII. That no person, shall be capable of holding any civil office, in this State, except he has acquired, and maintains a good moral character.

SECTION XXIX. All elections, whether by the people or in General Assembly, shall be by ballot, free and voluntary: and any elector who shall receive any gift or reward for his vote, in meat, drink, monies or otherwise, shall forfeit his right to elect at that time, and suffer such other penalty as future laws shall direct. And any person who shall, directly or indirectly, give, promise, or bestow, any such rewards to be elected, shall, thereby, be rendered incapable to serve for the ensuing year.

SECTION XXX. All fines, licence money, fees and forfeitures, shall be paid, according to the direction hereafter to be made by the General Assembly.

SECTION XXXI. All deeds and conveyances of land shall be recorded in the town clerk's office, in their respective towns.

SECTION XXXII. The printing presses shall be free to every person who undertakes to examine the proceedings of the legislature, or any part of government.

SECTION XXXIII. As every freeman, to preserve his independence (if without a sufficient estate) ought to have some profession, calling, trade or farm, whereby he may honestly subsist, there can be no necessity for, nor use in, establishing offices of profit, the usual effects of which are dependence and servility, unbecoming freemen, in the possessors or expectants; faction, contention, corruption and disorder among the people. But if any man is called into public service, to the prejudice of his private affairs, he has a right to a reasonable compensation; and whenever an office, through increase of fees, or otherwise, becomes so profitable as to occasion many to apply for it, the profits ought to be lessened by the legislature.

SECTION XXXIV. The future legislature of this State, shall regulate entails, in such manner as to prevent perpetuities.

SECTION XXXV. To deter more effectually from the commission of crimes, by continued visible punishment of long duration, and to make sanguinary punishments less necessary; houses ought to be provided for punishing, by hard labor, those who shall be convicted of crimes not capital; wherein the criminal shall be employed for the benefit of the public, or for reparation of injuries done to private persons; and all persons, at proper times, shall be admitted to see the prisoners at their labor.

SECTION XXXVI. Every officer, whether judicial, executive or military, in authority under this State, shall take the following oath or affirmation of allegiance, and general oath of office, before he enter on the execution of his office.

The Oath or Affirmation of Allegiance

"I —— do solemnly swear by the ever living God, (or affirm in presence of Almighty God,) that I will be true and faithful to the State of Vermont; and that I will not, directly or indirectly, do any act or thing, prejudicial or injurious, to the constitution or government thereof, as established by Convention."

The Oath or Affirmation of Office

"I —— do solemnly swear by the ever living God, (or affirm in presence of Almighty God) that I will faithfully execute the office of — for the — of —; and will do equal right and justice to all men, to the best of my judgment and abilities, according to law."

SECTION XXXVII. No public tax, custom or contribution shall be imposed upon, or paid by, the people of this State, except by a law for that purpose; and before any law be made for raising it, the purpose for which any tax is to be raised ought to appear clear to the legislature to be of more service to the community than the money would be, if not collected; which being well observed, taxes can never be burthens.

SECTION XXXVIII. Every foreigner of good character, who comes to settle in this State, having first taken an oath or affirmation of allegiance to the same, may purchase, or by other just means acquire, hold, and transfer, land or other real estate; and after one years residence, shall be deemed a free denizen thereof, and intitled to all the rights of a natural born subject of this State; except that he shall not be capable of being elected a representative, until after two years residence.

SECTION XXXIX. That the inhabitants of this State, shall have liberty to hunt and fowl, in seasonable times, on the lands they hold, and on other lands (not enclosed;) and, in like manner, to fish in all boatable and other waters, not private property, under proper regulations, to be hereafter made and provided by the General Assembly.

SECTION XL. A school or schools shall be established in each town, by the legislature, for the convenient instruction of youth, with such salaries to the masters, paid by each town; making proper use of school lands in each town, thereby to enable them to instruct youth at low prices. One grammar school in each county, and one university in this State, ought to be established by direction of the General Assembly.

SECTION XLI. Laws for the encouragement of virtue and prevention of vice and immorality, shall be made and constantly kept in force; and provision shall be made for their due execution; and all religious societies or bodies of men, that have or may be hereafter united and incorporated, for the advancement of religion and learning, or for other pious and charitable purposes, shall be encouraged and protected in the enjoyment of the privileges, immunities and estates which they, in justice, ought to enjoy, under such regulations, as the General Assembly of this State shall direct.

SECTION XLII. All field and staff officers, and commissioned officers of the army, and all general officers of the militia, shall be chosen by the General Assembly.

SECTION XLIII. The declaration of rights is hereby declared to be a part of the Constitution of this State, and ought never to be violated, on any pretence whatsoever.

SECTION XLIV. In order that the freedom of this Commonwealth may be preserved inviolate, forever, there shall be chosen, by ballot, by the freemen of this State, on the last Wednesday in March, in the year one thousand seven hundred and eighty-five, and on the last Wednesday in March, in every seven years thereafter, thirteen persons, who shall be chosen in the same manner the council is chosen—except they shall not be out of the Council or General Assembly—to be called the Council of Censors; who shall meet together, on the first Wednesday of June next ensuing their election; the majority of whom shall be a quorum in every case, except as to calling a Convention, in which two-thirds of the whole number elected shall agree; and whose duty it shall be to enquire whether the constitution has been preserved inviolate, in every part; and whether the legislative and executive branches of government have performed their duty as guardians of the people; or assumed to themselves, or exercised, other or greater powers, than they are entitled to by the constitution. They are also to enquire whether the public taxes have been justly laid and collected, in all parts of this Commonwealth—in what manner the public monies have been disposed of, and whether the laws have been duly executed. For these purposes they shall have power to send for persons, papers and records; they shall have authority to pass public censures—to order impeachments, and to recommend to the legislature the repealing such laws as appear to them to have been enacted contrary to the principles of the constitution. These powers they shall continue to have, for and during the space of one year from the day of their election, and no longer. The said Council of Censors shall also have power to call a

Convention, to meet within two years after their sitting, if there appears to them an absolute necessity of amending any article of this constitution which may be defective—explaining such as may be thought not clearly expressed, and of adding such as are necessary for the preservation of the rights and happiness of the people; but the articles to be amended, and the amendments proposed, and such articles as are proposed to be added or abolished, shall be promulgated at least six months before the day appointed for the election of such convention, for the previous consideration of the people, that they may have an opportunity of instructing their delegates on the subject.

Reference: Francis Newton Thorpe (ed.), *The Federal and State Constitutions, Colonial Charters, and Other Organic Laws of the States*, Vol. VI (Washington: GPO, 1909).

CONSTITUTION DEBATED, 1786; REVISED, MARCH 1787

WHEREAS all government ought to be instituted and supported for the security and protection of the community as such, and to enable the individuals, who compose it, to enjoy their natural rights, and the other blessings which the Author of existence has bestowed upon man: and whenever those great ends of government are not obtained, the people have a right, by common consent, to change it, and take such measures as to them may appear necessary to promote their safety and happiness.

And whereas the inhabitants of this State have (in consideration of protection only) heretofore acknowledged allegiance to the King of Great-Britain: and the said King has not only withdrawn that protection, but commenced and still continues to carry on, with unabated vengeance, a most cruel and unjust war against them; employing therein not only the troops of Great-Britain, but foreign mercenaries, savages, and slaves, for the avowed purpose of reducing them to a total and abject submission to the despotic domination of the British Parliament, with many more acts of

tyranny, (more fully set forth in the Declaration of Congress) whereby all allegiance and fealty to the said King and his Successors are dissolved and at an end; and all power and authority derived from him ceased in the American Colonies. And whereas the Territory, which now comprehends the State of Vermont, did antecedently of right belong to the government of New-Hampshire, and the former Governor thereof, viz. his excellency Benning Wentworth, Esq. granted many charters of lands and corporations within this State to the present inhabitants and others. And whereas the late Lieutenant-Governor Colden, of New York, with others, did, in violation, of the tenth command, covet those very lands: and by a false representation, made to the Court of Great-Britain, (in the year 1764, that for the convenience of trade and administration of justice, the inhabitants were desirous of being annexed to that government) obtained jurisdiction of those very identical lands, *ex parte*, which ever was and is disagreeable to the inhabitants. And whereas the Legislature of New-York ever have, and still continue, to disown the good people of this State, in their landed property, which will appear in the complaints hereafter inserted, and in the 36th section of their present Constitution, in which is established the Grants of Land made by that government.

They have refused to make re-grants of our lands to the original Proprietors and Occupants, unless at the exorbitant rate of 2,300 dollars fees for each township; and did enhance the quitrent three-fold, and demanded an immediate delivery of the title derived from New-Hampshire.

The Judges of their Supreme Court have made a solemn declaration, that the charters, conveyances, &c., of the lands included in the before-described premises, were utterly null and void, on which said title was founded. In consequence of which declaration, writs of possession have been by them issued, and the Sheriff of the county of Albany sent at the head of six or seven hundred men, to enforce the execution thereof.

They have passed an act, annexing a penalty thereto, of thirty pounds' fine, and six months' imprisonment, on any person who should refuse assisting the Sheriff, after being requested, for the purpose of executing writs of possession.

The Governors Dunmore, Tryon, and Colden, have made re-grants of several tracts of land included in the premises, to certain favourite land jobbers in the government of New-York, in direct violation of his Britannic Majesty's express prohibition, in the year 1767.

They have issued proclamations, wherein they have offered large sums of money for the purpose of apprehending those very persons, who have dared boldly and publickly to appear in defence of their just rights.

They did pass twelve acts of outlawry on the ninth day of March, A.D. 1774, empowering the respective Judges of their Supreme Court to award execution of death against those inhabitants in said district, that they should judge to be offenders, without trial.

They have and still continue an unjust claim to those lands, which greatly retards emigration into any settlement of this State.

They have hired foreign troops, emigrants from Scotland, at two different times, and armed them to drive us out of possession.

They have sent the Savages on our frontiers to distress us.

They have proceeded to erect the counties of Cumberland and Gloucester, and establish courts of justice there, after they were discountenanced by the authority of Great-Britain.

The free Convention of the State of New-York, at Harlem, in the year 1776, unanimously voted, "That all quitrents, formerly due to the King of Great-Britain, are now due, and owing to this Convention, or such future government as shall be hereafter established in this State."

In the several stages of the aforesaid oppressions, we have petitioned his Britannic Majesty in the most humble manner for redress, and have, at very great expense, received several reports in our favour: and in other instances, wherein we have petitioned the late legislative authority of New-York, those petitions have been treated with neglect. And whereas, the local situation of this State from New-York, which, at the extreme part, is upward of four hundred and fifty miles from the seat of that government, renders it extreme difficult to continue under the jurisdiction of said State;

Therefore it is absolutely necessary, for the welfare and safety of the inhabitants of this State, that it should be henceforth a free and independent State, and that a just, permanent, and proper form of government should exist in it, derived from and founded on the authority of the people only, agreeable to the direction of the honourable American Congress.

We the Representatives of the freemen of Vermont, in General Convention met, for the express purpose of forming such a government—confessing the goodness of the great Governor of the universe (who alone knows to what degree of earthly happiness mankind may attain by perfecting the arts of government) in permitting the people of this State, by common consent, and without violence, deliberately to form for themselves such just rules as they shall think best, for governing their future society; and being fully convinced, that it is our indispensable duty to establish such original principles of government as will best promote the general happiness of the people of this State, and their posterity, and provide for future improvements, without partiality for, or prejudice against, any particular class, sect, or denomination of men whatever; do, by virtue of authority vested in us by our constituents, ordain, declare and establish the following Declaration of Rights, and Frame of Government, to be the Constitution of this Commonwealth, and to remain in force therein forever unaltered, except in such articles as shall hereafter on experience be found to require improvement, and which shall, by the same authority of the people, fairly delegated, as this Frame of Government directs, be amended or improved, for the more effectual obtaining and securing the great end and design of all government, herein before mentioned.

Chapter I

A Declaration of The Rights of The Inhabitants of The State of Vermont

I. THAT all men are born equally free and independent, and have certain natural, inherent and unalienable rights; amongst which are, the enjoying and defending life and liberty—acquiring, possessing and protecting property—and pursuing and obtaining happiness and safety. Therefore, no male person, born in this country, or brought from over sea, ought to be holden by law to serve any person, as a servant, slave, or apprentice, after he arrives to the age of twenty-one years; nor female, in like manner, after she arrives to the age of eighteen years; unless they are bound by their own consent after they arrive to such age; or bound by law for the payment of debts, damages, fines, costs, or the like.

II. That private property ought to be subservient to public uses, when necessity requires it; nevertheless, whenever any particular man's property is taken for the use of the public, the owner ought to receive an equivalent in money.

III. That all men have a natural and unalienable right to worship Almighty God according to the dictates of their own consciences and understandings, as in their opinion shall be regulated by the word of God; and that no man ought, or of right can be compelled to attend any religious worship, or erect or support any place of worship, or maintain any minister, contrary to the dictates of his conscience; nor can any man be justly deprived or abridged of any civil right as a citizen, on account of his religious sentiments, or peculiar mode of religious worship; and that no authority can, or ought to be vested in, or assumed by any power whatsoever, that shall in any case interfere with, or in any manner control the rights of conscience, in the free exercise of religious worship: Nevertheless, every sect or denomination of Christians ought to observe the Sabbath or Lord's day, and keep up some sort of religious worship, which to them shall seem most agreeable to the revealed will of God.

IV. Every person within this Commonwealth ought to find a certain remedy, by having recourse to the laws, for all injuries or wrongs which he may receive in his person, property, or character: he ought to obtain right and justice freely, and without being obliged to purchase it—completely, and without any denial—promptly, and without delay; conformably to the laws.

V. That the people of this State, by their legal representatives, have the sole, exclusive and inherent right of governing and regulating the internal police of the same.

VI. That all power being originally inherent in, and consequently derived from the people; therefore, all officers of government, whether legislative or executive, are their trustees and servants, and at all times, in a legal way, accountable to them.

VII. That government is, or ought to be, instituted for the common benefit, protection and security of the people, nation, or community, and not for the particular emolument or advantage of any single man, family, or set of men, who are a part only of that community: and that the community hath an indubitable, unalienable, and indefeasible right, to reform or alter government, in such manner as shall be, by that community, judged to be most conducive to the public weal.

VIII. That those who are employed in the legislative and executive business of the State may be restrained from oppression, the people have a right, by their legal representatives, to enact laws for reducing their public officers to a private station, and for supplying their vacancies in a constitutional manner, by regular elections, at such periods as they may think proper.

IX. That all elections ought to be free and without corruption; and that all freemen, having a sufficient evident common interest with, and attachment to the community, have a right to elect officers, and be elected into office.

X. That every member of society hath a right to be protected in the enjoyment of life, liberty and property; and therefore is bound to contribute his proportion towards the expense of that protection, and yield his personal service, when necessary, or an equivalent thereto: but no part of a man's property can be justly taken from him, or applied to public uses, without his own consent, or that of the representative body of the freemen; nor can any man, who is conscientiously scrupulous of bearing arms, be justly compelled thereto, if he will pay such equivalent; nor are the people bound by any law, but such as they have in like manner assented to, for their common good. And previous to any law being made to raise a tax, the purpose, for which it is to be raised ought to appear evident to the Legislature to be of more service to the community, than the money would be if not collected.

XI. That in all prosecutions for criminal offences, a man hath a right to be heard by himself and his counsel—to demand the cause and nature of his accusation—to be confronted with the witnesses—to call for evidence in his favour, and a speedy public trial by an impartial jury of the country, without the unanimous consent of which jury he cannot be found guilty—nor can he be compelled to give evidence against himself—nor can any man be justly deprived of his liberty, except by the laws of the land, or the judgment of his peers.

XII. That the people have a right to hold themselves, their houses, papers and possessions, free from search or seizure: and therefore warrants, without oaths or affirmations first made, affording sufficient foundation for them, and whereby any officer or messenger may be commanded or required to search suspected places, or to seize any person or persons, his, her or their property not particularly described, are contrary to that right, and ought not to be granted.

XIII. That no warrant or writ to attach the person or estate of any freeholder within this State, shall be issued in civil action, without the person or persons, who may request such warrant or attachment, first make oath, or affirm before the authority who may be requested to issue the same, that he or they are in danger of losing his, her, or their debts.

XIV. That when an issue in fact, proper for the cognizance of a jury, is joined in a court of law, the parties have a right to a trial by jury; which ought to be held sacred.

XV. That the people have a right of freedom of speech and of writing and publishing their sentiments, concerning the transactions of government—and therefore the freedom of the press ought not to be restrained.

XVI. The freedom of deliberation, speech, and debate, in the legislature, is so essential to the rights of the people, that it cannot be the foundation of any accusation or prosecution, action or complaint, in any other court or place whatsoever.

XVII. The power of suspending laws, or the execution of laws, ought never to be exercised, but by the Legislature, or by authority derived from it, to be exercised in such particular cases only as the Legislature shall expressly provide for.

XVIII. That the people have a right to bear arms, for the defence of themselves and the State: and as standing armies, in the time of peace, are dangerous to liberty, they ought not to be kept up; and that the military should be kept under strict subordination to, and governed by the civil power.

XIX. That no person in this Commonwealth can, in any case, be subjected to law-martial or to any penalties or pains, by virtue of that law, except those employed in the army, and the militia in actual service.

XX. That frequent recurrence to fundamental principles, and a firm adherence to justice, moderation, temperance, industry, and frugality, are absolutely necessary to preserve the blessings of liberty, and keep government free; the people ought therefore to pay particular attention to these points, in the choice of officers and representatives; and have a right, in a legal way, to exact a due and constant regard to them, from their legislators and magistrats, in the making and executing such laws as are necessary for the good government of the State.

XXI. That all people have a natural and inherent right to emigrate from one State to another, that will receive them; or to form a new State in vacant countries, or in such countries as they can purchase, whenever they think that thereby they can promote their own happiness.

XXII. That the people have a right to assemble together, to consult for their common good—to instruct their representatives, and to apply to the Legislature for redress of grievances, by address, petition or remonstrance.

XXIII. That no person shall be liable to be transported out of this State, for trial for any offence committed within the same.

Chap. II

Plan or Frame of Government

SECT. I. THE Commonwealth or State of Vermont, shall be governed hereafter by a Governor, (or Lieutenant-Governor) Council, and an Assembly of the Representatives of the freemen of the same, in manner and form following:

II. The supreme legislative power shall be vested in a House of Representatives of the freemen, or Commonwealth, or State of Vermont.

III. The supreme executive power shall be vested in a Governor, (or, in his absence, a Lieutenant-Governor) and Council.

IV. Courts of justice shall be maintained in every county in this State, and also in new counties when formed; which courts shall be open for the trial of all causes proper for their cognizance, and justice shall be therein impartially administered, without corruption, or unnecessary delay. The Judges of the Supreme Court shall be Justices of the Peace throughout the State; and the several Judges of the County Courts, in their respective counties, by virtue of their offices, except in the trial of such causes as may be appealed to the County Court.

V. A future legislature may, when they shall conceive the same to be expedient and necessary, erect a Court of Chancery, with such powers as are usually exercised by that Court, or as shall appear for the interest of the Commonwealth: Provided they do not constitute themselves the Judges of the said Court.

VI. The legislative, executive and judiciary departments shall be separate and distinct, so that neither exercise the powers properly belonging to the other.

VII. In order that the freemen of this State may enjoy the benefit of election, as equally as may be, each town within this State, that consists or may consist of eighty taxable inhabitants, within one septenary or seven years next after the establishing this Constitution, may hold elections therein, and choose each two representatives; and each other inhabited town in this State may, in like manner, choose each one representative to represent them in General Assembly, during the said septenary or seven years; and after that, each inhabited town may, in like manner, hold such election, and choose each one representative forever thereafter.

VIII. The House of Representatives of the freemen of this State shall consist of persons most noted for wisdom and virtue, to be chosen by ballot by the freemen of every town in this State respectively, on the first Tuesday of September annually forever.

IX. The representatives, so chosen, (a majority of whom shall constitute a quorum for transacting any other business than raising a State tax, for which two thirds of the members elected shall be present) shall meet on the second Thursday of the succeeding October, and shall be styled, *The General Assembly of the State of Vermont*: they shall have power to choose their Speaker, Secretary of the State, their Clerk and other necessary officers of the house—sit on their own adjournments—prepare bills, and enact them into laws—judge of the elections and qualifications of their own members: they may expel members, but not for causes known to their constitutents antecedent to their election; they may administer oaths, or affirmations, in matters depending before them—redress grievances—impeach State criminals—grant charters of incorporation—constitute towns, boroughs, cities and counties: they may annually, in their first session after their election, and at other times when vacancies happen, choose Delegates to Congress: and shall also, in conjunction with the Council, annually, (or oftener if need be) elect Judges of the Supreme and several County and Probate Courts, Sheriffs and Justices of the Peace: and also with the Council, may elect Major-Generals and Brigadier-Generals, from time to time, as often as there shall be occasion; and they shall have all other powers necessary for the Legislature of a free and sovereign State: but they shall have no power to add to, alter, abolish, or infringe, any part of this Constitution.

X. The Supreme Executive Council of this State shall consist of a Governor, Lieutenant-Governor, and twelve persons, chosen in the following manner, viz. The freemen of each town shall, on the day of election for choosing representatives to attend the General Assembly, bring in their votes for Governor, with his name fairly written, to the Constable, who shall seal them up, and write on them, *Votes for the Governor,* and deliver them to the representative chosen to attend the General Assembly: and at the opening of the General Assembly, there shall be a committee appointed out of the Council and Assembly, who, after being duly sworn to the faithful discharge of their trust, shall proceed to receive, sort and count the votes for the Governor, and declare the person who has the major part of the votes to be Governor, for the year ensuing. And if there be no choice made, then the Council and General Assembly, by their joint ballot, shall make choice of a Governor.

The Lieutenant-Governor and Treasurer shall be chosen in the manner above directed. And each freeman shall give in twelve votes for twelve counsellors, in the same manner: and the twelve highest in nomination shall serve for the ensuing year a sellors.

XI. The Governor, and in his absence, the Lieutenant-Governor, with the Council, (a major part of whom, including the Governor or Lieutenant-Governor, shall be a quorum to transact business) shall have power to commissionate all officers—and also to appoint officers, except where provision is or shall be otherwise made by law, or this frame of government; and shall supply every vacancy in any office occasioned by death or otherwise, until the office can be filled in the manner directed by law or this Constitution. They are to correspond with other States—transact business with officers of government, civil and military, and to prepare such business as may appear to them necessary to lay before the General Assembly. They shall sit as Judges to hear and determine on impeachments, taking to their assistance, for advice only, the Judges of the Supreme Court; and shall have power to grant pardons, and remit fines in all cases whatsoever, except in treason and murder, in which they shall have power to grant reprieves but not to pardon, until after the end of the next session of Assembly, and except in cases of impeachment, in which there shall be no remission or mitigation of punishment, but by act of legislation. They are also to take care that the laws be faithfully executed. They are to expedite the execution of such measures as may be resolved upon by the General Assembly: and they may draw upon the Treasurer for such sums as may be appropriated by the House of Representatives. They may also lay embargoes, or prohibit the exportation of any commodity, for any time not exceeding thirty days, in the recess of the House only: they may grant such licenses as shall be directed by law, and shall have power to call together the General Assembly, when necessary, before the day to which they shall stand adjourned. The Governor shall be captain-general and commander-in-chief of the forces of the State, but shall not command in person, except advised thereto by the Council, and then only as long as they shall approve thereof: and the Lieutenant-Governor shall, by virtue of his office, be Lieutenant-General of all the forces of the State. The Governor, or Lieutenant-Governor, and the Council, shall meet at the time and place with the General Assembly: the Lieutenant-Governor shall, during the presence of the commander-in-chief, vote and act as one of the Council; and the Governor, and, in his absence, the Lieutenant-Governor, shall, by virtue of their offices, preside in Council, and have a casting, but no other vote. Every member of the Council shall be a Justice of the Peace for the whole State, by virtue of his office. The Governor and Council shall have a Secretary, and keep fair books of their proceedings, wherein any counsellor may enter his dissent, with his reasons to support it.

XII. The representatives, having met, and chosen their speaker and clerk, shall each of them, before they proceed to business, take and subscribe, as well the oath or affirmation of allegiance herein after directed (except where they shall produce certificates of their having heretofore taken and subscribed the same) as the following oath or affirmation, viz.

You—do solemnly swear, (or affirm) that, as a member of this Assembly, you will not propose or assent to any bill, vote, or resolution, which shall appear to you injurious to the people; nor do nor consent to any act or thing whatever, that shall have a tendency to lessen or abridge their rights and privileges as declared by the Constitution of this State; but will, in all things, conduct yourself as a faithful, honest representative and guardian of the people, according to the best of your judgment and abilities. (In case of an oath) So help you God. (And in case of an affirmation) Under the pains and penalties of perjury.

And each member, before he takes his seat, shall make and subscribe the following declaration, viz.

You do believe in one God, the Creator and Governor of the Universe, the rewarded of the good, and punisher of the wicked. And you do acknowledge the scriptures of the Old and New Testament to be given by divine inspiration; and own and profess the Protestant religion.

And no further or other religious test shall ever hereafter be required of any civil officer or magistrate, in this State.

XIII. The doors of the House, in which the General Assembly of this Commonwealth shall sit, shall be open for the admission of all persons who behave decently, except only when the welfare of the State may require them to be shut.

XIV. The votes and preceedings of the General Assembly shall be printed (when one third of the members think it necessary) as soon as conveniently may be, after the end of each session, with the yeas and nays on any question, when required by any member, (except where the votes shall be taken by ballot) in which case every member shall have a right to insert the reasons of his vote upon the minutes.

XV. The style of laws of this State, in future to be passed, shall be, *It is hereby enacted by the General Assembly of the State of Vermont.*

XVI. To the end that laws, before they are enacted, may be more maturely considered, and the inconvenience of hasty determinations as much as possible prevented, all bills which originate in the Assembly shall be laid before the Governor and Council for their revision and concurrence, or proposals of amendment; who shall return the same to the Assembly, with their proposals of amendment (if any) in writing: and if the same are not agreed to by the Assembly, it shall be in the power of the Governor and Council to suspend the passing of such bills until the next session of the Legislature. Provided, that if the Governor and Council shall neglect or refuse to return any such bill to the Assembly with written proposals of amendment, within five days, or before the rising of the Legislature, the same shall become a law.

XVII. No person ought, in any case, or in any time, to be declared guilty of treason or felony by the Legislature.

XVIII. Every man, of the full age of twenty-one years, having resided in this State, for the space of one whole year, next before the election of representatives, and is of a quiet and peaceable behaviour, and will take the following oath, (or affirmation) shall be entitled to all the privileges of a freeman of this State.

You solemnly swear, (or affirm) that whenever you give your vote or suffrage, touching any matter that concerns the State of Vermont, you will do it so as in your conscience you shall judge will most conduce to the best good of the same, as established by the Constitution, without fear or favour of any man.

XIX. The inhabitants of this Commonwealth shall be trained and armed for its defence, under such regulations, restrictions, and exceptions, as the General Assembly shall by law direct. The several companies of militia shall, as often as vacancies happen, elect their captains and other inferior officers; and the captains and subalterns shall nominate and recommend the field officers of their respective regiments, who shall appoint their staff-officers.

XX. All commissions shall be in the name of the freemen of the State of Vermont, sealed with the State seal, signed by the Governor, and in his absence the Lieutenant-Governor, and attested by the Secretary; which seal shall be kept by the Council.

XXI. Every officer of State, whether judicial or executive, shall be liable to be impeached by the General Assembly, either when in office, or after his resignation, or removal for mal-administration. All impeachments shall be before the Governor or Lieutenant-Governor, and Council, who shall hear and determine the same, and may award costs.

XXII. As every freeman, to preserve his independence, (if without a sufficient estate) ought to have some profession, calling, trade, or farm, whereby he may honestly subsist, there can be no necessity for, nor use in establishing offices of profit, the usual effects of which are dependence and servility, unbecoming freemen, in the possessors or expectants, faction, contention, corruption and disorder among the people. But if any man is called into public service, to the prejudice of his private affairs, he has a right to a reasonable compensation: and whenever an office, through increase of fees or otherwise, becomes so profitable as to occasion many to apply for it, the profits ought to be lessened by the legislature. And if any officer shall take greater or other fees than the laws allow him, either directly or indirectly, it shall ever after disqualify him from holding any office in this State.

XXIII. No person in this State shall be capable of holding or exercising more than one of the following offices at the same time, viz. Governor, Lieutenant-Governor, Judge of the Supreme Court, Treasurer of the State, member of the Council, member of the General Assembly, Surveyor-General, or Sheriff.

XXIV. The Treasurer of the State shall, before the Governor and Council, give sufficient security to the Secretary of the State, in behalf of the General Assembly; and each High Sheriff, before the first Judge of the County Court, to the Treasurer of their respective counties, previous to their respectively entering upon the execution of their offices, in such manner, and in such sums, as shall be directed by the Legislature.

XXV. The Treasurer's accounts shall be annually audited, and a fair state thereof laid before the General Assembly, at their session in October.

XXVI. Every officer, whether judicial, executive, or military, in authority under this State, before he enter upon the execution of his office, shall take and subscribe the following oath or affirmation of allegiance to this State, (unless he shall produce evidence that he has before taken the same) and also the following oath or affirmation of office, (except such as shall be exempted by the Legislature,) viz.

The Oath Or Affirmation Of Allegiance

You do solemnly swear (or affirm) that you will be true and faithful to the State of Vermont; and that you will not, directly nor indirectly, do any act or thing injurious to the Constitution or government thereof, as established by Convention. (If an oath) So help you God. (If an affirmation) Under the pains and penalties of perjury.

The Oath Or Affirmation Of Office

You——do solemnly swear, (or affirm) that you will faithfully execute the office of——for the—of—; and will therein do equal right and justice to all men, to the best of your judgment and abilities, according to law. (If an oath) So help you God. (If an affirmation) Under the pains and penalties of perjury.

XXVII. Any delegate to Congress may be superseded at any time, by the General Assembly appointing another in his stead. No man shall be capable of being a delegate to represent this State in Congress for more than three years, in any term of six years;—and no person, who holds any office in the gift of Congress, shall, during the time of his holding such office, be elected to represent this State in Congress.

XXVIII. Trials of issues, proper for the cognizance of a jury, in the Supreme and County Courts, shall be by jury, except where parties otherwise agree: and great care ought to be taken to prevent corruption or partiality in the choice and return, or appointment of juries.

XXIX. All prosecutions shall commence by the authority of the State of Vermont—all indictments shall conclude with these words, *Against the peace and dignity of the State.* And all fines shall be proportionate to the offences.

XXX. The person of a debtor, where there is not strong presumption of fraud, shall not be continued in prison after delivering up and assigning over, *bona fide*, all his estate, real and personal, in possession, reversion, or remainder, for the use ofe his creditors, in such manner as shall be hereafter regulated by law. And all prisoners, unless in execution, or committed for capital offences, when the proof is evident or presumption great, shall be bailable by sufficient sureties: nor shall excessive bail be exacted for bailable offences.

XXXI. All elections, whether by the people, or in General Assembly, shall be by ballot, free and voluntary: and any elector, who shall receive any gift or reward for his vote, in meat, drink, monies or otherwise, shall forfeit his right to elect at that time, and suffer such other penalty as the laws shall direct: and any person who shall, directly or indirectly, give, promise or bestow any such rewards to be elected, shall thereby be rendered incapable to serve for the ensuing year, and

be subject to such further punishment as a future Legislature shall direct.

XXXII. All deeds and conveyances of land shall be recorded in the Town Clerk's office, in their respective towns; and, for want thereof, in the County Clerk's office of the same county.

XXXIII. The Legislature shall regulate entails in such manner as to prevent perpetuities.

XXXIV. To deter more effectually from the commission of crimes, by continued visible punishment, of long duration, and to make sanguinary punishment less necessary, means ought to be provided for punishing by hard labour, those who shall be convicted of crimes not capital, whereby the criminal shall be employed for the benefit of the public, or for reparation of injuries done to private persons: and all persons, at proper times, ought to be permitted to see them at their labour.

XXXV. The estates of such persons as may destroy their own lives, shall not for that offence be forfeited, but descend or ascend in the same manner as if such persons had died in a natural way. Nor shall any article, which shall accidentally occasion the death of any person, be henceforth deemed a deodand, or in anywise forfeited on account of such misfortune.

XXXVI. Every person of good character, who comes to settle in this State, having first taken an oath or affirmation of allegiance to the same, may purchase, or by other just means, acquire, hold and transfer land, or other real estate; and, after one year's residence, shall be deemed a free denizen thereof, and entitled to all the rights of a natural born subject of this State, except that he shall not be capable of being elected Governor, Lieutenant-Governor, Treasurer, Counsellor, or Representative in Assembly, until after two years' residence.

XXXVII. The inhabitants of this State shall have liberty, in seasonable times, to hunt and fowl on the lands they hold, and on other lands not inclosed; and in like manner to fish in all boatable and other waters, not private property, under proper regulations, to be hereafter made and provided by the General Assembly.

XXXVIII. Laws for the encouragement of virtue, and prevention of vice and immorality, ought to be constantly kept in force, and duly executed; and a competent number of schools ought to be maintained in each town for the convenient instruction of youth; and one or more grammar schools be incorporated, and properly supported in each county in this State. And all religious societies, or bodies of men, that may be hereafter united or incorporated, for the advancement of religion and learning, or for other pious and charitable purposes, shall be encouraged and protected in the enjoyment of the privileges, immunities, and estates, which they in justice ought to enjoy, under such regulations as the General Assembly of this State shall direct.

XXXIX. The declaration of the political rights and privileges of the inhabitants of this State, is hereby declared to be a part of the Constitution of this Commonwealth; and ought not to be violated on any pretence whatsoever.

XL. In order that the freedom of this Commonwealth may be preserved inviolate forever, there shall be chosen by ballot, by the freemen of this State, on the last Wednesday in March, in the year one thousand seven hundred and eighty-five, and on the last Wednesday in March in every seven years thereafter, thirteen persons, who shall be chosen in the same manner the Council is chosen, except that they shall not be out of the Council or General Assembly, to be called the Council of Censors; who shall meet together on the first Wednesday of June next ensuing their election, the majority of whom shall be a quorum in every case, except as to calling a convention, in which two-thirds of the whole number elected shall agree: and whose duty it shall be to inquire whether the Constitution has been preserved inviolate in every part, during the last septenary (including the year of their service;) and whether the legislative and executive branches of government have performed their duty, as guardians of the people, or assumed to themselves, or exercised other or greater powers than they are entitled to by the Constitution: they are also to inquire, whether the public taxes have been justly laid and collected in all parts of this Commonwealth—in what manner the public monies have been disposed of—and whether the laws have been duly executed. For these purposes, they shall have power to send for persons, papers, and records; they shall have authority to pass public censures—to order impeachments—and to recommend to the Legislature the repealing such laws as appear to them to have been enacted contrary to the principles of the Constitution; these powers they shall continue to have, for, and during the space of one year from the day of their election, and no longer. The said Council of Censors shall also have power to call a Convention, to meet within two years after their sitting, if there appears to them an absolute necessity of amending any article of this Constitution which may be defective—explaining such as may be thought not clearly expressed—and of adding such as are necessary for the preservation of the rights and happiness of the people; but the articles to be amended, and the amendments proposed and such articles as are proposed to be added or abolished, shall be promulgated at least six months before the day appointed for the election of such Convention, for the previous consideration of the people, that they may have an opportunity of instructing their delegates on the subject.

By order of Convention, July 4th, 1786.
MOSES ROBINSON, *President.*
Attest: ELIJAH PAINE, *Secretary.*

Reference: Francis Newton Thorpe (ed.), *The Federal and State Constitutions, Colonial Charters, and Other Organic Laws of the States,* Vol. VI (Washington: GPO, 1909).

45

Massachusetts, June 16, 1780

The last state to ratify its constitution was Massachusetts. After the convention pledged to give the proposed constitution to the people for popular ratification, the citizenry turned it down. It was said that the towns did not think they received enough power in the constitution. Still, Massachusetts had a form of government, having adopted much of the plan John Adams had drafted for the federal constitution, before it finally ratified a constitution in 1780. The constitution of 1780, also based on Adams's previous draft, was noted for its declaration of rights, its emphasis on separation of powers, and its distrust of authority.

WHO MAY ENACT A CONSTITUTION, SEPTEMBER 17, 1776

In the House of Representatives, September 17th, 1776.

Resolved, That it be recommended to the male inhabitants of each town in this State, being free and twenty-one years of age or upwards, that they assemble as soon as they can in Town-Meeting, upon reasonable previous warning to be therefore given, according to law; and that in such Meeting, they consider and determine whether they will give their consent that the present House of Representatives of this State of the Massachusetts-Bay in New-England, together with the Council, if they consent in one Body with the House, and by equal voice, should consult, agree on, and enact such a Constitution and form of government for this State, as the said House of Representatives and Council as aforesaid, on the fullest and most mature deliberation, shall judge will most conduce to the safety, peace and happiness of this State, in all after successions and generations; and if they would direct that the same be made public for the inspection and perusal of the inhabitants, before the ratification thereof by the Assembly. . . .

J. WARREN, *Speaker*

Reference: Collections, Massachusetts Historical Society, Vol. CLXI (Boston: Charles C. Little and James Brown, 1801), 180.

VOTE ON FORMING CONSTITUTION, SEPTEMBER 27, 1776

Vote of Petersham Town Meeting, on forming a Constitution.
September 27, 1776

The question being put, whether this Town will consent that the present General Court shall form a Constitution of Government agreeable to their resolve of the 17th instant, and it passed in the negative, unanimously. Also unanimously voted, that the following draft be lodged in the Secretary's office, as the sense of this Town respecting that matter, agreeable to the resolve aforesaid.

The inhabitants, in order to express their mind respecting the forming a Constitution of Government for this State, would humbly show, that it is their opinion that it will be of little avail for this people to shed their blood and spend their treasure in opposing foreign tyranny, if, after all, we should fix a basis of Government partial, unsafe, and not fit for the enjoyment of free and virtuous men. We think that God, in his providence, has now opened a door, possibly the only one that this State will ever have, for the laying a foundation for its prosperity, peace and glory. A Constitution of Government, one levied on the laws of the people, cannot easily be altered (especially for the better), as the craftiness of designing men, if any errours are suffered to be fixed in its foundation in their favour, it will be next to impossible to remove them; therefore, in so momentous and important a matter, we would be willing to set out fair, and on the most likely ground to obtain the prize.

If we may be allowed to speak our minds freely, we apprehend that the present General Court of this State are not in a situation most likely to effect his great work to advantage, nor do we believe that when all the towns who have not sent a member, may have sent as many as the late law will allow them, that they will be in a proper situation for so great and important a business; for while the mercantile towns swarm with Representatives, the freehold interest of the country (in which we presume there is the most safety) have neglected to choose such a number as the late regulation entitles them; and the late resolve of Court does not empower any town who have a right to choose a number and have elected but one, to make any addition; and further a late General Court having taken it upon them in a thin House, constructed and without consulting the people, materially to alter the fundamental principles of representation, and as we apprehend much for the most sensibly affects us. . . .

Reference: Peter Force, *American Archives,* 5th Ser., Vol. II (Washington: GPO, 1836), 576–577.

NEW SALEM REJECTS CONSTITUTION, MAY 19, 1778

To the Honorable House of Representatives of the State of Massachusetts Bay. Gentlemen agreeable to your Resolve We have meet and Carfully Examiand the New form for a constetution and unanimasly Disaproved of it. The No Present at said meeting being, 74- - - - -

Because We conceive that there are some things contained *in it* that are Injures to the Rights of a free People—

1ly Because there is two Branches Proposed to make the Legaslative authority When we conceive that one Branch will *answer* all the Porposes of Good Government much Better then two.

2ly Because in said constetution mens worth of money seems to be Pointed out as Qualifycations But we think where the Great Auther of Natur hath furnished a man to the satisfaction of the Electors and he Legaly chosen he aught to have a *seat* and voice in any socity of men or to serve in any office whatever.

3ly Because said constetution as we conceive admitts of three times to Numeras a house since one third part the Number would Dispatch *Business* with Greater Briefness and be Less Burdensome to the State.

4ly Because the Eases method for the People Settleing their one civel Cases is Not Pointed out in this Constetution we conceive that it Would be more for the well Being of the People to have authority *in* Each town to settle their one civel affairs.- - - - -

5ly Because said Constitution Deprives the People of their just Rights of chusing their Civel and Military officers (viz) *Justices* Captains and Subboltons etc.- - - - -

6ly Because Said Constetution maks no Provision against Extravagences In Sallarys Pencions and fees we conceive that No Sallary ought to be granted Nor pencion Given or fee seet with a Less Majority then four to one.

BENJA. SOUTHWICK JUR
UR.L. PUTNAM *Selectmen*
JOHN KING

Reference: Collections, Massachusetts Historical Society, Vol. CLXI (Boston: Charles C. Little and James Brown, 1801), 366.

ESSEX RESULT, APRIL 29, 1778

Result of the Convention of Delegates holden at Ipswich in the County of Essex, who were Deputed to take into Consideration the Constitution and Form of Government proposed by the Convention of the State of Masachusetts-Bay. Newbury-Port: Printed and Sold by John Mycall. 1778.

In Convention of Delegates from the several towns of Lynn, Salem, Danvers, Wenham, Manchester, Gloucester, Ipswich, Newbury-Port, Salisbury, Methuen, Boxford, & Topsfield, holden by adjournment at Ipswich, on the twenty-ninth day of April, one thousand seven hundred & seventy-eight.

Peter Coffin Esq.; in the Chair.

The Constitution and form of Government framed by the Convention of this State, was read paragraph by paragraph, and after debate, the following votes were passed.

1. That the present situation of this State renders it best, that the framing of a Constitution therefor, should be postponed 'till the public affairs are in a more peaceable and settled condition.

2. That a bill of rights, clearly ascertaining and defining the rights of conscience, and that security of person and property, which every member in the State hath a right to expect from the supreme power thereof, ought to be settled and established, previous to the ratification of any constitution for the State.

3. That the executive power in any State, ought not to have any share or voice in the legislative power in framing the laws, and therefore, that the second article of the Constitution is liable to exception.

4. That any man who is chosen Governor, ought to be properly qualified in point of property—that the qualification therefor, mentioned in the third article of the Constitution, is not sufficient—nor is the same qualification directed to be ascertained on fixed principles, as it ought to be, on account of the fluctuation of the nominal value of money, and of property.

5. That in every free Republican Government, where the legislative power is vested in an house or houses of representatives, all the members of the State ought to be equally represented.

6. That the mode of representation proposed in the sixth article of the constitution, is not so equal a representation as can reasonably be devised.

7. That therefore the mode of representation in said sixth article is exceptionable.

8. That the representation proposed in said article is also exceptionable, as it will produce an unwieldy assembly.

9. That the mode of election of Senators pointed out in the Constitution is exceptionable.

10. That the rights of conscience, and the security of person and property each member of the State is entitled to, are not ascertained and defined in the Constitution, with a precision sufficient to limit the legislative power—and therefore, that the thirteenth article of the constitution is exceptionable.

11. That the fifteenth article is exceptionable, because the numbers that constitute a quorum in the House of Representatives and Senate, are too small.

12. That the seventeenth article of the constitution is exceptionable, because the supreme executive officer is not vested with proper authority—and because an independence between the executive and legislative body is not preserved.

13. That the nineteenth article is exceptionable, because a due independence is not kept up between the supreme legislative, judicial, and executive powers, nor between any two of them.

14. That the twentieth article is exceptionable, because the supreme executive officer hath a voice, and must be present in that Court, which alone hath authority to try impeachments.

15. That the twenty second article is exceptionable, because the supreme executive power is not preserved distinct from, and independent of, the supreme legislative power.

16. That the twenty third article is exceptionable, because the power of granting pardons is not solely vested in the supreme executive power of the State.

17. That the twenty eighth article is exceptionable, because the delegates for the Continental Congress may be elected by the House of Representatives, when all the Senators may vote against the election of those who are delegated.

18. That the thirty fourth article is exceptionable, because the rights of conscience are not therein clearly defined and ascertained; and further, because the free exercise and enjoyment of religious worship is there said to be *allowed* to all the protestants in the State, when in fact, that free exercise and enjoyment is the natural and uncontroulable right of every member of the State.

A committee was then appointed to attempt the ascertaining of the true principles of government, applicable to the territory of the Massachusetts-Bay; to state the non-conformity of the constitution proposed by the Convention of this State to those principles, and to delineate the general outlines of a constitution conformable thereto; and to report the same to this Body.

This Convention was then adjourned to the twelfth day of May next, to be holden at Ipswich.

The Convention met pursuant to adjournment, and their committee presented the following report.

The committee appointed by this Convention at their last adjournment, have proceeded upon the service assigned them. With diffidence have they undertaken the several parts of their duty, and the manner in which they have executed them, they submit to the candor of this Body. When they considered of what vast consequence, the forming of a Constitution is to the members of this State, the length of time that is necessary to canvass and digest any proposed plan of government, before the establishment of it, and the consummate coolness, and solemn deliberation which should attend, not only those gentlemen who have, reposed in them, the important trust of delineating the several lines in which the various powers of government are to move, but also all those, who are to form an opinion of the execution of that trust, your committee must be excused when they express a surprise and regret, that so short a time is allowed the freemen inhabiting the territory of the Massachusetts-Bay, to revise and comprehend the form of government proposed to them by the convention of this State, to compare it with those principles on which every free government ought to be founded, and to ascertain it's conformity or non-conformity thereto. All this is necessary to be done, before a true opinion of it's merit or demerit can be formed. This opinion is to be certified within a time which, in our apprehension, is much too short for this purpose, and to be certified by a people who, during that time, have had and will have their minds perplexed and oppressed with a variety of public cares. The committee also beg leave to observe, that the constitution proposed for public approbation, was formed by gentlemen, who, at the same time, had a large share in conducting an important war, and who were employed in carrying into execution almost all the various powers of government.

The committee however proceeded in attempting the task assigned them, and the success of that attempt is now reported.

The reason and understanding of mankind, as well as the experience of all ages, confirm the truth of this proposition, that the benefits resulting to individuals from a free government, conduce much more to their happiness, than the retaining of all their natural rights in a state of nature. These benefits are greater or less, as the form of government, and the mode of exercising the supreme power of the State, are more or less conformable to those principles of equal impartial liberty, which is the property of all men from their birth as the gift of their Creator, compared with the manners and genius of the people, their occupations, customs, modes of thinking, situation, extent of country, and numbers. If the constitution and form of government are wholly repugnant to those principles, wretched are the subjects of that State. They have surrendered a portion of their natural rights, the enjoyment of which was in some degree a blessing, and the consequence is, they find themselves stripped of the remainder. As an anodyne to compose the spirits of these slaves, and to lull them into a passively obedient state, they are told, that tyranny is preferable to no government at all; a proposition which is to be doubted, unless considered under some limitation. Surely a state of nature is more excellent than that, in which men are meanly submissive to the haughty will of an imperious tyrant, whose savage passions are not bounded by the laws of reason, religion, honor, or a regard to his subjects, and the point to which all his movements center, is the gratification of a brutal appetite. As in a state of nature much happiness cannot be enjoyed by individuals, so it has been comfortable to the inclinations of almost all men, to enter into a political society so constituted, as to remove the inconveniences they were obliged to submit to in their former state, and, at the same time, to retain all those natural rights, the enjoyment of which would be consistent with the nature of a free government, and the necessary subordination to the supreme power of the state. . . .

The freemen inhabiting the territory of the Massachusetts-Bay are now forming a political society for themselves. Perhaps their situation is more favourable in some respects, for erecting a free government, than any other people were ever favored with. That attachment to old forms, which usually embarrasses, has no place amongst them. They have the history and experience of all States before them. Mankind have been toiling through ages for their information; and the philosophers and learned men of antiquity have trimmed their midnight lamps, to transmit to them instruction. We live also in an age, when the principles of political liberty, and the foundation of governments, have been freely canvassed, and fairly settled. Yet some difficulties we have to encounter. Not content with removing our attachment to the old government, perhaps we have contracted a prejudice against some part of it without foundation. The idea of liberty has been held up in so dazzling colours, that some of us may not be willing to submit to that subordination necessary in the freest States. Perhaps we may say further, that we do not consider ourselves united as brothers, with an united interest, but have fancied a clashing of interests amongst the various classes of men, and have acquired a thirst of power, and a wish of domination, over some of the community. We are contending for freedom—Let us all be equally free—It is possible, and it is just. Our interests when candidly considered are one. Let us have a constitution founded, not upon party or prejudice—not one for to-day or to-morrow—but for posterity. . . .

A republican form is the only one consonant to the feelings of the generous and brave Americans. Let us now attend to those principles, upon which all republican governments, who boast any degree of political liberty, are founded, and which must enter into the spirit of a FREE republican constitution. For all republics are not FREE.

All men are born equally free. The rights they possess at their births are equal, and of the same kind. Some of those rights are alienable, and may be parted with for an equivalent. Others are unalienable and inherent, and of that importance, that no equivalent can be received in exchange. Sometimes we shall mention the surrendering of a power to controul our natural rights, which perhaps is speaking with more precision, than when we use the expression of parting with natural rights—but the same thing is intended. Those rights which are unalienable, and of that importance, are called the rights of conscience. We have duties, for the discharge of which we are accountable to our Creator and benefactor, which no human power can cancel. What those duties are, is determinable by right reason, which may be, and is called, a well informed conscience. What this conscience dictates as our duty, is so; and that power which assumes a controul over it, is an usurper; for no consent can be pleaded to justify the controul, as any consent in this case is void. The alienation of some rights, in themselves alienable, may be also void, if the bargain is of that nature, that no equivalent can be received. Thus, if a man surrender all his alienable rights, without reserving a controul over the supreme power, or a right to resume in certain cases, the surrender is void, for he becomes a slave; and a slave can receive no equivalent. Common equity would set aside this bargain.

When men form themselves into society, and erect a body politic or State, they are to be considered as one moral whole, which is in possession of the supreme power of the State. This supreme power is composed of the powers of each individual collected together, and VOLUNTARILY parted with by him. No individual, in this case, parts with his unalienable rights, the supreme power therefore cannot controul them. Each individual also surrenders the power of controuling his natural alienable rights, ONLY WHEN THE GOOD OF THE WHOLE REQUIRES IT. The supreme power therefore can do nothing but what is for the good of the whole; and when it goes beyond this line, it is a power usurped. If the individual receives an equivalent for the right of controul he has parted with, the surrender of that right is valid; if he receives no equivalent, the surrender is void, and the supreme power as it respects him is an usurper. If the supreme power is so directed and executed that he does not enjoy political liberty, it is an illegal power, and he is not bound to obey. . . .

Over the class of unalienable rights the supreme power hath no controul, and they ought to be clearly defined and ascertained in a BILL of RIGHTS, previous to the ratification of any constitution. The bill of rights should also contain the equivalent every man receives, as a consideration for the rights he has surrendered. This equivalent consists principally in the security of his person and property, and is also unassailable by the supreme power: for if the equivalent is taken back, those natural rights which were parted with to purchase it, return to the original proprietor, as nothing is more true, than that ALLEGIANCE AND PROTECTION ARE RECIPROCAL. . . .

That state, (other things being equal) which has reposed the supreme power in the hands of one or a small number of persons, is the most powerful state. An union, expedition, secrecy and dispatch are to be found only here. Where power is to be executed by a large number, there will not probably be either of the requisites just mentioned. Many men have various opinions: and each one will be tenacious of his own, as he thinks it preferable to any other; for when he thinks otherwise, it will cease to be his opinion. From this diversity of opinions results disunion; from disunion, a want of expedition and dispatch. And the larger the number to whom a secret is entrusted, the greater is the probability of it's disclosure. This inconvenience more fully strikes us when we consider that want of secrecy may prevent the successful execution of any measures, however excellently formed and digested.

But from a single person, or a very small number, we are not to expect that political honesty, and upright regard to the interest of the body of the people, and the civil rights of each individual, which are essential to a good and free constitution. For these qualities we are to go to the body of the people. The voice of the people is said to be the voice of God. No man will be so hardy and presumptuous, as to affirm the truth of that proposition in it's fullest extent. But if this is considered as the intent of it, that the people have always a disposition to promote their own happiness, and that when they have time to be informed, and the necessary means of information given them, they will be able to determine upon the necessary measures therefor, no man, of a tolerable acquaintance with mankind, will deny the truth of it. . . .

Yet, when we are forming a Constitution, by deductions that follow from established principles, (which is the only good method of forming one for futurity,) we are to look further than to the bulk of the people, for the greatest wisdom, firmness, consistency, and perseverance. These qualities will most probably be found amongst men of education and fortune. From such men we are to expect genius cultivated by reading, and all the various advantages and assistances, which art, and a liberal education aided by wealth, can furnish. From these result learning, a thorough knowledge of the interests of their country, when considered abstractedly, when compared with the neighbouring States, and when with those more remote, and an acquaintance with it's produce and manufacture, and it's exports and imports. All these are necessary to be known, in order to determine what is the true interest of any state; and without that interest is ascertained, impossible will it be to discover, whether a variety of certain laws may be beneficial or hurtful. From gentlemen whose private affairs compel them to take care of their own household, and deprive them of leisure, these qualifications are not to be generally expected, whatever class of men they are enrolled in.

Let all these respective excellencies be united. Let the supreme power be so disposed and ballanced, that the laws may have in view the interest of the whole; let them be wisely and consistently framed for that end, and firmly adhered to; and let them be executed with vigour and dispatch.

Before we proceed further, it must be again considered, and kept always in view, that we are not attempting to form a temporary constitution, one adjusted only to our present circumstances. We wish for one founded upon such principles as will secure to us freedom and happiness, however our circumstances may vary. One that will smile amidst the declensions of European and Asiatic empires, and survive the rude storms of time. It is not therefore to be understood, that all the men of fortune of the present day, are men of wisdom and learning, or that they are not. Nor that the bulk of the people, the farmers, the merchants, the tradesmen, and labourers, are all honest and upright, with single views to the public good, or that they are not. In each of the classes there are undoubtedly exceptions, as the rules laid down are general. The proposition is only this. That among gentlemen of education, fortune and leisure, we shall find the largest number of men,

possessed of wisdom, learning, and a firmness and consistency of character. That among the bulk of the people, we shall find the greatest share of political honesty, probity, and a regard to the interest of the whole, of which they compose the majority. That wisdom and firmness are not sufficient without good intentions, nor the latter without the former. The conclusion is, let the legislative body unite them all. The former are called the excellencies that result from an aristocracy; the latter, those that result from a democracy.

The supreme power is considered as including the legislative, judicial, and executive powers. The nature and employment of these several powers deserve a distinct attention.

The legislative power is employed in making laws, or prescribing such rules of action to every individual in the state, as the good of the whole requires, to be conformed to by him in his conduct to the governors and governed, with respect both to their persons and property, according to the several relations he stands in. What rules of action the good of the whole requires, can be ascertained only by the majority, for a reason formerly mentioned. Therefore the legislative power must be so formed and exerted, that in prescribing any rule of action, or, in other words, enacting any law, the majority must consent. This may be more evident, when the fundamental condition on which every man enters into society, is considered. No man consented that his natural alienable rights should be wantonly controuled: they were controulable, only when that controul should be subservient to the good of the whole; and that subserviency, from the very nature of government, can be determined but by one absolute judge. The minority cannot be that judge, because then there may be two judges opposed to each other, so that this subserviency remains undetermined. Now the enacting of a law, is only the exercise of this controul over the natural alienable rights of each member of the state; and therefore this law must have the consent of the majority, or be invalid, as being contrary to the fundamental condition of the original social contract. In a state of nature, every man had the sovereign controul over his own person.

He might also have, in that state, a qualified property. Whatever lands or chattels he had acquired the peaceable possession of, were exclusively his, by right of occupancy or possession. For while they were unpossessed he had a right to them equally with any other man, and therefore could not be disturbed in his possession, without being injured; for no man could lawfully dispossess him, without having a better right, which no man had. Over this qualified property every man in a state of nature had also a sovereign controul. And in entering into political society, he surrendered this right of controul over his person and property, (with an exception to the rights of conscience) to the supreme legislative power, to be exercised by that power, *when the good of the whole demanded it*. This was all the right he could surrender, being all the alienable right of which he was possessed. The only objects of legislation therefore, are the person and property of the individuals which compose the state. If the law affects only the persons of the members, the consent of a majority of any members is sufficient. If the law affects the property only, the consent of those who hold a majority of the property is enough. If it affects, (as it will very frequently, if not always,) but the person and property, the consent of a majority of the members, and of those members also who hold a majority of the property, is necessary. If the consent of the latter is not obtained, their interest is taken from them against their consent, and their boasted security of property is vanished. Those who make the law, in this case give and grant what is not theirs. The law, in it's principles, becomes a second stamp act. Lord Chatham very finely ridiculed the British house of commons upon that principle. 'You can give and grant, said he, only your own. Here you give and grant, what? The property of the Americans.' The people of the Massachusetts-Bay then thought his Lordship's ridicule well pointed. And would they be willing to merit the same? Certainly they will agree in the principle, should they mistake the application. The laws of the province of Massachusetts-Bay adopted the same principle, and very happily applied it. As the votes of proprietors of common

and undivided lands in their meetings, can affect only their property, therefore, the votes shall be collected according to the respective interests of the proprietors. If each member, without regard to his property, has equal influence in legislation with any other, it follows, that some members enjoy greater benefits and powers in legislation than others, when these benefits and powers are compared with the rights parted with to purchase them. For the property-holder parts with the controul over his person, as well as he who hath no property, and the former also parts with the controul over his property, of which the latter is destitute. Therefore to constitute a perfect law in a free state, affecting the persons and property of the members, it is necessary that the law be for the good of the whole, which is to be determined by a majority of the members, and that majority should include those, who possess a major part of the property in the state.

The judicial power follows next after the legislative power; for it cannot act, until after laws are prescribed. Every wise legislator annexes a sanction to his laws, which is most commonly penal, (that is) a punishment either corporal or pecuniary, to be inflicted on the member who shall infringe them. It is the part of the judicial power (which in this territory has always been, and always ought to be, a court and jury) to ascertain the member who hath broken the law. Every man is to be presumed innocent, until the judicial power hath determined him guilty. When that decision is known, the law annexes the punishment, and the offender is turned over to the executive arm, by whom it is inflicted on him. The judicial power hath also to determine what legal contracts have been broken, and what member hath been injured by a violation of the law, to consider the damages that have been sustained, and to ascertain the recompense. The executive power takes care that this recompense is paid.

The executive power is sometimes divided into the external executive, and internal executive. The former comprehends war, peace, the sending and receiving ambassadors, and whatever concerns the transactions of the state with any other independent state. The confederation of the United States of America hath lopped off this branch of the executive, and placed it in Congress. We have therefore only to consider the internal executive power, which is employed in the peace, security and protection of the subject and his property, and in the defence of the state. The executive power is to marshal and command her militia and armies for her defence, to enforce the law, and to carry into execution all the orders of the legislative powers.

A little attention to the subject will convince us, that these three powers ought to be in different hands, and independent of one another, and so ballanced, and each having that check upon the other, that their independence shall be preserved—If the three powers are united, the government will be absolute, *whether these powers are in the hands of one or a large number.* The same party will be the legislator, accuser, judge and executioner; and what probability will an accused person have of an acquittal, however innocent he may be, when his judge will be also a party.

If the legislative and judicial powers are united, the maker of the law will also interpret it; and the law may then speak a language, dictated by the whims, the caprice, or the prejudice of the judge, with impunity to him—And what people are so unhappy as those, whose laws are uncertain. It will also be in the breast of the judge, when grasping after his prey, to make a retrospective law, which shall bring the unhappy offender within it; and this also he can do with impunity—The subject can have no peaceable remedy—The judge will try himself, and an acquittal is the certain consequence. He has it also in his power to enact any law, which may shelter him from deserved vengeance.

Should the executive and legislative powers be united, mischiefs the most terrible would follow. The executive would enact those laws it pleased to execute, and no others—The judicial power would be set aside as inconvenient and tardy—The security and protection of the subject would be a shadow—The executive power would make itself absolute, and the government end in a tyranny— Lewis the eleventh of France, by cunning and treachery compleated the union of the executive and legislative powers of that kingdom, and upon that union established a system of tyranny. France was formerly under a free government.

The assembly or representatives of the united states of Holland, exercise the executive and legislative powers, and the government there is absolute.

Should the executive and judicial powers be united, the subject would then have no permanent security of his person and property. The executive power would interpret the laws and bend them to his will; and, as he is the judge, he may leap over them by artful constructions, and gratify, with impunity, the most rapacious passions. Perhaps no cause in any state has contributed more to promote internal convulsions, and to stain the scaffold with it's best blood, than this unhappy union. And it is an union which the executive power in all states, hath attempted to form: if that could not be compassed, to make the judicial power dependent upon it. Indeed the dependence of any of these powers upon either of the others, which in all states has always been attempted by one or the other of them, has so often been productive of such calamities, and of the shedding of such oceans of blood, that the page of history seems to be one continued tale of human wretchedness.

The following principles now seem to be established.

1. That the supreme power is limited, and cannot controul the unalienable rights of mankind, nor resume the equivalent (that is, the security of person and property) which each individual receives, as a consideration for the alienable rights he parted with in entering into political society.

2. That these unalienable rights, and this equivalent, are to be clearly defined and ascertained in a BILL of RIGHTS, previous to the ratification of any constitution.

3. That the supreme power should be so formed and modelled, as to exert the greatest possible power, wisdom, and goodness.

4. That the legislative, judicial, and executive powers, are to be lodged in different hands, that each branch is to be independent, and further, to be so ballanced, and be able to exert such

checks upon the others, as will preserve it from a dependence on, or an union with them.

5. That government can exert the greatest power when it's supreme authority is vested in the hands of one or a few.

6. That the laws will be made with the greatest wisdom, and best intentions, when men, of all the several classes in the state concur in the enacting of them.

7. That a government which is so constituted, that it cannot afford a degree of political liberty nearly equal to all it's members, is not founded upon principles of freedom and justice, and where any member enjoys no degree of political liberty, the government, so far as it respects him, is a tyranny, for he is controuled by laws to which he has never consented.

8. That the legislative power of a state hath no authority to controul the natural rights of any of it's members, unless the good of the whole requires it.

9. That a majority of the state is the only judge when the general good does require it.

10. That where the legislative power of the state is so formed, that a law may be enacted by the minority, each member of the state does not enjoy political liberty.

And

11. That in a free government, a law affecting the person and property of it's members, is not valid, unless it has the consent of a majority of the members, which majority should include those, who hold a major part of the property in the state.

It may be necessary to proceed further, and notice some particular principles, which should be attended to in forming the three several powers in a free republican government.

The first important branch that comes under our consideration, is the legislative body. Was the number of the people so small, that the whole could meet together without inconvenience, the opinion of the majority would be more easily known. But, besides the inconvenience of assembling such numbers, no great advantages could follow. Sixty thousand people could not discuss with candor, and determine with deliberation. Tumults, riots, and murder would be the result. But the impracticability of forming such an assembly, renders it needless to make any further observations. The opinions and consent of the majority must be collected from persons, delegated by every freeman of the state for that purpose. Every freeman, who hath sufficient discretion, should have a voice in the election of his legislators. To speak with precision, in every free state where the power of legislation is lodged in the hands of one or more bodies of representatives elected for that purpose, the person of every member of the state, and all the property in it, ought to be represented, because they are objects of legislation. All the members of the state are qualified to make the election, unless they have not sufficient discretion, or are so situated as to have no wills of their own; persons not twenty one years old are deemed of the former class, from their want of years and experience. The municipal law of this country will not trust them with the disposition of their lands, and consigns them to the care of their parents or guardians. Women what age soever they are of, are also considered as not having a sufficient acquired discretion; not from a deficiency in their mental powers, but from the natural tenderness and delicacy of their minds, their retired mode of life, and various domestic duties. These concurring, prevent that promiscuous intercourse with the world, which is necessary to qualify them for electors. Slaves are of the latter class and have no wills. But are slaves members of a free government? We feel the absurdity, and would to God, the situation of America and the tempers of it's inhabitants were such, that the slave-holder could not be found in the land.

The rights of representation should be so equally and impartially distributed, that the representatives should have the same views, and interests with the people at large. They should think, feel, and act like them, and in fine, should be an exact miniature of their constituents. They should be (if we may use the expression) the whole body politic, with all it's property, rights, and priviledges, reduced to a smaller scale, every part being diminished in just proportion. To pursue the metaphor. If in adjusting the representation of freemen, any ten are reduced into one, all the other tens should be alike reduced: or if any hundred should be reduced to one, all the other hundreds should have just the same reduction. The representation ought also to be so adjusted, that it should be the interest of the representatives at all times, to do justice, therefore equal interest among the people, should have equal interest among the body of representatives. The majority of the representatives should also represent a majority of the people, and the legislative body should be so constructed, that every law affecting property, should have the consent of those who hold a majority of the property. The law would then be determined to be for the good of the whole by the proper judge, the majority, and the necessary consent thereto would be obtained: and all the members of the State would enjoy political liberty, and an equal degree of it. If the scale to which the body politic is to be reduced, is but a little smaller than the original, or, in other words, if a small number of freemen should be reduced to one, that is, send one representative, the number of representatives would be too large for the public good. The expences of government would be enormous. The body would be too unwieldy to deliberate with candor and coolness. The variety of opinions and oppositions would irritate the passions. Parties would be formed and factions engendered. The members would list under the banners of their respective leaders: address and intrigue would conduct the debates, and the result would tend only to promote the ambition or interest of a particular party. Such has always been in some degree, the course and event of debates instituted and managed by a large multitude.

For these reasons, some foreign politicians have laid it down as a rule, that no body of men larger than a hundred, would transact business well: and Lord Chesterfield called the British house of commons a mere mob, because of the number of men which composed it.

Elections ought also to be free. No bribery, corruption, or undue influence should have place. They stifle the free voice of the people, corrupt their morals, and introduce a degeneracy of manners, a supineness of temper, and an inattention to their liberties, which pave the road for the approach of tyranny, in all it's frightful forms. . . .

The rights of representation should also be held sacred and inviolable, and for this purpose, representation should be fixed upon known and easy principles; and the constitution should make provision, that recourse should constantly be had to those principles within a very small period of years, to rectify the errors that will creep in through lapse of time, or alteration of situations. The want of fixed principles of government, and a stated regular recourse to them, have produced the dissolution of all states, whose constitutions have been transmitted to us by history.

But the legislative power must not be trusted with one assembly. A single assembly is frequently influenced by the vices, follies, passions, and prejudices of an individual. It is liable to be avaricious, and to exempt itself from the burdens it lays upon it's constituents. It is subject to ambition, and after a series of years, will be prompted to vote itself perpetual. The long parliament in England voted itself perpetual, and thereby, for a time, destroyed the political liberty of the subject. Holland was governed by one representative assembly annually elected. They afterwards voted themselves from annual to septennial; then for life; and finally exerted the power of filling up all vacancies, without application to their constituents. The government of Holland is now a tyranny *though a republic*.

The result of a single assembly will be hasty and indigested, and their judgments frequently absurd and inconsistent. There must be a second body to revise with coolness and wisdom, and to controul with firmness, independent upon the first, either for their creation, or existence. Yet the first must retain a right to a similar revision and controul over the second.

Let us now ascertain some particular principles which should be attended to, in forming the executive power.

When we recollect the nature and employment of this power, we find that it ought to be conducted with vigour and dispatch. It should be able to execute the laws without opposition, and to controul all the turbulent spirits in the state, who should infringe them. If the laws are not obeyed, the legislative power is vain, and the judicial is mere pageantry. As these laws, with their several sanctions, are the only securities of person and property, the members of the state can confide in, if they lie dormant through failure of execution, violence and oppression will erect their heads, and stalk unmolested through the land. The judicial power ought to discriminate the offender, as soon after the commission of the offence, as an impartial trial will admit; and the executive arm to inflict the punishment immediately after the criminal is ascertained. This would have an happy tendency to prevent crimes, as the commission of them would awaken the attendant idea of punishment; and the hope of an escape, which is often an inducement, would be cut off. The executive power ought therefore in these cases, to be exerted with union, vigour, and dispatch. Another duty of that power is to arrest offenders, to bring them to trial. This cannot often be done, unless secrecy and expedition are used. The want of these two requisites, will be more especially inconvenient in repressing treasons, and those more enormous offences which strike at the happiness, if not existence of the whole. Offenders of these classes do not act alone. Some number is necessary to the compleating of the crime. Cabals are formed with art, and secrecy presides over their councils; while measures the most fatal are the result, to be executed by desperation. On these men the thunder of the state should be hurled with rapidity; for if they hear it roll at a distance, their danger is over. When they gain intelligence of the process, they abscond, and wait a more favourable opportunity. If that is attended with difficulty, they destroy all the evidence of their guilt, brave government, and deride the justice and power of the state.

It has been observed likewise, that the executive power is to act as Captain-General, to marshal the militia and armies of the state, and, for her defence, to lead them on to battle. These armies should always be composed of the militia or body of the people. Standing armies are a tremendous curse to a state. In all periods in which they have existed, they have been the scourge of mankind. In this department, union, vigour, secrecy,

and dispatch are more peculiarly necessary. Was one to propose a body of militia, over which two Generals, with equal authority, should have the command, he would be laughed at. Should one pretend, that the General should have no controul over his subordinate officers, either to remove them or to supply their posts, he would be pitied for his ignorance of the subject he was discussing. It is obviously necessary, that the man who calls the militia to action, and assumes the military controul over them in the field, should previously know the number of his men, their equipments and residence, and the talents and tempers of the several ranks of officers, and their respective departments in the state, that he may wisely determine to whom the necessary orders are to be issued. Regular and particular returns of these requisites should be frequently made. Let it be enquired, are these returns to be made only to the legislative body, or a branch of it, which necessarily moves slow?—Is the General to go to them for information? intreat them to remove an improper officer, and give him another they shall chuse? and in fine is he to supplicate his orders from them, and constantly walk where their leading-strings shall direct his steps? If so, where are the power and force of the militia—where the union—where the dispatch and profound secrecy? Or shall these returns be made to him?—when he may see with his own eyes—be his own judge of the merit, or demerit of his officers—discern their various talents and qualifications, and employ them as the service and defence of his country demand. Besides, the legislative body or a branch of it is local—they cannot therefore personally inform themselves of these facts, but must judge upon trust. The General's opinion will be founded upon his own observations—the officers and privates of the militia will act under his eye: and, if he has it in his power immediately to promote or disgrace them, they will be induced to noble exertions. It may further be observed here, that if the subordinate civil or military executive officers are appointed by the legislative body or a branch of it, the former will become dependent upon the latter, and the necessary independence of either the legislative or executive powers upon the other is wanting. The legislative power will have that undue influence over the executive which will amount to a controul, for the latter will be their creatures, and will fear their creators.

One further observation may be pertinent. Such is the temper of mankind, that each man will be too liable to introduce his own friends and connexions into office, without regarding the public interest. If one man or a small number appoint, their connexions will probably be introduced. If a large number appoint, all their connexions will receive the same favour. The smaller the number appointing, the more contracted are their connexions, and for that reason, there will be a greater probability of better officers, as the connexions of one man or a very small number can fill but a very few of the offices. When a small number of men have the power of appointment, or the management in any particular department, their conduct is accurately noticed. On any miscarriage or imprudence the public resentment lies with weight. All the eyes of the people are converted to a point, and produce that attention to their censure, and that fear of misbehaviour, which are the greatest security the state can have, of the wisdom and prudence of its servants. This observation will strike us, when we recollect that many a man will zealously promote an affair in a public assembly, of which he is but one of a large number, yet, at the same time, he would blush to be thought the sole author of it. For all these reasons, the supreme executive power should be rested in the hands of one or of a small number, who should have the appointment of all subordinate executive officers. Should the supreme executive officer be elected by the legislative body, there would be a dependence of the executive power upon the legislative. Should he be elected by the judicial body, there also would be a dependence. The people at large must therefore designate the person, to whom they will delegate this power. And upon the people, there ought to be a dependence of all the powers in government, for all the officers in the state are but the servants of the people.

We have not noticed the navy-department. The conducting of that department is indisputably in the supreme executive power: and we suppose, that all the observations respecting the Captain-General, apply to the Admiral.

We are next to fix upon some general rules which should govern us in forming the judicial power. This power is to be independent upon the executive and legislative. The judicial power should be a court and jury, or as they are commonly called, the Judges and jury. The jury are the peers or equals of every man, and are to try all facts. The province of the Judges is to preside in and regulate all trials, and ascertain the law. We shall only consider the appointment of the Judges. The same power which appoints them, ought not to have the power of removing them, not even for misbehavior. That conduct only would then be deemed misbehavior which was opposed to the will of the power removing. A removal in this case for proper reasons, would not be often attainable: for to remove a man from an office, because he is not properly qualified to discharge the duties of it, is a severe censure upon that man or body of men who appointed him—and mankind do not love to censure themselves. Whoever appoints the judges, they ought not to be removable at pleasure, for they will then feel a dependence upon that man or body of men who hath the power of removal. Nor ought they to be dependent upon either the executive or legislative power for their salaries; for if they are, that power on whom they are thus dependent, can starve them into a compliance. One of these two powers should appoint, and the other remove. The legislative will not probably appoint so good men as the executive, for reasons formerly mentioned. The former are composed of a large body of men who have a numerous train of friends and connexions, and they do not hazard their reputations, which the executive will. It has often been mentioned that where a large body of men are responsible for any measures, a regard to their reputations, and to the public opinion, will not prompt them to use that care and precaution, which such regard will prompt one or a few to make use of. Let one more observation be now introduced to confirm it. Every man has some friends and dependents who will endeavor to snatch him from the public hatred. One man has but a few comparatively, they are not numerous enough to protect him, and he falls a victim to his own misconduct. When measures are conducted by a large number, their friends and connexions are numerous and noisy—they are dispersed through the State—their clamors stifle the execrations of the people, whose groans cannot even be heard. But to resume, neither will the executive body be the most proper judge when to remove. If this body is judge, it must also be the accuser, or the legislative body, or a branch of it, must be—If the executive body complains, it will be both accuser and judge—If the complaint is preferred by the legislative body, or a branch of it, when the judges are appointed by the legislative body, then a body of men who were concerned in the appointment, must in most cases complain of the impropriety of their own appointment. Let therefore the judges be appointed by the executive body—let their salaries be independent—and let them hold their places during good behaviour—Let their misbehaviour be determinable by the legislative body—Let one branch thereof impeach, and the other judge. Upon these principles the judicial body will be independent so long as they behave well and a proper court is appointed to ascertain their mal-conduct.

The Committee afterwards proceeded to consider the Constitution framed by the Convention of this State. They have examined that Constitution with all the care the shortness of the time would admit. And they are compelled, though reluctantly to say, that some of the principles upon which it is founded, appeared to them inconsonant, not only to the natural rights of mankind, but to the fundamental condition of the original social contract, and the principles of a free republican government. In that form of government the governor appears to be the supreme executive officer, and the legislative power is in an house of representatives and senate. It may be necessary to descend to a more particular consideration of the several articles of that constitution.

The second article thereof appears exceptionable upon the principles we have already attempted to establish, because the supreme executive officer hath a seat and voice in one branch of the legislative body, and is assisting in originating and framing the laws, the Governor being entitled to a seat and voice in the Senate, and to preside in it, and may thereby have that influence in the legislative body, which the supreme executive officer ought not to have.

The third article among other things, ascertains the qualifications of the Governor, Lieutenant Governor, Senators and Representatives respecting property—The estate sufficient to qualify a man for Governor is so small, it is hardly any qualification at all. Further, the method of ascertaining the value of the estates of the officers aforesaid is vague and uncertain as it depends upon the nature and quantity of the currency, and the encrease of property, and not upon any fixed principles. This article therefore appears to be exceptionable.

The sixth article regulates the election of representatives. So many objections present themselves to this article, we are at a loss which first to mention. The representation is grossly unequal, and it is flagrantly unjust. It violates the fundamental principle of the original social contract, and introduces an unwieldy and expensive house. Representation ought to be equal upon the principles formerly mentioned. By this article any corporation, however small, may send one representative, while no corporation can send more than one, unless it has three hundred freemen. Twenty corporations (of three hundred freemen in each) containing in the whole six thousand freemen, may send forty representatives, when one corporation, which shall contain six thousand two hundred and twenty, can send but nineteen. One third of the state may send a majority of the representatives, and all the laws may be enacted by a minority—Do all the members of the state then, enjoy political liberty? Will they not be controuled by laws enacted against their consent? When we go further and find, that sixty members make an house, and that the concurrence of thirty one (which is about one twelfth of what may be the present number of representatives) is sufficient to bind the persons and properties of the members of the State, we stand amazed, and are sorry that any well disposed Americans were so inattentive to the consequences of such an arrangement.

The number of representatives is too large to debate with coolness and deliberation, the public business will be protracted to an undue length and the pay of the house is enormous. As the number of freemen in the state encreases, these inconveniences will encrease; and in a century, the house of representatives will, from their numbers, be a mere mob. Observations upon this article croud upon us, but we will dismiss it, with wishing that the mode of representation there proposed, may be candidly compared with the principles which have been already mentioned in the course of our observations upon the legislative power, and upon representation in a free republic.

The ninth article regulates the election of Senators, which we think exceptionable. As the Senators for each district will be elected by all the freemen in the state properly qualified, a trust is reposed in the people which they are unequal to. The freemen in the late province of Main, are to give in their votes for senators in the western district, and so, on the contrary. Is it supposeable that the freemen in the county of Lincoln can judge of the political merits of a senator in Berkshire? Must not the several corporations in the state, in a great measure depend upon their representatives for information? And will not the house of representatives in fact chuse the senators? That independence of the senate upon the house, which the constitution seems to have intended, is visionary, and the benefits which were expected to result from a senate, as one distinct branch of the legislative body, will not be discoverable.

The tenth article prescribes the method in which the Governor is to be elected. This method is open to, and will introduce bribery and corruption, and also originate parties and factions in the state. The Governor of Rhode-Island was formerly elected in this manner, and we all know how long a late Governor there, procured his re-election by methods the most unjustifiable. Bribery was attempted in an open and flagrant manner.

The thirteenth article ascertains the authority of the general court, and by that article we find

their power is limited only by the several articles of the constitution. We do not find that the rights of conscience are ascertained and defined, unless they may be thought to be in the thirty fourth article. That article we conceive to be expressed in very loose and uncertain terms. What is a *religious* profession and worship of God, has been disputed for sixteen hundred years, and the various sects of christians have not yet settled the dispute. What is a free exercise and enjoyment of religious worship has been, and still is, a subject of much altercation. And this free exercise and enjoyment is said to be *allowed* to the protestants of this state by the constitution, when we suppose it to be an unalienable right of all mankind, which no human power can wrest from them. We do not find any bill of rights either accompanying the constitution, or interwoven with it, and no attempt is made to define and secure that protection of the person and property of the members of the state, which the legislative and executive bodies cannot withhold, unless the general words *of confirming the right to trial by jury*, should be considered as such definition and security. We think a bill of rights ascertaining and clearly describing the rights of conscience, and that security of person and property, the supreme power of the state is bound to afford to all the members thereof, ought to be fully ratified, before, or at the same time with, the establishment of any constitution.

The fifteenth article fixes the number which shall constitute a quorum in the senate and house of representatives—We think these numbers much too small—This constitution will immediately introduce about three hundred and sixty members into the house. If sixty make a quorum, the house may totally change its members six different times; and it probably will very often in the course of a long session, be composed of such a variety of members, as will retard the public business, and introduce confusion in the debates, and inconsistency in the result. Besides the number of members, whose concurrence is necessary to enact a law, is so small, that the subjects of the state will have no security, that the laws which are to controul their natural rights, have the consent of a majority of the freemen. The same reasoning applies to the senate, though not so strikingly, as a quorum of that body must consist of nearly a third of the senators. . . .

The judges by the twenty fourth article are to hold their places during good behaviour, but we do not find that their salaries are any where directed to be fixed. The house of representatives may therefore starve them into a state of dependence.

The twenty-eighth article determines the mode of electing and removing the delegates for Congress. It is by joint ballot of the house and Senate. These delegates should be some of the best men in the State. Their abilities and characters should be thoroughly investigated. This will be more effectually done, if they are elected by the legislative body, each branch having a right to originate or negative the choice, and removal. And we cannot conceive why they should not be elected in this manner, as well as all officers who are annually appointed with annual grants of their sallaries, as is directed in the nineteenth article. By the mode of election now excepted against, the house may choose their delegates, altho' every Senator should vote against their choice.

The thirty-fourth article respecting liberty of conscience, we think exceptionable, but the observations necessary to be made thereon, were introduced in animadverting upon the thirteenth article.

The Committee have purposely been as concise as possible in their observations upon the Constitution proposed by the Convention of this State—Where they thought it was non-conformable to the principles of a free republican government, they have ventured to point out the non-conformity—Where they thought it was repugnant to the original social contract, they have taken the liberty to suggest that repugnance—And where they were persuaded it was founded in political injustice, they have dared to assert it. . . .

[There follows a detailed scheme for the legislative, executive and judicial branches of government.]

The committee have only further to report, that the inhabitants of the several towns who deputed delegates for this convention, be seriously advised, and solemnly exhorted, as they value the political freedom and happiness of themselves and of their posterity, to convene all the freemen of their several towns in town meeting, for this purpose regularly notified, and that they do unanimously vote their disapprobation of the constitution and form of government, framed by the convention of this state; that a regular return of the same be made to the secretary's office, that it may there remain a grateful monument to our posterity of that consistent, impartial and persevering attachment to political, religious, and civil liberty, which actuated their fathers, and in defence of which, they bravely fought, chearfully bled, and gloriously died.

The above report being read was accepted.
Attest,
PETER COFFIN, *Chairman.*

Reference: Jack R. Pole (ed.), *The Revolution in America* (Stanford: Stanford University Press, 1970).

CONSTITUTION, JUNE 16, 1780

Preamble

The end of the institution, maintenance, and administration of government, is to secure the existence of the body politic, to protect it, and to furnish the individuals who compose it with the power of enjoying in safety and tranquillity their natural rights, and the blessings of life: and whenever these great objects are not obtained, the people have a right to alter the government, and to take measures necessary for their safety, prosperity, and happiness.

The body politic is formed by a voluntary association of individuals: it is a social compact, by which the whole people covenants with each citizen, and each citizen with the whole people, that all shall be governed by certain laws for the common good. It is the duty of the people, therefore, in framing a constitution of government, to provide for an equitable mode of making laws, as well as for an impartial interpretation and a faithful execution of them; that every man may, at all times, find his security in them.

We, therefore, the people of Massachusetts, acknowledging, with grateful hearts, the goodness of the great Legislator of the universe, in affording us, in the course of His providence, an opportunity, deliberately and peaceably, without fraud, violence, or surprise, of entering into an original, explicit, and solemn compact with each other; and of forming a new constitution of civil government, for ourselves and posterity; and devoutly imploring His direction in so interesting a design, do agree upon, ordain, and establish, the following *Declaration of Rights, and Frame of Government,* as the CONSTITUTION OF THE COMMONWEALTH OF MASSACHUSETTS.

Part the First

A declaration of the rights of the inhabitants of the commonwealth of massachusetts

ARTICLE I. All men are born free and equal, and have certain natural, essential, and unalienable rights; among which may be reckoned the right of enjoying and defending their fives and liberties; that of acquiring, possessing, and protecting property; in fine, that of seeking and obtaining their safety and happiness.

II. It is the right as well as the duty of all men in society, publicly, and at stated seasons, to worship the SUPREME BEING, the great Creator and Preserver of the universe. And no subject shall be hurt, molested, or restrained, in his person, liberty, or estate, for worshipping GOD in the manner and season most agreeable to the dictates of his own conscience: or for his religious profession of sentiments; provided he doth not disturb the public peace, or obstruct others in their religious worship.

III. a[As the happiness of a people, and the good order and preservation of civil government, essentially depend upon piety, religion, and morality; and as these cannot be generally diffused through a community but by the institution of the public worship of GOD, and of public instructions in piety, religion, and morality: Therefore, to promote their happiness, and to secure the good order and preservation of their government, the people of this commonwealth have a right to invest their legislature with power to authorize and require, and the legislature shall, from time to time, authorize and require, the several towns, parishes, precincts, and other bodies politic, or religious societies, to make suitable provision, at their own expense, for the institution of the public worship of GOD, and for the support and maintenance of public Protestant teachers of piety, religion, and morality, in all cases where such provision shall not be made voluntarily.

And the people of this commonwealth have also a right to, and do, invest their legislature with authority to enjoin upon all the subjects an attendance upon the instructions of the public teachers aforesaid, at stated times and seasons, if there be any on whose instructions they can conscientiously and conveniently attend.

Provided, notwithstanding, that the several towns, parishes, precincts, and other bodies politic, or religious societies, shall, at all times, have the exclusive right of electing their public teachers, and of contracting with them for their support and maintenance.

And all moneys paid by the subject to the support of public worship, and of the public teachers aforesaid, shall, if he require it, be uniformly applied to the support of the public teacher or teachers of his own religious sect or denomination, provided there be any on whose instructions he attends; otherwise it may be paid towards the support of the teacher or teachers of the parish or precinct in which the said moneys are raised.

And every denomination of Christians, demeaning themselves peaceably, and as good subjects of the commonwealth, shall be equally under the protection of the law: and no subordination of any one sect or denomination to another shall ever be established by law.]

IV. The people of this commonwealth have the sole and exclusive right of governing themselves, as a free, sovereign, and independent state; and do, and forever hereafter shall, exercise and enjoy every power, jurisdiction, and right, which is not, or may not hereafter be, by them expressly delegated to the United States of America, in Congress assembled.

V. All power residing originally in the people, and being derived from them, the several magistrates and officers of government, vested with authority, whether legislative, executive, or judicial, are their substitutes and agents, and are at all times accountable to them.

VI. No man, nor corporation, or association of men, have any other title to obtain advantages, or particular and exclusive privileges, distinct from those of the community, than what arises from the consideration of services rendered to the public; and this title being in nature neither hereditary, nor transmissible to children, or descendants, or relations by blood, the idea of a man born a magistrate, law-giver, or judge, is absurd and unnatural.

VII. Government is instituted for the common good; for the protection, safety, prosperity, and happiness of the people; and not for the profit, honor, or private interest of any one man, family, or class of men: Therefore the people alone have an incontestible unalienable, and indefeasible right to institute government; and to reform, alter, or totally change the same, when their protection, safety, prosperity, and happiness require it.

VIII. In order to prevent those who are vested with authority from becoming oppressors, the people have a right, at such periods and in such manner as they shall establish by their frame of government, to cause their public officers to return to private life; and to fill up vacant places by certain and regular elections and appointments.

IX. All elections ought to be free; and all the inhabitants of this commonwealth, having such qualifications as they shall establish by their frame of government, have an equal right to elect officers, and to be elected, for public employments.

X. Each individual of the society has a right to be protected by it in the enjoyment of his life, liberty, and property, according to standing laws.

He is obliged, consequently, to contribute his share to the expense of this protection; to give his personal service, or an equivalent, when necessary: but no part of the property of any individual can, with justice, be taken from him, or applied to public uses, without his own consent, or that of the representative body of the people. In fine, the people of this commonwealth are not controllable by any other laws than those to which their constitutional representative body have given their consent. And whenever the public exigencies require that the property of any individual should be appropriated to public uses, he shall receive a reasonable compensation therefor.

XI. Every subject of the commonwealth ought to find a certain remedy, by having recourse to the laws, for all injuries or wrongs which he may receive in his person, property, or character. He ought to obtain right and justice freely, and without being obliged to purchase it; completely, and without any denial; promptly, and without delay; conformably to the laws.

XII. No subject shall be held to answer for any crimes or offence, until the same is fully and plainly, substantially, and formally, described to him; or be compelled to accuse, or furnish evidence against himself. And every subject shall have a right to produce all proofs that may be favorable to him; to meet the witnesses against him face to face, and to be fully heard in his defence by himself, or his counsel, at his election. And no subject shall be arrested, imprisoned, despoiled, or deprived of his property, immunities, or privileges, put out of the protection of the law, exiled, or deprived of his life, liberty, or estate, but by the judgment of his peers, or the law of the land.

And the legislature shall not make any law that shall subject any person to a capital or infamous punishment, excepting for the government of the army and navy, without trial by jury.

XIII. In criminal prosecutions, the verification of facts, in the vicinity where they happen, is one of the greatest securities of the life, liberty, and property of the citizen.

XIV. Every subject has a right to be secure from all unreasonable searches, and seizures, of his person, his houses, his papers, and all his possessions. All warrants, therefore, are contrary to this right, if the cause or foundation of them be not previously supported by oath or affirmation, and if the order in the warrant to a civil officer, to make search in suspected places, or to arrest one or more suspected persons, or to seize their property, be not accompanied with a special designation of the persons or objects of search, arrest, or seizure; and no warrant ought to be issued but in cases, and with the formalities prescribed by the laws.

XV. In all controversies concerning property, and in all suits between two or more persons, except in cases in which it has heretofore been otherways used and practised, the parties have a right to a trial by jury; and this method of procedure shall be held sacred, unless, in causes arising on the high seas, and such as relate to mariners' wages, the legislature shall hereafter find it necessary to alter it.

XVI. The liberty of the press is essential to the security of freedom in a state it ought not, therefore, to be restricted in this conmouwealth.

XVII. The people have a right to keep and to bear arms for the common defence. And as, in time of peace, armies are dangerous to liberty, they ought not to be maintained without the consent of the legislature; and the military power shall always be held in an exact subordination to the civil authority, and be governed by it.

XVIII. A frequent recurrence to the fundamental principles of the constitution, and a constant adherence to those of piety, justice, moderation, temperance, industry, and frugality, are absolutely necessary to preserve the advantages of liberty, and to maintain a free government. The people ought, consequently, to have a particular attention to all those principles, in the choice of their officers and representatives: and they have a right to require of their lawgivers and magistrates an exact and constant observance of them, in the formation and execution of the laws necessary for the good administration of the commonwealth.

XIX. The people have a right, in an orderly and peaceable manner, to assemble to consult upon the common good; give instructions to their representatives, and to request of the legislative body, by the way of addresses, petitions, or remonstrances, redress of the wrongs done them, and of the grievances they suffer.

XX. The power of suspending the laws, or the execution of the laws, ought never to be exercised but by the legislature, or by authority derived from it, to be exercised in such particular cases only as the legislature shall expressly provide for.

XXI. The freedom of deliberation, speech, and debate, in either house of the legislature, is so essential to the rights of the people, that it cannot be the foundation of any accusation or prosecution, action or complaint, in any other court or place whatsoever.

XXII. The legislature ought frequently to assemble for the redress of grievances, for correcting, strengthening, and confirming the laws, and for making new laws, as the common good may require.

XXIII. No subsidy, charge, tax, impost, or duties ought to be established, fixed, laid, or levied, under any pretext whatsoever, without the consent of the people or their representatives in the legislature.

XXIV. Laws made to punish for actions done before the existence of such laws, and which have not been declared crimes by preceding laws, are unjust, oppressive, and inconsistent with the fundamental principles of a free government.

XXV. No subject ought, in any case, or in any time, to be declared guilty of treason or felony by the legislature.

XXVI. No magistrate or court of law shall demand excessive bail or sureties, impose excessive fines, or inflict cruel or unusual punishments.

XXVII. In time of peace, no soldier ought to be quartered in any house without the consent of the owner; and in time of war, such quarters ought not to be made but by the civil magistrate, in a manner ordained by the legislature.

XXVIII. No person can in any case be subject to law-martial, or to any penalties or pains, by virtue of that law, except those employed in the army or navy, and except the militia in actual service, but by authority of the legislature.

XXIX. It is essential to the preservation of the rights of every individual, his life, liberty, property, and character, that there be an impartial interpretation of the laws, and administration of justice. It is the right of every citizen to be tried by judges as free, impartial, and independent as the lot of humanity will admit. It is, therefore, not only the best policy, but for the security of the rights of the people, and of every citizen, that the judges of the supreme judicial court should hold their offices as long as they behave themselves well; and that they should have honorable salaries ascertained and established by standing laws.

XXX. In the government of this commonwealth, the legislative department shall never exercise the executive and judicial powers, or either of them: the executive shall never exercise the legislative and judicial powers, or either of them: the judicial shall never exercise the legislative and executive powers, or either of them: to the end it may be a government of laws and not of men.

Part the Second

The frame of government

The people, inhabiting the territory formerly called the Province of Massachusetts Bay, do hereby solemnly and mutually agree with each other, to form themselves into a free, sovereign, and independent body politic, or state, by the name of THE COMMONWEALTH OF MASSACHUSETTS.

Chapter I

The legislative power

SECTION I.—THE GENERAL COURT

ARTICLE I. The department of legislation shall be formed by two branches, a Senate and House of Representatives; each of which shall have a negative on the other.

The legislative body shall assemble every year [on the last Wednesday in May, and at such other times as they shall judge necessary; and shall dissolve and be dissolved on the day next preceding the said last Wednesday in May;] and shall be styled, THE GENERAL COURT OF MASSACHUSETTS.

II. No bill or resolve of the senate or house of representatives shall become a law, and have force as such, until it shall have been laid before the governor for his revisal; and if he, upon such revision, approve thereof, he shall signify his approbation by signing the same. But if he have any objection to the passing of such bill or resolve, he shall return the same, together with his objections thereto, in writing, to the senate or house of representatives, in whichsoever the same shall have originated; who shall enter the objections sent down by the governor, at large, on their records, and proceed to reconsider the said bill or resolve. But if after such reconsideration, two-thirds of the said senate or house of representatives, shall, notwithstanding the said objections, agree to pass the same, it shall, together with the objections, be sent to the other branch of the legislature, where it shall also be reconsidered, and if approved by two-thirds of the members present, shall have the force of law: but in all such cases, the votes of both houses shall be determined by yeas and nays; and the names of the persons voting for, or against, the said bill or resolve, shall be entered upon the public records of the commonwealth.

And in order to prevent unnecessary delays, if any bill or resolve shall not be returned by the governor within five days after it shall have been presented, the same shall have the force of a law.

III. The general court shall forever have full power and authority to erect and constitute judicatories and courts of record, or other courts, to be held in the name of the commonwealth, for the hearing, trying, and determining of all manner of crimes, offences, pleas, processes, plaints, actions, matters, causes, and things, whatsoever, arising or happening within the commonwealth, or between or concerning persons inhabiting, or residing, or brought within the same: whether the same be criminal or civil, or whether the said crimes be capital or not capital, and whether the said pleas be real, personal, or mixed; and for the awarding and making out of execution thereupon. To which courts and judicatories are hereby given and granted full power and authority, from time to time, to administer oaths or affirmations, for the better discovery of truth in any matter in controversy or depending before them.

IV. And further, full power and authority are hereby given and granted to the said general court, from time to time, to make, ordain, and establish, all manner of wholesome and reasonable orders, laws, statutes, and ordinances, directions and instructions, either with penalties or without; so as the same be not repugnant or contrary to this constitution, as they shall judge to be for the good and welfare of this commonwealth, and for the government and ordering thereof, and of the subjects of the same, and for the necessary support and defence of the government thereof; and to name and settle annually, or provide by fixed laws for the naming and settling, all civil officers within the said commonwealth, the election and constitution of whom are not hereafter in this form of government otherwise provided for; and to set forth the several duties, powers, and limits, of the several civil and military officers of this commonwealth, and the forms of such oaths or affirmations as shall be respectively administered unto them for the execution of their several offices and places, so as the same be not repugnant or contrary to this constitution; and to impose and levy proportional and reasonable assessments, rates, and taxes, upon all the inhabitants of, and persons resident, and estates lying, within the said commonwealth; and also to impose and levy reasonable duties and excises upon any produce, goods, wares, merchandise, and commodities, whatsoever, brought into, produced, manufactured, or being within the same; to be issued and disposed of by warrant, under the hand of the governor of this commonwealth for the time being, with the advice and consent of the council, for the public service, in the necessary defence and support of the government of the said commonwealth, and the protection and preservation of the subjects thereof, according to such acts as are or shall be in force within the same.

And while the public charges of government, or any part thereof, shall be assessed on polls and estates, in the manner that has hitherto been practised, in order that such assessments may be made with equality, there shall be a valuation of estates within the commonwealth, taken anew once in every ten years at least, and as much oftener as the general court shall order.

Chapter I

SECTION II.—SENATE

ARTICLE I. [There shall be annually elected, by the freeholders and other inhabitants of this commonwealth, qualified as in this constitution is provided, forty persons to be councillors and senators for the year ensuing their election; to be chosen by the inhabitants of the districts into which the commonwealth may, from time to time, be divided by the general court for that purpose: and the general court, in assigning the numbers to be elected by the respective districts, shall govern themselves by the proportion of the public taxes paid by the said districts; and timely make known to the inhabitants of the commonwealth the limits of each district, and the number of councillors and senators to be chosen therein; provided that the number of such districts shall never be less than thirteen; and that no district be so large as to entitle the same to choose more than six senators.

And the several counties in this commonwealth shall, until the general court shall determine it necessary to alter the said districts, be districts for the choice of councillors and senators, (except that the counties of Dukes County and Nantucket shall form one district for that purpose) and shall elect the following number for councillors and senators, viz.:—Suffolk, six; Essex, six; Middlesex, five; Hampshire, four; Plymouth, three; Barnstable, one; Bristol, three; York, two; Dukes County and Nantucket, one; Worcester, five; Cumberland, one; Lincoln, one; Berkshire, two.]

II. The senate shall be the first branch of the legislature; and the senators shall be chosen in the following manner, viz.: there shall be a meeting on the [first Monday in April,] annually, forever, of the inhabitants of each town in the several counties of this commonwealth; to be called by the selectmen, and warned in due course of law, at least seven days before the [first Monday in April,] for the purpose of electing persons to be senators and councillors; [and at such meetings every male inhabitant of twenty-one years of age and upwards, having a freehold estate within the commonwealth, of the annual income of three pounds, or any estate of the value of sixty pounds, shall have a right to give in his vote for the senators for the district of which he is an inhabitant.] And to remove all doubts concerning the meaning of the word "inhabitant" in this constitution, every person shall be considered as an inhabitant, for the purpose of electing and being elected into any office, or place within this state, in that town, district, or plantation where he dwelleth, or hath his home.

The selectmen of the several towns shall preside at such meetings impartially; and shall receive the votes of all the inhabitants of such towns present and qualified to vote for senators, and shall sort and count them in open town meeting, and in presence of the town clerk, who shall make a fair record, in presence of the selectmen, and in open town meeting, of the name of every person voted for, and of the number of votes against his name: and a fair copy of this record shall be attested by the selectmen and the town clerk, and shall be sealed up, directed to the secretary of the commonwealth for the time being, with a superscription, expressing the purport of the contents thereof, and delivered by the town clerk of such towns, to the sheriff of the county in which such town lies, thirty days at least before [the last Wednesday in May] annually; or it shall be delivered into the secretary's office seventeen days at least before the said [last Wednesday in May:] and the sheriff of each county shall deliver all such certificates by him received, into the secretary's office, seventeen days before the said [last Wednesday in May.]

And the inhabitants of plantations unincorporated, qualified as this constitution provides, who are or shall be empowered and required to assess taxes upon themselves toward the support of government, shall have the same privilege of voting for councillors and senators in the plantations where they reside, as town inhabitants have in their respective towns; and the plantation meetings for that purpose shall be held annually [on the same first Monday in April], at such place in the plantations, respectively, as the assessors thereof shall direct; which assessors shall have like authority for notifying the electors, collecting and returning the votes, as the selectmen and town clerks have in their several towns, by this constitution. And all other persons living in places unincorporated (qualified as aforesaid) who shall be assessed to the support of government by the assessors of an adjacent town, shall have the privilege of giving in their votes for councillors and senators in the town where they shall be assessed, and be notified of the place of meeting by the selectmen of the town where they shall be assessed, for that purpose, accordingly.

III. And that there may be a due convention of senators on the [last Wednesday in May] annually, the governor with five of the council, for the time being, shall, as soon as may be, examine the returned copies of such records; and fourteen days before the said day he shall issue his summons to such persons as shall appear to be chosen by [a majority of] voters, to attend on that day, and take their seats accordingly: provided, nevertheless, that for the first year the said returned copies shall be examined by the president and five of the council of the former constitution of government; and the said president shall, in like manner, issue his summons to the persons so elected, that they may take their seats as aforesaid.

IV. The senate shall be the final judge of the elections, returns and qualifications of their own members, as pointed out in the constitution; and shall, [on the said last Wednesday in May] annually, determine and declare who are elected by each district to be senators [by a majority of votes; and in case there shall not appear to be the full number of senators returned elected by a majority of votes for any district, the deficiency shall be supplied in the following manner, viz.: The members of the house of representatives, and such senators as shall be declared elected, shall take the names of such persons as shall be found to have the highest number of votes in such district, and not elected, amounting to twice the number of senators wanting, if there be so many voted for; and out of these shall elect by ballot a number of senators sufficient to fill up the vacancies in such district; and in this manner all such vacancies shall be filled up in every district of the commonwealth; and in like manner all vacancies in the senate, arising by death, removal out of the state, or otherwise, shall be supplied as soon as may be, after such vacancies shall happen.]

V. Provided, nevertheless, that no person shall be capable of being elected as a senator. [who is not seised of his own right of a freehold, within this commonwealth, of the value of three hundred pounds at least, or possessed of personal estate to the value of six hundred pounds at least, or both to the amount of the same sum, and] who has not been an inhabitant of this commonwealth for the space of five years immediately preceding his election, and, at the time of his election, he shall be an inhabitant in the district for which he shall be chosen.

VI. The senate shall have power to adjourn themselves, provided such adjournments do not exceed two days at a time.

VII. The senate shall choose its own president, appoint its own officers, and determine its own rules of proceedings.

VIII. The senate shall be a court with full authority to hear and determine all impeachments made by the house of representatives, against any officer or officers of the commonwealth, for misconduct and mal-administration in their offices. But previous to the trial of every impeachment the members of the senate shall respectively be sworn, truly and impartially to try and determine the charge in question, according to evidence. Their judgment, however, shall not extend further than to removal from office and disqualification to hold or enjoy any place of honor, trust, or profit, under this commonwealth; but the party so convicted shall be, nevertheless, liable to indictment, trial, judgment, and punishment, according to the laws of the land.

IX. [Not less than sixteen members of the senate shall constitute a quorum for doing business.]

Chapter I

SECTION III.—HOUSE OF REPRESENTATIVES

ARTICLE I. There shall be, in the legislature of this commonwealth, a representation of the people, annually elected, and founded upon the principle of equality.

II. [And in order to provide for a representation of the citizens of this commonwealth, founded upon the principle of equality, every corporate town containing one hundred and fifty ratable polls may elect one representative; every corporate town containing three hundred and seventy-five ratable polls may elect two representatives; every corporate town containing six hundred ratable polls may elect three representatives; and proceeding in that manner, making two hundred and twenty-five ratable polls the mean increasing number for every additional representative.

Provided, nevertheless, that each town now incorporated, not having one hundred and fifty ratable polls, may elect one representative; but no place shall hereafter be incorporated with the privilege of electing a representative, unless there are within the same one hundred and fifty ratable polls.]

And the house of representatives shall have power from time to time to impose fines upon such towns as shall neglect to choose and return members to the same, agreeably to this constitution.

The expenses of travelling to the general assembly, and returning home, once in every session, and no more, shall be paid by the government, out of the public treasury, to every member who shall attend as seasonably as he can, in the judgment of the house, and does not depart without leave.

III. Every member of the house of representatives shall be chosen by written votes; [and, for one year at least next preceding his election, shall have been an inhabitant of, and have been seised in his own right of a freehold of the value of one hundred pounds within the town he shall be chosen to represent, or any ratable estate to the value of two hundred pounds; and he shall cease to represent the said town immediately on his ceasing to be qualified as aforesaid.]

IV. [Every male person, being twenty-one years of age, and resident in any particular town in this commonwealth for the space of one year next preceding, having a freehold estate within the said town of the annual income of three pounds, or any estate of the value of sixty pounds, shall have a right to vote in the choice of a representative or representatives for the said town.]

V. [The members of the house of representatives shall be chosen annually in the month of May, ten days at least before the last Wednesday of that month.]

VI. The house of representatives shall be the grand inquest of this commonwealth; and all impeachments made by them shall be heard and tried by the senate.

VII. All money bills shall originate in the house of representatives; but the senate may propose or concur with amendments, as on other bills.

VIII. The house of representatives shall have power to adjourn themselves; provided such adjournment shall not exceed two days at a time.

IX. [Not less than sixty members of the house of representatives shall constitute a quorum for doing business.]

X. The house of representatives shall be the judge of the returns, elections, and qualifications of its own members, as pointed out in the constitution; shall choose their own speaker; appoint their own officers, and settle the rules and orders of proceeding in their own house. They shall have authority to punish by imprisonment every person, not a member, who shall be guilty of disrespect to the house, by any disorderly or contemptuous behavior in its presence; or who, in the town where the general court is sitting, and during the time of its sitting, shall threaten harm to the body or estate of any of its members, for any thing said or done in the house; or who shall assault any of them therefor; or who shall assault,

or arrest, any witness, or other person, ordered to attend the house, in his way in going or returning; or who shall rescue any person arrested by the order of the house.

And no member of the house of representatives shall be arrested, or held to bail on mean process, during his going unto, returning from, or his attending the general assembly.

XI. The senate shall have the same powers in the like cases; and the governor and council shall have the same authority to punish in like cases: provided, that no imprisonment on the warrant or order of the governor, council, senate, or house of representatives, for either of the above described offences, be for a term exceeding thirty days.

And the senate and house of representatives may try and determine all cases where their rights and privileges are concerned, and which, by the constitution, they have authority to try and determine, by committees of their own members, or in such other way as they may respectively think best.

Chapter II

Executive power

SECTION I.—GOVERNOR

ARTICLE I. There shall be a supreme executive magistrate, who shall be styled—THE GOVERNOR OF THE COMMONWEALTH OF MASSACHUSETTS; and whose title shall be—HIS EXCELLENCY.

II. The governor shall be chosen annually; and no person shall be eligible to this office, unless, at the time of his election, he shall have been an inhabitant of this commonwealth for seven years next preceding; [and unless he shall at the same time be seised, in his own right, of a freehold, within the commonwealth, of the value of one thousand pounds:] [and unless he shall declare himself to be of the Christian religion.]

III. Those persons who shall be qualified to vote for senators and representatives within the several towns of this commonwealth shall, at a meeting to be called for that purpose, on the [first Monday of April] annually, give in their votes for a governor, to the selectmen, who shall preside at such meetings; and the town clerk, in the presence and with the assistance of the selectmen, shall, in open town meeting, sort and count the votes, and form a list of the persons voted for, with the number of votes for each person against his name; and shall make a fair record of the same in the town books, and a public declaration thereof in the said meeting; and shall, in the presence of the inhabitants, seal up copies of the said list, attested by him and the selectmen, and transmit the same to the sheriff of the county, thirty days at least before the [last Wednesday in May]; and the sheriff shall transmit the same to the secretary's office, seventeen days at least before the said [last Wednesday in May]; or the selectmen may cause returns of the same to be made to the office of the secretary of the commonwealth, seventeen days at least before the said day; and the secretary shall lay the same before the senate and the house of representatives on the [last Wednesday in May], to be by them examined; and [in case of an election by a majority of all the votes returned], the choice shall be by them declared and published; [but if no person shall have a majority of votes, the house of representatives shall, by ballot, elect two out of four persons who had the highest number of votes, if so many shall have been voted for; but, if otherwise, out of the number voted for; and make return to the senate of the two persons so elected; on which the senate shall proceed, by ballot, to elect one, who shall be declared governor.]

IV. The governor shall have authority, from time to time, at his discretion, to assemble and call together the councillors of this commonwealth for the time being; and the governor with the said councillors, or five of them at least, shall, and may, from time to time, hold and keep a council, for the ordering and directing the affairs of the commonwealth, agreeably to the constitution and the laws of the land.

V. The governor, with advice of council, shall have full power and authority, during the session of the general court, to adjourn or prorogue the same to any time the two houses shall desire; [and to dissolve the same on the day next preceding the last Wednesday in May; and, in the recess of the said court, to prorogue the same from time to time, not exceeding ninety days in any one recess;] and to call it together sooner than the time to which it may be adjourned or prorogued, if the welfare of the commonwealth shall require the same; and in case of any infectious distemper prevailing in the place where the said court is next at any time to convene, or any other cause happening, whereby danger may arise to the health or lives of the members from their attendance, he may direct the session to be held at some other, the most convenient place within the state.

[And the governor shall dissolve the said general court on the day next preceding the last Wednesday in May.]

VI. In cases of disagreement between the two houses, with regard to the necessity, expediency, or time of adjournment or prorogation, the governor, with advice of the council, shall have a right to adjourn or prorogue the general court, not exceeding ninety days, as he shall determine the public good shall require.

VII. The governor of this commonwealth, for the time being, shall be the commander-in-chief of the army and navy, and of all the military forces of the state, by sea and land; and shall have full power, by himself, or by any commander, or other officer or officers, from time to time, to train, instruct, exercise, and govern the militia and navy; and, for the special defence and safety of the commonwealth, to assemble in martial array, and put in warlike posture, the inhabitants thereof, and to lead and conduct them, and with them to encounter, repel, resist, expel, and pursue, by force of arms, as well by sea as by land, within or without the limits of this commonwealth, and also to kill, slay, and destroy, if necessary, and conquer, by all fitting ways, enterprises, and means whatsoever, all and every such person and persons as shall, at any time hereafter, in a hostile manner, attempt or enterprise the destruction, invasion, detriment, or annoyance of this commonwealth; and to use and exercise, over the army and navy, and over the militia in actual service, the law-martial, in time of war or invasion, and also in time of rebellion, declared by the legislature to exist, as occasion shall necessarily require; and to take and surprise, by all ways and means whatsoever, all and every such person or persons, with their ships, arms, ammunition, and other goods, as shall, in a hostile manner, invade, or attempt the invading, conquering, or annoying this commonwealth; and that the governor be intrusted with all these and other powers, incident to the offices of captain-general and commander-in-chief, and admiral, to be exercised agreeably to the rules and regulations of the constitution, and the laws of the land, and not otherwise.

Provided, that the said governor shall not, at any time hereafter, by virtue of any power by this constitution granted, or hereafter to be granted to him by the legislature, transport any of the inhabitants of this commonwealth, or oblige them to march out of the limits of the same, without their free and voluntary consent, or the consent of the general court; except so far as may be necessary to march or transport them by land or water, for the defence of such part of the state to which they cannot otherwise conveniently have access.

VIII. The power of pardoning offences, except such as persons may be convicted of before the senate by an impeachment of the house, shall be in the governor, by and with the advice of council; but no charter of pardon, granted by the governor, with advice of the council before conviction, shall avail the party pleading the same, notwithstanding any general or particular expressions contained therein, descriptive of the offence or offences intended to be pardoned.

IX. All judicial officers, [the attorney-general,] the solicitor-general, b[all sheriffs,] coroners, [and registers of probate,] shall be nominated and appointed by the governor, by and with the advice and consent of the council; and every such nomination shall be made by the governor, and made at least seven days prior to such appointment.

X. The captains and subalterns of the militia shall be elected by the written votes of the train-band and alarm list of their respective companies, [of twenty-one years of age and upwards;] the field officers of regiments shall be elected by the written votes of the captains and subalterns

of their respective regiments; the brigadiers shall be elected, in like manner, by the field officers of their respective brigades; and such officers, so elected, shall be commissioned by the governor, who shall determine their rank.

The legislature shall, by standing laws, direct the time and manner of convening the electors, and of collecting votes, and of certifying to the governor, the officers elected.

The major-generals shall be appointed by the senate and house of representatives, each having a negative upon the other; and be commissioned by the governor.

And if the electors of brigadiers, field officers, captains or subalterns, shall neglect or refuse to make such elections, after being duly notified, according to the laws for the time being, then the governor, with advice of council, shall appoint suitable persons to fill such offices.

[And no officer, duly commissioned to command in the militia, shall be removed from his office, but by the address of both houses to the governor, or by fair trial in court-martial, pursuant to the laws of the commonwealth for the time being.]

The commanding officers of regiments shall appoint their adjutants and quartermasters; the brigadiers their brigade-majors; and the major-generals their aids; and the governor shall appoint the adjutant-general.

The governor, with advice of council, shall appoint all officers of the continental army, whom by the confederation of the United States it is provided that this commonwealth shall appoint, as also all officers of forts and garrisons.

The divisions of the militia into brigades, regiments, and companies, made in pursuance of the militia laws now in force, shall be considered as the proper divisions of the militia of this commonwealth, until the same shall be altered in pursuance of some future law.

XI. No moneys shall be issued out of the treasury of this commonwealth, and disposed of (except such sums as may be appropriated for the redemption of bills of credit or treasurer's notes, or for the payment of interest arising thereon) but by warrant under the hand of the governor for the time being, with the advice and consent of the council, for the necessary defence and support of the commonwealth; and for the protection and preservation of the inhabitants thereof, agreeably to the acts and resolves of the general court.

XII. All public boards, the commissary-general, all superintending officers of public magazines and stores, belonging to this commonwealth, and all commanding officers of forts and garrisons within the same, shall once in every three months, officially, and without requisition, and at other times, when required by the governor, deliver to him an account of all goods, stores, provisions, ammunition, cannon with their appendages, and small arms with their accoutrements, and of all other public property whatever under their care respectively; distinguishing the quantity, number, quality and kind of each, as particularly as may be; together with the condition of such forts and garrisons; and the said commanding officer shall exhibit to the governor, when required by him, true and exact plans of such forts, and of the land and sea or harbor or harbors, adjacent.

And the said boards, and all public officers, shall communicate to the governor, as soon as may be after receiving the same, all letters, despatches, and intelligences of a public nature, which shall be directed to them respectively.

XIII. As the public good requires that the governor should not be under the undue influence of any of the members of the general court by a dependence on them for his support, that he should in all cases act with freedom for the benefit of the public, that he should not have his attention necessarily diverted from that object to his private concerns, and that he should maintain the dignity of the commonwealth in the character of its chief magistrate, it is necessary that he should have an honorable stated salary, of a fixed and permanent value, amply sufficient for those purposes, and established by standing laws; and it shall be among the first acts of the general court, after the commencement of this constitution, to establish such salary by law accordingly.

Permanent and honorable salaries shall also be established by law for the justices of the supreme judicial court.

And if it shall be found that any of the salaries aforesaid, so established, are insufficient, they shall, from time to time, be enlarged, as the general court shall judge proper.

Chapter II

SECTION II.—LIEUTENANT-GOVERNOR

ARTICLE I. There shall be annually elected a lieutenant-governor of the commonwealth of Massachusetts, whose title shall be—HIS HONOR; and who shall be qualified, in point of [religion,] property, and residence in the commonwealth, in the same manner with the governor; and the day and manner of his election, and the qualifications of the electors, shall be the same as are required in the election of a governor. The return of the votes for this officer, and the declaration of his election, shall be in the same manner; [and if no one person shall be found to have a majority of all the votes returned, the vacancy shall be filled by the senate and house of representatives, in the same manner as the governor is to be elected, in case no one person shall have a majority of the votes of the people to be governor.]

II. The governor, and in his absence the lieutenant-governor, shall be president of the council, but shall have no vote in council; and the lieutenant-governor shall always be a member of the council, except when the chair of the governor shall be vacant.

III. Whenever the chair of the governor shall be vacant, by reason of his death, or absence from the commonwealth, or otherwise, the lieutenant-governor, for the time being, shall, during such vacancy, perform all the duties incumbent upon the governor, and shall have and exercise all the powers and authorities, which by this constitution the governor is vested with, when personally present.

Chapter II

SECTION III.—COUNCIL, AND THE MANNER OF SETTLING ELECTIONS BY THE LEGISLATURE

ARTICLE I. There shall be a council for advising the governor in the executive part of the government, to consist of [nine] persons besides the lieutenant-governor, whom the governor, for the time being, shall have full power and authority, from time to time, at his discretion, to assemble and call together; and the governor, with the said councillors, or five of them at least, shall and may, from time to time, hold and keep a council, for the ordering and directing the affairs of the commonwealth, according to the laws of the land.

II. [Nine councillors shall be annually chosen from among the persons returned for councillors and senators, on the last Wednesday in May, by the joint ballot of the senators and representatives assembled in one room; and in case there shall not be found upon the first choice, the whole number of nine persons who will accept a seat in the council, the deficiency shall be made up by the electors aforesaid from among the people at large; and the number of senators left shall constitute the senate for the year. The seats of the persons thus elected from the senate, and accepting the trust, shall be vacated in the senate.]

III. The councillors, in the civil arrangements of the commonwealth, shall have rank next after the lieutenant-governor.

IV. [Not more than two councillors shall be chosen out of any one district of this commonwealth.]

V. The resolutions and advice of the council shall be recorded in a register, and signed by the members present; and this record may be called for at any time by either house of the legislature; and any member of the council may insert his opinion, contrary to the resolution of the majority.

VI. Whenever the office of the governor and lieutenant-governor shall be vacant, by reason of death, absence, or otherwise, then the council, or the major part of them, shall, during such vacancy, have full power and authority to do, and execute, all and every such acts, matters, and things, as the governor or the lieutenant-governor might or could, by virtue of this constitution, do or execute, if they, or either of them, were personally present.

VII. [And whereas the elections appointed to be made, by this constitution, on the last Wednesday in May annually, by the two houses of the legislature, may not be completed on that day, the said elections may be adjourned from day to day until the same shall be completed. And the order of elections shall be as follows: the vacancies in the senate, if any, shall first be filled up; the governor and lieutenant-governor shall then be elected, provided there should be no choice of them by the people: and afterwards the two houses shall proceed to the election of the council.]

Chapter II

SECTION IV.—SECRETARY, TREASURER, COMMISSARY, ETC

ARTICLE I. [The secretary, treasurer, and receiver-general, and the commissary-general, notaries public, and] naval officers, shall be chosen annually, by joint ballot of the senators and representatives in one room. And, that the citizens of this commonwealth may be assured, from time to time, that the moneys remaining in the public treasury, upon the settlement and liquidation of the public accounts, are their property, no man shall be eligible as treasurer and receiver-general more than five years successively.

II. The records of the commonwealth shall be kept in the office of the secretary, who may appoint his deputies, for whose conduct he shall be accountable: and he shall attend the governor and council, the senate and house of representatives, in person, or by his deputies, as they shall respectively require.

Chapter III

Judiciary power

ARTICLE I. The tenure, that all commission officers shall by law have in their offices, shall be expressed in their respective commissions. All judicial officers, duly appointed, commissioned, and sworn, shall hold their offices during good behavior, excepting such concerning whom there is different provision made in this constitution: provided, nevertheless, the governor, with consent of the council, may remove them upon the address of both houses of the legislature.

II. Each branch of the legislature, as well as the governor and council, shall have authority to require the opinions of the justices of the supreme judicial court, upon important questions of law, and upon solemn occasions.

III. In order that the people may not suffer from the long continuance in place of any justice of the peace who shall fail of discharging the important duties of his office with ability or fidelity, all commissions of justices of the peace shall expire and become void, in the term of seven years from their respective dates; and, upon the expiration of any commission, the same may, if necessary, be renewed, or another person appointed, as shall most conduce to the well-being of the commonwealth.

IV. The judges of probate of wills, and for granting letters of administration, shall hold their courts at such place or places, on fixed days, as the convenience of the people shall require; and the legislature shall, from time to time, hereafter, appoint such times and places; until which appointments, the said courts shall be holden at the times and places which the respective judges shall direct.

V. All causes of marriage, divorce, and alimony, and all appeals from the judges of probate, shall be heard and determined by the governor and council, until the legislature shall, by law, make other provision.

Chapter IV

Delegates to congress

[The delegates of this commonwealth to the congress of the United States, shall, some time in the month of June, annually, be elected by the joint ballot of the senate and house of representatives, assembled together in one room; to serve in congress for one year, to commence on the first Monday in November then next ensuing. They shall have commissions under the hand of the governor, and the great seal of the commonwealth; but may be recalled at any time within the year, and others chosen and commissioned, in the same manner, in their stead.]

Chapter V

The university at cambridge and encouragement of literature, etc

SECTION I.—THE UNIVERSITY

ARTICLE I. Whereas our wise and pious ancestors, so early as the year one thousand six hundred and thirty-six, laid the foundation of Harvard College, in which university many persons of great eminence have, by the blessing of GOD, been initiated in those arts and sciences which qualified them for public employments, both in church and state; and whereas the encouragement of arts and sciences, and all good literature, tends to the honor of GOD, the advantage of the Christian religion, and the great benefit of this and the other United States of America,—it is declared, that the PRESIDENT AND FELLOWS OF HARVARD COLLEGE, in their corporate capacity, and their successors in that capacity, their officers and servants, shall have, hold, use, exercise, and enjoy, all the powers, authorities, rights, liberties, privileges, immunities, and franchises, which they now have, or are entitled to have, hold, use, exercise, and enjoy; and the same are hereby ratified and confirmed unto them, the said president and fellows of Harvard College, and to their successors, and to their officers and servants, respectively, forever.

II. And whereas there have been at sundry times, by divers persons, gifts, grants, devises of houses, lands, tenements, goods, chattels, legacies, and conveyances, heretofore made, either to Harvard College in Cambridge, in New England, or to the president and fellows of Harvard College, or to the said college by some other description, under several charters, successively; it is declared, that all the said gifts, grants, devises, legacies, and conveyances, are hereby forever confirmed unto the president and fellows of Harvard College, and to their successors in the capacity aforesaid, according to the true intent and meaning of the donor or donors, grantor or grantors, devisor or devisors.

III. And whereas, by an act of the general court of the colony of Massachusetts Bay, passed in the year one thousand six hundred and forty-two, the governor and deputy-governor, for the time being, and all the magistrates of that jurisdiction, were, with the president, and a number of the clergy in the said act described, constituted the overseers of Harvard College; and it being necessary, in this new constitution of government to ascertain who shall be deemed successors to the said governor, deputy-governor, and magistrates; it is declared, that the governor, lieutenant-governor, council, and senate of this commonwealth, are, and shall be deemed, their successors, who, with the president of Harvard College, for the time being, together with the ministers of the congregational churches in the towns of Cambridge, Watertown, Charlestown, Boston, Roxbury, and Dorchester, mentioned in the said act, shall be, and hereby are, vested with all the powers and authority belonging, or in any way appertaining to the overseers of Harvard College; provided, that nothing herein shall be construed to prevent the legislature of this commonwealth from making such alterations in the government of the said university, as shall be conducive to its advantage, and the interest of the republic of letters, in as full a manner as might have been done by the legislature of the late Province of the Massachusetts Bay.

Chapter V

SECTION II.—THE ENCOURAGEMENT OF LITERATURE, ETC

Wisdom and knowledge, as well as virtue, diffused generally among the body of the people, being necessary for the preservation of their rights and liberties; and as these depend on spreading the opportunities and advantages of education in the various parts of the country, and among the different orders of the people, it shall be the duty of legislatures and magistrates, in all future periods of this commonwealth, to cherish the interests of literature and the sciences, and all seminaries of them; especially the university at Cambridge, public schools and grammar schools in the towns; to encourage private societies and public institutions, rewards and immunities, for the promotion of agriculture, arts, sciences, commerce, trades, manufactures, and a natural history

of the country; to countenance and inculcate the principles of humanity and general benevolence, public and private charity, industry and frugality, honesty and punctuality in their dealings; sincerity, good humor, and all social affections, and generous sentiments, among the people.

Chapter VI

Oaths And Subscriptions; Incompatability Of And Exclusion From Offices; Pecuniary Qualifications; Commissions; Writs; Confirmation Of Laws; Habeas Corpus; The Enacting Style; Continuance Of Officers: Provision For A Future Revisal Of The Constitution, Etc

ARTICLE I. [Any person chosen governor, lieutenant-governor, councillor, senator, or representative, and accepting the trust, shall, before he proceed to execute the duties of his place or office, make and subscribe the following declaration, viz.:

"I, A. B., do declare, that I believe the Christian religion, and have a firm persuasion of its truth; and that I am seised and possessed, in my own right, of the property required by the constitution, as one qualification for the office or place to which I am elected."

And the governor, lieutenant-governor, and councillors, shall make and subscribe the said declaration, in the presence of the two houses of assembly; and the senators and representatives, first elected under this constitution, before the president and five of the council of the former constitution; and forever afterwards before the governor and council for the time being.

And every person chosen to either of the places or offices aforesaid, as also any person appointed or commissioned to any judicial, executive, military, or other office under the government, shall, before he enters on the discharge of the business of his place or office, take and subscribe the following declaration, and oaths or affirmations, viz.:

["I, A. B., do truly and sincerely acknowledge, profess, testify, and declare, that the Commonwealth of Massachusetts is, and of right ought to be, a free, sovereign, and independent state; and I do swear, that I will bear true faith and allegiance to the said commonwealth, and that

I will defend the same against traitorous conspiracies and all hostile attempts whatsoever; and that I do renounce and abjure all allegiance, subjection, and obedience to the king, queen, or government of Great Britain (as the case may be), and every other foreign power whatsoever; and that no foreign prince, person, prelate, state, or potentate, hath, or ought to have, any jurisdiction, superiority, pre-eminence, authority, dispensing or other power, in any matter, civil, ecclesiastical, or spiritual, within this commonwealth, except the authority and power which is or may be vested by their constituents in the congress of the United States; and I do further testify and declare, that no man or body of men hath or can have any right to absolve or discharge me from the obligation of this oath, declaration, or affirmation: and that I do make this acknowledgment, profession, testimony, declaration, denial, renunciation, and abjuration, heartily and truly, according to the common meaning and acceptation of the foregoing words, without any equivocation, mental evasion, or secret reservation whatsoever. So help me, GOD."]

"I, A. B., do solemnly swear and affirm, that I will faithfully and impartially discharge and perform all the duties incumbent on me as, according to the best of my abilities and understanding, agreeably to the rules and regulations of the constitution and the laws of the commonwealth. So help me, GOD."

Provided, always, that when any person chosen or appointed as aforesaid, shall be of the denomination of the people called Quakers, and shall decline taking the said oath[s], he shall make his affirmation in the foregoing form, and subscribe the same, omitting the words, ["*I do swear*," "*and abjure*," "*oath or*," "*and abjuration*," in the first oath, and in the second oath, the words] "*swear and*," and [in each of them] the words "*So help me*, GOD;" subjoining instead thereof, "*This I do under the pains and penalties of perjury*."

And the said oaths or affirmations shall be taken and subscribed by the governor, lieutenant-governor, and councillors, before the president of the senate, in the presence of the two houses of assembly; and by the senators and representatives first elected under this constitution, before the president and five of the council of the former constitution; and forever afterwards before the governor and council for the time being; and by the residue of the officers aforesaid, before such persons and in such manner as from time to time shall be prescribed by the legislature.

II. No governor, lieutenant-governor, or judge of the supreme judicial court, shall hold any other office or place, under the authority of this commonwealth, except such as by this constitution they are admitted to hold, saving that the judges of the said court may hold the offices of justices of the peace through the state; nor shall they hold any other place or office, or receive any pension or salary from any other state or government or power whatever.

No person shall be capable of holding or exercising at the same time, within this state, more than one of the following offices, viz.: judge of probate—sheriff—register of probate—or register of deeds; and never more than any two offices, which are to be held by appointment of the governor, or the governor and council, or the senate, or the house of representatives, or by the election of the people of the state at large, or of the people of any county, military offices, and the offices of justices of the peace excepted, shall be held by one person.

No person holding the office of judge of the supreme judicial court—secretary—attorney-general—solicitor-general—treasurer or receiver-general—judge of probate—commissary-general—[president, professor, or instructor of Harvard College]—sheriff—clerk of the house of representatives—register of probate—register of deeds—clerk of the supreme judicial court—clerk of the inferior court of common pleas—or officer of the customs, including in this description naval officers—shall at the same time have a seat in the senate or house of representatives: but their being chosen or appointed to, and accepting the same, shall operate as a resignation of their seat in the senate or house of representatives; and the place so vacated shall be filled up.

And the same rule shall take place in case any judge of the said supreme judicial court, or judge of probate, shall accept a seat in council; or any councillor shall accept of either of those offices or places.

And no person shall ever be admitted to hold a seat in the legislature, or any office of trust or importance under the government of this commonwealth, who shall, in the due course of law, have been convicted of bribery or corruption in obtaining an election or appointment.

III. In all cases where sums of money are mentioned in this constitution, the value thereof shall be computed in silver, at six shillings and eight pence per ounce; and it shall be in the power of the legislature, from time to time, to increase such qualifications, as to property, of the persons to be elected to offices, as the circumstances of the commonwealth shall require.

IV. All commissions shall be in the name of the Commonwealth of Massachusetts, signed by the governor and attested by the secretary or his deputy, and have the great seal of the commonwealth affixed thereto.

V. All writs, issuing out of the clerk's office in any of the courts of law, shall be in the name of the Commonwealth of Massachusetts; they shall be under the seal of the court from whence they issue; they shall bear test of the first justice of the court to which they shall be returnable, who is not a party, and be signed by the clerk of such court.

VI. All the laws which have heretofore been adopted, used, and approved in the Province, Colony, or State of Massachusetts Bay, and usually practised on in the courts of law, shall still remain and be in full force, until altered or repealed by the legislature; such parts only excepted as are repugnant to the rights and liberties contained in this constitution.

VII. The privilege and benefit of the writ of *habeas corpus* shall be enjoyed in this commonwealth, in the most free, easy, cheap, expeditious, and ample manner; and shall not be suspended by the legislature, except upon the most urgent and pressing occasions, and for a limited time, not exceeding twelve months.

VIII. The enacting style, in making and passing all acts, statutes, and laws, shall be—"Be it enacted by the Senate and House of Representatives, in General Court assembled, and by the authority of the same."

IX. To the end there may be no failure of justice, or danger arise to the commonwealth from a change of the form of government, all officers, civil and military, holding commissions under the government and people of Massachusetts Bay in New England, and all other officers of the said government and people, at the time this constitution shall take effect, shall have, hold, use, exercise, and enjoy, all the powers and authority to them granted or committed, until other persons shall be appointed in their stead; and all courts of law shall proceed in the execution of the business of their respective departments; and all the executive and legislative officers, bodies, and powers shall continue in full force, in the enjoyment and exercise of all their trusts, employments, and authority; until the general court, and the supreme and executive officers under this constitution, are designated and invested with their respective trusts, powers, and authority.

X. [In order the more effectually to adhere to the principles of the constitution, and to correct those violations which by any means may be made therein, as well as to form such alterations as from experience shall be found necessary, the general court which shall be in the year of our Lord one thousand seven hundred and ninety-five, shall issue precepts to the selectmen of the several towns, and to the assessors of the unincorporated plantations, directing them to convene the qualified voters of their respective towns and plantations, for the purpose of collecting their sentiments on the necessity or expediency of revising the constitution, in order to amendments.

And if it shall appear, by the returns made, that two-thirds of the qualified voters throughout the state, who shall assemble and vote in consequence of the said precepts, are in favor of such revision or amendment, the general court shall issue precepts, or direct them to be issued from the secretary's office, to the several towns to elect delegates to meet in convention for the purpose aforesaid.

The said delegates to be chosen in the same manner and proportion as their representatives in the second branch of the legislature are by this constitution to be chosen.]

XI. This form of government shall be enrolled on parchment, and deposited in the secretary's office, and be a part of the laws of the land; and printed copies thereof shall be prefixed to the book containing the laws of this commonwealth, in all future editions of the said laws.

Articles of Amendment

ARTICLE I. If any bill or resolve shall be objected to, and not approved by the governor; and if the general court shall adjourn within five days after the same shall have been laid before the governor for his approbation, and thereby prevent his returning it with his objections, as provided by the constitution, such bill or resolve shall not become a law, nor have force as such.

ART. II. The general court shall have full power and authority to erect and constitute municipal or city governments, in any corporate town or towns in this commonwealth, and to grant to the inhabitants thereof such powers, privileges, and immunities, not repugnant to the constitution, as the general court shall deem necessary or expedient for the regulation and government thereof, and to prescribe the manner of calling and holding public meetings of the inhabitants, in wards or otherwise, for the election of officers under the constitution, and the manner of returning the votes given at such meetings. Provided, that no such government shall be erected or constituted in any town not containing twelve thousand inhabitants, nor unless it be with the consent, and on the application of a majority of the inhabitants of such town, present and voting thereon, pursuant to a vote at a meeting duly warned and holden for that purpose. And provided, also, that all by-laws, made by such municipal or city government, shall be subject, at all times, to be annulled by the general court.

ART. III. Every male citizen of twenty-one years of age and upwards, excepting paupers and persons under guardianship, who shall have resided within the commonwealth one year, and

within the town or district in which he may claim a right to vote, six calendar months next preceding any election of governor, lieutenant-governor, senators, or representatives, [and who shall have paid, by himself, or his parent, master, or guardian, any state or county tax, which shall, within two years next preceding such election, have been assessed upon him, in any town or district of this commonwealth; and also every citizen who shall be, by law, exempted from taxation, and who shall be, in all other respects, qualified as above mentioned, shall have a right to vote in such election of governor, lieutenant-governor, senators, and representatives; and no other person shall be entitled to vote in such elections.]

ART. IV. Notaries public shall be appointed by the governor in the same manner as judicial officers are appointed, and shall hold their offices during seven years, unless sooner removed by the governor, with the consent of the council, upon the address of both houses of the legislature.

[In case the office of secretary or treasurer of the commonwealth shall become vacant from any cause, during the recess of the general court, the governor, with the advice and consent of the council, shall nominate and appoint, under such regulations as may be prescribed by law, a competent and suitable person to such vacant office, who shall hold the same until a successor shall be appointed by the general court.]

Whenever the exigencies of the commonwealth shall require the appointment of a commissary-general, he shall be nominated, appointed, and commissioned, in such manner as the legislature may, by law, prescribe.

All officers commissioned to command in the militia may be removed from office in such manner as the legislature may, by law, prescribe.

ART. V. In the elections of captains and subalterns of the militia, all the members of their respective companies, as well those under as those above the age of twenty-one years, shall have a right to vote.

ART. VI. Instead of the oath of allegiance prescribed by the constitution, the following oath shall be taken and subscribed by every person chosen or appointed to any office, civil or military, under the government of this common-wealth, before he shall enter on the duties of his office, to wit:—

"I, A.B., do solemnly swear, that I will bear true faith and allegiance to the Commonwealth of Massachusetts, and will support the constitu-tion thereof. So help me, GOD."

Provided, That when any person shall be of the denomination called Quakers, and shall decline taking said oath, he shall make his affirmation in the foregoing form, omitting the word "swear" and inserting, instead thereof, the word "affirm," and omitting the words "So help me, God," and subjoining, instead thereof, the words, "This I do under the pains and penalties of perjury."

ART. VII. No oath, declaration, or subscrip-tion, excepting the oath prescribed in the preced-ing article, and the oath of office, shall be required of the governor, lieutenant-governor, councillors, senators, or representatives, to qualify them to perform the duties of their respective offices.

ART. VIII. No judge of any court of this com-monwealth, (except the court of sessions,) and no person holding any office under the author-ity of the United States, (postmasters excepted,) shall, at the same time, hold the office of gover-nor, lieutenant-governor, or councillor, or have a seat in the senate or house of representatives of this commonwealth; and no judge of any court in this commonwealth, (except the court of sessions,) nor the attorney-general, solicitor-general, county attorney, clerk of any court, sheriff, treasurer, and receiver-general, register of probate, nor register of deeds, shall continue to hold his said office after being elected a member of the Congress of the United States, and accept-ing that trust; but the acceptance of such trust, by any of the officers aforesaid, shall be deemed and taken to be a resignation of his said office; and judges of the courts of common pleas shall hold no other office under the government of this commonwealth, the office of justice of the peace and militia offices excepted.

ART. IX. If, at any time hereafter, any specific and particular amendment or amendments to the constitution be proposed in the general court, and agreed to by a majority of the senators and two-thirds of the members of the house of representa-tives present and voting thereon, such proposed amendment or amendments shall be entered on the journals of the two houses, with the yeas and nays taken thereon, and referred to the general court then next to be chosen, and shall be pub-lished; and if, in the general court next chosen as aforesaid, such proposed amendment or amend-ments shall be agreed to by a majority of the sena-tors and two-thirds of the members of the house of representatives present and voting thereon, then it shall be the duty of the general court to submit such proposed amendment or amendments to the people; and if they shall be approved and rati-fied by a majority of the qualified voters, voting thereon, at meetings legally warned and holden for that purpose, they shall become part of the constitution of this commonwealth.

ART. X. The political year shall begin on the first Wednesday of January, instead of the last Wednesday of May; and the general court shall assemble every year on the said first Wednesday of January, and shall proceed, at that session, to make all the elections, and do all the other acts, which are by the constitution required to be made and done at the session which has heretofore commenced on the last Wednesday of May. And the general court shall be dissolved on the day next preceding the first Wednesday of January, without any proclamation or other act of the governor. But nothing herein contained shall prevent the general court from assembling at such other times as they shall judge neces-sary, or when called together by the governor. The governor, lieutenant-governor and council-lors, shall also hold their respective offices for one year next following the first Wednesday of January, and until others are chosen and quali-fied in their stead.

[The meeting for the choice of governor, lieu-tenant-governor, senators, and representatives, shall be held on the second Monday of November in every year; but meetings may be adjourned, if necessary, for the choice of representatives, to the next day, and again to the next succeeding day, but no further. But in case a second meeting shall be necessary for the choice of representatives, such meetings shall be held on the fourth Monday of the same month of November.]

All the other provisions of the constitution, respecting the elections and proceedings of the members of the general court, or of any other officers or persons whatever, that have reference to the last Wednesday of May, as the commencement of the political year, shall be so far altered, as to have like reference to the first Wednesday of January.

This article shall go into operation on the first day of October, next following the day when the same shall be duly ratified and adopted as an amendment of the constitution; and the governor, lieutenant-governor, councillors, senators, representatives, and all other state officers, who are annually chosen, and who shall be chosen for the current year, when the same shall go into operation, shall hold their respective offices until the first Wednesday of January then next following, and until others are chosen and qualified in their stead, and no longer; and the first election of the governor, lieutenant-governor, senators, and representatives, to be had in virtue of this article, shall be had conformably thereunto, in the month of November following the day on which the same shall be in force, and go into operation, pursuant to the foregoing provision.

All the provisions of the existing constitution, inconsistent with the provisions herein contained, are hereby wholly annulled.

ART. XI. Instead of the third article of the bill of rights, the following modification and amendment thereof is substituted:—

"As the public worship of GOD and instructions in piety, religion, and morality, promote the happiness and prosperity of a people, and the security of a republican government; therefore, the several religious societies of this commonwealth, whether corporate or unincorporate, at any meeting legally warned and holden for that purpose, shall ever have the right to elect their pastors or religious teachers, to contract with them for their support, to raise money for erecting and repairing houses for public worship, for the maintenance of religious instruction, and for the payment of necessary expenses; and all persons belonging to any religious society shall be taken and held to be members, until they shall file with the clerk of such society a written notice, declaring the dissolution of their membership, and thenceforth shall not be liable for any grant or contract which may be thereafter made, or entered into by such society; and all religious sects and denominations, demeaning themselves peaceably, and as good citizens of the commonwealth, shall be equally under the protection of the law; and no subordination of any one sect or denomination to another shall ever be established by law."

ART. XII. [In order to provide for a representation of the citizens of this commonwealth, founded upon the principles of equality, a census of the ratable polls, in each city, town, and district of the commonwealth, on the first day of May, shall be taken and returned into the secretary's office, in such manner as the legislature shall provide, within the month of May, in the year of our Lord one thousand eight hundred and thirty-seven, and in every tenth year thereafter, in the month of May, in manner aforesaid; and each town or city having three hundred ratable polls at the last preceding decennial census of polls, may elect one representative, and for every four hundred and fifty ratable polls in addition to the first three hundred, one representative more.

Any town having less than three hundred ratable polls shall be represented thus: The whole number of ratable polls, at the last preceding decennial census of polls, shall be multiplied by ten, and the product divided by three hundred; and such town may elect one representative as many years within ten years, as three hundred is contained in the product aforesaid.

Any city or town having ratable polls enough to elect one or more representatives, with any number of polls beyond the necessary number, may be represented, as to that surplus number, by multiplying such surplus number by ten and dividing the product by four hundred and fifty, and such city or town may elect one additional representative as many years, within the ten years, as four hundred and fifty is contained in the product aforesaid.

Any two or more of the several towns and districts may, by consent of a majority of the legal voters present at a legal meeting, in each of said towns and districts, respectively, called for that purpose, and held previous to the first day of July, in the year in which the decennial census of polls shall be taken, form themselves into a representative district to continue until the next decennial census of polls, for the election of a representative, or representatives; and such district shall have all the rights, in regard to representation, which would belong to a town containing the same number of ratable polls.

The governor and council shall ascertain and determine, within the months of July and August, in the year of our Lord one thousand eight hundred and thirty-seven, according to the foregoing principles, the number of representatives, which each city, town, and representative district is entitled to elect, and the number of years, within the period of ten years then next ensuing, that each city, town, and representative district may elect an additional representative; and where any town has not a sufficient number of polls to elect a representative each year, then, how many years within the ten years, such town may elect a representative; and the same shall be done once in ten years, thereafter, by the governor and council, and the number of ratable polls in each decennial census of polls, shall determine the number of representatives, which each city, town and representative district may elect as aforesaid; and when the number or representatives to be elected by each city, town, or representative district is ascertained and determined as aforesaid, the governor shall cause the same to be published forthwith for the information of the people, and that number shall remain fixed and unalterable for the period of ten years.

All the provisions of the existing constitution inconsistent with the provisions herein contained, are hereby wholly annulled.]

ART. XIII. [A census of the inhabitants of each city and town, on the first day of May, shall be taken, and returned into the secretary's office, on or before the last day of June, of the year one thousand eight hundred and forty, and of every tenth year thereafter; which census shall determine the apportionment of senators and representatives for the term of ten years.

The several senatorial districts now existing shall be permanent. The senate shall consist of forty members; and in the year one thousand eight hundred and forty, and every tenth year thereafter, the governor and council shall assign the number of senators to be chosen in each district, according to the number of inhabitants in the same. But, in all cases, at least one senator shall be assigned to each district.

The members of the house of representatives shall be apportioned in the following manner: Every town or city containing twelve hundred inhabitants may elect one representative; and two thousand four hundred inhabitants shall be the mean increasing number, which shall entitle it to an additional representative.

Every town containing less than twelve hundred inhabitants shall be entitled to elect a representative as many times within ten years as the number one hundred and sixty is contained in the number of the inhabitants of said town. Such towns may also elect one representative for the year in which the valuation of estates within the commonwealth shall be settled.

Any two or more of the several towns may, by consent of a majority of the legal voters present at a legal meeting, in each of said towns, respectively, called for that purpose, and held before the first day of August, in the year one thousand eight hundred and forty, and every tenth year thereafter, form themselves into a representative district, to continue for the term of ten years; and such district shall have all the rights, in regard to representation, which would belong to a town containing the same number of inhabitants.

The number of inhabitants which shall entitle a town to elect one representative, and the mean increasing number which shall entitle a town or city to elect more than one, and also the number by which the population of towns not entitled to a representative every year is to be divided, shall be increased, respectively, by one-tenth of the numbers above mentioned, whenever the population of the commonwealth shall have increased to seven hundred and seventy thousand, and for every additional increase of seventy thousand inhabitants, the same addition of one-tenth shall be made, respectively, to the said numbers above mentioned.

In the year of each decennial census, the governor and council shall, before the first day of September, apportion the number of representatives which each city, town, and representative district is entitled to elect, and ascertain how many years, within ten years, any town may elect a representative, which is not entitled to elect one every year; and the governor shall cause the same to be published forthwith.

[Nine councillors shall be annually chosen from among the people at large, on the first Wednesday of January, or as soon thereafter as may be, by the joint ballot of the senators and representatives, assembled in one room, who shall, as soon as may be, in like manner, fill up any vacancies that may happen in the council, by death, resignation, or otherwise. No person shall be elected a councillor, who has not been an inhabitant of this commonwealth for the term of five years immediately preceding his election; and not more than one councillor shall be chosen from any one senatorial district in the commonwealth.]

No possession of a freehold, or of any other estate, shall be required as a qualification for holding a seat in either branch of the general court, or in the executive council.

ART. XIV. In all elections of civil officers by the people of this commonwealth, whose election is provided for by the constitution, the person having the highest number, of votes shall be deemed and declared to be elected.

ART. XV. The meeting for the choice of governor, lieutenant-governor, senators, and representatives, shall be held on the Tuesday next after the first Monday in November, annually; but in case of a failure to elect representatives on that day, a second meeting shall be holden, for that purpose, on the fourth Monday of the same month of November.

ART. XVI. Eight councillors shall be annually chosen by the inhabitants of this commonwealth, qualified to vote for governor. The election of councillors shall be determined by the same rule that is required in the election of governor. The legislature, at its first session after this amendment shall have been adopted, and at its first session after the next state census shall have been taken, and at its first session after each decennial state census thereafterwards, shall divide the commonwealth into eight districts of contiguous territory, each containing a number of inhabitants as nearly equal as practicable, without dividing any town or ward of a city, and each entitled to elect one councillor: *provided, however*, that if, at any time, the constitution shall provide for the division of the commonwealth into forty senatorial districts, then the legislature shall so arrange the councillor districts, that each district shall consist of five contiguous senatorial districts, as they shall be, from time to time, established by the legislature. No person shall be eligible to the office of councillor who has not been an inhabitant of the commonwealth for the term of five years immediately preceding his election. The day and manner of the election, the return of the votes, and the declaration of the said elections, shall be the same as are required in the election of governor. [Whenever there shall be a failure to elect the full number of councillors, the vacancies shall be filled in the same manner as is required for filling vacancies in the senate; and vacancies occasioned by death, removal from the state, or otherwise, shall be filled in like manner, as soon as may be, after such vacancies shall have happened.] And that there may be no delay in the organization of the government on the first Wednesday of January, the governor, with at least five councillors for the time being, shall, as soon as may be, examine the returned copies of the records for the election of governor, lieutenant-governor, and councillors; and ten days before the said first Wednesday in January he shall issue his summons to such persons as appear to be chosen, to attend on that day to be qualified accordingly; and the secretary shall lay the returns before the senate and house of representatives on the said first Wednesday in January, to be by them examined: and in case of the election of either of said officers, the choice shall be by them declared and published; but in case there shall be no election of either of said officers, the legislature shall proceed to fill such vacancies in the manner provided in the constitution for the choice of such officers.

ART. XVII. The secretary, treasurer and receiver-general, auditor, and attorney-general, shall be chosen annually, on the day in November prescribed for the choice of governor; and each person then chosen as such, duly qualified in other respects, shall hold his office for the term of one year from the third Wednesday in January next thereafter, and until another is chosen and qualified in his stead. The qualification of the voters, the manner of the election, the return of the votes, and the declaration of the election, shall be such as are required in the election of governor. In case of a failure to elect either of said officers on the day in November aforesaid, or in case of the decease, in the mean time, of the person elected as such, such officer shall be chosen on or before the third Wednesday in January next thereafter, from the two persons who had the highest number of votes for said offices on the day in November aforesaid, by joint ballot of the senators and representatives, in one room; and in case the office of secretary, or treasurer and receiver-general, or auditor, or attorney-general, shall become vacant, from any cause, during an annual or special session of the general court, such vacancy shall in like manner be filled by choice from the people at large; but if such vacancy shall occur at any other time, it shall be supplied by the governor by appointment, with the advice and consent of the council. The person so chosen or appointed, duly qualified in other respects, shall hold his office until his successor is chosen and duly qualified in his stead. In case any person chosen or appointed to either of the offices aforesaid, shall neglect, for the space of ten days after he could otherwise enter upon his duties, to qualify himself in all respects to enter upon the discharge of such duties, the office to which he has been elected or appointed shall be deemed vacant. No person shall be eligible to either of said offices unless he shall have been an inhabitant of this commonwealth five years next preceding his election or appointment.

ART. XVIII. All moneys raised by taxation in the towns and cities for the support of public schools, and all moneys which may be appropriated by the state for the support of common schools, shall be applied to, and expended in, no other schools than those which are conducted according to law, under the order and superintendence of the authorities of the town or city in which the money is to be expended; and such moneys shall never be appropriated to any religious sect for the maintenance, exclusively, of its own school.

ART. XIX. The legislature shall prescribe, by general law, for the election of sheriffs, registers of probate, commissioners of insolvency, and clerks of the courts, by the people of the several counties, and that district-attorneys shall be chosen by the people of the several districts, for such term of office as the legislature shall prescribe.

ART. XX. No person shall have the right to vote, or be eligible to office under the constitution of this commonwealth, who shall not be able to read the constitution in the English language, and write his name: *provided, however,* that the provisions of this amendment shall not apply to any person prevented by a physical disability from complying with its requisitions, nor to any person who now has the right to vote, nor to any persons who shall be sixty years of age or upwards at the time this amendment shall take effect.

ART. XXI. A census of the legal voters of each city and town, on the first day of May, shall be taken and returned into the office of the secretary of the commonwealth, on or before the last day of June, in the year one thousand eight hundred and fifty-seven; and a census of the inhabitants of each city and town, in the year one thousand eight hundred and sixty-five, and of every tenth year thereafter. In the census aforesaid, a special enumeration shall be made of the legal voters; and in each city, said enumeration shall specify the number of such legal voters aforesaid, residing in each ward of such city. The enumeration aforesaid shall determine the apportionment of representatives for the periods between the taking of the census.

The house of representatives shall consist of two hundred and forty members, which shall be apportioned by the legislature, at its first session after the return of each enumeration as aforesaid, to the several counties of the commonwealth, equally, as nearly as may be, according to their relative numbers of legal voters, as ascertained by the next preceding special enumeration; and the town of Cohasset, in the county of Norfolk, shall, for this purpose, as well as in the formation of districts, as hereinafter provided, be considered a part of the county of Plymouth; and it shall be the duty of the secretary of the commonwealth, to certify, as soon as may be after it is determined by the legislature, the number of representatives to which each county shall be entitled, to the board authorized to divide each county into representative districts. The mayor and aldermen of the city of Boston, the county commissioners of other counties than Suffolk,—or in lieu of the mayor and aldermen of the city of Boston, or of the county commissioners in each county other than Suffolk, such board of special commissioners in each county, to be elected by the people of the county, or of the towns therein, as may for that purpose be provided by law,—shall, on the first Tuesday of August next after each assignment of representatives to each county, assemble at a shire town of their respective counties, and proceed, as soon as may be, to divide the same into representative districts of contiguous territory, so as to apportion the representation assigned to each county equally, as nearly as may be, according to the relative number of legal voters in the several districts of each county; and such districts shall be so formed that no town or ward of a city shall be divided therefor, nor shall any district be made which shall be entitled to elect more than three representatives. Every representative, for one year at least next preceding his election, shall have been an inhabitant of the district for which he is chosen, and shall cease to represent such district when he shall cease to be an inhabitant of the commonwealth. The districts in each county shall be numbered by the board creating the same, and a description of each, with the numbers thereof and the number of legal voters therein,

shall be returned by the board, to the secretary of the commonwealth, the county treasurer of each county, and to the clerk of every town in each district, to be filed and kept in their respective offices. The manner of calling and conducting the meetings for the choice of representatives, and of ascertaining their election, shall be prescribed by law. [Not less than one hundred members of the house of representatives shall constitute a quorum for doing business; but a less number may organize temporarily, adjourn from day to day, and compel the attendance of absent members.]

ART. XXII. A census of the legal voters of each city and town, on the first day of May, shall be taken and returned into the office of the secretary of the commonwealth, on or before the last day of June, in the year one thousand eight hundred and fifty-seven; and a census of the inhabitants of each city and town, in the year one thousand eight hundred and sixty-five, and of every tenth year thereafter. In the census aforesaid, a special enumeration shall be made of the legal voters, and in each city said enumeration shall specify the number of such legal voters aforesaid, residing in each ward of such city. The enumeration aforesaid shall determine the apportionment of senators for the periods between the taking of the census. The senate shall consist of forty members. The general court shall, at its first session after each next preceding special enumeration, divide the commonwealth into forty districts of adjacent territory, each district to contain, as nearly as may be, an equal number of legal voters, according to the enumeration aforesaid: *provided, however,* that no town or ward of a city shall be divided therefor; and such districts shall be formed, as nearly as may be, without uniting two counties, or parts of two or more counties, into one district. Each district shall elect one senator, who shall have been an inhabitant of this commonwealth five years at least immediately preceding his election, and at the time of his election shall be an inhabitant of the district for which he is chosen; and he shall cease to represent such senatorial district when he shall cease to be an inhabitant of the commonwealth. Not less than sixteen senators shall constitute a quorum for doing business; but a less number may organize temporarily, adjourn from day to day, and compel the attendance of absent members.

ART. XXIII. [No person of foreign birth shall be entitled to vote, or shall be eligible to office, unless he shall have resided within the jurisdiction of the United States for two years subsequent to his naturalization, and shall be otherwise qualified, according to the constitution and laws of this commonwealth: *provided*, that this amendment shall not affect the rights which any person of foreign birth possessed at the time of the adoption thereof; and, *provided, further,* that it shall not affect the rights of any child of a citizen of the United States, born during the temporary absence of the parent therefrom.]

ART. XXIV. Any vacancy in the senate shall be filled by election by the people of the unrepresented district, upon the order of a majority of the senators elected.

ART. XXV. In case of a vacancy in the council, from a failure of election, or other cause, the senate and house of representatives shall, by concurrent vote, choose some eligible person from the people of the district wherein such vacancy occurs, to fill that office. If such vacancy shall happen when the legislature is not in session, the governor, with the advice and consent of the council, may fill the same by appointment of some eligible person.

ART. XXVI. The twenty-third article of the articles of amendment of the constitution of this commonwealth, which is as follows, to wit: "No person of foreign birth shall be entitled to vote, or shall be eligible to office, unless he shall have resided within the jurisdiction of the United States for two years subsequent to his naturalization, and shall be otherwise qualified, according to the constitution and laws of this commonwealth: *provided*, that this amendment shall not affect the rights which any person of foreign birth possessed at the time of the adoption thereof; and *provided, further,* that it shall not affect the rights of any child of a citizen of the United States, born during the temporary absence of the parent therefrom," is hereby wholly annulled.

ART. XXVII. So much of article two of chapter six of the constitution of this commonwealth as relates to persons holding the office of president, professor, or instructor of Harvard College, is hereby annulled.

ART. XXVIII. No person having served in the army or navy of the United States in time of war, and having been honorably discharged from such service, if otherwise qualified to vote, shall be disqualified therefor on account of being a pauper; or, if a pauper, because of the nonpayment of a poll-tax.

ART. XXIX. The general court shall have full power and authority to provide for the inhabitants of the towns in this Commonwealth more than one place of public meeting within the limits of each town for the election of officers under the constitution, and to prescribe the manner of calling, holding and conducting such meetings. All the provisions of the existing constitution inconsistent with the provisions herein contained are hereby annulled.

ART. XXXI. Article twenty-eight of the Amendments of the Constitution is hereby amended by striking out in the fourth line thereof the words "being a pauper," and inserting in place thereof the words:—receiving or having received aid from any city or town,—and also by striking out in said fourth line the words "if a pauper," so that the article as amended shall read as follows: ARTICLE XXVIII. No person having served in the army or navy of the United States in time of war, and having been honorably discharged from such service, if otherwise qualified to vote, shall be disqualified therefor on account of receiving or having received aid from any city or town, or because of the non-payment of a poll tax.

ART. XXXII. So much of article three of the Amendments of the Constitution of the Commonwealth as is contained in the following words: "and who shall have paid, by himself, or his parent, master, or guardian, any state or county tax, which shall, within two years next preceding such election, have been assessed upon him, in any town or district of this Commonwealth; and also every citizen who shall be, by law, exempted from taxation, and who shall be, in all other respects, qualified as above mentioned," is hereby annulled.

ART. XXXIII. A majority of the members of each branch of the general court shall constitute a quorum for the transaction of business, but a less number may adjourn from day to day, and compel the attendance of absent members. All the provisions of the existing Constitution inconsistent with the provisions herein contained are hereby annulled.

ART. XXXIV. So much of article two of section one of chapter two of part the second of the Constitution of the Commonwealth as is contained in the following words: "and unless he shall at the same time, be seized in his own right, of a freehold within the Commonwealth of the value of one thousand pounds;" is hereby annulled.

ART. XXXV. So much of article two of section three of chapter one of the constitution of the commonwealth as is contained in the following words: "The expenses of travelling to the general assembly, and returning home, once in every session, and no more, shall be paid by the government, out of the public treasury, to every member who shall attend as seasonably as he can, in the judgment of the house, and does not depart without leave," is hereby annulled.

ART. XXXVI. So much of article nineteen of the articles of amendment to the constitution of the commonwealth as is contained in the following words: "commissioners of insolvency", is hereby annulled.

Reference: Francis Newton Thorpe (ed.), *The Federal and State Constitutions, Colonial Charters, and Other Organic Laws of the States,* Vol. III (Washington: GPO, 1909).

Part VIII

The Articles of Confederation:
Proposed, Debated, and Ratified

The major issues surrounding the writing and ratification of the first national constitution, the Articles of Confederation, are best seen in the debates in the Continental Congress. From the beginning, the division of powers between the national government and the state governments was central to the debates and the compromises that produced the Articles. The earliest drafts in Congress of the Articles probably came from the influence of John Adams, who envisioned a written national constitution even before independence. The collections of letters of the members of the Continental Congress as well as their printed procedures give full scope to the drafting, debates, and final version of the Articles. This is the principle focus of Chapter 46.

Chapter 47 of Part VIII presents the states as they discussed and moved to ratify the Articles of Confederation. The period covered is 1777–1781, when Maryland finally became the thirteenth state to authorize its delegates in the federal Congress to ratify the Articles. All of the states were required to ratify the Articles before that first Constitution became law. (The federal government, thus, had acted for some time without a formal constitution.) The arguments within the states over the need for a written national constitution and its contents focused almost entirely on the division of authority between the state and national governments. It is important to study the states' responses to the proposed Articles because they reveal much about the governance values and the historical precedence from the experiences in the colonial period. Unfortunately, not all of the states in their legislatures and conventions recorded their views. Fortunately, exchanges between leaders at home and their delegates in the federal Congress shed some light on these heated debates.

46

Drafts of the Articles of Confederation and Discussion in the Continental Congress

The drafts of the Articles of Confederation that the committee members proposed to the Continental Congress were built on John Adams, *Thoughts on Government* (Volume II, section III). Adams had replied to a letter from his South Carolina friend Edward Rutledge (1749–1800), who had enquired of Adams his views of John Dickinson's wording for the Articles. Rutledge was especially worried about two parts in the proposed constitution: popular sovereignty as a threat to quality leadership and fear that some states would be underrepresented in the new federal government. Dickinson's cautious concerns about leadership quality and fears that large states such as Pennsylvania, his own state, would not receive their fair share of delegates are also evident in Dickinson's writing. The second draft version of the Articles of Confederation, which Dickinson's committee presented to the delegates for debate, is presented here. The reader should look carefully at exactly what powers states had and whether the states or the national government had the most governance authority.

Though a number of the members of the Continental Congress commented on the proposed Articles, only the arguments of North Carolina's Thomas Burke (1747–1783) are presented here. Ill-tempered and suspicious, the Irish-born Burke was a brilliant student of political thought and an excellent orator. From April to November 1777, right up to the time the Articles were submitted to the state legislatures and conventions for discussion and ratification, Burke attempted to offer amendments to the document. His major objections, consistent with most other critics, were to the powers given the federal government. Burke believed the article binding all states to cooperate in national emergencies unaffordable and demeaning to the individual state's need for self-defense. On November 15, 1777, Burke offered detailed revisions to a number of the articles, including 4, 5, 6, 7, and 9. His most important concern was that members of the national congress could vote to override the objections of their fellow delegates from a specific state, because only they best knew the interests of their respective states. In what probably were debate notes, Burke expressed his concern of congressional power over the individual states. Burke had grasped the central dividing issue that would plague the members of the Continental Congress for its duration through 1787.

JOHN DICKINSON DRAFT OF THE ARTICLES, JUNE 17–JULY 11, 1776

The Congress shall have Authority to agree upon in the Manner herein directed proper Measures for the Defence & Security of the united Colonies & every of them against all their Enemies, and to carry the same into Execution so far forth as they are hereby permitted; to raise naval & land Forces for these purposes; to emit Money or Bills of Credit; to make Rules for governing & regulating such Forces; to appoint General Officers to command them; and other Officers necessary for managing the general Affairs of the Union under the Direction of Congress; to commission other Officers appointed by Virtue of the Article preceding (see pa. 4. last art of this Copy); to appoint a Council of Safety to act in the Recess of Congress, and such Committees and Officers as may be necessary for managing the general Affairs of the Union, under the Direction of Congress while sitting, and in their Recess, of the Council of *Safety* State, a Chamber of Accounts, an Office of Treasury, a Board of War, a Board of Admiralty, out of their own Body, and such Committees out of the same as shall be thought necessary. They may appoint one of their Number to preside, and a suitable person for Secretary. The Chamber of Accounts, the Office of Treasury, the Board of War and Board of Admiralty, shall always act under the Direction of Congress while sitting, and in their Recess, under that of the Council of Safety. . . .

But the Congress shall never impose or levy any Taxes or Duties, except in managing the Post offices, nor interfere in the internal Police of any Colony or Colonies, any farther than such Police may be *expressly* affected by this Confederation; nor shall any Alteration be at any Time hereafter made in the Terms of this Confederation or any of them, unless such Alteration be agreed to in *General Congress by the Delegates of every Colony of the Union and* an Assembly of the United States and be afterwards confirmed by the Legislature of every Colony.

The *Congress shall* United States assembled shall never engage the United Colonies in a War, nor conclude any Alliance or Treaty with any other Power, nor raise naval Forces, nor form a Resolution to raise land Forces, nor agree upon the coining Money & regulating the Value thereof, or the emitting Bills or borrowing money on the Credit of the United Colonies, unless the Delegates of nine Colonies freely assent to the same. No Question on any other Point except for adjourning shall be *put unless all the Colonies are actually represented in Congress when the Question is put* determined unless the Delegates of seven Colonies vote in the affirmative.

No person shall be capable of being a Delegate for more than three Years in any Term of six Years.

No person holding any Office under the United States, for which he receives any pay or Fees by himself or another for his Benefit, shall be capable of being a Delegate.

Art. [20]. The Council of *Safety* State shall consist of one Delegate from each Colony, *of whom in the first appointment, five shall be determined by Lott to serve for one Year, four for two Years, and four for three Years, and as the said Terms expire, the Vacancies shall be filled by appointments for three Years, from the Delegates of those Colonies, whose Delegates then go out of the said offices; and no person who has served the said Term of three Years as a Councillor, shall be elected again until after a Respite of three Years* annually to be named by the Delegates of each Colony, and where they cannot agree, by the Congress.

The Business and Duty of this Council, *of which seven Members shall be a Quorum,* shall be, *in Recess of Congress* To receive & open all Letters directed to the *Congress* United States, and to return proper Answers, but not to make any Engagements that shall be binding on the united Colonies, or any of them.

To correspond with the several Assemblies, Colonial Councils and Committees of Safety,

Governors and Presidents of Colonies, and all persons acting under the Authority of the Congress, or of the Legislature of any Colony.

To give Counsel to the Commanding officers of the Land and naval Forces in the Pay of the Continent whenever it may be expedient.

To supply the continental Forces by Sea and Land with all Necessaries from Time to Time.

To expedite *the Coining or Striking Money ordered by the Congress to be coined or struck and* the Execution of such Measures as the Congress is hereby impowered to resolve upon, and may by them be injoined.

To transmit to the several Commanding Officers, Paymasters & Commissaries, from Time to Time, such Sums of Money as may be necessary for the Pay and Subsistance of the Continental Forces, to draw upon the Treasurers for such Sums as may be appropriated by Congress, and to order Payment by them for such Contracts as the said Council may make in Pursuance of the Authorities hereby given them.

To take Charge of all military stores belonging to the united Colonies, to procure such further Quantities as may probably be wanted, and to order any part thereof wheresoever it may be most requisite for the Common Service.

To direct the safe keeping & comfortable Accommodation of all Prisoners of War.

To contribute their Counsel & Authority towards raising Recruits ordered by Congress.

To procure Intelligence of the Condition & Designs of Enemies.

To direct military operations by Sea and Land, not changing any Objects of Expeditions determined on by Congress, unless an Alteration of Circumstances which shall come to their Knowledge after the Recess of Congress, shall make such Change absolutely necessary.

To attend to the Defence and Preservation of Forts and strong Posts and to prevent the Enemy from acquiring new Holds.

To apply to the Legislatures or to such Officers in the several Colonies as are entrusted with the executive Powers of Government, for occasional Aid *of Minute Men & Militia>* whenever & wherever necessary.

In Case of the Death or Removal of any Officer within the Appointment of Congress, to employ a person to fulfill his Duties, untill the Meeting of Congress, unless the Office be of such a Nature as to admit a Delay of appointment untill such Meeting.

To suspend any Officer in the Land or naval Forces.

To examine public Claims & Accounts and make Report thereof to the Congress.

To superintend and controul or suspend all Officers civil & military acting under the Authority of the Congress.

To publish & disperse authentic Accounts of military operations.

To summon a Meeting of Congress at an earlier Day than is appointed for its next Meeting, if any great & unexpected Emergency should render it necessary for the Safety or Wellfare of the United Colonies or any of them.

To prepare Matters for the Consideration of Congress & To lay before the Congress at their next Meeting all Letters & Advices received by them, with a Report of their proceedings.

To appoint a proper person for their Clerk, who shall take an Oath of Secrecy & Fidelity, before he enters on the Exercise of his Office.

Seven Members shall have power to act.

In Case of the Death of any Member of the said Council, immediately to apply to his surviving Colleagues to appoint some one of themselves to be a Member of the said Council till the Meeting of Congress. If only one survives, to give him immediate notice that he may take his Seat as a Councillor, till such Meeting.

The Delegates while acting as Members of the Council to be supported at the Expence of the Union.

Art. [21]. *Any & every other of the British Colonies on this Continent, acceding to this Confederation and entirely joining in the Measures of the united Colonies, shall be admitted & entitled to all the Advantages & Priviledges of this Union.* Canada acceding to this Confederation and entirely joining in the Measures of the United Colonies, shall be admitted into & entitled to all the Advantages of this Union. But no other

Colony on this Continent shall be admitted into the same, unless such admission be agreed to by the Delegates of nine Colonies.

Art. [22]. These Articles shall be proposed to the Legislatures of all the united Colonies to be by them considered, and if approved by them they are advised to authorize their Delegates to ratify the same in Congress, which being done, the *Confederation and Union so agreed to is to be perpetual the foregoing* Articles of this Confederation shall be inviolably observed by every Colony, and the Union is to be perpetual.

Reference: Paul H. Smith (ed.), *Letters of Delegates to Congress, 1774–1789,* Vol. IV (Washington: Library of Congress, 1976–1990).

THOMAS BURKE OF NORTH CAROLINA OFFERS AMENDMENTS, APRIL 27, 1777

Agreeable to the order of the day, Congress resumed the consideration of the report from the Committee of the whole on the articles of confederation; and, after some time spent thereon,

Resolved, That the further consideration thereof be deferred till to morrow.

For the better managing the Interests of the United States, Shall be Instituted a General Council and Council of State to form a Congress.

The General Council Shall consist of Delegates chosen by the Several States in Such manner as is or Shall be provided by their respective Laws and Constitutions in the following proportions.

The Council of State Shall consist of one Delegate from every State to be chosen in manner provided by their respective Laws and Constitutions.

Every act Edict and ordinance Shall be first moved in the General Council and read three times and three times assented to by a majority of all the voices of which the Council ought to be composed. Every act, Edict and ordinance so assented to Shall also be assented [to] by a majority of all the voices of which the Council of State ought to consist before the Same Shall be binding on the States.

And every act, Edict and ordinance So assented to Shall be binding on all and Every of the United States: Provided, the Same Shall be within the Powers hereafter Expressly given to the United States in Congress assembled.

Except in the following cases, that is to say, Where any War is to be waged or acts of hostility commenced, or authorized against any Prince, State or People not having declared War against all or any of the United States, or invaded any of the Same by Acts of Hostility against the Coasts, Ports Fortresses or Dominions of any of the United States: every act, Edict or ordinance declaring Such War Shall be assented to by three fourths at the least of all the voices of which the general Council ought to consist, and of nine voices at the least in the Council of State before the Same Shall be held binding on the United States or any of them, to any intent or purpose, and every State dissenting from Such War Shall be no further bound thereby than to refuse any aid or protection to the Enemy with whom the other States may be at War, which Dissent every State Shall be at liberty to make by her delegate in the Council of State, and every Such State Shall be Excluded from all Benefits resulting from Such War, and Exempted from all Expences attending the Same.

(Endorsement)

Burke's amendments to Confederation proposed on the Qu: Shall the Congress consist of two houses, passed in the Negative. So whole dropt.

1. Delays in Execution
Congress Executive Body resembling King &c:
2. No Combination Except one or the other
Idea of Distinctions resembling British Constitution.

Reference: Worthington Chauncey Ford (ed.), *Journal of the Continental Congress, 1774–1789,* Vol. IV (Washington: GPO, 1906).

THOMAS BURKE, NOTES ON THE PROPOSED ARTICLES, NOVEMBER 1777

Article 4th

The Constitution of No. Carolina permits not the Privilege of Citizens to any who have not resided therein 12 months, and paid Taxes. (local protection is given to all within the Territory) the Legislature therefore cannot ratify an artikle which gives such priviliges to persons residing in other States. Our Commons are voted for by all free Citizens, and if the Inhabitants of our Neighboring States have the priviliges of Citizens in ours they might insist upon the right of voting for Members of Our Legislature which would be a political absurdity. it seems therefore proper that this article should be Amended by adding after the clause refer'd to—*not inconsistant with their respective Constitutions:* The Provisionary clause of this article, in my opinion, deprives the States of every power to increase or regulate their particular Commerce, Agriculture or Manufactures. they cannot prevent by Duties or restrictions importations, or Exportations Injurious to any of them. this surely is what no staple state ought to admit, and that of all ours, who has so many Staples.

Article 5th

This article supposes that the appointment of delegates is at the will of the Legislature. tis an Error with respect to No. Carolina. Those officers are the creatures of the Constitution, are to be annually chozen by ballot, and if superceded must be in the same way. no choice can be made for less than one year. this article wants alteration if all the states are circumstanced as ours. for us I think the following would do "Delegates Constitutionally appointed and Controlled by the respective States shall annually meet in Congress on the first Monday in November" The remaining part of this article tho unjust[?] in the mode of determining Questions, must be submitted to for the sake of public convenience, but if the latter clause exempts the Delegates from Prosecutions in their respective states for their misdemeanors in Congress, it takes away the control of the States, and being contrary to our Constitution cannot be admitted.

Article 6th

The first clause of this article in my opinion imposes very unnecessary restraints upon the States. the various affairs of a free commercial People will require them often to enter into Conferences and agreements with foreign states, and the commercial Interests of each state ought to be its own peculiar care; and subject [to] no control or Interposition from others I can see no propriety in such a Restraint as each State ought, in my opinion, to be at least at liberty to enter into any Commercial Treaty it may think proper so that it be not inconsistent with Treaties entered into by the United States. These seem to me to be of Importance to the Staple States. there can be no reason for subjecting them to restraints which may arise from the Jealousy or ambition of others. each should be at liberty to increase its wealth and strength as much as possible. tis sufficient that they be restrained from using them to the Injury of their Neighbors, and that they be obliged to contribute in Just proportion to the Common defence. The latter part of the first section of this article is right.

The second Section goes too far. the Word Treaty ought to be left out. the States will often have occasion to Treat on subjects which concern none but those engaged in it; and there can be no reason for restraining them from it, if the United States have [power to?] prevent any alliance or Compact injurious to the whole it is sufficient, and this purpose will be answered by giving them a negative on all Compacts between two or more States.

The third section is right.

The fourth section so far as it regards the Navy appears to me to be impolitic. it speaks a Jealousy which I fear will forever prevent the United States from having a powerful Navy, tho' nothing is more Essential to its future Security against foreign Enemies. the Emulation of the States in this particular ought to be encouraged by every Means, for that Emulation will be the most powerful Instrument for giving to the whole a formidable Navy, and with such they will be secure against the World. I see no reason for the Jealousy. the fleet of one state cannot endanger another because they are accessable to each other by Land, and a Sea Invasion might very readily be counteracted by a Land Invasion. the rest of this Section is right.

The fifth Section is right in everything but what relates to Indian Wars, and it will be difficult to frame an article to suit in this particular. I am inclined to think this might be left for the subject of partial alliances, for all the States are not Interested in it and yet Several States have one common Interest in it, and there are still some particular Interests in which but one or few states are concerned,

Article 7th

I have no objection to this provided the provision recommended by Connecticut takes place.

Article 9th

This article is exceedingly Comprehensive, its matter is of the greatest Importance, but its arrangement seems to me much too Complicated. My own Idea of the Power which Congress ought to possess is founded on the following proposition

The United States ought to be as one Sovereign with respect to foreign Powers, in all things that relate to War or where the States have one Common Interest. But in all commercial or other peaceful Intercourse they ought to be as separate Sovereigns.

The first is Necessary, because no one can be defended from the evils of war but by the united force of all, and to make this force the more Effectual their union for its Exertions should be as close and simple as possible.

The Second is Necessary, in order that each may acquire strength to as great a degree as its circumstances may admit, without being subject to restraints which may arise from the Jealousy of its neighbors. and as the growth of each is its own proper concern, and cannot be prejudicial to the whole, but on the contrary advantageous to them as long as the force acquired is still subject to be applied for the common security, by one common Magistrate, I can perceive no reason for a power in any Common Council which can restrain the Commercial or other peaceful intercourse of the States, among themselves, or separately with foreign Powers, and it can answer no purpose but to

subject the Property of the States to partial combinations in the common council.

A private citizen who embarques a part of his fortune in a Copartnership would be deemed very unwise should he suffer the members of that partnership to possess a power that might restrain him from [improving] the remaining part of his Fortune to what extent he pleased consistent with the Common Interest. equally unwise in my opinion is it for a State who unites with others for common defence to submit to a power which may prevent the growth of her Strength and Oppulence. pursuant to these propositions my Ideas of the powers which ought to be in Congress are as follow.

In General they should have the Power of declaring War, and peace. But wherever a war should be declared before actual Invasion or commencement or Threatening of some actual Hostilities, any State ought to be at Liberty to renounce the War and become a Neutral power but when Hostilities are actually commenced against any of the States, it ought to be deemed common cause, and none should withhold assistance.

Also they should have the Power of Concluding Treaties of Alliance equally binding and affecting the whole for the purpose of strengthening the common security. this should be restrained like the former to defence, for it ought always to be in the Power of each state to remain Neuter in all offensive wars whether the United States be principles or allies in it.

These Powers necessarily require that the Congress should send and receive Embassadors, but not that this Power should be sole and exclusive. I should like an Amendment to this purpose "shall have the sole and exclusive Power of declaring War and concluding Peace, and of sending, and receiving ambassadors *in the name of the United States* of Entering into Treaties and Alliances *equally binding upon, and affecting the whole.* here the Exceptions to those general rules should come by way of provision. The remaining powers in the first section of this article are Incident to the power of declaring War, they are only an execution of the Law of Nations *quoad hoc*

The second section is [b]adly worded, "the United States shall be the last resort on appeal in all disputes between the States." I have no Idea of an appeal, or last resort unless their be some prior Jurisdiction and prior resort, and I know of no such thing between the States. but my objection to this section is more substantial. if the Congress are to nominate the persons who Constitute the Judicatory I can easily foresee it will not always if ever be impartial. the Congress cannot know any persons to appoint, but such as are Suggested by the parties and that State which has the prevailing Interest in Congress will thus nominate all the Judges. their being drawn from each State and afterwards drawn by Lot is no Security, because three persons in each State are easily corrupted. if this article were amended by giving the Nomination by ballot to the States not Interested it would answer better to my Idea of an Impartial arbiter between the States, and the Congress should have this Power only as the Official Instrument for erecting the occasional Tribunal, and for carrying its decrees into Execution. as it now stands they have it too much in their power to Influence the decisions which they themselves are to execute which in my Opinion is dangerous in any political Community.

The third section might be easily fitted to the Amendment I propose

The four[th] section includes many powers which I cannot perceive either to be necessary or proper for Congress. regulating the alloy of coin struck by authority of any of the States, fixing the standard of weights and measures, regulating the Trade and affairs with Indians, and all that Appertains to the Naval force which ought never in my opinion to be under any restraint or authority of Congress except in time of public War. the first is dangerous, because it gives to a council which is composed of but very few members from each state and which is without control an unlimited power over the property of Individuals. the power to increase the alloy is a power to pay off any Debt with less than the sum contracted for, and involves an extensive power over property.

In the fifth Section the power to borrow money and emit Bills, is an unlimited power over all property. it is a power to Tax at pleasure, and ought never to be in Congress but when given by the States upon special Occasions. it is Contrary to the fundamental Maxims of our Constitution, vizt [No] Man is to be subject to any Imposition but by [consent of] his representatives. the Congress is not the representative of any one community. the members are delegates from the Legislatures, not represent[at]ives of the people, and the Delegates of one State are not the choice of the other states nor has any state a check on the Delegates of another state. if the Legislature can delegate their power to tax to any person they may Delegate it to the Executive Magistrate, and may make him absolute, by giving him the power over the property of the Community if they cannot delegate to him they cannot delegate to any other the delegation in any case is transferring that power to others which the Constitution vests solely in the Legislative Magistrate and is as unconstitutional as if the Governor or Judges were to substitute other persons to exercise their respective powers, or as if the assembly were to appoint substitutes to Enact Laws or impower the Delegates in Congress to enact Law

[Endorsed:]

Some Notes on the Articles of Confederation while in Congress.

Reference: Edmund C. Burnett (ed.), *Letters of Members of the Continental Congress*, Vol. II (8 vols.; Washington: Carnegie Institution, 1921–1936).

THOMAS BURKE, REMARKS CONCERNING THE PROPOSED ARTICLES, NOVEMBER 15, 1777

I consider the Congress at present as a General Council of America instituted for the purpose of opposing the usurpations of Britain, conducting the war against her, and forming foreign alliances as necessary thereto. Incident to this must be the General direction of the Army and Navy, because they are the instruments of the war.

Also for the providing the necessary funds for the disbursements, because without them neither Army or Navy can subsist.

Also the making Treaties with Foreign Powers, to be binding on all the States alike and equally to affect them, because this is the essence of foreign alliance.

This Idea of the Powers, use and authority of Congress, excludes all coercive Interpositions within the States respectively, except with respect to the Army and Navy because the States are competent to every exertion of power within themselves. Also the appointment of ways and means for supplying the Contingents of men, money or other things otherwise than by recommendation which always implies a power in the State to reject.

Also the power of imprisoning or otherwise punishing any Citizen, because that is not necessary for the end of their Institution, and every individual is to be tried and punished only by those Laws to which he consents. The Congress for this reason can give no authority to any man or set of men to arrest or punish a Citizen, nor can it Lawfully be done but by the authority of the particular States.

Also all pretence for continuance of a Congress after the war is concluded, or of assuming a power to any other purposes—than that are above expressed. The Congress now determines by a majority which need not be more than five, and of which seven is always conclusive if the last mentioned exclusion be not right, the Congress might engage the States in confederacies, injurious to all but the continued majority 'Tis my opinion that every State has a right to control the Cantonment of Soldiers within their Territories, but as all the Governments, are not yet settled, it might be inconvenient to say any thing of it, and it is not necessary. Whenever a State finds occasion to exercise this right, I think none will be hardy enough to dispute it. But I believe it will be necessary for every established State to provide a mode whereby the Civil authority can interpose to prevent Courts Martial from exceeding their Jurisdiction.

Tis true a Soldier expressly consents to be bound by the articles of war, and to submit to the martial Jurisdiction, but in all trials, the first question is the Identity which must raise in this case the enquiry Soldier or Citizen? If the Court Martial can determine this question, it is in their power to call any Citizen a Soldier, and to subject him to Military Law. This evidently points out the necessity of the check of the civil authority. This Confederation is a subject of the highest importance, but not having yet passed the House, except when in Committee, it seems it must not be laid before the Assemblies. I shall deem it my duty to examine every article of it with the most critical scrutiny, and submit my thoughts to the Assembly, and receive their Instructions. But I am told by the President that it will violate my obligation of Secrecy to do this before it has passed the House.

If the Assembly agree with me in the foregoing Ideas, of the Power, use and authority of Congress, I beg leave to recommend that they instruct their Delegates not to depart from them, nor to consent to any act or resolve which shall tend to exempt the Courts Martial from the control of the civil power in the States.

I am not desirous of these Instructions in order to restrain the Delegates. I believe none of them even without Instructions would vote contrary to those Ideas, but as all questions are carried by a Majority in Congress, the state may perhaps be bound, tho' her Delegates should dissent, especially where the Instructions are so general and Powers so indefinite as ours. I wish the state therefore to instruct, and by some public act to disclaim being bound by any resolves contrary to her Instructions. Without some thing of this kind, according to the present Constitution of Congress it may be impossible for the Delegates to preserve the Independence of the State from Encroachments, for by that constitution they are not allowed to protest or enter their Dissent.

These thoughts are humbly submitted to the Honorable the General Assembly of North Carolina by their most respectful humble Serv't

THOS. BURKE.

Reference: Edmund C. Burnett (ed.), *Letters of Members of the Continental Congress,* Vol. II (8 vols.; Washington: Carnegie Institution, 1921–1936).

47

The States and Ratification of the Articles of Confederation

The Articles of Confederation were sent to the states for debate and ratification on November 15, 1777. All of the states debated the Articles and key discussions are presented here to show the concerns of the states. Some of the states responded to their delegates in the Continental Congress who had asked for speedy favorable instructions for their votes. In most cases, even those state legislatures with reservations authorized their delegates to vote in favor of the Articles.

On July 9, 1778 delegates from eight states, New Hampshire, Massachusetts, Rhode Island, Connecticut, New York, Pennsylvania, Virginia, and South Carolina, voted to ratify the Articles. On July 21, 1778 North Carolina's delegates ratified, followed by Georgia on July 24, New Jersey on November 26, and Delaware on May 5, 1779. Only Maryland refused to ratify, supposedly because of worries over the disposition of western lands. Indeed, when Virginia's legislature gave up conflicting western land claims, Maryland's legislature instructed its delegates to vote favorably, which they did on January 30, 1781. All of the states had had some reservations, especially over separation of power between the states and the central government. By the time Maryland ratified the Articles of Confederation, some of the states and a number of national congressmen had ceased to have much confidence in the national government they had created.

ARTICLES PROPOSED TO THE STATES, NOVEMBER 15, 1777

To all to whom these Presents shall come, we the undersigned Delegates of the States affixed to our Names send greeting.

Whereas the Delegates of the United States of America in Congress assembled did on the fifteenth day of November in the Year of our Lord One Thousand Seven Hundred and Seventyseven, and in the Second Year of the Independence of America agree to certain articles of Confederation and perpetual Union between the States of Newhampshire, Massachusetts-bay, Rhodeisland and Providence Plantations, Connecticut, New York, New Jersey, Pennsylvania, Delaware, Maryland, Virginia, North-Carolina, South-Carolina and Georgia in the Words following, viz.

"Articles of Confederation and perpetual Union between the States of Newhampshire, Massachusetts-bay, Rhodeisland and Providence Plantations, Connecticut, New-York, New-Jersey, Pennsylvania, Delaware, Maryland,

Virginia, North-Carolina, South-Carolina and Georgia.

ARTICLE I. The stile of this confederacy shall be "The United States of America."

ARTICLE II. Each State retains its sovereignty, freedom and independence, and every power, jurisdiction and right, which is not by this confederation expressly delegated to the United States, in Congress assembled.

ARTICLE III. The said States hereby severally enter into a firm league of friendship with each other, for their common defence, the security of their liberties, and their mutual and general welfare, binding themselves to assist each other, against all force offered to, or attacks made upon them, or any of them, on account of religion, sovereignty, trade, or any other pretence whatever.

ARTICLE IV. The better to secure and perpetuate mutual friendship and intercourse among the people of the different States in this Union, the free inhabitants of each of these States, paupers, vagabonds and fugitives from justice excepted, shall be entitled to all privileges and immunities of free citizens in the several States; and the people of each State shall have free ingress and regress to and from any other State, and shall enjoy therein all the privileges of trade and commerce, subject to the same duties, impositions and restrictions as the inhabitants thereof respectively, provided that such restrictions shall not extend so far as to prevent the removal of property imported into any State, to any other State of which the owner is an inhabitant; provided also that no imposition, duties or restriction shall be laid by any State, on the property of the United States, or either of them.

If any person guilty of, or charged with treason, felony, or other high misdemeanor in any State, shall flee from justice, and be found in any of the United States, he shall upon demand of the Governor or Executive power, of the State from which he fled, be delivered up and removed to the State having jurisdiction of his offence.

Full faith and credit shall be given in each of these States to the records, acts and judicial proceedings of the courts and magistrates of every other State.

ARTICLE V. For the more convenient management of the general interests of the United States, delegates shall be annually appointed in such manner as the legislature of each State shall direct, to meet in Congress on the first Monday in November, in every year, with a power reserved to each State, to recall its delegates, or any of them, at any time within the year, and to send others in their stead, for the remainder of the year.

No State shall be represented in Congress by less than two, nor by more than seven members; and no person shall be capable of being a delegate for more than three years in any term of six years; nor shall any person, being a delegate, be capable of holding any office under the United States, for which he, or another for his benefit receives any salary, fees or emolument of any kind.

Each State shall maintain its own delegates in a meeting of the States, and while they act as members of the committee of the States.

In determining questions in the United States, in Congress assembled, each State shall have one vote.

Freedom of speech and debate in Congress shall not be impeached or questioned in any court, or place out of Congress, and the members of Congress shall be protected in their persons from arrests and imprisonments, during the time of their going to and from, and attendance on Congress, except for treason, felony, or breach of the peace.

ARTICLE VI. No State without the consent of the United States in Congress assembled, shall send any embassy to, or receive any embassy from, or enter into any conferrence, agreement, alliance or treaty with any kind prince or state; nor shall any person holding any office of profit or trust under the United States, or any of them, accept of any present, emolument, office or title of any kind whatever from any king, prince or foreign state; nor shall the United States in Congress assembled, or any of them, grant any title of nobility.

No two or more States shall enter into any treaty, confederation or alliance whatever between them, without the consent of the United States in Congress assembled, specifying accurately the purposes for which the same is to be entered into, and how long it shall continue.

No State shall lay any imposts or duties, which may interfere with any stipulations in treaties, entered into by the United States in Congress assembled, with any king, prince or state, in pursuance of any treaties already proposed by Congress, to the courts of France and Spain.

No vessels of war shall be kept up in time of peace by any State, except such number only, as shall be deemed necessary by the United States in Congress assembled, for the defence of such State, or its trade; nor shall any body of forces be kept up by any State, in time of peace, except such number only, as in the judgment of the United States, in Congress assembled, shall be deemed requisite to garrison the forts necessary for the defence of such State; but every State shall always keep up a well regulated and disciplined militia, sufficiently armed and accoutred, and shall provide and constantly have ready for use, in public stores, a due number of field pieces and tents, and a proper quantity of arms, ammunition and camp equipage.

No State shall engage in any war without the consent of the United States in Congress assembled, unless such State be actually invaded by enemies, or shall have received certain advice of a resolution being formed by some nation of Indians to invade such State, and the danger is so imminent as not to admit of a delay, till the United States in Congress assembled can be consulted: nor shall any State grant commissions to any ships or vessels of war, nor letters of marque or reprisal, except it be after a declaration of war by the United States in Congress assembled, and then only against the kingdom or state and the subjects thereof, against which war has been so declared, and under such regulations as shall be established by the United States in Congress assembled, unless such State be infested by pirates, in which case vessels of war may be fitted out for that occasion, and kept so long as the danger shall continue, or until the United States in Congress assembled shall determine otherwise.

ARTICLE VII. When land-forces are raised by any State for the common defence, all officers of or under the rank of colonel, shall be appointed by the Legislature of each State respectively by whom such forces shall be raised, or in such manner as such State shall direct, and all vacancies shall be filled up by the State which first made the appointment.

ARTICLE VIII. All charges of war, and all other expenses that shall be incurred for the common defence or general welfare, and allowed by the United States in Congress assembled, shall be defrayed out a common treasury, which shall be supplied by the several States, in proportion to the value of all land within each State, granted to or surveyed for any person, as such land and the buildings and improvements thereon shall be estimated according to such mode as the United States in Congress assembled, shall from time to time direct and appoint.

The taxes for paying that proportion shall be laid and levied by the authority and direction of the Legislatures of the several States within the time agreed upon by the United States in Congress assembled.

ARTICLE IX. The United States in Congress assembled, shall have the sole and exclusive right and power of determining on peace and war, except in the cases mentioned in the sixth article—of sending and receiving ambassadors—entering into treaties and alliances, provided that no treaty of commerce shall be made whereby the legislative power of the respective States shall be restrained from imposing such imposts and duties on foreigners, as their own people are subjected to, or from prohibiting the exportation or importation of any species of goods or commodities whatsoever—of establishing rules for deciding in all cases, what captures on land or water shall be legal, and in what manner prizes taken by land or naval forces in the service of the United States shall be divided or appropriated—of granting letters of marque and reprisal in times of peace—appointing courts for the trial of piracies and felonies committed on the high seas and establishing courts for receiving and determining finally appeals in all cases of captures, provided that no member of Congress shall be appointed a judge of any of the said courts.

The United States in Congress assembled shall also be the last resort on appeal in all disputes and differences now subsisting or that hereafter may arise between two or more States concerning boundary, jurisdiction or any other cause whatever; which authority shall always be exercised in the manner following. Whenever the legislative or executive authority or lawful agent of any State in controversy with another shall present a petition to Congress, stating the matter in question and praying for a hearing, notice thereof shall be given by order of Congress to the legislative or executive authority of the other State in controversy, and a day assigned for the appearance of the parties by their lawful agents, who shall then be directed to appoint by joint consent, commissioners or judges to constitute a court for hearing and determining the matter in question: but if they cannot agree, Congress shall name three persons out of each of the United States, and from the list of such persons each party shall alternately strike out one, the petitioners beginning, until the number shall be reduced to thirteen; and from that number not less than seven, nor more than nine names as Congress shall direct, shall in the presence of Congress be drawn out by lot, and the persons whose names shall be so drawn or any five of them, shall be commisioners or judges, to hear and finally determine the controversy, so always as a major part of the judges who shall hear the cause shall agree in the determination: and if either party shall neglect to attend at the day appointed, without showing reasons, which Congress shall judge sufficient, or being present shall refuse to strike, the Congress shall proceed to nominate three persons out of each State, and the Secretary of Congress shall strike in behalf of such party absent or refusing; and the judgment and sentence of the court to be appointed, in the manner before prescribed, shall be final and conclusive; and if any of the parties shall refuse to submit to the authority of such court, or to appear or defend their claim or cause, the court shall nevertheless proceed to pronounce sentence, or judgment, which shall in like manner be final and decisive, the judgment or sentence and other proceedings being in either case transmitted to Congress, and lodged among the acts of Congress for the security of the parties concerned: provided that every commissioner, before he sits in judgment, shall take an oath to be administered by one of the judges of the supreme or superior court of the State where the cause shall be tried, "well and truly to hear and determine the matter in question, according to the best of his judgment, without favour, affection or hope of reward:" provided also that no State shall be deprived of territory for the benefit of the United States.

All controversies concerning the private right of soil claimed under different grants of two or more States, whose jurisdiction as they may respect such lands, and the States which passed such grants are adjusted, the said grants or either of them being at the same time claimed to have originated antecedent to such settlement of jurisdiction, shall on the petition of either party to the Congress of the United States, be finally determined as near as may be in the same manner as is before prescribed for deciding disputes respecting territorial jurisdiction between different States.

The United States in Congress assembled shall also have the sole and exclusive right and power of regulating the alloy and value of coin struck by their own authority, or by that of the respective States.—fixing the standard of weights and measures throughout the United States,—regulating the trade and managing all affairs with the Indians, not members of any of the States, provided that the legislative right of any State within its own limits be not infringed or violated—establishing and regulating post-offices from one State to another, throughout all the United States, and exacting such postage on the papers passing thro' the same as may be requisite to defray the expenses of the said office—appointing all officers of the land forces, in the service of the United States, excepting regimental officers—appointing all the officers of the naval forces, and commissioning all officers whatever in the service of the United States—making rules for the government and regulation of the said land and naval forces, and directing their operations.

The United States in Congress assembled shall have authority to appoint a committee, to sit in the recess of Congress, to be denominated "a Committee of the States," and to consist of one delegate from each State; and to appoint such other committees and civil officers as may be necessary for managing the general affairs of the United States under their direction—to appoint one of their number to preside, provided that no person be allowed to serve in the office of president more than one year in any term of three years; to ascertain the necessary sums of money to be raised for the service of the United States, and to appropriate and apply the same for defraying the public expenses—to borrow money, or emit bills on the credit of the United States, transmitting every half year to the respective States an account of the sums of money so borrowed or emitted,—to build and equip a navy—to agree upon the number of land forces, and to make requisitions from each State for its quota, in proportion to the number of white inhabitants in such State; which requisition shall be binding, and thereupon the Legislature of each State shall appoint the regimental officers, raise the men and cloath, arm and equip them in a soldier like manner, at the expense of the United States; and the officers and men so cloathed, armed and equipped shall march to the place appointed, and within the time agreed on by the United States in Congress assembled: but if the United States in Congress assembled shall, on consideration of circumstances judge proper that any State should not raise men, or should raise a smaller number of men than the quota therof, such extra number shall be number of men that the quota thereof, such extra number shall be raised, officered, cloathed, armed and equipped in the same manner as the quota of such State, unless the legislature of such State shall judge that such extra number cannot be safely spared out of the same, in which case they shall raise officer, cloath, arm and equip as many of such extra number as they judge can be safely spared. And the officers and men so cloathed, armed and equipped, shall march to the place appointed, and within the time agreed on by the United States in Congress assembled.

The United States in Congress assembled shall never engage in a war, nor grant letters of marque and reprisal in time of peace, nor enter into any treaties or alliances, nor coin money, nor regulate the value thereof, nor ascertain the sums and expenses necessary for the defence and welfare of the United States, or any of them, nor emit bills, nor borrow money on the credit of the United States, nor appropriate money, nor agree upon the number of vessels of war, to be built or purchased, or the number of land or sea forces to be raised, nor appoint a commander in chief of the army or navy, unless nine States assent to the same: nor shall a question on any other point, except for adjourning from day to day be determined, unless by the votes of a majority of the United States in Congress assembled.

The Congress of the United States shall have power to adjourn to any time within the year, and to any place within the United States, so that no period of adjournment be for a longer duration than the space of six months, and shall publish the journal of their proceedings monthly, except such parts thereof relating to treaties, alliances or military operations, as in their judgment requiry secresy; and the yeas and nays of the delegates of each State on any question shall be military operations, as in their judgment require secresy; and the delegates of a State, or any of them, at his or their request shall be furnished with a transcript of the said journal, except such parts as are above excepted, to lay before the Legislatures of the several States.

ARTICLE X. The committee of the States, or any nine of them, shall be authorized to execute, in the recess of Congress, such of the powers of Congress as the United States in Congress assembled, by the consent of nine States, shall from time to time think expedient to vest them with; provided that no power be delegated to the said committee, for the exercise of which, by the articles of confederation, the voice of nine States in the Congress of the United States assembled is requisite.

ARTICLE XI. Canada acceding to this confederation, and joining in the measures of the United States, shall be admitted into, and entitled to all the advantages of this Union: but no other colony shall be admitted into the same, unless such admission be agreed to by nine States.

ARTICLE XII. All bills of credit emitted, monies borrowed and debts contracted by, or under the authority of Congress, before the assembling of the United States, in pursuance of the present confederation, shall be deemed and considered as a charge against the United States, for payment and satisfaction whereof the said United States, and the public faith are hereby solemnly pledged.

ARTICLE XIII. Every State shall abide by the determinations of the United States in Congress assembled, on all questions which by this confederation are submitted to them. And the articles of this confederation shall be inviolably observed by every State, and the Union shall be perpetual; nor shall any alteration at any time hereafter be made in any of them; unless such alteration be agreed to in a Congress of the United States, and be afterwards confirmed by the Legislatures of every State.

And whereas it has pleased the Great Governor of the world to incline the hearts of the Legislatures we respectively represent in Congress, to approve of, and to authorize us to ratify the said articles of confederation and perpetual union. Know ye that we the undersigned delegates, by virtue of the power and authority to us given for that purpose, do by these presents, in the name and in behalf of our respective constituents, fully and entirely ratify and confirm each and every of the said articles of confederation and perpetual union, and all and singular the matters and things therein contained: and we do further solemnly plight and engage the faith of our respective constituents, that they shall abide by the determinations of the United States in Congress assembled, on all questions, which by the said confederation are submitted to them. And that the articles thereof shall be inviolably observed by the States we re[s]pectively represent, and that the Union shall be perpetual.

In witness whereof we have hereunto set our hands in Congress. Done at Philadelphia in the State of Pennsylvania the ninth day of July in the year of our Lord one thousand seven hundred and seventy-eight, and in the third year of the independence of America.

On the part & behalf of the State of New Hampshire

JOSIAH BARTLETT,
JOHN WENTWORTH, Junr.,

August 8th, 1778.
On the part and behalf of the State of Massachusetts Bay

JOHN HANCOCK,
SAMUEL ADAMS,
ELBRIDGE GERRY,
FRANCIS DANA,
JAMES LOVELL,
SAMUEL HOLTEN.

On the part and behalf of the State of Rhode Island and Providence Plantations

WILLIAM ELLERY,
HENRY MARCHANT,
JOHN COLLINS.

On the part and behalf of the State of Connecticut

ROGER SHERMAN,
SAMUEL HUNTINGTON,
OLIVER WOLCOTT,
TITUS HOSMER,
ANDREW ADAMS.

On the part and behalf of the State of New York

JAS. DUANE,
FRA. LEWIS,
WM. DUER,
GOUV. MORRIS.

On the part and in behalf of the State of New Jersey, Nov. 26, 1778

JNO. WITHERSPOON,
NATHL. SCUDDER.

On the part and behalf of the State of Pennsylvania

ROBT. MORRIS,
DANIEL ROBERDEAU,
JONA. BAYARD SMITH,
WILLIAM CLINGAN,
JOSEPH REED, 22d July, 1778.

On the part & behalf of the State of Delaware

THO. M'KEAN,

Feby. 12, 1779.

JOHN DICKINSON,

May 5th, 1779.

NICHOLAS VAN DYKE.

On the part and behalf of the State of Maryland

JOHN HANSON,

March 1, 1781.

DANIEL CARROLL,

Mar. 1, 1781.
On the part and behalf of the State of Virginia

RICHARD HENRY LEE,
JOHN BANISTER,

THOMAS ADAMS,
JNO. HARVIE,
FRANCIS LIGHTFOOT LEE.

On the part and behalf of the State of No. Carolina

JOHN PENN, July 21st, 1778.
CORNS. HARNETT,
JNO. WILLIAMS.

On the part & behalf of the State of South Carolina

HENRY LAURENS,
WILLIAM HENRY DRAYTON,
JNO. MATHEWS,
RICHD. HUTSON,
THOS. HEYWARD, Junr.

On the part & behalf of the State of Georgia

JNO. WALTON,

24th July, 1778.

EDWD. TELFAIR,
EDWD. LANGWORTHY.

Reference: Francis Newton Thorpe (ed.), *The Federal and State Constitutions, Colonial Charters, and Other Organic Laws of the States*, Vol. I (Washington: GPO, 1909).

CONGRESS URGES STATES TO RATIFY ARTICLES, NOVEMBER 17, 1777

The committee appointed to arrange the articles of confederation, and prepare a circular letter to accompany it to the several states, brought in the following draught:

IN CONGRESS, YORK TOWN, 17 November, 1777.

Congress having agreed upon a plan of confederacy for securing the freedom, sovereignty, and independence of the United States, authentic copies are now transmitted for the consideration of the respective legislatures.

This business, equally intricate and important, has, in its progress, been attended with uncommon embarrassments and delay, which the most anxious solicitude and persevering diligence could not prevent. To form a permanent union, accommodated to the opinion and wishes of the delegates of so many states, differing in habits, produce, commerce, and internal police, was found to be a work which nothing but time and reflection, conspiring with a disposition to conciliate, could mature and accomplish.

Hardly is it to be expected that any plan, in the variety of provisions essential to our union, should exactly correspond with the maxims and political views of every particular State. Let it be remarked, that, after the most careful enquiry and the fullest information, this is proposed as the best which could be adapted to the circumstances of all; and as that alone which affords any tolerable prospect of a general ratification.

Permit us, then, earnestly to recommend these articles to the immediate and dispassionate attention of the legislatures of the respective states. Let them be candidly reviewed under a sense of the difficulty of combining in one general system the various sentiments and interests of a continent divided into so many sovereign and independent communities, under a conviction of the absolute necessity of uniting all our councils and all our strength, to maintain and defend our common liberties: let them be examined with a liberality becoming brethren and fellow-citizens surrounded by the same imminent dangers, contending for the same illustrious prize, and deeply interested in being forever bound and connected together by ties the most intimate and indissoluble; and finally, let them be adjusted with the temper and magnanimity of wise and patriotic legislators, who, while they are concerned for the prosperity of their own more immediate circle, are capable of rising superior to local attachments, when they may be incompatible

with the safety, happiness, and glory of the general Confederacy.

We have reason to regret the time which has elapsed in preparing this plan for consideration: with additional solicitude we look forward to that which must be necessarily spent before it can be ratified. Every motive loudly calls upon us to hasten its conclusion.

More than any other consideration, it will confound our foreign enemies, defeat the flagitious practices of the disaffected, strengthen and confirm our friends, support our public credit, restore the value of our money, enable us to maintain our fleets and armies, and add weight and respect to our councils at home, and to our treaties abroad.

In short, this salutary measure can no longer be deferred. It seems essential to our very existence as a free people, and without it we may soon be constrained to bid adieu to independence, to liberty and safety; blessings which, from the justice of our cause, and the favour of our Almighty Creator visibly manifested in our protection, we have reason to expect, if, in an humble dependence on his divine providence, we strenuously exert the means which are placed in our power.

To conclude, if the legislature of any State shall not be assembled, Congress recommend to the executive authority to convene it without delay; and to each respective legislature it is recommended to invest its delegates with competent powers ultimately in the name and behalf of the state to subscribe articles of confederation and perpetual union of the United States; . . .

Reference: Worthington Chauncey Ford (ed.), *Journal of the Continental Congress, 1774–1789*, Vol. IX (Washington: GPO, 1906).

WILLIAM H. DRAYTON OF SOUTH CAROLINA, JANUARY 20, 1778

The speech of the hon. William Henry Drayton, esq. chief justice of South Carolina, delivered on the twentieth January, 1778, in the general assembly—resolved into the committee of the whole upon the articles of the confederation of the United States of America.

Mr. Chairman—A plan of a confederation of the United States of America, is at length by congress, given to the continent: A subject of as high importance as can be presented to their attention. Upon the wise formation of this, their independence, glory and happiness ultimately depend. The plan is delivered abroad for private and public information: It is sent to us for consideration. Sir, my mind labors under the load that is thus thrown upon it.—Millions are to experience the effects of the judgment of those few, whom the laws permit to think and to act for them in this grand business. Millions—posterity innumerable, will bless or curse our conduct!—Their happiness or misery depend upon us—their fate is now in our hands! I almost tremble, while I assist in holding the important balance!—But sir, the great Disposer of all things, has placed us in this important period, pregnant with vast events. He has called us forth to legislate for the new world; and to endeavor to bind the various people of it in durable bands of friendship and union. We must obey: and I trust we shall obey, with courage and integrity. Actuated by these principles, I am incapable of receding from my duty. And conscious that I am bound to consider the subject of a confederation of the United States, upon the broad basis of equality, I shall endeavor to discharge this obligation, first, by viewing the plan before us, with liberality, and with that decency and respect, due to the high authority from which it is derived; and then, by taking the liberty of throwing out my ideas of such terms, as in my opinion are desirable, attainable, and likely to form a beneficial confederation.

The best writers upon government, agree in this as a political truth; that where the liberties of the people are to be preserved, the legislative and executive should ever be separate and distinct; and that the first should consist of parts mutually forming a check upon each other. The consuls, senate and people, constituted such a government in Rome. The kings, lords and commons, erected such a government in Britain. The first, one of the best of antiquity—the last, the most perfect system, the wit of man ever devised: But

both, as it is the case with all things temporal, lost their capability of action, and changed their very nature.

We are about to establish a confederated government which I religiously hope will last for ages. And, I must be pardoned when I say, that this government does not appear likely to be formed upon those principles, which the wisest men have deemed, and which long and invariable experience prove, to be the most secure defences to liberty. The congress seem to have lost sight of this wise mode of government. At least it is certain, that they have rejected it. I lament their decision: I have apprehension for the consequences. Into their own hands, they appear inclined to assume almost all the important powers of government. The second article speaks of the sovereignty of the respective states, but by the time we arrive at the last, scarce the shadow of sovereignty remains to any. "No two or more states shall enter into any treaty," but by consent of congress—"nor shall any body of forces be kept up by any state, in time of peace, except such number only," as congress shall deem requisite—"no vessels of war, shall be kept up in time of peace by any state, except such number only," as congress shall deem necessary—"nor shall any state grant commissions to any ships or vessels of war, except it be after a declaration of war by," Congress—and, these are great and humiliating restrictions upon their sovereignty. It is of necessity, that the sovereignty of the states should be restricted—but I would do this with a gentle hand. Cannot a good confederation be had, without these humiliating restrictions? I think it may. However, independent of the settlement of this point; the two last restrictions require another observation. From the first of them it ought to be presumed, that upon a vacancy in any of the vessels of war, kept up by any state in the time of peace by the permission of congress, the state to which they belong shall in time of peace, be at liberty to issue a new commission. But if this is to be presumed, the sentiment ought to have been precisely expressed; for it is obvious, a doubt upon this matter, may arise from the restriction, that no state shall grant commissions to any ships or vessels of war, except it be after a declaration of war. These clauses, if we give due efficacy to the signification of words, really clash—at least displaying an ambiguity, they require a rule of construction, that must destroy the peremptoriness of words. A rule which ought not to be admitted into an instrument of this kind; for it should be maturely considered; and it may be precisely worded, without the formality of a statute law.

There seems to be a dangerous inaccuracy in that part of the sixth article, prohibiting the states respectively from entering into any conference with any king, prince or state. I presume this ought to be understood, to respect a foreign state only: But it may be insisted upon, that the prohibition includes even the United States. And why should not two or more of these have any conference? I would have the doubt absolutely destroyed.

The third section of the article now under my observation, declares, that "no state shall lay any imposts or duties, which may interfere with any stipulations in treaties, entered into by congress with any king, prince or state, in pursuance of any treaties already proposed by congress to the courts of France and Spain:" And I must contrast this with the provision in the ninth article, "that no treaty of commerce shall be made whereby the legislative power of the respective states shall be restrained from imposing such imposts and duties on foreigners, as their own people are subject to, or from prohibiting the exportation or importation of any species of goods or commodities whatsoever."—I am of opinion, we are to understand from the first of these clauses, that no state shall lay any imposts or duties, which may interfere with the present foreign stipulations of congress, in treaties already proposed; and that such stipulations, free of such interference, may be concluded by treaty: But this latter meaning is not expressed. Indeed a great doubt arises, whether this be the true intent of that clause, when we consider the subsequent proviso, worded in these most peremptory terms, that "no treaty of commerce shall be made whereby the legislative power of the respective states shall be restrained from imposing such imposts and duties on foreigners, as their own people are subject to, or from prohibiting the exportation or importation of any species of goods or commodities whatsoever." I know, that the rule of construction in law, is capable of warranting the meaning I have extended to the first clause, and of giving efficacy to both: But then it must destroy the positive terms in the second, qualifying by giving them an operation only respecting treaties of commerce, which shall be made exclusive and independent of the foreign stipulations of congress in treaties already proposed. And unless this rule takes place, the first clause is absolutely in effect repealed, by that which is subsequent. We experimentally know, that men will not always admit that to be reason, which really is so; and that where there is a doubt, they will obstinately contend for, and persist in opposite constructions. Those two clauses will undoubtedly admit of contention; and the least consequence that can arise, will be, either that the first clause must be considered as repealed, or the natural import of the positive terms in the last must be destroyed, and qualified. And independent of these disagreeable alternatives, the last clause appears to be an intolerable clog to foreign negotiation—I could wish here to finish particularizing matter of doubt: but it is necessary to select one instance more, and then I will shew the main tendency of these objections.

In the fourth section of the ninth article, congress is vested with the power of "regulating the trade and managing all affairs with the Indians, not members of any of the states, provided that the legislative right of any state within its own limits, be not infringed or violated." I much approve the grant, but I confess I do not understand the grant and proviso combined. For I cannot conceive, in what manner the legislative right of a state within its own limits, can be infringed, by an act of congress relative to Indians not members of any state: and therefore not within the limits of any so as to be subject to the operation of its legislative right.

It is of no moment with me, whether the doubts I have raised, are deemed obvious and important, or rather refined and of little consequence. Grant, and it must be admitted, that they have the appearance of doubts—I ask no more. The honor and interest of America require, that their grand act of confederation, should be a noble monument, free, as far as human wisdom can enable it to be from defect and flaw: Every thing unnecessary should be critically removed—every appearance of doubt should be carefully eradicated out of it. It is not to be thought, but that the present congress clearly understand the confederation. But other congresses will look for the spirit of the law. This "will then be the result of their good or bad logic: and this will depend on their good or bad digestion; on the violence of their passions; on the rank and condition of the parties, or on their connections with congress; and on all those little circumstances, which change the appearance of objects in the fluctuating mind of man." Thus thought the illustrious marquis Beccaria, of Milan, a sublime philosopher, reasoning on the interpretation of laws.—I must be permitted to continue his ideas, yet a little further upon this subject—they are so exactly in point. He says, "there is nothing more dangerous than the common axiom: The spirit of the laws is to be considered. To adopt it, is to give way to the torrent of opinions." "When the code of laws is once fixed, it should be observed in the literal sense." "When the rule of right which ought to direct the actions of the philosopher, as well as the ignorant, is a matter of controversy, not of fact, the people are slaves to the magistrates."—Is it not the intention of the confederation, that the people shall be free?—Let it then be adapted to the meanest capacity—let the rule of right be not matter of controversy, but of fact—let the confederation be understood according to that strict rule by which we understand penal laws. The confederation is of at least as much importance to America, as penal laws are in a small society—safety to the people is the object of both. In a word, the spirit of laws, lays down this maxim, that "in republics, the very nature of the constitution requires the judges to follow the letter of the law."

The fourth article declares, "that the free inhabitants of each of these states, paupers, vagabonds and fugitives from justice excepted, shall be entitled to all privileges and immunities of free citizens in the several states:" A position, in my opinion, absolutely inadmissible. Would the people of Massachusetts have the free negroes of Carolina eligible to their general court? Can it be intended, that the free inhabitants of one state shall have power to go into another, there to vote for representatives in the legislature?—And yet these things are clearly included in that clause. I think there ought to be no doubt, but that the free inhabitants should be white, and that such of one state, should be entitled to the privileges and immunities in another, only by the same means through which the free white inhabitants of that state are by law entitled—This article also provides for the "removal of property imported into any state;" but the removal of property acquired in it, into that "of which the owner is an inhabitant," is neglected. Has not the owner an equal right to enjoy at home, the last kind of property as the first? The provision in behalf of the congress, or a state, is manifestly in contradistinction to that in favor of a private owner.

The fifth article directs, that delegates shall be annually appointed to meet in congress, on the first Monday in November; and this is a matter requiring particular attention. Our climate instructs us, that the general assembly should make their long and important session in winter; and but a short one in summer, rather to finish than begin even common business. Indeed this is assented to by the members, and of course but few, and those too, in the vicinity of Charleston, attend the summer sitting, which cannot even with prudence be had between the months of July and November. When then, sir, are the delegates to be elected for the November congress? Are they to be chosen in the summer session; and in a very thin house of course? Congress cannot intend this—our country cannot admit of it; because such delegates, a representation of the highest nature, should ever be chosen in a full house, as the most obvious sign that they are the real delegates of the people. Nor can it be expected they should be chosen in January, the time which the climate and local circumstances point out, as the most proper for beginning our long and important session. For this would be reducing us to the necessity of appointing del-egates, almost twelve months before they were to serve—a measure neither necessary, nor to be admitted, if we can avoid it. Those months com-prehend an inclement summer and autumn; and death or sickness may destroy the intended rep-resentation: In which case the state may not, by the united voice of the people, be represented in congress from the begining of November to the middle of February—an event, that might be of fatal consequences. I shall therefore be very glad to see, either the month of February, March or April substituted instead of November. These rea-sons will also support me, in objecting to that part of the same article, relative to the recall of del-egates, within their year. A thin house may cast an unmerited censure upon a worthy delegate. I do not wish to see such a power existing. Not that I expect if there was such, that it would be abused, but we ought, as far as we can, to guard against the possible abuse of power. And, in addition to these principal objections against the fifth article, I must add, that I think it is utterly impolitic, to exclude a member of congress from being nomi-nated to a commission under the United States: The clause upon this subject is rather dark. Many a delegate, may be able to render much more important service to the confederacy, in such a station, than in congress—the occasion of such service may be pressing—as fit a person out of congress may not then be known—a member of congress may be most capable of the station because possessed of the secrets of congress—and shall the service of such a man be lost to the con-federacy, merely because he is a member of con-gress? The answer is obvious, I think—No, but let his acceptance of the commission vacate his seat and render him incapable of a re-election during the time he holds it.

I have already said, the sovereignty of the states should be restricted with a gentle hand: I now add it ought to be restrioted, only in cases of absolute necessity.—What absolute necessity is there, that congress should have the power of causing the value of all granted land, to be "estimated accord-ing to such mode, as they shall from time to time direct?" Congress should have no power, but

what is clearly defined in the nature of its opera-tion.—But I am absolutely against the position, that the public aids shall be raised by the several states, in proportion to the value of their granted lands, buildings and improvements. At the first blush of this proposition, nothing seems more equitable. But viewing the subject with more attention, I think I see, that it is unequal, injuri-ous and impolitic. It is unequal, because it seems to be in vain to expect, that such lands, etc. will be equally assessed in their true value. To have any chance of doing this, the assessors must actu-ally know every acre; and the multitude of them must have an equal judgment: But can either be even hoped for? Do we not positively know, that this mode of assessment does not answer the end—an equal and just assessment of the value? The assessors in Charleston, are men of knowl-edge, diligence and integrity, and is it not noto-rious, that the landed property in Charleston, although minutely known, and within a small circle, is unequally valued. Shall we, with our rea-son in full vigor, wish to extend to an immense circle, a principle that we are sensible fails us even in a small one? Is there any certain criterion of value? Does not value altogether depend on opinion, imagination, caprice? Hence it is, that we see the ideas of men upon this matter, infi-nitely wide. How then can it be expected, that a general assessment will ascertain, the true value? More or less than this, ought not to be rated: In the first case, the state would be injured—in the last, the other states would be defrauded; and that course should be taken, which seems most likely to avoid this Scylla and Charybdis. All move-ments in politics, as in mechanics, are difficult and hazardous in proportion to their complexed-ness. Now, in order to raise the general aid, a complex motion of government is necessary. First to assess the value of the land—then to ascertain the sum to arise from it—and then, to raise the sum, by a variety of taxes, according to the dis-cretion of the legislature. Is such a complicated motion to raise the aid desirable, especially when it cannot possibly be done with equality to the several states; and also when another principle is at hand, perfectly simple in its nature, just and equal in its operation, and is the allowed criterion to ascertain the proportion that is desired? I have been given to understand, that a capitation throughout the United States, was in contemplation of congress; and I have ever understood from the most approved writers upon this subject, that the true riches and strength of a state were to be rated in proportion to the number of people sustained in it. I would then have this the criterion of the public aid from each state. It is, in my humble opinion, in every respect preferable to the other. The criterion may be ascertained, and the tax raised by one act of government. Such a criterion and mode of taxation, has long been in use in some parts of this continent; and it is best, under a new government, to continue customs in use under the old, as long as they are salutary and practicable—this is the north point in my political compass. If we can attach the people, by exempting them from old impositions, such as quit rents in particular, it is the soundest policy to do so; for this interests them in support of the new establishment: But we cannot be too cautious in trying projects of a contrary nature. I said, the capitation criterion of proportion, was in every respect preferable to the land assessment: I now add, that it will be an important check upon the numeration of the white inhabitants to be taken in order to rate the military quota of each state; and this is a very material reason in support of the capitation criterion—we cannot well have too many proofs, to establish the true number of white inhabitants.

The mode of trial of disputes between any two or more states seems full of delay, and therefore it ought to be amended. The fifth article provides, that the representation of each state, shall not be less than two delegates; But the mode of trial specifies, that in a certain case, "congress shall name three persons out of each of the United States, from whom the judges shall be selected. Now a state may be represented by only two delegates, and then, the trial cannot be had, and considering the expense of paying delegates—the inconvenience of their attendance upon congress at a distance from their private affairs, and from constant experience, a bare representation is oftener

to be expected, than a supernumerary one. If it is meant, the three shall be taken from the people at large, which I will not imagine to be the case, a court may be picked; and therefore, that plan ought not to be heard of—In this case, I would prefer judges during good behavior, eminent for their knowledge in the law of nations; and who should be obliged to assign at large, the reasons upon which they ground their decrees.

The congress would be vested with the sole and exclusive right and power of regulating the alloy and value of coin struck by the authority of the respective states; and of fixing the standard of weights and measures throughout the United States: But I see no necessity for such delegation. To regulate the alloy and value of coin is one of the most distinguished prerogatives of sovereignty, nor can any of the United States part with it without exposing itself to be drained of specie. Did we not a few years ago, increase the value of dollars and half johanneses, in order to retain those coins; and shall we now part with the very ability of retaining coin among us? The balance of trade may be against us, then remittances will be made in coin, and our produce will be left upon our hands. It is our business to endeavor to reverse the case, and I hope we shall, by refusing to vest the congress with a power that we have hitherto been able to exercise ourselves with advantage in a time of necessity.—Nor do I see any reason for our resigning the power of fixing the standard of our weights and measures. The states are very competent to this business. Let the weights and measures be ever so variable in the several states, the price of commodities will ever be adequate to the variation in the respective markets.

Congress desire to be invested with the "appointing all officers in the land forces, excepting regimental officers." And far from seeing any absolute necessity for their having such a power, I can see no degree of common propriety to warrant the claim. The several states are to raise the regiments composing the land forces. Deputy staff officers in particular are absolutely necessary to each of the quotas; and they rank with regimental officers. I cannot see the shadow of a good reason, why the states should not have the appointment of all officers necessary to complete their respective quotas. Their honor, interest and safety are immediately and primarily affected, by the proper formation and regulation of their quotas. Their respective spheres of action, being within a very small circle, in comparison of that, in which the congress preside; they must of consequence be enabled to view objects at a nearer distance—to penetrate into the characters and abilities of candidates, and to make a proper choice with more accuracy and precision, than congress can be supposed to do. They will have enough upon their hands, in actuating the great machine of government. Their attention necessarily engaged in general and important affairs, ought not to be permitted to be drawn off, by those inferior objects which can more minutely and therefore better be examined by the respective states. This ought to be a fundamental maxim in the confederated policy. There is justice in it; and I will be bold to say, it arises from principles of true wisdom. It will display a confidence on the part of congress in the several states; and this must be the grand basis of their independency and freedom. We do not mean, unnecessarily to delegate any part of our sovereignty: We are willing to sacrifice only such parts of it, as are necessary to be sacrificed for the general safety. In short, we enter into this confederacy, on the same principle only, that men enter into society.

But independent of this position, as a matter of right, I will consider the claim upon the footing of common prudence and experience. Whenever congress sit, there will be a number of persons, especially from the nearer states, soliciting offices; They will form acquaintances with the members; and we know the common effect of such connections. In consequence, congress may appoint even an unexceptionable person, as to his character and capacity, to a post in a state in which he has no connections, and of which he is not a member: This may occasion an envy against the officer, even to the detriment of the public service; and a displeasure against congress, for having made, as it may be deemed, an appointment injurious to those individuals of that state, who were in every respect capable of the office, and whom the

public would wish to see in it. Or congress may be induced to appoint a member of the state, but such a one as the people never would have chosen, because they know him to be unequal to the trust. To say such things ought not to be supposed, is to say but little: Every page in history—the known disposition of the human heart inform us, that nothing is more likely to happen. I am therefore clearly against the clause—all officers excepting regimental officers. And indeed I am of opinion, that of as many brigades as the quota of any state may consist, so many brigadiers general should that state nominate; the eldest of whom should command the whole, while in the state, and not therein actually assisted by the major part of another quota, commanded by a superior officer. Let congress appoint a generalissimo and major generals—these are proper to command two or more quotas when in conjunction: And the states being divided into departments, a proper number of major-generals may command in them.

In a confederacy of states, for the purpose of general security of arms, I cannot but conceive that there ought of prudence and necessity, to be a clause, at least obliging the parties to furnish their respective quotas, beyond the possibility of a neglect or evasion with impunity. But, I see no such clause in the confederation before us—the main pillar of security therefore is not in it. It is true, there is a long clause respecting quotas. But, it is only directory. And how many such laws are there, which are regarded as nugatory, merely for the want of a penal clause? Have we not had sufficient experience, of the inefficacy of that clause relating to quotas? Before it was inserted in the plan of confederation, did not congress act upon the very principles contained in it? The present quotas of the respective states were arranged upon a computation of their respective abilities. The numbers were sufficient, with the favor of Heaven, nay abundantly sufficient almost without effusion of blood, to captivate all the British forces in America. But, when they ought to have crushed the ungenerous foe, they were not even raised in the most populous states. These principles, even in the hour of the most pressing necessity, have been neglected with impunity, at our hands, to the imminent hazard of the liberties of America. Are we not to be instructed, even by a bloody experience? Shall we not receive light, even from the conflagrations spread over our land? Oh! why has our beneficent Creator endowed us with recollection!—Mr. Chairman, pardon me; I am hurt—pierced to the quick, at an omission of the most fatal nature. It is a symptom filling me with torturing apprehensions.

Upon such principles was the allied army to be formed, under the great duke of Marlborough. The quotas were specified, I may say even in a more positive manner. Yet the emperor and Holland were yearly more and more deficient. The war was of necessity to proceed; and as the other allies failed in their quotas, so England was obliged to increase her exertions: and to such a degree was the one and the other, that at length England almost entirely supported the war, while the emperor had but little more than a single regiment at his own expense, that could be said properly to act against the common enemy. Mankind are not more honest in their principles, or faithful to their engagements than they then were nor will they be so. Honor, duty and our most essential interests, have loudly and in vain called upon the Americans to complete their quotas. They are as strongly bound by the principles upon which the quota clause is formed as they can possibly be, if that clause without aid, become a part of the confederation. Shall we shut our eyes, and absolutely trust our liberties and safety to a clause, that as it stands, we experimentally know will fail us in the hour of necessity? While I retain my proper senses, I cannot.

Nor are these my only objections against that clause in its present state. There is a degree of injustice in its tendency. I do not mean that it was designed. By there not being any thing compelling in it, it has a tendency to expose an unequal proportion of the strength of some states, to the hazards of war in defence of the confederation. And the first principles of justice direct, that this danger should be provided against as far as may be. We well know, that man is so selfish and ungenerous a being, that he will, when he can, throw his load upon the shoulder

of his neighbor. Men form states—these act upon the same principle; and accordingly we find, that the emperor and Holland unjustly placed a load upon England, that almost crushed her. It is against such an evasion of duty, and such a forced assumption of burden, that I wish to provide—and they ought to be guarded against by every possible means. Let it not be said, the confederated treasury is to pay the whole expense incurred—that is not the point. But if it was, is there the least security that there *shall* be money in that treasury?—My aim is to protect the states from a more fatal injury—to preserve them from the necessity of sacrificing an unreasonable proportion of the flower of their people. An ardor for the public weal, may involve generous states, in the utmost distress; and throw them a century or two behind those ungenerous ones they saved. Nor can the confederation make them amends for that loss, which, of all that can happen is the greatest. Valerius Maximus said, severity is the sure preserver and avenger of liberty.

Sir, when I consider the extent of territory possessed by the thirteen states—the value of that territory; and that the three most southern, must daily and rapidly increase in population, riches and importance. When I reflect, that from the nature of the climate, soil and produce of the several states, a northern and southern interest in many particulars naturally and unavoidably arise; I cannot but be displeased with the prospect, that the most important transactions in congress, may be done contrary to the united opposition of Virginia, the two Carolinas and Georgia: States possessing more than one half of the whole territory of the confederacy; and forming, as I may say, the body of the southern interest. If things of such transcendent weight, may be done notwithstanding such an opposition; the honor, interest and sovereignty of the south, are in effect delivered up to the care of the north. Do we intend to make such a surrender? I hope not, there is no occasion for it. Nor would I have it understood, that I fear the north would abuse the confidence of the south: But common prudence, sir, admonishes me, that confidence should not wantonly be placed any where—it is but the other day, that we thought our liberties secure in the care of Britain. I am assisting to form the confederation of the United States: It is my duty to speak, and to speak plainly: I engage in this great work with a determined purpose, to endeavor, as far as my slender abilities enable me, to render it equal, just and binding, I presume, that all my coadjutors in the several states, in and out of congress, act upon this sentiment; nor can I admit a contrary idea. When all mean fair, equitable terms are not difficult to be adjusted. I therefore hope, I shall not be thought unreasonable, because I object to the nine voices in congress; and wish that eleven may be substituted, to enable that body to transact their most important business. The states general of Holland must be unanimous: Their government is accounted a wise one; and although it causes their proceedings to be slow, yet, it secures the freedom and interest of its respective states. Is not this our great aim?

For the present, I here, sir, limit my particular objection to the plan under consideration: I have made these with the highest reluctance. In a word, I cannot admit of any confederation that gives congress any power, that can with propriety, be exercised by several states—or any power, but what is clearly defined beyond a doubt. Nor can I think of entering into any engagements, which are not as equal as may be, between the states—engagements of a compelling nature, and the whole to be understood according to the letter only. Without these five leading principles, a confederation is not a desirable object in my opinion.

Thus, Mr. Chairman, have I complied with the first division of my subject—to perform the second is a much more arduous task: But before I proceed I must crave the kind indulgence of your honor, and the house; I fear I have too long intruded upon your attention.

It is with the greatest diffidence, sir, that I presume to throw out my ideas of such terms as in my opinion are desirable, attainable and likely to form a beneficial confederation. In doing this, I flatter myself, it will not be understood, that I am so weak as to think them unexceptionable. Indeed I declare, that sketch I shall draw, will not be such an one, as I would prefer, and think the most perfect. From the complexion of the present plan, and the labor and time spent upon it, I fear, that which I would wish, cannot be attained: And hence, I mean to conform my ideas to the scheme laid down by congress; with design respectfully and zealously to endeavor to render as little liable to objection as I can, the scheme likely to take effect. I shall therefore sketch the plan of a confederation in the following order. The appellation of the country in which the confederacy is formed—a confederated union, and its objects declared—the style of the confederacy—the constitution of its legislature and executive—the powers of each described and limited, and their respective duties pointed out—the public faith plighted for past engagements of congress—the engagements of the several states to each other, and declaration of their rights, a declaration of the capability of admission into the confederacy—the penalty of violating the articles of confederation—the obligatory nature of the confederation; and in what manner only it is capable of alteration—the rule by which the confederation shall be understood.

Reference: Hezebiah Niles (ed.), *Principles and Arts of the Revolution in America* (New York: A.S. Barner, 1876).

CONNECTICUT URGES REVISIONS AND AUTHORIZES DELEGATES TO RATIFY ARTICLES, FEBRUARY 1778

The Articles of Confederation and Perpetual Union proposed by Congress to be entered into by the thirteen United States of America being laid before this Assembly by his Excellency the Governor were read and maturely considered: Whereupon,

Resolved, as the opinion of this Assembly, That said articles in general appear to be well adapted to cement and preserve the union of said States, to secure their freedom and independence and promote their general welfare: but that with some amendments they may be rendered more perfect, equitable and satisfactory. Wherefore the Delegates of this State are hereby instructed to propose to the consideration of Congress the following amendments, *viz:*

1. That in the eighth Article, as a rule for determining each State's proportion of the common expence, instead of the value of the lands, buildings &c., as expressed in said Article, be inserted the number of inhabitants in each State; this being in the opinion of this Assembly a more certain, equitable and practicable rule than the other. Trade and manufactures, which employ and support great numbers of inhabitants, being sources of wealth to a State as well as the produce of lands; besides it will be very difficult, if not impossible, to obtain such an estimate of the value of the lands and buildings in the United States as would do justice or give satisfaction to the several States.

2. That next after the fifth paragraph in the 9th Article be inserted the following clause, *viz:* Provided, that no land army shall be kept up by the United States in time of peace, nor any officers or pensioners kept in pay by them who are not in actual service, except such as are or may be rendered unable to support themselves by wounds received in battle in the service of said States, agreeable to the provision already made by a resolution of Congress.

The foregoing amendments being agreed to in substance may be made in such manner and form as Congress shall think proper.

And whereas other amendments may be proposed by some of the other States, and it being highly expedient for the welfare and security of the said States that the Articles of Confederation be finally concluded and ratifyed as soon as possible: Therefore,

Resolved, That the Delegates of this State who shall be present in Congress be and they are hereby fully authorized and impowered in behalf of this State. to agree to and ratify the said Articles of Confederation with such amendments, if any be, as by them in conjunction with the Delegates of the other States in Congress shall be thought proper.

Reference: Charles J. Hoadly (ed.), *The Public Records of the State of Connecticut,* Vol. I (Hartford: Case, Lockwood & Brainard Co., 1894).

RHODE ISLAND OBJECTS TO ARTICLES, YET AUTHORIZES RATIFICATION, FEBRUARY 1778

Instructions to the Honorable Stephen Hopkins, William Ellery and Henry Marchant, Esqs., Delegates from Rhode Island in Congress, respecting the proposed Articles of Confederation and perpetual Union between the Thirteen United States.

1st. By the fifth article, no state can be represented by less than two members. As it will be inconvenient and burthensome for the small states to keep in Congress more than two or three members, it may happen from sickness, death, or some other unavoidable accident, that such state may have not more than one member present in Congress; and thereby be deprived of a voice, which may be highly prejudicial. You are therefore instructed to move in Congress for an alteration in that article; so that in case by sickness, death, or any other unavoidable accident, but one of the members of a state can attend Congress, such state may be represented in Congress by one member, for such reasonable space of time as shall be agreed upon by Congress, and ascertained by the articles of confederation.

2d. Taxes ought to be assessed equally; and nothing will have a greater tendency to induce freemen to submit to heavy burthens, than an opinion that they are justly proportioned; and as very material alterations may happen in the abilities of the different states to pay taxes in the course of a few years, you are instructed to move in Congress for the following addition to the eighth article: "That such estimate be taken and made once in every five years, at least."

3d. The King of Great Britain, before the present war, was vested with the property of great quantities of land; and enjoyed large revenues arising from quit-rents within the United States. By commencing and carrying on this unnatural war, with the avowed design of reducing the United States to the most debasing and ignominious servitude, that crown hath justly forfeited such lands and revenues. If the forfeiture takes place, it will be in consequence of the exertions of all the United States, by whom the war is supported. Consequently, all the United States ought to be proportionably benefitted by the forfeiture. But should the several states in which such lands lie, and revenues are raised, appropriate them to their separate use, they will at the end of the war, be possessed of great funds to reimburse themselves their expenses; while those states which are not in that situation, although at a proportionable expense of blood and treasure, in recovering such forfeiture, not receiving any benefit therefrom, will be left to struggle with an immense debt, which is unequal and unjust. The claim of the crown of Great Britain to such lands and revenues, was uncontested before the present war; none of the states having formed any pretensions thereto, which is another cogent argument why the forfeiture ought to be vested all the United States. Omitting many things which your attention to this important object will suggest to you, it is proper to eserve that Congress have promised lands to the army; and that, unless they be provided out of such forfeiture, several of the states, and this in particular, will be in a very unhappy predicament. You are therefore instructed to move in Congress that it be inserted in the articles of confederation, that all such lands and revenues be forfeited to the United States, to be disposed of, and appropriated by Congress, for

the benefit of the whole confederacy. It is not meant, by this instruction, that Congress should claim the jurisdiction of the forfeited lands; but that the same should remain to the state in which it lies.

4th. Although this Assembly deem the amendments and alterations herein proposed, of very great importance, yet the completion of the union, is so indispensably necessary, that you are instructed, after having used your utmost influence to procure them to be made, in case they should be rejected, not to decline acceding, on the part of this state, to the articles of confederation; taking care that these proposed amendments and alerations be previously entered upon the records of the Congress, that it may appear they were made before the signing of the contederation; and that this state intends hereafter to renew the motion for them. This Assembly, trusting that Congress, at some future time, convinced of their utility and justice, will adopt them; and that they will be confirmed by all the states.

It is further voted and resolved, that an exemplification of this act be made and transmitted by the secretary, to the delegates appointed to represent this state in Congress, who are indispensably to observe and follow the said instructions.

This Assembly having taken into consideration the articles of confederation and perpetual union between the states of New Hampshire, Massachusetts Bay, Rhode Island and Providence Plantations, Connecticut, New York, New Jersey, Pennsylvania, Delaware, Maryland, Virginia, North Carolina, South Carolina and Georgia, transmitted by Congress to this state; and having had them repeatedly read, and having maturely weighed, and most seriously deliberated upon them, as their importance to this and the other states, and to posterity, deserves; and considering also the pressing necessity of completing the union, as a measure essential to the preservation of the independence and safety of the said states,—

Do vote and resolve, and it is voted and resolved, that the Honorable Stephen Hopkins,

Esq., William Ellery, Esq., and Henry Marchant, Esq., the delegates to represent this state in Congress, or any one of them, be, and they are hereby, fully authorized and empowered, on the part and behalf of this state, to accede to and sign the said articles of confederation and perpetual union, in such solemn form and manner, as Congress shall think best adapted to a transaction so important to the present and future generations; provided, that the same be acceded to by eight of the other states.

And in case any alterations in, or additions to, the said articles of confederation and perpetual union, shall be made by nine of the said states, in Congress assembled, that the said delegates, or any one of them, be, and they are hereby, authorized and empowered, in like manner, to accede to and sign the said articles of confederation and perpetual union, with the alterations and additions which shall be so made.

It is further voted and resolved, that this Assembly will, and do hereby, in behalf of the said state of Rhode Island and Providence Plantations, in the most solemn manner, pledge the faith of the said state to hold and consider the acts of the said delegates, or any one of them, in so acceding to and signing the said articles of confederation and perpetual union,

as valid and binding upon the said state in all future time.

And it is further voted and resolved, that a fair copy of this act be made, and authenticated under the public seal of this state, with the signature of His Excellency the Governor, and be transmitted to said delegates; and that the same shall be sufficient warrant and authority to the said delegates, or any one of them, for the purposes aforesaid.

It is voted and resolved, that the Honorable Henry Marchant, Esq., be, and he is hereby, requested to give his attendance on Congress by the 20th of March next.

That when a report shall be made by the several legislatures, of the articles of confederation proposed to them by Congress, he may, with our other delegate, procure such alterations therein, as are agreeable to the instructions given them by this Assembly.

It is further voted and resolved, that a copy hereof, with an exemplification of said instructions, be transmitted to the said Henry Marchant, Esq., that he may proceed therewith, accordingly.

Reference. J.R. Bartlett (ed.), *Records of the Colony and State of Rhode Island*, Vol. VIII (10 vols.; Providence: A.C. Greene, 1856–1865).

J.B. SMITH TO GEORGE BRYAN, FEBRUARY 3, 1778

Dr. Sir,

I wrote you a few days ago by Nothing since has occurred worth your notice. The Assembly of Virginia has acceded to the Confederation. I do not think, however, they have treated the matter with form equal to its importance. Does it appear proper to raise so great a fabrick on the slender basis of a simple resolution of the two houses? Will not *legal consequences* follow from this confederation? I apprehend it would be not only proper, but that it would answer many

valuable purposes if more form were used, at least if the articles were approved & acceded to by a law of each State solemnly enacted, & in which law perhaps it may be expedient to insert certain matters connected therewith. It is a question in this house, whether suits can be supported for the recovery of particular moneys in the several States. What think you of this? This may be one object in the act I speak of.

Reference: Samuel Hazard (ed.), *Pennsylvania Archives*, Vol. VI (Philadelphia: J. Severns, 1853).

COUNCIL TO PENNSYLVANIA DELEGATES, APRIL 30, 1778

Sirs,

The Supreme Executive Council of Pennsylvania, thoroughly persuaded that the compleat establishment of the Confederation of said States must greatly consolidate the union, & invigorate the Negotiations of Congress at this important Conjuncture, do hereby add their concurrence in the Articles of Confederation, now under public consideration, to the acceptance & consent of the Legislature of this State; & do recommend to you, Gentlemen, to use your best endeavours & influence in forwarding the said business, which Council consider as of the highest importance to the honour, advantage & safety of the united Body of North America.

I am,
Sirs,
your most obed[t]
& very humble Serv[t].

Reference: Samuel Hazard (ed.), *Pennsylvania Archives,* Vol. VI (Philadelphia: J. Severns, 1853).

NATHANIEL SCUDDER TO SPEAKER OF NEW JERSEY ASSEMBLY, JULY 13, 1778

MY DEAR SIR,—I do myself the honor to address you upon an affair to me of the most serious and alarming importance. The honorable Council and Assembly of this state have not thought proper to invest their delegates with power to ratify and sign the confederation, and it is obvious that unless every of the thirteen states shall accede to it we remain an unconfederated people. These states have actually entered into a treaty with the court of Versailles as a confederated people, and Monsieur Girard, their Ambassador Plenipotentiary to Congress is now on our coast with a powerful fleet of ships, which have taken a pilot on board for Delaware. He probably may be landed by this time, and will at all events be in Philadelphia in a few days. How must he be astonished and confounded, and what may be the fatal consequences to America when he discovers (which he will immediately do,) that we are ipso facto unconfederated, and consequently what our enemies have called us, "a rope of sand."

Will he not have just cause to resent the deception? and may not insidious Britain, knowing the same, take advantage of your disunion? for my own part I am of opinion she will never desist from her nefarious designs, nor ever consider her attempts upon our liberties fruitless and vain, until she knows the golden knot is actually tied. I left Congress last Wednesday evening. The affair of confederation was to be taken up next day. The magna charta of America was amply engrossed and prepared for signing. Ten states had actually authorized their delegates to ratify: a delegate from an eleventh (viz. Georgia) declared he was so fully possessed of the sense of his constituents, that he should not hesitate to subscribe it. New Jersey and Maryland only stood it out. Mr. Chase, one of the delegates from that state, told me the day I left Philadelphia, that he imagined the determination of Maryland would depend much upon that of New Jersey, and thought if our state should accede, theirs would also. He therefore concluded to go immediately down and try what could be done. I at the same time assured him I would write you on the subject on my return.

I ought to inform you, sir, that the objections stated by New Jersey were read and considered in Congress, and after being entered at large on their minutes, a question was taken whether Congress at that time judged it expedient to take up the said objections so as to admit any emendations in the plan of confederation or not? and it passed in the negative. In consequence of which they remain both upon the journal and files to be taken up and considered at any future time when they may be called for. I expect my colleagues will soon address you on this subject. I left Doct. Witherspoon, Doct. Elmer and Mr. Boudinot at Philadelphia, whither I expect to return in a few days. I should have been much more uneasy when I was last at Princeton, and should have taken more pains to convince the members of the necessity of granting the powers of ratification to their delegates, had I not been encouraged to expect that the Legislature would not rise without doing it; at the same time supposing the reason why they withheld at that juncture to be, that their objections might have the greater weight with Congress. Indeed I all along expected Doct. Witherspoon would have brought on such powers with him, especially as I hoped the honorable houses would be clearly of opinion that it were better to confederate under all the disadvantages they apprehended, than that the general union should be broken or even greatly endangered.

I know not whether I ought to say anything respecting the objections themselves: some of them are perhaps not very essential. The obtaining an admission of several of them would doubtless be of great local advantage to this state; but every state must expect to be subjected to considerable local disadvantages in a general confederation. Indeed upon the whole I am fully of opinion that no plan can or will ever be adopted more equal or less generally injurious to the confederated states than the present. I also declare it as my opinion that, if the general business of emendation were to be fairly taken up in Congress to-morrow, several alterations would be made exceedingly disadvantageous to the smaller circumscribed states, and which perhaps might more than counterbalance the obtaining what we apply for. As to the grand and capital objection respecting the lands, &c., I will only observe that in case we never obtain an original quota of them, we shall only lose a share in the prime sale of them, which will probably be very low, while we shall inevitably reap a permanent and increasing benefit from the rapid and enormous growth of the larger states; for surely in proportion to their extent and population, their quota of the public expense and debt will be increased, while ours will be proportionably diminished. What avails it therefore to us, whether five pounds of our national debt be paid by the accession of a subject to this state, or whether our quota be really lessened five pounds by the settlement of a person in the state of Virginia at the distance of a thousand miles from the Atlantic? for my own part, I think we shall have greatly the advantage of these enormous, unwieldly governments; nor do I judge it unlikely they will soon find it necessary to sue for the curtailing their extravagant jurisdiction.

In the settlement of our soldiery, and the foreign deserters at the expiration of the war, we shall incur considerable disadvantage; however, as the larger states will doubtless rejoice to have their frontiers immediately enlarged, and will vie with each other in courting so great an accession of inhabitants, there will probably be no greater expense than barely that of locating the lands, our quota of which cannot be any very considerable sum.

I congratulate you on the signal success of our arms in this neighborhood on the 28th of June. Great plunder and devastation have been committed among my friends in this quarter, but through the distinguishing goodness of Providence, my family and property escaped, and that almost in a miraculous manner.

I wish you to take the above representation into your serious consideration, and if with me you shall judge it a matter of sufficient importance, that the Legislature may be as speedily as possible convened to deliberate and determine thereon.

I am, dear Sir, with great esteem, your most obed't h'ble servant,

NATH. SCUDDER.
Hon'ble John Hart, Esq.

Reference: Selection from the Correspondence of the Executive of New Jersey, From 1776 to 1786 (Newark: Newark Daily Advertiser Office, 1848).

GENERAL ASSEMBLY OF CONNECTICUT, MAY 7, 1779

(L. S:) At a general assembly of the governor and company of the state of Connecticut, in America, holden at Hartford, by special order of the governor of the said state, on Wednesday, the 7th day of April, Anno Domini 1779.

It appearing to this assembly to be essentially necessary for the preservation, safety, independence, and sovereignty of the United States of America, that the articles of confederation and perpetual union be acceded to, ratified and confirmed: and whereas all of the said states, except Maryland, have agreed to and confirmed said articles of confederation, and Maryland hath not acceded to said articles as drawn up, for reasons heretofore published; and whereas the confederation of thirteen states may not be considered as obligatory on twelve states only:

Resolved, That the delegates of this state in Congress be directed and empowered, and full power and authority is hereby given and granted to the said delegates, in the name and behalf of this state, to enter into, ratify and confirm said articles of confederation and perpetual union with the states of New Hampshire, Massachusetts Bay, Rhode Island, and Providence Plantations, New York, New Jersey, Pennsylvania, Delaware, Virginia, North Carolina, South Carolina, and Georgia, in the most full and ample manner; always provided that the state of Maryland be not thereby excluded from acceding to said confederation at any time hereafter. A true copy of record:

Examined by
GEORGE WYLLYS, *Secretary.*

References: Worthington Chauncey Ford (ed.), *Journal of the Continental Congress, 1774–1789,* Vol. XIV (Washington: GPO, 1909).

INSTRUCTIONS OF THE GENERAL ASSEMBLY OF MARYLAND, MAY 21, 1779

The delegates of Maryland informed Congress, that they have received instructions respecting the articles of confederation, which they are directed to lay before Congress, and to have entered on their journals; the instructions being read are as follows:

Instructions of the general assembly of Maryland, to George Plater, William Paca, William Carmichael, John Henry, James Forbes and Daniel of St. Thomas Jenifer, esqrs;

GENTLEMEN, Having conferred upon you a trust of the highest nature, it is evident we place great confidence in your integrity, abilities and zeal to promote the general welfare of the United States, and the particular interest of this state, where the latter is not incompatible with the former; but to add greater weight to your proceedings in Congress, and to take away all suspicion that the opinions you there deliver, and the votes you give, may be the mere opinions of individuals, and not resulting from your knowledge of the sense and deliberate judgment of the state you represent, we think it our duty to instruct you as followeth on the subject of the confederation, a subject in which, unfortunately, a supposed difference of interest has produced an almost equal division of sentiments among the several states composing the union: We say a supposed difference of interests; for, if local attachments and prejudices, and the avarice and ambition of individuals, would give way to the dictates of a sound policy, founded on the principles of justice, (and no other policy but what is founded on those immutable principles deserves to be called sound,) we flatter ourselves this apparent diversity of interests would soon vanish; and all the states would confederate on terms mutually advantageous to all; for they would then perceive that no other confederation than one so formed can be lasting. Although the pressure of immediate calamities, the dread of their continuance from the appearance of disunion, and some other peculiar circumstances, may have induced some states to accede to the present confederation, contrary to their own interests and judgments, it requires no great share of foresight to predict, that when those causes cease to operate, the states which have thus acceded to the confederation will consider it as no longer binding, and will eagerly embrace the first occasion of asserting their just rights and securing their independence. Is it possible that those states, who are ambitiously grasping at territories, to which in our judgment they have not the least shadow of exclusive right, will use with greater moderation the increase of wealth and power derived from those territories, when acquired, than what they have displayed in their endeavours to acquire them? we think not; we are convinced the same spirit which hath prompted them to insist on a claim so extravagant, so repugnant to every principle of justice, so incompatible with the general welfare of all the states, will urge them on to add oppression to injustice. If they should not be incited by a superiority of wealth and strength to oppress by open force their less wealthy and less powerful neighbours, yet the depopulation, and consequently the impoverishment of those states, will necessarily follow, which by an unfair construction of the confederation may be stripped of a common interest in, and the common benefits derivable from, the western country. Suppose, for instance, Virginia indisputably possessed of the extensive and fertile country to which she has set up a claim, what would be the probable consequences to Maryland of such

an undisturbed and undisputed possession? they cannot escape the least discerning.

Virginia, by selling on the most moderate terms a small proportion of the lands in question, would draw into her treasury vast sums of money, and in proportion to the sums arising from such sales, would be enabled to lessen her taxes: lands comparatively cheap and taxes comparatively low, with the lands and taxes of an adjacent state, would quickly drain the state thus disadvantageously circumstanced of its most useful inhabitants, its wealth; and its consequence in the scale of the confederated states would sink of course. A claim so injurious to more than one half, if not to the whole of the United States, ought to be supported by the clearest evidence of the right. Yet what evidences of that right have been produced? what arguments alleged in support either of the evidence or the right; none that we have heard of deserving a serious refutation.

It has been said that some of the delegates of a neighbouring state have declared their opinion of the impracticability of governing the extensive dominion claimed by that state: hence also the necessity was admitted of dividing its territory and erecting a new state, under the auspices and direction of the elder, from whom no doubt it would receive its form of government, to whom it would be bound by some alliance or confederacy, and by whose councils it would be influenced: such a measure, if ever attempted, would certainly be opposed by the other states, as inconsistent with the letter and spirit of the proposed confederation. Should it take place, by establishing a sub-confederacy, *imperium in imperio*, the state possessed of this extensive dominion must then either submit to all the inconveniences of an overgrown and unwieldy government, or suffer the authority of Congress to interpose at a future time, and to lop off a part of its territory to be erected into a new and free state, and admitted into the confederation on such conditions as shall be settled by nine states. If it is necessary for the happiness and tranquillity of a state thus overgrown, that Congress should hereafter interfere and divide its territory; why is the claim to that territory now made and so pertinaciously insisted on? we can suggest to ourselves but two motives; either the declaration of relinquishing at some future period a portion of the country now contended for, was made to lull suspicion asleep, and to cover the designs of a secret ambition, or if the thought was seriously entertained, the lands are now claimed to reap an immediate profit from the sale. We are convinced policy and justice require that a country unsettled at the commencement of this war, claimed by the British crown, and ceded to it by the treaty of Paris, if wrested from the common enemy by the blood and treasure of the thirteen states, should be considered as a common property, subject to be parcelled out by Congress into free, convenient and independent governments, in such manner and at such times as the wisdom of that assembly shall hereafter direct. Thus convinced, we should betray the trust reposed in us by our constituents, were we to authorize you to ratify on their behalf the confederation, unless it be farther explained: we have coolly and dispassionately considered the subject; we have weighed probable inconveniences and hardships against the sacrifice of just and essential rights; and do instruct you not to agree to the confederation, unless an article or articles be added thereto in conformity with our declaration: should we succeed in obtaining such article or articles, then you are hereby fully empowered to accede to the confederation.

That these our sentiments respecting the confederation may be more publicly known and more explicitly and concisely declared, we have drawn up the annexed declaration, which we instruct you to lay before Congress, to have it printed, and to deliver to each of the delegates of the other states in Congress assembled, copies thereof, signed by yourselves or by such of you as may be present at the time of the delivery; to the intent and purpose that the copies aforesaid may be communicated to our brethren of the United States, and the contents of the said declaration taken into their serious and candid consideration.

Also we desire and instruct you to move at a proper time, that these instructions be read to Congress by their secretary, and entered on the journals of Congress.

We have spoken with freedom, as becomes freemen, and we sincerely wish that these our representations may make such an impression on that assembly as to induce them to make such addition to the articles of confederation as may bring about a permanent union.

A true copy from the proceedings of December 15, 1778.

Test,

J. DUCKETT, C. H. D.

Reference: Worthington Chauncey Ford (ed.), *Journal of the Continental Congress, 1774–1789,* Vol. XIV (Washington: GPO, 1909).

THEODORICK BLAND TO RICHARD HENRY LEE, MARCH 5, 1781

D'r S'r,

. . . The Confederation was signed and completely ratified on thursday last, and was accompanied with every demonstration of Joy by all ranks of People in this Place. I thought I had acknowledged the Rect of yrs. enclosing Col. Masons Sentiments. I have little doubt of the Grant's being accepted by Congress on the terms mentioned in the act of Cession which I see nearly corresponds with those in that Paper. I believe the Covert manoeuvers of the land Jobbing Companies are so well known, and so fully discovered, that few

of their abettors will be hardy enough to oppose it in its fullest latitude. Congress seems at this time more Unanimous, and less torn by factions than (from the best Information I can obtain from the Oldest Members) it has ever been since its first meeting. . . .

Reference: Edmund C. Burnett (ed.), *Letters of Members of the Continental Congress,* Vol. VI (8 vols.; Washington: Carnegie Institution, 1921–1936).

Part IX

Continental Congress as the National Government

This last part of Volume III is divided into two chapters. Chapter 48 looks at the internal governance reforms within the Congress from 1776 to 1787. These activities point to how the federal Congress attempted to alleviate the fears and worries of the states about its ability to govern. The Congress knew that the central issue of its governance had become the right to tax and raise revenue. Those members who worried about the ability to pay national debts desired the appointment of a national revenue officer. Also of concern to the Congress was the governance of western lands. Perhaps the Congress's finest accomplishments were the Northwest Ordinances that organized governance in the territories.

Chapter 49 presents a dialogue between criticism and defense of the Congress's governance activities. Between 1781 and 1787, delegates in Congress, state leaders, and theorists of governance debated and discussed how to reform the Articles of Confederation. These discussions and debates carried into the convention of 1785 in Annapolis and, upon its failure, the calling of a convention to meet in Philadelphia during the summer of 1787. The reader should look carefully at these debates and ask which position best defended the governing system that had developed during the previous two hundred years. Central to those discussions was the issue of where sovereignty lay: in the states or in the national government.

Congress at Work and Changes Made in Governance, 1776–1787

Frustrations about the functioning of Congress and its changes in the structure of governance are the central documents in this Chapter. The first document shows the federal Congress's frustrations with states' border disputes, in particular that between New Hampshire and New York. Congress also concerned itself with its internal governance structure when it created an executive office, the Treasurer of the United States. The ability to collect taxes and finance government initiatives was behind the creation of the executive office. The delegates argued at length about organizing that office (the first Treasurer was the controversial Robert Morris [1735–1806] of Pennsylvania). Attendance at Congress even became an issue because some delegates refused to attend because they believed the national government was of little use to the governing needs of the young nation. Even the issue of a code of behavior in Congress divided the members. An inability to oversee member behavior, such as the case of Rhode Island's David Howell (1747–1824), shows a growing frustration over Congress's effectiveness.

Still, the Congress did manage to pass some governance legislation of great importance to the country's future growth. Its central accomplishment was the creation of a governing system for the western territories. The two Northwest Ordinances, 1784 and 1787, are included in this Chapter. How closely did those ordinances conform to the long established patterns of governance in the individual colonies and confirmed in the original state constitutions?

DISPUTE OVER NEW YORK–NEW HAMPSHIRE BORDER, AUGUST 27, 1779; CONGRESSIONAL RESOLUTION, SEPTEMBER 24, 1779

Instructions of the New York Legislature

To its delegates in congress relative to the disorders prevailing in the north eastern parts of the state of new york.

Gent[n].

We anxiously expected that, by an effectual Interposition of Congress, our deluded Fellow Citizens in the North Eastern Parts of the State would before our present meeting have peaceably returned to their duty, and prevented the necessity of coercive Measures to compel a submission to the authority of Legal Government. This we were the more readily induced to hope as we conceive the Terms we have offered to them to be not only perfectly just and equitable but even generous; these pacific Overtures have been disregarded, violence and Outrage are daily committed upon, and the Severest punishment threatened against (the latter of which will appear from the inclosed Copy of an Act of the Legislature of the pretended State of Vermont) our good subjects in Brattleborough and other well affected Towns, who now claim from us that Protection which we have Solemnly promised to them and which consistent with justice we can no longer withhold.

While on the one hand we view with a degree of Horror the dreadful consequences of having Recourse to Force, not only to this State, and especially to the unhappy People who will be its immediate Object, but also to the common cause of America—yet on the other we are persuaded our Successful efforts, to expel a foreign Tyranny will avail us little while we remain Subject to the domestic Usurpation; earnestly wishing however by every attempt to Peace, to prevent the evils of a Civil War, we must direct you to entreat once more the mediation of Congress.

A Quorum of the Committee, appointed by the Resolution of the first of June last, having never met, and as we have not been informed that Congress have since proceeded in the business we presume it is remaining before them in the same State it was prior to that day upon this supposition we shall take the Liberty of suggesting several matters for their consideration and proposing certain measures, not only just and satisfactory in themselves, but such as we believe will be effectual in restoring the Peace of the State.

It is to be observed that all the Lands in that District of Country, which has attempted a Separation from this State under the name of Vermont, is 1st either unpatented and unoccupied or 2dly unpatented and actually occupied or 3dly Patented by New Hampshire or Massachusetts Bay and not afterwards patented by New York or 4thly Patented by New York prior to any Patent under New Hampshire or Massachusetts Bay or 5 Patented by New Hampshire or Massachusetts Bay and afterwards patented by New York.

With respect to the first Case the Lands must remain for the future Disposition of Government

with respect to the second we have engaged to confirm to the Occupants their respective Possessions together with as much vacant adjoining Land as to form convenient Farms not exceeding three hundred acres each.

With respect to the third we have engaged to confirm the Patents under New Hampshire or Massachusetts Bay as fully as if they had been made under New York without taking any advantage of a non performance of Condition.

With respect to the fourth and fifth Cases we have engaged besides confirming such Possessions as were made under New Hampshire or Massachusett's Bay prior to any Patent for the same Lands under New York to submit the Determination of the Right of Soil to Commisrs. to be appointed by Congress who are to determine agreeable to Equity and Justice without adhering to the strict Rules of Law Provided nevertheless that the actual Occupants under New York shall be confirmed in their respective Possessions.

It is further to be observed that every part of the above District was indisputably included within the Jurisdiction either of New York or New Hampshire or Massachusett's Bay and that the Right of Jurisdiction as Congress themselves have declared was not altered by these Communities respectively becoming Independant States.

Having made these observations we would premise further that in order to remove every objection fully to evince the Uprightness of our Intentions and our earnest desire for an accommodation We are willing that if Congress should deem the above mode of determining the Right of Soil between interfering Claimants under New Hampshire or Massachusets Bay on the one and under New York on the other part ineligible we will consent that it shall be determined either immediately by Congress themselves or in such other manner as they shall think proper we will also concede that on all Questions relative to such Right of Soil this State shall not vote in Congress, that Congress shall guaranty to the Inhabitants on the Grants the Performance of these Terms and that no Proceeding of Congress requiring or recommending it to the Inhabitants to submit to the Authority of this State shall be construed to injure any Right of Jurisdiction which the States of New Hampshire or Massachusets Bay may respectively have to the above Territory or any part thereof.

This last Proposal does not arise from an apprehension that probably these States will claim the jurisdiction of any of the Grants lying West of Connecticut River but is mentioned solely with a view that nothing would remain which can possibly have even the appearance of a Difficulty We will at all Times chearfully submit the Right of Jurisdiction to the decision of Congress agreeable to the 9th Article of Confederation.

Those Terms and Proposals We conceive must satisfy every Claim either upon our Justice or Generosity and we trust they will appear to Congress to whom we instruct and authorise you immediately to communicate them, to pledge the public Faith of this State for the Performance of them and thereupon to sollicit the immediate Interference of Congress recommending to such of the Inhabitants of the Grants who at the Commencement of the present War were within the Jurisdiction of New York again to submit to the Government & Authority of this State, with a Proviso (should the same be deemed necessary) that such Interference shall not be construed to injure a Right of Jurisdiction existing in any other of the United States.

We presume it will be needless at this time particularly to recapitulate all the Reasons which induced this State to apply to Congress for a Declaration of their Sence of the Conduct of our revolted fellow subjects, as they are fully contained in the numberless Papers which we have from time to time transmitted to Congress respecting this matter let it suffice to mention as a principal Inducemt that the Revolters asserted and their adherents believed that their attempts to a separation from this State were agreeable to and favored by Congress or some Members of Weight and Influence.

Every Delay on the Part of Congress explicitly to disavow and disapprove of is construed by these People as countenancing and has a manifest tho' we do not say a designed Tendency to establish and confirm the secession—Their

Pretended Legislature has already confiscated and are now disposing of the Estates of Persons who have joined the Enemy and probably will soon proceed to grant the unappropriated Lands—By these means they raise moneys for the Support of their Government and obtain a great and dayly accession of Strength not only by an additional number of Settlers but every other Purchaser will be interested to maintain an authority upon which their Title depends—These Proceedings also will increase the Confusion and render the Restoration of Peace at a future day more difficult as They bear no Share in the present public Burthens that part of the Country is become an Assylum for all Persons who wish to avoid Military Duty or the Payments of Taxes and Numbers are daily emigrating thither influenced merely by this Motive—They will also attempt to enforce their cruel Edict and oblige the Inhabitants of Brattleborough and the other Towns who have remained in Allegiance to this State to submit to their usurpation—These Inhabitants will resist and the Justice Peace and Safety of the State demand that we should and we are resolved to assist and protect them—In short for we cannot enter into particulars, Matters are bro't to a Crisis and we must in this session determine with Decision upon the important Question of protecting our faithful Subjects and supporting the rightful Jurisdiction of the State What the Consequences will be we forbear to mention—They may easily be imagined and Congress can prevent them.

One principal Design of our present Meeting was to deliberate upon this momentuous Subject. We shall notwithstanding suspend all further proceedures and continue sitting till we are favored with the Sentiments of Congress which you will transmit to us by the messenger who convey's this and whom you will detain for that purpose.

Should we however be disappointed and Congress decline to interpose by an express Recommendation as above proposed we do in such Case direct Mr. Jay to whom we have in a special manner committed this Business immediatly to withdraw and attend us at this Place.

Gent^n

With this you will receiv a Letter in the nature of Instructions which you will observe is wrote upon a Presumption that no Proceedings relative to the Vermont Business have been had in Congress since the appointment of the Committee on the 1st of June last. Should subsequent measures however have been adopted by Congress which you may conceive equally effectual and beneficial to the State with those we have instructed you to propose you are in such Case at Liberty to suspend the Communication of these Instructions till our further Direction and immediately inform us of the measures by a special messenger.

> We are with due Respect
> Gentlemen your most obedient Servants
> By order of the Senate
> By order of the Assembly

Resolutions of the Continental Congress

1 Whereas on the first Day of June last Congress by a certain Resolution, reciting that "Whereas divers applications had been made to Congress on the part of the State of New York and of the State of New Hampshire relative to Disturbances, & animosities among Inhabitants of a certain District known by the name of "the New Hampshire Grants" praying their Interference for quieting thereof did resolve that a Committee be appointed to repair to the New Hampshire Grants & enquire into the reason why they refuse to continue Citizens of the respective States which heretofore exercised Jurisdiction over the said District; for that as Congress are in duty bound on the one hand to preserve inviolate the Rights of the several States, so on the other they will always be careful to provide that the Justice due to the States, does not interfere with the Justice which may be due to Individuals.

That the said Committee confer with the said Inhabitants, & that they take every prudent measure to promote an amicable Settlement of all Differences & prevent Divisions & Animosities so prejudicial to the United States and did further resolve that the further Consideration of this subject be postponed until the said Committee shall have made report."

2 And whereas it so happened that a Majority of the Committee appointed in pursuance of the aforementioned Resolutions did not meet in the said District and therefore have never executed the Business committed to them, or made a regular Report thereupon to Congress, Ordered that the said Committee be discharged.

3 And Whereas the animosities aforesaid have lately proceeded so far and & risen so high as to endanger the internal Peace of the United States which renders it indispensably necessary for Congress to interpose for the Restoration of quiet and good order.

4 And Whereas one of the great objects of the Union of the United States of America is the mutual Protection and Security of their respective Rights.

5 And Whereas it is of the last Importance to the said Union that all Causes of Jealousy & Discontent between the said States should be removed, and therefore that their several Boundaries and Jurisdiction be ascertained and settled.

6 And whereas Disputes at present subsist between the States of New Hampshire, Massachusetts Bay & New York on the one part, and the People of a District of Country called New Hampshire Grants on the other, which People deny the Jurisdiction of each of the said States over the said District; and each of the said States claim the said District against each other as well as against the said People, as appertaining in the whole or in part to them respectively.

7th Resolved unanimously, That it be and hereby is most earnestly recommended to the States of New Hampshire, Massachusetts Bay & New York forthwith to pass Laws expressly authorising Congress to hear & determine all Differences between them relative to their respective Boundaries in the mode prescribed by the Articles of Confederation so that Congress may proceed thereon by the First Day of February next at farthest.

8 And *further* that the said States of New Hampshire, Massachusetts Bay & New York do by Express Laws for the Purpose refer to the decision of Congress all Differences or Disputes relative to Jurisdiction, which they may respectively have with the People of the District aforesaid, so that Congress may proceed thereon on the said first day of February next.

9 *And also* to authorise Congress to proceed to hear & determine all Disputes subsisting between the Grantees of the several States aforesaid with one another or with either of the said States respecting Title to Lands lying in the said District to be heard and determined in the mode prescribed for such Cases by the Articles of Confederation aforesaid: And further to provide that no Advantage be taken of the Non-performance of the Condition of any of the Grants of the said Lands, but that further reasonable Time be allowed for fulfilling such Conditions.

10 Resolved unanimously That Congress will and hereby do Pledge their Faith to carry into Execution & support their Decisions & Determinations in the Premises in favour of whichsoever of the Parties the same may be, to the end that permanent Concord & Harmony may be established between them, & all cause of uneasiness removed.

11 Resolved unanimously, that Congress will on the said first Day of February next proceed without Delay to hear & examine into the Disputes & Differences relative to Jurisdiction aforesaid between the said three States respectively, or such of them as shall pass the Laws before mentioned on the one Part & the People of the District aforesaid who claim to be a seperate Jurisdiction on the other; And after a full and fair hearing will decide & determine the same according to Equity, and that *neither of the said States shall vote on any question relative to the Decision thereof.* And Congress do hereby pledge their Faith to execute & support their Decisions & Determination in the Premises.

And Whereas it is essential to the Interest of the whole Confederacy that all intestine Dissentions be carefully avoided & domestic Peace & good Order maintained.

12 Resolved unanimously That it is the Duty of the People of the District aforesaid who deny the Jurisdiction of all the aforenamed States to abstain in the meantime from exercising any Power over any of the Inhabitants of the said District who profess themselves Citizens of or to owe Allegiance to any or either of the said States: But that none of the Towns either on the East or West side of Connecticut River be considered as included within the said District, but such as have heretofore actually joined in denying the Jurisdiction of either of the said States, and have assumed a separate Jurisdiction, which they call the State of Vermont. And further that in the opinion of Congress the said three States afore-named ought in the mean time to suspend executing their Laws over any of the Inhabitants of the said District except such of them as shall profess Allegiance to and confess the Jurisdiction of the same respectively.—And further that Congress will consider any violences committed against the Tenor true Intent & meaning of this Resolution as a Breach of the Peace of the Confederacy which they are determined to keep and maintain: And to the end that all such violences & breaches of the public Peace, may be the better avoided in the said District; It is hereby recommended to all the Inhabitants thereof to cultivate Harmony & Concord among themselves to forbear vexing each other at Law or otherwise & give as little occasion as possible to the Interposition of Magistrates.

13 Resolved unanimously, That in the Opinion of Congress, no unappropriated Lands or Estates which are or may be adjudged forfeited or confiscated lying in the said District, ought until the final Decision of Congress in the Premises to be granted or sold.

Ordered, That Copies of the aforegoing Resolutions be sent by express to the States of New York New Hampshire and Massachusetts Bay, and to the People of the District aforesaid; and that they be respectively desired to loose no time in the appointing their Agent or Agents & otherwise preparing for the hearings aforesaid.

The aforesaid Resolution being read over and a Question taken to agree to the whole,

Resolved unanimously in the affirmative. Extract from the minutes.

CHA. THOMSON, Sec'y.

Reference: E. B. O'Callaghan (ed.), *The Documentary History of the State of New York,* Vol. IV (12 vols.; Albany: Charles Van Bentkeyren, 1851).

CONGRESS DISCUSSES EXECUTIVE COMMITTEE, FEBRUARY 1781

Congress then resumed the consideration of the plan for the arrangement of the civil executive departments of the United States; and thereupon,

Resolved, That there be a Superintendant of Finance, a Secretary at War, and a Secretary of Marine:

That it shall be the duty of the [Superintendant of Finance], to examine into the state of the public debt, the public expenditures, and the[1] public revenue, to digest and report plans for improving and regulating the finances, and for establishing order and economy in the expenditure of the public money; to direct the execution of all plans which shall be adopted by Congress respecting revenue and expenditure; to superintend and control the settlement of all public accounts; to direct and control all persons employed in procuring supplies for the public service, and in the expenditure of public money; to obtain accounts of all the issues of the specific supplies furnished by the several states; to compel the payment of all moneys due to the United States, and in his official character, [or in such manner as the laws of the respective states shall direct,] to prosecute on behalf of the United States, for all delinquencies [respecting the public revenue and expenditures]; to report to Congress the officers which shall be necessary for assisting him in the various branches of his department.

That the powers and duty of the Secretary at War shall be as follows:

To examine into the present state of the war-office, the returns and present state of the troops, ordnance, arms, ammunition, cloathing, and supplies of the armies of these United States,

and report the same to Congress; to obtain and keep exact and regular returns of all the forces of the United States, and of all the military stores, equipments, and supplies in the magazines of United States, or in other places for their use; and to take the immediate care of all such as are not in actual service; to form estimates of all such stores, equipments and supplies as may be requisite for the military service, and for keeping up competent magazines, and to report the same to the [Superintendant of Finance], that he may take measures for procuring the same in such manner as may best suit the finances of these states; to prepare estimates for paying and recruiting the armies of these United States, and lay them before the [Superintendant of Finance], so seasonably as to enable him to make provision without delay or derangement; to execute all the resolutions of Congress respecting military preparations, and transmit all orders and resolutions relative to the military land forces of these United States; to make out, seal, and countersign all military commissions, keep registers thereof, and publish annually a list of all appointments; to report to Congress the officers necessary for assisting him in the business of his department.[1]

The Committee to whom was re-committed a plan for the arrangement of the Civil Executive Departments of the United States so far as it respects the marine, submit the following Report:

Resolved, That it shall be the duty of the Secretary of Marine, to examine into and report to Congress the present state of the navy, a register of the officers in and out of command, and the dates of their respective commissions; and an account of all the naval and other stores belonging to that department; to form estimates of all pay, equipments and supplies necessary for the navy; and from time to time to report such estimates to the Superintendant of Finance, that he may take measures for providing for the expences, in such manner as may best suit the condition of the public treasury; to superintend and direct the execution of all resolutions of Congress respecting naval preparations; to make out, seal and countersign all marine commissions, keep registers thereof, and publish annually a list of all appointments; to report to Congress the officers and agents necessary to assist him in the business of his department; and in general to execute all the duties and powers specified in the act of Congress constituting the Board of Admiralty.

Reference: Galliard Hunt (ed.), *Journals of the Continental Congress,* Vol. XIX (Washington: GPO, 1912).

PLAN OF SUPPLEMENTAL ACTS OF CONGRESS, AUGUST 1781

The Committee appointed to prepare an Exposition of the Confederation, a plan for its complete execution and supplemental articles report,

That they ought to be discharged from the exposition of the Confederation because such a comment would be voluminous if coextensive with the subject, the omission to enumerate any Congressional powers become an argument against their existence, and it will be early enough to insist upon them, when they shall be exercised and disputed.

They farther report that the Confederation requires execution in the following manner

1 By adjusting the mode and proportions of the Militia aid to be furnished to a sister State labouring under Invasion.

2 By describing the privileges and immunities to which the citizens of one State are entitled in another.

3 By setting forth the conditions upon which a criminal is to be deliv^d up by one State upon the demand of the executive of another.

4 By declaring the method of exemplifying records and the operation of the Acts and judicial proceedings of the Courts of one State contravening those of the States in which they are asserted.

5 By a form to be observed in the notification of the appointment or suspension of Delegates.

6 By an oath to be taken by every Delegate against secret trusts of salaries.

7 By specifying the privileges of delegates from arrests, imprisonments, questioning for free speech and debates in Congress saving as well their amenability to their constituents, as protesting against the authority of individual legislatures to absolve them from obligations to secrecy.

8 By instituting an oath to be taken by the Officers of the U.S. or any of them against presents, emoluments, office or title of any kind from a King Prince or Foreign State.

9 By one universal plan of equipping, training and governing the Militia.

10 By a scheme for estimating the value of all land within each State granted to or surveyed for any person or persons together with the buildings and improvements thereon: and the appointment of certain periods at which payment shall be made.

11 By establishing rules for captures on land and the distribution of the sales.

12 By ascertaining the jurisdiction of Congress in territorial questions.

13 By erecting a mint.

14 By fixing a Standard of weights and measures throughout the U.S.

15 By appointing a Com^{ee}. for Indian affairs.

16 By regulating the Post-Office.

17 By establishing a Census of white Inhabitants in each State.

18 By publishing the Journal of Congress monthly.

19 By registering seamen.

20 By liquidation of old accounts against the U. S. and

21 By providing means of animadverting on delinquent States.

Resolved, that of the preceding articles, the 9th. be referred to the Board of War, the 13th. 14th. and 16th. to the Sup^t of Finance and the others to a Com^ee. in order that the subject matter thereof may be extended in detail for the consideration of Congress.

And Your Committee further report,

That as America became a Confederate Republic to crush the present and future foes of her Independence;

As of this Republic a general Council is a necessary organ;

And without the extension of its power in the cases hereinafter enumerated War may receive a fatal inclination and peace be exposed to daily convulsion;

It be resolved to recommend to the Several States to authorise the U.S. in Congress assembled,

1 To lay Embargoes in time of war without any limitation.

2 To prescribe rules for impressing property into the service of the U.S. during the present war.

3 To appoint the Collectors of and direct the mode of accounting for taxes imposed according to the requisitions of Congress.

4 To recognise the Independence of and admit into the federal Union any part of one or more of the U.S., with the consent of the dismembered State.

5 To stipulate in treaties with foreign nations for the establishment of consular power, without reference to the States individually.

6 To destrain the property of a State delinquent in its assigned proportion of Men and Money.

7 To vary the rules of suffrage in Congress, taking care that in questions for waging war

Granting letters of marque and reprisal in time of peace

Concluding or giving instructions for any alliance

Coining money

Regulating the value of coin

Determining the total number of land and sea forces and allotting to each State its quota of men or money.

Emitting bills of credit.

Borrowing money.

Fixing the number and force of Vessels of War, and appointing a Commander in Chief of the Army and Navy. At least two thirds of the U.S. shall agree therein.

Resolved, That a Com^ee. be appointed to prepare a representation to the several States of the necessity of these supplemental powers and of pursuing in the modification thereof, one uniform plan.

Reference: Galliard Hunt (ed.), *Journals of the Continental Congress,* Vol. XX (Washington: GPO, 1912).

NEW YORK DELEGATES TO GOVERNOR GEORGE CLINTON, MARCH 29, 1782

Sir

We were honored with your Excellency's Letter of the 20th instant by Major Hale; and doubt not of your Endeavor speedily to procure one of the absent delegates to supply Colonel Floyd's place; which We beg may be done as early in the next Month as possible. Tho, probably there will be as great difficulty in furnishing him with the necessary Money, as there will be in supplying Mr Scott for his Continuance here. When it is considered how much inferior the allowance made by our State is to that of all the other States, We cannot but think our Legislature ought, if a Representation be necessary, to make every Exertion for a bare decent Support of their delegates; who, tho' they chearfully submit to the Loss and Inconvenience necessarily arising from their Absence from home and Neglect of their domestic Concerns, cannot possibly maintain themselves in the public Service at their own private Expence. When the Jealousy of the smaller concerning the larger States, the political Views of three of the New England States to increase their Weight in the Scale of the Union, by the Junction of a new one, which will closely coalesce with them, and the Influence of the private Interest of Many Members or their Friends, who have been land-jobbing under the usurped Government of the Grants are duly considered, we apprehend their can be little cause for astonishmt that Members of Congress, should countenance that usurpation and that Congress itself should suffer persons confessedly their Leaders & Instruments in League with the Enemy, to attend the public Councils & depart unmolested. It is not even pretended, to be believed that their Negotiations with the Enemy were calculated to deceive them. But it is alledged that the Difficulty of subduing the Grants by the Arms of the united States, the probability that the Attempt would compel them to take an active part with the Enemy, the immediate danger of our State, in such Case, and the Injury that would thence result to the united States in general, are sufficient Inducements in sound policy to countenance and Establish the Independence of the Grants. In short it is easy for Men to find reasons to justify a Measure suited to their Wishes.

We think, Sir, it would be well were we furnished with proofs of the Original & Progressive Extent & Objects of the criminal Negotiations of the Leaders of the Grants, with the Enemy & particularly of the Countenance given by them for recruiting for the British Service. We might perhaps Use them to advantage. We too well know the understanding, Sagacity & Integrity of your informant to doubt any part of his Intelligence and could wish to have it all minutely detailed in proof. And while we place the greatest Confidence in his Information we heartily join with him in Opinion that conciliatory Overtures such

as You mention, followed by a spirited and vigorous Exertion of the civil Authority of the State would produce the most happy Effects, by enabling the Friends to our Govt. to shew themselves and vindicating our public Conduct to the World. These Steps notwithstanding the sinister Views of too many, it is to be hoped would induce Congress formally to pronounce agt. the Independence of the Grants. We are happy to find that our Legislature are disposed to pursue every Measure calculated to restore peace and good Govt. in that Quarter. The Acts You mention meet with our hearty Approbation because they will in our Opinion have the salutary Effects You expect. But we beg Leave to suggest that perhaps, however justly the Conduct of some may deserve the severest punishment, sound policy may forbid any Exception in the Act of Grace to make it more palatable to some in high Station who have countenanced the Revolt & Treason of the Grants.

We heard of the narrow Escape of Allen & Fay. Laying aside our Just Resentments, it may, peradventure, have been better so, than otherwise.

Having foiled our Adversaries in the attempt to carry into Execution the Report of the Committee of last to establish the Independence of the Grants, within the bounds therein limited we most impatiently wait for the Concurrent Resolutions of our Legislature. For tho nothing has since been attempted agt. Us; yet we know their Advocates only wait for a Change of Members to renew the Attempt. This Change will shortly happen. We therefore wish for those Resolutions & every Conciliatory Step of our Legislature that We may anticipate the renewal of the Subject.

In a Conference with the Secretary at War he advised that the State should exercise the Authority reserved to them in the Articles of Confederation by appointing Colonel Willet to his former Continental Rank which he said had been done in other Instances; & assured us that on being certified of this, he will do every Thing necessary on his part, and will by Letter to the Commr. in Chief (which he flatters himself with take Effect) endeavor to have the Command on our Frontiers so arranged, if it be requested by our Governmt. that Colonel Willet shall have no superior but a General Officer in that department of Service.

Colonel Vanschaick's affair is also in good Train with the Secry. He considers him and several other Officers as greatly injured by the promotion of General Hazen; and tho' he does not much like Brevets, he thinks it in the present Instance but a just Expedient to restore the Colonel to his Rank. These he say are his present Sentiments, that Congress should either thus reinstate him, which can be done without any Expence to the public; or permit him to retire on the expected Emoluments. The latter however we think would be a precarious dependence; because several of the States are determined agt. an half pay establishment; we shall therefore indeavor very shortly to obtain his matured Sentiments on the former; and should they be in its favor, We will move it in Congress. In the Interim we should be glad to be informed whether, if we should not succeed, the Colonel would wish to risk retiring on half pay.

We inclose a Copy of the Journals of on the Subject of promotions to the Rank of Major-General. They speak plainly for themselves; and

therefore need no Comment. We wish General Clinton may be immediately informed of them. Brigadiers Moultrie & McIntosh who are both on the Spot are much mortified by the preference they exhibit. They mean speedily as we are informed to signify it to Congress. We think they may be prevailed on to suspend this Step for a short Time; and should General Clinton Incline to make common Cause with them, We wish to be furnished by him without delay with the Means of doing it—a Memorial from him to Congress on the Subject may perhaps be proper.

The new Commissioners from the Grants are arrived and their Accession to the Terms of August last is known, tho' not announced to Congress. It has leaked out that the Changes in that country are favorable for Us; & that their Leaders are held in detestation. A Short Time will perhaps furnish Us with particulars which We shall not fail to communicate.

We are your Excellency's most obedt. and humble Servts.

Wm. Floyd.
Jno. Morin Scott.

Reference: Paul H. Smith (ed.), *Letters of Delegates to Congress,* Vol. XVIII (Washington: Library of Congress, 1991).

DAVID HOWELL TO GOVERNOR WILLIAM GREENE, JULY 30, 1782

Sir,

It being impracticable for a new member of Congress soon to comprehend our great national concernments & the views & purposes of Principal men in the various Departments and especially the complicated System of European Policy you will not expect such profitable communications from me at present as are to be expected from my Colleague, who has every advantage to be derived from

experience in military & political life. I shall, however, neglect no opportunity of transmitting every intelligence from time to time which may be in my power & affect the Interests of my constituents.

Eleven States have transmitted copies of their acts vesting Congress with a power to levy and collect a duty of 5 per Cent. on Imports & Prize goods; all of which acts are passed on the express condition that the measure shall be universally adopted throughout the United States and some of them have other conditions annexed; Such as the following. That after a term of years it shall be in the power of the State to substitute some other revenue equally productive and which shall be approved of by Congress. That no part of the revenue shall ever be appropriated to the discharge of half-pay, pensions, &c. That the State retain a right of appointing, or suspending the Train of revenue officers, within its jurisdiction, &c. &c. Whereon I shall only observe that a reluctance against the measure appears from the mode of compliance therewith in some instances.

A Committee was lately appointed in Congress to enquire into the reasons why the other States had not complied with this recommendation before whom, on notice & request, the Delegates for the States of Georgia & R. I. & P. Ps. appeared to give Information.

Having discovered on my arrival in this City that all the members of Congress, as well as the Inhabitants, were universally in favour of the Impost, and concluding that my single voice would be unavailing against the general current: I cautiously avoided entring unnecessarily into the discussion of the Subject, but being called on this occasion to assign the reasons which induced a delay on the part of my Constituents, a fair opportunity opened, I embraced it with pleasure, to lay before the Committee the following representations.

That the maritime Situation of our State peculiarly exposeth us to the attacks of an enemy in a time of War. By a *coup de main* an enemy may lay waste our Sea-port towns all around the Naragansett-bay, destroy our Navigation and plunder the whole treasure of our little State; in which sad Catastrophe the value of the State would be reduced to that of a County in the neighbouring States: and yet we should have no claim in virtue of any compact, or Stipulation, on the fœderal Union for a reimbursement. That in fact this had partially taken place; our State had been invaded & plundered, our Towns partly burnt, & partly torn down, & our Navigation reduced to a very low

ebb—So that out of the ancient & once wealthy Town of New-Port, which in the year 1774 sent to Sea nearly 150 Sail, three only were at Sea in March 1782: WHEREFORE, if any substantial revenue could be derived from a duty on trade, this benefit ought, in all right & justice, to belong solely & exclusively to the State in Compensation for losses already sustained, and as a Security against still more fatal evils to be apprehended in all future Wars. That this was the voice of nature, the voice of reason & the voice of *Confederation*, the Constitution of the Ud. Ss. which had in this particular, secured to us our Birthright, Viz, THE WHOLE, ENTIRE EMOLUMENTS OF OUR OWN TRADE. It was moreover represented—That, in fact, the measure in its present form tended to raise a revenue within our State & from the earnings of its Inhabitants to be carried to the general credit of the Ud. Ss.: Inasmuchas, not only in the first instance, would the Merchant be compelled to pay the duty at all events on Importation, which it might, or might not be in his power to Superadd to the price of his merchandize; but admitting the duty to be superadded, and the revenue to be wholly drawn out of the consumer, the first consequence would be an obvious inequality in respect to individuals, & the second a no less obvious inequality in respect to the Several States. And that our State would feel this grievance more sensibly than any other State in the Union, as consisting more of Merchants, manufacturers & tradesmen who are chiefly subsisted on imported goods and consuming a greater proportion of duties articles would pay an unequal part of a revenue to be appropriated to the common benefit of the Union. Another consequence would be the rise of the prices of such articles of country produce as may be substituted in lieu of imported articles, which would no doubt continue to bear nearly their usual proportion to each other, & being drawn from our neighbouring States although by an Inland communication, they would thus in fact come charged with the five per Cent. duty, which would be pernicious to our intrests & increasingly so in all future time. And, moreover, that inland duties, imposed at the pleasure of our neighbours, on specific articles in addition to their prices thus unnaturally raised, (which by the way the Confederation authorised them to impose) and temporary Embargoes, the effects of which we had sorely felt during the State-bill, might lay us wholly at their mercy and precipitate our ruin; while, on the contrary, should trade remain unfettered with duties, & free to all the world, while our Ports continued open, supplies might be drawn from any part of the World, whereby we might be enabled to treat with our neighbours, however extensive their territory, or however overbearing their temporary insolence, upon terms of equality.

It was further represented—That it derogated from the Sovereignty & Independance of the State for the Ud. Ss. to draw a Revenue for their benefit out of our State & to collect it by their officers—For that all monies raised in a Sovereign State ought to pass to the credit of that Sovereignty exclusively; and all civil officers acting in a Sovereign State ought to be authorised by & accountable to that Sovereignty—the contrary being a Solecism in Politicks, and in this case injurious to the State.

That such was the State of mankind that the experience of ages evinced the extreme difficulty of collecting duties on trade. That this difficulty would be less should the duty proposed be laid on by the State for its own benefit and greater in the measure proposed. In the former case it would be the interest of every citizen to aid in the collecting with a view of lightening his own Tax thereby: in the latter, he would not only promote his own particular intrest by avoiding the duty in his own case, but the intrest of his State in abetting others in the practice: Therefore it was not probable that the measure proposed was practicable, at least so as to afford any considerable net produce, after deducting the vast expences of the numerous officers necessary in the collecting & after management thereof.

That the term of its duration was exceptionable and precluded the State from the possibility of revoking their grant in any future Period, should experience prove it ever so unproffitable & ruinous.

That Congress were not to be accountable for the amount or expenditure of this revenue; but on the contrary it was to be absolutely at their disposal, during a term of time which would be wholly in their power. That perhaps it might really be the Intrest of the Ud. Ss. never to discharge all the debts contracted, and to be contracted during this War, and if so the duty, by the terms of the grant, was to remain to perpetuity.

That however safely this extraordinary, uncontroulable & unaccountable power might be granted to the present Congress, a change of times & of men—might bring forth abuses at present unthought of, and cause us to rue the fatal day when we so rashly devested ourselves & that irrevocably, of a power naturally inherent in the several States & guaranteed & secured to us in CONFEDERATION.

It was further represented—That the measure proposed in addition to all the evils aforsd. had an unpromising aspect upon the morals of the Community at large, by multiplying oaths, by increasing temptations to perjury both in officers of the customs & in citizens, & by nourishing in idleness & Luxury a numerous train of Collectors, Comptrollers, Searchers, tide-waiters, Clerks, &c. &c. whereby the country would loose the benefit of their industry & incur the additional charge of their support & that not to *create* a revenue but only in order to throw taxation out of its *present channel* & to bring the weight thereof upon particular setts, or descriptions of men in the community to their great & lasting injury.

That it did not appear as yet in what manner Congress would enforce the Law proposed, whether prosecutions were to be commenced or penalties were to be recoverable in the common Courts of justice, or whether the Maritime Courts were to be impowered to have cognizance hereof & that the general plan for the execution of the Law might affect the propriety of making the grant in question.

That I had lately received pointed instructions to make urgent application to Congress in behalf of my Constituents for a participation in the *vacant*, or *backlands*, to which they claimed, for reasons the most substantive, a good right in common with their Sister States. That Congress had hitherto delayed to come to an ultimate decision hereon—And as some States pertinaciously persisted in claiming exclusive rights to sd lands: it was not to be expected that our State would part with all the benefits of its maritime Situation untill some assurance could be obtained of a Participation in common with other States in the back lands, which ought to be considered as a continental acquisition & to be appropriated accordingly—but this was thrown out as a reason of the delay in question only conjecturally, not being so assigned in the instructions referred to.

After proposing the following alterations, Viz,

1st. That each State retain the power of chusing the officers of the revenue to be collected within its own jurisdiction.

2. That the revenue arising from this duty be carried to the credit of each State, wherein it shall be collected respectively, and deducted from their annual *Quotas* of continental requisitions. I withdrew, not a little mortified at having been opposed rather than seconded by my Colleague.

It ought also to be noted that on this occasion, the extraordinary exertions of our State during the whole contest, and on the opening of the present campaign in special were mentioned & not contested & added much weight to the aforegoing representations in behalf of the State; And that the Committee have not yet made their report, which no doubt will produce a renewed application to the State: For, the same reasons, which make it against our intrest, to make this grant, make it the intrest of the whole Union to solicit it, which you may expect will be done with the most unremitting importunity. After the part I have taken

in this matter, which has been done with views the most disinterested, so far as I am personally concerned, my Constituents will not expect any direct advice on the Subject; and knowing they possess integrity & abilities sufficient for the places they respectively fill, in all events, I shall always endeavour to reconcile myself to their determinations & govern myself by their instructions, however contrary to my private opinion.

A grand Committee for the support of public credit has lately been appointed in Congress, and I shall endeavour as one of that Committee to bring on a decision respecting the *backlands*. They would undoubtedly be a means in our hands of reviving public credit; they are of vast extent & value, beyond what is generally known or conjectured. A gentleman of no mean Talents in Finance thinks well of this plan, & that, in a course of time, they would enable us to discharge a great part of our national debt. So much in answer to the Instruction on that head referred to in your Excellencys Letter of 17 June last. The Commissioners appointed by the resolve of the 20 of February last are to liquidate and put on the list of the funded debt, which is to draw Interest, all the Certificates issued on account of the Continent in the Several States. And it is proposed that in the Settlement to be made by the sd Commissioners the States have credit for their taxes of old money actually collected & paid in, & be charged with their deficiencies—but this arrangement is not compleated, nor fixed as it would affect individuals in possession of sd Bills as I can yet discover.

The recommendation of Congress of Feby. 20 last for empowering them to settle the several States Quota's of expences incurred before Janry 1 1782, otherwise than by articles of the Confederation, has been formally rejected by an act of the Legislature of Virginia; whether they fear the deviation would be made against their intrest, or mean to procrastinate a Settlement, I shall not undertake to determine.

Several reductions in public expenditures have taken place since I have had the Honor of a Seat in Congress. Œconomy is the present plan; the good work is begun, & going on, I perceive, can yet be done; & my exertions, such as they are, will not be wanting on this Subject. Could prompt pay be made to the army, many reductions might take place with propriety & without inconvenience. Is not this an object worthy our attention?

By a resolve of the 23 October 1780, the officers, who shall continue in the Service to the end of the War shall be entitled to half-pay during life; as well as those who are reduced by the resolve of the same day; & others deranged by other resolves & permitted to retire; whereby the Ud. Ss. are loaded with half-pay officers, even during the war, and that which was intended as an antidote against depreciation is continued, even now when the army is paid in hard money & having been originally intended as a motive to keep officers in the army, is now become a temptation for them to leave it. And what is still more extraordinary by another resolve, half-pay is to be made in all cases in proportion to full pay, so that a M.G. and B. Gl. draw their respective half pays, instead of the half-pay of a Colonel—against the universal custom in all European nations, where there are half-pay establishments. A Major General &

a Brigadier General lately applied to Congress for leave to retire on the half-pay establishment & obtained it, and officers of inferior grades in the Line are daily retiring on half pay and others advanced to take their places, whereby we have duplicates & triplicates of officers in some instances and an enormous expence is incurred. This in my opinion calls loudly on the Legislatures of the States either to provide Funds, inaddition to the 5 per Cent, which will be insufficient, or to instruct their Delegates to discontinue the practice. I the rather wish for instructions on this head as I am so unhappy as to differ from my worthy Colleague on these points, tho' I do it with much diffidence & reluctance.

A report lies for Congress from the office of Finance recommending the 5 per Cent., a Land tax of one Dollar per hundred acres & a Capitation tax. From this report Congress have taken & recommended only the 5 per Cent. QUERE—Would either of the other two be eligible?

Reference: Paul H. Smith (ed.), *Letters of Delegates to Congress,* Vol. XVIII (Washington: Library of Congress, 1991).

CONGRESS ATTEMPTS TO DISCIPLINE DAVID HOWELL, DECEMBER 1782

The committee to whom were referred a motion of Mr. Arnold, for transmitting to the executive of Rhode Island sundry extracts of public letters from Europe, and some subsequent motions thereon, report:—

That, in their opinion, it would be improper for Congress to concur in the object of that motion, as with respect to a part of the extracts specified relating merely to the general growing political importance of these states, the injunction of secrecy being taken off, any member who inclines to communicate them to his state, may take copies of them; and more especially, as Mr. Howell was furnished with complete copies

of letters, from which particular detached sentences are now requested. And with respect to such extracts as relate to the subject of foreign loans, they are already within the purview of the resolution of the 20th of December last, directing the secretary for foreign affairs to transmit to the executive of the state of Rhode Island an authenticated state of the applications for foreign loans, and the result. That the same observation applies to that part of the motion which relates generally to the transmission of the letters from our foreign ministers on the subject of loans, not under the injunction of secrecy; with this additional consideration, that such of those letters as would in fact throw light upon the subject, comprehend many delicate transactions which it is the duty of Congress, at the present juncture, to conceal. The committee, notwithstanding, are of opinion that, to obviate misrepresentation, it will be advisable to transmit to the executive of the state of Rhode Island a copy of Mr. Arnold's motion, and the proceedings thereupon, with a request that precautions may be taken to prevent their appearing in the public prints.

On the question—Resolved, that Congress agree to the said report.

CHARLES THOMSON, Secretary.

Reference: J.R. Bartlett (ed.), *Records of the Colony and State of Rhode Island,* Vol. IX (10 vols.; Providence: A.C. Greene, 1856–1865).

REPORT BY CONGRESS ON DAVID HOWELL, JANUARY 14, 1783

December 12th, 1782.

The committee, consisting of Mr. Williamson, Mr. Carroll and Mr. Madison, appointed to consider how far the honor of Congress and the finances of the United States may be affected by some late publications on the subject of foreign loans, &c., report:—

"That among the different publications which have lately been made, concerning foreign loans, they have particularly attended to a very remarkable extract of a letter published in the Boston Gazette, of November 10th, 1782, under the Providence head, which is there said to be an 'extract of a letter from a gentleman in Philadelphia, to his friend in that town, dated October 16th,' in which are the following observations: 'This day letters have been read in Congress, from Mr. Adams, of the 16th of August, and Mr. Dumas, his secretary, of the 19th. The loan he is negotiating fills as fast as could be expected. The national importance of the United States is constantly rising in the estimation of European powers and the civilized world. Such is their credit, that they have of late failed in no application for foreign loans; and the only danger on that score, is that of contracting too large a debt.'

"Your committee have examined the several letters that have been received from Mr. Adams, your minister at the Hague, in the course of the last six months, as well as those from Mr. Dumas, and the sundry letters which have been received from your ministers at Versailles and Madrid, on the subject of loans, in the course of the present year, and they are sorry to observe that the positions just referred to on the subject of loans, are not only ill founded, but some of them are expressly contradicted by the letters of your ministers at foreign courts. And whereas, the above extract, from its date and particular mention of other dates, is so drawn as to give reason to suspect that it was written by a member of Congress, or by some person officially entrusted with their papers; and as the duty and honor of Congress require that they should endeavor to detect and prevent misrepresentations of this kind,—

"Resolved, that the secretary for foreign affairs be instructed to write to the executive of Rhode Island, requesting them to inquire through what channel the above communication was made, or who is the supposed author of the extract referred to, and report accordingly."

Resolved, that Congress agree to the said report.

December 18th, 1782.

A motion being before the house in the following words, "That the secretary for foreign affairs be discharged from the instruction given him on the 12th instant, Mr. Howell, a delegate from the state of Rhode Island, having acknowledged himself the author of the extract of the letter quoted in the report of the committee," a motion was made by Mr. Howell to postpone the consideration of the motion before the house, to make way for one he read in his place, in the words following: "David Howell, of Providence, in the state of Rhode Island and Providence Plantations, now a delegate in Congress for the said state, having in his place made the following declaration, viz.: That he hath, in sundry letters to his constituents, written largely on the public affairs, both foreign and domestic, of the United States, particularly in a letter of fifteen pages in folio, directed to His Excellency William Greene, Esq., governor of said state, and in another, less copious, directed to John Carter, Esq., printer of the Providence Gazette, from one of which he doubts not was extracted a certain paragraph in the Providence Gazette, of the 2d day of November last, as follows, viz.: 'This day letters have been read in Congress, from Mr. Adams, of the 16th of August, Mr. Dumas, his secretary, of the 19th. The loan he is negotiating fills as fast as can be expected. * * * The national importance of the United States is constantly arising in the estimation of European powers and the civilized world. * * * Such is their credit, that they have of late failed in no application for foreign loans; and the danger on that score, is that of contracting too large a debt.' * * * Desunt von nulla. * * * But not having copies of said letters, he is at present unable to identify the words and sentences;—the substance he avows to have written, not only in said letters, but others on sundry occasions. At the same time absolutely protesting generally against any power exercised, or claimed by Congress, to call any member of their body to account for any information which he may think proper to communicate to his constituents, (the secrets only of Congress excepted,) and more especially against any power in the present Congress to call to account a member of the late Congress. Further alleging and protesting, that the resolve of the—day of December instant, appointing a committee of Congress on late publications, is a departure from the dignity of Congress, and tends to establish a precedent dangerous to the freedom of the press, the palladium of liberty, civil and religious; and that the resolve of the—day of December instant, accepting the report of said committee, against a certain paragraph in a newspaper, and demanding the writer thereof to be delivered up by the executive of the state of Rhode Island, is in effect an infraction of the fifth article of the confederation, which allows

freedom of speech and debate in Congress, and of course a free communication of such speeches and debates to their constituents, by the members of Congress, without being accountable to that body for the propriety of what is said, debated or communicated. And declaring that the facts stated in said paragraph, respecting foreign loans, are substantially true, and can be established by authentic documents in possession of Congress, there having been no eventual and final failure in any late application. That the opinions advanced were such as he entertained and declared on the floor of Congress, when the sum of a foreign loan was agitated, as the yeas and nays on the journal will manifest, and such as he still retains, and in which he is not alone. That great injustice may be done to the most cautious writer, by publishing a single paragraph only of a letter, (of which, however, he does not in this case complain;) and still greater by a committee of Congress reporting only a part of such paragraphs, and thereby fixing it on the journals in such a detached and maimed condition, of which he does complain, and alleges that such proceeding threatens the privileges and endangers the characters of members of Congress. That such a mode of inquisition, established by authority of Congress, has a tendency to erect a system of despotism, by deterring the minority from writing freely to their constituents such things as they have a right to know, lest their letters should be intercepted, published, and in detached paragraphs injuriously fixed on the journals of Congress, by an overbearing majority. That it is well known that in his private opinion he is, has been, and has a right to be, against the five per cent. impost. His constituents expected him to oppose it; that he has been faithful to them in that particular, will not be denied. He is happy to find that the state he has the honor to represent has unanimously rejected that dangerous measure, by a solemn determination of the lower house of Assembly, on the 1st day of November last, fifty-three members being present. If the part he has taken in that regard, has drawn on him the resentment of any, he will endeavor to sustain it with a fortitude becoming the cause of freedom and his country, which in every part of his conduct he has uniformly supported, and for proof appeals to the journals of Congress. His constituents have hitherto approved his conduct, and he trusts they will not fail to support him. He considers himself as their servant, and to them alone he is accountable for his doings; and under them, the servant of the United States, and not the servant of Congress."

The declaration and protest aforegoing being duly considered,—

Resolved, that the resolution of—, in the words following, viz.: "Resolved, that the secretary for foreign affairs be instructed to write to the executive of Rhode Island, requesting them to inquire through what channel the above communication was made, or who is the supposed author of the extract referred to, and report accordingly," be, and the same is hereby, revoked.

This motion of Mr. Howell being seconded by Mr. Arnold, and on the question to agree to it the yeas and nays being required by Mr. Howell, it was decided in the negative.

A question was then taken on the motion before the house, whereupon it was—

Resolved, that the secretary for foreign affairs be discharged from the instruction given him on the 12th instant, Mr. Howell, a delegate from the state of Rhode Island, having acknowledged himself the author of the extract of the letter quoted in the report of the committee of that day.

A motion was then made by Mr. Hamilton, seconded by Mr. Carroll, in the words following: "Congress having, in respect to the articles of confederation, admitted on their journals an entry of a motion made by Mr. Howell, seconded by Mr. Arnold, highly derogatory to the honor and dignity of the United States in Congress assembled,—

Resolved, that a committee be appointed to report such measures as it will be proper for Congress to take thereupon.

A motion was made by Mr. Arnold, seconded by Mr. Howell, to strike out the words "highly derogatory to the honor and dignity of the United States in Congress assembled." And on the question, Shall the words moved to be struck out stand, the yeas and nays being required by Mr. Arnold, it was carried in the affirmative.

On the question to agree to the motion— Resolved in the affirmative.

Members chosen for the foregoing committee— Mr. Gilman, Mr. Hamilton and Mr. Madison.

December 20th, 1782.

On the report of the committee appointed to report such measures as it will be proper for Congress to take in consequence of the motion made by Mr. Howell, on the 18th instant,—

Resolved, that the said motion, with the preceding resolutions of Congress to which it refers, be transmitted by the secretary for foreign affairs to the executive authority of the state of Rhode Island, with an authenticated state of the several applications for foreign loans, and the result thereof.

Extract from the minutes.

GEO. BOND, Dep. Sec'y.

The United States in Congress assembled.

December 12th, 1782.

A letter of the 30th of November, from the speaker of the lower house of Assembly of the state of Rhode Island, being read, a motion was made by Mr. Howell, seconded by Mr. Arnold, in the words following:—

"Whereas, a letter to His Excellency the President of Congress, from the lower house of Assembly of the state of Rhode Island and Providence Plantations, hath been this day read in Congress, in the words and figures following, to wit:—

'East Greenwich, 30th November, 1782.

'Sir:—In obedience to the direction of the lower house of Assembly of this state, I have the honor to enclose to your Excellency their unanimous resolution on the recommendation of Congress, respecting an impost on imported goods, &c., and to state some of the principal reasons which produced that resolution. The recommendation was rejected, first, because it would be unequal in its operation, bearing hardest on the most commercial states, and so would press peculiarly hard upon this state, which draws its chief support from commerce.

Secondly, because it proposes to introduce into this and the other states officers unknown and unaccountable to them, and so is against the constitution of this state. And thirdly, because, by granting to Congress a power to collect monies from the commerce of these states, indefinitely as to time and quantity, and for the expenditure of which they are not to be accountable to the states, they would become independent of their constituents, and so the proposed impost is repugnant to the liberty of the United States. Many more reasons might be offered, and the subject drawn out to a great length, by descending to particulars; but these are sufficient to answer the main design of the house, which is to show a decent respect to the states which have differed from them in opinion upon this subject. This state may be justly ranked among the foremost in the common cause, having furnished in support of it as many men and as much money, in proportion to its abilities, as any state in the Union, and much more than most of them; and it is still disposed to continue its exertions; but it will raise and collect its quota of public taxes in such a way as shall be judged most proper. And it is hoped that when its resolutions are founded on the great principles of liberty and a general interest, it will not be thought to suspect the public virtue of the present Congress, by withholding from them or their servants a

power of which their successors might make a dangerous use.

'With the highest sentiments of respect for your Excellency, and the Honorable Assembly over which you preside, I am your Excellency's most obedient servant,

WILLIAM BRADFORD, Speaker.'

"Wherefore—Resolved, that the resolution of the 6th of December instant, for appointing a deputation to be sent to the state of Rhode Island, for the purpose of making a full and just representation of the public affairs of the United States, and of urging the absolute necessity of a compliance with the resolution of Congress of the 3d day of February, 1781, respecting the duty on imports and prizes, as a measure essential to the safety and reputation of these states, be, and the same is hereby repealed."

On this motion, the previous question was moved by the state of New York, seconded by the state of New Hampshire, that the question be not now put; and on the question to agree to the previous question, the yeas and nays being required by Mr. Howell, it was resolved in the affirmative, and the main question was set aside.

Extract from the minutes.
GEO. BOND, Dep. Sec'y.

Reference: J. R. Bartlett (ed.), *Records of the Colony and State of Rhode Island,* Vol. IX (10 vols.; Providence: A. C. Greene, 1856–1865).

NORTHWEST ORDINANCES OF 1784 AND 1787

Report of a committee, on a plan for a temporary government of the Western territory, adopted April 23, 1784

Resolved, That so much of the territory ceded or to be ceded by individual states to the United States, as is already purchased or shall be purchased of the Indian inhabitants, and offered for sale by Congress, shall be divided into distinct states, in the following manner, as nearly as such cessions will admit; that is to say, by parallels of latitude, so that each State shall comprehend from north to south two degrees of latitude, beginning to count from the completion

of forty-five degrees north of the equator; and by meridians of longitude, one of which shall pass through the lowest point of the rapids of Ohio, and the other through the western cape of the mouth of the Great Kanhaway: but the territory eastward of this last meridian, between the Ohio, Lake Erie, and Pensylvania, shall be one State whatsoever may be its comprehension of latitude. That which may lie beyond the completion of the 45th degree between the said meridians, shall make part of the State adjoining it on the south: and that part of the Ohio, which is between the same meridians coinciding nearly with that parallel as a boundary line.

That the settlers on any territory so purchased, and offered for sale, shall, either on their own petition or on the order of Congress, receive authority from them, with appointments of time and place, for their free males of full age within the limits of their State to meet together, for the purpose of establishing a temporary government, to adopt the constitution and laws of any one of the original States; so that such laws nevertheless shall be subject to alteration by their ordinary legislature; and to erect, subject to a like alteration, counties, townships, or other divisions, for the election of members for their legislature.

That when any such State shall have acquired twenty thousand free inhabitants, on giving due proof thereof to Congress, they shall receive from them authority with appointments of time and place, to call a convention of representatives to establish a permanent constitution and government for themselves. Provided that both the temporary and permanent governments be established on these principles as their basis:

First. That they shall for ever remain a part of this confederacy of the United States of America.

Second. That they shall be subject to the Articles of Confederation in all those cases in which the original states shall be so subject, and to all the acts and ordinances of the United States in Congress assembled, conformable thereto.

Third. That they in no case shall interfere with the primary disposal of the soil by the United states in Congress assembled, nor with the ordinances and regulations which Congress may find necessary, for securing the title in such soil to the bona fide purchasers.

Fourth. That they shall be subject to pay a part of the federal debts contracted or to be contracted, to be apportioned on them by Congress, according to the same common rule and measure by which apportionments thereof shall be made on the other states.

Fifth. That no tax shall be imposed on lands, the property of the United States.

Sixth. That their respective governments shall be republican.

Seventh. That the lands of non-resident proprietors shall, in no case, be taxed higher than those of residents within any new State, before the admission thereof to a vote by its delegates in Congress.

That whensoever any of the said states shall have, of free inhabitants, as many as shall then be in any one the least numerous of the thirteen Original states, such State shall be admitted by its delegates into the Congress of the United States, on an equal footing with the said original states; provided the consent of so many states in Congress is first obtained as may at the time be competent to such admission. And in order to adapt the said Articles of Confederation to the state of Congress when its numbers shall be thus increased, it shall be proposed to the legislatures of the states, originally parties thereto, to require the assent of two-thirds of the United States in Congress assembled, in all those cases wherein, by the said articles, the assent of nine states is now required, which being agreed to by them, shall be binding on the new states. Until such admission by their delegates into Congress, any of the said states, after the establishment of their temporary government, shall have authority to keep a member in Congress, with a right of debating but not of voting.

That measures not inconsistent with the principles of the Confederation, and necessary for the preservation of peace and good order among the settlers in any of the said new states, until they shall assume a temporary government as aforesaid, may, from time to time, be taken by the United States in Congress assembled.

That the preceding articles shall be formed into a charter of compact; shall be duly executed by the President of the United States in Congress assembled, under his hand, and the seal of the United States; shall be promulgated; and shall stand as fundamental constitutions between the thirteen original states, and each of the several states now newly described, unalterable from and after the sale of any part of the territory of such State, pursuant to this resolve but by the joint consent of the United States in Congress assembled, and of the particular State within which such alteration is proposed to be made. . . .

—

An Ordinance for the government of the territory of the United States North West of the river Ohio, 1787

Be it ordained by the United States in Congress Assembled that the said territory for the purposes of temporary government be one district, subject however to be divided into two districts as future circumstances may in the Opinion of Congress make it expedient.

Be it ordained by the authority aforesaid, that the estates both of resident and non resident proprietors in the said territory dying intestate shall descend to and be distributed among their children and the descendants of a deceased child in equal parts; the descendants of a deceased child or grand child to take the share of their deceased parent in equal parts among them; and where there shall be no children or descendants then in equal parts to the next of kin in equal degree and among collaterals the children of a deceased brother or sister of the intestate shall have in equal parts among them their deceased parent's share and there shall in no case be a distinction between kindred of the whole and half blood; saving in all cases to the widow of the intestate her third part of the real estate for life, and one third part of the personal estate; and this law relative to descents and dower shall remain in full force until altered by the legislature of the district. And until the governor and judges shall adopt laws as hereinafter mentioned estates in the said territory may be devised or bequeathed by wills in writing signed and sealed by him or her in whom the estate may be, being of full age, and attested by three witnesses, and real estates may be conveyed by lease and release or bargain and sale signed, sealed and delivered by the person being of full age in whom the estate may be and attested by two witnesses provided such wills be duly proved and such conveyances be acknowledged or the execution thereof duly proved and be recorded within one year after proper magistrates, courts and registers shall be appointed for that purpose and personal property

may be transferred by delivery saving however to the french and canadian inhabitants and other settlers of the Kaskaskies, Saint Vincents and the neighbouring villages who have heretofore professed themselves citizens of Virginia, their laws and customs now in force among them relative to the descent and conveyance of property.

Be it ordained by the authority aforesaid that there shall be appointed from time to time by Congress a governor, whose commission shall continue in force for the term of three years, unless sooner revoked by Congress; he shall reside in the district and have a freehold estate therein, in one thousand acres of land while in the exercise of his office. There shall be appointed from time to time by Congress a secretary, whose commission shall continue in force for four years, unless sooner revoked; he shall reside in the district and have a freehold estate therein in five hundred acres of land while in the exercise of his office; It shall be his duty to keep and preserve the acts and laws passed by the legislature and the public records of the district and the proceedings of the governor in his executive department and transmit authentic copies of such acts and proceedings every six months to the Secretary of Congress. There shall also be appointed a court to consist of three judges any two of whom to form a court, who shall have a common law jurisdiction and reside in the district and have each therein a freehold estate in five hundred acres of land while in the exercise of their offices, and their commissions shall continue in force during good behaviour.

The governor, and judges or a majority of them shall adopt and publish in the district such laws of the original states criminal and civil as may be necessary and best suited to the circumstances of the district and report them to Congress from time to time, which laws shall be in force in the district until the organization of the general assembly therein, unless disapproved of by Congress; but afterwards the legislature shall have authority to alter them as they shall think fit.

The governor for the time being shall be Commander in chief of the militia, appoint and commission all officers in the same below the rank of general Officers; All general Officers shall be appointed and commissioned by Congress.

Previous to the Organization of the general Assembly the governor shall appoint such magistrates and other civil officers in each county or township, as he shall find necessary for the preservation of the peace and good order in the same. After the general Assembly shall be organized, the powers and duties of magistrates and other civil officers shall be regulated and defined by the said Assembly; but all magistrates and other civil officers, not herein otherwise directed shall during the continuance of this temporary government be appointed by the governor.

For the prevention of crimes and injuries the laws to be adopted or made shall have force in all parts of the district and for the execution of process criminal and civil, the governor shall make proper divisions thereof, and he shall proceed from time to time as circumstances may require to lay out the parts of the district in which the indian titles shall have been extinguished into counties and townships subject however to such alterations as may thereafter be made by the legislature.

So soon as there shall be five thousand free male inhabitants of full age in the district upon giving proof thereof to the governor, they shall receive authority with time and place to elect representatives from their counties or townships to represent them in the general assembly, provided that for every five hundred free male inhabitants there shall be one representative and so on progressively with the number of free male inhabitants shall the right of representation encrease until the number of representatives shall amount to twenty five after which the number and proportion of representatives shall be regulated by the legislature; provided that no person be eligible or qualified to act as a representative unless he shall have been a citizen of one of the United States three years and be a resident in the district or unless he shall have resided in the district three years and in either case shall likewise hold in his own right in fee simple two hundred acres of land within the same; provided also that a freehold in fifty acres of land in the

district having been a citizen of one of the states and being resident in the district; or the like freehold and two years residence in the district shall be necessary to qualify a man as an elector of a representative.

The representative thus elected shall serve for the term of two years and in the case of the death of a representative or removal from office, the governor shall issue a writ to the county or township for which he was a member, to elect another in his stead to serve for the residue of the term.

The general assembly or legislature shall consist of the governor, legislative council and a house of representatives. The legislative council shall consist of five members to continue in Office five years unless sooner removed by Congress any three of whom to be a quorum and the members of the council shall be nominated and appointed in the following manner, to wit; As soon as representatives shall be elected, the governor shall appoint a time and place for them to meet together, and when met they shall nominate ten persons residents in the district and each possessed of a freehold in five hundred acres of Land and return their names to Congress; five of whom Congress shall apppoint and commission to serve as aforesaid; and whenever a vacancy shall happen in the council by death or removal from office, the house of representatives shall nominate two persons qualified as aforesaid, for each vacancy, and return their names to Congress, one of whom Congress shall appoint and commission for the residue of the term, and every five years, four months at least before the expiration of the time of service of the Members of the Council, the said house shall nominate ten persons qualified as aforesaid, and return their names to Congress, five of whom Congress shall appoint and commission to serve as Members of the council five years, unless sooner removed. And the governor, legislative council, and house of representatives, shall have authority to make laws in all cases for the good government of the district, not repugnant to the principles and Articles in this Ordinance established and declared. And all bills having passed by a majority in the house, and by a majority in the council, shall be referred to the Governor for his assent; but no bill or legislative Act whatever, shall be of any force without his assent. The Governor shall have power to convene, prorogue and dissolve the General Assembly, when in his opinion it shall be expedient.

The Governor, Judges, legislative Council, Secretary, and such other Officers as Congress shall appoint in the district shall take an Oath or Affirmation of fidelity, and of Office,; the Governor before the president of Congress, and all other Officers before the Governor. As soon as a legislature shall be formed in the district, the Council and house assembled in one room, shall have authority by joint ballot to elect a Delegate to Congress, who shall have a seat in Congress, with a right of debating, but not of voting, during this temporary Government.

And for extending the fundamental principles of civil and religious liberty, which form the basis whereon these republics, their laws and constitutions are erected; to fix and establish those principles as the basis of all laws, constitutions and governments, which forever hereafter shall be formed in the said territory; to provide also for the establishment of States and permanent government therein, and for their admission to a share in the federal Councils on an equal footing with the original States, at as early periods as may be consistent with the general interest,

It is hereby Ordained and declared by the authority aforesaid, That the following Articles shall be considered as Articles of compact between the Original States and the people and States in the said territory, and forever remain unalterable, unless by common consent, *to wit,*

Article the First. No person, demeaning himself in a peaceable and orderly manner shall ever be molested on account of his mode of worship or religious sentiments in the said territory.

Article the Second. The inhabitants of the said territory shall always be entitled to the benefits of the writ of habeas corpus, and of the trial by Jury; of a proportionate representation of the people in the legislature, and of judicial proceedings according to the course of the common law; all persons shall be bailable unless for capital offences, where the proof shall be evident, or

the presumption great; all fines shall be moderate, and no cruel or unusual punishments shall be inflicted; no man shall be deprived of his liberty or property but by the judgment of his peers, or the law of the land; and should the public exigencies make it necessary for the common preservation to take any persons property, or to demand his particular services, full compensation shall be made for the same; and in the just preservation of rights and property it is understood and declared; that no law ought ever to be made, or have force in the said territory, that shall in any manner whatever interfere with, or affect private contracts or engagements, bona fide and without fraud previously formed.

Article the Third. Religion, Morality and knowledge being necessary to good government and the happiness of mankind, Schools and the means of education shall forever be encouraged. The utmost good faith shall always be observed towards the Indians, their lands and property shall never be taken from them without their consent; and in their property, rights and liberty, they never shall be invaded or disturbed, unless in just and lawful wars authorised by Congress; but laws founded in justice and humanity shall from time to time be made, for preventing wrongs being done to them, and for preserving peace and friendship with them.

Article the Fourth. The said territory, and the States which may be formed therein shall forever remain a part of this Confederacy of the United States of America, subject to the Articles of Confederation, and to such alterations therein as shall be constitutionally made; and to all the Acts and Ordinances of the United States in Congress Assembled, conformable thereto. The Inhabitants and Settlers in the said territory, shall be subject to pay a part of the federal debts contracted or to be contracted, and a proportional part of the expences of Government, to be apportioned on them by Congress, according to the same common rule and measure by which apportionments thereof shall be made on the other States; and the taxes for paying their proportion, shall be laid and levied by the authority and direction of the legislatures of the district or districts or new States, as in the original States, within the time agreed upon by the United States in Congress Assembled. The Legislatures of those districts, or new States, shall never interfere with the primary disposal of the Soil by the United States in Congress Assembled, nor with any regulations Congress may find necessary for securing the title in such soil to the bona fide purchasers. No tax shall be imposed on lands the property of the United States; and in no case shall non resident proprietors be taxed higher than residents. The navigable Waters leading into the Mississippi and St. Lawrence, and the carrying places between the same shall be common highways, and forever free, as well to the Inhabitants of the said territory, as to the Citizens of the United States, and those of any other States that may be admitted into the Confederacy, without any tax, impost or duty therefor.

Article the Fifth. There shall be formed in the said territory, not less than three nor more than five States, and the boundaries of the States, as soon as Virginia shall alter her act of cession and consent to the same, shall become fixed and established as follows, to wit: The Western State in the said territory, shall be bounded by the Mississippi, the Ohio and Wabash rivers; a direct line drawn from the Wabash and post Vincents due North to the territorial line between the United States and Canada, and by the said territorial line to the lake of the Woods and Mississippi. The middle State shall be bounded by the said direct line, the Wabash from post Vincents to the Ohio; by the Ohio, by direct line drawn due North from the mouth of the great Miami to the said territorial line, and by the said territorial line. The eastern State shall be bounded by the last mentioned direct line, the Ohio, Pensylvania, and the said territorial line;

provided however, and it is further understood and declared, that the boundaries of these three States, shall be subject so far to be altered, that if Congress shall hereafter find it expedient, they shall have authority to form one or two States in that part of the said territory which lies north of an east and west line drawn through the southerly bend or extreme of lake Michigan [see Map 3]; and whenever any of the said States shall have sixty thousand free Inhabitants therein, such State shall be admitted by its Delegates into the Congress of the United States, on an equal footing with the original States, in all respects whatever; and shall be at liberty to form a permanent constitution and State government, provided the constitution and government so to be formed, shall be republican, and in conformity to the principles contained in these Articles; and so far as it can be consistent with the general interest of the Confederacy, such admission shall be allowed at an earlier period, and when there may be a less number of free Inhabitants in the State than sixty thousand.

Article the Sixth. There shall be neither Slavery nor involuntary Servitude in the said territory otherwise than in the punishment of crimes, whereof the party shall have been duly convicted; provided always that any person escaping into the same, from whom labor or service is lawfully claimed in any one of the original States, such fugitive may be lawfully reclaimed and conveyed to the person claiming his or her labor or service as aforesaid.

References: Galliard Hunt (ed.), *Journals of the Continental Congress*, Vol. XXVI (Washington: GPO, 1929), 274–279 and Vol. XXXI (Washington: GPO: 1934), 334–343.

SECRETARY OF CONGRESS TO ROBERT LIVINGSTON, MARCH 1, 1786

SIR,—As many states in the Union continued to be unrepresented in Congress, or to be represented by only two members, notwithstanding the many recommendations of Congress for remedying these defects, particularly those of 1st of

November, 1783, and the 19th of April, 1784; and as from the want of a complete representation, the great interests of the Union had frequently been, and continued to be, neglected or delayed, and the confederation itself or the administration thereof might be considered as the cause of evils which solely resulted from an incomplete representation, Congress judging it incumbent upon them to prevent opinions so derogatory to their honor, and so dangerous to the public welfare, did on the 17th of August last, pass a resolve whereby it became the duty of the Secretary of Congress once in every month to transmit to the Legislatures of the respective states a list of the states represented, and of those unrepresented in Congress, and of the members from each state. The object of this resolution was, that effectual measures might from time to time be taken by such states as were unrepresented or represented only by two members, to remedy these defects.

In the execution of this duty I have had the honor every month since of transmitting to your Excellency a monthly statement of the representation of the states in Congress to be laid before your Legislature. The statement which accompanies this, and which I have to request the favor of your Excellency to communicate to the Legislature, is for the month of February last. By this and the three other statements transmitted since the meeting of Congress on the first Monday in November last, your Excellency and the Legislature will see that there has not been for a single day, a number of states assembled sufficient to proceed on the great business of the Union; indeed, for half the time, not a number sufficient to do more than to adjourn from day to day.

With the greatest respect, I have the honor to be your Excellency's most obedient and most humble servant,

CHAˢ THOMSON.

Reference: Edmund C. Burnett (ed.), *Letters of Members of the Continental Congress,* Vol. VIII (8 vols.; Washington: Carnegie Institution, 1921–1936), 311–312.

Criticism and Defense of Congress Under the Articles

This final Chapter of Part IX presents the debates (never formal) over governance structures under the Articles of Confederation. Almost all of these documents are regarded as major critiques of the national government, especially over national leadership and the rights of the states. The reader should ask whether the arguments against or the arguments for the Articles of Confederation best reflect the system of governance created in the colonial and revolutionary periods.

The first and perhaps major critique comes from Alexander Hamilton (1757–1804), the principal architect of a strong national government. Hamilton probably also wrote the call for a convention to amend the Articles. He believed that the Articles too narrowly defined the powers of the national congress. In 1785, the Englishman Richard Price (1723–1791), a supporter of the American Revolution, wrote that congress had no power to enforce its acts. The Address of the Annapolis Convention, probably drafted by James Madison (1751–1836) who was then a trenchant critic of weak national governance, revealed frustration over Congress's inability to reform itself. In September 1786, James Manning (1739–1791) and Nathan Miller (1743–1790), delegates from Rhode Island, told their governor that the federal government had no power. Finally, and most tellingly, on the eve of the convention in Philadelphia, James Madison wrote that corrupt state legislatures were resisting federal unity by sending weak leaders to the national congress. All of those critics wanted major changes in the Articles of Confederation and some wanted to abandon the Articles altogether.

Others in public life only wanted minor revisions of the Articles of Confederation. They feared changes to a document that they believed represented the system of governance under which they and their forebears had lived. On September 3, 1785, the Massachusetts delegation to the federal Congress wrote to Governor James Bowdoin (1726–1790) with some reservations about the Congress (but they assured him they opposed any substantive changes). Others wanted some reforms, such as giving the national Congress authority over commercial trade deals between states. Of course, the delegates as representatives of their states never would approve issues of regulating commerce between the states.

Lack of support for the Annapolis Convention frustrated James Madison and elated the defenders of the status quo. Madison and his friends found a means to confront the problems they saw in the national Congress by calling a convention in Philadelphia in 1787. In the belief that the proposed convention was a threat to the existing system of governance, Richard Henry Lee (1733–1794) wrote to his fellow Virginian, George

Mason, that he would not accept selection to that convention. He believed that the national government was as strong as the people and the states wanted it to be. As an eloquent defender of the colonial and revolutionary foundations of governance, Lee has the last word in this volume.

ALEXANDER HAMILTON, "THE CONTINENTALIST," AUGUST 1781–JULY 1782

No. I

It would be the extreme of vanity in us not to be sensible, that we began this revolution with very vague and confined notions of the practical business of government. To the greater part of us it was a novelty; of those who under the former constitution had had opportunities of acquiring experience, a large proportion adhered to the opposite side, and the remainder can only be supposed to have possessed ideas adapted to the narrow colonial sphere, in which they had been accustomed to move, not of that enlarged kind suited to the government of an independent nation.

There were, no doubt, exceptions to these observations; men in all respects qualified for conducting the public affairs with skill and advantage; but their number was small—they were not always brought forward in our councils; and when they were, their influence was too commonly borne down by the prevailing torrent of ignorance and prejudice.

On a retrospect, however, of our transactions, under the disadvantages with which we commenced, it is perhaps more to be wondered at, that we have done so well, than that we have not done better. There are, indeed, some traits in our conduct, as conspicuous for sound policy, as others for magnanimity. But, on the other hand, it must also be confessed, there have been many false steps, many chimerical projects and utopian speculations, in the management of our civil as well as of our military affairs. A part of these were the natural effects of the spirit of the times, dictated by our situation. An extreme jealousy of power is the attendant on all popular revolutions, and has seldom been without its evils. It is to this source

we are to trace many of the fatal mistakes, which have so deeply endangered the common cause; particularly that defect which will be the object of these remarks—A want of power in Congress.

The present Congress, respectable for abilities and integrity, by experience convinced of the necessity of change, are preparing several important articles, to be submitted to the respective States, for augmenting the powers of the Confederation. But though there is hardly at this time a man of information in America, who will not acknowledge, as a general proposition, that in its present form, it is unequal, either to a vigorous prosecution of the war, or to the preservation of the union in peace; yet when the principle comes to be applied to practice, there seems not to be the same agreement in the modes of remedying the defect; and it is to be feared, from a disposition which appeared in some of the States, on a late occasion, that the salutary intentions of Congress may meet with more delay and opposition, than the critical posture of the States will justify.

It will be attempted to show, in a course of papers, what ought to be done, and the mischiefs of a contrary policy.

In the first stages of the controversy, it was excusable to err. Good intentions, rather than great skill, were to have been expected from us. But we have now had sufficient time for reflection, and experience as ample as unfortunate, to rectify our errors. To persist in them becomes disgraceful, and even criminal, and belies that character of good sense, and a quick discernment of our interests, which, in spite of our mistakes, we have been hitherto allowed. It will prove, that our sagacity is limited to interests of inferior moment; and that we are incapable of those enlightened and liberal views, necessary to make us a great and a flourishing people.

History is full of examples, where in contests for liberty, a jealousy of power has either defeated the attempts to recover or preserve it, in the first instance, or has afterwards subverted it by clogging government with too great precautions for its felicity, or by leaving too wide a door for sedition and popular licentiousness. In a government framed for durable liberty, not less regard must be paid to giving the magistrate a proper degree of authority, to make and execute the laws with rigor, than to guard against encroachments upon the rights of the community. As too much power leads to despotism, too little leads to anarchy, and both, eventually, to the ruin of the people. These are maxims well known, but never sufficiently attended to, in adjusting the frames of governments. Some momentary interest or passion is sure to give a wrong bias, and pervert the most favorable opportunities.

No friend to order or to rational liberty, can read without pain and disgust, the history of the Commonwealths of Greece. Generally speaking, they were a constant scene of the alternate tyranny of one part of the people over the other, or of a few usurping demagogues over the whole. Most of them had been originally governed by kings, whose despotism (the natural disease of monarchy) had obliged their subjects to murder, expel, depose, or reduce them to a nominal existence, and institute popular governments. In these governments, that of Sparta excepted, the jealousy of power hindered the people from trusting out of their own hands a competent authority, to maintain the repose and stability of the Commonwealth; whence originated the frequent revolutions and civil broils, with which they were distracted. This, and the want of a solid federal union to restrain the ambition and rivalship of the different cities, after a rapid succession of bloody wars, ended in their total loss of liberty, and subjugation to foreign powers.

In comparison of our governments with those of the ancient republics, we must, without hesitation, give the preference to our own; because every

power with us is exercised by representation, not in tumultuary assemblies of the collective body of the people, where the art or impudence of the *Orator* or *Tribune*, rather than the utility or justice of the measure could seldom fail to govern. Yet, whatever may be the advantage on our side, in such a comparison, men who estimate the value of institutions, not from prejudices of the moment, but from experience and reason, must be persuaded, that the same *jealousy* of *power* has prevented our reaping all the advantages, from the examples of other nations, which we ought to have done, and has rendered our Constitutions in many respects, feeble and imperfect.

Perhaps the evil is not very great in respect to our State Constitutions; for, notwithstanding their imperfections, they may, for some time, be made to operate in such a manner, as to answer the purposes of the common defence, and the maintenance of order; and they seem to have, in themselves, and in the progress of society, among us the seeds of improvement.

But this is not the case with respect to the Federal Government; if it is too weak at first, it will continually grow weaker. The ambition and local interests of the respective members, will be constantly undermining and usurping upon its prerogatives, till it comes to a dissolution; if a partial combination of some of the more powerful ones does not bring it to a more *speedy* and *violent end*.

No. IV

August 30, 1781

The preceding numbers are chiefly intended to confirm an opinion, already pretty generally received, that it is necessary to augment the powers of the confederation. The principal difficulty yet remains to fix the public judgment definitively on the points which ought to compose that augmentation.

It may be pronounced with confidence that nothing short of the following articles can suffice.

1st.—THE POWER OF REGULATING TRADE, comprehending a right of granting bounties and premiums by way of encouragement, of imposing duties of every kind as well for revenue as regulation, of appointing all officers of the customs, and of laying embargoes in extraordinary emergencies.

2d.—A moderate-levied tax, throughout the United States, of a specific rate per pound or per acre, granted to the Federal Government in perpetuity; and, if Congress think proper, to be levied by their own collectors.

3d.—A moderate capitation-tax on every male inhabitant above fifteen years of age, exclusive of common soldiers, common seamen, day laborers, cottagers, and paupers, to be also vested in perpetuity, and with the same condition of collection.

4th.—The disposal of all unlocated land for the benefit of the United States (so far as respects the profits of the first sale and the quit-rents), the jurisdiction remaining to the respective States in whose limits they are contained.

5th.—A certain proportion of the product of all mines discovered, or to be discovered, for the same duration, and with the same right of collection as in the second and third articles.

6th.—The appointment of all land (as well as naval) officers of every rank.

The three first articles are of IMMEDIATE NECESSITY; the three last would be of great present, but of much greater future utility; the whole combined would give solidity and permanency to the Union.

The great defect of the confederation is, that it gives the United States no property; or, in other words, no revenue, nor the means of acquiring it, inherent in themselves and independent on the temporary pleasure of the different members. And power without revenue, in political society, is a name. While Congress continue altogether dependent on the occasional grants of the several States, for the means of defraying the expenses of the Federal Government, it can neither have dignity, vigor, nor credit. Credit supposes specific and permanent funds for the punctual payment of interest, with a moral certainty of the final redemption of the principal.

In our situation, it will probably require more, on account of the general diffidence which has been excited by the past disorders in our finances.

It will perhaps be necessary, in the first instance, to appropriate funds for the redemption of the principal in a determinate period, as well as for the payment of interest.

It is essential that the property in such funds should be in the contractor himself, and the appropriation dependent on his own will. If, instead of this, the possession or disposal of them is dependent on the voluntary or occasional concurrence of a number of different wills not under his absolute control, both the one and the other will be too precarious to be trusted. The most wealthy and best established nations are obliged to pledge their funds to obtain credit, and it would be the height of absurdity in us, in the midst of a revolution, to expect to have it on better terms. This credit being to be procured through Congress, the funds ought to be provided, declared, and vested in them. It is a fact that verifies the want of specific funds—a circumstance which operates powerfully against our obtaining credit abroad is, not a distrust of our becoming independent, but of our continuing united, and with our present confederation the distrust is natural. Both foreigners and the thinking men among ourselves, would have much more confidence in the duration of the Union, if they were to see it supported on the foundation here proposed.

There are some among us ignorant enough to imagine, that the war may be carried on without credit, defraying the expenses of the year with what may be raised within the year. But this is for want of a knowledge of our real resources and expenses.

It may be demonstrated, that the whole amount of the revenue, which these States are capable of affording, will be deficient annually five or six millions of dollars for the support of civil government and of the war.

This is not a conjecture hazarded at random, but the result of experiment and calculation; nor can it appear surprising, when it is considered that the revenues of the United Provinces, equal to these States in population, beyond comparison superior in industry, commerce, and riches, do not exceed twenty-five millions of guilders, or about nine millions and a half of dollars. In times of war, they have raised a more considerable sum, but it has been chiefly by gratuitous combinations of rich individuals, a resource we cannot employ, because there are few men of large fortunes in this country, and these for the most part in land. Taxes in the United Provinces are carried to an extreme which would be impracticable here. Not only the living are made to pay for every necessary of life, but even the dead are tributary to the public for the liberty of interment at particular hours. These considerations make it evident that we could not raise an equal amount of revenue in these States. Yet, in '76, when the currency was not depreciated, Congress emitted, for the expenses of the year, fourteen millions of dollars. It cannot be denied, that there was a want of order and economy in the expenditure of public money, nor that we had a greater military force to maintain at that time than we now have; but, on the other hand, allowing for the necessary increase in our different civil lists, and for the advanced prices of many articles, it can hardly be supposed possible to reduce our annual expense very much below that sum. This simple idea of the subject, without entering into details, may satisfy us, that the deficiency which has been stated is not to be suspected of exaggeration.

Indeed, nations the most powerful and opulent are obliged to have recourse—loans in time of war, and hence it is that most of the States of Europe are deeply immersed in debt. France is among the number, notwithstanding her immense population, wealth, and resources. England owes the enormous sum of two hundred millions sterling. The United Provinces, with all their prudence and parsimony, owe a debt of the generality of fifty millions, besides the particular debts of each province. Almost all the other powers are more or less in the same circumstances.

While this teaches us how contracted and uninformed are the views of those who expect to carry on the war without running in debt. It ought to console us with respect to the amount of that which we now owe, or may have occasion to incur, in the remainder of the war. The whole, without burthening the people, may be paid off in twenty years after the conclusion of peace.

The principal part of the deficient five or six millions must be procured by loans from private persons at home and abroad. Every thing may be hoped from the generosity of France, which her means will permit, but she has full employment for her revenues and credit in the prosecution of the war on her own part. If we judge of the future by the past, the pecuniary succors from her must continue to be far short of our wants; and the contingency of a war on the continent of Europe makes it possible they may diminish rather than increase.

We have in a less degree experienced the friendship of Spain in this article.

The government of the United Provinces, if disposed to do it, can give us no assistance. The resources of the Republic are chiefly mortgaged for former debts. Happily, it has extensive credit, but it will have occasion for the whole to supply its own exigencies.

Private men, either foreigners or natives, will not lend to a large amount, but on the usual security of funds properly established. This security Congress cannot give, till the several States vest them with revenue, or the means of revenue, for that purpose.

Congress have wisely appointed a superintendent of their finances—a man of acknowledged abilities and integrity, as well as of great personal credit and pecuniary influence.

It was impossible, that the business of finance could be ably conducted by a body of men however well composed or well intentioned. Order in the future management of our moneyed concerns, a strict regard to the performance of public engagements, and of course the restoration of public credit, may be reasonably and confidently expected from Mr. Morris's administration, if he is furnished with materials upon which to operate; that is, if the Federal Government can acquire funds as the basis of his arrangements. He has very judiciously proposed a National Bank, which, by uniting the influence and interest of the moneyed men with the resources of Government, can alone give it that durable and extensive credit of which it stands in need. This is the best expedient he could have devised for relieving the public embarrassments; but to give success to the plan, it is essential that Congress should have it in their power to support him with unexceptionable funds. Had we begun the practice of funding four years ago, we should have avoided that depreciation of the currency which has been pernicious to the morals and to the credit of the nation; and there is no other method than this to prevent a continuance and multiplication of the evils flowing from that prolific source.

No. VI

July 4, 1782

Let us see what will be the consequences of not authorizing the Federal Government to regulate the trade of these States. Besides the want of revenue and of power, besides the immediate risk to our independence, the dangers of all the future evils of a precarious Union, besides the deficiency of a wholesome concert, and provident superintendence, to advance the general prosperity of trade, the direct consequence will be that the landed interest and the laboring poor, will in the first place fall a sacrifice to the trading interest, and the whole eventually to a bad system of policy, made necessary by the want of such regulating power.

Each State will be afraid to impose duties on its commerce, lest the other States, not doing the same, should enjoy greater advantages than itself, by being able to afford native commodities cheaper abroad, and foreign commodities cheaper at home.

A part of the evils resulting from this would be, a loss to the revenue of those moderate duties, which, without being injurious to commerce, are allowed to be the most agreeable species of taxes to the people. Articles of foreign luxury, while they would contribute nothing to the income of the State, being less dear by an exemption from duties, would have a more extensive consumption.

Many branches of trade, hurtful to the common interest, would be continued for want of proper checks and discouragements. As revenues must be found to satisfy the public exigencies in peace and in war, too great a proportion of taxes will fall directly upon land, and upon the necessaries of life—the produce of that land. The influence of these evils will be to render landed property fluctuating and less valuable—to oppress the poor by raising the prices of necessaries—to injure commerce by encouraging the consumption of foreign luxuries—by increasing the value of labor—by lessening the quantity of home productions, enhancing their prices at foreign markets, of course obstructing their sale, and enabling other nations to supplant us.

Particular caution ought at present to be observed in this country not to burthen the soil itself and its productions with heavy impositions, because the quantity of unimproved land will invite the husbandmen to abandon old settlements for new, and the disproportion of our population for some time to come will necessarily make labor dear, to reduce which, and not to increase it, ought to be a capital object of our policy.

Easy duties, therefore, on commerce, especially on imports, ought to lighten the burthens which will unavoidably fall upon land. Though it may be said that, on the principle of a reciprocal influence of prices, whereon the taxes are laid in the first instance, they will in the end be borne by all classes, yet it is of the greatest importance that no one should sink under the immediate pressure. The great art is to distribute the public burthens well, and not suffer them, either first or last, to fall too heavily on parts of the community; else, distress and disorder must ensue—a shock given to any part of the political machine vibrates through the whole.

As a sufficient revenue could not be raised from trade to answer the public purposes, other articles have been proposed. A moderate land and poll tax being of easy and unexpensive collection, and leaving nothing to discretion, are the simplest and best that could be devised.

It is to be feared the avarice of many of the landholders will be opposed to a perpetual tax upon land, however moderate. They will ignorantly hope to shift the burthens of the national expense from themselves to others—a disposition as iniquitous as it is fruitless—the public necessities must be satisfied; this can only be done by the contributions of the whole society. Particular classes are neither able nor will be willing to pay for the protection and security of the others, and where so selfish a spirit discovers itself in any member, the rest of the community will unite to compel it to do its duty.

Indeed, many theorists in political economy have held, that all taxes, wherever they originate, fall upon land, and have therefore been of opinion, that it would be best to draw the whole revenue of the State immediately from that source, to avoid the expense of a more diversified collection, and the accumulations which will be heaped in their several stages, upon the primitive sums advanced in those stages which are imposed on our trade. But though it has been demonstrated, that this theory has been carried to an extreme, impracticable in fact; yet it is evident, in tracing the matter, that a large part of all taxes, however remotely laid, will, by an insensible circulation, come at last to settle upon land—the source of most of the materials employed in commerce.

It appears, from calculation made by the ablest master of political arithmetic, about sixty years ago, that the yearly product of all the lands in England amounted to £42,000,000 sterling, and the whole annual consumption at that period, of foreign as well as domestic commodities, did not exceed £49,000–000 and the surplus of the exportation above the importation £2,000,000, on which sums arise all the revenues in whatever shape, which go into the Treasury.

It is easy to infer from this, how large a part of them must, directly or indirectly, be derived from land.

Nothing can be more mistaken, than the collision and rivalship which almost always subsist between the landed and trading interests, for the truth is, they are so inseparably interwoven that one cannot be injured without injury nor benefited without benefit to the other. Oppress trade, lands sink in value, make it flourish, their value rises; incumber husbandry, trade declines, encourage agriculture, commerce revives. The progress of this mutual reaction might be easily delineated, but it is too obvious to every man, who turns his thoughts, however superficially,

upon the subject, to require it. It is only to be regretted, that it is too often lost sight of, when the seductions of some immediate advantage or exemption tempt us to sacrifice the future to the present.

But perhaps the class is more numerous of those, who, not unwilling to bear their share of public burthens, are yet averse to the idea of perpetuity, as if there ever would arrive a period when the State would cease to want revenues, and taxes become unnecessary. It is of importance to unmask this delusion, and open the eyes of the people to the truth. It is paying too great a tribute to the idol of popularity, to flatter so injurious and so visionary an expectation. The error is too gross to be tolerated any where but in the cottage of the peasant. Should we meet with it in the Senate House, we must lament the ignorance or despise the hypocrisy on which it is ingrafted. Expense is in the present state of things entailed upon all governments; though, if we continue united, we shall be hereafter less exposed to wars by land than most other countries; yet while we have powerful neighbors on either extremity, and our frontier is embraced by savages, whose alliance they may without difficulty command, we cannot, in prudence, dispense with the usual precautions for our interior security; as a commercial people, maritime power must be a primary object of our attention, and a navy cannot be created or maintained without ample revenues. The nature of our popular institutions requires a numerous magistracy, for whom competent provision must be made, or we may be certain our affairs will always be committed to improper hands, and experience will teach us that no government costs so much as a bad one.

We may preach, till we are tired of the theme, the necessity of disinterestedness in republics, without making a single proselyte. The virtuous declaimer will neither persuade himself nor any other person to be content with a double mess of pottage, instead of a reasonable stipend for his services. We might as soon reconcile ourselves to the Spartan community of goods and wives, to their iron coin, their long beards, or their black broth. There is a total dissimilarity in the circumstances, as well as the manners of society among us, and it is as ridiculous to seek for models in the small ages of Greece and Rome, as it would be to go in quest of them among the Hottentots and Laplanders.

The public, for the different purposes that have been mentioned, must always have large demands upon its constituents, and the only question is, whether these shall be satisfied by annual grants, perpetually renewed by a perpetual grant, once for all, or by a compound of permanent and occasional supplies. The last is the wisest course. The Federal Government should neither be independent nor too much dependent. It should neither be raised above responsibility or control, nor should it want the means of maintaining its own weight, authority, dignity and credit. To this end, permanent funds are indispensable, but they ought to be of such a nature, and so moderate in their amount as never to be inconvenient. Extraordinary supplies can be the objects of extraordinary emergencies, and in that salutary medium will consist our true wisdom.

It would seem as if no mode of taxation could be relished, but the worst of all modes, which now prevails by assessment. Every proposal for a specific tax is sure to meet with opposition. It has been objected to a poll tax at a fixed rate, that it will be unequal, and the rich will pay no more than the poor. In the form in which it has been offered in these papers, the poor, properly speaking, are not comprehended, though it is true, that beyond the exclusion of the indigent, the tax has no reference to the proportion of property, but it should be remembered that it is impossible to devise any specific tax that will operate equally on the whole community. It must be the province of the Legislature to hold the scales with a judicious hand, and balance one by another. The rich must be made to pay for their luxuries, which is the only proper way of taxing their superior wealth.

Do we imagine that our assessments operate equally? Nothing can be more contrary to the fact. Wherever a discretionary power is lodged in any set of men over the property of their neighbors, they will abuse it; their passions, prejudices, partialities, dislikes, will have the principal lead

in measuring the abilities of those over whom their power extends; and assessors will ever be a set of petty tyrants, too unskilful, if honest, to be possessed of so delicate a trust, and too seldom honest to give them the excuse of want of skill.

The genius of liberty reprobates every thing arbitrary or discretionary in taxation. It exacts that every man, by a definite and general rule, should know what proportion of his property the State demands; whatever liberty we may boast in theory, it cannot exist in fact while assessments continue.

The admission of them among us is a new proof, how often human conduct reconciles the most glaring opposites; in the present case, the most vicious practice of despotic governments, with the freest constitutions and the greatest love of liberty.

The establishment of permanent funds would not only answer the public purposes infinitely better than temporary supplies, but it would be the most effectual way of easing the people.

With this basis for procuring credit, the amount of present taxes might be greatly diminished. Large sums of money might be borrowed abroad, at a low interest, and introduced into the country, to defray the current expenses and pay the public debts; which would not only lessen the demand for immediate supplies, but would throw more money into circulation, and furnish the people with greater means of paying the taxes.

Though it be a just rule that we ought not to run in debt to avoid present expense, so far as our faculties extend, yet the propriety of doing it cannot be disputed, when it is apparent that these are incompetent to the public necessities. Efforts beyond our abilities can only tend to individual distress and national disappointment. The product of the three foregoing articles will be as little as can be required, to enable Congress to pay their debts, and restore order into their finances. In addition to them—

The disposal of the unlocated lands will hereafter be a valuable source of revenue, and an immediate one of credit. As it may be liable to the same condition with the duties on trade, that is, the product of the sales within each State to be credited to that State, and as the rights of jurisdiction are not infringed, it seems to be susceptible of no reasonable objection.

Mines in every country constitute a branch of the revenue. In this, where nature has so richly impregnated the bowels of the earth, they may in time become a valuable one; and as they require the care and attention of government to bring them to perfection, this care and a share in the profits of it will very properly devolve upon Congress. All the precious metals should absolutely be the property of the Federal Government, and with respect to the others it should have a discretionary power of reserving, in the nature of a tax, such part as it may judge not inconsistent with the encouragement due to so important an object. This is rather a future than a present resource.

The reason of allowing Congress to appoint its own officers of the customs, collectors of the taxes, and military officers of every rank, is to create in the interior of each State, a mass of influence in favor of the Federal Government. The great danger has been shown to be, that it will not have power enough to defend itself, and preserve the Union, not that it will ever become formidable to the general liberty; a mere regard to the interests of the confederacy will never be a principle sufficiently active to crush the ambition and intrigues of different members. Force cannot effect it. A contest of arms will seldom be between the common sovereign and a single refractory member, but between distinct combinations of the several parts against each other. A sympathy of situations will be apt to produce associates to the disobedient. The application of force is always disagreeable—the issue uncertain. It will be wise to obviate the necessity of it, by interesting such a number of individuals in each State, in support of the Federal Government, as will be counterpoised to the ambition of others, and will make it difficult for them to unite the people in opposition to the first and necessary measures of the Union.

There is something noble and magnificent in the perspective of a great Federal Republic, closely linked in the pursuit of a common interest, tranquil and prosperous at home—respectable abroad; but there is something proportionably diminutive and contemptible in the prospect of a number of petty States, with the appearance only of union, jarring, jealous, and perverse, without any determined direction, fluctuating and unhappy at home, weak and insignificant by their dissensions in the eyes of other nations.

Happy America, if those to whom thou hast intrusted the guardianship of thy infancy, know how to provide for thy future repose, but miserable and undone, if their negligence or ignorance permits the spirit of discord to erect her banner on the ruins of thy tranquillity!

Reference: John C. Hamilton (ed.), *The Works of Alexander Hamilton*, Vol. II (New York: John F. Trow, 1830).

UNSUBMITTED RESOLUTIONS TO AMEND ARTICLES, JULY 1783

Whereas in the opinion of this Congress the confederation of the United States is defective in the following essential points, to wit:

First and generally in confining the power of the fœderal government within too narrow limits, withholding from it that efficacious authority and influence in all matters of general concern which are indispensable to the harmony and welfare of the whole—embarrassing general provisions by unnecessary details and inconvenient exceptions incompatible with their nature tending only to create jealousies and disputes respecting the proper bounds of the authority of the United States and of that of the particular states, and a mutual interference of the one with the other.

Secondly. In confounding legislative and executive powers in a single body, as that of determining on the number and quantity of force, land and naval, to be employed for the common defence, and of directing their operations when raised and equipped with that of ascertaining and making requisitions for the necessary sums or quantities of money to be paid by the respective states into the common treasury; contrary to the most approved and well founded maxims of free government which require that the legislative executive and judicial authorities should be deposited in distinct and separate hands.

Thirdly. In the want of a Fœderal Judicature having cognizance of all matters of general concern in the last resort, especially those in which foreign nations, and their subjects are interested; from which defect, by the interference of the local regulations of particular states militating directly or indirectly against the powers vested in the Union, the national treaties will be liable to be infringed, the national faith to be violated and the public tranquillity to be disturbed.

Fourthly. In vesting the United States in Congress assembled with the *power of general taxation*, comprehended in that of "ascertaining the necessary sums of money to be raised for the common defence and of appropriating and applying the same for defraying the public expences"—and yet rendering that power, so essential to the existence of the union, nugatory, by witholding from them all controul over either the imposition or the collection of the taxes for raising the sums required; whence it happens that the inclinations not the abilities of the respective states are in fact the criterion of their contributions to the common expence; and the public burthen has fallen and will continue to fall with very unequal weight.

5thly. In fixing a rule for determining the proportion of each state towards the common expence which if practicable at all, must in the execution be attended with great expence inequality uncertainty and difficulty.

6thly. In authorising Congress "to borrow money or emit bills on the credit of the United States" without the power of establishing funds to secure the repayment of the money borrowed or the redemption of the bills emitted; from which must result one of these evils, either a want of sufficient credit in the first instance to borrow, or to circulate the bills emitted, whereby in great national exigencies the public safety may be endangered, or in the second instance, frequent infractions of the public engagements, disappointments to lenders, repetitions of the calamities of depreciating paper, a continuance of the injustice and mischiefs of an unfunded debt, and first or last the annihilation of public credit. Indeed, in authorising Congress at all to emit an *unfunded* paper as the sign of value, a resource which though useful in the infancy, of this country, indispensable in the commencement of the revolution, ought not to continue a formal part of the constit[u]tion, nor ever hereafter to be employed, being in its nature pregnant with abuses and liable to be made the engine of imposition and fraud, holding out temptations equally pernicious to the integrity of government and to the morals of the people.

7thly. In not making proper or competent provision for interior or exterior defence: for interior defence, by leaving it to the individual states to appoint all regimental officers of the land forces, to raise the men in their own way, to cloath arm and equip them at the expence of the United States; from which circumstances have resulted and will hereafter result, great confusion in the military department, continual disputes of rank, languid and disproportionate levies of men, an enormous increase of expence for want of system and uniformity in the manner of conducting them, and from the competitions of state bounties; by an ambiguity in the 4th clause of the 6th article, susceptible of a construction which would devolve upon the particular states in time of peace the care of their own defence both by sea and land and would preclude the United states from raising a single regiment or building a single ship, before a declaration of war, or an actual commencement of hostilities; a principle dangerous to the confederacy in different respects, by leaving the United states at all times unprepared for the defence of their common rights, obliging them to begin to raise an army and to build and equip a navy at the moment they would have occasion to employ them, and by putting into the hands of a few states, who from their local situations are more immediately exposed, all the standing forces of the country; thereby not only leaving the care of the safety of the whole to a part which will naturally be both unwilling and unable to make effectual provision at its particular expence, but also furnishing grounds of jealousy and distrust between the states; unjust in its operation to those states, in whose hands they are by throwing the exclusive burthen of maintaining those forces upon them, while their neighbours immediately and all the states ultimately would share the benefits of their services: For exterior defence, in authorising Congress "to build and equip a navy" without providing any means of manning it, either by requisitions of the states, by the power of registering and drafting the seamen in rotation, or by embargoes in cases of emergency to induce them to accept employment on board the ships of war; the omission of all which leaves no other resource than voluntary inlistment, a resource which has been found ineffectual in every country, and for reasons of peculiar force in this.

8thly. In not vesting in the United States a general superintendence of trade, equally necessary in the view of revenue and regulation; of revenue because duties on commerce, when moderate, are one of the most agreeable and productive species of it, which cannot without great disadvantages be imposed by particular states, while others refrain from doing it, but must be imposed in concert, and by laws operating upon the same principles, at the same moment, in all the states, otherwise those states which should not impose them would engross the commerce of such of their neighbours as did; of regulation because by general prohibitions of particular articles, by a judicious arrangement of duties, sometimes by bounties on the manufacture or exportation of certain commodities, injurious branches of commerce might be discouraged, favourable branches encouraged, useful products and manufactures promoted; none of which advantages can be as effectually attained by separate regulations, without a

general superintending power; because also, it is essential to the due observance of the commercial stipulations of the United States with foreigner powers, an in[ter]ference with which will be unavoidable if the different states have the exclusive regulation of their own trade and of course the construction of the treaties entered into.

9thly. In defeating essential powers by provisos and limitations inconsistent with their nature; as the power of making treaties with foreign nations, "provided that no treaty of commerce shall be made whereby the legislative power of the respective states shall be restrained from imposing such imposts and duties on foreigners as their own people are subjected to, or from prohibitting the importation or exportation of any species of goods or commodities whatsoever," a proviso susceptible of an interpretation which includes a constitutional possibility of defeating the treaties of commerce entered into by the United States: As also the power "of regulating the trade and managing all affairs with the Indians not members of any of the states *provided* that the legislative right of any state within its own limits be not infringed or violated"—and others of a similar nature.

10thly. In granting the United States the sole power "of regulating the alloy and value of coin struck by their own authority, or by that of the respective states" without the power of regulating the foreign coin in circulation; though the one is essential to the due exercise of the other, as there ought to be such proportions maintained between the national and foreign coin as will give the former a preference in all internal negotiations; and without the latter power, the operations of government in a matter of primary importance to the commerce and finances of the United States will be exposed to numberless obstructions.

11thly. In requiring the assent of *nine* states to matters of principal importance and of seven to all others, except adjournments from day to day; a rule destructive of vigour, consistency or expedition in the administration of affairs, tending to subject the *sense* of the majority to *that* of the minority, by putting it in the power of a small combination to retard and even to frustrate the most necessary measures and to oblige the greater number, in cases which require speedy determinations, as happens in the most interesting concerns of the community, to come into the views of the smaller, the evils of which have been felt in critical conjunctures and must always make the spirit of government, a spirit of compromise and expedient, rather than of system and energy.

12thly. In vesting in the Fœderal government the sole direction of the interests of the United States in their intercourse with foreign nations, without empowering it to pass all general laws in aid and support of the laws of nations; for the want of which authority, the faith of the United States may be broken, their reputation sullied, and their peace interrupted by the negligence or misconception of any particular state.

And Whereas experience hath clearly manifested that the powers reserved to the Union in the Confederation are unequal to the purpose of effectually d[r]awing forth the resources of the respective members for the common welfare and defence; whereby the United States have upon several occasions been exposed to the most critical and alarming situations; have wanted an army adequate to their defence and proportioned to the abilities of the country—have on account of that deficiency seen essential posts reduced, others eminently endangered, whole states and large parts of others overrun and ravaged by small bodies of the enemy's forces—have been destitute of sufficient means of feeding, cloathing, paying and appointing that army, by which the troops, rendered less efficient for military operations, have been exposed to sufferings, which nothing but unparalleled patience perseverance and patriotism could have endured—whereby also the United States have been too often compelled to make the administration of their affairs a succession of temporary expedients, inconsistent with order œconomy energy or a scrupulous adherence to the public engagements; and now find themselves at the close of a glorious struggle for independence, without any certain means of doing justice to those who have been its principal supporters—to an army which has bravely fought and patiently suffered—to citizens who

have chearfully lent their money, and to others who have in different ways contributed their property and their personal service to the common cause; obliged to rely for the only effectual mode of doing that justice, by funding the debt on solid securities, on the precarious concurrence of thirteen destinct deliberations, the dissent of either of which may defeat the plan and leave these states at this early period of their existence involved in all the disgrace and mischiefs of violated faith and national bankruptcy.

And Whereas notwithstanding we have by the blessing of providence so far happily escaped the complicated dangers of such a situation, and now see the object of our wishes secured by an honorable peace, it would be unwise to hazard a repetition of the same dangers and embarrassments in any future war in which these states may be engaged, or to continue this extensive empire under a government unequal to its protection and prosperity.

And Whereas it is essential to the happiness and security of these states, that their union, should be established on the most solid foundations, and it is manifest that this desireable object cannot be effected but by a government capable both in peace and war of making every member of the Union contribute in just proportion to the common necessities, and of combining and directing the forces and wills of the several parts to a general end; to which purposes in the opinion of Congress the present confederation is altogether inadequate.

And Whereas on the spirit which may direct the councils and measures of these states at the present juncture may depend their future safety and welfare; Congress conceive it to be their duty freely to state to their constituents the defects which by experience have been discovered in the present plan of the Fœderal Union and solemnly to call their attention to a revisal and amendment of the same:

Therefore Resolved that it be earnestly recommended to the several states to appoint a convention to meet at on the day of with full powers to revise the confederation and to adopt and propose such alterations as to them shall appear necessary to be finally approved or rejected by the states respectively—and that a Committee of be appointed to prepare an address upon the subject.

Reference: Harold C. Sysett (ed.), *The Papers of Alexander Hamilton*, Vol. III (New York: Columbia, 1962).

MASSACHUSETTS DELEGATES TO GOVERNOR JAMES BOWDOIN, SEPTEMBER 3, 1783

Sir,

We have deferred a Communication of the Reasons which urged Us to suspend the Delivery to Congress, of your Excellency's Letter to them for revising and altering the Confederation, and to each of the Executives of the States on the same Subject; in Expectation of an answer to the Letter which We had the Honour of addressing to you the 18th of August last:[2] but lest any Inconvenience should result from a longer Delay, We now beg Leave to suggest our Sentiments on the Subject:

It may be necessary previously to observe, that many are of Opinion, the States have not yet had Experience sufficient to determine the Extent of powers vested in Congress by the Confederation; and therefore, that every Measure at this Time, proposing an Alteration, is premature. but admitting the Necessity, of immediately investing Congress with more commercial powers, it may be expedient to enquire,

first. Whether good policy does not require, that those powers should be temporary? in determining this question, We are led to consider, the commercial Evils to be remedied: the Efficacy of temporary powers for this purpose: and the Disposition of the several States touching the Subject—the Evils principally consist, in the Impositions. Restrictions, and prohibitions, of foreign powers on our Commerce; and the Embarrassments resulting from the commercial Regulations of our own States. how far temporary powers can remedy these Evils, perhaps Time and Experience, can only determine. Thus much may nevertheless be suggested, that as the several Treaties, which are now negotiating by our Commissioner in Europe, are not to exceed the Term of fifteen years; if the commercial powers

to be vested in Congress should be of a similar Duration, they may remedy the Evils for that Term: and at the Expiration thereof, a new commercial Epoch will commence, when the States will have a more clear and comprehensive View of their commercial Interests, and of the best Means for promoting the same, whether by Treaties abroad, or by the Delegation and exercise of greater commercial Powers at Home. Whatever the Disposition of the States may be, it can only be known by their Acts: but the different Views which they have had of the Subject give Reason to suppose, that some Legislatures will think temporary commercial powers eligible under present Circumstances; and should this be the Opinion of but one, an attempt immediately to delegate perpetual commercial powers, must fail, and may prevent a delegation of temporary powers—for in politics as in private Life by aiming at too much, We oft-times accomplish nothing.

secondly. If the States are unanimously disposed to increase the commercial powers of the Confederacy; should not the additional powers be in the first Instance temporary; and the Adoption of them as part of the Confederation, depend on their beneficial Effects?—this is a question on which We propose not to venture a decided Opinion; but Experience teaches us, that in the Formation of Constitutions and Laws, the wisest Men have not been able to foresee the Evasions and Abuses, which in the Operation have resulted from vague Terms and Expressions; latent consistencies, artful Constructions, and from too full and unguarded a Delegation of powers. Whether the Subject of Commerce, and the Danger to which the States may be exposed by a Surrender to the Union of their commercial Authority, are so fully understood as to justify the Consideration of an immediate Alteration of the Confederation, is a Matter that the Legislatures alone are competent to determine. any of them, who may not be clear with respect to either of those points, will probably (as in the other Case) be in the first Instance in Favour of temporary commercial powers, and, if approved by Experience, of adopting them as part of the Confederation. but should all the States be in Favour of an immediate Alteration of the Articles, will it not be expedient for them, previously to consider? that, however great the abuse of this Trust may hereafter be; however grievous to a considerable part of the Union; the powers, once delegated in the Confederation, cannot be revoked without the *unanimous Consent* of the States—that *this* may be earnestly sought for, but never obtained—that the federal and State Constitutions, are the great Bulwarks of Liberty—that if they are subject, on trivial or even important Occasions, to be revised, and re-revised, altered and re-altered, they must cease to be considered as effectual and sacred Barriers; and like land Marks frequently changed, will afford no certain Rule for ascertaining the Boundaries, no criterion for distinguishing between the Rights of Government and those of the people, and therefore, that every Alteration of the Articles, should be so thoroughly understood and digested, as scarcely to admit the *possibility* of a Disposition for a Reconsideration.

Thirdly—Shall any Alteration, either temporary or perpetual be proposed in a Way, not *expressly* pointed out by the Confederation?—the thirteenth Article provides, "that the Articles of this Confederation shall be inviolably observed by every State, and the Union shall be perpetual; nor shall any Alteration at any Time hereafter be made in any of them: unless such Alteration be agreed to in a Congress of the united States and be afterwards confirmed by the Legislature of every State." here, no provision is made, for or against a Convention and therefore it may be said not to be inconsistent with this Article; but as the proceedings of a Convention would not be binding on Congress, should the latter think themselves under the Necessity of rejecting the Report of the former, would not the States, after having

thus incurred a considerable Expence be dissatisfied on the Occasion? would not the Members of the Convention, who, it must be supposed, would be Men of the first Abilities and Influence in the several States, be hurt, and opposed in this Instance to Congress? and would not parties, in the Legislatures and amongst the people, be the Consequence?—if so, may not an Apprehension of these Evils, have a Tendency to influence some Members of Congress to give up their Opinion respecting the Report, rather than to be considered as pertinacious, and involved in contentions? And if such are the prospects of a Convention, will not Congress consider it as being contrary to the Spirit of the Confederation?—indeed, We are doubtful, whether a Measure of this Kind, would not be viewed as manifesting a Want of Confidence in Congress, and on this Ground, meet their Disapprobation.

Fourthly. If an Alteration, either temporary or perpetual, of the commercial powers of Congress, is to be considered by a Convention, shall the latter be authorized to revise the Confederation *generally,* or only for express purposes?—the great object of the Revolution, was the Establishment of good Government, and each of the States, in forming their own, as well as the federal Constitution, have adopted republican principles. notwithstanding this, plans have been artfully laid, and vigorously pursued, which had they been successful, We think would inevitably have changed our republican Governments, into baleful Aristocracies. Those plans are frustrated, but the same Spirit remains in their abettors: And the Institution of the Cincinnati, honourable and beneficent as the Views may have been of the Officers who compose it, We fear, if not totally abolished, will have the same fatal Tendency. What the Effect then may be, of calling a Convention to revise the Confederation generally, We leave with your Excellency and the honorable Legislature to determine. We are apprehensive and it is our Duty to declare it, that such a Measure would produce thro'out the Union, an Exertion of the Friends of an Aristocracy, to send Members who would promote a Change of Government: and We can form some Judgment of the plan, which such members would report to Congress.—but Should the Members be altogether republican, such have been the Declamations of designing Men against the Confederation generally: against the Rotation of Members, which perhaps is the best Check to Corruption And against the Mode of altering the Confederation by the unanimous Consent of the Legislatures, which effectually prevents Innovations in the Articles, by Intrigue or Surprise, that we think there is great Danger of a Report which would invest Congress with powers, that the honorable Legislature have not the most distant Intention to delegate. perhaps it may be said, this can produce no ill Effect; because Congress may correct the Report however exceptionable, or if passed by them, any of the States may refuse to ratify it—true it is, that Congress, and the States have such powers, but would not such a Report, affect the Tranquility and weaken the Government of the Union? We have already considered the Operation of the Report as it would respect Congress; and if animosities and parties would naturally arise from their rejecting it, how much would these be increased, if the Report approved by Congress and some of the States, should be rejected by other States? would there not be Danger of a party Spirit's being thus more generally diffused and warmly Supported?—far distant We know it to be from the honorable Legislature of Massachusetts, to give up a single principle of Republicanism, but when a general Revision Shall have proceeded from their Motion, and a Report which to them may be highly offensive, shall have been confirmed by seven States in Congress, and ratified by several Legislatures, will not these be ready to charge Massachusetts with Inconsistency, in being the first to oppose a Measure, which the State will be said to have originated? Massachusetts has great Weight, and is considered as one of the most republican States in the Union; and when it is known, that the Legislature have proposed a general Revision, there can be no Doubt, that they will be represented as being convinced of the Necessity of increasing generally, the powers of Congress, and the Opinion of the State will be urged with such Art, as to convince Numbers

that the Articles of the Confederation are altogether exceptionable. thus, whilst Measures are taken to guard against the Evils arising from the Want in one or two particulars, of power in Congress, we are in great danger of incurring the other Extreme—"more power in Congress" has been the Cry from all quarters; but especially of those whose Views, not being confined to a Government that will best promote the Happiness of the people, are extended to one that will afford lucrative Employments, civil and military. such a government is an Aristocracy, which would require a standing Army, and a numerous Train of pensioners and placemen to prop and support its exalted Administration. to recommend ones self to such an Administration, would be to secure an Establishment for Life and at the same Time to provide for his posterity. these are pleasing prospects, which republican Governments do not afford, And it is not to be wondered at, that many persons of elevated Views and idle Habits in these States are desirous of the Change. We are for increasing the power of Congress, as far as it will promote the Happiness of the people; but at the same Time are clearly of Opinion that every Measure should be avoided which would strengthen the Hands of the Enemies to a free Government: And that an Administration of the present Confederation with all its Inconveniences, is preferable to the Risque of general Dissentions and Animosities, which may approach to Anarchy and prepare the Way to a ruinous System of Government.

Having thus, from a Sense of the Duty We owe to the United States as well as to our Constituents, communicated to your excellency, our Sentiments on this important Subject; We request You to lay them before the honorable Legislature at their next Session, and to inform them, that their Measures for a general Revision of the Confederation, if confirmed shall be immediately communicated to Congress; that no Time will be lost by the Suspension, since the Requisition and other important Matters before Congress, would have prevented them from an early Attention to the *propositions* of Massachusetts; and that, if these had been approved by Congress, many of the Legislatures, being now adjourned, could not take the same into Consideration.

Reference: Edmund C. Burnett (ed.), *Letters of Members of the Continental Congress*, Vol. VIII (8 vols.; Washington: Carnegie Institution, 1921–1936).

CRITICISM BY RICHARD PRICE, 1785

Observations, &c

Of the IMPORTANCE *of the* REVOLUTION *which has established the Independency of the United States.*

HAVING, from pure conviction, taken a warm part in favour of the *British* colonies (now the United States of America) during the late war; and been exposed, in consequence of this, to *much* abuse and *some* danger; it must be supposed that I have been waiting for the issue with anxiety.—I am thankful that my anxiety is removed; and that I have been spared to be a witness to that very issue of the war which has been all along the object of my wishes. With heartfelt satisfaction, I see the revolution in favour of universal liberty which has taken place in *America*;—a revolution which opens a new prospect in human affairs, and begins a new æra in the history of mankind;—a revolution by which *Britons* themselves will be the greatest gainers, if wise enough to improve properly the check that has been given to the despotism of their ministers, and to catch the flame of virtuous liberty which has saved their American brethren.

The late war, in its *commencement and progress*, did great good by disseminating just sentiments of the rights of mankind, and the nature of legitimate government; by exciting a spirit of resistance to tyranny which has emancipated one *European* country, and is likely to emancipate others; and by occasioning the establishment in *America* of forms of government more equitable and more liberal than any that the world has yet known. But, in its *termination*, the war has done still greater good by preserving the new governments from that destruction in which they must have been involved, had Britain conquered; by providing, in a sequestered continent possessed of many singular advantages, a place of refuge for opprest men in every region of the world; and by

laying the foundation there of an empire which may be the seat of liberty, science and virtue, and from whence there is reason to hope those sacred blessings will spread, till they become universal, and the time arrives when kings and priests shall have no more power to oppress, and that ignominious slavery which has hitherto debased the world is exterminated. I therefore, think I see the hand of Providence in the late war working for the general good.

Reason, as well as tradition and revelation, lead us to expect that a more improved and happy state of human affairs will take place before the consummation of all things. The world has hitherto been gradually improving. Light and knowledge have been gaining ground, and human life *at present* compared with what it *once* was, is much the same that a youth approaching to manhood is compared with an infant.

Such are the natures of things that this progress must continue. During particular intervals it may be interrupted, but it cannot be destroy'd. Every present advance prepares the way for farther advances; and a single experiment or discovery may sometimes give rise to so many more as suddenly to raise the species higher, and to resemble the effects of opening a new sense, or of the fall of a spark on a train that springs a mine. For this reason, mankind may at last arrive at degrees of improvement which we cannot now even suspect to be possible. A dark age may follow an enlightened age; but, in this case, the light, after being smothered for a time, will break out again with a brighter lustre. The present age of increased light, considered as succeeding the ages of *Greece* and *Rome* and an intermediate period of thick darkness, furnishes a proof of the truth of this observation. There are certain kinds of improvement which, when once made, cannot be entirely lost. During the dark ages, the improvements made in the ages that preceded them remained so far as to be recovered immediately at the resurrection of letters, and to produce afterwards, that more rapid progress in improvement which has distinguished modern times.

There can scarcely be a more pleasing and encouraging object of reflection than this. An accidental observation of the effects of gravity in a garden has been the means of discovering the laws that govern the solar system, and of enabling us to look down with pity on the ignorance of the most enlightened times among the antients. What new dignity has been given to man, and what additions have been made to his powers, by the invention of optical glasses, printing, gunpowder, &c. and by the late discoveries in navigation, mathematics, natural philosophy, &c.?

But among the events in modern times tending to the elevation of mankind, there are none probably of so much consequence as the recent one which occasions these observations. Perhaps, I do not go too far when I say that, next to the introduction of Christianity among mankind, the American revolution may prove the most important step in the progressive course of human improvement. It is an event which may produce a general diffusion of the principles of humanity, and become the means of setting free mankind from the shackles of superstition and tyranny, by leading them to see and know "that nothing is *fundamental* but impartial enquiry, an honest mind, and virtuous practice—that state policy ought not to be applied to the support of speculative opinions and formularies of faith."—"That the members of a civil community are *confederates*, not *subjects*; and their rulers, *servants*, not *masters*.—And that all legitimate government consists in the dominion of equal laws made with common consent; that is, in the dominion of men over *themselves*; and not in the dominion of communities over communities, or of any men over other men."

Happy will the world be when these truths shall be every where acknowledged and practised

upon. Religious bigotry, that cruel demon, will be then laid asleep. Slavish governments and slavish Hierarchies will then sink; and the old prophecies be verified, "that the last universal empire upon earth shall be the empire of reason and virtue, under which the gospel of peace (better understood) *shall have free course and be glorified, many will run to and fro and knowledge be increased, the wolf dwell with the lamb and the leopard with the kid, and nation no more lift up a sword against nation.*"

It is a conviction I cannot resist, that the independence of the *English* colonies in America is one of the steps ordained by Providence to introduce these times; and I can scarcely be deceived in this conviction, if the United States should escape some dangers which threaten them, and will take proper care to throw themselves open to future improvements, and to make the most of the advantages of their present situation. Should this happen, it will be true of them as it was of the people of the Jews, that *in them all the families of the earth shall be blessed*. It is scarcely possible they should think too highly of their own consequence. Perhaps, there never existed a people on whose wisdom and virtue more depended; or to whom a station of more importance in the plan of Providence has been assigned. They have begun nobly. They have fought with success for themselves and for the world; and, in the midst of invasion and carnage, established forms of government favourable in the highest degree to the rights of mankind.—But they have much more to do; more indeed than it is possible properly to represent. In this address, my design is only to take notice of a few *great* points which seem particulary to require their attention, in order to render them permanently happy in themselves and useful to mankind. On these points, I shall deliver my sentiments with freedom, conscious I mean well; but, at the same time, with real diffidence, conscious of my own liableness to error. . . .

I must not, however, forget that there is ONE of their debts on which no sinking fund can have any effect; and which it is impossible for them to discharge:—A debt, greater, perhaps, than has been ever due from any country; and which will be deeply felt by their latest posterity.—But it is a debt of GRATITUDE only—Of GRATITUDE to that General, who has been raised up by Providence to make them free and independent, and whose name must shine among the first in the future annals of the benefactors of mankind.

The measure now proposed may preserve America for ever from too great an accumulation of debts; and, consequently, of taxes—an evil which is likely to be the ruin not only of *Britain*, but of other *European* States.—But there are measures of yet greater consequence, which I wish ardently to recommend and inculcate.

For the sake of mankind, I wish to see every measure adopted that can have a tendency to preserve PEACE in America; and to make it an open and fair stage for discussion, and the seat of PERFECT LIBERTY.

Of Peace

And the Means of perpetuating it

CIVIL GOVERNMENT is an expedient for collecting the wisdom and force of a community or confederacy, in order to preserve its peace and liberty against every hostile invasion, whether from *within* or from *without*.—In the latter of these respects, the United States are happily secured; but they are far from being equally happy in the *former* respect. Having now, in consequence of their successful resistance of the invasion of *Britain*, united to their remoteness from *Europe*, no external enemy to fear, they are in danger of fighting with one another.—This is their *greatest* danger; and providing securities against it is their *hardest* work. Should they fail in this, America may some time or other be turned into a scene of blood; and instead of being the hope and refuge of the world, may become a terror to it.

When a dispute arises among *individuals* in a State, an appeal is made to a *court* of law; that is, to the wisdom and justice of the State. The court decides. The losing party acquiesces; or, if he does not, the power of the State *forces* him to submission; and thus the effects of contention are

supprest, and peace is maintained.—In a way similar to this, peace may be maintained between any number of confederated States; and I can almost imagine, that it is not impossible but that by such means *universal* peace may be produced, and all war excluded from the world.—Why may we not hope to see this begun in America?—The articles of confederation make considerable advances towards it. When a dispute arises between any of the States, they order an appeal to Congress—an enquiry by Congress,—a hearing,—and a decision.—But here they stop.—What is most of all necessary is omitted. No provision is made for enforcing the decisions of Congress; and this renders them inefficient and futile. I am by no means qualified to point out the best method of removing this defect. Much must be given up for this purpose, nor is it easy to give up *too* much. Without all doubt the powers of Congress must be enlarged. In particular, a power must be given it to collect, on certain emergencies, the force of the confederacy, and to employ it in carrying its decisions into execution. A State against which a decision is made, will yield of course when it knows that such a force exists, and that it allows no hope from resistance.

By this force I do not mean a STANDING ARMY. God forbid, that standing armies should ever find an establishment in America. They are every where the grand supports of arbitrary power, and the chief causes of the depression of mankind. No wise people will trust their defence out of their own hands, or consent to hold their rights at the mercy of armed *slaves*. Free States ought to be bodies of armed *citizens*, well regulated and well disciplined, and always ready to turn out, when properly called upon, to execute the laws, to quell riots, and to keep the peace. Such, if I am rightly informed, are the citizens of America. Why then may not CONGRESS be furnished with a power of calling out from the confederated States, *quotas* of *militia* sufficient to force at once the compliance

Reference: Richard Price, *Observations on the Importance of the American Revolution* (Dublin: L. White, 1785).

PROPOSED AMENDMENTS TO THE ARTICLES OF CONFEDERATION, AUGUST 7, 1786

The Grand Committee consisting of M^r. [Samuel] Livermore, M^r. [Nathan] Dane, M^r. [James] Manning, M^r. [William Samuel] Johnson, M^r. [Melancton] Smith, M^r. [John Cleves] Symmes, M^r. [Charles] Pettit, M^r. [William] Henry, M^r. [Henry] Lee, M^r. [Timothy] Bloodworth, M^r. [Charles] Pinckney and M^r. [William] Houstoun appointed to report such amendments to the confederation, and such resolutions as it may be necessary to recommend to the several states for the purpose of obtaining from them such powers as will render the federal government adequate to the ends for which it was instituted.

Beg leave to submit the following Report to the consideration of Congress:

Resolved, That it be recommended to the Legislatures of the several States to adopt the following Articles as Articles of the Confederation, and to authorise their Delegates in Congress to sign and ratify the same severally as they shall be adopted, to wit:

ART. 14. The United States in Congress Assembled shall have the sole and exclusive power of regulating the trade of the States as well with foreign Nations as with each other and of laying such prohibitions and such Imposts and duties upon imports and exports as may be Necessary for the purpose; provided the Citizens of the States shall in no instance be subjected to pay higher duties and Imposts that those imposed on the subjects of foreign powers, provided also, that all such duties as may be imposed shall be collected under such regulations as the united States in Congress Assembled shall establish consistent with the Constitutions of the States Respectively and to accrue to the use of the State in which the same shall be payable; provided also, that the Legislative power of the several States shall not be restrained from laying embargoes in time of Scarcity and provided lastly that every Act of Congress for the above purpose shall have

the assent of Nine States in Congress Assembled, and in that proportion when there shall be more than thirteen in the Union.

ART. 15. That the respective States may be induced to perform the several duties mutually and solemnly agreed to be performed by their federal Compact, and to prevent unreasonable delays in any State in furnishing her just proportion of the common Charges of the Union when called upon, and those essential evils which have heretofore often arisen to the Confederacy from such delays, it is agreed that whenever a requisition shall be made by Congress upon the several States on the principles of the Confederation for their quotas of the common charges or land forces of the Union Congress shall fix the proper periods when the States shall pass Legislative Acts complying therewith and give full and compleat effect to the same and if any State shall neglect, seasonably to pass such Acts such State shall be charged with an additional sum to her quota called for from the time she may be required to pay or furnish the same, which additional sum or charge shall be at the rate of ten per Cent pr. annum on her said Quota, and if the requisition shall be for Land forces, and any State shall neglect to furnish her quota in time the average expence of such quota shall be ascertained by Congress, and such State shall be charged therewith, or with the average expence of what she may be deficient and in addition thereto from the time her forces were required to be ready to act in the field with a farther sum which sum shall be at the rate of twelve per Cent per Annum on the amount of such expences.

ART. 16. And that the resources of any State which may be negligent in furnishing her just proportion of the Common expence of the Union may in a reasonable time be applied, it is further agreed that if any State shall so Neglect as aforesaid to pass laws in compliance with the said Requisition and to adopt measures to give the same full effect for the space of Ten months, and it shall then or afterwards be found that a Majority of the States have passed such laws and adopted such measures the United States in Congress Assembled shall have full power and authority to levy, assess, and collect all sums and duties with which any such state so neglecting to comply with the requisition may stand charged on the same by the Laws and Rules by which the last State tax next preceeding such requisition in such State was levied, assessed and Collected, to apportion the sum so required on the Towns or Counties in such State to order the sums so apportioned to be assessed by the assessors of such last State tax and the said assessments to be committed to the Collector of the same last State tax to collect and to make returns of such assessments and Commitments to the Treasurer of the United States who by himself or his deputy, when directed by Congress shall have power to recover the monies of such Collectors for the use of the United States in the same manner and under the same penalties as State taxes are recovered and collected by the Treasurers of the respective States and the several Towns or Counties respectively shall be responsible for the conduct of said Assessors and Collectors and in case there shall be any vacancy in any of said Offices of Assessors or Collectors by death, removal, refusal to serve, resignation or otherwise, then other fit persons shall be chosen to fill such Vacancies in the usual manner in such Town or County within Twenty days after Notice of the assessment, and in case any Towns or Counties, any assessor, Collectors or Sheriffs shall Neglect or refuse to do their duty Congress shall have the same rights and powers to compel them that the State may have in assessing and collecting State Taxes.

And if any state by any Legislative Act shall prevent or delay the due Collection of said sums as aforesaid, Congress shall have full power and authority to appoint assessors and Collectors thereof and Sheriffs to enforce the Collections under the warrants of distress issued by the Treasurer of the United States, and if any further opposition shall be made to such Collections by

the State or the Citizens thereof, and their conduct not disapproved of by the State, such conduct on the part of the State shall be considered as an open Violation of the federal compact.

ART. 17. And any State which from time to time shall be found in her payments on any Requisition in advance on an average of the payments made by the State shall be allowed an interest of—per Cent pr. annum on her said advanced sums or expences and the State which from time to time shall be found in arrear on the principles aforesaid shall be charged with an Interest of—per Cent pr. annum on the sums in which she may be so in arrear.

ART. 18. In case it shall hereafter be found Necessary by Congress to establish any new Systems of Revenue and to make any new regulations in the finances of the U.S. for a limited term not exceeding fifteen years in their operation for supplying the common Treasury with monies for defraying all charges of war, and all other expences that shall be incurred for the common defence or general welfare, and such new Systems or regulations shall be agreed to and adopted by the United States in Congress Assembled and afterwards be confirmed by the Legislatures of eleven States and in that proportion when there shall be more than thirteen States in the Union, the same shall become binding on all the States, as fully as if the Legislatures of all the States should confirm the same.

ART. 19. The United States in Congress Assembled shall have the sole and exclusive power of declaring what offences against the United States shall be deemed treason, and what Offences against the same Mis-prison of treason, and what Offences shall be deemed piracy or felony on the high Seas and to annex suitable punishments to all the Offences aforesaid respectively, and power to institute a federal Judicial Court for trying and punishing all officers appointed by Congress for all crimes, offences, and misbehaviour in their Offices and to which Court an Appeal shall be allowed from the Judicial Courts of the several States in all Causes wherein questions shall arise on the meaning and construction of Treaties entered into by the United States with any foreign power, or on the Law of Nations, or wherein any question shall arise respecting any regulations that may hereafter be made by Congress relative to trade and Commerce, or the Collection of federal Revenues pursuant to powers that shall be vested in that body or wherein questions of importance may arise and the United States shall be a party—provided that the trial of the fact by Jury shall ever be held sacred, and also the benefits of the writ of *Habeas Corpus;* provided also that no member of Congress or officer holding any other office under the United States shall be a Judge of said Court, and the said Court shall consist of Seven Judges, to be appointed from the different parts of the Union to wit, one from New Hampshire, Rhode Island, and Connecticut, one from Massachusetts, one from New York and New Jersey, one from Pennsylvania, one from Delaware and Maryland, one from Virginia, and one from North Carolina, South Carolina and Georgia, and four of whom shall be a quorum to do business.

ART. 20. That due attention may be given to the affairs of the Union early in the federal year, and the sessions of Congress made as short as conveniently may be each State shall elect her Delegates annually before the first of July and make it their duty to give an Answer before the first of September in every year, whether they accept their appointments or not, and make effectual provision for filling the places of those who may decline, before the first of October yearly, and to transmit to Congress by the tenth of the same month, the names of the Delegates who shall be appointed and accept their appointments, and it shall be the indispensable duty of Delegates to make a representation of their State in Congress on the first Monday in November annually, and if any Delegate or Delegates, when required by Congress to attend so far as may be Necessary to keep up a Representation of each State in Congress, or having taken his or their Seat, shall with-draw without leave of Congress, unless recalled by the State, he or they shall be proceeded against as Congress shall direct, provided no punishment shall be further extended than to disqualifications any longer to be members of Congress, or to hold any Office of trust or profit under the United States or any individual State, and the several States shall adopt regulations effectual to the attainment of the ends of this Article.

Reference: Galliard Hunt (ed.), *Journals of the Continental Congress,* Vol. XXXI (Washington: GPO, 1934).

ADDRESS OF THE ANNAPOLIS CONVENTION, SEPTEMBER 4, 1786

To the Honorable the Legislatures of Virginia, Delaware Pennsylvania, New Jersey, and New York.

The Commissioners from the said states, respectively assembled at Annapolis, humbly beg leave to report.

That, pursuant to their several appointments, they met, at Annapolis in the State of Maryland, on the eleventh day of September Instant, and having proceeded to a Communication of their powers; they found, that the States of New York, Pennsylvania and Virginia had, in substance, and nearly in the same terms, authorised their respective Commissioners "to meet such commissioners as were, or might be, appointed by the other States in the Union, at such time and place, as should be agreed upon by the said Commissioners to take into consideration the trade and Commerce of the United States, to consider how far an uniform system in their commercial intercourse and regulations might be necessary to their common interest and permanent harmony, and to report to the several States, such an Act, relative to this great object, as when unanimously ratified by them would enable the United States in Congress assembled effectually to provide for the same."

That the State of Delaware, had given similar powers to their Commissioners, with this difference only that the Act to be framed in virtue of those powers, is required to be reported "to the United States in Congress Assembled, to be agreed to by them, and confirmed by the Legislatures of every State."

That the State of New Jersey had enlarged the object of their Appointment, empowering their Commissioners, "to consider how far an uniform system in their commercial regulations and *other important matters*, might be necessary to the common interest and permanent harmony of the several States," and to report such an Act on the subject, as when ratified by them "would enable the United States in Congress Assembled, effectually to provide for the exigencies of the Union."

That appointments of Commissioners have also been made by the States of New Hampshire, Massachusetts, Rhode Island, and North Carolina, none of whom however have attended; but that no information has been received by your Commissioners of any appointments having been made by the States of Connecticut, Maryland, South Carolina, or Georgia.

That the express terms of the powers to your Commissioners supposing a deputation from all the States, and having for object the Trade and Commerce of the United States, Your Commissioners did not conceive it advisable to proceed on the business of their mission, under the Circumstance of so partial and defective a representation.

Deeply impressed however with the magnitude and importance of the object confided to them on this occasion, your Commissioners cannot forbear to indulge an expression of their earnest and unanimous wish, that speedy measures may be taken, to effect a general meeting, of the States, in a future Convention, for the same and such other purposes, as the situation of public affairs, may be found to require.

If in expressing this wish, or in intimating any other sentiment, your Commissioners should seem to exceed the strict bounds of their appointment, they entertain a full confidence, that a conduct, dictated by an anxiety for the welfare, of the United States, will not fail to receive an indulgent construction.

In this persuasion your Commissioners submit an opinion, that the Idea of extending the powers of their Deputies, to other objects, than those of Commerce, which has been adopted by the State of New Jersey, was an improvement on the original plan, and will deserve to be incorporated into that of a future Convention; they are the more naturally led to this conclusion, as in the course of their reflections on the subject, they have been induced to think, that the power of regulating trade is of such comprehensive extent, and will enter so far into the general System of the foederal government, that to give it efficacy, and to obviate questions and doubts concerning its precise nature and limits, may require a correspondent adjustment of other parts of the Foederal System.

That there are important defects in the system of the Foederal Government is acknowledged by the Acts of all those States, which have concurred in the present Meeting; That the defects, upon a closer examination, may be found greater and more numerous, than even these acts imply, is at least so far probable, from the embarrassments which characterise the present State of our national affairs—foreign and domestic, as may reasonably be supposed to merit a deliberate and candid discussion, in some mode, which will unite the Sentiments and Councils of all the States. In the choice of the mode your Commissioners are of opinion, that a Convention of Deputies from the different States, for the special and sole purpose of entering into this investigation, and digesting a plan for supplying such defects as may be discovered to exist, will be entitled to a preference from consideration, which will occur, without being particularised.

Your Commissioners decline an enumeration of those national circumstances on which their opinion respecting the propriety of a future Convention with more enlarged powers, is founded; as it would be an useless intrusion of facts and observations, most of which have been frequently the subject of public discussion, and none of which can have escaped the penetration of those to whom they would in this instance be addressed. They are however of a nature so serious, as, in the view of your Commissioners to render the Situation of the United States delicate and critical, calling for an exertion of the united virtue and wisdom of all the members of the Confederacy.

Under this impression, Your Commissioners, with the most respectful deference, beg leave to suggest their unanimous conviction, that it may essentially tend to advance the interests of the union, if the States, by whom they have been respectively delegated, would themselves concur, and use their endeavours to procure the concurrence of the other States, in the appointment of Commissioners, to meet at Philadelphia on the second Monday in May next, to take into consideration the situation of the United States, to devise such further provisions as shall appear to them necessary to render the constitution of the Fœderal Government adequate to the exigencies of the Union; and to report such an Act for that purpose to the United States in Congress Assembled, as when agreed to, by them, and afterwards confirmed by the Legislatures of every State will effectually provide for the same.

Though your Commissioners could not with propriety address these observations and sentiments to any but the States they have the honor to Represent, they have nevertheless concluded from motives of respect, to transmit Copies of this report to the United States in Congress assembled, and to the executives of the other States.

By order of the Commissioners
Dated at Annapolis
September 14th. 1786

Reference: Harold C. Sysett (ed.), *The Papers of Alexander Hamilton,* Vol. III (New York: Columbia, 1962).

JAMES MANNING AND NATHAN MILLER TO THE GOVERNOR OF RHODE ISLAND, SEPTEMBER 28, 1786

Sir:—Permit your delegates to address Your Excellency in your official character, and give you a short detail of the business now before Congress, with some observations upon the present state of the federal government, etc.

An important national matter, which has for some time past engaged the attention of Congress, will probably soon come into public view. That body have now before them a report of a grand committee for granting to your federal government additional powers necessary to render it efficient. This, after the subject has undergone the necessary investigations, will be laid before the respective legislatures. An ordinance for the establishing a colonial government in the western territory is also nearly completed; as also for the establishment of a mint for the United States, with many other matters of less magnitude.

Your delegates wish to be informed whether the accounts of the State against the United States are ready for adjustment, Mr. Chinn having informed the treasury board that they are not ready; nor can they be got ready for a long time.

As that gentleman's salary still goes on, your delegates wish to be possessed of such official documents as may set that subject in its true point of view.

It is highly necessary that all payments made by the state to the federal government, whether on requisitions or otherwise, should be carried to its credit on the books of the treasury, therefore all these accounts ought, without loss of time, to be sent forward.

Your Excellency will be made acquainted, by Congress, that no paper emitted by the states will answer federal purposes. Will not this evince it to be mistaken policy in our legislature to order payments for the late requisition in their own paper currency?

When gentlemen reflect, but for a moment, on the exhausted state of the federal treasury; that no monies are expected but what come in from requisitions on the different states; that these are either all stopped, or so slow in their operations that nothing can be calculated upon with certainty; that the moment is arrived that our credit with foreign powers is *lost;* that an enemy on our frontiers stands prepared to take every advantage of our prostrate situation; that an enemy more despicable is embarrassing our most beneficial commerce, and carrying our fellow citizens into slavery for life, (about thirty at present being in that unhappy situation,) does it require the spirit of prophecy to predict what will and must inevitably be the consequence? Or will arguments be necessary to draw forth the most vigorous exertions of every friend to American liberty, to arrest the sacred palladium, and prevent our total ruin as a nation?

Amidst, however, these gloomy scenes, we have the pleasure to inform you that Her Majesty of Portugal has ordered a squadron of five sail of men-of-war to cruise at the mouth of the Straits for the protection of her trade, and that she has ordered her officers to give the same protection to the American flag as to her own; of this her minister has given official information to Mr. Adams at the court of London. An instance of magnanimity, this, which is worthy of imitation, and demands our grateful acknowledgments, as we have nothing better to offer her in payment.

While foreign potentates take such an interested part in our favor, does it not call for unanimity and exertions at home, amongst every class of our citizens, to rescue the commonwealth from impending ruin? Should not these considerations reconcile the mercantile and landed interests in the state of Rhode Island, and produce a repeal of those penal laws which have already convulsed and still threaten ruin to the state?

It is now agreed by all that our federal government is but a name; a mere shadow without any substance; and we think it our duty to inform the state that it is totally inefficient for the purposes of the Union; and that Congress, without being vested with more extensive powers, must prove totally nugatory. Should it be imagined that your delegates, as individuals, wish for an increment of power, be assured that we hold ourselves servants of the state of Rhode Island, and in readiness to relinquish the exalted station in which you have placed us, and return with pleasure to the shade of retirement, provided we can see such a degree of energy infused into your federal government as may render it adequate to the great ends of its original institution.

We need not, sir, inform you how it wounds our feelings, in every company, as well as in the gazettes, to hear and see the proceedings of our legislature burlesqued and ridiculed; and to find that Congress and all men of sober reflection reprobate, in the strongest terms, the principles which actuate our administration of government. We are citizens of Rhode Island, and are most sensibly affected with everything which militates to the dishonor of the state. Your delegates further beg leave to observe, that if those measures are continued which have for the last six months been pursued, in their opinion they will infallibly terminate in the ruin of the state, and have no inconsiderable share in the subversion of the Union.

We conclude by observing that the necessary supplies for our support are expected, and will be provided by the legislature, as we greatly need them; while we have the honor to be,

Your Excellency's most obedient and most humble servants,

JAMES MANNING,
NATHAN MILLER.

Reference: J.R. Bartlett (ed.), *Records of the Colony and State of Rhode Island,* Vol. X (10 vols.; Providence: A.C. Greene, 1856–1865).

JAMES MADISON, *THE VICES OF THE POLITICAL SYSTEM OF THE UNITED STATES,* APRIL 1787

1. *Failure of the States to Comply with the Constitutional Requisitions.* This evil has been so fully experienced both during the war and since the peace, results so naturally from the number and independent authority of the States and has been so uniformly exemplified in every similar

Confederacy, that it may be considered as not less radically and permanently inherent in than it is fatal to the object of the present system.

2. *Encroachments by the States on the Federal Authority.* Examples of this are numerous and repetitions may be foreseen in almost every case where any favorite object of a State shall present a temptation. Among these examples are the wars and treaties of Georgia with the Indians. The unlicensed compacts between Virginia and Maryland, and between Pena. & N. Jersey—the troops raised and to be kept up by Massts.

3. *Violations of the Law of Nations and of Treaties.* From the number of Legislatures, the sphere of life from which most of their members are taken, and the circumstances under which their legislative business is carried on, irregularities of this kind must frequently happen. Accordingly not a year has passed without instances of them in some one or other of the States. The Treaty of Peace—the treaty with France—the treaty with Holland have each been violated. [See the complaints to Congress on these subjects.] The causes of these irregularities must necessarily produce frequent violations of the law of nations in other respects.

As yet foreign powers have not been rigorous in animadverting on us. This moderation, however cannot be mistaken for a permanent partiality to our faults, or a permanent security agst. those disputes with other nations, which being among the greatest of public calamities, it ought to be least in the power of any part of the community to bring on the whole.

4. *Trespasses of the States on the Rights of Each Other.* These are alarming symptoms, and may be daily apprehended as we are admonished by daily experience. See the law of Virginia restricting foreign vessels to certain ports—of Maryland in favor of vessels belonging to her *own citizens*—of N. York in favor of the same—

Paper money, instalments of debts, occlusion of Courts, making property a legal tender, may likewise be deemed aggressions on the rights of other States. As the Citizens of every State aggregately taken stand more or less in the relation of Creditors or debtors, to the Citizens of every other State, Acts of the debtor State in favor of debtors, affect the Creditor State, in the same manner as they do its own citizens who are relatively creditors towards other citizens. This remark may be extended to foreign nations. If the exclusive regulation of the value and alloy of coin was properly delegated to the federal authority, the policy of it equally requires a controul on the States in the cases above mentioned. It must have been meant 1. to preserve uniformity in the circulating medium throughout the nation. 2. to prevent those frauds on the citizens of other States, and the subjects of foreign powers, which might disturb the tranquillity at home, or involve the Union in foreign contests.

The practice of many States in restricting the commercial intercourse with other States, and putting their productions and manufactures on the same footing with those of foreign nations, though not contrary to the federal articles, is certainly adverse to the spirit of the Union, and tends to beget retaliating regulations, not less expensive and vexatious in themselves than they are destructve of the general harmony.

5. *Want of Concert in Matters Where Common Interest Requires It.* This defect is strongly illustrated in the state of our commercial affairs. How much has the national dignity, interest, and revenue, suffered from this cause? Instances of inferior moment are the want of uniformity in the laws concerning naturalization & literary property; of provision for national seminaries, for grants of incorporation for national purposes, for canals and other works of general utility, wch may at present be defeated by the perverseness of particular States whose concurrence is necessary.

6. *Want of Guaranty to the States of their Constitutions & Laws against Internal Violence.* The confederation is silent on this point and therefore by the second article the hands of the federal authority are tied. According to Republican Theory. Right and power being both vested in the majority, are held to be synonimous. According to fact and experience a minority may in an appeal to force, be an overmatch for the majority. 1. if the minority happen to include all such as possess the skill and habits of military life, & such as possess the great pecuniary resources, one-third only may

conquer the remaining two-thirds. 2. one-third of those who participate in the choice of the rulers, may be rendered a majority by the accession of those whose poverty excludes them from a right of suffrage, and who for obvious reasons will be more likely to join the standard of sedition than that of the established Government. 3. where slavery exists the republican Theory becomes still more fallacious.

7. *Want of Sanction to the Laws and of Coercion in the Government of the Confederacy.* A sanction is essential to the idea of law, as coercion is to that of Government. The federal system being destitute of both, wants the great vital principles of a Political Constitution. Under the form of such a constitution, it is in fact nothing more than a treaty of amity of commerce and of alliance, between independent and Sovereign States. From what cause could so fatal an omission have happened in the articles of Confederation? from a mistaken confidence that the justice, the good faith, the honor, the sound policy, of the several legislative assemblies would render superfluous any appeal to the ordinary motives by which the laws secure the obedience of individuals: a confidence which does honor to the enthusiastic virtue of the compilers, as much as the inexperience of the crisis apologizes for their errors. The time which has since elapsed has had the double effect, of increasing the light and tempering the warmth, with which the arduous work may be revised. It is no longer doubted that a unanimous and punctual obedience of 13 independent bodies, to the acts of the federal Government ought not to be calculated on. Even during the war, when external danger supplied in some degree the defect of legal & coercive sanctions, how imperfectly did the States fulfil their obligations to the Union? In time of peace, we see already what is to be expected. How indeed could it be otherwise? In the first place, Every general act of the Union must necessarily bear unequally hard on some particular member or members of it, secondly the partiality of the members to their own interests and rights, a partiality which will be fostered by the courtiers of popularity, will naturally exaggerate the inequality where it exists,

and even suspect it where it has no existence, thirdly a distrust of the voluntary compliance of each other may prevent the compliance of any, although it should be the latent disposition of all. Here are causes & pretexts which will never fail to render federal measures abortive. If the laws of the States were merely recommendatory to their citizens, or if they were to be rejudged by County authorities, what security, what probability would exist, that they would be carried into execution? Is the security or probability greater in favor of the acts of Congs. which depending for their execution on the will of the State legislatures, wch. are tho' nominally authoritative, in fact recommendatory only?

8. *Want of Ratification by the People of the Articles of Confederation.* In some of the States the Confederation is recognized by, and forms a part of the Constitution. In others however it has received no other sanction than that of the legislative authority. From this defect two evils result:

1. Whenever a law of a State happens to be repugnant to an act of Congress, particularly when the latter [former] is of posterior date to the former, [latter] it will be at least questionable whether the latter [former] must not prevail; and as the question must be decided by the Tribunals of the State, they will be most likely to lean on the side of the State.

2. As far as the union of the States is to be regarded as a league of sovereign powers, and not as a political Constitution by virtue of which they are become one sovereign power, so far it seems to follow from the doctrine of compacts, that a breach of any of the articles of the Confederation by any of the parties to it, absolves the other parties from their respective Obligations, and gives them a right if they chuse to exert it, of dissolving the Union altogether.

9. *Multiplicity of Laws in the Several States.* In developing the evils which viciate the political system of the U.S., it is proper to include those which are found within the States individually, as well as those which directly affect the States collectively, since the former class have an indirect influence on the general malady and must not be overlooked in forming a compleat remedy.

Among the evils then of our situation may well be ranked the multiplicity of laws from which no State is exempt. As far as laws are necessary to mark with precision the duties of those who are to obey them, and to take from those who are to administer them a discretion which might be abused, their number is the price of liberty. As far as laws exceed this limit, they are a nuisance; a nuisance of the most pestilent kind. Try the Codes of the several States by this test, and what a luxuriancy of legislation do they present. The short period of independency has filled as many pages as the century which preceded it. Every year, almost every session, adds a new volume. This may be the effect in part, but it can only be in part, of the situation in which the revolution has placed us. A review of the several Codes will shew that every necessary and useful part of the least voluminous of them might be compressed into one tenth of the compass, and at the same time be rendered ten fold as perspicuous.

10. *Mutability of the Laws of the States*. This evil is intimately connected with the former yet deserves a distinct notice, as it emphatically denotes a vicious legislation. We daily see laws repealed or superseded, before any trial can have been made of their merits, and even before a knowledge of them can have reached the remoter districts within which they were to operate. In the regulations of trade this instability becomes a snare not only to our citizens, but to foreigners also.

11. *Injustice of the Laws of the States*. If the multiplicity and mutability of laws prove a want of wisdom, their injustice betrays a defect still more alarming: more alarming not merely because it is a greater evil in itself; but because it brings more into question the fundamental principle of republican Government, that the majority who rule in such governments are the safest Guardians both of public Good and private rights. To what causes is this evil to be ascribed?

These causes lie 1. in the Representative bodies. 2. in the people themselves.

1. Representative appointments are sought from 3 motives. 1. ambition. 2. personal interest. 3. public good. Unhappily the two first are proved by experience to be most prevalent. Hence the candidates who feel them, particularly, the second, are most industrious, and most successful in pursuing their object: and forming often a majority in the legislative Councils, with interested views, contrary to the interest and views of their constituents, join in a perfidious sacrifice of the latter to the former. A succeeding election it might be supposed, would displace the offenders, and repair the mischief. But how easily are base and selfish measures, masked by pretexts of public good and apparent expediency? How frequently will a repetition of the same arts and industry which succeeded in the first instance, again prevail on the unwary to misplace their confidence?

How frequently too will the honest but unenlightened representative be the dupe of a favorite leader, veiling his selfish views under the professions of public good, and varnishing his sophistical arguments with the glowing colours of popular eloquence?

2. A still more fatal if not more frequent cause, lies among the people themselves. All civilized societies are divided into different interests and factions, as they happen to be creditors or debtors—rich or poor—husbandmen, merchants or manufacturers—members of different religious sects—followers of different political leaders—inhabitants of different districts—owners of different kinds of property &c &c. In republican Government the majority however composed, ultimately give the law. Whenever therefore an apparent interest or common passion unites a majority what is to restrain them from unjust violations of the rights and interests of the minority, or of individuals? Three motives only 1. a prudent regard to their own good as involved in the general and permanent good of the community. This consideration although of decisive weight in itself, is found by experience to be too often unheeded. It is too often forgotten, by nations as well as by individuals, that honesty is the best policy. 2dly. respect for character. However strong this motive may be in individuals, it is considered as very insufficient to restrain them from injustice. In a multitude its efficacy is diminished in proportion to the number which

is to share the praise or the blame. Besides, as it has reference to public opinion, which within a particular Society, is the opinion of the majority, the standard is fixed by those whose conduct is to be measured by it. The public opinion without the Society will be little respected by the people at large of any Country. Individuals of extended views, and of national pride, may bring the public proceedings to this standard, but the example will never be followed by the multitude. Is it to be imagined that an ordinary citizen or even Assemblyman of R. Island in estimating the policy of paper money, ever considered or cared, in what light the measure would be viewed in France or Holland; or even in Massts or Connect? It was a sufficient temptation to both that it was for their interest; it was a sufficient sanction to the latter that it was popular in the State; to the former, that it was so in the neighbourhood. 3dly. will Religion the only remaining motive be a sufficient restraint? It is not pretended to be such on men individually considered. Will its effect be greater on them considered in an aggregate view? quite the reverse. The conduct of every popular assembly acting on oath, the strongest of religious ties, proves that individuals join without remorse in acts, against which their consciences would revolt if proposed to them under the like sanction, separately in their closets. When indeed Religion is kindled into enthusiasm, its force like that of other passions, is increased by the sympathy of a multitude. But enthusiasm is only a temporary state of religion, and while it lasts will hardly be seen with pleasure at the helm of Government. Besides as religion in its coolest state is not infallible, it may become a motive to oppression as well as a restraint from injustice. Place three individuals in a situation wherein the interest of each depends on the voice of the others; and give to two of them an interest opposed to the rights of the third? Will the latter be secure? The prudence of every man would shun the danger. The rules & forms of justice suppose & guard against it. Will two thousand in a like situation be less likely to encroach on the rights of one thousand? The contrary is witnessed by the notorious factions & oppressions which take place in

corporate towns limited as the opportunities are, and in little republics when uncontrouled by apprehensions of external danger. If an enlargement of the sphere is found to lessen the insecurity of private rights, it is not because the impulse of a common interest or passion is less predominant in this case with the majority; but because a common interest or passion is less apt to be felt and the requisite combinations less easy to be formed by a great than by a small number. The Society becomes broken into a greater variety of interests, of pursuits of passions, which check each other, whilst those who may feel a common sentiment have less opportunity of communication and concert. It may be inferred that the inconveniences of popular States contrary to the prevailing Theory, are in proportion not to the extent, but to the narrowness of their limits.

The great desideratum in Government is such a modification of the sovereignty as will render it sufficiently neutral between the different interests and factions, to controul one part of the society from invading the rights of another, and at the same time sufficiently controuled itself, from setting up an interest adverse to that of the whole Society. In absolute Monarchies the prince is sufficiently, neutral towards his subjects, but frequently sacrifices their happiness to his ambition or his avarice. In small Republics, the sovereign will is sufficiently controuled from such a sacrifice of the entire Society, but is not sufficiently neutral towards the parts composing it. As a limited monarchy tempers the evils of an absolute one; so an extensive Republic meliorates the administration of a small Republic.

An auxiliary desideratum for the melioration of the Republican form is such a process of elections as will most certainly extract from the mass of the society the purest and noblest characters which it contains; such as will at once feel most strongly the proper motives to pursue the end of their appointment, and be most capable to devise the proper means of attaining it.

Reference: Galliard Hunt (ed.), *The Writings of James Madison*, Vol. II (New York: G. P. Putnam, 1900–1910), 361–369.

BENJAMIN RUSH, *ON THE DEFECTS OF THE CONFEDERATION*, MAY 1787

THERE IS nothing more common than to confound the terms of the American Revolution with those of the late American War. The American War is over: but this is far from being the case with the American Revolution. On the contrary, nothing but the first act of the great drama is closed. It remains yet to establish and perfect our new forms of government; and to prepare the principles, morals, and manners of our citizens, for these forms of government, after they are established and brought to perfection.

The Confederation, together with most of our state constitutions, were formed under very unfavorable circumstances. We had just emerged from a corrupted monarchy. Although we understood perfectly the principles of liberty, yet most of us were ignorant of the forms and combinations of power in republics. Add to this, the British army was in the heart of our country, spreading desolation wherever it went: our resentments, of course, were awakened. We detested the British name, and unfortunately refused to copy some things in the administration of justice and power, in the British government, which have made it the admiration and envy of the world. In our opposition to monarchy, we forgot that the temple of tyranny has two doors. We bolted one of them by proper restraints: but we left the other open, by neglecting to guard against the effects of our own ignorance and licentiousness.

Most of the present difficulties of this country arise from the weakness and other defects of our governments.

My business at present shall be only to suggest the defects of the Confederation. These consist, 1st, In the deficiency of coercive power. 2d, In a defect of exclusive power to issue paper money, and regulate commerce. 3d, In vesting the sovereign power of the United States in a single legislature: and 4th, In the too frequent rotation of its members.

A convention is to sit soon for the purpose of devising means of obviating part of the two first

defects that have been mentioned. But I wish they may add to their recommendations to each state, to surrender up to Congress their power of emitting money. In this way, uniform currency will be produced, that will facilitate trade, and help to bind the states together. Nor will the states be deprived of large sums of money by this means when sudden emergencies require it: for they may always borrow them as they did during the war, out of the treasury of Congress. Even a loan-office may be better instituted in this way in each state, than in any other.

The two last defects that have been mentioned, are not of less magnitude than the first. Indeed, the single legislature of Congress will become more dangerous from an increase of power than ever. To remedy this, let the supreme federal power be divided, like the legislatures of most of our states, into two distinct, independent branches. Let one of them be styled the Council of the States, and the other the Assembly of the States. Let the first consist of a single delegate,—and the second, of two, three, or four delegates, chosen annually by each state. Let the president be chosen annually by the joint ballots of both houses, and let him possess certain powers in conjunction with a privy council, especially the power of appointing most of the officers of the United States. The officers will not only be better when appointed this way, but one of the principal causes of faction will be thereby removed from congress. I apprehend this division of the power of Congress will become more necessary, as soon as they are invested with more ample powers of levying and expending public money.

The custom of turning men out of power or office, as soon as they are qualified for it, has been found to be as absurd in practice, as it is virtuous in speculation. It contradicts our habits and opinions in every other transaction of life. Do we dismiss a general—a physician—or even a domestic as soon as they have acquired knowledge enough to be useful to us, for the sake of increasing the number of able generals—skilful physicians—and faithful servants? We do not. Government is a science; and can never be perfected in America, until we encourage men to devote not only three years, but their whole lives to it. I believe the principal reason why so many men of abilities object to serving in Congress, is owing to their not thinking it worth while to spend three years in acquiring a profession which their country immediately afterwards forbids them to follow.

There are two errors or prejudices on the subject of government in America, which lead to the most dangerous consequences.

It is often said that "the sovereign and all other power is seated *in* the people." This idea is unhappily expressed. It should be—"all power is derived *from* the people." They possess it only on the days of their elections. After this, it is the property of their rulers, nor can they exercise or resume it, unless it is abused. It is of importance to circulate this idea, as it leads to order and good government.

The people of America have mistaken the meaning of the word sovereignty: hence each state pretends to be sovereign. In Europe it is applied only to those states which possess the power of making war and peace—of forming treaties, and the like. As this power belongs only to Congress, they are the only sovereign power in the United States.

We commit a similar mistake in our ideas of the word independent.—No individual state as such has any claim to independence. She is independent only in a union with her sister states in Congress.

To conform the principles, morals, and manners of our citizens to our republican forms of government, it is absolutely necessary that knowledge of every kind, should be disseminated through every part of the United States.

For this purpose, let Congress, instead of laying out half a million of dollars in building a federal town, appropriate only a fourth part of that sum, in founding a federal university. In this university, let every thing connected with government, such as history—the law of nature and nations—the civil law—the municipal laws of our country—and the principles of commerce, be taught by competent professors. Let masters be employed likewise to teach gunnery—fortification—and every thing connected with defensive and offensive war.— Above all, let a professor, of what is called in the European universities, economy, be established in this federal seminary. His business should be to unfold the principles and practice of agriculture and manufactures of all kinds; and to enable him to make his lectures more extensively useful, Congress should support a travelling correspondent for him, who should visit all the nations of Europe, and transmit to him, from time to time, all the discoveries and improvements that are made in agriculture and manufactures. To this seminary young men should be encouraged to repair, after completing their academical studies in the colleges of their respective states. The honors and offices of the United States should, after a while, be confined to persons who had imbibed federal and republican ideas in this university.

For the purpose of diffusing knowledge, as well as extending the living principle of government to every part of the United States; every state—city—county—village—and township in the union, should be tied together by means of the postoffice.—This is the true non-electric wire of government. It is the only means of conveying heat and light to every individual in the federal commonwealth. Sweden lost her liberties, says the Abbé Raynal, because her citizens were so scattered, that they had no means of acting in concert with each other. It should be a constant injunction to the postmasters to convey newspapers free of all charge for postage.—They are not only the vehicles of knowledge and intelligence, but the sentinels of the liberties of our country.

The conduct of some of those strangers who have visited our country, since the peace, and who fill the British papers with accounts of our distresses, shows as great a want of good sense, as it does of good nature. They fear nothing; but the foundations and walls of the temple of liberty, and yet they undertake to judge of the whole fabric.

Our own citizens act a still more absurd part, when they cry out, after the experience of three or four years, that we are not proper materials for republican government. Remember, we assumed these forms of government in a hurry, before we were prepared for them. Let every man exert himself in promoting virtue and knowledge in our country, and we shall soon become good republicans. Look at the steps by which governments have been changed or rendered stable in Europe. Read the history of Great Britain. Her boasted government has risen out of wars—and rebellions that lasted above sixty years. The United States are travelling peaceably into order and good government. They know no strife—but what arises from the collision of opinions: and in three years, they have advanced further in the road to stability and happiness, than most of the nations in Europe have done, in as many centuries.

There is but one path that can lead the United States to destruction, and that is their extent of territory. It was probably to effect this, that Great Britain ceded to us so much waste land. But even this path may be avoided. Let but one new state be exposed to sale at a time; and let the land office be shut up till every part of this new state is settled.

I am extremely sorry to find a passion for retirement so universal among the patriots and heroes of the war. They resemble skilful mariners, who, after exerting themselves to preserve a ship from sinking in a storm, in the middle of the ocean, drop asleep as soon as the waves subside, and leave the care of their lives and property, during the remainder of the voyage to sailors without knowledge or experience. Every man in a republic is public property. His time and talents—his youth—his manhood—his old age—nay more, life, all, belong to his country.

Patriots of 1774, 1775, 1776,—heroes of 1778, 1779, 1780! come forward! your country demands your services.—Philosophers and friends to mankind, come forward! your country demands your studies and speculations! Lovers of peace and order, who declined taking part in the late war, come forward! your country forgives your timidity, and demands your influence and advice!—Hear her proclaiming in sighs and groans, in her governments, in her finances, in her trade, in her manufactures, in her morals, and in her manners, *"The revolution is not over!"*

Reference: Dagobert D. Runer (ed.), *The Selected Writings of Benjamin Rush* (New York: Philosophical Library, 1947).

RICHARD HENRY LEE TO GEORGE MASON, MAY 15, 1787

DEAR SIR—

It has given me much pleasure to be informed that General Washington and yourself, have gone to the convention. We may hope, from such efforts, that alterations beneficial will take place in our federal constitution, if it shall be found, on deliberate inquiry, that the evils now felt do flow from errors in that constitution; but, alas! sir, I fear it is more in vicious manners, than mistakes in form, that we must seek for the causes of the present discontent. The present causes of complaint seem to be, that Congress cannot command the money necessary for the just purposes of paying debts, or for supporting the federal government; and that they cannot make treaties of commerce, unless power unlimited, of regulating trade, be given. The confederation now gives right to name the sums necessary, and to apportion the quotas by a rule established. This rule is, unfortunately, very difficult of execution, and, therefore, the recommendations of Congress on this subject, have not been made in federal mode; so that states have thought themselves justified in non-compliance. If the rule were plain and easy, and refusal were then to follow demand, I see clearly, that no form of government whatever, short of force, will answer; for the same want of principle that produces neglect now, will do so under any change not supported by power compulsory; the difficulty certainly is, how to give this power in such manner as that it may only be used to good, and not abused to bad, purposes. Whoever shall solve this difficulty will receive the thanks of this and future generations. With respect to the want of power to make treaties of trade, for want of legislation, to regulate the general commerce, it appears to me, that the right of making treaties, and the legislative power contended for, are essentially different things; the former may be given and executed, without the danger attending upon the states parting with their legislative authority, in the instance contended for. If the third paragraph of the sixth article were altered, by striking out the words, in pursuance of any treaties already proposed by Congress, to the courts of France and Spain; and the proviso stricken out of the first section in the ninth article, Congress would then have a complete and unlimited right of making treaties of all kinds, and, so far, I really think it both right and necessary; but this is very different from, and in danger far short of, giving an exclusive power of regulating trade. A minister of Congress may go to a foreign court with full power to make a commercial treaty; but if he were to propose to such court that the eight northern states in this union, should have the exclusive right of carrying the products of the five southern states, or of supplying these states with foreign articles; such a proposition of monopoly would be rejected; and, therefore, no danger here from the power of making treaty; but a legislative right to regulate trade through the states, may, in a thousand artful modes, be so abused as to produce the monopoly aforesaid, to the extreme oppression of the staple states, as they are called. I do not say that this would be done, but I contend that it might be done; and, where interest powerfully prompts, it is greatly to be feared that it would be done. Whoever has served long in Congress, knows, that the restraint of making the consent of nine states necessary, is feeble and incompetent. Some will sometimes sleep, and some will be negligent, but it is certain that improper power not given, cannot be improperly used. The human mind is too apt to rush from one extreme to another; it appears, by the objections that came from the different states, when the confederation was submitted for consideration, that the universal apprehension was, of the too great, not the defective powers of Congress. Whence this immense change of sentiment, in a few years? for now the cry is power, give Congress power. Without reflecting that every free nation, that hath ever existed, has lost its liberty by the same rash impatience, and want of necessary caution. I am glad, however, to find, on this occasion, that so many gentlemen, of competent years, are sent to the convention, for, certainly, "youth is the season of credulity, and confidence a plant of slow growth in an aged bosom." The states have been so unpardonably remiss, in furnishing their federal quotas, as to make impost necessary, for a term of time, with a provisional security, that the money arising shall be unchangeably applied to the payment of their public debts: that accounts of the application, shall be annually sent to each state; and the collecting officers appointed by, and be amenable to the states; or, if not so, very strong preventives and correctives of official abuse and misconduct, interpose, to shield the people from oppression. Give me leave, sir, to detain you a moment longer, with a proposition that I have not heard mentioned. It is that the right of making paper money shall be exclusively vested in Congress; such a right will be clearly within the spirit of the fourth section of the ninth article of the present confederation. This appears to me, to be a restraint of the last importance to the peace and happiness of the Union, and of every part of it. Knaves assure, and fools believe, that calling paper money, and making it tender, is the way to be rich and happy; thus the national mind is kept in constant ferment; and the public councils in continual disturbance by the intrigues of wicked men, for fraudulent purposes, for speculating designs. This would be a great step towards correcting morals, and suppressing legislative frauds, which, of all frauds, is the most fatal to society. Do you not think, sir, that it ought to be declared, by the new system, that any state act of legislation that shall contravene, or oppose, the authorized acts of Congress, or interfere with the expressed rights of that body, shall be *ipso facto* void, and of no force whatsoever. My respects, if you please, to your brethren of the convention, from this state, and pardon me for the liberty I have taken of troubling you with my sentiments on the interesting business that calls you to Philadelphia. I have the honour to be, with affectionate esteem and regard,

Your friend and servant,

GEORGE MASON, Esq.

Reference: James Curtis Ballagh (ed.), *The Letters of Richard Henry Lee*, Vol. II (New York: Macmillan, 1914).

Afterword: The Meaning of Governance in America

These three volumes of America's foundational documents tell us how and even why our system of governance has developed the way it has throughout the course of some two hundred years. Included in the three volumes of documents are theories on the structure of governance, views of why we have a governing system, and arguments for what is worth protecting in that system. Theoretical writings appear in all of these volumes because, especially in Volumes II and III, they examine the governing systems. Early theories of governance soon gave way to the practical charters, or, the institutional documents that set up systems of governance from the beginning of British settlement in North America. Also included are English documents that gave instructions to the executives or governors and established the colonial legislative systems. Other institutional documents include the first state constitutions and the Articles of Confederation, our first national Constitution. Essential to understanding the growing powers of the legislature are the documents of statutes and laws passed in those legislatures. The struggles between growing colonial legislative authority and the powers of the crown-appointed governors are included in those statutes. Through their laws, mostly seen in Volume II, the colonial legislative leaders created a unique system of governance. They then defended their own system of governance against what they called British aggression. Theories of governance, institutional charters, governance directives, state and national constitutions, and the statutes at large and other legislative laws, are the documents printed in these volumes.

Volume I includes the earliest English theories of overseas governance, and the importance of governance in setting up viable settled and economically successful colonies. To attract settlers to the new lands and to make that economic system, many of the charters included promises of popular participation in the political process. The structures of governance contained in the original charters clearly were based on the precedent of English governance practices. But these early charters soon were revised as the colonial governance systems created a governance structure to fit the needs of the new lands. Instructions from the crown to the new governors vied with the early statutes that the new legislatures adapted. At the end of Volume I, England attempted to organize the colonies into one dominion system, and the failure of this attempt highlighted the viability and growing independence of the separate colonies' systems of governance.

Volume II begins around 1689 with the results of the colonies' resistance to dominion status and charter revisions. The powers given to the executive branch of governance soon vied with the growing legislative systems in the colonies. The legislatures of the eighteenth century wrote statutes confirming the growth of local governance and establishing an independent judiciary. The legislatures regulated elections, extended voting rights, and attempted to clean up corrupt politics in the local centers of power. The more the people realized their stake in social order, the more the statutes reflected concerns with the voters and their rights. If the people did not always exercise their voting rights, the legislatures nevertheless looked to them for legitimacy. Intense struggles, especially after 1763, broke out between crown representatives and the legislatures, as revealed in the laws passed in those legislatures, and the restrictions the crown placed on the legislatures.

Also, Volume II prints the documents that studied the political structure—the theories of governance—similar to the first theoretical documents used in Volume I. Those documents, written texts and reproductions of speeches, summed up colonial leaders' views of their system of governance and their privileges of participation in that governance. Almost two centuries of movement toward forms of self-governance were discussed and defended in those writings. Those efforts also reveal how the leaders and the people distrusted one another as they moved toward independence. The disagreements within the colonies about representation and apportionment and the fears the colonies had of each other are seen in these documents. Slowly, the colonial leaders realized that they must come together for mutual defense and Volume II ends with a declaration of independence.

Volume III begins with a nation declared but a governing system lacking clarity and cohesion of purpose. By building on the historical charters of governance and two centuries of self-governing experience, the states began to write constitutions that delineated specific systems of governance. Reflecting past tensions and accomplishments in governing, most of the state constitutions limited executive authority, gave clear power to state legislatures, stressed the importance of local government, and made many reforms that expanded suffrage. No doubt those insecure new governments had come to believe what their forebears had taught them: Popular support gave governance legitimacy.

From the experience of state making by writing Constitutions, the new Continental Congress understood that it must have its own constitutional guide to national governance. Struggles in the national Congress over writing a national Constitution, and state debates over its ratification, revealed a fiercely independent people distrustful of the national government. Founded as separate colonies, suspicious of England's desire to unite them, and with years of experience in self-governance, the states were wary of giving too much power to a national government. Volume III ends with leaders debating and discussing the functioning of the national government under its first federal Constitution. The precedents of colonial and revolutionary governance clearly had clashed with those who wanted an entirely new system of governance not made up of separate colonies and states but of a united states.

So what have these many documents on the origins of our governing system taught us about our values as a people and our views of government? In one regard, this has been the seedy story of a people who were racist, male-dominated, and divided among themselves, yet who brought forth a federal republic based on hostility to government oppression and on popular sovereignty (the consent of the governed). Surrounded by natives whom they pushed from their land, successful in part because of the exploitation of imported African slaves, and restricting the governance participation of many non-English–speaking immigrants, the colonists' desire for material success and social order nevertheless led them to establish the freest system of governance then known to Western civilization. What those English colonists created more than two hundred years ago, despite its birth in freedom for some and not for others, has lasted until today. Those freedoms, that social order, and even that complex view of support for and fear of government are now called into question. Perhaps the reprinting of these founding documents will be of some service to help understand what is at stake today.

Let there be one last word on the meaning of governance as revealed in our founding documents. Human beings have always required some kind of social order, some kind of system of governance. There are those who say that our very nature requires governing order. Throughout history, certainly the leaders and sometimes the people have debated the creation and management of the systems of governance best suited to their existence. This collection of founding documents has charted the origins of, theories on, growth of, and defining moments of governance in the British North American colonies down to the creation of a second national Constitution in 1787. Our system of governance that exists today is beholden to those ancestors who recognized the necessity of a governing order for themselves and future generations.

Essay on Sources Consulted

VOLUME 1

Primary Sources

There are a number of major printed collections of sources on colonial governance. Among the most important are Alexander Brown (ed.), *Genesis of the United States* (2vols., Boston: Houghton, Mifflin,1890); Jack P. Greene (ed.), *Settlement to Society, 1584–1763: A Documentary History of Colonial America* (New York: Norton, 1975); David F. Hawke (ed.), *United States Colonial History: Readings and Documents* (New York: Bobbs Merrill, 1966); Peter Force (ed.), *Tracts and Other Papers* (2 vols., Washington, DC: Government Printing Office, 1836); Michael Kammen, *Deputies and Libertyes: The Origins of Representative Government in America* (New York: Alfred Knopf, 1969); W. Keith Kavenagh (ed.), *Foundations of Colonial America: A Documentary History* (3 vols., New York: Chelsea House, 1973); Donald P. Lutz (ed.), *Origins of American Constitutionalism* (Indianapolis: Liberty Fund, 1996); Frank Moore (ed.), *The American Experience* (2 vols., New York: D. Appleton and Co., 1858); Ben Perley Poore (ed.), *The Federal and State Constitutions, Colonial Charters, and Other organic Laws* (2 vols., Washington, DC: Government Printing Office, 1877); and Francis Newton Thorpe (ed.), *American Charters, Constitutions, and Organic Laws, 1492–1908* (7 vols., Washington, DC; Government Printing Office, 1909).

The early writings of the explorers and political thinkers include *The Works of Sir Walter Raleigh* (8 vols., Oxford: Oxford University Press, 1829); G. E. Hadow (ed.), *Sir Walter Raleigh: Selections from his Histoire of the World* (Oxford: The Clarendon Press, 1917); Gerald Hammond (ed.), *Sir Walter Raleigh: Selected Writings* (Manchester: Carrant Press, 1984); Samuel Harvey Reynolds (ed.), *The Essays on Counsels, Civil an Moral of Sir Francis Bacon* (Oxford: The Clarendon Press, 1890); Brian Vickers (ed.), *Francis Bacon* (Oxford: Oxford University Press, 1996); and David B. Quinn (ed.), *The Hakluyt Handbook* (London: The Hakluyt Society, 1974).

Although many of the primary sources on the early colonies will be included in Volume II, the reader should look at the many individual colonies' publications that collected the early statutes. I include some of the most important for the seventeenth century. Warren M. Billings (comp.), *The Old Dominion in the Seventeenth Century: A Documentary History of Virginia 1606–1689* (Chapel Hill: University of North Carolina Press, 1975); Samuel M. Bemiss (ed.), *The Three Charters of the Virginia Company London* (Williamsburg: Virginia Historical Society, 1957); William H. Whitmore (ed.), *Bibliographical Sketch of the Laws of the Massachusetts Colony from 1630 to 1686* (Boston: Rockwell and Churchill, 1890); Nathaniel B. Shurtleff (ed.), *The Records of the Government and Company of Massachusetts Bay in New England, 1628–1686* (5 vols., Boston: William White, 1853–1854); Charles J. Hoadley (ed.), *Records of the Colony and Plantation of New Haven from 1635 to 1649* (Hartford, CT: Case, Tifffary and Co.,1857); Aaron Leamesig and Jacob Spicer (eds.), *Grants, Concessions, and Original Constitutions of the Province of New Jersey, 1664–1682* (Somerville, NJ: Honeyman and Co., 1881); Alexander Salley (ed.), *Narratives of Early Carolina, 1650–1708* (New York: Charles Scribner's Sons, 1911); and N. B. Shurtleff and David Pularfer (eds.), *Records of the Colony of New Plymouth in New England* (12 vols., Boston: William White, 1855–1861).

Secondary Sources

The general secondary sources that cover the origins and development of the early colonies are: John E. Pomfret, *Founding the American Colonies* (New York: Harper and Row, 1970); Joshua J. Miller, *The Rise and Fall of Democracy in Early America, 1630–1789* (University Park: Pennsylvania State University Press, 1991); Wesley Frank Craven, *The Colonies in Transition, 1660–1713* (New York: Harper and Row, 1968); Robert M. Bliss, *Revolution and Empire: English Politics and the American Colonies in the Seventeenth Century* (Manchester: Manchester University Press, 1990); Clarence L. Ver Steeg, *The Formative Years, 1607–1763* (New York: Hill and Wang, 1964); Charles MacLean Andrews, *The Colonial Period of American History* (4 vols., New Haven, CT: Yale University Press, 1934); George Beer, *Origins of the British Colonial Systems, 1578–1660* (New York: Macmillan, 1908); and Herbert L Osgood, *The American Colonies in the Seventeenth Century* (3 vols., Gloucester, MA: Peter Smith, 1967). See also, George A. Billias (ed.), *Law and Authority in Colonial America* (Barre, MA: Barre Publishers, 1963).

Important studies of the early explorers and theorists of settlement are: Raleigh Trevelyan, *Sir Walter Raleigh* (New York: Henry Holt, 2002); David Beers Quinn, *The Voyages and Colonizing Expeditions of Sir Humphrey Gilbert* (Glasgow: Hakluyt Society, 1940); Anthony Pagden (ed.), *The Language of Political Theory in Early Modern England* (Cambridge: Cambridge University Press, 1987); John Racin, *Sir Walter Raleigh as Historian* (Salzburg: Institut fur Englishe Sprache und Literatur, 1974); and, E.G.R. Taylor (ed.), *Writings and Correspondence of the Two Richard Hakluyts* (London; University Press, 1881).

Of the many secondary studies on specific topics exploration and early settlement that have been useful, a few stand out. See Stephen Greenblatt (ed.), *New World Encounters* (Berkeley: University of California Press, 1993); A. L. Rowse, *The Elizabethans and America* (New York: Harper and Row, 1959); David Beers Quinn, *Raleigh and the British Empire* (New York: Alfred Knopf, 1949); especially David Beers Quinn, *England and the Discovery of America* (New York: Alfred Knopf, 1974); and, intriguingly, Robert Appelbaum and John Wood Sweet (eds.), *Envisioning an English Empire: Jamestown and the Making of the North Atlantic World* (Philadelphia: University of Pennsylvania Press, 2005).

Most useful on the individual colonies in regards to settlement and the growth of governance are: John Gilman Kolp, *Gentlemen and Freeholders: Electoral Politics in Colonial*

Virginia (Baltimore: Johns Hopkins University Press, 1998); Thomas J. Wertenbaker, *The Government of Virginia in the Seventeenth Century* (Williamsburg, VA: 350th Annual celebration Fund, 1957); Warren M. Billings, *A Little Parliament: The Virginia General Assembly in the Seventeenth Century* (Richmond, VA: Jamestown-Yorktown Foundation, 2004); and David Grayson Allen, *In English Ways* (Chapel Hill: University of North Carolina Press, 1981). Secondary sources that deal with both the seventeenth and eighteenth century developments are listed in Volume II.

Valuable secondary histories on events surrounding the Glorious Revolution are: James Peacey, *Politics and Pamphleteers: Propaganda During the English Civil War and Interregnum* (Aldershot, England: Ashgate Publisher Limited, 2004); Jack M. Sosin, *English America and the Restoration Monarchy of Charles II* (Lincoln: University of Nebraska Press, 1980); and David S. Lovejoy, *The Glorious Revolution in America* (New York: Harper and Row, 1972). Two studies of use in the transition period after 1689 are Philip S. Haffenden, *New England in the English Nation, 1689–1713* (Oxford: Oxford University Press, 1974); and Lawrence H. Leder, *Liberty and Authority: Early American Political ideology, 1689–1763* (Chicago: Quadrangle Books, 1968).

VOLUME 2

A few primary collections giving an overview of developments of colonial governance have been discussed in Volume I. Eric Kavenagh's splendid three-volume collection is largely of documents on the seventeenth century with the most helpful being a few colony-wide and local documents taken from the statutes at large. Kavenagh does include a few key statutes from the early eighteenth century Thorpe, always useful, has all of the charters of the eighteenth century: *American Charters, Constitutions, and Organic Laws, 1492–1908* (7 vols., Washington, DC: Government Printing Office, 1909). (Thorpe is most helpful to this book in the third volume because there he reprints all of the first state constitutions.) The best multivolume collection of documents pertaining to eighteenth century governance is William MacDonald (ed.), *Select Charters and Other Documents Illustrative of American History, 1606–1775* (22 vols., New York: Macmillan, 1904). See also, Merrill Jensen (ed.), *English Historical Documents: American Colonial Documents to 1776* (London: Eyre and Spottswoodie, 1955); and Hezekiah Niles (ed.), *Principles and Acts of the Revolution in America* (Baltimore: Published for the Editor, 1822).

The marvelous collections the states made of their colonial statutes and proceedings of the legislatures, and therefore the governance of the individual colonies, provide the heart of any study of governance. For Virginia see William Waller Hening (ed.), *The Statutes at Large of Virginia* (13 vols., New York: Printed for the Editor, 1809–1823). For Massachusetts see Max Farrand (ed.), *Laws and Liberties of Massachusetts* (Cambridge: Harvard University Press, 1929); and John G. Palfrey (ed.), *The Acts and Resolves, Public and Private, of the Province of Massachusetts Bay, 1692–1780* (21 vols., Boston: Wright and Potter, 1869–1922). For Maryland see William H. Browne (ed.), *Archives of Maryland* (65 vols., Baltimore: Maryland Historical Society, 1883–1952). For Connecticut see, J. H. Trumbull and C. J. Hoadley (eds.), *The Public records of the Colony of Connecticut, 1636–1776* (15 vols., Hartford, CT: Lockwood and Brainard Co., 1850–1890). For Rhode Island see J. R. Bartlett (ed.), *Records of the Colony of Rhode Island. . . . in New England, 1636–1792* (10 vols., Providence, RI: A. C. Greene, state printer, 1856–1865). For New York see *Colonial Records of New York from the Year 1664 to the Revolution* (5 vols., Albany, NY: J.S. Lyon, 1894); and Edmund B. O'Callaghan (ed.), *Documents Relative to Colonial New York* (15 vols., Albany, NY: Weed, Parsons, and Co., 1853–1887). For New Jersey see W. A. Whitehead et al. (eds.), *Archives of the State of New Jersey* (33 vols., Newark, NJ: The State Historical Society, 1888–1928). For North Carolina see William L. Saunders (ed.), *The Colonial Records of North Carolina* (10 vols., Raleigh, NC: State Archives, 1886–1890). South Carolina has a number of major printed collections dating back to the early nineteenth century. See especially, Thomas Cooper and David J. McCord (eds.), *Statutes at Large of South Carolina* (10 vols., Columbia, SC: A.S. Johnston, 1836–1841); and J. H. Easterby (ed.), *The Colonial Records of South Carolina* (3 vols., Columbia, SC: Historical Commission, 1951–1953). For New Hampshire see Albert S. Batchellor and H. H. Metcalf (eds.), *Laws of the New Hampshire Province* (3 vols., Manchester, NH: The John B. Clarke Co., 1904–1915). Pennsylvania has collected its past quite well; see J. T. Mitchell and Henry Flanders (eds.), *Statutes at Large of Pennsylvania from 1682 to 1801* (15 vols., Harrisburg, PA: Clarence M. Busch, State printer, 1896–1908); and *The Colonial Records of Pennsylvania, 1683–1790* (16 vols., Philadelphia: J. Severns, 1852–1853). For Delaware see *Laws of the State of Delaware, 1700–1797* (2 vols., New Castle, DE: Samuel and John Adams, 1797–1816). For Georgia see Allen D. Candler et al. (eds.), *Colonial Records of the State of Georgia* (26 vols., Atlanta: State Printer, 1904–1916).

Aside from the two essays on the colonies' governance in the eighteenth century, there are a few other works worth citing. See Cotton Mather, *The First Book of New-English History* (Vol. I, Hartford, CT: Silas Anderson and Son, 1855); Robert Beverley, *The History and Present State of Virginia* (London: Richard Parker, 1705); and Clarence L. Ver Steeg (ed.), *A True and Historical Narrative of the Colony of Georgia* (Athens: University of Georgia Press, 1960).

There are only a few collections of pamphlets and speeches in defense of the colonies. See, Frank Moore (ed.), *American Eloquence: A Collection of Speeches and Addresses. . .* (2 vols., New York: D. Appleton and Co., 1858). The most thorough collection is Bernard Bailyn (ed.), *Pamphlets of the American Revolution* (Cambridge: Harvard University Press, 1965). Bailyn promised a multivolume collection of the pamphlets of the Revolution, but only one volume appeared. There is much need for those editions because most of the pamphlets lay uncollected in the Rare Book Room of the Library of Congress and the Houghton Library of Harvard College.

Some of the most important writers on defending governance in the colonies have appeared in print. See Charles F. Mullett (ed.), *Some Political Writings of James Otis* (Vol. IV, Columbia, MO: The University of Missouri Studies, July 1929); Paul Leicester Ford (ed.), *The Writings of John Dickinson* (Philadelphia: Historical Society of Pennsylvania, 1895); Henry Alonzo Cushing (ed.), *The Writings of Samuel Adams* (New York: Octogan Press, 1968); James DeWitt Andrews (ed.), *Works of James Wilson* (Chicago: Callaghan and Co., 1896); George A. Peek, Jr., *The Political Writings of John Adams* (Indianapolis: The Bobbs-Merrill Co., 1954); and Adrienne Koch and William Peden (ed.), *Life and Selected Writings of Thomas Jefferson* (New York: Random House, 1944).

The primary works cited in the text on the Albany Plan and the unity and divisions within the colonies will suffice for the readers' understanding of how the late colonial leaders viewed their interrelations. For the events around the Declaration of Independence, see the William Peden edition of *The Life and Selected Writings of Thomas Jefferson* (New York: Random House, 1944).

Of the major secondary general studies of the nature of colonial governance and the coming of the American Revolution I will cite only the books that give a comprehensive account of those events. See Herbert L. Osgood, *The American Colonies in the Eighteenth Century* (4 vols., New York: Columbia University Press, 1924–1925); Charles M. Andrews, *The Colonial Background to the American Revolution* (New Haven: Yale University Press, 1931); Lawrence Henry Gibson, *The British Isles and the American Colonies* (New York: Alfred Knopf, 1958); and Merrill Jensen, *The Founding of a Nation: A History of the American Revolution* (New York: Oxford University Press, 1968).

Some other general studies on governance as a factor in the American Revolution are Jack P. Greene, *Peripheries and Center: Constitutional Development in the Extended Politics of the British Empire and the United States, 1607–1788* (Athens: University of Georgia Press, 1986); Jack P. Greene, *Negotiated Authorities: Essays in Colonial Political and Constitutional History* (Charlottesville: University Press of Virginia, 1994); Edmund S. Morgan, *Inventing the People: The Rise of Popular Sovereignty in England and America* (New York: W.W. Norton, 1989); Richard R. Beeman, *The Varieties of Political Experience in Eighteenth Century America* (Philadelphia: University of Pennsylvania Press, 2004); Alison Gilbert Olson, *Making the Empire Work* (Cambridge: Harvard University Press, 1992); Jack M. Sosin, *English America and Imperial Inconstancy* (Lincoln: University of Nebraska Press, 1985); Alan Rogers, *Empire and Liberty: American Resistance to British Authority, 1755–1763* (Berkeley: University of California Press, 1974); Leonard Woods Labaree, *Royal Government in America: A Study of the British Colonial System Before 1783* (New Haven: Yale University Press, 1930); Michael G. Kammen, *A Rope of Sand: The Colonial Agents, British Politics, and the American Revolution* (Ithaca: Cornell University Press, 1968); and Jack R. Pole, *The Gift of Government: Political Responsibility from the English Restoration to American Independence* (Athens: University of Georgia Press, 1983).

Separate studies of the colonies as they evolved systems of governance in the Revolutionary era abound. Some of the best are Percy Scott Flippin, *The Royal Government in Virginia, 1624–1775* (New York: Columbia University Press, 1919); A.G. Roeber, *Faithful Magistrates and Republican Lawyers: Creators of Virginia Legal Culture* (Chapel Hill: University of North Carolina Press, 1981); Kenneth Colgrove, *New England Town Mandates* (Cambridge: John Wilson and Son, 1920); John Fairfield Sly, *Town Government in Massachusetts* (Cambridge: Harvard University Press, 1930); Richard L. Bushman, *King and People in Provincial Massachusetts* (Chapel Hill: University of North Carolina Press, 1985); John M. Williams, *New England's Crisis and Cultural Memory* (Cambridge: Cambridge University Press, 2004); Lois Green Carr and David William Jordan, *Maryland's Revolution of Government, 1689–1692* (Ithaca: Cornell University Press, 1974); George Edward Fisher, *Laboratory for Liberty: The South Carolina Legislative Committee System, 1719–1776* (Lexington: University Press of Kentucky, 1970); Clarence Ver Steeg, *Origins of a Southern Mosaic: Studies of Early Carolina and Georgia* (Athens: University of Georgia Press, 1975); Bruce C. Daniels (ed.), *Power and Status: Officeholding in Colonial America* (Middletown, CT: Wesleyan University Press, 1968); and Alfred F. Young, *The Democratic Republicans of New York, the Origins, 1763–1797* (Chapel Hill: University of North Carolina Press, 1967). In classes by themselves because of how well they articulate the issues of legislative growth and autonomy are Jack P. Greene, *The Quest for Power: The Lower Houses of Assembly in the Southern Royal Colonies, 1689–1776* (Chapel

Hill: University of North Carolina Press, 1963); and Alan Tully, *Forming American Politics: Ideals, Interests, and Institutions in Colonial New York and Pennsylvania* (Baltimore: Johns Hopkins University Press, 1994).

Specific books that study suffrage developments in the eighteenth-century colonies include John Phillip Reid, *The Concept of Representation in the Age of the American Revolution* (Chicago: University of Chicago Press, 1987); Albert E. McKinley, *The Suffrage Franchise in the Thirteen English Colonies in America* (Philadelphia: Ginn and Co., 1905); Hubert Phillips, *The Development of a Residential Qualification for Representation in Colonial Legislatures* (Cincinnati: The Abingdon Press, 1921); and Cortland F. Bishop, *History of Elections in the American Colonies* (New York: Columbia College, 1893).

Still the finest general study of the theories of governance and the defense of colonial prerogatives of self-governance is Clinton Rossiter, *Seedtime of the Republic: The Origin of the American Tradition of Political Liberty* (New York: Harcourt, Brace, 1953). See also, Isaac Kramnick, *Republicanism and Bourgeois Radicalism: Political Ideology in Late Eighteenth-Century England and America* (Ithaca: Cornell University Prss, 1990); Barry Alam Shain, *The Myth of Amrican Individualism: The Protestant Origins of American Political Thought* (Princeton: Princeton University Press, 1994); Thomas L. Pangle, *The Spirit of Modern Republicanism: The Moral Vision of the American Founders and the Philosophy of Locke* (Chicago: University of Chicago Press, 1988); Mark E. Kann, *A Republic of Men: The American Founders, Gendered Language, and Patriarchal Politics* (New York: New York University Press, 1997); Annabel Patterson, *Early Modern Liberalism* (Cambridge: Cambridge University Press, 1997); William R. Everdell, *The End of Kings: A History of Republics and Republicanism* (Chicago: University of Chicago Press, 2000); and Jerrilyn Green Marston, *Kings and Congress: The Transfer of Political Legitimacy, 1774–1776* (Princeton: Princeton University Press, 1987).

The issue of division and unity in the run up to the Revolutionary War may best be seen in the documents selected for Part VI of Volume II. There is some commentary on the Albany Plan of 1754 and on relations among the colonies in Harry M. Ward, *"Unite or Die": Intercolonial Relations, 1690–1763* (Port Washington, NY: Kennikat Press, 1971); and Robert C. Newbold, *The Albany Congress and the Plan of Union of 1754* (New York: Vantage Press, 1955). For further study of internal dissent on the eve of the Revolution, including the problems in North Carolina, see Gary B. Nash, *The Unknown American Revolution* (New York: Viking Press, 2005); and Elisha P. Douglass, *Rebels and Democrats* (Chapel Hill: University of North Carolina Press, 1955).

VOLUME 3

The most important primary source collection for this volume is Francis W. Thorpe, *American Charters, Constitutions, and Organic Laws, 1492–1908* (7 vols., Washington, DC: Government Printing Office, 1909). Thorpe printed all of the first state constitutions as well as the Articles of Confederation and the Ordinances of 1784 and 1787. Another useful collection of state and federal constitutions are in Peter Force (ed.), *American Archives* (4th and 5th Series, Washington, DC: Peter Force, 1837–1853).

The various volumes on the individual state's statutes, laws, legislative, and convention proceedings are indispensable to an understanding of how the states made their constitutions. See especially Nathaniel Bouton (ed.), *New Hampshire Provincial, Town, and State Papers* (21 vols., Concord, NH: George E. Jenks, 1867–1943); James H. Easterby (ed.), *The Journal of the South Carolina Common House of Assembly* (5 vols., Columbia: Historical

Commission of South Carolina, 1951); James Ballagh (ed.), *The Letters of Richard Henry Lee* (New York: Macmillan Co., 1911); W. A. Whitehead et al. (eds.), *Archives of the State of New Jersey* (33 vols., Newark, NJ: State Historical Society, 1850–1928); *Laws of the State of Delaware* (2 vols., New Castle, DE: Samuel and John Adams, 1797–1816); *Votes and Proceedings of the House of Representatives of the Province of Pennsylvania, 1682–1776* (6 vols., Philadelphia: B. Franklin, Printer, 1752–1776); H. M. Chapin (ed.), *Documentary History of Rhode Island* (2 vols., Providence, RI: Preston and Rounds, Co., 1876–1919); Gair M. Brumbaugh (ed.), *Maryland Records* (2 vols., Baltimore: Maryland Historical Society, 1915); Walter Clark (ed.), *The State Records of North Carolina*, Vol. XII, 1777–1778 (Winston, NC: J.C. Stewart, 1895); Allen D. Candler (ed.), *The Revolutionary Records of the State of Georgia*, Vol. I (Atlanta: The Franklin-Turner Co., 1908); Edmund. B. O'Callaghan (ed.), *The Documentary History of the State of New York*, Vol. IV (Albany, NY: Charles Van Benthupen, 1851); and *The Acts and Resolves, Public and Private of the Province of Massachusetts Bay, 1692–1780* (21 vols., Boston: Wright and Potter, 1869–1922).

For the best collections on the activities of the Continental Congress, including the debates over the Articles of Confederation, see Edmund Cody Burnett (ed.), *Letters of Members of the Continental Congress* (8 vols., Washington, DC: The Carnegie Institution of Washington, 1921–1936); Worthington Chauncey Ford (ed.), *Journals of the Continental Congress* (34 vols., Washington, DC; Government Printing Office, 1904–1937); and Paul H. Smith et al. (eds.), *Letters of Delegates to Congress, 1774–1789* (Washington, DC: Library of Congress, 1976–1990).

Criticism and support for the Congress and the Articles of Confederation may be found in Merrill Jensen (ed.), *Documentary History of the Ratification* (16 vols., esp. Vol. 1, Madison: University of Wisconsin Press, 1976). Of the numbers of commentators who discussed the problems of the Articles, and defended the Articles, some stand out. See L. H. Butterfield (ed.), *Letters of Benjamin Rush* (esp. Vol 1, Princeton: Princeton University Press, 1951); Mark DeWolfe Howe (ed.), *The Warren-Adams Letters* (Vol. 2, Boston: Massachusetts Historical Society, 1925); Gaillard P. Hunt (ed.), *The Writings of James Madison* (New York: G.P. Putnam Sons, 1910); Harold C. Syrett (ed.), *The Papers of Alexander Hamilton* (New York: Columbia University Press, 1961–1979); and Randolph G. Adams (ed.), *Selected Political Essays of James Wilson* (New York: Alfred Knopf, 1930).

There are a number of important secondary studies on the first state constitutions. The best include, Donald S. Lutz, *Popular Consent and Popular Control: Whig Political Theory in the Early State Constitutions* (Baton Rouge: Louisiana State University Press, 1980); Jackson Turner Main, *The Sovereign States, 1775–1783* (New York: Franklin Watts, 1973); Willi Paul Adams, *The First American Constitutions* (Chapel Hill: University of North Carolina Press, 1980); and Marc W. Kruman, *Between Authority and Liberty* (Chapel Hill: University of North Carolina Press, 1997).

Specific state studies are uneven in quality but a few have been most helpful in understanding the procedures of writing and ratifying those constitutions. Among them are, Chilton Williamson, *Vermont in Quandry: 1763–1825* (Montpelier: Vermont Historical Society, 1949); J. Paul Simon, *The Pennsylvania Constitution of 1776* (Philadelphia: University of Pennsylvania Press, 1956); Jere Daniell, *Experiment in Republicanism: New Hampshire* (Cambridge: Harvard University Press, 1970); Charles R. Erdman, *The New Jersey Constitution of 1776* (Princeton: Princeton University Press, 1940); Fletcher Green, *Constitutional Developments in the South Atlantic States* (Chapel Hill: University of North Carolina Press, 1940); Philip A. Crowl, *Maryland During and After the Revolution* (Baltimore: Johns Hopkins University Press, 1943); Griffith John McRee,

Life and Correspondence of James Iredell (New York: Peter Smith, 1949); Albert B. Sayre, *Constitutional History of Georgia* (Athens: University of Georgia Press, 1948); and Charles Z. Lincoln, *Constitutional History of New York* (esp. Vol. 3, Rochester, NY: The Lawyers Co., 1905).

The best general studies of the Continental Congress and the Articles of Confederation are: Merrill Jensen, *The Articles of Confederation* (Madison: University of Wisconsin Press, 1940); Merrill Jensen, *The New Nation: A History of the United States During the Confederation, 1781–1789* (Boston: Northeastern University Press, 1981); H. James Ferguson, *Party Politics in the Continental Congress* (New York: McGraw-Hill, 1974); Jack N. Rakove, *The Beginnings of National Politics* (New York: Alfred Knopf, 1979); Keith L. Dougherty, *Collective Action Under the Articles of Confederation* (New York: Cambridge University Press, 2001); and Robert W. Hoffert, *A Politics of Tension: The Articles of Confederation and American Political Ideas* (Boulder: University of Colorado Press, 1992). In a class by itself as a seminal reconstruction of the period building up to the federal union and the years before the Constitution of 1787 is Charles A. Kromkowski, *Recreating the American Republic: Rules of Apportionment, Constitutional Change, and American Political development* (New York: Cambridge University Press, 2002).

For changes in governance and governance developments during the Confederation period, subjects much neglected, see Jennings B. Sanders, *Evolution of the Executive Department of the Continental Congress* (Gloucester, MA: Peter Smith, 1971); Peter S. Onuf, *Statehood and Union: History of the Northwest Ordinances* (Bloomington: Indiana University Press, 1987); Frederick D. Williams (ed.), *The Northwest Ordinances: Essays on Its Formulation, Provisions and Legacy* (East Lansing: Michigan State University Press, 1989); and Rosemarie Zagarri, *The Politics of Size: Representation in the United States, 1776–1850* (Ithaca: Cornell University Press, 1987).

Index

Absence: councilor's, 348, 400, 419; governor's, 177, 412, 427, 474; officer's, 165, 400, 419; president's, 730. *See also* Vacancy

Abuse, 632–35; of employment contracts, 76; of land grant, 53; of person/goods, 144; of power, 419–23, 540, 542, 632–35

Accounting, 36

Act of Navigation, 285

Acts of Assembly, violating state constitution, 749–53

Acts of Congress, supplemental, 905–6

Acts of Parliament, 285, 369–70, 583, 600–601; altering Massachusetts Bay constitution, 603–4, 606; colonies against, 643–46; Congress listing, 647, 649; Jefferson on, 583, 585; New York legislature suspension by, 583; oaths of, 306, 308; remission of, 62

Adams, John, 556, 607–11, 638, 822, 863, 865; preamble of, 656–57

Addington, Isaac, 325

Adjournment, 321

Admiralty/Admiral's court, 226, 408, 522, 649

Adultery, 167

Adventurer(s), 39, 43, 44, 46, 49–55; land grants and, 74

Affirmation, 476; Quaker, as recognized, 360, 406, 819

Africa, 337, 352; trade with, 352, 409

Age, 107, 954; governor's, 261; officers', 228, 238; voting, 95, 728

Agent, 543–45; at Imperial Seat, 355–59

Agriculture, law and, 235–38

Aid, 274–75, 364, 581; during invasions, 274–75, 364; to jury, justice as, 192; during rebellion, 191

Albany, 162, 180

Albany Plan of Union, 615–28; considered/rejected, 621–28

Aldermen, 388, 391

Allegiance: dissolved, 726; to king, 183, 202, 206, 644, 726; oaths of supremacy and, 43, 47, 76, 306, 308, 326

Alliances/enemies, of Crown, Pennsylvania and, 254

Amendments: Articles of Confederation, 854–62, 941–43; state constitutional, 735–53, 742, 744–46

America. *See* United States

Americaments, 166

American Revolution, 938–41, 951

Ammunition, 63, 205; for Indians, 170

Andros, Edmund, 283, 286–87, 372

Animals, 149, 170, 172, 212, 265, 315

Anne (Queen), to Dudley, 331–39

Annexing: government to Crown, 542; objection to charter, 281, 285

Annual liberty, 103

Appeal(s), 128–29, 132, 430; cases having no, 227; charges for, 228; courts of, 442, 706–13; criminal case, 163, 166, 245, 251; Crown receiving, 163, 245, 251, 286, 328, 430

Appointment(s): by congress, 886; election v., 833–35; by governor, 233, 390, 467–70; of jurors, 443–44

Arbitrator, 165

Arms, 336, 351, 610–11; at elections, 502; for Protestants, 293; required, 232; right to bear, 198

Army, 933; payment of, 912; standing, 292–93, 833, 940

Arnold, Benedict, 153

Arrows, as seal, 111

Articles of Amendment, Massachusetts, 854–62

Articles of Confederation, 661, 662, 873–79; amendments to, 854–62, 941–43; Burke on, 865, 868–72; defects/alteration of, 923–31, 935–38; Dickinson's draft of, 866–68; Drayton on, 880–88; formation of, circumstances of, 951; land and, 889; ratification of, debated, 873, 879–96; Rush on, 951–53; voting and, 883. *See also* Confederation; National Government plan

Arts committee, 260

Assembly. *See* Acts of Assembly; County(ies); General Assembly; Grand Assembly

Assessors, 341–42, 942; oaths required by, 341

Assistants: to Company, 87; court of, 87, 101, 103, 135, 154, 227, 364; oath of, 315

Assizes, court of, 167, 229

Atheism, 200

Attorney(s), 82, 443, 801–2

Authority: abuse of, 542, 632–35; burgesses', 301; of General Assembly, 192–94, 457; governor's, 42, 72, 330–31, 340, 364, 375, 378–83, 433, 461–66, 534–35; granted to Bradford, 79–82; to grant free inhabitancy/citizenship, 392; of king/parliament, voided, 649–51; king's, 534–35, 606; land grant, governor's, 330; of legislature, 28, 299, 371, 376, 457, 537; of lords proprietors, 454; New York/Albany, 162; over Negro slaves, 232; of parliament, 590–92, 594–95; of Plymouth council, 70–72; state v. Congress/national, 863, 870, 871–72, 925; tax, of president-general, 367

Bacon, Francis, 6, 12–17, 28

Bacon's Rebellion, 28

Badge of office, staff as, 168

Bail, 166, 263; excessive, 293

Bailiff, wages of, 50

Balance of Power, 549–50, 551, 609, 665–66

Ballot(s): joint, 499, 500; for jurors, 443; secret, 371; voting by voice v., 788, 793–94

Baltimore, Lord, 115; land dispossession of, 117–18; petition against, 117–18; tyranny of, 344–47

Bankruptcy, 338

Barbados, ships from, 204

Barclay, Robert, 196

Battle of Lexington, 652

Beans, voting with, 103

Bear-baiting, 265

Beaver skins, as Crown payment, 163, 250, 387

Beccaria of Milan, on law, 883

Benchers of guild hall, 310, 312

Bennett, Richard, 63, 64

Berkeley, William, 63–64

Bernard, Francis, 413–18

Bill of Rights, 664, 700–701; England's, 292–96; violations of state constitution and, 749–53

Bills: into laws, 261, 425, 740–41; posting of, 266, 752

Birth records, 58, 230, 263

Bishop of London, 256, 433

Bland, Richard, 554–55, 569–80

Body politick, 70, 87, 136

The Book of Common Prayer: use of, 63, 106, 350–51

Books, forbidden, 338

Boston: British military in, 652; tea rebellion, 584, 601

Boundary(ies): of Carolinas, 214, 775–76; disputes over state, 899–904; of Georgia, 515–16; of Maryland, 110; of Massachusetts Bay, 323–24; of New England, 73, 139; of New Hampshire, 461; of New Plymouth, 79; of new states, 921; of New York, 163, 902–3; towns', 173; of Virginia territory, 52–53

Bowdoin, James, 935–38

Bradford, William, 79–82

Bribery, 197, 262, 263, 369, 543

Bristol, 38

Britain. *See* England; Great Britain

British: alliance of Indians with, 337; trade regulation by, 601

British military: in Boston, 652; soldiers, sent to United States, 367

British Parliament. *See* Parliament

Bull, 172, 265

Burgess(es), 27; authority of, 301; church and, 131, 132; electing magistrates, 131; elections and, 64, 131, 132, 302, 303; house of, 455; payment to, 320; taxes/salary and, 301; voting and, 28, 132

Burke, Thomas, on Articles of Confederation, 865, 868–72

Burleigh, Lord, 20

Bushmen, Richard L., 300

Byrd, William, 531–32

Calvert, Caecilius. *See* Baltimore, Lord

Calvert family, 109, 114. *See also* Baltimore, Lord

Cape Comfort, 44

Cape Merchant, 36; magazine and, 57, 58

Cape Romania, 205

Capital offense(s), 167, 199, 263, 264; Negroes/Indians' murder as, 338

Capitol building, 705

Captives, 113, 372

Carolinas, 203–39; boundaries of, 214, 775–76; chief officers of, 222; land grants of, 206, 209, 210; lords proprietors of, 204, 216, 237, 419–23; as non-democratic, 222; as parliament, 225–26; temporary laws of, 233–35

Case(s): charges for, 263; of criminal appeal, 163, 166, 245, 251; hearing, 100; jury for all, 192; with no appeal, 227; partiality in, 105; pleading own, 192, 201, 229, 262. *See also* Pleading(s)

Casting, for land, 208

Casting voice, 128

Catholic. *See* Roman Catholic(s)

Cattle, 50, 58, 63, 95–96; straying, 186–87, 210; value/rating of, 172

Cazique, 223, 225

Cecill, William, 20

Certificates, ministers', 404, 433

Chamberlain's court, 227

Charges/fees: for all cases, 263; for appeals, 228; exorbitant, 358, 629–30; plantation, for lords proprietors, 237; for trials, 165

Charles (King), 65–66; Massachusetts Bay charter issued by, 82–93

Charles City, 50

Charles II (King), 106–7, 134–40, 151–60, 162–65; Carolinas

charter of, 214–22; to James, Duke of York, 174–80; to Penn, 249–56; religious freedom granted by, 152–53; renaming Narragansett country, 160; restraining New Hampshire, 244

Charter(s), 147; annexing, 281, 285; Carolinas, 214–22; King James I, greeting of, 37, 43; lost, 273; Massachusetts Bay, 82–93, 603–4; Penn restoring, 480; to Raleigh, 21–24; sacred, 371; as state constitutions, 663, 754. *See also specific states*

Charter of Civil Incorporation and Government, 147

Charter of Liberties (Privileges), 467, 479–83

Chicohomini (Indians), 55–56

Children, 96, 264

Chimneys, 315

Christianity: churches of, 180; conversion of Indians to, 43, 56, 152; dissenters from, 231; Indians and, 28, 34, 37; servants and, 211

Christian People, territory and, 21

Christian Prince, territory and, 21, 22

Church(es), 20, 180, 350–51, 437; burgesses and, 131, 132; construction of, by parliament, 231; freemen and, 103, 105; governor and, 126; intolerance of, 598–99; law and, 98; Roman Catholics and, 344; slaves in, 232

Church of England, 20

Church wardens, heading elections, 436

Citizen. *See* Inhabitant(s)

Citizenship. *See* Inhabitancy

Clayborne, William, 63, 64

Clergymen, 696

Clerk(s), 36, 799–801; jurors and, 443–44

Clinton, George, 906–8

Coast of New England, 92–93

Cockfights, 265

Coin, 30; alloy regulation of, 871, 876, 934

Colony(ies), 153; allegiance to George III of, 644; Congress

delegates of, 638–43, 755, 808, 820, 866, 906–7, 921–22; defense of, 185; first, 28; government of, Congress and, 654–56; governor of, choosing own, 125; against Great Britain, 643–46; as Hundreds, 52, 57; inhabitants of, holding office, 306; laws of, Crown voiding, 252, 315, 340; oppressed, 602; petition of united, 651–52; position of, as unique, 593; in rebellion, 649–51; reputation of, 600; rights of, 569–80, 589–95; seal of, Crown's v., 308; as slaves, 592; territories' separation from, 497; travel within, 59, 160, 189; trials of, in Britain, 593; union of, 67–68, 107–8, 141, 271, 274; waging war beyond, 220, 338. *See also* New England; Plantation(s); State(s)

Commerce, 882, 928; between states, 947

Commission(s): to alter constitution, 606; from Crown, as illegal, 651

Committee(s): on constitution as inviolate, 746; four, in Pennsylvania council, 259–60; Mecklenburg, 649–51; of South Carolina, 596–600; for state constitutional amendments, 735–53; of the States, 877

Commodities, custom/duty of, 402

Common pleas, court of, 393

Common Seal, Plymouth council and, 71

Commons House. *See* Lower House

Company, governor and, 87, 88

Company of Adventurers for Virginia, 44, 46; instructions of, on land grants, 49–55

Company's Land, 50

Confederation: of New England, 273–81; as United States of America, 874

Confederation era: court of appeals in, 706–13; lower house in, 664, 699; voting in, 728

Confession, 34–35

Conflict of interest. *See* Partiality

Congress (Continental), 637, 718, 886, 904–5, 912–13, 945–46; acts of parliament listed by, 647, 649; acts of, supplemental, 905–6; Burke on power of, 871–72; Council of State/General Council forming, 866–67, 868; debt of, 917, 927; defects of, 923–31; defense and, 932; delegates in, 638–43, 755, 808, 820, 866, 906–7, 921–22; executive departments of, 904–5; levying of duty by, 908–11; money and, 934, 951, 954; national government plan of, 656; power of, 863, 870, 871–72, 925; precious metals, owning of, 926, 931; provincial government and, 654–56; resolution/declaration of rights by, 646–49; revenue system of, 926, 930, 942; state under-representation in, 921–22; tax levied by, 910, 926, 930; trade, regulating, 925–26, 928, 933, 941. *See also* Union; United American Colonies

Connecticut, 125–42, 363–70, 663, 754–57; New Haven uniting with, 141; ratification of, 888–89

Constable(s), 165, 194, 243, 524; court of, 226; petty, 391; of towns, 168

Constitution. *See* State Constitution(s); *specific states*

Construction: of churches, by parliament, 231; highway, 97; of ports, 218; street, 214; water and, 312

Contempt of court, 104

Continental Congress. *See* Congress

Contracts: employment, 76; between servants, tenants, 57, 264

Convention(s): Essex constitutional, 824–37; Pennsylvania, 600–607; state constitutional, 719, 724–26, 788–89, 825–37

Conversion, to Christianity, of Indians, 43, 56, 152

Convict, voting of, 303
Copley, Lionel, 343; instructions to, 347–53
Copper mines, 30
Corn: planting, 56; voting with, 103
Cornwall county, 181
Coronation, 296
Corporation: plantation as, 513–14; term of, 520
Correspondence, 432
Corruption, 542, 632–35; proprietors', 419–23, 540. *See also* Abuse
Council(s), 46, 517, 736; authority of Plymouth, 72; in England, 30, 33, 61; of four, 20, 24; freemen in, 197; general, 866–67, 868; Georgia's common, 517–18; governor and, 60, 93–94, 191, 197; governor appointing members of, 461; grievances, governor and, 214; Indians' treatment by, 28, 34, 37; Massachusetts Bay, 93–94; members, suspension of, 348; New Plymouth, forty-member, 79; Pennsylvania's, 258–62; planters on, 94; at Plymouth, forty-member, 70, 71; quorum in, 259, 260, 266, 348, 353, 400, 478; rotation of members, 498, 736; supporting Governor, creation of, 60, 93–94, 191, 197; vacancy in, 235, 287; in Virginia, 29–30, 33, 34, 61. *See also* Council of Estate; Council of State
Council of Estate, 50, 57
Council of State, 60, 120, 866–67, 868
Councilor(s), 45; absence/suspension of, 348, 400, 419; Lord Chancellor of England and, 39; of Massachusetts Bay, 84–85, 325
County(ies): assemblies of, 207; of Carolinas, 216, 222; defense of, 208; Narragansett, 160; of New York, 180–81, 376, 793; representatives of, 376, 793. *See also* Court(s)
Court(s), 46, 88, 169, 171, 226, 292, 306, 443; adjournment of,

321; admiralty, 226, 408, 522, 649; of appeals, 442, 706–13; of assistants, 87, 101, 103, 135, 154, 227, 315, 364; of assizes, 167, 229; chamberlain's, 227; of common pleas, 393; county, 440–48; days, 51, 52, 59, 65, 119–20, 261, 264, 805; of elections, 126; of England, 521; four quarter, 54, 100, 226–27, 228; magistrate's, 133, 161; of magistrates, 133, 161; open to public, 192; palatine's, 224, 228; standing, 268; steward's, 226; treasurer's, 226. *See also* General court; High Court of Chancery; Pleading(s); Supreme court
Court days, 51, 52, 59, 65, 119–20, 261, 264, 805
Court of Commissioners for Ecclesiastical Causes, 292
Covenant, 46, 130; of Puritans, 67
Cradocke, Mathew, 87
Credit, 446, 878, 926–27, 932
Crown, 334, 547–48; Agent of, 355–59; appeals received by, 163, 245, 251, 286, 328, 430; arms required by, 232; attorneys appointed by, 82; beaver skins to, 163, 250, 387; commissions from, as illegal, 651; Company designated by, 87, 88; defense and, 407; dependence on, value of, 547–48, 551; duty/subsidy paid to, 31, 38–39, 41, 74; enemies/alliances of, 254; fairs and, 315, 392; forbidding printing/books, 338; government annexed to, 542; grievances and, 245, 584; import/export regulated by, 81, 218, 230, 253–54, 402, 408; market days and, 393; Maryland seized by, 343–47; ministers of, oppression and, 606–7; money/aid from, 581; name of, on all laws, 332, 411; negative voice of, 340, 586–87; oaths of, replaced, 306, 308; offices/ministers approved by, 404; parliament v., 293, 591, 606; petition to, from United American Colonies, 651–52; precious metals, mines and, 30,

40, 73, 140, 159, 215; salaries and, 405; seal of, colony's v., 308; Speaker/House of Representatives negated by, 340; successors of, 295; tax and, 41, 74; travel restricted by, 59, 160, 189; voiding colony laws, 252, 315, 340; war and, 220, 338. *See also* Allegiance; British
Cryer, 707
Culpepper, Thomas, 65–66
Curtis, Edmon, 63, 64
Custom/duty, 31, 38–39, 41, 74; commodities', 402; levied by Congress, 908–11, 928; punishment for not paying, 411
Cutt, John, 244

Davenport, John, 129
Death: of governor, 474; records of, 230, 263
Debate: constitutional, 799–802, 822–37; ratification, of Articles of Confederation, 873, 879–96; separation of power, 863, 865, 869–71, 932
Debt(s), 446–47; of Congress, 917, 927; discharge of, 446; neighbors', 165
Declaration of Independence, 637, 657–59
Declaration of Rights: by Congress, 646–49; of Maryland, 758–61; North Carolina's, 771, 774–76; of Pennsylvania, 726–28; Vermont's, 805–6, 814–16
Deed, 179, 750
Defense, 185, 186, 198, 199, 208, 336; Congress and, 932; Crown informed of, 407
Delaware, 162–81, 494–510; 1776 new constitution of, 719–23; George III's constitution of, 502–10
The Delaware State, naming of, 498
Delegate(s): election of, 755, 820, 943; freemen as, 123; pay of, 906–7; sent to Congress, 638–43, 755, 808, 820, 866, 906–7, 921–22
Democracy, 145, 150, 222

Deputy(ies), 541; age and, 228; election of, by freemen, 102; freeholders as, 184; freemen as, 123, 127; meeting place of, 541; number of, 541; oaths and, 47; in separate house from magistrate, 161; treasurer and, 39
Despotism, 925
Dickinson, John, 555, 589–96; Articles draft of, 866–68
Discharge, of debt, 446
A Discourse on Western Planting (Hakluyt), 6–9
Discovery of Guiana (Raleigh), 9–11
Dishonor, 77
Dispossession, land, 117–18, 134, 455–56, 890, 893, 894–96
Dispute(s), 165; boundary, 899–904; Isle of Kent, 118; land, 118, 241, 247, 397–99, 756, 803–4, 890, 893, 894–96
Dissent, 780; against amendments, 742, 744–46; from Christianity, 231; meeting minutes excluding, 738; from War, of states, 868
Dissolution, of General Assembly, 322, 418, 587, 602
Distraction (mental illness), 170
Divorce, 101, 750
Dogma, Laurens on, 598–600
Dongan, Thomas, George II to, 385–94
Drayton, William H., 880–88
Drunkenness, 56
Duchess's county, 180
Dudley, Joseph, 323; Queen Anne's instructions to, 331–39
Due course of law, 178
Duke's county, 181
Dunkers/Menonists, 761
Dutch Fleet, 250
Duty: neglecting, 243. See also Custom/duty

Easter, general court on, 88
East Jersey, West Jersey and, 182
Education, 52, 96; of children, trade/skills, 264; useful sciences in, 267. See also School(s)
Election(s), 101–2, 317, 391; annual, Adams on, 610; appointment v., 833–35; arms at place of, 502; bribery in, 197, 262,

263, 369; of burgesses, 64, 302, 303; burgesses in, 131, 132; church wardens and, 436; of Company officers, 88; of constables, 168; of councilor, 39; court of, 126; of delegates to Congress, 755, 820, 943; of deputy, 102; disorderly, 491; freemen in, 109, 363–64, 365; of General Assembly, 435–40; of governor, 143, 363–64, 365, 754; inheritance v., 280, 393–94; by papers, 148, 485; poll copies of, 304; of president, 784; of town officers, 341–42, 373–75
Elizabeth, Queen: letters patent issued by, 18–24; protection of, 19, 21; to Raleigh, 21–24; Raleigh's praise of, 12
Employment, 12–13; of children, 96; contracts, 76; in New World, 6–8, 9; of poor/indigent, 338
Endecott, John, governor selection of, 93–94
Enemies/alliances, of Crown, Pennsylvania and, 254
England, 929; agent residing in, 543–45; Bill of Rights of, 292–96; Church of, 20; cities of, in Virginia, 38; constitution of, 571, 572, 573; contracts made in, 57; council of Virginia in, 30, 61; general courts, courts of, 521; Glorious Revolution of, 271, 292, 371, 375; goods transported from, 20, 22, 24, 73; king's Council in, 33; land and, 179; Lord Chancellor of, 39; offenders sent to, 245; protection of, 19, 21, 137, 158; tax and, 41, 74; tobacco shipped to, 58; trials in, 245, 593; voyages from, 74, 158, 204. See also Crown; Great Britain
English, pleadings in, 263
Enlisting, of youth from abroad, 366
Entertainment, 265; house of, 482; of servants/slaves, 445
Escape, prisoners', 276, 447
Essay on the Constitutional Power of Great Britain (Dickinson), 589–96

An Essay on the Government of the Colonies (Kennedy), 532, 545–53
An Essay upon the government of the English Plantations (Anonymous), 531, 532–45
Essex County, constitutional convention of, 824–37
Estate(s), 33; of capital offenders, 264; of freeholders, 304, 401, 448; governor's, 50, 538; inheritance of, 223–24, 255, 482, 918; of jurors, 338; rating of, 172
Evidence, 171
Excess of apparel, 56
Excommunication, 59
Execution, of Raleigh, 5
Executive department: of Congress, 904–5
Exeter, 38, 240
Expeditions, Raleigh's, 5, 9–12
Export. See Import/export

Fairs: Crown disallowing, 315; Crown regulating, 392
False witness, 167, 202
Family, government and, 550
Farmers, merchants v., 758
Fear, 608
Feast days, religious, 390; excommunication on, 59; payments made on, 51, 52, 65
Feast of St. Michael the Archangel: appointing of mayor/sheriff, 390; excommunication on day of, 59; rent paid on day of, 51, 52
Federal constitution. See Articles of Confederation
Federal government. See Congress; Government
Fees. See Charges/fees
Felony, stealing as, 59
Feme covert, 179
Fifth part/fourth part (payment): for precious metals, 30, 40, 73, 140, 159, 215
Fines, 95–96, 165; birth/death record-keeping, 230; for neglect of duty, 243; tobacco as payment for, 302, 317; for town-meeting misbehavior, 95; voting, 373, 526–27

Fire, 146
Fish, 311
Fishing: on New England coast, 92–93; rights, 81, 85, 92–93, 104
Flesh. *See* Meat
Fletcher, Benjamin, 375; William, Mary to, 378–83
Forfeiture: of animals, 212; of land, 202, 212, 890, 893
Fortification, of ports, 337
Fowling, 104, 269
Franklin, Benjamin, 734, 752
Frank Pledge, 115
Free citizen, 392
Freedom: from oaths, 63; of press, 914; to print, 732; of speech, 128, 293, 914. *See also* Liberties Common; Religion
Freeholder(s), 191; as deputies/representatives, 184; estates of, 304, 401, 448; in general assemblies, 454, 716; on jury, 228, 294; lawmaking of, 112; oath of, 318–19, 384; as voters, 27, 64, 177, 304, 318–19, 348–49, 448
Freemen, 67, 68, 197; allegiance to king of, 183; church and, 103, 105; in council, land and, 197; as Deputy/Delegate, 123, 127; election of deputy by, 102; election of governor by, 363–64, 365; housing soldiers by, 179; land grants of, freewomen and, 210; in legislature, 95, 109, 116, 123, 738–39; Negro slaves of, 232; non-, 95, 99; voting of, 95, 177
Free rent. *See* Rent
French, 203, 432; killing Indians, 368; ships taken by, 408
French Huguenot, 203
French, John, 504
Fugitives, 18

Gambling. *See* Gaming; Vice
Games, 265
Gaming (gambling), 56. *See also* Vice
General Assembly, 88, 136, 184, 192–94, 320, 498–99, 698; au-

thority of, 192–94, 457; county, 207; dissolution of, 322, 418, 587, 602; elections of members to, 435–40; freeholders in, 454, 716; governor and, 184, 191, 195–96, 424–30, 461; Maryland's, 116; of New Jersey, 184, 192–94, 715–16, 717, 718; New York's, 375–78; quorum in, 259, 260, 266, 478; Rhode Island's, 154, 155, 156, 161; time limit of, 395–96. *See also* Grand Assembly; Legislature
General court, 104; covenant and, 46, 67; England's courts compared to, 521; Georgia's, 521–22, 523; Virginia's, 306; yearly/Easter meeting of, 88
George II (King), 353–55, 385–94, 502–10; Delaware constitution ratified by, 502–10; Georgia charter of, 511–21
George III (King), 715; colonial allegiance to, 644; Delaware constitution of, 502–10; land of, ratification by states and, 890, 893, 894–96
Georgia, 511–27; boundaries of, 515–16; constitution of, 781–87; as corporation, 513–14
Gilbert, Humphrey: in letters patent, 18–21; territory of, 19
Glorious Revolution, 271, 292; New York and, 375; Rhode Island and, 371
Goats/swine, 149
God: denying, 167; freedom of religion and, 200; government and, 256, 546–47; Indians and, 110; in oaths of constitutions, 729, 807, 811; Penn on law and, 256; presence of, 97–98, 145; public worship of, 231, 696; word of, 99, 141, 142. *See also* Christianity; Church(es); Religion; Scripture
Gold. *See* Precious metals
Goods: abuse of, 144; from piracy, 405; sale of, 32, 42, 57, 58; transport out of England of, 20, 22, 24, 73
Governance. *See* Government

Government, 225–26, 654–56; absolute, Massachusetts Bay as, 93–95; Adams on, 607–11; annexed to Crown, 542; Bacon on, 13; body of, number of people in, 832; Crown and, 542; democratic, 145, 150, 222; in family, 550; God and, 256, 546–47; King James II abdicating, 295; mayor/council, New Castle's, 494; ministers in, 799; mixed monarchy, 545; New Hampshire without, 458–60; Penn on, 256–58; proprietary, 467, 511; provincial, Congress advising, 654–56; religion and, 59, 99, 141, 142, 195, 257, 433, 950; republican, 608, 826, 937, 948–50, 953; Roman, 666; seats of, 704; state v. national, 863, 870, 871–72, 925; temporary, 916–21
Government by magistracy, 50
Governor, 93–94, 542–43, 782, 906–8; absence of, 177, 412, 427, 474; abuse of power by, 542; age of, 261; appointing council members, 461; appointments by, 233, 390, 467–70; approval of bills and, 740–41; authority of, 42, 72, 330–31, 340, 364, 375, 378–83, 433, 461–66, 534–35; church and, 126; colony choosing own, 125; company and, 87, 88; council supporting, 60, 93–94, 197; Culpepper as, 65–66; death of, 474; drunkenness punishment for, 56; election of, 363–64, 365, 666, 754; estates/land of, 50, 538; General Assembly and, 184, 191, 195–96, 424–30, 461; grievances, council and, 214; invasion of New York's, into New Jersey, 284; king and, 534–35; land grants by, 330; lawmaking of, 88; legislature v., 28, 371, 418, 419–23, 457, 458, 467; martial law and, 42; Maryland's constitution and, 765; of Massachusetts Bay, 87, 93–94; nominating, 126, 363–64; oaths

and, 89, 128; palatine appointing, 233; position of, as reward, 538; President, replacing, 741; property of, 835; Rhode Island electing own, 143; as Roman Catholic, 344; salary of, 65, 301, 373–74; solicitation for, 196; term of, 65, 196

Governor's House, 51

Grand Assembly, 62

Great and General Courts of the Council, 46

Great Britain: colonies against, 643–46, 651–52; constitution of, 589–95, 604–5; merchandise of, 645; North Carolina and, 653; oppression of, colonial response to, 602; regulating/restricting trade, 601; soldiers of, 367; trials in, 245, 593

Green, Jonas, 362

Greeting, of King James, 37, 43

Grievance(s): Crown and, 245, 584; governor/council and, 214; Maryland's, Baltimore and, 343–47

Ground, for housing, 214

Guild hall, 310

Guns. See Ammunition

Habeas corpus, 712

Hakluyt, Richard, 5, 6–9, 28

Hamilton, Alexander, 923–31

Hearing, 100

Hemp, 57

Henrico, 50–51

Hereditaments/tenements, 32–33

High Constable, 165

High Court of Chancery, 707–8, 709, 710–11

Highway, 97, 149

Hoc Ithacus velit, 278

Honors, 113, 220

Hopkins, Stephen, 618–20; Philolethes' answer to, 624–28

House(s), 825, 932; of Burgesses, 455; deputy/magistrate, 133, 161; of entertainment, 482; governor's, 51; lower/upper, 121, 143, 161, 361, 363, 364–65, 737; separate, 161; single, 664, 724, 728; Spiritual,

Temporal, 292, 293, 294, 295; work-, prisons as, 263, 810

House of Representatives, 394–95, 466; Crown negating, 340; quorum in, 836–37

Housing: grounds allotted to, 214; of soldiers, by freemen, 179

Howell, David, 908–12, 913–16; Congress and, 912–13

Hue/cries, 168

Hundreds, colonies as, 52, 57

Hunting (fowling), 104, 269

Husband, Herman: on lawyers/excessive fees, 629–30

Idleness, 56, 446

Immigrant, 308

Imparlance, 302

Impeachment, 586

Imperial Seat, agent of, 355–59

Import/export: ceasing of, 601, 603; Crown and, 81, 210, 218, 230, 253–54, 402, 408; into other countries, as forbidden, 253; of salt, 309; of slaves/servants, 309. See also Transport

Imprisonment, 100, 122, 192, 263, 810; bail and, 166, 263, 293; bailiff and, 50; of poor, 446; of Protestants, by Roman Catholics, 346

In capite, 39

Indenture, 54

Independence. See Declaration of Independence

Indian(s), 13, 21, 28, 34, 37, 55, 273, 368; ammunition for, 170; British alliance of, 337; Chicohomini, 55–56; conversion of, 43, 56, 152; French killing, 368; God and, 110; invasion by, 245; killing, 338; land for, 21, 237; land purchase from, 404, 916; Maryland's invasion by, Jesuits and, 346; Narragansett, 152; in office, disallowed, 305; property rights of, 920; as slaves, 234, 237; stealing from, 59; trade with, 58, 217; university for, 52; war, in South Carolina, 420

Indian corn. See Corn

Indictments, language of, 501

Inhabitancy, 42, 46, 306, 716

Inhabitant(s): illegal Virginia, 55; as king's subjects, 185, 206; New England and, 74; new, rules for, 58, 185, 243; of North Carolina, abused, 632–35; number of, land parcels and, 236; offices held by, 306; Protestant, 242; against public officers, 630–31; of states in other states, 905; unauthorized new, 96

Inheritance: estate, 223–24, 255, 482, 918; political, 280, 393–94; wills and, 263

Inns, 445, 481

An Inquiry into the Rights of the British Colonies (Bland), 569–80

Interpretation, letters patent, 49

Invasion, 245, 274–75, 364; of Maryland, 346; of New Jersey, by New York governor, 284

Isle of Kent: dispute over, 118; New Hampshire, 247

James (King), 68–78; greeting of, 37, 43; Raleigh and, 5, 11–12

James City, 59, 302

James, Duke of York, 162, 174–80; Protestants and, 292; union attempts of, 271. See also James II, King

James II (King): abdicating government, 295; Protestants and, 292, 293; violations of, 293

Jamestown, 50

Jay, John, 799–802

Jealousy, 924, 925, 931

Jefferson, Thomas, 555, 580–89, 637

Jehovah, 141

Jencks, Joseph, 373

Jesuit, conducting invasion of Maryland, 346

Jew, as dissenter of Christianity, 231

Johnson, Samuel, 771

John the Baptist, 279; feast day of, 65

Judge(s), 118–19, 664; divorce, 750; partiality of, 105; salary of, 552

Judicial laws of Moses, 98

Juror(s): appointment of, 443–44; estates required of, 338

Jury: freeholders on, 228, 294; freemen on, 95; for land disputes, 241; majority verdict of, 229; trial by, 178, 192, 242, 731; twelve on, 178; of Virginia, 34

Justice(s) (position), 194; absence/payment of, 165; jurors and, 192, 443–44

Justice of the peace, 439

Kennedy, Archibald, 532, 545–53

King, 540, 590; allegiance to, 183, 202, 206, 644, 726; authority of, 534–35, 606; authority of, as null/void, 649–51, 726; land and, 588, 890, 893, 894–96; natural subjects of, 185, 206; officer of, murdered, 344; unaware of plantations' condition, 538. *See also specific kings/queens*

King and People in Provincial Massachusetts (Bushmen), 300

King Charles. *See* Charles (King)

King James. *See* James (King)

Kings Bench, 521

King's Council of Virginia, 33

King's county, 181, 793

King's Province, Narragansett renamed as, 160

Lading, 230, 253–54

Land, 50, 179, 183, 188, 533, 540, 899–904; Articles and, 889; for Capitol building, 705; casting lots for, 208; deeds of, 179, 750; dispossession of, 117–18, 134, 455–56, 890, 893, 894–96; disputes, 118, 241, 247, 397–99, 756, 803–4, 890, 893, 894–96; forfeiture of, 202, 212, 890, 893; freemen and, right to be in council, 197, 210; for Indians, 21, 237; Indians', purchase of, 404, 916; jury and, 228; king and, 588, 890, 893, 894–96; neglect of, 129; for new planters, 187, 205; oaths and, 526; parcels, in Carolinas, 235–38; parliament membership and,

229; possession of, 202, 212; proprietorship of, 186, 188–89, 190, 222–24; as ratification obstacle, 890, 893, 894–96; right to purchase/take, 87, 588; sale of, 219, 314; for servants/slaves, 187–88, 211, 212; surveys of, 431; treason and, 202; unappropriated, 903; voting and, 190, 316, 448; of widow, 179; women and, 210, 224, 263. *See also* Estate(s)

Land grants, 32–33, 49–55, 53–54, 63, 146, 238, 519, 803–4; abuse of, 53; adventurers and, 74; Carolinas', 206, 209, 210; councilors of Massachusetts Bay, 84–85; of freemen/freewoman, 210; of Georgia's common council, 518; governor's authority to make, 330; Maryland, by Baltimore, Lord, 115; Massachusetts Bay, 83–85; New York, 387–88; tenants and, 50, 57, 264, 316, 540

Landgrave, as proprietor, 223, 225, 237

Language: of indictments, 501; of pleadings, 263

Laurens, Henry, 555–56, 596–600

Law(s), 883; agrarian, Carolinas', 235–38; capital, 167, 199, 263, 264; church and, 98; Crown's name on all posted, 332, 411; Crown's voiding of colony, 252, 315, 340; due course of, 178; God and, 256, 546–47; governor/company creating, 88; intermixing of, 425; limited time of, 333; Lower house creating, 699; multiplicity/mutability of, 202, 230, 949; of nature, 588; passing bills into, 261, 425, 740–41; of Penn, 256–62; proposing, in parliament system, 239; publication of, 313, 361–62; reading of, 783; during rebellion, 649–51; religion and, 98; scripture on, 98, 142, 256, 257, 546–47; society and, 572; style of, 769; temporary, 233–35; Touching, 150–51;

without limit, 350, 403; word of God and, 99, 141, 142. *See also* Right(s)

Lawmaking, 401; of freeholders, 112; of freemen, 95, 123; of townships, 96, 148

Law Martial. *See* Martial law

Law of Christ, 99

Laws of Oleron, 149

Lawyers, fees of, 629–30

League of friendship, 274

Ledger book, 129

Lee, Richard Henry, 923–24, 953–55

Leet-man, 224

Leet-woman, 224

Legislature, 592, 664, 669, 747–48, 825, 932; authority of, 28, 299, 371, 376, 457, 537; Company as, Crown and, 87, 88; freemen in, 95, 109, 116, 123; governor v., 28, 371, 457, 458, 467; proprietary governor v., 418, 419–23; schools paid for/established by, 779, 786; single-house, 664, 724, 728; state, 663; suspended, 583; two-house, 121, 143, 161, 361, 363, 364–65, 737; under William/Mary, 376. *See also* House(s); Parliament

Letters, of delegates to governor, 906–8

Letters Patent, 18–24, 49

Levy(ies): Baltimore's exorbitant, 344, 358; Congress's power to, duty and, 908–11, 926, 928, 930; on sea vessels, 358

The Liberties (Anonymous), 98

Liberties Common, 104

Liberty, 103, 887; obedience and, 258

Liberty of conscience: in religion, 195, 536, 539; Roman Catholics excluded from, 327, 335, 406

License: of attorneys, 801–2; for inns/taverns, 445

Life, limb or banishment, 99

Livingston, Robert, 799–802

Locke, John, 203

London, 38; Bishop of, 256

Lord Baltimore. *See* Baltimore, Lord

Lord Chancellor of England, 39
Lord's Day, 59, 261, 264, 805
Lords Proprietors, 188–89, 190; of Carolinas, 204, 216, 237, 419–23; eldest, as palatine, 238; limiting authority of, 454
Lords Spiritual and Temporal, 292, 293, 294, 295
Lots, 48–49; constables chosen by, 524; land, 208
Lottery. *See* Lots
Lower House, 121, 143, 361, 363, 524–25; in Confederation period, 664, 699
Lying in bolts, 56
Lyttelton, William Henry, 448

Madison, James, 946–50
Magazine: Cape Merchant and, 36; sales of goods from, 57, 58
Magistrate, 100, 131, 134; court/house of, 133, 161; oath of governor and, 128
Maiming, 352
Majority rule, 949–50; aldermen/petty constables elected by, 390; clergymen elected by, 696; jury's verdict as, 229; magistrates and, 134
Manning, James, 945–46
Manufacturing, 583, 603; in United States only, 646
Map, 335
Mapscock, 52
Market/Market Day, 311, 509; Crown defining, 393; posting of statutes/ordinances in, 312, 313
Marriage, 59, 201, 433; record of, 58, 230; to Roman Catholic, 295
Marshal, in constable's court, 226
Martial law, 42, 139, 221
Martin's Hundred, 52
Mary, (Princess), 294
Maryland, 109–24, 343–62, 663–64, 758–70; 1776 constitution of, 758–70; Calvert family and, 109; Council of State and, 120; Declaration of Rights, 758–61; General Assembly in, 116; grievances of, 343–47; land dispute, ratification and, 894–96;

naming of, 111; ratification by, delayed, 894; taxes in, 114
Mason, George, 698–700
Mason, Roberd, 247
Massachusetts Bay, 67–108, 323–42, 822–62; acts of parliament altering, 603–4; articles of amendment of, 854–62; boundaries of, 323–24; constitution of, 603–4, 606, 663, 664, 837–62; convention for constitution of, 825–37; councilors of, 84–85, 325; governor of, 87, 93–95; King Charles issuing charter of, 82–93; land grant of, 83–85; offices of, 88; Puritan proprietors of, 67; rejection/postponement of constitution of, 823–37; William/Mary to, 323–31
Master of Chancery, 136
Maximus, Valerius, 887
May-games, 265
Mayor: appointed by governor, 390; of New Castle, 494
Mayor/council system, 494
Meat, 311
Mechanics of New York, 636
Mecklenburg, resolutions of, 649–51
Meeting Minutes, excluding dissent, 738
Menonists/Dunkers, 761
Mental illness. *See* Distraction
Merchandise, British, 645
Merchant(s): Cape, 36; farmers v., 758; Otis on, 567; planters v., 421
Military, 768, 933; British, 367, 652; nominated, 367. *See also* Standing Army
Miller, Nathan, 945–46
Mining: Congress paid from, 926; Crown's fifth part from, 30, 40, 73, 140; Crown's fourth part from, 215; profit division of, 202
Minister(s): certificates for, 404, 433; of Crown, oppression and, 606–7; first, of Great Britain, 651–52; government offices and, 799; poll copies to, 317; punishment of, 536; wages/salary of, 51, 536

Minority, 949
Mixed monarchy, 545
Money, 581; Congress and, 934, 951, 954; foreign, 428; illegal/private use of, 357; public, 349, 426, 749; valuing of, 402. *See also* Coin
Mulatto, 305, 306; voting of, 305
Mulberry trees, 56
Murder, of king's officer, 344
Mutiny, aid during, 191

Name(s)/Naming, 160; Crown's, on laws, 332, 411; of states, 111, 498; of United Colonies of New England, 274; voting by written, 525
Narragansett county, renamed, 160
Narragansett Indians, 152
National Bank, 927
National Government Plan, 656
Natives. *See* Indian(s); Inhabitant(s)
Naturalization, of immigrants, 308
Negative voice, 340, 366, 379, 586–87
Neglect: of duty, 243, 407; of land, 129
Negro: killing of, as capital offense, 338; as mulatto, 305; slaves, 232, 445
Neighbor, debt and, 165
The New Atlantis (Bacon), 6, 14–17
New Castle, 494, 498–502
New England: boundaries of, 73, 139; confederation of, 273–81; General Assembly of, 136; inhabitants of, illegal/legal, 74; population of, 80; taxes in, 74; trade on coast of, 92–93; trafficking in, 41, 75
New Hampshire, 43, 240–48, 458–66, 654; 1776 constitution of, 666–67; 1783 constitution of, 670–83; boundaries of, 461, 902
New Haven, uniting with Connecticut, 141
New Jersey, 182–202, 397–417; 1776 constitution of, 715–18; General Assembly in, 184,

192–94, 715–16, 717, 718;
invasion of, by governor of
New York, 284; land dispute in,
397–99; proprietors' oppression
of, 397–99; urging ratification
by, 892; without governor, 412
New Plymouth: boundaries of, 79;
council of forty at, 79
Newport, 154
New World, 6–8, 9
New York, 162–81, 375–96; 1777
constitution of, 789–99; boundaries of, 163, 902–3; as central
authority, Albany and, 162;
counties of, 180–81, 376, 793;
General Assembly of, 375–78;
Glorious Revolution and, 375;
governor letter from delegates
of, 906–8; governor of, invading New Jersey, 284; legislature
of, suspended, 583; mechanics
union of, 636
Nicholson, Francis, 418, 423–35
Nomination(s): governor, 126,
363–64; military officers', 367
Non compotes mentis, 731
North Carolina, 451–57, 663, 664,
771–80; Declaration of Rights/
constitution, 771, 774–80;
inhabitants of, abused, 632–35;
petition of inhabitants, 630–31;
resolutions during rebellion,
649–51; warning to, 653. See
also Carolinas
Northwest Ordinances, 916–21

Oath(s), 36, 37, 43, 47, 76, 89,
145, 341–42, 378, 449, 467–68;
affirmation as substitute for,
360, 406, 476, 819; alteration
of, 399; of assistants, 315; of
bencher, 312; in constitutions,
729, 752, 807, 811; of fidelity,
in Virginia courts, 708; freedom
from, 63; of freeholder, 318–19,
384; God in, 729, 807, 811;
governor and, 89, 128; of land
ownership, 526; Massachusetts
Bay, 94; against Pope/Catholic
church, 487–88; replacing
Crown's, 306, 308; retaking
of, 327; of secrecy, 785; in Virginia, 306, 307, 308, 312

Oath of Allegiance and Supremacy, 43, 47, 76, 306, 308, 326
Oath of obedience, 36, 37, 76; replaced, 306, 308
Obedience: blind, 278; liberty and,
258
Occupier, 53
Offenders: false pursuit of, 144;
sent to England, 245
Offense(s), 34–35, 56, 59, 104,
309, 311, 361, 445; capital,
167, 199, 263, 264, 338; pardon
of, 199, 251, 825
Office(s): badge of, 168; colony inhabitants holding, 306; Crown
approving, 404; excluded from
holding, 305, 799; ministers
barred from, 799; more than
one, 750, 866; residency and,
305; tenure of, 952
Officer(s), 610; absence of, 165,
400, 419; admiralty, 226,
408, 522, 649; age of, 228,
238; chief, of Carolinas, 222;
chosen by General Assembly,
194; Company, elections of,
88; military, 367, 768, 933;
murder of king's, 344; petition
against, 630–31; prison, 192;
prudential, of New Hampshire,
243; revenue, 911; suits against,
320; town election of, 341–42,
373–75; warrant, 290
Of Plantations (Bacon), 12–14
Oglethorpe, James, 511
Oppression: British, colonies' response to, 602; of Crown ministers, 606–7; of New Jersey by
proprietors, 397–99
Orange county, 180, 793
Ordinance(s): Northwest, 916–21;
publication of, 313, 361–62
Orphans, 446
Otis, James, 554, 556–69
Overseer, 173–74
Ox, 172

Palatine, 233; eldest lord proprietor
as, 238; naming governor, 233
Palatine's court, 224, 228
Paper(s): election by, 148, 485;
money, 951, 954; voting, 126,
363–64

Parcels, of Carolinas, 235–38
Pardon, 199, 251, 825
Parliament, 564–65; authority
of, 590–92, 594–95; Carolinas' government as, 225–26;
churches and, 231; commission
of, to alter state constitution,
606; Crown v., 293, 591, 606;
land and, Carolinas', 229; proposing laws in, 239; remission
of acts of, 62; representation in,
570–74, 576–78; two houses of,
294; voiding of king and, 649–
51; voting for British members
of, 570–71. See also Acts of
Parliament
Partiality, 105, 422, 423; voting
and, 242
Pawcawtuck River, 159
Payment: for absence from office,
165; army, 912; beaver skins
as, 163, 250, 387; to burgess,
for General Assembly, 320;
for court days, towns', 169; to
delegates in Congress, 906–7;
fifth part, 30, 40, 73, 140, 159;
fourth part, 215; for pleading,
229; to prison officers, 192; on
religious days, 51, 52, 65; in tobacco, 302, 317. See also Profit
Pennsylvania, 249–69, 467–93,
600–607, 724–54; 1776 constitution of, 726–34, 747–49;
constitutional amendments of,
735–53; council of, 258–62;
Crown enemies/alliances and,
254
Penn, William, 467–70, 479–83;
charter restoration of, 480; on
God, law, 256; on government,
256–58; King Charles II to,
249–56; laws framed by, 256–62
Perjury, 361
Perpetual Succession, 71
Peryn, Joseph, 214
Petition(s), 117–18, 293, 342; to
Crown, from United American
Colonies, 651–52; of poor,
against public officers, 630–31
Petty larceny, 311
Philolethes, on Albany Union
Plan/Hopkins, 624–28
Pillory, 446

Piracy, 334, 405

Plantation(s): Bacon on, 12–14; benefit of, 533; as corporation, 513–14; failure or, dishonor and, 77; king unaware of condition of, 538; lords proprietors' charges for, 237; New England's increasing, 80; owners, 52; proximity between, 52; start of, 233–35

Planter(s), 252; on council, 94; land for new, 187, 205; merchants v., 421; as parliament representatives, 570–74, 576–78; poor as, 511–12; potential, 534; prior, Gilbert's instructions on, 19; as slaves, 592; transport of, 74, 158, 204; trials for, in Britain, 593. *See also* Adventurer(s)

Planters of the City of London, 44; land grant instructions of, 49–55

Planting: corn, 56; householders' mandatory, 57

Pleading(s), 393; in English, 263; own cases, 192, 201, 229, 262; payment for, 229

Plymouth, 38, 67–108; Council at, 70–72; uniting with Massachusetts Bay, 67–68

Political system, of United States, Madison, J. on, 946–50

Poll/polling, 318; copy of, 304, 317

Poor, 630–31; employment of, 338, 511–12; imprisonment of, 446; maintenance of, 96–97; overseers of, 503; as planters, 511–12

Pope: marriage to, 295; oaths against, 487–88

Population, 80

Port(s): approved, 253, 314; construction of, 218; fortification of, 337

Port Royal, 204

Portsmouth, 154

Portugal, 946

Posting: of bills, 266, 752; of statutes/ordinances, 312, 313, 332, 411

Post office, 952

Power, 671, 831; abuse of, 542; executive, Essex convention on,

832–35; judicial, 750; national v. state, 863, 870, 871–72, 925; right v., 578, 588; separation of, 863, 865, 869–71, 932; supreme v. derived, 772; usurped, 583. *See also* Authority; Balance of Power

Preachers, for teaching, 256

Preamble, Adams', 656–57

Precedents, constitution and, 594–95

Precious metals: Congress owning, 926, 931; Crown's payment from, 30, 40, 73, 140, 159, 215; division of, in Jersey, 202; Jersey's division of, 202

Preface to the History of the World (Raleigh), 11–12

President, 615, 616, 917; absence of, 730; election of, 784; governor replacing, 741; of Virginia councils, 34

President-General: in Albany Plan of Union, 615, 616; tax authority of, 367

Price, Richard, 923, 938–41

Prince of Wales, pretended, 308

Printing, 732, 810; Crown forbidding, 338

Prison(s), 100; officers of, payment to, 192; poor in, 446; as workhouses, 263, 810

Prisoners, 122; bail of, 263; escape of, 276, 447

Privy Council, 61

Profit, mining, 202

Property: governor's, 835; Indians' rights of, 920

Property rights, 387, 397–99, 403–4, 814; of Congress, 931; Dickinson on, 589

Proprietor(s), 27, 200; corruption of, 419–23, 540; landgraves as, 223, 225, 237; New Jersey's, 397–99; Puritans as, 67; vote by proxy of, 199. *See also* Lords Proprietors

Proprietorship: land, 186, 188–89, 190, 222–24. *See also* Lords Proprietors

Protection: England's, 19, 21, 137, 158; Queen Elizabeth's, 19, 21; United States, by Portugal, 946

Protestant(s), 347; arms disallowed for, 293; dominated by Catholics, 344; inhabitants required to be, 242; on James' attempt to subvert, 292; Roman Catholics imprisoning, 346

Providence, 148, 150, 161

Province. *See* Colony(ies)

Provost/provost marshal, 227, 447

Proxy, vote by, 199

Prudential officers, 243

Public: court/trial open to, 192; prisons open to, 810; seal of, 379

Public affairs, record-keeping of, 182, 206

Publication: of laws, 313, 361–62; of polls, 304. *See also* Posting

Public office(s): absence from, 165; of Massachusetts Bay, 88; more than one, 201; religion, eligibility for, 195; staff as badge of, 168

Public service, mandatory, 104, 133

Punishment, 35, 133, 352, 446, 536; Council of Estate's discretion in, 57; custom/duty negligence, 411; lying in bolts, 56; pillory, 446; stocks as, 132, 373; whipping, 132, 170, 445. *See also* Pardon

Purchase, land, rights of, 87, 588

Puritans, as proprietors, 67

Pursuit, false, of offenders, 144

Quaker(s), 106, 318; affirmation of, 360, 406, 476, 819; Penn as, 249

Quarter court(s), 226–27, 228; land grants and, 54, 100

Queen Anne/Elizabeth. *See* Anne (Queen); Elizabeth (Queen)

Queen's Creek, 52

Quitrent, 63, 312, 403

Quorum, 353, 737, 836–37; in council/General Assembly, 259, 260, 266, 306, 348, 400, 478; increasing, 400

Quo warranto, 284

Raleigh, Walter: charter to, 21–24; expeditions of, 5, 9–12

Ratification: of Articles of Confederation, 873, 879–96; of Delaware constitution, 502–10; by General Assembly, 184; land as obstacle to, 890, 893, 894–96; need for, 892–94

Rating: of cattle/bull/ox, 172; of estates, 172; of foreign money, 428

Rebellion: aid during, 191; Bacon's, 28; Boston tea, 584, 601; colonies in state of, 649–51; inciting, 451–52. See also Resistance

Reconciliation, with England, provided for, 718

Record-keeping, 36, 129, 144, 263, 333, 402–3; birth/death, 230, 263; in Congress, 905; land grant, 54, 146, 519; of marriages/religious activities, 58, 230; of public affairs, 182, 206

Reinstatement, of oaths of allegiance/supremacy, 326

Religion, 51, 52, 58, 65, 103, 107, 198, 231, 277, 335; freedom of, 8, 125, 152–53, 195, 200, 480, 536; government and, 59, 99, 141, 142, 195, 257, 433, 950; laws and, 98; liberty of conscience in, 195, 536, 539; Protestant, Maryland's, 347; rent and, 51, 52; slaves and, 232. See also Christianity; Scripture

Religious days, 51, 52, 59, 65

Remission, of acts against Parliament, 62

Renaming, of Narragansett country, 160

Rent, 53, 185; paid on religious day, 51, 52; quit-, 63, 312, 403

Repair, highway, 97, 149

Repeal, 121, 202, 537; stamp act, 369–70

Reporter, 264

Representation, 648, 831–32; colonists' parliament, 570–74, 576–78; in Congress, states', 638–43, 755, 808, 820, 866, 906–7, 921–22; right of, 648; under-, 921–22

Representatives, 793; choosing, 376, 608; county, 376; freeholders as, 184

Republic/republican government, 608, 826, 937, 948–50, 953; Adams on, 608

Reputation, of colonists, 600

Resistance, 590

Resolution(s): of Congress, 646–49; of North Carolina 1775 committee, 649–51

Retirement, servants', 264

Revenue, of Congress system of, 926, 930, 942

Revenue officers, 911

Reward, governorship as, 538

Rhode Island, 143–61, 371–74; as democracy, 145, 150; electing own governor, 143; General Assembly of, 154, 155, 156, 161; Howell as delegate of, 913–16; ratification by, 889–90; state constitutions and, 663; travel to other colonies from, 160

Richard, Earle of Bellomont, 460

Richmond county, 181

Right(s), 559–69, 938; to bear arms, 198; of colonies, 569–80, 589–95; of dissent, 780; fishing, 81, 85, 92–93, 104; Indians' property, 920; inhabitants', in other states, 905; land acquisition, 87, 588; minority, 949; natural, 572, 573, 578, 580–81, 588, 726; power v., 578, 588; property, 387, 397–99, 403–4, 589, 814, 920; of representation, 648, 831–32; to wage war, 113, 220, 276. See also Bill of Rights; Declaration of Rights; Freedom; Liberties Common

Robbery, 77

Roman Catholic(s) (papists), 109; dominating Protestants, 344; excluded from liberty of conscience, 327, 335, 406; imprisoning Protestants, 346; marriage to, 295; oaths against, 487–87; voting of, denied, 343

Rome, 666

Rotation, 498, 719, 736, 937

Royal African Company of England, 337, 352

Royal Fishes, 85

Rule of Judicature, 119

Rush, Benjamin, 951–53

Sabbath days, 59, 261, 264, 805

Salary(ies): Crown and, 405; of governor, 65, 301, 373–74; of judges, 552; ministers', 51, 536; tobacco as, 536

Sale(s): of fish/meat, 311; of goods, 32, 42; land, 219, 314; of magazine goods, 57, 58; of tobacco, 58, 61–62; unauthorized, 90

Salem, 101

Salt, 309

Savages. See Indian(s)

School(s): legislature establishing, 779, 786; science in, 267

Science, in public schools/education, 267

Scripture, 130, 142; on law, 98, 142, 256, 257, 546–47; in oaths, 729

Scudder, Nathaniel, 892–94

Seacunck River, 159

Seal, 71, 146, 212, 500; arrows, 111; colony's, v. Crown's, 308; public, 379. See also Badge of office

Seamen, pressed into service, 407

Sea vessels, 80, 358. See also Laws of Oleron

Secrecy, oath of, 785

Secretary at War, 904

Secretary of Marine, 904–5

Seizure, 113, 645, 760; of Andros, 372; by piracy, recovered goods from, 405; of unauthorized ships, 75

Senate, quorum in, 836–37

Sentence, 35, 133

Separation: of houses, 161; of power, 863, 865, 869–71, 932; of territories, 497

Servants, 59; Christianity required of, 211; contracts of, 57, 264; entertainment/taverns and, 445; importing of, 309; land and, 187–88, 211, 212; retirement of, 264; running away of, 276; treatment of, inhumane, 338

Settlement. See Plantation(s)

Settlers. See Planter(s)

Sheriff, 119, 169, 383–84, 390, 767–68

Ships: from Barbados, 204; captains of, 407; safety of, 408; unauthorized, seizure of, 75

Shipwreck, prizes/spoils of, 22–23
Silk flax, 57
Silver. *See* Precious metals
Sixth commandment, 280
Slave(s): in church, 232; colonies
    as, 592; entertainment/taverns
    and, 445; importing of, 309;
    Indian, 234, 237; land for,
    187–88; Negro, 232, 445
Slavery, Jefferson on, 583
Smith, J. B., 891
Smith, John, 52
Smith, Thomas, 39
Smuggling, 309
Soccage, 159
Society: government and, 608;
    laws and, 572
Society of Smith's Hundred, 52
Soldiers, 179, 185, 198; British,
    sent to United States, 367;
    mandatory service as, 232
Solicitation, governor, 196
South Carolina, 418–50, 775–76;
    1776 constitution of, 684–89;
    1778 constitution of, 689–97;
    committee of, Laurens and,
    596–600; Georgia as separate
    from, 516; Indian war in, 420.
    See also Carolinas
South Carolina Committee, Lau-
    rens to, 596–600
Speaker of the House of Represen-
    tatives, 466; Crown negating,
    340
*Speech Delivered in the Convention
    of Pennsylvania, 1775* (Wilson),
    600–607
Speech, freedom of, 128, 293, 914
Spoil, 77
Staff, as badge of office, 168
Stamp act, 369–70, 600–601
Standing Army, 292–93, 833, 940
Standish, Miles, 82
State(s), 111, 274, 868, 877, 905,
    917; boundary disputes of,
    899–904; choosing revenue of-
    ficers, 911; commerce between,
    947; Congress formed by coun-
    cils of, 866–67, 868; council of,
    60, 120, 866–67, 868; delegates
    in Congress, 638–43, 755,
    808, 820, 866, 906–7, 921–22;
    George III's land and, 890,

893, 894–96; national power
    v., 863, 870, 871–72, 925; new,
    917, 921; trials out of, 806;
    underrepresented in Congress,
    921–22; war and, 868. *See also
    specific states*
State constitution(s), 663–64,
    668–69; altering of Massachu-
    setts Bay, 603–4, 606; British,
    589–95, 604–5; charter as, 663,
    754; conventions, 719, 724–26,
    788–89, 825–37; debates on,
    799–802, 822–37; of England,
    571, 572, 573; establishing,
    difficulty in, 771; as inviolate,
    committee to determine, 746;
    knowledge of, 550; Maryland
    governor and, 765; oaths of,
    729, 752; precedents and,
    594–95; violations of, 749–53;
    voting and, 664. *See also* State
    Constitutional amendments;
    specific states
State Constitutional amendments:
    dissent against, 738, 742, 744–
    46; Massachusetts, 854–62;
    Pennsylvania, 735–53
Statute of Quia emptores Ter-
    rarum, 219, 255
Statute, publication of, 312, 313,
    361–62
Stealing, 59
Steward's court, 226
Stocks/stocking, 132, 373
Storage. *See* Magazine
Style, of laws, 769
Subjects, of king, inhabitants',
    185, 206
Subpoena, 447
Subsidy, paid to Crown, 31, 38–39,
    41, 74
Successors: of council of forty, 71;
    of Crown, 295
Suffolk Resolves, 643–46
Suits, 320
Sullivan, John, 665–68
*A Summary View of the Rights of
    British America* (Jefferson),
    580–89
Summons, 443
Sundays, 483. *See also* Lord's Day
Superintendent of Finance, 904–5
Superstition, 486

Supreme court, 731, 767–57; attor-
    neys licensed by, 801–2
Survey: highway, 149; land, 431
Surveyor General, 183, 188
Suspension: of councilors, 348,
    400; of suits against officers,
    320
Swearing, 59
Swine, 149

Talbot, William, 123–24
Tales de circumstanibus, 444
Tavern, 445, 481; servants/slaves
    and, 445
Tax(es), 41, 52, 74, 547, 580, 589;
    burgesses control of, 301; in
    Calvert's Maryland, 114; Con-
    gress levying, 910, 926, 930;
    New England's, 74; petition
    and, 342; President-General
    setting, 367; stamp act and,
    369–70, 600–601; tobacco,
    310; towns setting, 96. *See also*
    Custom/duty; Levy(ies)
Tea, 584, 601; Boston rebellion
    and, 584
Teaching, of preachers, 256
Tenants, 540; contracts between
    servants and, 57, 264; on Gov-
    ernor's Land, 50; joint, 316
Tenements/hereditaments, 32–33
Tenure, 952; of freemen in office,
    738–39; of Georgia's corpora-
    tion, 520
Term. *See* Tenure
Territory(ies): 1606, 28, 29; 1612,
    44; enlargement of/undiscov-
    ered, 44; Gilbert's, 19; Indian,
    21, 237; of Jamestown, 50;
    of Massachusetts Bay, 1629,
    83–85; of New England, 73,
    139; Raleigh's, 22; separation
    of, 497; of Virginia, 51; West-
    ern, 916–21
Thanksgiving, 370
Thoughts on Government (Adams),
    607–11
Throne. *See* Crown
Ties: casting voice in, 128; elec-
    tion, of burgess, 303
Timing, of court sessions, 171
Tip-staff, 707
Title, of governor, 782

Tobacco, 58, 61–62, 536; as fines payment, 302, 317; foreign, 62; as salary, 536; tax, 310

To South Carolina Committee, 1775 (Laurens), 596–600

Town(s)/township(s), 174, 243; announcing/paying for court, 169; boundaries of, 173; children from other, 96; constables of, 168; deputy of, 102, 161; lawmaking of, 96, 148; mayor of, in Carolinas, 230; meetings/fines for misbehaving in, 95; officers of, election of, 341–42, 373–75; setting taxes, 96

Trade, 42, 59, 81, 92–93, 577; with Africa, 352, 409; British regulation of, 601; children learning skill and, 264; Congress regulating, 925–26, 928, 933, 941; with Indians, 58, 217; Jefferson on restricted, 582, 584, 589; on New England coast, 92–93. *See also* Commerce; Merchant(s); Smuggling

Tradesman, 52

Trafficking, 41, 75

Training, of soldiers, 185, 198

Transport: of goods out of England, 20, 22, 24, 73; of people, to plantations, 74, 158, 204

Travel, Crown restricting, 59, 160, 189

Treason, 241, 942; property/land and, 202

Treasurer: colony, 31, 36, 39, 44; deputy replacing, 39; land grant instructions of, 49–55; oaths and, 47; of United States, 942

Treasurer's court, 226

Treaties, 892, 933, 954

Treaty of Versailles, 892

Trespassing, 104, 445

Trial(s), 34–35, 122, 144, 171; charges for, 165; in England/Great Britain, 245, 593; by jury, 178, 192, 242, 731; out of state, 806; as public, 192

Tyranny: Hamilton, A. on, 930; Kennedy on, 549; of Lord Baltimore, 344–47; of minister of Great Britain, 651–52

Ulster county, 180

Union, 107–8, 141, 271, 274; Mechanics of New York, 636; of New Haven/Connecticut, 141; opposing, 365–66; of Plymouth, Massachusetts Bay, 67–68. *See also* Albany Plan of Union

United American Colonies, petition from, to Great Britain, 651–52

United Colonies of New England: naming of, 274. *See also* Union; United States

United Provinces, credit system compared to United States, 927

United States, 365–69, 874, 946; credit system of United Provinces compared to, 927; Madison, J. on political system of, 946–50; manufacturing solely in, 646; new states joining, 917; petition of, 651–52; treasurer, 942; Vermont joining, 803. *See also* Articles of Confederation; New World; Union

United States of America: confederation as, 874

University, in Virginia, 52

Upper House, 121, 143, 363, 364–65

U.S. Constitution. *See* Articles of Confederation

Usurpation, 583

Vacancy, 235, 287, 453

Vermont: 1777 constitution of, 803–12; boundary dispute and, 900–904; revised constitution of, 812–21

Verplank, Philip, 394–95

Vessels. *See* Sea Vessels

Vice, 246

A Vindication of the British Colonies (Otis), 556–69

Violations: of constitution/bill of rights, 749–53; by King James II, 293

Virginia, 27–66, 301–22, 705–14; in 1776, constitution of, 698–700, 701–4, 713–14; Bill of Rights of, 700–701; boundaries of, 51; councils of, 29–30,

33, 34, 61; Crown voiding laws of, 315; as first colony, 28, 29; general court of, 306; illegal inhabitants of, 55; proprietors in, 27; trafficking in, 41, 75; treasurer of, 31, 34, 39, 44

Virgin Mary, 486

Voice: casting, 128; negative, 340, 366, 379, 586–87; voting ballots v., 788, 793–94

Voiding: of king/parliament authority, 649–51; of laws, 252, 315, 340

Voting, 27, 64, 140, 174, 363, 373–75, 449, 883; age for, 95, 728; Articles of Confederation and, 883; ballot v. viva voce, 788, 793–94; for British Parliament members, 570–71; burgesses and, 28, 132; confederation era, 728; corn/beans for, 103; excluded from, 303, 305, 343; fines for illegal, 373, 526–27; freeholders, 27, 64, 177, 304, 318–19, 348–49, 448; freemen/non-freemen, 95, 177; of joint tenants, 316; land and, 190, 316, 448; in Maryland, 123–24; more than once, 373; Mulatto not, 305; name writing as, 525; papers used for, 126, 363–64; partiality and, 242; by proxy, 199; Roman Catholics denied right of, 343; sheriff in, 383–84; state constitution and, 664; Sullivan on, 667; women denied right of, 303

Voyage(s), 59; to New England, from England, 74; oath of supremacy and, 43

The Voyages (Hakluyt), 5

Wages: bailiff's, 50; minister's, 51, 536. *See also* Salary

Walker, Thomas, 214

War, 420, 432, 938; Crown permission to declare, 338; right to wage, 113, 220, 276; Secretary of, 904; states dissenting from, 868

Warehouses, 309, 315

Warrant Officer, 290

Warwick, 148, 154
Water, construction and, 312
Weekes, John, 153
Weights and Measures, 509
Westchester county, 180, 793
Western territory, 916–21
West Jersey, East Jersey and, 182
Whipping, 132, 170, 445
Widow, land of, 179
Will. *See* Inheritance
William, (Prince), 294
William and Mary (King and
    Queen), 378–83; legislature
under, 376; to Massachusetts
    Bay, 323–31; to Pennsylvania
    governor, 470–74
William III (King), 460–66
Wilson, James, 556, 600–607
Winslowe, Edward, 82
Winthrop, John, 135
Witness, 202, 263, 447; false, 167,
    202
Wolves, 170
Women: inheritance of, 224; land
    of, 210, 263; voting of, disal-
    lowed, 303

Woodbridge, 190
Woods, for Crown's use, 334
Worship, public, 231, 696
Writ of Habeas corpus, 712

Year of the dominion of Cecilius
    &c Annoq Domini, 124
Youth, enlisting, from abroad, 366

About the Author

JON L. WAKELYN is Professor Emeritus of History at Kent State University. He is the author or editor of eleven books, including *The Politics of Literary Man, Southern Pamphlets on Secession, Leaders of the American Civil War, Southern and Unionist Pamphlets of the Civil War, Confederates against the Confederacy,* and *Birth of the Bill of Rights: Encyclopedia of the Antifederalists*.